This is the first comprehensive study for nearly 200 years of what remains of the writings of the Presocratic philosopher Philolaus of Croton (*c*. 470–385 BC). These fragments are crucial to our understanding of one of the most influential schools of ancient philosophy, the Pythagoreans; they also show close ties with the main lines of development of Presocratic thought, and represent a significant response to thinkers such as Parmenides and Anaxagoras.

Professor Huffman presents the fragments and testimonia (including the spurious fragments in a separate section for reference) with accompanying translations and introductory chapters and interpretive commentary. He not only produces further arguments for the authenticity of much that used to be neglected, but also undertakes a critique of Aristotle's testimony, opening the way for a quite new reading of fifth-century Pythagoreanism in general and of Philolaus in particular. Philolaus is revealed as a serious natural philosopher.

This book is a major contribution to Presocratic studies and provides an authoritative edition and definitive treatment of material of central importance to scholars working on early Greek philosophy.

PHILOLAUS OF CROTON

Pythagorean and Presocratic

CARL A. HUFFMAN
ASSOCIATE PROFESSOR OF CLASSICS,
DEPAUW UNIVERSITY

PHILOLAUS

OF

CROTON

Pythagorean and Presocratic

*

A COMMENTARY

ON THE

FRAGMENTS AND TESTIMONIA

WITH

INTERPRETIVE

ESSAYS

*

CAMBRIDGE UNIVERSITY PRESS
Cambridge, New York, Melbourne, Madrid, Cape Town, Singapore, São Paulo

Cambridge University Press
The Edinburgh Building, Cambridge CB2 2RU, UK

Published in the United States of America by Cambridge University Press, New York

www.cambridge.org
Information on this title: www.cambridge.org/9780521415255

First published 1993
This digitally printed first paperback version 2006

A catalogue record for this publication is available from the British Library

Library of Congress Cataloguing in Publication data
Huffman, Carl A.
Philolaus of Croton: Pythagorean and presocratic:
a commentary on the fragments and testimonia
with interpretive essays / Carl A. Huffman.
p.   cm.
Includes original Greek texts with English translation.
Includes bibliographical references and indexes.
ISBN 0 521 41525 X
1. Philolaus, of Croton, b. ca. 470 BC
2. Philosophy – Early works to 1800.
I. Philolaus, of Croton, b. ca. 470 BC
Selections. English & Greek.   1993.   II. Title.
B235.P44H84   1993
182′.2 – dc20   92-11194   CIP

ISBN-13 978-0-521-41525-5 hardback
ISBN-10 0-521-41525-X hardback

ISBN-13 978-0-521-02471-6 paperback
ISBN-10 0-521-02471-4 paperback

For My Father

The student of Plato will do well to
turn the page when he meets the
name Pythagoras in a commentator.

CONTENTS

ix

Part IV

SPURIOUS OR DOUBTFUL FRAGMENTS
AND TESTIMONIA

CONTENTS

PREFACE

Since the last book devoted exclusively to Philolaus was written by Boeckh in 1819, little apology seems necessary for presenting the scholarly world with a new commentary on his fragments and an interpretation of his philosophy. It is my hope that the present study will provide a basis on which Philolaus and early Pythagoreanism can enter the mainstream of scholarship both on the Presocratics and also on ancient philosophy as a whole. At present, despite the recent work of Schofield (KRS 1983), Barnes (1982), Nussbaum (1978), and Kahn (1974), it would appear that many scholars, at least tacitly, take the advice of Shorey which I print as an epigraph. They seem to feel that it is impossible to talk rigorously about the Pythagoreans in the way that we can about other Presocratics. "Pythagoreanism" seems to mean too much and to be hopelessly vague. The remedy for this problem is to focus detailed attention on the earliest Pythagorean texts we have, the fragments of Philolaus, and to use them as the foundation for our thinking about Pythagoreanism. It will be up to the reader to judge whether I have written any pages to which Shorey's dictum should not apply.

The giant on whose shoulders my work stands is Walter Burkert's magnificent *Lore and Science in Ancient Pythagoreanism*. Although I disagree with Burkert about the authenticity of a few fragments and although the interpretation of Philolaus' philosophy which I present is radically different from his, the reader will have a hard time finding a page on which I do not owe a debt to his work.

Since Philolaus is, in my opinion, the foremost of the early Pythagoreans, this book should give a good picture of the dominant themes of fifth-century Pythagoreanism. However, it is not intended as a comprehensive study of fifth-century Pythagoreanism and has little to say about Pythagoras himself, largely because the relationship between Pythagoras and Philolaus belongs almost totally to the realm of conjecture. In general my tendency has been to see Philolaus as as much a Presocratic as a Pythagorean.

There are many people without whose kindness and insight this book would never have been written. First and foremost I would like to thank Alex Mourelatos who first suggested the project to me, who directed my dissertation on the topic, and who has been unfailingly supportive. The Joint Graduate Program in Ancient Philosophy at the University of Texas at Austin, which he directs, provided a wonderful environment in which to work and I owe much to discussion with fellow students there, notably Larry Shrenk and Steve Strange. Jonathan Barnes, Martha Nussbaum, David Furley, and Charles Kahn were kind enough to discuss earlier versions of my work with me. A generous Fellowship for Independent Study and Research from the National Endowment for the Humanities in 1983–4 allowed me to develop important parts of my work. During the tenure of my fellowship I resided in Cambridge, England, where my ideas were greatly improved by the comments and advice of Myles Burnyeat and David Sedley. Malcolm Schofield discussed my work with me extensively and has given unstinting support. Geoffrey Lloyd provided a great number of valuable comments which particularly helped to improve the section on Philolaus' medical theory. He also organized The Cambridge Conference on Early Greek Mathematics in Spring 1984 at which I gave an earlier version of the chapter on the role of number in Philolaus. DePauw University has supported my work by providing a Fisher Time Out in Fall 1987 and a sabbatical leave in 1989–90. A fellowship from the Howard Foundation for 1989–90 allowed me to take the entirety of my sabbatical year off and thus finally bring the project to completion. Many other scholars have helped with comments and encouragement. In particular I would like to thank Andrew Barker for his detailed comments on the sections dealing with music theory. My wife Martha has taken time from her own work to help with the task of proofreading and without her support this book would still not be done. My sons David, Peter, and John have been very patient with my rantings about Philolaus. The comments of the Press's anonymous readers were very useful and my editor Pauline Hire and copy-editor Peter Singer have been both helpful and patient. It goes without saying that the flaws that remain are my own responsibility. An earlier version of the chapter on number and harmony (Pt. II, ch. 2) appeared as "The role of number in Philolaus' philosophy" in *Phronesis* 33 (1988) 1–30. The chapter on Philolaus' cosmogony (Pt. III, ch. 3) is a revised version of a paper given at the First International Conference on Greek Philosophy: Ionian Philosophy, organized by K. Boudouris on Samos, Greece in August 1988 and published in Boudouris 1989.

TEXTS AND ABBREVIATIONS

For the fragments and testimonia of Philolaus, as well as other Presocratics, I have generally followed the text in the edition of Diels, revised by Kranz, *Die Fragmente der Vorsokratiker* (6th edn., 1951–2 – referred to as DK). However, I have also made reference to the standard editions of the sources quoted in DK and on occasion print a slightly different text or add additional information in the apparatus. In addition I have recollated some manuscripts of the sources for the central metaphysical fragments of Philolaus (Frs. 1–7). Fragments 2 and 4–7 are all derived from the *Eclogae* of Stobaeus. Wachsmuth's text is based solely on manuscripts F and P which he regards as the only two independent sources for the text (see the introduction to his edition and his separate monograph [1882: 55–89]). I have collated the sections on Fragments 2 and 4–7 in all nine manuscripts of the *Eclogae* known to me. The results of this collation have been largely negative. They confirm Wachsmuth's view that all the other manuscripts are derived from F and P. The apparatus which I have provided for these fragments gives a complete report of the important variants in the manuscripts which I collated, although the collation has not led to any change in the final text. Only F, G, V, M, and E have the entirety of Fragments 2 and 4–7. P, H, R, and Y include only F2 and the first sentence of F4. In the case of F1 I have recollated the three primary manuscripts of Diogenes Laertius (B, F, and P). For F3 I have rechecked manuscript F of Iamblichus, *In Nic.* which is the primary witness for the text and the basis of Pistelli's edition. In both of these cases my results were similarly negative. I have made no attempt to solve the problem of Philolaus' dialect and early Doric prose in general and have tended to choose between the forms the manuscripts present us with rather than restoring Doric forms (on Doric prose see recently Cassio [1988]).

In general I have followed the numbering of DK for the fragments and testimonia of Philolaus on the grounds that to introduce a new numbering of my own would only confuse matters. However, in a few cases I have added new testimonia or divided other fragments and testimonia in different ways while still staying close to the numbering in DK. Thus, I have distinguished Fragments 6, 6a, and 6b all of which are listed under F6 in DK. Likewise I have distinguished the spurious and genuine parts of Testimonia A16 and A17 by designating the spurious parts 16b and 17b. The citations about the names Philolaus supposedly gave to the number 10 (from Lydus and the *Theol. ar.*) which DK prints at the end of A13 have been renumbered as Fragments 20b and 20c, because they clearly belong with the other arithmological citations from Lydus (F20 and 20a in DK). I have included a text from Syrianus about god creating limit and unlimited, which is not in DK, as F8a. What I have called Testimonium A26b, from Proclus, *In Ti.*, is only mentioned by DK in the apparatus to A26. The references to Philolaus as an author of a work on military matters which DK includes without any number at the end of the collection of fragments have been numbered A30.

In a number of cases it is difficult to be sure whether a given text should be regarded as a literal quotation of Philolaus' words and hence a fragment or rather a second-hand report of his views and thus a testimonium. Where these issues arise I have discussed them in the commentary on individual texts. All of the genuine fragments are clearly presented as fragments and often marked by the Doric dialect, although even in these cases we can not be sure how accurate the quotation is. However, there are a number of cases in the spurious material presented in the appendix where DK present a text as a fragment (i.e. they include it in the B section) which is clearly only a testimonium. Although I have continued to refer to these texts as "fragments" in order to keep close to the numbering in DK, I have pointed out their true status in the commentary. Only texts that refer to Philolaus by name have been included among the fragments and testimonia (but see F10). Identifying unascribed Philolaic material in the morass of later Pythagoreanism is a daunting task and I doubt that there is much to be found given the Platonizing tendency of the later tradition. Moreover, what is needed for Philolaus at the moment is a delineation and interpretation of a set of texts that we can confidently regard as genuine, not a presentation of questionable material.

I have referred to the works of Plato according to Burnet's Oxford text; the treatises of Aristotle according to Bekker's Berlin edition; the fragments of Aristotle according to the numbering of the third edition of Rose (1886). Where possible I have tried to cite the Greek medical texts according to the *Corpus medicorum Graecorum* (*CMG*) editions, but in many cases the references are to the edition of E. Littré, *Œuvres complètes d'Hippocrate*, 10 vols. (Paris, 1839–61 – referred to as L). Other Greek authors are cited according to the editions mentioned in the *Greek–English Lexicon* of H. G. Liddell and R. Scott, revised by H. S. Jones, with Supplement (1968 – referred to as LSJ), although I have in some cases made reference to more recent editions. Abbreviations are generally those used in LSJ.

Modern works are generally referred to by the author's last name and publication date. The abbreviations used for periodicals are generally those of *L'Année philologique*. I have referred to the first edition of Kirk and Raven, *The Presocratic Philosophers*, and the second edition revised by Malcolm Schofield, as KR and KRS. A complete list of modern works referred to will be found in the bibliography.

The translations are usually my own, although I have made use of a variety of other translations as indicated.

SIGLA

Stobaeus, *Eclogae*
F = Farnesinus III D 15
P = Parisinus 2129
G = Farnesinus III D 16
V = Vaticanus 201
M = Monacensis 396
H = Harleianus 6318
E = Escurialensis T-11-2
R = Escurialensis R-1-11
Y = Escurialensis Y-1-16

Diogenes Laertius
B = Neapolitanus Burbonicus III B 29
F = Laurentianus 69.13
P = Parisinus 1759

Iamblichus, *In Nicomachi Arithmeticam Introductionem*
F = Laurentianus 86.3

Part I

INTRODUCTION

1. LIFE AND WRITINGS

Ἐν τοῖς Ἕλλησι τοῖς πάλαι μακρᾷ τῇ δόξῃ διέπρεπε Γοργίας ὁ
Λεοντῖνος Φιλολάου καὶ Πρωταγόρας Δημοκρίτου, τῇ δὲ σοφίᾳ
τοσοῦτον ἐλείποντο ὅσον ἀνδρῶν παῖδες. (Aelian, *VH* 1.23)

*Among the ancient Greeks Gorgias of Leontini far exceeded Philolaus in
reputation as Protagoras did Democritus, but in wisdom they fell as far
short [of Philolaus and Democritus] as boys do of men.*

Scholarship on the Presocratics has, in recent years, restored to
Democritus some of the reputation that he lacked in the ancient
world but Philolaus still resides in a limbo of uncertainty. It is one of
the goals of this book to determine what reputation Philolaus should
have and there is little doubt that he deserves at least as much fame
as Gorgias. However, Aelian's remark about Philolaus' lack of fame
in the ancient world is confirmed by the paucity of evidence about
his life. As is the case with most Presocratics any chronology constructed for his life is a fabric of the loosest possible weave. Nonetheless it is important to try to get an idea of the possibilities for
the chronology of his life in order to see his relationship to other
Presocratics and his position in the intellectual history of the fifth
and early fourth century BC.

The crucial text for any reconstruction of Philolaus' life is Plato's
reference to him at *Phaedo* 61d. Cebes expresses surprise at Socrates'
statement that on the one hand it is not lawful for someone to commit suicide, but on the other hand a philosopher would be willing to
follow those who have died. The conversation then continues:

τί δέ, ὦ Κέβης; οὐκ ἀκηκόατε σύ τε καὶ Σιμμίας περὶ τῶν τοιούτων
Φιλολάῳ συγγεγονότες; Οὐδέν γε σαφές, ὦ Σώκρατες. . . . Κατὰ
τί δὴ οὖν ποτε οὔ φασι θεμιτὸν εἶναι αὐτὸν ἑαυτὸν ἀποκτεινύναι,
ὦ Σώκρατες; ἤδη γὰρ ἔγωγε, ὅπερ νυνδὴ σὺ ἤρου, καὶ Φιλολάου
ἤκουσα, ὅτε παρ᾽ ἡμῖν διῃτᾶτο, ἤδη δὲ καὶ ἄλλων τινῶν, ὡς οὐ

I

δέοι τοῦτο ποιεῖν· σαφὲς δὲ περὶ αὐτῶν οὐδενὸς πώποτε οὐδὲν ἀκήκοα.

What, Cebes? Have you and Simmias not heard about such things in your association with Philolaus? Nothing definite, at least, Socrates ... Why ever then do they deny that it is lawful to kill oneself, Socrates? For, to answer the question that you were just now asking, I already heard from Philolaus, when he was spending time with us, and before that from some others as well, that it was not right to do this. But I have never yet heard anything definite from anyone.

This passage makes clear that Philolaus had spent time in Thebes where he was heard by Simmias and Cebes (ὅτε παρ' ἡμῖν διῃτᾶτο) sometime before the dramatic date of the *Phaedo*, 399. It is implied that Philolaus is no longer in Thebes, but there is no suggestion that he is dead. If Philolaus had the stature to be the teacher of Simmias and Cebes sometime before 399, it seems reasonable to conclude that he was at least forty and hence 440 becomes the *terminus ante quem* for his birth, although he could have been born considerably earlier on this evidence. Likewise 399 becomes the *terminus post quem* for his death.

Other testimonia increase the likelihood that he was born considerably earlier than 440. In the scholia to this passage of the *Phaedo* (DK A1a) Olympiodorus says that Philolaus fled Italy because of the burning (of the Pythagorean meeting place) instigated by Cylon. This must refer to the second of two major attacks on the Pythagoreans, which is dated by Minar to around 454.[1] Cylon was only directly involved in the first attack (509), which occurred in the lifetime of Pythagoras himself, but the second attack, which involves the burning of the house of Milo, is regularly confused with the earlier one. Olympiodorus also says that Philolaus and Hipparchus (Archippus?) were the only Pythagoreans to escape from the burning. Plutarch (*De genio Soc.* 13, 583a) gives a similar report except that Lysis is named as Philolaus' companion, the story is explicitly set in Metapontum, and they are said to have escaped because of their youthful strength and quickness. Philolaus is reported to have fled to Lucania and to have met up with other Pythagoreans

---

[1] Minar 1942: 50–94. He bases the date of 454 for the second uprising against the Pythagoreans on the unlikelihood that Sybaris would have been restored in 453–452, if Croton had not been weakened. While this is not certain it is better than von Fritz's assertion (1940: 78–9) that the revolt was between 450 and 440, based on the very uncertain dating of Lysis.

who were already starting to prevail over the Cylonians. If these reports could be accepted, it would suggest that Philolaus was a young man in 454 which would point to a birth date around 475. However, there are problems.

Our oldest authority for the attacks on the Pythagoreans is Aristoxenus, the pupil of Aristotle, as preserved in Iamblichus, *VP* 248ff. After describing the origin of Cylon's hostility to Pythagoras and Pythagoras' consequent departure from Croton to Metapontum, he goes on to detail the continuing hostility of the Cylonians to the Pythagoreans.

τέλος δὲ εἰς τοσοῦτον ἐπεβούλευσαν τοῖς ἀνδράσιν, ὥστε ἐν τῇ Μίλωνος οἰκίᾳ ἐν Κρότωνι συνεδρευόντων τῶν Πυθαγορείων καὶ βουλευομένων περὶ πολιτικῶν πραγμάτων ὑφάψαντες τὴν οἰκίαν κατέκαυσαν τοὺς ἄνδρας πλὴν δυεῖν, Ἀρχίππου τε καὶ Λύσιδος· οὗτοι δὲ νεώτατοι ὄντες εὐρωστότατοι διεξεπαίσαντο ἔξω πως.

(249–50)

Finally they became so hostile to the men [the Pythagoreans] that when the Pythagoreans were meeting in the house of Milo in Croton and taking council about affairs of the city they set fire to the house and burned all the men except two, Archippus and Lysis. These men, since they were the youngest and strongest, somehow got out.

There is no mention of Philolaus at all here and the setting is Croton, but in other respects the story is very much the same. It is possible that Philolaus was involved in a separate escape from an attack in Metapontum since that is where Plutarch sets the story, but Plutarch is presenting a romantic story and is much less likely to be providing accurate information than Aristoxenus. He may simply have substituted "Philolaus" for the more obscure "Archippus" which he found in Aristoxenus. Olympiodorus' report then appears to be a confused compilation of Plutarch and Aristoxenus.[2] It is thus doubtful that Philolaus is really to be associated with the story of the burning of the house of Milo.

However, there are a number of other reports that indicate that Philolaus was born some time before 440. First, Aristoxenus (D.L.

---

[2] Minar (1942: 82 n. 108) says that it is possible that Philolaus escaped from another revolt in Metapontum shortly after the revolt in Croton, but warns that "caution is indicated by the romantic character of Plutarch's whole tale." Burkert (1972: 228 n. 48) argues that in the face of Aristoxenus' report "Plutarch's novelistic treatment has no value." That Aristoxenus is the source for Iamblichus, *VP* 249 is secured by the reference to him by name at *VP* 251.

8.46 = DK A4) reportedly saw the last of the Pythagoreans who were said to be students of Philolaus and Eurytus of Tarentum. It is difficult to date these figures, but Echecrates of Phlius is used by Plato in the *Phaedo*. If Aristoxenus (born 375–360) saw these Pythagoreans, it suggests that they were alive in the mid fourth century and must therefore be rough contemporaries of Plato (428–348). Philolaus could be their teacher if he were born in 440, but it seems more likely that, like Socrates, he was born around 470. This suspicion is strengthened by the fact that, while he and Eurytus are said to be the teachers of the last of the Pythagoreans, Philolaus is in turn said to be the teacher of Eurytus (Iamblichus, *VP* 139, 148). In the catalogue of Pythagoreans in Iamblichus, *VP* 267 Philolaus is listed before Eurytus. In order to be the teacher of these last Pythagoreans Eurytus must be born in 440 or more likely 450. If Philolaus is his teacher he should be at least twenty years older and thus born in 460 or more likely 470. Philolaus is also said to have been the teacher of Archytas (Cic. *De or.* 3.139), but the two are not joined as overlapping teachers as Eurytus and Philolaus are. All of this would make sense if we supposed that Philolaus was born *c.* 470, Eurytus *c.* 450, and Archytas *c.* 430. Philolaus would thus be the contemporary of Socrates and bear the same chronological relationship to Archytas that Socrates did to Plato. One last report seems to confirm this scheme. Apollodorus of Cyzicus, who should probably be dated before the time of Epicurus, reports that Democritus studied with Philolaus.[3] If Democritus was born around 460, this would push Philolaus' birth to the earliest possible date of about 480.

When we turn to Philolaus' death things are even more uncertain, but nonetheless intriguing. It is common to refer to the Pythagorean influence on Plato, but the Pythagorean named is usually Plato's contemporary Archytas, who is mentioned in the seventh letter although not in any of the dialogues. Yet, there are persistent reports that make a connection between Plato and Philolaus. A

---

[3] Olympiodorus in the scholia to *Phaedo* 61e (= DK 44A1a) makes Lysis the teacher of Philolaus, which would make it difficult for Philolaus to be born before 460, since Lysis cannot be born much earlier than 480 and still teach Epaminondas. However, the purpose of the scholia is clearly to explain the visit of Philolaus to Thebes mentioned in the *Phaedo* and it says that he does so in order to make libations at the tomb of Lysis. However, since Olympiodorus' report is a late compilation influenced by Plutarch's novelistic treatment, the story does not inspire much confidence. Apollodorus (or Apollodotus) of Cyzicus is a shadowy figure associated with Hecataeus of Abdera and Nausiphanes who is reported to be a teacher of Epicurus. See DK 73, 74, and 75. For the dating see Burkert 1972: 228–9 n. 51.

report by Hermippus (third century BC – D.L. 8.85) has Plato himself buying a book from Philolaus' relatives or else given the book as a reward for saving one of Philolaus' students from Dionysius the tyrant of Syracuse. Plato is said to have transcribed his *Timaeus* from this book which probably is to be understood as written by Philolaus. Timon's verses which accuse Plato of having cribbed the *Timaeus* from someone are probably based on this same story and show that it is early (DK A8). The connection between Plato and Philolaus could have been invented in this case because of similarities between the *Timaeus* and Philolaus' book, and the suggestion that Plato got the book from relatives would support the idea that Plato did not have direct contact with Philolaus. However, the other version of the story, that makes the book a reward for saving a pupil of Philolaus, suggests that Philolaus himself was alive when Plato first visited Sicily around 388. This possibility is made more attractive by an additional intriguing testimonium. In Diogenes' life of Plato (3.6) Hermodorus is cited for a report that after Socrates' death, when Plato was 28, he went to Euclides in Megara with some other Socratics. The report continues to say that he visited Theodorus in Cyrene and Philolaus and Eurytus in Italy. Finally, he is said to have visited the prophets in Egypt in the company of Euripides! Scholars accept the trip to Megara which is based on the excellent authority of Hermodorus, who was a student of Plato, and are rightly amused by the absurd story that Euripides went to Egypt with Plato. But, what about the report that Plato visited Philolaus and Eurytus in Italy? Is it also based on the authority of Hermodorus or does it come from the tradition that makes Euripides Plato's companion? The text of Diogenes does not allow us to be certain, but if the report were drawn from Hermodorus it would fit very well with Plato's supposed contact with Philolaus on his first visit to Sicily. It also would explain the mention of Philolaus in the *Phaedo* which many scholars regard as being written around the time of Plato's first visit to Sicily.[4]

The most likely date for Philolaus' birth would then appear to be

---

[4] Calder (1983) has recently suggested that the reading Euripides in the text of D.L. 3.6 is a mistaken expansion of the abbreviation Εὐ., and that the likely reading is Eudoxus rather than Euripides. This is very appealing and, if accepted, it would remove a major obstacle to regarding the whole report, including the mention of Plato's visit with Philolaus, as based on the very good authority of Hermodorus. See Guthrie for Plato's first trip to Sicily and for the date of the *Phaedo* (1975: 17ff, 325).

around 470, although he could have been born as early as 480 or as late as 440. He appears to have lived into the 380s and at the very least until 399.

The sources are also mixed as to his city of origin. Our two oldest sources disagree. Meno, the pupil of Aristotle, in his history of medicine says that Philolaus is from Croton (Anon. Lond. 18.8 = DK A27). The last Pythagoreans that Aristoxenus, also the pupil of Aristotle, saw are said to be students of Philolaus and Eurytus of Tarentum (D.L. 8.46 = DK A4). Aristoxenus is clearly the source for this list of the last Pythagoreans and hence it is likely that he is also the source for the statement that Philolaus is from Tarentum. However, Aristoxenus is clearly most interested in the last generation of Pythagoreans and might well be giving Philolaus' home in the later part of his life while Meno is referring to his city of origin. It is certainly clear that Croton was the main Pythagorean center up to the attack on the society in 454, whereas Tarentum grows in importance later and as the home of Archytas is important in fourth-century Pythagoreanism.[5]

Beyond this chronological outline the details of Philolaus' life are unknown to us.[6] However, it is important to look at his chronological relationship first to other Pythagoreans and then to other thinkers in the Presocratic tradition. The most likely dating for Pythagoras himself (569–494) would have him dying twenty-five years before Philolaus' birth. There is no good evidence that he wrote anything.[7] Hippasus of Metapontum seems to have been active in the first part of the fifth century so that he may have been in his old age while Philolaus was growing up. Hippasus is joined to Heraclitus by Aristotle (*Metaph.* 1, 984a7) as believing that fire is the basic principle. He is associated with experiments showing the relationship between the whole number ratios and the basic musical intervals. In a number of ways he is portrayed as a maverick. He argues for democratic reforms at Croton during the first uprising against the Pythagoreans (509) and is tied to the split between *mathematici* and *acusmatici*. He is

[5] For Tarentum as the center of Pythagoreanism in the later period see Minar 1942: 86ff. Wuilleumier (1939: 567) suggests the view that I adopt in the text. Burkert (1972: 228 n. 48) leaves the matter undecided.

[6] The story at D.L. 84 that Philolaus was killed because he was thought to be aiming at a tyranny is clearly a confusion with Dion who is mentioned in the context and did have such a death.

[7] For the chronology of Pythagoras' life see Minar 1942: 133–5 and Burkert 1972: 110ff. For the evidence about Pythagoras' writings or the lack of them see Burkert 1972: 218–20.

grouped with the *mathematici* whom the *acusmatici* even say to be followers of Hippasus rather than Pythagoras. In some reports he is said to be punished for revealing mathematical secrets. Demetrius of Magnesia (D.L. 8.84) says that he wrote nothing, although others said that he wrote a Μυστικὸς λόγος to traduce the master (D.L. 8.7), but even were this later story true it is clear that he wrote no philosophical treatise. His name is often confused with that of Hipparchus. If Hipparchus is an historical figure he seems to belong to the time of Lysis.[8]

Lysis would appear to be a contemporary, perhaps slightly older, of Philolaus. Unlike Hippasus we have no evidence for any philosophical beliefs of Lysis at all. After his escape from the burning of Milo's house in Croton (454), he went to Thebes. He is most famous in the tradition as the teacher, in his old age, of Epaminondas, the great Theban general of the fourth century. Epaminondas was probably born around 410 and thus could have been taught by Lysis in the 390s and 380s when Lysis was in his 70s and 80s. He seems to have died and been buried in Thebes sometime before 379. A spurious letter of his addressed to Hipparchus survives and one report says that a book under Pythagoras' name was really by Lysis, but we have no good evidence of his writing a book. It is significant that in the *Phaedo* it is Philolaus that Socrates mentions as the teacher of Simmias and Cebes at Thebes rather than Lysis.[9] It may be that Plato knew more of Philolaus from his visit to Sicily or it may indicate that Lysis was more famous for his mode of life than for any philosophical beliefs.

As mentioned above Eurytus seems to be both the pupil of Philolaus and a fellow teacher and thus was probably born about 450 or 440. Archytas seems to be the source for the famous story of Eurytus' identification of man or horse with a specific number and illustration of this identification by making pebble drawings of men and horses. A spurious work *On Luck* is assigned to a Eurysus but there is no good evidence that Eurytus wrote anything.[10]

Archytas of Tarentum is the last of the famous Pythagoreans and

---

[8] For Hippasus see DK 18 and Burkert 1972: 206ff. For the correct account of the relationship between Hippasus and the *acusmatici* and *mathematici* see Burkert 1972: 193–4. For Hipparchus see Burkert 1972: 459 n. 63.

[9] For Lysis see DK 46. There is a spurious letter of Lysis to Hipparchus (Hippasus D.L. 8.42) for which see Burkert 1961.

[10] For Eurytus see DK 45. See Thesleff 1965: 87–8 for Eurysus Περὶ τύχας.

is presented as a pupil of Philolaus in some reports (Cic. *De or.* 3.334.139 = DK 44 A3). He is most famous as the contemporary and friend of Plato (428–348) for which the major evidence is the Platonic letters. Aristoxenus wrote a life of Archytas and Aristotle wrote three books on the philosophy of Archytas. He served as general of Tarentum seven times and supposedly was never defeated. He is credited with being the first to make the study of mechanics systematic. There are charming stories told about his love for children including his invention of a rattle to keep them entertained. He was a formidable mathematician and we have some fragments both from mathematical and philosophical treatises.[11]

Ecphantus and Hicetas of Syracuse are two rather shadowy figures that some have thought to be the literary creation of Heraclides of Pontus. However, since their views seem to have been mentioned by Theophrastus, it seems probable that they are historical figures. It is difficult to date them, but they seem to be later than both the atomists and Philolaus and may be contemporaries of Archytas. Ecphantus is reported to have explained all things in terms of atoms and void, although he said that atoms were limited in number. Both Hicetas and Ecphantus said that the earth moved, but they put it in the center of the cosmos and made its movement axial rotation. They may have written books but we have no evidence for them.[12]

Thus after Pythagoras himself there are really just three prominent names in Pythagoreanism: Hippasus (*c.* 530–450?), Philolaus (*c.* 470–385), and Archytas (*c.* 430–350). There is no good evidence for any Pythagorean, including Pythagoras himself, writing a book before Philolaus (see further below) and after Philolaus it is only in the case of Archytas that we can be sure of some writings. There were of course many other Pythagoreans in these years, but most of them are just names and do not seem to have contributed much to philosophical speculations.

Turning from the specifically Pythagorean tradition to the broader tradition of Presocratic philosophy, it is clear that Philolaus belongs to almost the very last generation of that tradition, since he is the older contemporary of Democritus (b. *c.* 460). When Philolaus was

---

[11] For Archytas see DK 47, Guthrie 1962: 333–6 and Lloyd 1990. Despite Burkert's doubts (1972: 379–80 n. 46) F1 of Archytas is likely to be genuine. See Huffman 1985.

[12] For Ecphantus and Hicetas see Burkert 1972: 341 n. 17 and Guthrie 1962: 323–9.

thirty (*c.* 440) both Anaxagoras (*c.* 500–428) and Empedocles (*c.* 495–435) will have published their work and it is these figures who will have represented the forefront of philosophy as Philolaus was developing into a mature philosopher. In fact the fragments of Philolaus do show some clear ties to Anaxagoras (see F3). If the tradition of Zeno (b. *c.* 490) publishing his book early in his career is true, it would be a little older than these works. Philolaus would look back to Parmenides (b. *c.* 515) and Heraclitus (*c.* 540–480?) as belonging to the previous generation and Pythagoras himself as even older. Alcmaeon came from the same polis as Philolaus and is sometimes mistakenly identified as a Pythagorean in the later tradition. Alcmaeon's dates are controversial, but he probably does belong to the fifth century and flourished in the first rather than the second half of it so that one would expect that Philolaus would become familiar with his views while growing up in Croton. Alcmaeon is known for his views on medicine and in particular for his account of the composition of the human body in terms of a balance of opposites and for his account of the senses in which he identifies the brain as the seat of sensation.[13]

If we turn from Presocratic philosophers to mathematics and science, it is important to note that Philolaus is a contemporary of Hippocrates of Chios and Theodorus of Cyrene, two pioneering figures in Greek mathematics, the former of whom may have been the first to write an *Elements*. The astronomers Oenopides of Chios, who discovered the angle of the obliquity of the ecliptic, and Euctemon and Meton of Athens are also contemporaries. Medical theory was also making important advances in Philolaus' lifetime. Hippocrates of Cos is once again his contemporary and some of the treatises in the Hippocratic corpus date to Philolaus' lifetime.[14]

With Philolaus' position in both the Pythagorean and the Presocratic tradition before us, it is important to raise the question of what it means to be a Pythagorean rather than simply a Presocratic or *physikos*. A number of people get called Pythagorean in the ancient tradition whom few modern scholars would recognize as

[13] For the dates of Anaxagoras see Sider 1981: 1–11 and Mansfeld 1979–80 who argues for a late arrival in Athens and late publication of the book. For Alcmaeon see Mansfeld 1975 and Lloyd 1975.

[14] For the dates of Hippocrates and Theodorus see Proclus, *in Euc.* 66.4 = DK 42A1. See also Burnyeat 1978: 499 n. 33.

Pythagoreans. Empedocles, Parmenides and Alcmaeon are clear examples.[15] These later figures come to be associated with the Pythagoreans in part simply because they come from southern Italy. In some cases, notably Empedocles, there is enough similarity in their thinking to reputed Pythagorean views for them to earn the label. However, we must be wary of supposing a great deal of orthodoxy in philosophical beliefs among supposed Pythagoreans. If we compare figures who are universally recognized as Pythagoreans such as Hippasus, Philolaus, and Archytas, we see that their philosophical views and interests differ considerably. All show some interest in mathematics, but, while Archytas is clearly interested in genuine mathematical problems such as the duplication of the cube and Hippasus may have worked on the problem of incommensurability, there is no evidence that Philolaus was a serious mathematician.[16] Instead Philolaus wants to apply basic mathematical ideas to philosophy in the same way that Plato does in the *Timaeus* and elsewhere. Again, Philolaus has a strong interest in medicine that does not appear in Hippasus or Archytas. While Philolaus posits limiters and unlimiteds as the foundation of all reality, Hippasus makes fire the basic principle. There is not time here to do an exhaustive comparison of these three figures, but the point is that the Pythagorean tradition admits a wide range of philosophical ideas and interests and we should be wary of assuming that there was a rigid set of philosophical dogmas accepted by all Pythagoreans.

Plato's mention of the contribution of Pythagoras in the *Republic* (10, 600b) first and foremost emphasizes the way of life that he handed on to his followers. What I would like to suggest is that it is in living a certain sort of life that one becomes a Pythagorean. Following such a life may presuppose accepting certain beliefs that may be loosely called philosophical, but it need not include any very extensive philosophical account of the nature of reality. This way of life may have been constituted by certain rules about food and clothing as are famous from the Pythagorean tradition, notably the ban

---

[15] For Empedocles as a Pythagorean see D.L. 8.54. Alcmaeon is called a pupil of Pythagoras in D.L. 8.83 and simply a Pythagorean in Iamblichus, *VP* 104, 267 and Philoponus *in de An.* 88, despite the fact that Aristotle clearly distinguishes him from the Pythagoreans (*Metaph.* 986a27ff), Iamblichus includes Parmenides in his list of Pythagoreans (*VP* 267).

[16] For Hippasus' mathematics see von Fritz 1945b. For Archytas on the duplication of the cube see Heath 1921 1. 246–9. For Philolaus see Huffman (1988).

on eating beans. However, it undoubtedly also included certain moral principles such as the exhortation to live a simple life and to practice temperance and may have called for some sort of communal living.[17] In the modern world we may say that someone is a Catholic without therefore being at all clear what he believes on a whole range of philosophical issues. Being a Pythagorean in the ancient world may entail more in terms of philosophical beliefs than being a Catholic does in the modern world, but we should be wary of assuming that too much is entailed. The reason that Philolaus is a Pythagorean and Alcmaeon is not is that Philolaus lived a Pythagorean life while Alcmaeon did not. However, within the Pythagorean life very few people were interested in abstract philosophy as were Hippasus and Philolaus. At least we have a wealth of names of Pythagoreans who seem to have made no contribution in these areas. A Pythagorean could become a philosopher of the Presocratic sort (a *physikos*), a mathematician, a physician or even a leading general, but none of these pursuits were demanded of him as a Pythagorean. When Philolaus came to write his book he probably looked to Anaxagoras, Alcmaeon, Empedocles, and Parmenides as his predecessors as much as to any Pythagorean. Plato's *Phaedo* with its discussion of a variety of views about the soul and the clearly open-minded consideration of them by supposed Pythagoreans such as Simmias, Cebes, and Echecrates shows that not even precise philosophical views on the nature of the soul are dictated to those who live a Pythagorean life.

In the tradition several types or grades of Pythagoreanism are distinguished. The most prominent distinction is that between the *mathematici* and the *acusmatici*. The accounts of this split are somewhat confused in the sources, but Burkert has brilliantly shown that the original version is that found at Iamblichus, *Comm. math.* 76.19ff and that this account ultimately goes back to the excellent authority of Aristotle.[18] The *acusmatici* are said to be recognized as genuine Pythagoreans by the *mathematici*, but the *acusmatici* are said not to regard the *mathematici* as real Pythagoreans but to say that they are really followers of Hippasus. The *mathematici* deny this and say that "all things come from that man [Pythagoras] ". When he first came

---

[17] For the way of life of fourth-century Pythagoreans see Burkert 1972: 204ff.
[18] Burkert 1972: 192–208.

to Italy, they say, Pythagoras was unable to teach the older men proofs for all he said because they were wrapped up in public affairs and did not have the time. Accordingly they only learned the precepts governing the proper way of life without learning the arguments for them. The young, on the other hand, having the time to devote themselves to μαθήματα (mathematical studies including music) learned the proofs and arguments. These later became the *mathematici* and the former the *acusmatici*. Since this split is associated with the name of Hippasus, it is probably to be dated in the first half of the fifth century, although these internal troubles could be tied to the external troubles around 454.

Philolaus will have come to maturity after this split arose and is clearly to be placed on the side of the *mathematici*, given the emphasis on mathematics (including music) in the fragments. However, it need not be assumed that the *mathematici* completely abandoned the way of life followed by the *acusmatici*. The fact that they recognized the *acusmatici* as genuine Pythagoreans suggests that there was something common to the two groups and this common ground might include shared notions as to the proper way to live one's life. In the *Phaedo* Philolaus is reported to teach that one should not commit suicide, which shows his interest in ethical matters that would be shared with the *acusmatici*, but this is very likely to be oral teaching and not to have appeared in his book *On Nature*.

There are two main traditions about Philolaus' publication of books and it is crucial not to get them confused.[19] Both are reported in Diogenes' life of Philolaus, but are also found in other sources. In one tradition Philolaus is reported to have written just one book, from which Plato is supposed to have copied the *Timaeus*. Diogenes cites Hermippus (third century BC) as the authority for this story:

γέγραφε δὲ βιβλίον ἕν, ὅ φησιν Ἕρμιππος λέγειν τινὰ τῶν συγγραφέων Πλάτωνα τὸν φιλόσοφον παραγενόμενον εἰς Σικελίαν πρὸς Διονύσιον ὠνήσασθαι παρὰ τῶν συγγενῶν τοῦ Φιλολάου ἀργυρίου Ἀλεξανδρινῶν μνῶν τετταράκοντα καὶ ἐντεῦθεν μεταγεγραφέναι τὸν Τίμαιον. ἕτεροι δὲ λέγουσι τὸν Πλάτωνα λαβεῖν αὐτά, παρὰ Διονυσίου παραιτησάμενον ἐκ τῆς φυλακῆς νεανίσκον ἀπηγμένον τῶν τοῦ Φιλολάου μαθητῶν.

(D.L. 8.85)

---

[19] Burkert (1972: 223ff n. 27) points out that Wiersma (1942) first correctly analyzed the tradition.

He has written one book which, according to Hermippus, some one of the prose authors said Plato the philosopher bought from the relatives of Philolaus for forty Alexandrine (!) minae, when he was visiting Dionysius in Sicily, from which he copied the Timaeus. *Others say that Plato received it because he had procured from Dionysius the release from prison of a young disciple of Philolaus who had been arrested.*

This story is current even earlier than Hermippus, as is shown by the following lines of Timon the sillographer (320–230) which say in reference to Plato:

πολλῶν δ' ἀργυρίων ὀλίγην ἠλλάξαο βίβλον,
ἔνθεν ἀπαρχόμενος τιμαιογραφεῖν ἐδιδάχθης.   (F54 = DK 44 A8)

You paid a lot of silver for a little book, starting from which you learned to write the Timaeus.

Once again there is the emphasis on one book and a connection to the *Timaeus*. Although the plagiarism story is of course absurd, that is no reason to reject the existence of Philolaus' book. The fragments we have from that book do show a general similarity in content to the *Timaeus*. This may have been enough to start the slander of Plato which probably goes back into the fourth century with other such accusations.[20]

The second tradition consistently refers to *three* books rather than one and has Plato asking Dion in a letter to buy them for 100 minae. There is no mention of the *Timaeus* in this tradition and the wording suggests that these books were not written by Philolaus himself, but are simply in his possession. This story is mentioned in Diogenes' life of Philolaus and a number of other sources but is stated most fully in Diogenes' life of Plato (3.9).[21]

λέγουσι δέ τινες, ὧν ἐστι καὶ Σάτυρος, ὅτι Δίωνι ἐπέστειλεν εἰς Σικελίαν ὠνήσασθαι τρία βιβλία Πυθαγορικὰ παρὰ Φιλολάου μνῶν ἑκατόν.

Some say, among them Satyrus [second half of third century], that he wrote Dion in Sicily to buy three Pythagorean books from Philolaus for 100 minae.

That these three books are not by Philolaus is made even clearer at

---

[20] On the charges of plagiarism against Plato see Burkert 1972: 226–7 n. 40 and 41.
[21] See also D.L. 8.84, Gellius 3.17.1, Iamblichus, *VP* 199 and Cic. *Resp.* 1.16.

D.L. 8.15:

μέχρι δὲ Φιλολάου οὐκ ἦν τι γνῶναι Πυθαγόρειον δόγμα· οὗτος
δὲ μόνος ἐξήνεγκε τὰ διαβόητα τρία βιβλία, ἃ Πλάτων ἐπέστειλεν
ἑκατὸν μνῶν ὠνηθῆναι.

*Until the time of Philolaus it was not possible at all to learn the Pytha-
gorean teaching. But he alone brought forth the famous three books which
Plato asked in a letter to be bought for 100 minae.*

Here Philolaus is said to "bring forth" (ἐξήνεγκε) the three books,
which surely indicates that he made them public rather than that he
wrote them. It is now recognized that the three Pythagorean books
in question must be the tripartitum referred to at D.L. 8.6 consisting
of *On Education, On Statesmanship*, and *On Nature* and supposedly written by Pythagoras himself, but which are really forgeries of the third
century. The letter of Plato to Dion asking him to purchase the
books from Philolaus was probably a forgery used to establish the
authenticity of the tripartitum.[22]

This second tradition then is likely to be a fabrication of the third
century. However, the first tradition, according to which Philolaus
wrote one book that bore some resemblance to the *Timaeus*, should
be accepted. Menon, the pupil of Aristotle, is clearly using a written
source for the rather detailed account of Philolaus' medical views
that he gives in his history of medicine so that the book must have
been available still in the later part of the fourth century.[23] As
Burkert points out, Aristotle also had the book and was not just
relying on oral sources, as is made clear by the language he uses in
discussing Pythagorean cosmogony:

οἱ μὲν οὖν Πυθαγόρειοι πότερον οὐ ποιοῦσιν ἢ ποιοῦσι γένεσιν
οὐδὲν δεῖ διστάζειν· φανερῶς γὰρ λέγουσιν ὡς…

(Metaph. 1091a13ff)

*There is no need to dispute whether or not the Pythagoreans make a
generation [of things eternal], for they clearly say…*

Aristotle's remark only has force if he is pointing to a text to support
his point. (The text is in fact preserved as F7 of Philolaus.)

---

[22] For the tripartitum see Burkert 1972: 225, Diels 1890, and Thesleff 1965: 170–2. For the
letter of Plato to Dion as a forged preface to the tripartitum see Burkert 1972: 224 n. 30.
[23] DK 44A27.

This book of Philolaus is also likely to be the first book written by a Pythagorean. The idea that Philolaus was the first to make Pythagorean ideas public is found in the report at D.L. 8.15 quoted above and is repeated in several other sources all in connection with the suspect story of Plato's purchase of the three books.[24] But the idea that Philolaus was the first Pythagorean to publish a book is supported by testimonia that do not mention the three books. Thus D.L. 8.55 joins Empedocles to Philolaus as the first to make Pythagorean ideas public. But most important is a statement made in Diogenes' life of Philolaus (8.85) on the authority of Demetrius of Magnesia (fl.50 BC):

τοῦτόν φησι Δημήτριος ἐν Ὁμωνύμοις πρῶτον ἐκδοῦναι τῶν Πυθαγορικῶν Περὶ φύσεως, ὧν ἀρχὴ ἥδε...

According to Demetrius in his work Men of the Same Name, *Philolaus was the first of the Pythagoreans to publish* On Nature, *of which the beginning is as follows...* [F1]

This statement, combined with the fact that we also have good ancient evidence that neither Pythagoras himself nor the most prominent Pythagorean thinker of the early part of the fifth century, Hippasus, wrote anything, makes it likely that Philolaus' book, perhaps entitled *On Nature* and appearing sometime in the later part of the fifth century, was in fact the first book written by a Pythagorean.[25]

With the passage of time a number of books came to be forged

---

[24] Iamblichus, *VP* 199 and Eusebius, *adv. Hierocl.* 64 = DK 44A8.

[25] Zhmud', in an interesting article with which I agree in many respects, casts doubt on the assertion that Philolaus was the first to write a book (1989: 272). He refers to "the evidence for the existence of writings by Hippasus, Alcmaeon, Menestor, Hippon and some other Pythagoreans..." But there are problems with all of these figures. Alcmaeon probably did write a book, but is almost surely not a Pythagorean. We do have enough reports about Hippasus to suggest that he could have written a book, but how are we to deal with the assertion at D.L. 8.85 that Philolaus was the first Pythagorean to write a book and the corresponding statement at D.L. 8.84 which states explicitly that Hippasus wrote nothing? Menestor is a very shadowy figure. He probably did write a book, but so far as we can tell it was limited to botanical topics. His identification as a Pythagorean is based only on Iamblichus' catalogue (which includes Parmenides and Melissus as Pythagoreans). Furthermore, the evidence for his date is so insecure that he may just as easily have written after Philolaus as before. I would be the first to admit that we cannot be certain that Philolaus was the first Pythagorean to write a book, but that hypothesis makes the best sense of the evidence which we have.

in Philolaus' name, perhaps beginning as early as the late fourth century BC. Demetrius of Magnesia in the first century BC still knows that Philolaus wrote only one book Περὶ φύσεως (D.L. 8.85), but Claudianus Mamertus in the fifth century AD refers to "many volumes" written by Philolaus (2.3 = F22). The central genuine fragments dealing with limiters and unlimiteds, and agreeing with Aristotle's testomony (Frs. 1, 2, 4–7) are referred to by Demetrius (F1) and by Nicomachus (*Ench.* 9 = F6) as coming from the book Περὶ φύσεως. Stobaeus (*Eclogae* 1.21.7) presents F2 and 4–7 under the title of *On the Cosmos* (Περὶ κόσμου), but this appears to be a variation introduced because Stobaeus' own chapter heading is Περὶ κόσμου. Likewise the genuine F13 is cited as from *On Nature* in the *Theologumena arithmeticae* (25.17). Theo Smyrnaeus also refers to the title *On Nature* (106.10).

On the other hand late sources give us titles of what are probably forged books. Stobaeus presents the spurious F21 as from a work titled *On the Soul* (Περὶ ψυχῆς – 1.20.2). Claudianus Mamertus quotes a spurious fragment from the third book of *On Rhythms and Measures* (Περὶ ῥυθμῶν καὶ μέτρων – or Περὶ ἀριθμῶν καὶ μέτρων? – see F22). But the most intriguing title is the Βάκχαι which is referred to by both Proclus and Stobaeus. Proclus (*in Euc.* 22.9 = F19) regards the *Bacchae* as presenting a secret teaching about the gods, and this would fit well with the spurious material relating gods to geometrical figures which he assigns to Philolaus elsewhere (*in Euc.* 130.8 etc. – see A14). The problem is that Stobaeus assigns F17, which appears to be genuine, to the *Bacchae*. One might use this to argue against the authenticity of F17, but too much is unknown about the later external tradition to use it to rule against a fragment that appears genuine on internal grounds. Perhaps *Bacchae* is a late title given to *On Nature* (and Proclus' material about gods did not come from it), or more likely Stobaeus (or some excerptor) who was working with many books of Philolaus in front of him simply made a mistake in assigning F17 (and the missing F18) to the *Bacchae*.

2. AUTHENTICITY

The controversy about the authenticity of the fragments of Philolaus has been raging since the publication of the first and only book-length interpretive study of the fragments by Boeckh in 1819. As late as 1962 the question was still undecided, with scholarly opinion about equally divided between the two sides, so that Guthrie in the first volume of his *History of Greek Philosophy* leaves the question in doubt, although he admits that "those who impugn the fragments do not seem to be at their best on the subject" (331). However, Walter Burkert's masterful treatment of the question in *Weisheit und Wissenschaft* published in German that same year (English translation by Minar [1972]) has produced a new consensus that a core of the fragments (1–7, 13, and 17) is genuine. Thus Barnes (1982), Kahn (in Mourelatos [1974] 161–85), and Schofield (KRS 1983) in the main accept Burkert's conclusions.[1] I hope that the discussion of Philolaus' philosophy based on Fragments 1–7, 13, and 17 which is provided in the body of this book will further strengthen this consensus.

However, although I agree with Burkert on the authenticity of these central fragments and accept the criteria he uses to determine the authenticity or spuriousness of individual fragments, there are a few important cases where I differ in the application of those criteria. Thus, while I accept as spurious everything Burkert does, there are a few cases where it does not seem to me that we can accept as

---

[1] Barnes confuses matters somewhat in the introduction to the second edition where he confesses to doubts about the authenticity (1982: xx). His reasons for doubt are (1) his rejection of one of Burkert's grounds for authenticity, the argument that Philolaus' book appears to be the basis for Aristotle's account of the Pythagoreans and (2) his impression, on rereading the fragments, of the strong similarity between them and the Pythagorean pseudepigrapha. He says that he will remain skeptical pending a thorough philological study of the fragments. I have attempted to provide the latter in my commentaries on each of the fragments.

authentic fragments and testimonia which he regarded as authentic, notably F6b and testimonia A14 and A26. The authenticity of these fragments and testimonia, which have to do with Philolaus' supposed geometrical theology (A14) and arithmology disguised as music theory (F6b and A26), is crucial to Burkert's overall view of the nature of Philolaus' philosophy and in particular to his claim that early Pythagorean philosophy is based much more on number mysticism than it is on rigorous mathematics. My rejection of these fragments naturally leads to a different assessment of the role of number in Philolaus' philosophy, but is not based on an assumption of that role, but rather arises out of detailed consideration of the contents of those testimonia and fragments. The authenticity question must be addressed for each individual fragment and I have done that below for both the genuine and spurious fragments. However, there are certain general problems having to do with the tradition about and authenticity of Philolaus' book and the tradition of Pythagorean pseudepigrapha which will be addressed in this introduction. I will begin by examining the general nature of the pseudepigraphical writings and then consider the specific case of Philolaus in light of this tradition in an attempt to respond to the major arguments that have been brought against their authenticity.

It sometimes seems as if most of the questions about the authenticity of ancient works are the results of over-zealous philologists who determine that a given work is not "worthy" of one of the great classical authors.[2] Indeed, in the case of most ancient authors the presumption is that anything handed down in their name is authentic and a large onus of proof must be placed on any scholar who is doubtful. However, the situation is almost reversed in the case of ancient Pythagorean writings. In this case there is a large body of demonstrably spurious material, but only a very meagre number of texts that can with some confidence be regarded as genuine works of Pythagorean authors of the fifth and fourth century. For the sake of a rough comparison it is enough to note that Thesleff's collection of the pseudepigrapha is over 200 pages long while the fragments of early Pythagoreans in DK which are likely to be authentic (i.e.

---

[2] Bywater applies this nebulous criterion of "worthiness of a great mind" to Philolaus when he requires, as one of the standards of authenticity, that the fragments show "the coherence by which an original effort of mind is distinguished from a mere compilation" (1868: 29).

some of Archytas and Philolaus) cover only ten or twenty pages at most. In the face of this evidence, any fragment that purports to be by an early Pythagorean has to be regarded with the most extreme skepticism and subjected to minute analysis.

Just how obviously spurious most of the pseudepigrapha are can be seen from a few noteworthy examples. The *Timaeus Locrus* is the most famous case. It is correctly described as a precis of Plato's *Timaeus* and follows the main outlines of that dialogue very closely, but does nonetheless "correct" Plato in light of Aristotle's criticisms. Yet it is presented as a treatise by the Timaeus whom Plato used as the main speaker in his dialogue and is accepted as the model Plato followed by later Neoplatonists such as Proclus. It may be that the *Timaeus Locrus*, at least in part, arose not too long after Plato. There are intriguing connections with Aristotle and the early Academy, although it is first quoted by Nicomachus in the second century AD.[3] What is most important to note is that, apart from a Doric coloring to the language, there is no real attempt to make the treatise archaic. It uses Platonic and Aristotelian terminology freely and presupposes Platonic and Aristotelian concepts. Needless to say there is nothing in it that corresponds with the more "archaic" Pythagoreanism of the fifth century as Aristotle reports it.

The situation is much the same with the most famous of the other forgeries, the writing ascribed to Ocellus.[4] In this case the treatise is not simply a precis of a specific Platonic or Aristotelian work, but nonetheless it does contain several passages that are taken word for word from Aristotle's *On Generation and Corruption*, so that it was regarded as the work which was the original of Aristotle's treatise by some of the Neoplatonists (Syrianus, *in Metaph.* 175.11). Similarly, two different treatises are ascribed to Archytas on the topic of "universal assertions," which put forth a theory of categories.[5] While these treatises do show some differences in treatment both among themselves and from Aristotle's *Categories*, they nevertheless put forward a theory of exactly ten categories with exactly the same names

---

[3] See Marg's text and commentary (1972), Thesleff (1961), and Ryle (1965). The latter's account of the origins of the *Timaeus Locrus* is fantastic, but his study of its characteristics is valuable.

[4] See Thesleff (1961) and the edition by Harder (1926).

[5] See Thesleff (1965) and (1961) and Szlezak (1972) who dates Περὶ τοῦ καθόλου λόγου between 50 BC and AD 150 while Καθολικοὶ λόγοι δέκα is much later still.

as Aristotle's categories. Once again some figures in the later tradition regarded them as the originals on which Aristotle based his work (see Thesleff 1965: 21). The vast majority of the pseudo-Pythagorean texts fit this pattern of relatively obvious dependence on Platonic and Aristotelian conceptions with only the Doric dialect to speak for their authenticity. Similarly they have little in common with the Pythagoreans that Aristotle describes as working in the fifth century.

It is of course natural to ask why such forgeries arose. Who thought they were fooling whom about what and when? This is a complex question that cannot be treated in full here.[6] Certainly there is enough variety in the texts that one explanation will hardly be sufficient to explain the whole mass. However, some important general observations can be made. First, it is one of the most salient doctrines of the Pythagoreanizing Neoplatonic tradition that the truth about reality was given as a revelation of the gods very early on in human history to certain important figures, most notably Pythagoras, who then brought that view to humanity. Greek philosophy is then, in so far as it is true, seen as the unfolding of the original Pythagorean revelation with some false steps, mostly by Aristotle. What in effect happens is that Platonism comes to be identified with the divine revelation given to Pythagoras and hence as Pythagoreanism. O'Meara (1989) has carefully traced this tradition from Numenius in the second century AD through Iamblichus' central work, *On Pythagoreanism* (third–fourth century AD), to Syrianus and Proclus in the fifth century AD. It is obvious that such an attitude towards the history of philosophy provides a fertile soil in which forgeries may grow. All the texts of Plato and Aristotle which unfold the Pythagorean revelation survived, but there was precious little to point to in the way of original Pythagorean texts to support the thesis that philosophy was ultimately of Pythagorean origin. Certainly Aristotle's characterization of early Pythagoreanism as just a rather odd variety of Presocratic thought could not be accepted.

However, despite the fact that the Neoplatonic attitude to Pythagoras provided an ideal motive for forgeries, most of the pseudepi-

---

[6] Thesleff (1961) gives a thorough discussion. While his edition of the texts and introduction to them is invaluable, and his view that the texts mostly belong to the Hellenistic period is convincing, the details of his account of the origin of the treatises go far beyond the evidence we have.

grapha are clearly earlier than the Neoplatonists we have talked about so far. The *Timaeus Locrus* is referred to already in the second century AD and the first mention of Ocellus goes back even further, to the first century BC. Nonetheless, even if the forgeries do not arise among the Neoplatonists, the Neoplatonic attitude towards Pythagoras and hence the motive for forgery could go back much earlier.

It does not go back to Aristotle. Aristotle does startle us, in the account of his predecessors' views on causation in Book I of the *Metaphysics* (987a29), when he asserts that Plato's philosophy followed that of the Pythagoreans in most things. However, he also says that there were features that were unique to Plato and in his account of the origins of Plato's philosophy he emphasizes Cratylus, the follower of Heraclitus, and Socrates. Indeed, the Platonic theory of forms is explained as originating from these influences without any mention of the Pythagoreans, although it is true that Aristotle connects Plato's theory of the "participation" of things in forms with a Pythagorean theory of things "imitating" numbers. Nonetheless, Aristotle is crystal clear that there are crucial points that distinguish the Pythagoreans from Plato. First, while Plato is said to agree with the Pythagoreans in regarding numbers as the causes of being of everything else, he posited a separate realm of mathematicals between forms and sensibles, whereas the Pythagoreans did not separate numbers from things or posit a separate realm of mathematicals. Secondly, Plato is said to resemble the Pythagoreans in regarding the one as a substance rather than a predicate of some other entity, but whereas the Pythagoreans postulate a single unlimited, Plato uniquely regards the unlimited as a dyad consisting of the great and the small. Thus while Aristotle sees a clear connection between Plato and the Pythagoreans and even sees advantages to the Pythagorean system in some ways (e.g. the fact that they did not separate numbers from things) he presents a clear distinction between Plato and the Pythagoreans and certainly does not regard the Pythagorean system as worthy of veneration as a divinely inspired revelation of the truth. Indeed, he is constantly complaining of its shortcomings.

As has been shown above, this Aristotelian account of things did not win favor in the later Neoplatonic tradition and was explicitly repudiated in some places (Syrianus, *in Metaph.* 104.9ff). Burkert

(1972: 53ff) has shown that Aristotle's account of the Pythagoreans is sometimes represented in the doxographical tradition in reports on the Pythagoreans. However, alongside these reports are testimonia that refer to Pythagoras himself (whom Aristotle seldom mentions) and which completely ignore Aristotle's careful distinctions between Plato and the Pythagoreans. These testimonia, in direct contradiction to Aristotle, assign to "Pythagoras and Plato" the Platonic doctrine of the one and the indefinite dyad as first principles (so the Pythagorean *Memoirs* at D.L. 8.25, Aetius 1.3.8, and especially Sextus *P.* 3.151–67 and *M.* 10.248–309). Thus, something like the Neoplatonic attitude to Pythagoreanism already exists in the doxographical tradition alongside the Aristotelian point of view. How far back can this attitude be traced?

There is in fact good evidence that it already existed in one of the main sources of the doxographical tradition, Aristotle's pupil Theophrastus, and that he derived it from members of the early Academy of the late fourth and early third centuries BC. Thus, something like the Neoplatonic view of Pythagoras existed already at the time of Aristotle and in contrast to Aristotle's view. At the end of his short *Metaphysics* (11a27) Theophrastus makes the following statement:

> *Plato and the Pythagoreans make the distance between the real and the things of nature a great one, but hold that all things wish to imitate the real; yet since they make a sort of opposition between the One and the indefinite dyad, on which essentially depends what is indefinite and disordered and, so to speak, all shapelessness, it is absolutely impossible that for them the nature of the whole should exist without the indefinite dyad; they say that it has an equal share in things with, or even predominates over, the other principle; whereby they make even the first principles contrary to one another.*
> (tr. Ross-Fobes)

This is a clear break with Aristotle's account of the tradition in so far as Theophrastus joins the Pythagoreans with Plato as (1) positing "a great distance" between the real and the things of nature (Aristotle consistently portrays the Pythagoreans as not postulating any gap between their first principles and the things of nature) (2) adopting the one and the indefinite dyad (which Aristotle labels as specifically Platonic) as first principles, and (3) arguing that it was impossible for the world to arise unless the indefinite dyad is postulated along with the one. This virtual identification of Pythagoreans with Plato regarding first principles also seems to have been shared by Plato's immediate successor, Speusippus. In William of Moerbeke's Latin translation of Proclus' commentary on Plato's *Parmenides* there is a passage in which Proclus quotes from Speusippus (F48T). Proclus introduces the quotation by saying that Speusippus is reporting the views of "the ancients" and then continues:

> *What does he [i.e. Speusippus] say? "For they held that the One is higher than being and is the source of being; and they delivered it from that status which is in accord with (its being) a principle. On the other hand, they held that given the One, in itself, conceived as separate and alone, without the other things, with no additional element, nothing else would come into existence. And so they introduced the indefinite duality as the principle of beings."*
>
> (tr. after Anscombe and Labowsky in Klibansky and Labowsky 1953: 39–41)

Although there is some controversy in interpreting this passage, it appears that Speusippus regarded these ancients as having first posited the one as a principle that was above being and the source of being. However, they then realized that, if this principle alone were posited, nothing else would come to be and accordingly introduced the indefinite dyad as a principle of beings.[7] This seems to be exactly what Theophrastus is saying when he reports that the Pythagoreans and Plato posited a principle at a great distance from reality (i.e. the one), but then recognized that it was impossible for the nature of the whole to exist unless there were also another principle, the indefinite dyad. Thus, there can hardly be any doubt that the ancients to whom Speusippus was referring are the Pythagoreans, and it seems likely that Theophrastus is following Speusippus rather than Aristotle in his report on the Pythagoreans in the *Metaphysics*. Accordingly it is clear that already among Plato's immediate successors in the Academy there was a tendency to equate Plato's mature philo-

---

[7] Burkert (1972: 63) first brought attention to the importance of this passage. Taran (1981: 350ff) argues against Burkert's interpretation, but despite showing some difficulties in interpreting the text does not produce a convincing reading. He takes Proclus' statement that Speusippus is producing the views of the ancients to mean simply that Proclus, not Speusippus, regards these as views of the ancients. However, Proclus' remark makes much more sense as an explanation of who Speusippus is referring to with the plural subjects in the passage. Burkert's reading of Speusippus is also supported by the tie to Theophrastus (*Metaph.* 11a27)

sophy with Pythagoreanism. Certainly there is also abundant evidence that the early Academy was fascinated by Pythagoreanism.

In addition to Speusippus' statement above which ties the Pythagoreans to what Aristotle tells us is the Platonic pair of principles, the one and the indefinite dyad, we have evidence that Speusippus wrote a book entitled *On Pythagorean Numbers* (Philolaus A13 = F28 Taran). His successor as head of the Academy, Xenocrates, wrote two works on numbers and also a work on things Pythagorean (D.L. 4.13). There is also one direct statement by Xenocrates about Pythagoras himself (F9) in which he ascribes to the master the discovery that the musical intervals have their origin in number. It is also clear that the Platonic dialogue with some of the strongest connections to the Pythagoreans, the *Timaeus*, was central in the early Academy and Crantor, a member of the Academy in the early third century, is reported to have written the first commentary on it.

Our knowledge of the early Academy is too meagre to be sure of all the nuances of the Academic view of the relation between Pythagoreans and Plato, but it is clear that the tendency is to identify the doctrines of Plato and Pythagoras even more closely than Aristotle does and there is no evidence for the clear distinctions on specific points which Aristotle develops. The most plausible reading of these divergent views is that Aristotle, based on whatever Pythagorean writings and oral traditions he had access to, felt it was possible to distinguish Plato clearly from the Pythagoreans. The Academic tradition on the other hand seems to have felt that Platonic ideas were really just developments of what was already implicit in the Pythagorean position. This latter view certainly would contribute to confusion as to what is original to Plato and what is taken from the Pythagoreans. What we have is another version of the Socratic question, but this time in regard to the Pythagoreans. As Burkert points out, the problem clearly has its origin, at least in part, in Plato's use of the dialogue form and his reluctance to identify himself clearly with any one point of view (1972: 93).

There may in fact be a sense in which the Academic and Neoplatonic attitude towards Pythagoras originates in Plato himself. Certainly Proclus (*Plat. Th.* 1.5) quotes Plato's description of those who first made the limit and the unlimited basic principles (i.e. the Pythagoreans) as "dwellers with the gods" (*Philebus* 16c8) as evidence for the view that a divine revelation of the truth was given to the Pythagoreans and that Plato took over "the complete science of the gods" from them. Most modern scholars would take Plato's assertion as a literary fashion of some sort and note that he clearly seems to take a basic distinction of the Pythagoreans (limiters and unlimiteds) and make it his own by developing it within his own system, but the Neoplatonists obviously took Plato's remark quite literally and, as the evidence given above shows, the early Academy appears closer to the Neoplatonist point of view. Given the literary form of the *Philebus*, it is simply very hard to be sure to what extent Plato sees himself as simply explicating Pythagorean ideas as opposed to using them just as a starting point for his own original insights.

Thus the environment of the early Academy was such that several different views on the relation between Plato and the Pythagoreans could well develop which would contribute to the development of treatises written in the name of supposed early Pythagoreans. First, those who were hostile to Plato for whatever reason would be interested in showing him as a mere copier of earlier Pythagorean wisdom and hence be motivated to construct the Pythagorean treatises which he copied. Such an attitude to Plato is clear in the story current in the third century that he bought a book from Philolaus and copied the *Timaeus* from it.[8] Others who are not hostile to Plato, but still anxious to glorify Pythagoras and Pythagoreans, would also have a motive to develop texts which show Pythagoreans anticipating Platonic ideas, perhaps even in response to Aristotle's claims that Plato developed ideas that went beyond Pythagoreanism. Finally, there is the possibility that some members of the Academy or other adherents of the Academic view on Pythagoreanism might conceive of themselves as writing in the Pythagorean tradition and therefore present their own contributions to the Pythagorean tradition under the name of an early Pythagorean.[9] There are probably other variations on these motivations that could be developed and we cannot be sure of the relative importance of these various motives given our ignorance about the Academy. There is an important

[8] Charges of copying by Plato do not inevitably mean that his alleged models are forgeries; such charges also arise from the "clever" discovery of Platonic ideas in a genuinely early text (Burkert 1972: 227).

[9] Thesleff (1961: 76) argues that most of the pseudepigrapha which are in Archytas' name and various Italiote names are not really forgeries. He ascribes them to Pythagoreans writing in southern Italy in the third century who adopt a literary fashion of writing in the name of Archytas or other early Pythagoreans.

point to note about all these motivations, however. All of them would lead to documents that show the Pythagoreans working with sophisticated Platonic and Aristotelian concepts. It is just such documents that we find in the Pythagorean pseudepigrapha collected by Thesleff. There would be no reason to show them as members of the Presocratic milieu taking the tentative first steps towards important later distinctions, nor to show them as the Pythagoreans whom Aristotle presents as the somewhat confused predecessors of Plato. Indeed this sort of text is not to be found among the pseudepigrapha.

With this account of the character of the Pythagorean pseudepigrapha and some of the likely reasons for the genesis of such writings as background, it is now appropriate to turn to the specific case of Philolaus. The two most prominent reasons that have led scholars to reject the authenticity of the fragments are (1) Aristotle's failure to mention Philolaus' book and (2) the assumption that the fragments are either all genuine or all spurious. I will discuss Aristotle's relation to Philolaus' book below and focus on the mistaken assumption of unity of the fragments first. Boeckh (1819: 38) introduced this pernicious assumption as part of his defence of the authenticity of the fragments and opponents of the authenticity have been quick to follow (e.g. Burnet, Bywater, Raven, Frank).[10] Indeed, it makes their case against the fragments very easy; simply focus on the most problematic fragments, show that they cannot be genuine and dismiss the rest with little discussion.[11] The justification for this assumption seems to be that, since some of the testimonia about Philolaus' book mention only one book, all the fragments that survive must be from that one book. However, while the one-book tradition for Philolaus is fairly early (third century BC) and thus confirms that there was only one *genuine* book of Philolaus, the later tradition gives

---

[10] Bywater (1868: 50) and Burnet (1948: 282) state the assumption explicitly and refer to Boeckh. Raven is not so explicit, but in responding to Mondolfo's defense of the fragments he concedes that that defense works in many cases, but argues that the spuriousness of the fragments is likely because of "the unduly large number of such suspicious or unusual features" (KR: 309). But this latter point only makes sense if one assumes that all the fragments must be taken together to form a unity. Frank was more careful in that he did not *assume* that there was only one book, but his attempt to show the unity of the spurious F21 with Fragments 1–7 is incredibly weak.

[11] Bywater's study is particularly deceptive in this way. For example, when he is examining anachronisms in the use of expressions found in the fragments, of the eleven examples that he gives no less than nine come from one fragment, F21, which almost everyone regards as spurious (1868: 52). Burnet (1948: 283) takes it as self-evident that F12 is spurious and on this basis rejects the rest of the fragments, which he hardly discusses.

26

clear evidence that other books were circulating in Philolaus' name (see Pt. I, ch. 1 above). Moreover, given the massive amount of forgery in the Pythagorean tradition, it is extremely unlikely that there should not be some works forged in the relatively famous name of Philolaus to go along with the fragments of the book he actually wrote. The case of Archytas provides good evidence for this suggestion. There are forty-six pages of spurious fragments of Archytas in Thesleff's collection (1965: 2–48) in comparison with eight short pages of fragments likely to be authentic in DK. Thus, in the face of both the later tradition about Philolaus' "many volumes" and also the luxuriant Pythagorean pseudepigrapha, it is totally unjustified simply to assume that all the fragments preserved in Philolaus' name came from one book and must stand or fall together. We must judge the authenticity of each fragment of Philolaus individually and argue for its connections to other fragments rather than assuming them.

In developing criteria to decide the authenticity or spuriousness of individual fragments, it must be recognized that the crucial feature which characterizes the Pythagorean pseudepigrapha is the use of mature Platonic and Aristotelian distinctions and language. These treatises do not try to make the Pythagoreans speak in the terms one would expect of Presocratics writing in the fifth century, but rather show them as conversant with the developed philosophy of the Platonic and Aristotelian schools. Particularly prominent are the Platonic ideas of the one and indefinite dyad, the demiurge, tripartite structure of the soul, and the world soul, as are the Aristotelian distinctions of form and matter, and the distinction between the supra- and sublunary spheres.[12] A coloring of Doric dialect is the only evidence of an attempt to make these texts appear "authentic."[13] Most of the scholars who have attacked the fragments of Philolaus have done so by attempting to show that like other pseud-

---

[12] Bywater felt that the presence of *any* metaphysical significance for number or any sophistication in addressing epistemological questions (1868: 33, 35) was evidence that a fragment was spurious, and uses these criteria against the fragments that agree with Aristotle. However, it is surely rash to deny the Pythagoreans any interest in the metaphysical questions raised by the Presocratic tradition.

[13] The fact that the fragments of Philolaus are also in Doric need not mean that they are forgeries. Burnet (1948: 282) particularly emphasized that Philolaus was unlikely to have written in Doric since Ionic was the dialect of philosophy and science until the latter part of the fifth century. However, Burkert (1972: 222ff.) points out that the physician Acron of Acragas (fl. *c.* 430) is supposed to have written in Doric as did the rhetoricians Tisias and Corax. Most scholars (including Burnet) accept that Archytas wrote in Doric. He could have been following Philolaus' earlier example.

epigraphical treatises they assume Platonic and Aristotelian ideas. Such attacks are naturally successful since many of the fragments assigned to Philolaus do have such ideas and are spurious. Where such attacks fall down is in their attempt to show that *all* the fragments fit this pattern.

Particularly problematic for these attacks on authenticity is a group of fragments (1–7) which have long been recognized as showing strong similarities to Aristotle's reports on the Pythagoreans, even by opponents of authenticity. However, very recently both Barnes and Philip have tried to argue that Aristotle's reports cannot in fact be meaningfully connected with these fragments and on these grounds Barnes has been led to doubt their authenticity once again. The problem with both Philip's and Barnes's arguments is that they do not sufficiently take account of the fact that Aristotle is reporting Pythagorean views, but always under an interpretation. What Barnes and Philip see as differences between Aristotle's Pythagoreans and Philolaus 1–7 are really just differences between Aristotle's interpretation of Philolaus and Barnes's and Philip's interpretation. The type of argument which they develop could equally show that Aristotle's reports on Parmenides or even Plato are not really based on Parmenides or Plato, because his interpretations differ so much from modern readings.

The crucial point is that all the basic conceptual terms which Aristotle assigns to the Pythagoreans are also found in Fragments 1–7 of Philolaus. The main group of Pythagoreans that Aristotle discusses in the first book of the *Metaphysics* and elsewhere are clearly said to have posited the limited and unlimited as first principles (e.g. 987a13ff and 990a9ff) and are constantly compared with Plato for doing so. These Pythagoreans are also said to have emphasized the role of number in explaining the world and to have recognized two types of number, the even and the odd, along with a third type, the even-odd, which is identified with the one (986a19). Aristotle connects the even and the odd with the unlimited and the limited respectively. These Pythagoreans are also consistently shown as interested in cosmology and are said to have seen the whole cosmos as a *harmonia* (986a3), to have explicitly talked about the generation of the cosmos (1091a13), and to have introduced a system with the earth orbiting around the central fire where a tenth orbiting body, the counter-earth, was introduced simply to fill out the perfect number 10 (986a12). However, it is precisely these concepts of limit, unlimited, harmony, number (divided into the even, the odd, and the even-odd), and the generation of a cosmos around a central fire that are prominent in Fragments 1–7 of Philolaus.[14]

Raven, having correctly recognized that these fragments agreed not with the later Platonic account of Pythagoreanism but with Aristotle's reports, attacked the fragments on different grounds than previous critics, arguing that they were forged on the basis of Aristotle. In the abstract it is not impossible to assume that someone finding no book of Philolaus in existence might accept Aristotle's account of the Pythagoreans and compose a book in Philolaus' name in accord with Aristotle's evidence. However, the concrete reality of the tradition of Pythagorean pseudepigrapha shows that this was not in fact the motive for the forgeries and is in fact antithetical to the motivation for those forgeries (i.e. to show that Pythagoreans anticipated Platonic and Aristotelian ideas). If these fragments of Philolaus were in fact forgeries which tried to be true to early Pythagoreanism and thus followed Aristotle's account, they would be a unique example of such a forgery among the pseudepigrapha. Moreover, as Raven himself notes, while many of these fragments are clearly closely tied to Aristotle's reports, some of them, although using the same conceptual matrix as Aristotle's Pythagoreans, introduce

---

[14] In the face of these clear connections between Philolaus 1–7 and Aristotle, Barnes nonetheless rejects Philolaus as the main source for Aristotle, because the connections which Aristotle gives between the unlimited and the even and the limited and the odd do not "lead to any clear overall understanding of Philolaus' theory of principles" (1982: 390). But this is most likely to be a difference between Barnes's and Aristotle's interpretation of Philolaus. Philip (1966: 121) argues that Aristotle is not drawing on Philolaus for three reasons: (1) for Philolaus limit and unlimited are not the first principles, but rather "an eternal being/substance from which they proceed"; (2) in Aristotle "harmonia refers especially to numerical relations in the musical chord (985b31) and in the heavens (986a2)" while in Philolaus it has an ordering function in the cosmos; (3) for Aristotle Pythagorean numbers are things while "for Philolaus things are limited, unlimited or a mixture and number makes them knowable (B4)." But (1) and (2) rest on misreadings of Philolaus. I agree with (3), but it does not seem to me that this discrepancy is best resolved by positing a different source than Philolaus for Aristotle, but rather by supposing that it is a result of Aristotelian interpretation (see Huffman 1988). Even if we were to accept Barnes's and Philip's view that Aristotle is not using Philolaus, but some other unknown Pythagorean of the fifth century, as his primary source, this would not have the disastrous results for Burkert's arguments for authenticity which Barnes suggests. If we followed Philip and Barnes and posited Pythagorean X as the source, it would still remain true that Philolaus 1–7 are much more closely connected to Pythagorean X than they are to the Pythagorean pseudepigrapha and hence that they are likely to be authentic.

ideas which Aristotle did not mention and that therefore could not be the work of a forger working from Aristotle (note particularly the epistemological theme in F3 and 4 which is lacking in Aristotle). Thus, it surely becomes more plausible to assume that these fragments agree with Aristotle's reports on the Pythagoreans because they are genuine and derived from Philolaus' book which was one of Aristotle's sources.

We have one important piece of evidence which is independent of Aristotle and which shows that there was a genuine book by Philolaus in existence in the fourth century to which Aristotle could have referred. Aristotle's pupil, Meno, put together a history of medicine sometime around the end of the fourth century. Parts of this treatise are preserved in a papyrus known as the Anonymus Londinensis and they include a discussion of Philolaus' views about the origin of diseases (DK A27). This discussion is detailed and technical enough that it is surely based on a written text which is overwhelmingly likely to be a book by Philolaus. It is true, as has been shown above, that the situation in the Academy in the late fourth century is such that attribution of Platonic and Aristotelian ideas to early Pythagoreans is already a possibility, but it is very implausible that Meno, who was a contemporary, would accept Academic ideas as belonging to Philolaus when trying to write the history of earlier medicine. Moreover, the Academy does not seem to have been strongly interested in medical theory and the ideas which Meno assigns to Philolaus are very plausible for a figure of the fifth century and show no suspicious connections with the Academy. This book which Meno consulted in the late fourth century is also likely to be the "one" book that Philolaus is supposed to have written and which Plato supposedly bought from Philolaus' relatives (D.L. 8.85). It is possible that this book was a forgery developed under the influence of the Academy's interest in Pythagoreanism, but the emphasis on Philolaus' having written only *one* book is perhaps a reaction to the appearance of works forged in Philolaus' name and suggests that the book in question is the one which Meno had consulted earlier. The additional fact that the book is described as small would fit with the typically small size of a Presocratic treatise. Thus, starting from the time of Meno there is good evidence, independent of Aristotle, for the existence of a single book by Philolaus.

We thus arrive at the criteria for determining authenticity which

Burkert follows in his defense of the fragments. Fragments which belong to the conceptual world of the Pythagoreans as Aristotle describes them are likely to be authentic. On the other hand, fragments which use mature Platonic and Aristotelian ideas and show strong similarities to other Pythagorean pseudepigrapha in style and content are drawn from works forged in Philolaus' name. Close connection to the ideas of figures from the early Academy such as Speusippus and Xenocrates and the tradition of commentary on the *Timaeus* are also grounds for suspicion. The results of the application of these criteria which are arrived at by Burkert, and with which I agree in the main, show that only something like a third of the material, in terms of number of lines, is likely to be authentic. This result is not at all surprising given the pseudepigraphical tradition as a whole.

The only remaining reason for rejecting this strong cumulative evidence for a book by Philolaus, which survived into the fourth century and which Aristotle used, is the fact that neither Plato nor Aristotle mentions the book directly. Plato's mention of Philolaus in the *Phaedo* is very brief and only alludes to his prohibition on suicide, which could easily be derived from an oral source, and in fact would be unlikely to be included in the subject matter of *On Nature*. Similarly, Aristotle only mentions Philolaus by name once, in a passage in the *Eudemian Ethics*, which assigns the gnomic sentence "there are *logoi* which are too strong for us" to Philolaus. Clearly this too is most likely based on oral tradition rather than anything written. However, there is nothing in the *Phaedo* that indicates that Philolaus did *not* write a book either, nor is it surprising that he does not mention Philolaus elsewhere given that he makes no direct mention at all in the dialogues of important figures such as Democritus, whom he probably saw as an opponent, or even his good friend Archytas who is mentioned in the letters.

Aristotle's silence is more puzzling. Both Raven (KR 310) and Burnet (1948: 284 n. 2) thought it was "inconceivable" that he could have used Philolaus' book and yet only referred to him once. However, Aristotle is famous for mentioning few Pythagoreans by name and more commonly ascribing doctrines to "the so-called Pythagoreans" (οἱ καλούμενοι Πυθαγόρειοι). However, as Burkert points out (1972: 236), the detailed nature of Aristotle's reports (see especially *Metaph.* 1091a14) presupposes use of some written text and that text can hardly have had "the so-called Pythagoreans" as its author. Aristotle must have used a text (or texts) by a specific author in addition to oral reports, and the similarity with the Philolaus fragments shows that Philolaus' book was an important source. Indeed, even if nothing of Philolaus' book survived to compare with Aristotle, study of the Pythagorean tradition would lead to the same conclusion. The tradition shows that no one is likely to have written before Philolaus, and Archytas is the only figure that we can be sure wrote a book after him. Since Aristotle wrote separate books about Archytas and the Pythagoreans, it is clear that Archytas is not the source for the main body of the reports, leaving Philolaus' book as the only likely candidate. This means that Aristotle chose to report much of what he read in Philolaus as the views of "the so-called Pythagoreans" rather than just as the views of Philolaus. But why should Aristotle do this? The answer will hinge on what is implied by Aristotle's strange phrase.

Considerable attention has been paid to this question, but there is no uniformly accepted interpretation (see Burkert 1972: 29 ff). Clearly the addition of "so-called" (καλούμενοι) indicates some sort of reservation about the use of "Pythagoreans" to describe the people whose views Aristotle discusses and is roughly equivalent to the modern use of quotation marks. Most people would reject Frank's contention that the phrase shows that these people were not really Pythagoreans at all. Frank used this interpretation to support his idea that the Pythagorean views which Aristotle discusses really refer to Archytas in the fourth century or to members of the Academy (1923: 77). However, this is pure fancy on Frank's part, since Aristotle clearly identifies these Pythagoreans as living before or contemporaneously with the atomists. In response to Frank's interpretation of the phrase, Cherniss aptly points to *Politics* 1290b40 where Aristotle is talking about the various parts of the state and refers to one of them as "the so-called farmers" (οἱ καλούμενοι γεωργοί) and where he cannot be calling into question that they are really farmers. Cherniss then concludes that the addition of the participle shows that Aristotle is using the substantives "as designations in the currently designated sense" (1959: 37–8). This makes the important point that in calling these people Pythagoreans Aristotle is following the current practice, but Cherniss does not explain why Aristotle feels that he has to point this out.

The case of the farmers at *Politics* 1290b40 needs to be examined further. The context shows that the reason Aristotle uses "so-called" (καλούμενοι) here is that the commonly used term "farmer" does not literally apply to all the members of this part of the state. Aristotle defines this part of the state as τὸ περὶ τὴν τροφὴν πλῆθος ("the mass of people concerned with feeding [the state]"). Farmers clearly are the leading members of this class and this is why current usage refers to the whole group as "farmers," but there are members of the food-providing class who are not farmers in the literal sense, for example hunters and fishermen. The exact same thing is happening when Aristotle goes on in the next sentence (1291a1) to call the second class τὸ καλούμενον βάναυσον. This class Aristotle then defines as "the class that has to do with the arts" (τὸ περὶ τὰς τέχνας). Here the problem is that the current technical term for this class τὸ βάναυσον suggests that all of its members work with a forge (βαῦνος) while many craftsmen will not literally use one. Thus, these two cases clearly suggest that Aristotle is pointing to current technical terms that do not literally apply to all members of the class that they designate.

In the most extreme case it might suggest that the term does not literally apply to any of the members. This seems to be the case in two passages where Aristotle refers to views expressed ἐν τοῖς καλουμένοις 'Ορφέως ἔπεσιν ("in the so-called verses of Orpheus," *GA* 734a19; *De an.* 410b27). In these cases Aristotle is surely suggesting that although the verses are said to be by Orpheus he does not think they really are and refers to them as Orphic because that is the technical term in common use to refer to them. This is the way Philoponus reads Aristotle in his commentary on the passage, and Philoponus reports that Aristotle says this explicitly in his dialogue *On Philosophy.*

If we return now to the Pythagoreans, it is clear that Aristotle felt that the use of the term "Pythagoreans" did not literally describe either all or some of the class of people to whom it was usually applied. Both Zeller and Minar have suggested that properly the term Πυθαγόρειοι refers to a political association and Aristotle is pointing out that some members of the group had philosophical and religious ties and not just political ones (Zeller 1923: 446 n. 1; Minar 1942: 21). There may well be some truth in this, but the old view adopted by Ross is probably also at the heart of the matter. Ross thought that Aristotle was simply indicating that he regarded Pythagoras as a largely legendary figure and "... will not vouch for the origin of any of their doctrines in Pythagoras himself" (1924: 143). I would suggest that the use of terms such as "Pythagoreans," "Anaxagoreans," and "Heraclitaeans" (Πυθαγόρειοι, Ἀναξαγόρειοι, Ἡρακλείτειοι) normally suggested very close ties to the master and his doctrines. Aristotle then is recognizing that at least some of the people commonly designated as "Pythagoreans" really are developing their own ideas and that their connections to Pythagoras himself either politically or philosophically are problematic. Philolaus would seem to fit this description very well. Since he is the first Pythagorean to publish a book, he might well be supposed to be presenting original ideas whose connection with Pythagoras himself are problematic. The other "so-called Pythagoreans" with whom he is grouped would be known through oral tradition and would be likely to include Hippasus, Lysis, Eurytus, and whoever originated the theory of the *sustoicheia* which Aristotle reports.

Why it should become standard practice to refer to Philolaus as simply one of the Pythagoreans remains unclear, but Aristotle makes clear that the practice was not his invention, but one he found already in use. It may well be that the society did have a tendency to ascribe all of its discoveries to the founder, or that such a tendency had developed in the fourth century in the Platonic Academy. Aristotle "sees through" this fashion in his use of the phrase οἱ καλούμενοι Πυθαγόρειοι. Certainly such a tendency is present in much of the later tradition and is probably a major force in the creation of the Pythagorean pseudepigrapha. Thus, in the end, Aristotle's failure to mention Philolaus by name represents the common fashion of referring to the Pythagoreans at that time, a fashion that may well have arisen in the school itself, and one that Aristotle is uncomfortable with perhaps in large part because he had a book in Philolaus' name in front of him, the contents of which he could not believe went back to the shadowy figure of Pythagoras himself.

Fragments 1–7 and Testimonia 9, 16 (part), 17 (part), 18–21 are almost surely from that book because of their similarity to Aristotle's reports. Likewise the testimonia on Philolaus' medical views (A27–8) are guaranteed by Meno's authority. Fragments 13 and 17 cannot be closely paralleled in Aristotle's reports, but they show none of the signs of the Pythagorean pseudepigrapha and seem conceptually closer to Aristotle's Pythagoreans and should therefore be accepted as genuine. It is this group of fragments and testimonia, then, that form the basis on which Philolaus' philosophy must be reconstructed. Another group of testimonia and fragments are of uncertain authenticity largely because they are too brief to make a confident judgment on (A10, 11, 22, 23, 24; F8, 9, 20c). Each is discussed below in detail.

I have given all of the spurious fragments along with a detailed discussion of the grounds for regarding them as spurious. These fall into three main classes that overlap with one another to some extent. One class in characterized by clear use of Platonic and Aristotelian ideas and has strong parallels in the pseudo-Pythagorean tradition both in terms of content and also of style. The most obvious examples here are Fragments 21 and 11 although 12 and 23 also fall into this class. A second class show very strong connections with figures from the early Academy, especially with Xenocrates and the tradition of commentary on the *Timaeus* (A13: Speusippus; A14, F20a: Xenocrates; A12, A16b, A17b, A25, A26, F6b, F19, F20b: *Timaeus* interpretation and general Academic doctrines). F14 cannot be tied directly to the Academy, but is working with a concept of the soul that is too late for Philolaus. Finally, the third class is represented by Fragments 15 and 22 which seem to be based on an overreading of the passage on Philolaus in Plato's *Phaedo*.

Part II
PHILOLAUS' PHILOSOPHY

1. LIMITERS AND UNLIMITEDS

Philolaus' book begins with a statement of his central thesis:

> Nature in the world-order was fitted together both out of things which are unlimited (ἀπείρων) and out of things which are limiting (περαινόντων), both the world-order as a whole and everything in it.

Thus, right from the beginning the major problem in interpreting the fragments of Philolaus is easy to identify, although very difficult to answer: What is meant by "things which are unlimited" ("unlimiteds" – ἄπειρα) and "things which are limiting" ("limiters" – περαίνοντα). It is a difficult question because, although he uses the terms limiters and unlimiteds repeatedly in Fragments 1–3 and 6, Philolaus simply does not tell us what he means by limiters and unlimiteds, nor does he provide even a single explicit example of either class in the fragments which we possess. Yet, if we cannot answer this fundamental question there is little hope of gaining any real understanding of Philolaus' philosophical system.

There have been several recent hypotheses about the nature of limiters and unlimiteds. However, given the lack of clarity in the fragments, scholars have tended to put forth only brief speculations on the topic without sustained argumentation to support them. As might be expected there is quite a variety in the proposed answers. Thus, Burkert suggests that the limiters and unlimiteds correspond to material atoms and the empty interstices between atoms, but, while the ancient tradition does make a few connnections between atomists and Pythagoreans, there is no clear evidence for such atoms in anything Philolaus says, and Burkert does not in fact develop the thesis in detail (1972: 258–9). Schofield in KRS argues that Philolaus assumes knowledge on the part of his readers of Pythagorean number doctrine and accordingly intends limiters to be understood as odd numbers and unlimiteds as even numbers (1983: 326). Finally, Jonathan Barnes puts forth the hypothesis that limiters are shapes and unlimiteds are stuffs, but has no argument for the hypothesis beyond the fact that it gives Philolaus an interesting thesis without any obvious conflict with what is stated in the fragments (1982: 387ff).

All of these interpretations have the virtue of at least being based on the actual fragments of Philolaus. There is another pervasive interpretation of limiters and unlimiteds that is primarily based on Aristotle's account of the Pythagoreans and hence is heavily influenced by Platonic and Aristotelian ideas. This sort of interpretation is well represented by Guthrie (1962: 240ff) who is in turn influenced by Raven (1948). Since this interpretation is based largely on Aristotle, limiters and unlimiteds are assigned a secondary role to the real star of Pythagorean metaphysics according to Aristotle, number. The first thing that happens to limiters and unlimiteds, and this is very important, is that they become singular instead of plural and accordingly become something like "the principle of limit" and "the principle of the unlimited." This is the direct influence of Plato and Aristotle who always use the singular in discussing these terms. This principle of the unlimited and principle of limit then become totally detatched from the phenomenal world around us. They are admitted to be in fact the basic principles of number, but little attention is paid to them, since it is number that is used to explain reality. Limit and Unlimited serve the strange function of generating, or perhaps just being equivalent to, odd and even, which in turn generate numbers, which in turn generate things. Limit and Unlimited in fact appear to be largely redundant principles that explain nothing which odd and even do not.

The radical problem with this sort of interpretation is that it is not based on the actual words of any Pythagorean and it is heavily distorted by Platonic and Aristotelian conceptions of first principles. Despite Guthrie's remark that Philolaus' fragments on limiters and unlimiteds "in any case add little to our sketch of fifth-century Pythagoreanism" (1962: 333 – Guthrie is agnostic on their authenticity), taking the genuine fragments of Philolaus seriously in fact produces a radically different picture of Pythagoreanism than what we can derive from Aristotle. In what follows I will develop an interpretation of limiters and unlimiteds that is grounded as much as possible in the actual fragments of Philolaus. While the interpretations of Burkert, Barnes, and Schofield are partially based on those fragments, I do not think that they have been fully mined for information that will help to solve the problem of limiters and unlimiteds. It appears to me that Philolaus' reticence in giving examples of limiters and unlimiteds at the beginning of his book is in fact purposeful, but that if we look beyond Fragments 1–6, where limiters and unlimiteds are introduced, to examples of things which are fitted together in Philolaus' cosmogony as well as in his musical and medical theory, some possible examples of limiters and unlimiteds emerge. It will turn out that Philolaus' use of the terms limiter and unlimited can be seen not as arising out of esoteric Pythagorean doctrine, but as understandable in terms of the development of Presocratic philosophy and in response to figures such as Parmenides and Anaxagoras. Once Philolaus' limiters and unlimiteds are seen in this Presocratic context, we can appreciate his very original contribution to Greek speculation on the nature of reality.

There are five crucial things to notice about Philolaus' treatment of limiters and unlimiteds in the fragments. First, it is limiters and unlimiteds which are primary, and not number as in Aristotle's account of Pythagoreanism. When Philolaus states his central thesis about the cosmos in F1, he does not say that "all things are numbers," but rather that both the world-order as a whole and everything in it were fitted together out of limiters and unlimiteds. Indeed, in all three fragments in which Philolaus discusses the basic nature of reality (1, 2, 6) limiters and unlimiteds are mentioned repeatedly, while the word number does not even appear. Number does play an important role for Philolaus, but in the fragments, at least, number is only discussed in an epistemological context: it is what allows us to know things (F4 and F5). Of course such an epistemological role is not unrelated to considerations of the nature of the ultimate principles of reality, but, in the fragments we have, Philolaus always states his basic thesis about the nature of reality in terms of limiters and unlimiteds.

The second point to emphasize is that Philolaus always refers to limiters and unlimiteds in the plural. He uses the neuter plural of the Greek adjective "unlimited" (ἄπειρος) to refer to the unlimiteds (literally "the unlimited [things]") and the neuter plural of the present active participle of the Greek verb "to limit" (περαίνω) to refer to limiters ("the limiting [things]"). This is in direct contrast to Plato in the *Philebus* or Aristotle in the *Metaphysics* who regularly use an expression in the singular. Limit is expressed by the abstract noun πέρας ("limit") or by the perfect passive participle of the verb to limit, τὸ πεπερασμένον ("the limited"), and unlimited by the neuter singular adjective with an article, τὸ ἄπειρον ("the unlimited"). In some cases even more abstract periphrases with the word nature are used, once again always in the singular (ἡ περαίνουσα φύσις – "the limiting nature", Arist. F47; ἡ τοῦ ἀπείρου φύσις – "the nature of the unlimited", *Philebus* 24e4). Any account of limiters and unlimiteds in Philolaus should be able to explain his insistence on the use of the plural.

The third characteristic of Philolaus' limiters and unlimiteds is that they are not treated as abstract principles divorced from the world, but rather as manifest features of the world. In F2 Philolaus makes clear appeal to our direct experience of the world when he says that it is manifest (φαίνεται ... ἐόντα) that the world-order and the things in it are not from limiting things alone or unlimited things alone, but that it is clear (δῆλον) that they were fitted together from both limiting and unlimited things. The next sentence again makes an appeal to the phenomena in so far as he adduces what is clear from the way things act (δηλοῖ δὲ καὶ τὰ ἐν τοῖς ἔργοις). Some things from limiting constituents limit, others from both limiting and unlimited constituents both limit and do not limit, while some from unlimited constituents will be manifestly unlimited (ἄπειρα φανέονται). It is impossible to be sure whether these manifest features of the world are conceived of as something like sense data or whether they are only obvious once we assume the correct (i.e. Philolaic) interpretation, but limiters and unlimiteds are presented as in some sense "clear" aspects of the world.

The fourth point about Philolaus' treatment of limiters and unlimiteds in the fragments is that his failure to be more precise about what exactly counts as a limiter or an unlimited is to some extent a result of real philosophical scruple and a virtue rather than a vice in his system, when properly understood. This becomes clear from the interpretation of F6. In that fragment Philolaus eschews consideration of "nature in itself" and "eternal being" as beyond human knowledge. The only proviso that Philolaus adds is that none of the things that are and are known by us could have come to be unless we suppose the preexistence of limiters and unlimiteds. What Philolaus seems to be saying (see Pt. II, ch. 3) is that our knowledge of the ultimate reality from which the world has arisen is very limited and that attempts to define it as fire or air, etc. really go beyond what we can know. All that we can legitimately say about the ultimate reality is that it must embody the minimum conditions necessary for the world as we know it to arise. According to Philolaus, then, specifying a set of elements such as earth, air, fire, and water goes beyond (and probably also falls short of) what we are justified in supposing about the ultimate nature of reality. All Philolaus feels justified in saying is that the world around us could not have arisen without some sort of limiters and some sort of unlimiteds. Our knowledge does not allow us to specify in any more detail which limiters or unlimiteds preexist.

The final point about limiters and unlimiteds in Philolaus is that they are not in fact sufficient to explain the world-order. Philolaus goes on in F6 to argue that, since limiters and unlimiteds are inherently unlike, they would never have come together to form the world-order unless some third principle had supervened to bind them together in an order. This third principle is *harmonia* or fitting together and it was present in Philolaus' initial statement of his thesis in F1 when he asserted that all things in the cosmos are "fitted together (ἁρμόχθη) from unlimiteds and limiters." Thus, when we look at the world around us we should see limiters and unlimiteds, but also a third feature, the glue that holds them together when they are combined. The role of *harmonia* also suggests a further strategy for determining what Philolaus meant by limiters and unlimiteds. If we can find examples of things that are explicitly said by Philolaus to have been "fitted together" or "harmonized," we should be able to identify what is limiting and what unlimited in such a compound, since the explicit function of *harmonia* for Philolaus is to hold together limiters and unlimiteds.

The natural place to turn in order to find such compounds of limiters and unlimiteds is Philolaus' account of the generation of the world-order. Indeed, F7 starts with a reference to "the first thing fitted together":

The first thing fitted together (τὸ πρᾶτον ἁρμοσθέν), the one in the center of the sphere, is called the hearth.

41

This first thing that is fitted together, which is located in the center of the sphere and called the hearth, is clearly the central fire around which the earth orbits in Philolaus' astronomical system. What then are the limiters and unlimiteds from which it is fitted together? Just two elements seem to be involved, "fire" and the "center of the sphere." Thus, I would want to argue that the name "central fire" (πῦρ ἐν μέσῳ, A16; τὸ πῦρ μέσον, A17) wears on its face Philolaus' point that things in the world-order have both limiting and un-limited elements. The fire, which can be viewed as in itself a stuff undetermined by quantitative or spatial notions, can be seen as the unlimited, while the notion of the middle of the sphere in fact deter-mines the fire's position spatially and hence can reasonably be called a limiter. Locating something in the middle of a sphere clearly de-limits its relation to other parts of the sphere. Further, the fact that something is in the middle of a sphere as opposed to the middle of a cube delimits a set of relationships it can have to other parts of the cosmos, relationships that are governed by the geometrical prop-erties of the sphere. It might seem that fire and "middle" are fea-tures of the cosmos in radically different senses, but it is well to remember that Philolaus is a Presocratic author writing before Plato and Aristotle and just a little later than Anaxagoras and Empedocles who were ready to see Mind, and Love and Strife, respectively, as some sort of components of the cosmos.

The only other surviving fragment of Philolaus' book which deals with cosmogony is F17. This fragment does not refer to any "fit-ting together," nor is there any direct reference to limiters and un-limiteds. However, it can give more insight into the role of limit in Philolaus. The first section of the fragment runs as follows:

> The world-order is one, it began to come to be right up at the middle and from the middle [came to be] upwards in the same way as downwards.

The point is, as Burkert puts it, that "the cosmos develops from the center out, in each direction equally" (1972: 268). This initial state-ment is supported in the last part of the fragment by a laborious statement of the point that there is no absolute top or bottom of the sphere, but that what is up or down depends on the observer's par-ticular position in the cosmos. Thus by a principle of sufficient rea-son it is argued that there is no reason for the world-order to develop differently in one direction than in another. This fragment is in fact likely to have preceded F7 and has no reference to anything that might be called an unlimited, but rather seems to provide a set of limiting notions that will govern the generation of the cosmos. What is at issue is not the fitting together of any specific body in the cosmos, that will begin with F7, but rather the general plan of development. The limiting notion of development in all directions equally from the center, which is inherent in the spherical shape, is one of the important limiters that is combined with a variety of unlimiteds in order to generate the actual cosmic order.

There is one other important piece of evidence about Philolaus' cosmogony which can shed considerable light on what he meant by unlimiteds. This is a fragment from Aristotle's special treatise on the Pythagoreans. It appears to be based on Philolaus' cosmogony because, after describing the cosmos as one (cf. Philolaus F17), the fragment describes the cosmos as drawing things in from outside, a clear reference to Philolaus' notion of the cosmos breathing in like the new-born child. Aristotle says:

> The universe is one and it drew in (ἐπεισάγεσθαι) from the unlimited time, breath, and void which in each case distinguishes the place of each thing. (F201)

The crucial question to ask here is what it means to say that time, breath, and the void came from the unlimited. It could just mean that they came from the boundless region outside the cosmos; however, it is just as likely that time, breath, and void come from the unlimited precisely because they are unlimiteds. It seems to me that this passage of Aristotle is as close as we get to a series of examples of what Philolaus meant by unlimiteds. Certainly, breath (= air?) fits easily alongside of fire as a material which in its own nature is not determined by quantitative or spatial concepts. Void and especially time, however, show that Philolaus' unlimiteds cannot simply be identified with stuffs as Barnes suggested. Nonetheless, there is still common ground between fire and breath on the one hand and time and void on the other, which allows them all to be included together in the class of unlimiteds. Each in itself defines a continuum, but none of them is defined by any set quantity or boundaries within that continuum. They could perhaps be called quantifiables in that, although an account of their own essence would make no mention

43

of any specific quantity, each of them does admit of the imposition of boundaries or quantities from without. Sections of void can be bounded by the insertion of bodies into it, and time can be divided into segments just as fire can be enclosed in a certain shape and given a specific position. Aristotle turns this point on its head when he says that it is void that distinguishes (διορίζει) the places of things. The point presumably is that by intervening between bits of stuff void distinguishes them from each other. However, since void fits so well as a quantifiable alongside time, breath, and fire, and since Aristotle himself describes it as coming from the unlimited, it seems more likely that the notion of void "distinguishing" or setting limits is really just a careless Aristotelian formulation, whereas Philolaus would have seen the void as that in which limits are set. Thus, we now have a list of four unlimiteds (fire, breath, time, and void) which Philolaus saw as having a role in cosmogony as well as some of the limiters which structure them (the properties of a sphere including the notion of a center).

F6a presents another helpful example of what Philolaus may have meant by a fitting together of limiters and unlimiteds. After arguing in F6 for the necessity of a *harmonia* or "fitting together" in order to hold limiters and unlimiteds together, Philolaus goes on to specify the "size of the fitting together" (ἁρμονίας δὲ μέγεθος). What follows is an account of the structure of the "Pythagorean" diatonic scale or attunement that is identical to the scale that is presupposed in the *Timaeus*. What are the limiters and unlimiteds here? In accordance with what we have seen so far it would seem quite plausible to see the undefined continuum of possible musical pitches as the unlimited involved. On the other hand the limiters would be the boundaries we establish in this continuum by picking out specific pitches. If we think in terms of a monochord for illustration (begging the question of whether such an instrument was used in the fifth century), the string and the indefinite number of pitches it can produce can be compared to the unlimited, while stops placed along it to determine specific pitches are the limiters. What this example interestingly shows is the point that Philolaus is making in the first part of F6, namely that limiters and unlimiteds alone will not produce an ordered system. We can have an unlimited continuum of pitches and can set various limits to that continuum by picking out a set of pitches, but not just any set of pitches will produce a musically ordered set; such a set only results when the unlimited continuum is limited in accordance with a *harmonia* which determines a pleasing set of limits in the unlimited in accordance with number.

None of the other genuine fragments of Philolaus refer explicitly to a "fitting together" or to limiters and unlimiteds. However, Philolaus' account of the structure of the human body in F13 and his medical theories reported in A27 are both very amenable to interpretation in terms of limiters and unlimiteds. F13 divides the human body into four regions which are in turn tied to a set of distinct faculties. The head is the seat of intellect, the heart of life and sensation, the navel of rooting and first growth, the genitals of the sowing of seed and generation. The organs in these four regions are in turn associated with a hierarchy of living things; the brain being the origin (ἀρχή) of humans, the heart of animals, the navel of plants, and the genitals common to all three. The overwhelming emphasis here is on structure. F13 works for human beings as F17 did for the cosmos as a whole; it provides the structural framework within which unlimiteds will be constrained. Limiting notions are most clearly seen in the four-part structure of the human body. Indeed, it is here that Philolaus shows the most originality in comparison with other Presocratic thinkers. We have good evidence that other Presocratics were concerned to determine the seat of the intellect and we have evidence that some of them went much farther than Philolaus in trying to explain the mechanism of sensation (e.g. Empedocles and his pores). However, Philolaus is unique in providing such a detailed structural account of the human body and its faculties and in fact anticipates Plato and Aristotle in some ways, so that it is easy to suppose that this results from his interest in limiters.

The testimonium on Philolaus' medical views provided by Aristotle's pupil Meno (A27) clearly shows the corresponding role of unlimiteds in Philolaus' account of human beings. Meno emphasizes Philolaus' insistence that human beings are constituted from the hot. This appears to mean that the human embryo is composed only of the hot, which then comes to be tempered by the cold upon birth by the process of breathing. The analogy with the cosmos starting from the heat of the central fire and then drawing in breath is clear. Once again the hot can well take its place alongside fire as an unlimited,

45

since in its own nature it simply defines a continuum without being defined by a specific quantity. However, Philolaus clearly suggests that part of the process that leads to the development of a mature human being is the tempering of this heat by the breathing which starts at birth. Thus, the development of the human being can be in part viewed as the fitting together of the original human heat with cooling breath. In this case the limiter would seem to be precisely the process of breathing or the desire for breath (ὄρεξις τοῦ ἐκτὸς πνεύματος – A27) and the balance of hot and cold that results is the *harmonia* (Philolaus alludes to this balance by describing exhaling as paying back what is owed – καθαπερεὶ χρέος). Meno goes on in A27 to talk of Philolaus' theory of disease and at first sight it appears that unlimiteds dominate in that substances such as bile, blood, and phlegm are said to be the origins of disease. However, once again at the end of the testimonium limiting notions appear, in that excess and defect are cited as additional causes of disease, and it would appear that disease was in fact explained in terms of noxious substances arising in the body (bile, phlegm, unhealthy blood), when the unlimiteds and limiters in the body are not in fact governed by a *harmonia*.

The suggestion that an action like breathing might be conceived of as a limiter leads us to reconsider F13 and wonder whether each of the faculties there might also be viewed as limiters. Certainly, intellect, perception, rooting, and the sending forth of seed all could be conceptualized as activities that in some way determine limits. Rooting defines the place and structure of a plant and the sowing of seed determines the development of a structure in the womb. That intellectual activity was viewed as a process of setting limits by Philolaus is in fact strongly supported by F3. In that fragment he argues that if all things were unlimited "there will not be anything that will know." The most likely interpretation of this (see F3) is that the process of knowing in fact is a limiter and hence could not exist if we only appealed to unlimiteds in our account of the cosmos. Thus, it appears plausible that certain activities such as knowing, perceiving, breathing, and the sending forth of roots and seed were viewed by Philolaus as limiters.

Now that the major evidence for the nature of limiters and unlimiteds in the fragments and testimonia has been examined, it is perhaps appropriate to draw some conclusions.[1] It would appear that limiters and unlimiteds should not be identified with shapes and stuffs as Barnes suggests, although shapes and stuffs are certainly good examples of limiters and unlimiteds. The spherical shape of the cosmos and the properties of the sphere are limiters for Philolaus, but so are the limits that are placed in a musical continuum to determine an attunement, and so is a process like breathing or knowing, none of which are shapes. What they have in common is that they all provide boundaries of some sort in a continuum. Once again unlimiteds include as prominent members stuffs such as fire and air. However, besides including opposites such as hot and cold, and light and dark, both of which many Presocratics seemed to think of as stuffs, but which seem immaterial to us, unlimiteds for Philolaus included continuums such as that of the void, time, and sound. It would also appear that certain features of the world can be conceived of as either limiters or unlimiteds, depending on the perspective from which they are viewed. Thus, breath (= air) can be described both as an unlimited and as a limiter (as a cooling agent in the body).

It is important to note that unlimiteds and limiters turn out to be a natural pair, as Philolaus' language suggests; the unlimiteds define a continuum without any boundaries while the limiters establish boundaries in these continuums. This explanation of limiters and unlimiteds fits the constraints developed above by looking at the use of the terms in Fragments 1, 2, 3, and 6. There is clearly a plurality of such limiters and unlimiteds and they are readily observable features of our world as F2 suggests. We can pick out unlimiteds like fire, breath, and time as well as limiters such as shapes, stops on a string, and activities like knowing. Moreover, we can see why Philolaus does not want to identify any unique set of such limiters and

[1] At *EN* 1106b Aristotle says that the Pythagoreans associated what is bad with the unlimited and what is good with the limited. Such a doctrine clearly was held by the Pythagoreans who set out the table of opposites which Aristotle describes at *Metaph.* 986a22ff, since good is put in the same column with limit and bad in the same column with unlimited. However, Aristotle sharply distinguishes these Pythagoreans from the Pythagoreans he has been discussing previously, who clearly included Philolaus because of the reference to the counter-earth. Indeed, throughout the fragments of Philolaus, limiters and unlimiteds are presented on completely equal terms and it would appear that Philolaus, at least, saw both as necessary for the world-order to arise and did not consider either category as good or bad.

unlimiteds as elements. Their variety is such that it would be illegitimate to specify one as prior to another and it is precisely in their nature as unlimited or limiting that they have anything in common.

At the same time, while the world can intelligibly be seen as a combination of such limiters and unlimiteds, they do not in fact seem to be adequate to explain the order which we see in the world. The world is not a jumbled conglomeration of limiters and unlimiteds. Limiters and unlimiteds are bound together in a pleasing way; they have been fitted together. This raises an important point. It is sometimes hard to distinguish between limiters and unlimiteds and their concrete manifestations in the world, which are brought about through *harmonia*. In particular we may be tempted to equate limit with the fitting together in accordance with number which Philolaus calls *harmonia*. However, the two concepts can be distinguished logically and Philolaus always keeps them distinct, never equating number or harmony with limit. Thus, a random set of boundaries within a continuum of pitches does constitute a set of limits, but they are only a *harmonia* if they are a musically pleasing set of pitches determined by number. Limiters are simply things that set boundaries within a continuum, but in their own nature they do not necessarily produce an order; that is the role of *harmonia* in Philolaus' system.

This theory of what limiters and unlimiteds are for Philolaus can be supported by a different argument. Another way of trying to solve the problem of limiters and unlimiteds is to assume that Philolaus is using these terms in accordance with the philosophical tradition in which he is writing. Schofield takes this approach when he assumes that Philolaus is writing in an esoteric Pythagorean tradition and hence that he means nothing more by limiters and unlimiteds than odd and even numbers. However, this reading does not work very well with two features of the fragments. First, far from a simple identification of limiters and unlimiteds with numbers, what we find in the fragments is a sharp separation between the two, so sharp that limiters and unlimiteds are never mentioned in the same fragment with number. Second, it is hard to see why limiters and unlimiteds are introduced at all if they are simply equivalent to even and odd. There is a better context in which to read Philolaus' remarks on limiters and unlimiteds than a narrowly Pythagorean one. The rest of Philolaus' language in the genuine fragments is not the language

48

of an esoteric school, but rather abounds in terms that have had a long history in Presocratic thought. Nature (φύσις), world-order (κόσμος), and *harmonia* are all crucial concepts for earlier Presocratics. Similarly, Philolaus' astronomical system and his medical thought, although containing much that is original, clearly work with the concepts common in the general Presocratic and Hippocratic tradition. Thus it only makes sense to see if Philolaus' use of limiters and unlimiteds can be illuminated by studying the use of these terms in earlier Presocratics. Certainly even a superficial survey of Presocratic thought shows that the concept of the unlimited has played a central role, and Parmenides has something important to say about limit.

Indeed, I would argue that a close reading of F2 and F3 of Philolaus reveals that he is in fact arguing against a specific thesis about limiters and unlimiteds in the earlier Presocratic tradition. In F2 Philolaus pointedly rejects the thesis that the world can be explained solely in terms of unlimiteds ("[the things that are are] not in every case unlimited alone" – ἄπειρα δὲ μόνον οὐκ ἀεί). That fragment goes on to emphasize that both limiters and unlimiteds are manifest features of the world and that therefore both must be recognized as basic components of it, since one cannot be derived from the other. In F3 Philolaus seems to further attack the thesis that all things are unlimited. He argues that if all things are unlimited a knower will not arise. This can be plausibly read as an attack on Anaxagoras who believes both that the world is composed out of things that are all unlimited (F1) and also that there is a knower in the world, namely the famous Anaxagorean Νοῦς ("intelligence").

It makes sense then to turn back to this Presocratic tradition in order to see if the seeds of Philolaus' conception of unlimiteds can be found there. There certainly is no lack of reference to the unlimited in Presocratic thought prior to Philolaus. Anaximander is famous for positing the unlimited (τὸ ἄπειρον) as the starting point from which the cosmos arose. It is not completely clear what Anaximander meant by this unlimited, but it appears to be a limitless expanse of indeterminate nature (see e.g. Furley 1987: 29) out of which emerge the basic elements which constitute our world. He seems to have laid particular emphasis on the opposites, such as hot and cold and dry and wet, as emerging from the unlimited, and pictures the world as arising in part out of the balanced conflict of these opposites, although it is doubtful that he had a clearly defined set of elements. The opposition between limited and unlimited could be seen in the contrast between the unlimited and the distinct things which emerge from it. However, it also seems not impossible to see these opposites (hot, cold, etc.) which emerge from the unlimited as instead resembling their parent, and hence as unlimiteds themselves, although not of course being without any qualitative determination (i.e. they are hot or cold, etc.), as the unlimited itself is often supposed to be. These opposites would then come to be quantitatively limited by their conflict with one another which Anaximander describes in terms of retribution paid to each other for their injustices (F1). If we turn from Anaximander to his pupil Anaximenes, we find an even clearer example of an unlimited, in that Anaximenes probably labeled his basic stuff, air, as unlimited (A1 and 6). However, it is with Anaxagoras that we get the clearest picture of a plurality of unlimiteds. In F1 Anaxagoras asserts that all things were together unlimited (ἄπειρα) both in respect of number and smallness. It is possible to come up with a considerable list of these things which Anaxagoras considered to be unlimited. The list includes air, aither (F1), dry, wet, hot, cold, bright, dark (F4), dense, and rare (F12). It thus seems not implausible to assume that, when Philolaus mentions unlimiteds, a reader in the Presocratic tradition would think of a list of things something like this.

On the other hand the adjective unlimited was also applied by Melissus to his one being and in doing so he is in a sense just agreeing with the Presocratic tradition just discussed, that what is is unlimited, although he of course argues that there can only be one such unlimited. Philolaus, on the other hand, makes the same sort of pluralist assumption that Anaxagoras does. He assumes that the explanandum is the plural world we see around us and therefore recognizes that it will have to arise from origins that are plural. However, Philolaus is also sharply critical of Anaxagoras as well as Melissus for trying to explain the world just in terms of what is unlimited. Parmenides has argued that what is must be held in the bonds of limit in order for it to be intelligible (F8). Moreover, when he comes to give an image for these limits he refers to nothing less than a geometrical shape, the sphere. So once again, in a Presocratic context, when Philolaus refers to limiters or limits, what may well come to mind is the sphere of Parmenides. However, what is strikingly new in Philolaus is the assertion that both what is unlimited and what limits must be invoked in order to explain reality, and given his pluralist assumptions we get limiters and unlimiteds. I have treated complicated matters in the interpretation of Presocratic thought somewhat superficially in this survey, but my purpose here is not to show the full complexity of the dialectic, but rather to demonstrate that Philolaus' invocation of limiters and unlimiteds as basic principles can in fact be seen as a natural development out of earlier Presocratic thought. Moreover, I hope to have shown that, when interpreted in this way, limiters and unlimiteds in fact turn out to be very similar to what they appear to be just on the basis of the fragments of Philolaus themselves, although Philolaus has developed the concepts in important ways. In conclusion then I will outline what I take to be Philolaus' original contribution to this dialectic on limit and the unlimited and to Presocratic accounts of the cosmos as a whole.

Philolaus is original, first of all, in his explicit definition of a class of unlimiteds. Earlier thinkers, such as Anaxagoras, had labeled their basic principles as unlimited, so that when Philolaus mentions unlimiteds we are reminded of things such as air, aither, hot, and cold, but earlier thinkers had not identified this as the defining characteristic of one whole class of entities. Philolaus on the other hand does not think of these things as primarily defined by their qualitative features such as hot and cold, but rather as all having in common the fact that in themselves they are not determined by any quantity, but rather simply mark out a continuum of possible quantities. At the same time this definition allows him to include not just the very wide range of stuffs recognized by Presocratics such as Anaxagoras (i.e. not just air and aither but light and dark), but also some other features of the world that fall into the class of unlimiteds newly defined, such as time, void, and musical pitch.

This new recognition of a distinct class of unlimiteds is probably the indirect result of the most original feature of Philolaus' system, the introduction of limiters alongside of unlimiteds as basic constituents of reality. It is certainly true that Greek philosophy before Philolaus is full of references to structure, from Anaximander's three rings, to Heraclitus' *logos*, to Empedocles' formula for the composition of bone, to Anaxagoras' Mind. Indeed, the whole idea of the world's being a cosmos shows the Greek absorption with order and structure. However, with the possible exception of Parmenides, no one before Philolaus had argued that these structural features were just as much origins of the world as the much invoked opposites or the material elements such as Empedocles' earth, air, fire, and water. It is Philolaus' recognition of a distinct class of limiters which must be postulated as components of the world that probably led him to see unlimiteds as a unified class, unified by the fact that they provide the boundaryless continuum in which limiters establish boundaries. Thus Philolaus, while clearly drawing on the Presocratic tradition, produces a very original and coherent development of that tradition. It should be clear that this response to the Presocratic thought of his day is the work of a serious thinker and much more than a "melange of myth and φυσιολογία" or a bizarre attempt to "express Pythagorean lore in the form of Ionian φυσιολογία" as Burkert has argued (1972: 350, 400).

It is striking of course that Philolaus is willing to treat limiters such as the spherical shape or particular pitches in a continuum as just as much components of the world-order as unlimiteds such as air or fire. His conception is at one and the same time dazzlingly abstract and almost absurdly concrete. It may be that he shows some awareness of the oddity of thinking of a spherical shape and the stuff put in that shape (e.g. earth) as both equal components of things, when he emphasizes that limiters and unlimiteds are not alike or even related (F6 – οὐχ ὁμοῖαι οὐδ' ὁμόφυλοι). Still, he does throughout treat limiters on a par with unlimiteds. It should be clear that, while Philolaus is approaching something akin to a distinction between form and matter, his thinking is still very much in the Presocratic mode and in fact exactly accords with the point that Aristotle makes repeatedly, that the Pythagoreans, despite developing principles suited for a different sort of reality, talk about nothing but the sensible world as do most of the Presocratics (*Metaph.* 989b29ff). Still, Plato was fascinated by this distinction between limiters and unlimiteds, and in the *Philebus* presents it as something handed down from his forefathers who lived closer to the gods.

Thus, Philolaus' adoption of limiters and unlimiteds as principles makes sense as precisely a development of Presocratic ideas which anticipates Aristotelian and Platonic distinctions in interesting ways, but which is innocent of distinctions, such as that between the intelligible and the sensible, which become important later. Thus the use of limiters and unlimiteds in the fragments can in no way be seen as a post-Aristotelian forgery. But Philolaus, while arguing that the world we know can be made sense of as a combination of limiters and unlimiteds, recognized that he also had to explain how it was that these limiters and unlimiteds came to be combined in the specific order we see around us rather than an incoherent jumble, and in order to do this he called in another principle with a good Presocratic pedigree, *harmonia*, and associated it with number in a way that solved some of Parmenides' problems about the intelligibility of the sensible world. It is to these concepts of number and harmony that I will turn in the next chapter.

2. NUMBER AND *HARMONIA*

F6 of Philolaus argues that limiters and unlimiteds are not enough to explain the world-order which we know and *harmonia* is introduced as a third necessary factor whose role is to bind together limiters and unlimiteds into an order. I have already suggested that *harmonia* is tightly connected to yet another explanatory principle of Philolaus, number, and will return to this connection below. However, consideration of the role of number and *harmonia* in Philolaus' philosophy leads into the long-vexed topic of the role of the Pythagoreans in the development of Greek mathematics. Burkert's work has taught us that the history of Greek mathematics can be told very well with hardly any mention of the early Pythagoreans and he concludes that serious Pythagorean achievement in mathematics does not appear until the work of certain anonymous Pythagoreans in geometry in the late fifth century and the work of Archytas in the first half of the fourth century (1972: 401ff and esp. 449ff).

Indeed an overview of the genuine fragments and testimonia of Philolaus reveals that he is not primarily a mathematician. No important advance in mathematics is attributed to him, unlike his contemporary Hippocrates of Chios, or indeed figures such as Theaetetus and Archytas in the next generation. However, the fragments and testimonia show plenty of interest in mathematics. In F6a Philolaus shows awareness of the whole-number ratios that govern the concordant intervals in music, and in Testimonium A24 he is plausibly said to have known the "musical proportion" (12, 9, 8, 6), which in turn presupposes knowledge of the arithmetic and harmonic means. A29 and A7a suggest that he recognized a certain set of mathematical sciences (probably including arithmetic, geometry, astronomy and music, as in Archytas F1) and that he even established a hierarchy of sciences with geometry as the basic science. In F5 he presents

54

a threefold classification of numbers and in F4 he identifies numbers as the basis of our knowledge of reality. A22 may show an attempt mathematically to reconcile the solar and lunar year. What all of this suggests is a figure something like Plato, who is not a professional mathematician, but who is familiar with the work of mathematicians of his day and who is convinced that mathematics is crucial both in providing an account of the physical world and also in addressing important philosophical questions. In fact I will argue that Philolaus deserves a prominent place in the history of Greek philosophy, as the first thinker self-consciously and thematically to employ mathematical ideas to solve philosophical problems.

The primary question concerning the relation between Philolaus and Greek mathematics then becomes, "What sort of philosophical problems did Philolaus think mathematics could solve and what type of mathematics is presupposed by his book?" Walter Burkert has argued that the type of mathematics that finds expression in Philolaus' book is not the rigorous deductive mathematics that was beginning to take shape at the hands of Philolaus' contemporaries Hippocrates of Chios and Theodorus of Cyrene, but a reverence for and interpretation of number that arise from the same context as the Pythagorean *acusmata* and find their parallels in the numerology of numerous primitive peoples around the globe (1972: 465ff).

Burkert views Philolaus as trying to bridge the gap between a Pythagorean number lore that has its ultimate origin in the distant past and the recent tradition of Ionian *physiologia*. He regards Pythagorean mathematics in Philolaus' time as having literally nothing to do with the main line of Ionian mathematics represented by Hippocrates of Chios. The assumptions of Pythagorean number mysticism, Burkert argues, are directly contrary to those of rigorous mathematical proof. Accordingly, proofs such as that of incommensurability would have had no impact on Philolaus and his contemporaries, because they were concerned with number in a different sense (1972: 463).

Burkert's case is forceful, but there are difficulties. First, it is not clear that we have to accept his conclusion that "reverence" for numbers is completely incompatible with an outlook that emphasizes deductive proof. Given that Philolaus had belief in the power of certain numbers, it is not necessary that he have no interest in a tradition that tries to prove certain properties of numbers. Burkert's point is that proof makes the properties non-mystical by showing that they simply follow from other more basic principles: "A scheme of proof could hardly be anything but annoying because it would show the result as a logical consequence of the preconceptions, and reduce it to banality" (1972: 433). This is a possible outlook, but would someone fascinated by numbers really have no interest in relationships proved about them? Would it really diminish some-one's belief in the power of number to see the proof of Euclid 1.47? Second, and more important, Burkert bases his argument that Philolaus was primarily involved in number mysticism, rather than rigorous mathematics, heavily on fragments and testimonia which should not in fact be regarded as genuine (see especially A14, A26, F6b and my arguments against Burkert's account of Philolaus' as-tronomy). Moreover, another large part of Burkert's case is based on Aristotle's testimony. In particular he emphasizes Aristotle's ref-erences to the Pythagorean identification of ideas such as justice, mind, and opportunity with certain numbers, but it is not clear that this is the whole story for Philolaus. Moreover, the thesis that "all is number," which is assigned to the Pythagoreans by Aristotle and which underlies Burkert's thesis, when taken as implying a reverential attitude to number, can be shown not to hold for Philolaus.

The remainder of this chapter will fall into three parts. First, I will discuss Philolaus' relationship to Aristotle's statement that the Pythagoreans believed that all things were numbers. My thesis is that Aristotle himself formulated the doctrine in this way as a conve-nient way of summarizing his interpretation of the Pythagoreans. The fragments of Philolaus show that he did not believe that all things are numbers, but rather that all things that are known are *known* through number. In the second part, I will show how Philolaus thought that number could solve epistemological problems first posed by Parmenides and why he connected number with *harmonia*. Finally, I will examine the way in which Philolaus' program of searching for the numbers which give us knowledge of things manifests itself in other aspects of his philosophy such as astronomy and medicine. The upshot of these last two points will be the conclusion that Philolaus was drawing on the rigorous mathematics of figures like Theodorus and Hippocrates rather than number lore.

Did the Pythagoreans believe that things are numbers?

In both histories of Greek philosophy and also histories of Greek mathematics the doctrine that "all things are numbers" is commonly regarded as the foundation of Pythagorean philosophy.[1] The reason for this is clear. Aristotle, the most valuable secondary source available for early Pythagoreanism, states flatly that the Pythagoreans say that "all things are numbers." In fact this doctrine is at the center of Aristotle's account of early Pythagoreanism and is ascribed to them many times. The ascription takes two basic forms in Aristotle: (1) in five instances the Pythagoreans "say," "make," or "suppose" that τὰ πράγματα ("things"), τὰ ὄντα ("the things that are"), or τὸν ὅλον οὐρανόν ("the whole heaven") are number or numbers. (2) In seven cases the Pythagoreans are said to "make" or "construct" τὰ ὄντα ("the things that are"), τὰ σώματα ("bodies"), τὰς αἰσθητὰς οὐσίας ("perceptible reality"), τὴν φύσιν ("nature"), or τὸν κόσμον ("the world-order") out of (ἐκ) number or numbers.[2] Now Aristotle clearly had a considerable amount of information about the Pythagoreans, for we know that he wrote a treatise devoted exclusively to the Pythagoreans as well as three separate books on Archytas.[3] The *prima facie* case for accepting his repeated statement that the Pythagoreans thought that things were numbers is thus very strong. But what sort of evidence is likely to be behind Aristotle's statements? The most natural supposition is that he had a Pythagorean text in which the doctrine was directly stated or that he had unambiguous oral reports. Now the only written Pythagorean works that we know to have existed before Aristotle are Philolaus' book and the writings of Archytas.[4] Since Archytas seems to be treated separately by

---

[1] Heath 1921: 1.67 and Guthrie 1962: 229ff.

[2] For the formulation "things are numbers" see *Metaph.* 986a3, 986a21, 987b28, 1083b17. Things are said to be "out of numbers" at *Metaph.* 990a21, 1080b16ff(2), 1083b11, 1090a24, 1090a32 and *De caelo* 300a16. At *De caelo* 303a8 Aristotle says that in a way the atomists too say that all things are numbers. He admits that they may not show it clearly, but goes on to say ὅμως τοῦτο βούλονται λέγειν. Although in this case Aristotle is careful to indicate that the atomists did not actually say that "all things are numbers," the passage still shows his tendency to interpret other philosophical systems in formulations of his own devising.

[3] See Burkert (1972: 28 n. 5) on the evidence for Aristotle's books on the Pythagoreans. Aristotle's works on Archytas are listed in Hesychius' catalogue of Aristotle's writings. See DK 47A13.

[4] For Philolaus as the first Pythagorean to write a book see Pt. I, ch. 1.

Aristotle, Philolaus' book would be likely to be an important source for Aristotle. Indeed, there are undeniable similarities between the fragments and testimonia of Philolaus and Aristotle's account which show that Philolaus was a primary source for Aristotle.[5] What then does Philolaus say about number?

There is no place in the testimonia or genuine fragments of Philolaus where the thesis that all things are number is advanced. To be sure number is mentioned prominently, but it is never assigned the role which Aristotle says the Pythagoreans gave it. Based on Aristotle's evidence we might well have expected that Philolaus' book would have begun with the assertion that "the cosmos and everything in it was constructed out of numbers." Instead, as we have seen, Philolaus' book actually begins "Nature in the world-order was fitted together out of limiters and unlimiteds, both the world-order as a whole and everything in it" (F1). Now there are several possible ways to resolve this conflict between the fragments of Philolaus and Aristotle's evidence. First, since only a small part of Philolaus' book survives it is possible that he did say that all things are numbers in a passage that does not survive. However, such a statement would most naturally occur where Philolaus is setting out the basic principles of his system. Fragments 1, 2, and 6 are just such passages and the basic principles invoked are always limiters and unlimiteds, not numbers. Indeed, F4 states straightforwardly what the role of number was for Philolaus: "Indeed, everything that is known has number, for nothing is either understood or known without this." Thus number plays an epistemological role for Philolaus. He says that things cannot be known without number, not that they are numbers.

Another way to avoid the apparent contradiction between Philolaus and Aristotle is to suppose that Philolaus is not after all Aristotle's source for this doctrine. Thus Schofield argues that Philolaus is Aristotle's source only for the technical features of Pythagoreanism such as the astronomical system, but that since Philolaus makes limiters and unlimiteds the basic constituents of things rather than numbers, Aristotle must be using another source for the doctrine that things are numbers (KRS 330–1). This is a possible view, but it is hard to

[5] See Pt. I, ch. 2.

say who Aristotle's sources would have been in that case. Moreover, some texts in Aristotle indicate that he is ascribing both the astronomical system and the doctrine that all things are numbers to the same source, which is likely to be Philolaus. Thus, in his description of the Pythagoreans in *Metaphysics* 1, Aristotle says that they supposed that the elements of number were the elements of all things and that the whole heaven was a harmony and a number. Although the language that Aristotle uses here is slightly different than in some other passages, the Pythagoreans that he is discussing are clearly those who are elsewhere said to think that all things are numbers. However, Aristotle then describes the procedure of such Pythagoreans when they encounter phenomena that go counter to their theories, and his example is the invention of the counter-earth to make the number of heavenly bodies equal to the perfect number ten. But this is the astronomical system of Philolaus, so that it would appear that Aristotle includes him among those who think that all things are number.[6]

I would like to propose a different explanation for the discrepancy between Aristotle and Philolaus.[7] My thesis is that the doctrine that all things are numbers was not stated in any of Aristotle's sources, including Philolaus, whom I believe to be Aristotle's main source. Instead the doctrine represents Aristotle's own succinct formulation of the Pythagorean outlook. He is saying that what Pythagorean philosophy *amounts to* is the doctrine that all things are numbers. Following the fundamental work of Cherniss (1935) many other detailed studies have shown that Aristotle is very prone to reformulate earlier philosophy in his own terminology and for his own dialectical purposes. In the case of Pythagoreanism it has been harder to see to what extent this is true because of the lack of any pre-Aristotelian Pythagorean texts, but now that a core of the Philolaus fragments are accepted as authentic we do have a check on Aristotle's testimony. It may perhaps seem extreme to assert that Aristotle went so far as to assign his own formulation repeatedly to the Pythagoreans

---

[6] Aristotle refers to the astronomical system as of the Pythagoreans in general (*De caelo* 2.13), but the later tradition represented in Aetius assigns it to Philolaus (A16).

[7] Another way of solving the contradiction would be to suppose that limiters and unlimiteds in Philolaus just are odd and even numbers. This is Schofield's suggestion. For an argument against this thesis see Pt. II, ch. 1 above.

themselves. However, detailed examination of Aristotle's reports will show that this is a very strong possibility and that there was a clear dialectical motive for him to do so.

First, it is important to note the remarkable variety of ways in which Aristotle formulates the Pythagorean position. He commonly says that the Pythagoreans believe that all things are numbers or that they construct things out of numbers, but in some passages they are portrayed as interested in resemblances (ὁμοιώματα) between things and numbers, and in one famous passage (987b10–13) we are told that the Pythagoreans thought that things exist by "imitation" of numbers, this being only verbally different from Plato's notion of "participation." Thus in Aristotle's account of the Pythagoreans things are said to have three different relations to numbers: (1) things are made of numbers; (2) things display resemblances to numbers; (3) things exist by imitation of numbers. In light of this Heidel suggested that Aristotle could hardly be doing justice to the Pythagorean outlook.[8] Of course it is quite possible that the ambiguity in Aristotle's reports is based on a lack of clarity in the Pythagorean sources he was working with. However, whether Aristotle or the Pythagoreans are responsible for the confusion, we should be wary of accepting one version of the relation of things to numbers, e.g. that things are numbers, as the only or most likely interpretation of what the Pythagoreans were about.

A passage in Aristotle's *Metaphysics* allows us to go further. In book 13 at 1083b16 Aristotle first states flatly that the Pythagoreans say that all things are numbers, but then continues in the next sentence "at least (γοῦν) they apply θεωρήματα ("mathematical theories") to bodies as if they (the bodies) consisted of those numbers" (τὰ γοῦν θεωρήματα προσάπτουσι τοῖς σώμασιν ὡς ἐξ ἐκείνων ὄντων τῶν ἀριθμῶν).[9] There are some problems in discovering what Aris-

---

[8] Heidel 1940 in Furley and Allen 1970: 362. Others, notably Cherniss (1935: 386), have recognized the seeming contradiction in Aristotle's reports. For an attempt to explain it away see Guthrie 1962: 229ff.

[9] The central meaning of θεώρημα in Aristotle seems to be "a subject or topic of consideration by the mind" (*EN* 9.4, 1166a26; *Po.* 1456b19; *EE* 1214a9; etc.), but the reference can also be to the theory that results from such consideration (*Somn. vig.* 455a25; *Mete.* 345b2). The best parallel for the use of θεωρήματα here at *Metaph.* 1083b18 is the μαθηματικῶν θεωρημάτων at *Metaph.* 1093b15–16 which should be translated "mathematical speculations." θεώρημα rarely approaches the meaning "theorem" (*MA* 701a10).

totle means here, but the crucial point is that the doctrine that all
things are numbers is not presented as something that the Pythagoreans explicitly stated, rather it is presented as Aristotle's own
deduction from the way the Pythagoreans proceed.[10] Aristotle sees the
Pythagoreans applying mathematical speculations to bodies in a
way that suggests that they think that the bodies are composed of
numbers, and on this basis he ascribes to them the thesis that all
things are numbers. What Aristotle found in the Pythagoreans was
an attempt to relate properties of number to properties of things, an
attempt which for Aristotle did not make clear enough the relative
ontological status of numbers and things. He did not find an assertion that all things were numbers.

There is another passage, in *Metaphysics* 14, which points to the
same conclusion. Aristotle frequently says that the Pythagoreans
constructed bodies *out of* numbers. He no less frequently complains
that in doing so they have confused things which have no magnitude, numbers, with bodies which do. In *Metaphysics* 14 (1091a12ff)
Aristotle attacks those who assign generation to things that are eternal. The Pythagoreans are mentioned in the following passage and
the specific complaint in their case seems to be that they treat numbers as if they were bodies subject to generation. However, the
phrasing of the passage is very revealing. Aristotle begins by saying
that there is no reason to doubt whether the Pythagoreans make
such a generation or not. Aristotle's language here might suggest
that someone had raised the question as to whether the Pythagoreans
deserved Aristotle's criticism or not. But what is most interesting
is the evidence that Aristotle provides to put an end to any such
doubts. He gives the impression that he is referring to a specific
Pythagorean text:

---

[10] There is a difficulty of grammar. A majority of translators render the ὡς clause so that
ὄντων modifies σωμάτων which is understood from the first part of the sentence, while
ἐκείνων goes with ἀριθμῶν, leading to the translation "as if they (the bodies) were out of
those numbers." This translation does agree well with the numerous other passages in
Aristotle where he talks of things being constituted out of numbers. However, the structure
of the sentence would be smoother if ὄντων went with τῶν ἀριθμῶν and ἐκείνων referred to
bodies, giving the translation "as if the numbers were (constructed) from those (bodies)."
It is awkward on this view that ἐκείνων should refer to the immediately preceding "bodies,"
so that the previous translation seems more likely. Whether Aristotle is saying that the
Pythagoreans proceeded as if numbers were composed of bodies or bodies of numbers will
not materially affect the thesis which I am developing.

> For *they clearly state* that when the one had been constituted
> – whether out of planes or superficies or seed or out of
> something they cannot explain – immediately the nearest part
> of the infinite began to be drawn in and limited by the limit.

By using such a text to support his case Aristotle indirectly indicates
that he could find no explicit assertion in a Pythagorean text to the
effect that numbers are corporeal. Instead he draws the conclusion
that they must have held such a doctrine given the way they talk in
certain cosmogonic passages. Evidently what he found in a Pythagorean text was a passage in which "the one" appeared to be constructed (συσταθέντος) in some sense. The speculation that Aristotle
provides as to how the one was constituted shows clearly that the
text before him did not itself say how the one was constructed, just
that it was. I am almost certain that we have at least part of the
Pythagorean text to which Aristotle is referring and can thus get yet
a clearer idea of how he uses his Pythagorean sources.

Stobaeus preserves the following fragment of Philolaus (F7):

> The first thing fitted together, the one in the middle of the
> sphere, is called the hearth.

F7 is the beginning of Philolaus' account of the generation of the
cosmos from limiters and unlimiteds. Aristotle's comments could very
easily be understood as a commentary on this fragment. Philolaus
explicitly mentions a one and says that it has been "fitted together"
(ἁρμοσθέν), which must mean that it has been put together out of
limiters and unlimiteds. This would correspond to Aristotle's claim
that the one is constructed. Further, the usage of τὸ πρᾶτον (the
first) in Philolaus clearly suggests the temporal generation that Aristotle is assigning to the Pythagoreans. Immediately after Aristotle's
description of the construction of "the one" in *Metaphysics* 14 he dis-
misses the Pythagoreans from further consideration because "they
are constructing a cosmos and wish to speak in terms of physics."[11]
It is just such a context from which Philolaus F7 seems to derive.

How should we then describe Aristotle's use of his Pythagorean
source in this case? Certainly Philolaus F7 does discuss a one and

---

[11] However, Aristotle never does take the Pythagoreans as serious theorists on matters of
physics. The vast majority of passages in Aristotle dealing with the Pythagoreans come
from the *Metaphysics*. The Pythagoreans are only mentioned in two passages in the *Physics*
(3.4, 203a1 and 4.6, 213b22) for their views on the ἄπειρον and the void respectively.

relate it to the first step in the generation of the cosmos, the emergence of the central fire. Aristotle's claim that Philolaus is here generating the number one is a plausible interpretation of the passage, although I do not think it is correct (see Pt. III, ch. 3). However, if this passage is one of Aristotle's main reasons for ascribing the doctrine that all things are constructed out of numbers to the Pythagoreans, it is clear that his testimony about the Pythagoreans must be used with extreme caution. When this passage of the *Metaphysics* is taken together with the earlier passage discussed above (1083b16), it appears to be a very strong possibility that Aristotle had seen no Pythagorean text that said that all things were numbers or that all things were composed of numbers. It seems most likely that he had Philolaus' book and perhaps some other writing or oral reports such as that about Eurytus, in which similarities between properties of numbers and properties of things were emphasized. Aristotle's interpretation of all this led him to summarize Pythagorean doctrine as teaching that all things are numbers. It should be clear then that the relation between things and numbers in early Pythagoreanism is not decisively resolved by Aristotle's evidence. When interpreting the fragments of Philolaus we need not take the doctrine that all things are number as an undisputed starting-point, but should realize that it is in fact an Aristotelian interpretation of Philolaus, not one of his own axioms.[12]

One final point should be made about Aristotle's presentation of Pythagoreanism. In a great number of instances the Pythagoreans are introduced into Aristotle's discussion in connection with Plato.[13] In particular he likes to emphasize the contrast between Plato's separation of numbers from things and his postulation of mathematicals between forms and sensibles on the one hand, and the Pythagorean identification of things with numbers on the other.[14] The contrast

---

[12] It might perhaps seem that by undermining Aristotle's authority as a witness for early Pythagoreanism I am undercutting the basis used by Burkert to distinguish between authentic early Pythagorean thought and the later Platonizing tradition. However, even if the "all things are number" doctrine is taken as an example of Aristotelian interpretation, this does not alter the fact that Aristotle's evidence allows us to distinguish early Pythagoreans from Plato. For instance, his evidence will still show that the one–indefinite dyad opposition and the derivation sequence of point, line, surface, and solid are Platonic and not Pythagorean.

[13] *Metaph.* 1.6, 987b1off.; 3.1, 996a5; 3.4, 1001a9; 10.2, 1053b9; 13.8, 1083b8; *Physics* 3.4, 203a1.

[14] *Metaph.* 13.8, 1083b8.

with Plato, given Aristotle's interest in seeing dialectical connections between his predecessors, would provide Aristotle with a strong motive to interpret the Pythagorean talk about things and numbers as identification of things and numbers. It in fact seems likely that the issue of the ontological status of numbers and the question of what mathematical propositions are about, what they correspond to in reality, first arose in Plato's thought of the time of the *Republic* or a little earlier and developed into an important issue in the Academy.[15] Philolaus, writing thirty to fifty years before Plato raised these questions, probably did not clearly recognize them or directly address them. Aristotle's attempt to put the Pythagoreans into debate with Plato and himself thus distorts their view. Philolaus is at the very beginning of the tradition that considers the relation between mathematics and things and is thus unlikely to fit into the later dialectic neatly.

The recognition that the thesis that "all things are numbers" is not Pythagorean can have far-reaching implications for some traditional problems in the study of Pythagoreanism. For instance, in a system like Philolaus', where numbers are not identified with things, the discovery of incommensurability may not have in fact generated the great problems for the Pythagoreans which scholars have often assumed it would (see Huffman 1988: 14–19). However, this is not the time to examine all such repercussions for the study of Pythagoreanism, and I will now turn back from Aristotle's account of the Pythagoreans to Philolaus.

The role of number in Philolaus' system

What role, then, do numbers play in Philolaus' system and what can that role tell us about the type of mathematics that lies behind it? F4 provides a relatively clear answer to the first part of this question:

> And indeed all the things that are known have number (πάντα ...τὰ γιγνωσκόμενα ἀριθμὸν ἔχοντι). For it is not possible that anything whatsoever be understood (νοηθῆμεν) or known (γνωσθῆμεν) without this.

Number is necessary for knowledge. It solves an epistemological

---

[15] Burnyeat 1987.

problem. The very appearance of an epistemological concern at such an early point in Greek thought caused some older scholars to regard the fragment as spurious (KR 311), but recent scholarship has recognized a clear epistemological strain in Presocratic thought, and surely Barnes is right when he asserts that already in the time of Parmenides epistemology was "... a young discipline but not an infant" (1982: 296).

This is not the place to provide a critical history of Presocratic epistemology, but since number and mathematics are invoked to solve a specifically epistemological problem in Philolaus, it is necessary to give a brief overview of some of the strains in Presocratic epistemology and how Philolaus fits into those trends. From the beginning, both the Greek literary and philosophical traditions show interest in the limitations of the human mind (e.g. Homer's appeal to the Muses), and it is often noted that there is an innate skeptical tinge to Greek thought. It is characteristic of this tradition that clear or exact knowledge is denied to human beings in certain domains, which is not to say that we cannot have more or less well founded beliefs in these areas and even certain knowledge in other domains.

Philolaus F6 displays a skepticism that is similar to this. In just the same manner as his predecessors Philolaus denies human knowledge in a certain domain. However, the area in which clear knowledge is not possible is specified in a new way.

> Concerning inner nature and harmony the situation is this: to begin with, the being of things (ἁ μὲν ἐστὼ τῶν πραγμάτων) which is eternal, and inner nature in itself (αὐτὰ μὲν ἁ φύσις) admit of divine and not of human knowledge, except that it was impossible for any of the things that are and are known by us to come to be if the being of the things from which the ordered world came together, both the limiting things and the unlimited things, did not preexist.

For Philolaus it is "the being of things" and "inner nature in itself" that admit only of divine and not of human knowledge. This would seem to allow that humans can have knowledge about areas such as cosmology and natural science (*pace* Xenophanes and the author of *On Ancient Medicine*), but that the ultimate basis of reality is beyond our grasp. At this point Philolaus is clearly siding with thinkers like Empedocles, Anaxagoras, and the atomists, who assume the existence of the world of our experience, a world consisting of a plurality of things. The question is how he thinks we can gain secure knowledge of this world.

Once again there is clear background to this question in Presocratic thought. A number of Presocratics show strong skepticism about the reliability of our senses, but with the exception of the Eleatics they also agree that the senses are the indispensable starting-point in our attempt to discover the truth. Usually the idea is that the senses provide us with valuable information, but only if we know how to interpret it. Thus in F55 Heraclitus says "I prefer those things of which there are seeing, hearing, and perception." But he tempers this praise of the senses in F107: "The eyes and ears are bad witnesses for those men who have barbarian souls (i.e. souls that do not understand the language of the senses)." In general Heraclitus' view of the phenomenal world seems to be that it is like the oracle at Delphi which, in the words of F93, neither speaks out nor conceals, but gives a sign. What it gives a sign of is the underlying λόγος which Kirk describes well as a "unifying formula or proportionate method of arrangement of things" (KRS 187). It is this λόγος which is really knowable. The same notion of sense experience as pointing to a less obvious, but more cognitively reliable reality may be behind Anaxagoras' famous statement that "the phenomena are the vision of unclear things" (F21a). Democritus reportedly approved of Anaxagoras' dictum, and indeed in his system he distinguishes sharply between a bastard knowing that arises through the senses and a legitimate knowledge that arises through the intellect (F9 and F11). At the same time he recognizes that sense experience is indispensable (F125). It is, at any rate, clear that in atomism what our senses present to us (e.g. a sweet taste) is based on an invisible reality of quite a different kind, atoms and void (F9).

Philolaus once again has a clear place in this tradition. There is no direct assessment of the senses in the fragments, but F2 at least seems to rely on direct appeal to sense experience to establish the existence of limiters and unlimiteds. While this suggests that Philolaus assigns some value to the evidence of the senses, it is clear that he too thinks that such evidence requires proper interpretation and that it is crucial to go beyond the superficial message of the senses in order to see what further understanding that evidence points to:

Number, indeed, has two proper kinds, odd and even, and a
third from both mixed together, the even-odd. Of each of the
two kinds there are many forms, of which each thing itself gives
signs.   (F5)

There are a number of obscure points in this fragment, but what I
want to focus on here is the last clause. The reference of ἕκαστον
(each thing) is not completely clear, but the most plausible explanation is that it refers to individual things in the world. The idea would
then be that individual things in the world "give signs of" or "point
to" something else, in this case not Heraclitus' *logos*, but numbers or
"forms of numbers." Indeed it is with the introduction of number at
this point that we can see Philolaus' very original response to the
most illustrious of his predecessors, Parmenides.

What I want to suggest is that, in specifying number as the
reality to which phenomena point, Philolaus is trying to solve the
same problem that Parmenides addressed in his poem. I agree with
scholars such as Mourelatos and Kahn who have argued that
Parmenides' problem is primarily epistemological and that his main
goal is to determine what the object of knowledge is like.[16] The
conclusion is that it must both exist and exist as a determinate state
of affairs. The problem with the route that Parmenides rejects, the
route of "is not," is that it is completely indeterminate and hence
incurably vague. Philolaus accepts Parmenides' claim that the object of knowledge must be a determinate state of affairs, but wants
to preserve a plurality. The bold step he takes is to argue that numerical relationships in particular and mathematical relationships
in general solve the problem. They possess the requisite determinacy
and at the same time they relate a plurality of entities and thus are
capable of explaining a world that consists of a plurality of entities.

The extent to which Philolaus' appeal to mathematical relationships conforms to Parmenides' restrictions on the character of a possible object of knowledge can be seen by considering the extent to
which mathematical relations satisfy the famous "signposts" on the
way of truth that Parmenides outlines in F8. Parmenides says that
the object of inquiry must be uncreated and imperishable, continuous, unchangeable, and perfect. If we consider a geometrical proof

---

[16] Mourelatos 1970 and 1979. Kahn 1968/9.

such as the so-called Pythagorean theorem (Euclid 1.47) or the numerical proportions that govern the concordant intervals in the octave they do in fact seem to be uncreated and imperishable. To be sure individual instances of the concordant intervals (e.g. two particular taut strings, one twice the length of the other) may come to be and pass away, but it seems quite plausible to argue that the relationship between the whole number proportions $\frac{1}{2}$, $\frac{2}{3}$, $\frac{3}{4}$ and concordant sounds, or the relationship between the hypotenuse and the sides of a right triangle, did not come into existence at any point nor will they pass away. Similarly there seems little problem in saying that mathematical relationships are unchangeable. Further, since mathematical relationships are completely determinate, they are perfect in Parmenides' sense of being complete and not deficient. It is more difficult to see how the signpost of being continuous (ξυνεχές) applies to mathematics. Of course this part of Parmenides' poem is taken by some to argue that all of reality is one, and if Philolaus is trying to save a plural world while accepting Parmenides' requirements for intelligibility, it is precisely at this point that we might expect some difficulties. However, Philolaus might well argue that, although there are a plurality of entities, they each individually are completely determinate in the way required by Parmenides. Philolaus would then have affinities to the atomists who are often seen as positing a plurality of entities which individually satisfy the requirements of Parmenidean being. However, Philolaus chooses mathematical relationships rather than atoms, because he appeals to number to solve the problem of a reliable object of knowledge. The world is known through number, not made up of number.

Having placed Philolaus' epistemology in this context I now want to turn to deal with the problems presented by F4 in more detail and in doing so explain further how knowledge and number are tied together for Philolaus. Since we do not have any further explanation of the simple statement that nothing is known without number (if there was any), a number of points remain obscure and controversial. First, what sort of knowledge is number meant to explain? Second, what does it mean for something to "have number"? Finally, how does knowing something's number allow us to know it?

In order to answer the first question it is necessary to consider the verbs of knowing which Philolaus uses in F4, νοεῖν and γιγνώσκειν. Nussbaum and later Schofield have argued that Philolaus is giving the conditions necessary for anything merely to be apprehended.[17] Something must have number in the sense of being countable, i.e. distinguishable from other somethings, in order to be recognized as a distinct entity at all. On this view Philolaus is concerned to explain how it is that we can recognize distinct objects in the world, not how we can have secure knowledge of those objects. Such a view relies heavily on taking γιγνώσκω as suggesting mere recognition and νοεῖν as referring to thinking in a vague psychological sense, i.e. something going on between the ears. However, the typical Presocratic usage of these verbs argues against this interpretation (see F3 and F4). It is much more likely that, when used without any limiting modifiers, γιγνώσκειν refers to successful recognition or knowledge of things and that νοεῖν indicates "understanding" and not mere thought. Indeed, in F6, when Philolaus describes the divine knowledge that is not accessible to humans, the word he uses is the noun formed from γιγνώσκειν (γνῶσις), and surely what is in question here is the gods' secure knowledge and not mere apprehension of things.

Furthermore, as we have already seen, it is clear in several places in the fragments that Philolaus is perfectly able to talk and think about the world with no mention of number. As I have argued above, the basic principles in Philolaus' system are not numbers, but limiters and unlimiteds. The existence of and our perception of distinct objects are explained in terms of the combination of limiters and unlimiteds. F5, quoted above, supports this in saying that individual things "give signs of" or "point to" numbers. For this surely suggests that number is introduced to explain how it is we can have "real" or "secure" knowledge of entities which are initially apprehended by simple perception. F13 again supports this general outlook in assigning sense perception to both animals and humans, but understanding (νοῦς) to humans alone. Animals share with humans the ability to pick out distinct objects in the world through perception, but sure knowledge of things is reserved for humans alone in so far as they grasp the number that each thing "has". Thus the evidence from the fragments of Philolaus, combined with the common use of νοεῖν and γιγνώσκειν in Presocratic contexts in the sense of "understand" and "know", makes it overwhelmingly likely that Philolaus is talking

[17] Nussbaum 1979; KRS 327.

69

about conditions for understanding and not just conditions for any thought at all.

Granted, then, that Philolaus is trying to explain how it is that we can "really" know something, the next major problem is to explain what it means to say that things that are known must "have number". Number (ἀριθμός) in Greek typically has a more concrete sense than we are used to and commonly refers to an ordered plurality of things. Thus it works more like our word "dozen" which always conjures up an image of a specific collection of things (e.g. eggs). In the simplest sense, then, "having number" means that something is an ordered plurality that can be counted. It is possible that it is this meaning of "having number" that lies behind the strange story of Eurytus, a Pythagorean who was a slightly younger contemporary of Philolaus, who is reported to have drawn a picture of a man and filled it in with pebbles and then identified the man with the number of pebbles used. However, there are many other examples in Greek thought (see the commentary on F4) which suggest a less puerile interpretation and treat "having number" as equivalent to "having an order or structure that can be specified in terms of the relationships between numbers." To say that something "has number" then becomes equivalent to saying that it has a structure which can be described in terms of mathematics.

This slide from discussing number to the consideration of structure in so far as it can be described mathematically is, interestingly enough, found in a passage from Aristotle's book on the Pythagoreans.

> The Pythagoreans having devoted themselves to mathematics, and admiring the accuracy of its reasonings, because it alone among human activities knows of proofs, and seeing the facts about harmony, that they happen on account of numbers, generally admitted ... they deemed these (facts of mathematics) and their principles to be, generally, causative of existing things, so that whoever wishes to comprehend the true nature of existing things should turn his attention to these, that is to numbers and proportions, because it is by them that everything is made clear.[18]

---

[18] Iamblichus, *Comm. math.* 78.8–18. For the argument that this is a fragment of Aristotle see Burkert 1972: 49–50 and n. 112.

What is remarkable in this passage is that, while it starts out talk-ing about mathematics in general and in particular mathematical proofs, it ends up by saying that to understand things we must study number and proportion. The study of number has become equiva-lent to the study of the structure of the cosmos in so far as it can be expressed in mathematical relationships. At the same time this passage from Aristotle's special work on the Pythagoreans provides excellent support for my position on the role of number in Philolaus. For clearly Aristotle is saying in this passage that the key role of mathematics for the Pythagoreans is epistemological ("it is by them [numbers and proportions] that everything is made clear").

What all of this suggests is that in F4 of Philolaus "having num-ber" may mean much more than simply "having count." It may well mean "having structure that can be described mathematically." If this is so the role of number in Philolaus' epistemology starts to become clear. Philolaus is arguing that we only really understand something when we understand the structure of and relationships between its various parts. The best example is our understanding of the octave. Philolaus would argue that we only really know it when we can specify the intervals that go to make it up and the rela-tionships between those intervals, and can express them in terms of numerical ratios.[19]

I would now like to return to some of the issues raised at the beginning of this chapter about the role of mathematics in Philolaus' philosophy and the nature of that mathematics. What is revolution-ary in the philosophy of Philolaus is the thematic use of number and mathematics to solve philosophical problems. Someone might well object that from the beginning Presocratic philosophy has been characterized by notions of balance, proportion and harmony, and so it has. Nonetheless, no previous Presocratic had dared to invoke "number" as an explanatory concept. Philolaus does so because he does not just wish to describe the world as being a cosmos (order)

---

[19] On this view Philolaus' epistemology does have some very interesting similarities to the Pythagoreanizing passages of Plato's *Philebus*, where we are told not to be content with just grasping the one or moving right away to the unlimited, but enjoined to find the number between them. There is nothing in the phrasing of Fragments 1–7 of Philolaus to make us think that they were modelled on Plato, but quite the reverse. Plato makes it clear that he is drawing on Pythagoreans in this passage but it remains unclear what is Plato and what is Philolaus.

or as having a *logos* (proportionate method of arrangement). He specifically refers to number because what he wants to emphasize, in response to Parmenides, is the cognitive reliability of numerical and mathematical relations; that is why number is brought in to solve a question of epistemology. The sort of mathematics that Philolaus is invoking then is mathematics that relies on proof. It is only this sort of mathematics that can solve the problem that Parmenides posed. This account of Philolaus' endeavor gains support from the excerpt from Aristotle's account of the Pythagoreans which I have quoted above. There Aristotle says that it is the accuracy of the reasoning of mathematics and the fact that it alone of human endeavors admitted of proof that impressed the Pythagoreans. The picture of a Philolaus deeply impressed by the accuracy and reliability of the type of mathematical reasoning which must have characterized the work of Hippocrates and Theodorus is further supported by two brief testimonia about Philolaus. Testimonium A7a, which in fact is probably a brief quotation, says that Philolaus regarded geometry as the "mother-city" of the mathematical sciences (μαθημάτων). This clearly suggests that Philolaus had identified a set of mathematical sciences and more importantly that he was sufficiently aware of the work in those sciences to recognize that it was in the geometry of his time that there was the greatest progress. Again the brief statement in Sextus (A29) that Philolaus regarded the *logos* which arises from study of the mathematical sciences as the criterion of truth, while cast in terms of later philosophy, gives another small indication that coheres with the idea that Philolaus was *au courant* with the work that was going on in rigorous mathematics in his day.

In the end the greatest argument against Burkert's claim that the mathematics that Philolaus invokes is simply number mysticism is the way Philolaus' fragments fit into the Presocratic debate about the basis for knowledge. Number is not invoked in the fragments as an all-powerful explanatory concept. Limiters and unlimiteds are introduced to explain many aspects of the world. Number and mathematics are introduced because of their cognitive reliability, because they satisfy Parmenides' requirements for a proper way of knowing while still applying to a plural world. But this type of mathematics is what Hippocrates was laboring on in his *Elements* (whatever that term may mean), not the number mysticism found in folklores around the world.

Now that the questions of the role of number in Philolaus' philosophy as well as the type of mathematics that is likely to have inspired him have been discussed, it is important to investigate a little further the connection between the role of number in Philolaus' philosophy and his two fundamental explanatory principles, limiters and unlimiteds. Of course I have already made a number of points that are relevant to this connection, but it can be most dramatically seen by pointing to F6. In the second half of that fragment Philolaus argues that limiters and unlimiteds are essentially unlike and would never come together to form an ordered whole unless some third principle bound them together. This principle is *harmonia* or "fitting together." This concept of course has a prominent role in Presocratic thought before Philolaus. Philolaus takes over from his predecessors (Heraclitus, Empedocles) the idea of harmony as something that holds together elements that are in some way in conflict with one another. What is new in Philolaus is the fact that he almost seems to identify *harmonia* with number. Thus, after he has introduced the concept of *harmonia* in F6 he immediately goes on to discuss it in quantitative terms (he refers to its size – μέγεθος) and that discussion turns out to be a discussion of the system of whole-number ratios that determine a diatonic scale. The first actual numbers we meet in the fragments of Philolaus are this system of ratios that is said to determine the size of the *harmonia* of the cosmos. There is in fact some precedent for this connection of number and *harmonia* in Empedocles (F96 where *harmonia* is associated with the proportions of elements which are combined to make bone), but Philolaus seems to have made the connection even tighter and to conceive of all "fitting together" of limiters and unlimiteds in terms of numerically specifiable relations.

But there are some indications that Philolaus tried to make an even closer tie between numbers and limiters and unlimiteds. Aristotle's testimony clearly says that there was a specific connection between limiters and odd numbers and unlimiteds and even numbers, and F5, while not explicitly making this connection, does divide numbers into three classes (even, odd, and even-odd) which seem to be parallel to the division of things in the world into limiters, unlimiteds, and things that both set limits and are unlimited (F2). It is possible that, as Barnes suggests (1982: 390), there is no connection to be made here and we could suppose that Aristotle simply saw the parallelism and assumed the connection between limiters and odd numbers, etc., even though Philolaus made no such connection. Certainty is not possible here; however, it seems not at all unlikely that Philolaus did try to connect these two triads. He may have simply thought that numbers like everything else were manifestations of limiters and unlimiteds and hence identified one class of numbers with limiters and the other with unlimiteds.

Philolaus' program

If, then, Philolaus thought that we only really know things by grasping the numerical structure according to which the limiters and unlimiteds which compose them are combined, this suggests a clear program for the rest of Philolaus' book. In so far as he is trying to present us with the truth about the world-order and the individual things in it, his treatment of topics such as cosmogony, astronomy, psychology, and medicine should show him at least searching for the numbers in things, just as Plato said that the Pythagoreans searched for numbers in heard harmonies (*R.* 531c1–2). Lloyd has made this point very well. He argues that, while in some cases the Pythagorean interest in numbers may "reflect ethical, symbolic, or aesthetic considerations," the theory that "all things are numbers" (or as I would prefer to say "all things are known by numbers") "could and did act as a stimulus to find those numbers, by measurement, in the phenomena" (1987: 276). Lloyd is thinking primarily of the reports about the various experiments carried out by Pythagoras and his followers in order to demonstrate the correspondence of whole-number ratios to the musical concords of the octave, fourth, and fifth. These experiments are problematic in several ways, but the point is that, even if they would not have worked, they still reflect the ambition of carrying out precise measurement of phenomena. In Philolaus' case we know of no such experiments, but F6 and F6a show that harmonic science was the area in which he was successful in finding the numbers which give us knowledge of things, and the remarkable success of Philolaus' thesis in this regard is undoubtedly what led him to the general thesis that all things are known in so far as we understand the number that determines their structure.

When we turn to the rest of Philolaus' account of the world-order and the things in it we certainly find evidence of the ambition to find numbers in a variety of phenomena, but there are also many aspects of the world which Philolaus does not seem to try to explain in terms of number. Thus, in his astronomical system we find evidence that he tried numerically to reconcile the solar and lunar year (A22) to arrive at a great year of fifty-nine years, and it seems likely that he took advantage of the best information available on the periods of the planets in order to determine their ordering, although he made no attempt to account for planetary movement in any sophisticated way. There is some suggestion in his theory of the great year that he may have manipulated the actual data slightly in favor of arriving at particularly pleasing numbers, and Aristotle certainly suggests that this is exactly what he did in positing the existence of the invisible counter-earth in order to bring the number of bodies orbiting the central fire to 10, because 10 is a more significant number than 9. This sort of procedure drives some modern scholars to conclude that Philolaus is a number mystic after all, but Philolaus' thesis that the phenomena point to numbers (F5) makes it very clear that the phenomena require interpretation and that the apparent answer may not be the correct one. Just as the modern scientist will many times call his data and experimental procedure into question before abandoning his theory, so Philolaus may have felt that it was legitimate in some cases to assume that further study will reveal that the cosmos is in fact constructed according to the significant numbers he expected, rather than the less significant number that actually appears to be the case.

When we turn to other areas of Philolaus' thought, we find considerably less reference to number. F13 may suggest that Philolaus saw the human body as structurally determined by the number 4 in so far as the body has four crucial centers corresponding to the four basic psychic faculties of the mature human being. However, while testimonia about Philolaus' medical theory are amenable to interpretation in terms of limiters and unlimited, there are only indirect hints of any specific role for number (i.e. the mention of a role for excess and defect in accounting for disease and the image of breathing as paying back a debt). This may be partially the result of the state of our sources and it is important to remember that until the discovery of the medical papyrus known as the *Anonymus Londinensis* we had no idea that Philolaus had any medical views at all. Certainly there is considerable evidence in the writings of the Hippocratic corpus which suggests that the role of number and measurement in medicine was a topic that was being canvased in Philolaus' day (Lloyd 1987: 247–70) and we might suppose that Philolaus had a role in this development. However, I do not think that we should be surprised if Philolaus was simply not able to say anything about the precise role of number in his account of many aspects of the cosmos, as it was simply beyond his ability to do so. Indeed, a great number of the prominent theses in Presocratic thought, as well as in early Greek medicine, are characterized by a tremendous amount of bluff which simply cannot be backed up in detail. As Lloyd says "we clearly need to suspend disbelief, if not our critical judgement entirely, when we are solemnly told, as by the author of *On Breaths*, that air is the cause of every illness..." (1987: 15–16; see also 28 and 335).

It appears that the search for the numbers in things may have led Philolaus to try to find numbers which defined certain abstract concepts as well. Aristotle reports Pythagorean attempts to identify certain numbers with concepts such as justice, opportunity, and mind, and this may well have been some sort of attempt at definition. It is not completely clear how much of this should be attributed to Philolaus, but there is some indication that he made some such identifications (see F20 and Pt. III, ch. 4, pp. 283–8). This seems to me to be only an attempt to follow out the implications of his general thesis about knowledge. If everything that is known has number, then the only way we can be said to come really to understand concepts such as justice will be by grasping the number to which justice points. These are certainly the least appealing manifestations of Philolaus' thesis about number from our point of view. However, one has only to look at the very luxuriant development of the connection of numbers and things in the later Pythagorean tradition, as exemplified by such works as the *Theologumena arithmeticae*, in order to realize that, so far as we can tell, Philolaus was in comparison the model of restraint in carrying out his program. What we have of the fragments of Philolaus suggests a much stronger similarity to Plato's use of number in dialogues such as the *Timaeus* or *Republic* than to figures in the later Greek arithmological tradition such as Philo and Anatolius. The fact that Philolaus' medicine is not an exercise in number theory and that he evidently did not try to impose an elaborate artificial numerical scheme in articulating a doctrine such

76

as the harmony of the spheres shows that, while his interest in pleasing numerical structure could lead him to question observation in some cases, his project was nonetheless to find the numbers in things where he could and not to put them there at all costs.

3. PHILOLAUS' USE OF ἀρχαί
AND THE METHOD OF HYPOTHESIS

Lloyd has made the suggestion that the author of the Hippocratic treatise *On Ancient Medicine* (henceforth *VM*) had Philolaus in mind when he launched his virulent attack on the use of hypotheses in medicine. These "hypotheses" are "postulates or assumptions used as the basis of philosophical or medical theories" (Lloyd 1963: 111) and the author of *VM* particularly complains about the practice of trying to explain the great complexity of phenomena concerning diseases in terms of just one or two such postulates (*VM* 1). He repeatedly uses the hot, the cold, the dry, and the wet as examples of these hypotheses and particularly focuses on the hot (15ff). Philolaus is a plausible target of attack because he is presented in the medical papyrus known as the *Anonymus Londinensis* as arguing precisely that the body is constituted out of "the hot." Further, Philolaus evidently also used such postulates in his cosmology, the prime example being the central fire. This is significant because *VM* seems to be attacking someone who used hypothesis both in cosmology and medicine. As Lloyd puts it "the author of *VM* concedes, ironically, that ὑποθέσεις have a place in the study of things in the heaven and under the earth which are beyond empirical verfication, while at the same time strenuously maintaining that they should be excluded from the study of medicine" (1963: 125). Two further points give some support to the idea that Philolaus used a method of hypothesis: (1) when hypothesis is first mentioned in Plato's *Phaedo* it is Simmias, a pupil of Philolaus, who uses it; (2) ὑποτίθεσθαι is used twice in the description of Philolaus' views in the *Anon. Lond.* (A27), although the word is used only once elsewhere in the *Anon. Lond.* All of this is circumstantial evidence and not enough to prove that Philolaus is the object of attack in *VM* or that he used a method of hypothesis.

Indeed, as Lloyd points out, *VM* seems to be attacking someone who explains *disease* by postulating the hot or the cold, whereas the *Anon. Lond.* only says that Philolaus thought that *the body was constituted from the hot* and assigns him a more complicated theory of disease. Still, it may well be that the hot was also central in Philolaus' account of disease, as Lloyd suggests, and it is plausible to see Philolaus as influential in developing a type of medical theory that used hypotheses and as a possible object of attack in *VM*.

In what follows I will give further support for connecting Philolaus and the type of medicine attacked in *VM*. However, I will also go on to argue that Philolaus' use of hypotheses in medicine is just one manifestation of a more general methodology which Philolaus self-consciously develops in F6 in his account of the basic nature of the cosmos and which he also applies in his account of psychic faculties in F13. This method has similarities to the "method of hypothesis" that *VM* attacks and that Plato says he borrowed from the geometers in the *Meno*, but the word hypothesis does not occur in the extant fragments of Philolaus. Instead, the word that is prominent is ἀρχή, "origin," "starting-point," "cause." In each area of investigation Philolaus tries to determine the minimum number of ἀρχαί that must be assumed to exist (or preexist – ὑπάρχειν) in order to explain the cosmos as we know it. This prominent use of ἀρχαί is one of the most striking things about the genuine fragments of Philolaus and I will discuss in more detail below exactly what Philolaus was trying to do methodologically. However, it is first necessary to confront the problems sometimes raised for the authenticity of the fragments on the basis of such a use of ἀρχαί. In the course of answering this problem by examining the uses of ἀρχή plausible in Philolaus' time we will also be able to see the background against which Philolaus developed his methodology.

Both Bywater (1868: 51) and von Fritz (1973: 481) have pointed out the use of ἀρχή in Philolaus in what they regard as the Aristotelian sense of "principle" and have used this as one basis for doubting the authenticity of some or all of the fragments. It is true that Aristotle uses the term ἀρχή in this way and it is particularly noteworthy that he uses it in this sense and as roughly equivalent to αἰτία ("cause") throughout his account of Presocratic philosophy (including the Pythagoreans) in the first book of the *Metaphysics*. I would not deny that Philolaus' usage of the term approaches

Aristotle in some ways, although the contexts in Philolaus make clear that it has not become simply a technical term for "principle" yet. However, it is not true that the use of ἀρχή in this sense of "starting-point" in explanation or "explanatory principle" is impossible before Aristotle. This use of ἀρχή is not found in the fragments of the other Presocratics, but it would appear that Hippocrates of Chios, the mathematician who is a contemporary of Philolaus, may have used it in this way. Even more significantly ἀρχή is used extensively in the Hippocratic corpus and there are a number of important texts dating around 400 in which it is used to mean "cause" and others in which it is used in discussions of methodology in a way which is reminiscent of Philolaus. Philolaus' use of ἀρχή thus fits into the general development of notions of explanation in the late fifth century and is a precursor of Aristotle's use and not part of a forgery composed after Aristotle.

In order to support this point I will now look at the texts of the Presocratics, the Hippocratic corpus, and Hippocrates of Chios in more detail. However, before doing so it is worth noting that, even apart from the parallels between Philolaus and this other late fifth-century evidence, comparison with the Pythagorean pseudepigrapha also suggests that what we have in Philolaus does not fit the pattern of the forgeries. While it is surely true that ἀρχή is used very prominently in the pseudepigrapha, its use is not isolated as in Philolaus, but combined with a wealth of other developed Platonic and Aristotelian terms. Thus, for example, there is a treatise attributed to Archytas entitled *On Principles* (Περὶ ἀρχῶν – Thesleff 1965: 19.3) in which ἀρχαί occurs frequently. But, when it comes to specifying what the ἀρχαί are, the Platonic and Aristotelian influence becomes clear. There are said to be three ἀρχαί which turn out to be god as the active principle (τὸν μὲν θεὸν...τὸν κινέοντα), matter (τὰν δ᾽ ἐστὼ τὰν ὕλαν), and form (τὰν δὲ μορφώ...). Such patently Platonic and Aristotelian terminology is lacking in the contexts in which ἀρχή occurs in Philolaus. This, in itself, does not prove that the Philolaus texts are authentic, but it does distance them from the typical Pythagorean pseudepigrapha and should make us look very closely at Philolaus' use of ἀρχή before simply labelling it as Aristotelian and classifying it with uses such as those in pseudo-Archytas.

In Presocratic texts other than Philolaus ἀρχή is commonly used with the simple meaning "beginning" and set in contrast to τέλος ("end"). See for example Melissus F2: "it does not have a beginning or end, but is unlimited" (ἀρχὴν οὐκ ἔχει οὐδὲ τελευτήν, ἀλλ' ἄπειρόν ἐστι). Melissus F4 and Heraclitus F103 are similar. Of course, there is a long-standing debate as to whether Theophrastus indicates that Anaximander used ἀρχή with reference to his "unlimited" (ἄπειρον) from which all things come (see Kirk in Furley and Allen 1970: 324–7 and Kahn 1960/85: 30–2). However, even if we accept the interpretation that Anaximander did use the term ἀρχή, it is not likely that he used it in the Aristotelian sense of "principle" (Kahn 1960/85: 235ff.). Its most probable meaning would be the "starting-point," in both a temporal and spatial sense, from which the world came to be. One final use of ἀρχή in the Presocratics that should be noted is found at the beginning of Diogenes of Apollonia's book: "It seems to me that in beginning any treatise (λόγου) it is necessary to provide a starting-point that is beyond dispute" (τὴν ἀρχὴν ἀναμφισβήτητον παρέχεσθαι). In this case ἀρχή to some extent just refers to the literal "beginning" of the book, but the fact that Diogenes specifies that this beginning should be "indisputable" shows that he is also thinking of it as a "starting-point" or "premise" in an argument.

That this use of ἀρχή is somewhat of a *topos* in the late fifth century becomes clear from a number of parallel passages in the Hippocratic corpus. Thus, in On the Art 4 the author says that "the beginning of his discourse" (ἀρχὴ τοῦ λόγου) will be agreed to by all. This beginning turns out to be the proposition that some people treated by medicine are healed. Diseases 1.9 (6.156.14ff L) asserts that there is no "demonstrated starting-point" of medicine (ἀρχὴ ἀποδεδειγμένη), nor second point, nor middle, nor end. Here the reference does not seem to be an initial premise as a starting-point, but rather to a more general question of whether it is best to begin by speaking or by acting. Yet a slightly different sense is found in Decent. 9 (CMG. 1.1.28.11), where the memory of the use of certain drugs is said to be the beginning (ἀρχή), middle, and end of medicine. Here the reference is to the learning or knowledge of medicine. The uses in this paragraph to some extent rely on the commonplace that the beginning of any endeavor is crucial. However, it is also clear that this has led to some serious reflection on methodology and the significant use of ἀρχή to refer to an initial premise in an argument. A further development of this idea of initial premise in the direction of explanatory principle can be seen in other texts.

Thus in the first chapter of *Fleshes* the author asserts that a common starting-point (κοινὴν ἀρχὴν) must be postulated (ὑποθέσθαι), by which he means a starting-point common to the opinions of men. This sounds very much like the call for an indisputable initial premise which was seen in the texts above, but it is less clear what the author of *Fleshes* regards as the common starting-point. In the treatise itself a four-element theory is advocated with some emphasis on the hot as well as a prominent role for the fatty and the glutinous. It is at least a possibility that it is the four-element theory or the role of the hot that he regards as the common starting-point, since these elements were surely prominent in a great number of medical and philosophical theories. What is also striking about the passage is that the verb "postulate" or "hypothesize" (ὑποθέσθαι), which Lloyd emphasized in the connection between *VM* and Philolaus, is used and is connected with ἀρχή which figures so largely in the Philolaus fragments. The idea that the ἀρχή in medicine might be something like the four elements rather than an initial premise, and hence that ἀρχή is developing a meaning much closer to cause or explanatory principle, becomes much clearer in a number of other texts.

The least explicit of these texts are those which refer to accounts of a given subject matter as being "from the beginning" (ἐξ ἀρχῆς). Thus *Regimen* 1.2 (*CMG* 1.2.4. 122.22–5) asserts that to treat human regimen properly it is necessary to know the nature of man and in particular from what things man was constituted "from the beginning" (ἀπὸ τίνων συνέστηκεν ἐξ ἀρχῆς), and a few lines later refers to the "primary constitution" (τὴν ἐξ ἀρχῆς σύστασιν). *VM* 20 rejects this view and says that the inquiry about the nature of man is irrelevant to medicine and belongs to philosophy and to those like Empedocles who have written on "what man is from the beginning" (ἐξ ἀρχῆς ὅ τί ἐστιν ἄνθρωπος). In these cases the constituents from which man is constituted are not literally called ἀρχαί, but once again it is significant that accounts that did begin by isolating a set of basic components or explanatory principles were labeled as being "from the beginning" (ἐξ ἀρχῆς). The final group of Hippocratic texts which I will consider goes on explicitly to use ἀρχαί to refer to the explanatory principles or causes of medical phenomena.

Thus in *Breaths* 1 the author refers to the question of the cause (αἴτιον) of diseases and glosses it as the search for "the beginning and source" (ἀρχὴ καὶ πηγή) of affections (παθῶν) of the body. *Diseases* 4 (7.542.14 L) promises to show "what are the ἀρχαί of diseases" where ἀρχαί may still have connotations of "beginnings," but where it clearly also means "causes." Thus, in chapter 50 (7.581.21 L) the author refers to the three "causes" (ἀρχαί) of disease which turn out to be the excess of one of the humors, violence, and intemperate weather (see also *Diseases* 1.26, 2.8; *Affections* 25; *Places in Man* 31). In *VM* 10 changes in diet are said to be "the cause/origin of a serious illness for many" (πολλοῖσιν ἀρχὴ νούσου αὕτη μεγάλης – see also the end of the same chapter). A skeptic might maintain that ἀρχή means nothing more than "beginning" in these passages, but the frequent combination with αἴτιον ("cause"), which is exactly what we find in Aristotle *Metaphysics* 1, surely suggests that it is coming to be understood not simply as a temporal beginning, but as a causal and explanatory factor. Indeed, "cause" is clearly the most natural reading of most of the uses in *Diseases* 1, 2, and 4 as well as *Affections*.

In summary, then, amongst the very numerous uses of ἀρχή in the Hippocratic corpus (there are some 369 in total – the most common use being the simple spatial/temporal sense of "beginning") there are: (1) a number of passages where the word takes on a methodological significance and means something like "initial premise" or "starting-point" in a discussion; (2) a number of other passages where it is closely tied to αἰτία ("cause") and refers to the factors or principles that are seen as the beginnings or causes of diseases or even of the constitution of a human being.

If we turn to the mathematician Hippocrates of Chios, who is contemporaneous with these medical texts or somewhat earlier (430 BC), we find a significant use of ἀρχή that has close connections to the methodological use of "initial premise" found in the medical writers. Not much is known about Hippocrates of Chios, but we do have one extended account of his work on the quadrature of lunes which is probably from the history of mathematics by Aristotle's pupil Eudemus and is preserved in Simplicius (*in Ph.* 60.22–68.32). For present purposes there are two things to note about Hippocrates. First of all he is reported by Proclus (*in Euc.* 66.7) to be the first person to compose an *Elements* (στοιχεῖα). What is important about this is that it indicates that in the latter part of the fifth century mathematics had advanced far enough to distinguish between more and less fundamental propositions and was concerned to try to determine a set of first principles. Second, in the account of Hippocrates' work on lunes preserved in Simplicius the word ἀρχή is used to refer to a proposition (that similar segments of circles have the same ratios as the squares on their bases) that is the starting-point of a given demonstration, but which is itself proved from prior propositions. It is not certain that this use of ἀρχή really belongs to Hippocrates rather than Eudemus or Simplicius, but it is plausible that it does (Lloyd 1979: 109ff). Its use to refer to a proposition that is the basis of a given demonstration, but not among the basic axioms of Hippocrates' *Elements* as a whole, goes beyond the medical use of "initial premise" of medical science, but will have some interesting connections with Philolaus' methodology, as will be shown below.

My contention then is that Philolaus' use of the word ἀρχαί, while going beyond most of the uses in the preserved texts of other Presocratic philosophers, has interesting connections with the development of the term in Greek medicine and mathematics in the later part of the fifth century which I have outlined above. Philolaus differs from these texts in so far as he is more self-conscious about developing a consistent methodology of ἀρχαί than the medical writers and in so far as he applies that methodology over a wider range of topics. Nonetheless, his usage has more in common with the writers of the later fifth century than with Aristotle, and the discussion of ἀρχαί makes better sense in a fifth-century context than as a forgery after the time of Aristotle. But what is this method of ἀρχαί which I keep ascribing to Philolaus?

The crucial text is F6. Philolaus begins by asserting that knowledge of ultimate reality ("the being of things and nature itself") is beyond human ability with one exception. The exception is that "it was impossible for any of the things that are and are known by us to have come to be, if the being of the things from which the world-order came together, both the limiting things and the unlimited things, did not preexist (ὑπαρχούσας). But since these beginnings (ἀρχαί) preexisted (ὑπᾶρχον)..." The first thing to note about Philolaus' use of ἀρχαί here is that it is connected to the verb ὑπάρχειν ("to preexist"). This connection is one of the things which shows that for Philolaus ἀρχή has not become simply a technical term for "principle," but rather that the original sense of "origin" or

"beginning" is still strong. For Philolaus ἀρχαί are preexistent beginnings or origins. The second thing to note is the way in which
Philolaus determines the nature of these beginnings or origins. They
are beginnings without which the world as we know it would not
come to be as we know it. Thus for Philolaus the ἀρχαί are something like "explanatory origins" or "explanatory principles." The
final important point to note is that Philolaus is taking a reductionist
stance in specifying these principles. He is hesitant to say anything
at all about the ultimate principles of the cosmos, and the exception
which he makes is to say what are the minimum principles that must
preexist in order to explain the cosmos. His answer then is very
schematic and unspecific. No further statement is made about which
limiters or which unlimiteds must preexist. All we are justified in concluding is that some limiters and unlimiteds preexisted. The point is
that you can give an account of the cosmos in terms of limiters and
unlimiteds, while it is not clear that such an account can be given
just in terms of any other preexistent principle such as, say, water or
fire.

This use of ἀρχαί by Philolaus clearly has some connections with
the Hippocratic texts which have been discussed above. Both the
sense of "cause" or "origin" and also the sense of an accepted
"starting-point" or "premise" in an argument, which are prominent in the Hippocratics, are involved in F6, since the ἀρχαί are
presented as both the "cause" of the coming-to-be of cosmos and as
the "starting-point" in Philolaus' explanation of it. What is distinctive about F6 is that it defines the nature of the ἀρχαί much more
explicitly and self-consciously than any text in the Hippocratic corpus. Philolaus explicitly identifies the ἀρχαί as the minimum starting-
points or principles required to explain the phenomena. But the
other striking thing about Philolaus' procedure is that he does not
just try to determine the ultimate ἀρχαί of the whole cosmos, but
goes on in other parts of his book to define other ἀρχαί that serve as
explanatory principles of certain defined sets of phenomena, such as
diseases or psychic capabilities.

Thus, in F13 Philolaus says that "the brain [provides] the origin
(ἀρχή) of man, the heart the origin of animals, the navel the origin
of plants, the genitals the origin of all (living things). For all things
both flourish and grow from seed." I want to argue that ἀρχή is
being used here in just the same way as in F6 and that Philolaus is

85

following the method of explanation which he introduced there. When trying to define the sense of ἀρχή in F13, the first clue is found in the last sentence of the fragment. In order to explain why the genitals are the ἀρχή of all things Philolaus asserts that "all things both flourish and grow from seed." Thus, the point seems to be that the ἀρχή is "that from which a given thing develops" and since all things develop from their respective seeds and since the genitals produce seed, the genitals can be said to be the ἀρχή of all living things. This emphasis on the ἀρχή as referring to the starting-point from which something develops is the same emphasis Philolaus achieved in F6 by using the verb ὑπάρχειν ("preexist") to describe the ἀρχαί. But the connection is closer than that. In F13 the ἀρχαί are not just preexisting starting-points from which something develops. Once again, as in F6, they are the minimum starting-points required in order to explain the relevant phenomena. Thus, the brain is not simply the temporal or spatial starting-point from which the human develops (although it may be that too), it is what we have to appeal to in order to explain the specific organism known as a human being. Without appealing to the brain, which is the seat of intellect for Philolaus, it is impossible to give an account of what distinguishes a human being from any other organism. Similarly, the heart as the seat of sensation is the indispensable explanatory principle in any account of animals, the navel as the seat of rooting is the explanatory principle for plants, and the genitals are the explanatory principle necessary to distinguish living things in general from non-living things. Aristotle interestingly gives support for use of ἀρχή among his predecessors in just such a context during his account of the meaning of the term in Book 5 of the *Metaphysics*. At 1013a4 he gives as the third meaning of ἀρχή, "that from which, by its preexistence (ὑπάρχοντος), a thing first comes to be." As one of the examples of this use he mentions those who suppose that the heart is the beginning of animals and others who suppose that it is the head.

There is a striking parallel between Philolaus' use of ἀρχή in F13 and the use of ἀρχή by Hippocrates of Chios, the contemporary of Philolaus, which I discussed above. Hippocrates used ἀρχή to refer to a proposition which was the starting-point of a specific demonstration, but which was itself proved in terms of other propositions and which was thus in no way an ultimate starting-point or axiom in Hippocrates' *Elements*. Similarly, in F13 Philolaus describes the brain as providing the starting-point of humans, the heart of animals, etc., where once again ἀρχή is not an ultimate principle in Philolaus' system, but rather a principle necessary to explain one circumscribed field of phenomena (e.g. humans or animals), and which will itself need to be explained in terms of more basic principles (i.e. limiters and unlimiteds). The method which I am attributing to Philolaus is in fact the practice of determining the minimum number of ἀρχαί or starting-points necessary for explanation for each major area of phenomena. We have seen that he follows this procedure for the cosmos as a whole where limiters and unlimiteds are posited as the ἀρχαί, and in F13 he uses it in his account of living things, positing one ἀρχή which explains their difference from inanimate nature, and a separate ἀρχή for each of the three major types of living things. The fragments do not allow us to prove that he followed this procedure everywhere, but the fact that it can be shown that he used the procedure in two other cases strongly suggests that it was a general methodology.

The least clear of the two other cases is found in A7a. There Philolaus is reported as having said that "Geometry is the mother city and ἀρχή of the other sciences (μαθήματα)." As in the case of F6 and F13 Philolaus once again emphasizes the role of the ἀρχή as the preexisting origin, this time by using the image of the mother city which is the origin from which a colony is sent forth. Of course the mother city also "explains" the colony in the sense that it provided not only the people that made up the colony, but also its constitution. It seems clear that Philolaus is postulating some sort of hierarchy of sciences, but much remains unclear. What exactly did Philolaus include among the sciences (μαθήματα)? How did Philolaus conceive of geometry as necessary to explain all other sciences? But, it is still striking that even when it came to discussing the sciences Philolaus tried to order them in a hierarchy in terms of his methodology of ἀρχαί.

At this point we can return to where we began, Philolaus' medical theory, to see the final example of his application of the method of ἀρχαί. It appears that Philolaus called bile, blood, and phlegm the ἀρχαί of diseases (A27). This is a clear example of the same approach as in Fragments 6 and 13. All diseases are conceived of as explicable in terms of these three substances. Blood causes disease when it becomes abnormally thick or thin, while bile and phlegm seem to be simply noxious substances in the body whose presence generates disease.

A problem arises, however, concerning the connection between the theories attacked in *VM* and Philolaus. As noted above *VM* particularly responds to a theory that explains disease in terms of the hot. However, it is bile, blood, and phlegm that Philolaus has labeled the ἀρχαί of disease, and not the hot. This problem can be somewhat overcome by recognizing that several levels of explanation may be involved, so that in one sense the hot is the cause of all disease and in another sense it is bile, blood, and phlegm. To show this it will be necessary to examine Philolaus' account of the origin of the human body. It is clear that heat had the central role in Philolaus' embryology and that it is the original constituent of the human body. We have no direct evidence that Philolaus called the hot the ἀρχή of the embryo, but his arguments for saying that the embryo is constituted of the hot are very reminiscent of his discussion of ἀρχαί elsewhere. He shows for instance that upon birth the child draws in the cold through breath as something foreign to it. The point is that, since the cold only enters after birth, it is not a necessary principle of explanation for the embryo. Once again Philolaus looks at those things which must be postulated in order for the embryo to come to be, the sperm and the womb, and determines that both of these are hot. But this is just the move to determine the minimum number of preexisting principles necessary to explain a phenomenon which was so clear in F6 and F13. It is thus not at all implausible that Philolaus called the hot the ἀρχή of the human body, but what has this got to do with disease?

Philolaus may well have thought that the body's innate heat is the cause of disease when it is not properly kept in check by the activity of breathing, or when other factors such as excess nutriment produce more heat than can be tempered by breath. That this is so is clearly implied by two features of the description of his medical views by Meno. First of all, it is explicitly said that the function of breathing is to cool the body which is too hot (θερμότερα – A27). Second, at the end of the section on Philolaus' account of disease, Meno mentions that excesses and deficiencies of nutriment, hot, and cold also have a role in disease, which would certainly be consistent with the idea that the proper amount of innate heat accounts for health, whereas heat that is out of balance in some way causes disease. This is a very appealing interpretation of Philolaus' theory because it can be easily tied to his most fundamental principles, limiters, unlimiteds, and *harmonia*. In itself hot is an unlimited and can cause disease, but heat that is limited in accordance with *harmonia* produces health.

But if this is Philolaus' theory why did he not simply say that the hot is the ἀρχή of disease? Why bother to introduce bile, blood, and phlegm? The problem may simply be that while Philolaus thought that the hot, when not in proper balance, was at the root of disease, he recognized that by itself heat is simply not sufficient to explain the great variety of diseases. His method first outlined in F6 calls for postulating principles that are sufficient to explain how the phenomena as we know them came to be as we know them. If imbalances in the hot were taken as the only ἀρχή of disease, it would simply not be an explanatory principle of sufficient power to account for all the phenomena of disease; it could not distinguish between, say, dysentery and pleurisy. However, postulating three different ἀρχαί may well allow us to distinguish between the main types of disease. Certainly, bile, blood, and phlegm are constantly appealed to in explanations of disease in the Hippocratic corpus, even if no text explains all disease just in terms of the triad Philolaus proposes. Moreover, the connection with the hot does not have to be given up. Bile, blood, and phlegm can all be seen as different manifestations of imbalances of heat in the body, and this explains Philolaus' treatment of phlegm as hot, although it is usually regarded as cold. It is true that the accounts given of the origin of bile, phlegm, and abnormally thick or thin blood make no mention of heat. Yet these accounts are clearly drastically compressed in Meno's report and hard to make sense of at all. So that even here it remains possible that heat had a role and that e.g. thin blood, which is said to be produced by compression of flesh, might be the result of heat which causes the flesh to contract.

If Philolaus' theory was anything like what I have described above, it is clear that properly speaking bile, blood, and phlegm are the ἀρχαί of disease, because they would have the explanatory power required by Philolaus' method of ἀρχαί. However, if we turn around and ask how we are to explain the appearance of each of these, it may be that heat had the central role. Thus, to a critic like the author of *VM* it may well have appeared that Philolaus' account of disease was all based on excess and deficiency of heat. Certainly, it is such a theory that *VM* spends most of its time attacking. As long as we lack Philolaus' account of disease in his own words, it will be impossible to be sure how specifically he was the target of *VM*. However, that Philolaus had a central role in the type of medicine decried by *VM* becomes even clearer now that we have seen the nature of Philolaus' theory of ἀρχαί. It is the search for a minimum number of explanatory features that characterizes Philolaus' method and is precisely what is attacked by the author of *VM*, who argues that a much wider variety of explanatory factors must be employed. It is at this point that we can see how striking the connection between Philolaus' method and the object of attack in *VM* is. The language that *VM* 1 uses to characterize the pernicious trend in medicine which it is attacking not only emphasizes "hypothesis," but in fact uses the key word in Philolaus' method, ἀρχή. Philolaus is a very good target indeed for someone who complains against those who "narrow down the originating cause of diseases (ἐς βραχὺ ἄγοντες τὴν ἀρχὴν τῆς αἰτίης... νούσων)..., and make it the same in all cases, postulating one thing or two..."

At this point I hope to have given a tolerably clear account of Philolaus' use of ἀρχαί in his method of explanation, and to have shown the connection of that method both to texts in the Hippocratic corpus and also to the work of Hippocrates of Chios, as well as strengthening the case for seeing him as the object of the attack in *VM*. I would like to conclude by pointing out that the close connection between the terms ἀρχή and ὑπόθεσις which my account of Philolaus' method embraces is supported by some texts in Plato. Before looking at those texts, though, it is worthwhile to note again that the two terms are used together both in *Fleshes* 1 where the author talks of "postulating a common starting-point" (κοινὴν ἀρχὴν ὑποθέσθαι) and in *VM* 1 where the complaint is that only one or two causal principles are postulated (ἐς βραχὺ ἄγοντες τὴν ἀρχὴν τῆς αἰτίης... νούσων... ἓν ἢ δύο ὑποθέμενοι...).

The close connection between the terms ἀρχή and ὑπόθεσις in the late fifth and early fourth century is abundantly clear from Plato. Thus, at *Phaedo* 101d1ff Socrates makes a careful distinction between an hypothesis as an initial assumption and the results which follow from it, and stresses the importance of not confusing the discussion of the starting-point with the discussion of what follows from it. The word used at the outset of the passage to refer to the initial assumption is ὑπόθεσις, but at the end of the discussion (101e1) ἀρχή is introduced as a virtual synonym. Further, in *Republic* 6 (511b2ff) Plato mentions ὑπόθεσις and ἀρχή together, although this time he makes a distinction between them, calling an ὑπόθεσις a "footing" (ἐπίβασις) or "springboard" (ὁρμή) in contrast to an ἀρχή which is said to have more stability and permanence. It seems to me that this distinction between an ἀρχή and a ὑπόθεσις is likely to be Plato's own and presupposes a situation in which ὑποθέσεις are commonly regarded as ἀρχαί. It is thus tempting to suppose that Philolaus' use of ἀρχαί is in fact an early form of a method of hypothesis which forms part of the background for Plato's theory. (It is not at all unlikely that Philolaus used both terms since the testimony of Meno suggests that he used ὑποτίθημι in the medical section of his book.)

This is not the place to try to examine the complexities of Plato's discussion of hypothesis (see Lloyd 1979: 113ff for references), but it is significant that two of Plato's criticisms of the use of hypothesis by earlier thinkers could be applied to Philolaus. First, Plato criticizes thinkers who treat hypotheses as if they were firm starting-points rather than as provisional "footings" (*R.* 511b5–6). This would fit Philolaus' practice so far as we know it, in that there is never any hint that he treated any of his ἀρχαί as in any way provisional. Second, in the *Phaedo* Simmias, a follower of Philolaus, distinguishes those theories which are based only on plausible arguments from those which are based on an hypothesis worthy of acceptance (92d6). It is significant that Simmias here rejects as an unworthy hypothesis that the soul is a harmony, a doctrine that has some connections to Philolaus, in favor of the Platonic doctrine of recollection. These two criticisms could be seen as directed against Philolaus for adopting ἀρχαί too uncritically and for being unwilling to correct them in light of problems that arise.

Whether or not Philolaus is a partial object of attack in Plato, it is clear that the background of Plato's remarks on hypothesis must be much broader than just Philolaus' book, since he explicitly says in the *Meno* (86e4–5) that he is borrowing the method from the geometers, and Philolaus is not a geometer. However, he seems to be the precursor of Plato in that, under the influence of the practice of mathematicians and medical writers, he first explicitly tried to develop a general philosophical method that applied to every area of inquiry, a method which called for an attempt to identify a minimum set of explanatory principles necessary for a given domain of phenomena.

Part III
GENUINE FRAGMENTS
AND TESTIMONIA

1. BASIC PRINCIPLES

Fragment 1

Diogenes Laertius 8.85 τοῦτόν [Φιλόλαον] φησι Δημήτριος ἐν
Ὁμωνύμοις πρῶτον ἐκδοῦναι τῶν Πυθαγορικῶν Περὶ φύσεως,
ὦν ἀρχὴ ἥδε· **ἁ φύσις δ' ἐν τῷ κόσμῳ ἁρμόχθη ἐξ ἀπείρων**
τε καὶ περαινόντων καὶ ὅλος ⟨ὁ⟩ κόσμος καὶ τὰ ἐν αὐτῷ
5 **πάντα.**

2 post Πυθαγορικῶν ⟨βιβλία καὶ ἐπιγράψαι⟩ Diels ⟨τὰ⟩ Reiskius   Περὶ FP^pc om.
BP^ac   3 ἀρχὴ BP^ac ἡ ἀρχὴ FP^pc   ἥδε· ἁ Diels ἥδε α BP^ac ἥδε FP^pc   ἐν τῷ κόσμῳ
MSS τῷ κόσμῳ Heidel   4 τε FP om. B   ⟨ὁ⟩ Cobet

Demetrius, in *People of the Same Name*, says that he [Philolaus] was
the first of the Pythagoreans to publish an *On Nature*, of which this is
the beginning: "Nature in the world-order was fitted together both
out of things which are unlimited and out of things which are limiting, both the world-order as a whole and all the things in it."

AUTHENTICITY

The authenticity of this fragment is very likely for two reasons: (1) It cele-
brates precisely those concepts which Aristotle assigns to the Pythagoreans
of the fifth century (i.e. limiters and unlimiteds). (2) It betrays none of the
features of the pseudepigrapha either in content or style. The usage of the
terms "nature" (φύσις) and "world-order" (κόσμος) exactly accords with
what we would expect from a fifth-century author, while there are no
distinctively Platonic or Aristotelian ideas.

COMMENTARY

The context in Diogenes: Diogenes Laertius (third century AD) says
that, according to Demetrius of Magnesia (first century BC), Philolaus

93

was the first Pythagorean to publish an *On Nature* (ἐκδοῦναι Περὶ φύσεως). Diogenes uses Demetrius frequently as a source and refers to him shortly before this passage (8.84) for the information that Philolaus' predecessor Hippasus wrote nothing, which is consistent with the report here that Philolaus was the first Pythagorean to publish (see Pt. I, ch. 1).

It is clear in numerous places in Diogenes that he regarded the phrase "On Nature" (περὶ φύσεως) as a book title (e.g. 9.46; 10.27). Thus Burkert is probably right that Diogenes (and Demetrius) regarded περὶ φύσεως as the title of Philolaus' book and that it should be understood as the object of the verb ἐκδοῦναι ("publish"). Burkert (1972: 241 n. 10) gives as parallels Plut. *Rom.* 8 ([ὁ Πεπαρήθιος Διοκλῆς] ὃς δοκεῖ πρῶτος ἐκδοῦναι Ῥώμης κτίσιν) and Strabo 1.15. Diels thought that this passage was parallel to the story at D.L. 8.15 where Philolaus is said to have brought forth the three famous books (of Pythagoras), and therefore suggested that something to that effect had fallen out at 8.85. He suggests that we supplement the passage to read "... he was the first to publish the Pythagorean books and give them the title *On Nature*..." One piece of evidence that might appear to support such an emendation is the use of the plural ὧν ("of which") in the next sentence when Diogenes goes on to give the first sentence of Philolaus' book. But the plural is just a vague form of reference ("of which things") and does not require that more than one book was referred to in the preceding sentence. If it did we would expect more than one first line to be given (Burkert 1972: 241 n. 10). Thus, it is unjustified to insert the words Diels proposes, without any manuscript authority or palaeographical likelihood, in order to homogenize the tradition about Philolaus' publications. There is a tradition that merely has him publish the supposed works of Pythagoras, but he is also said to have published his own book (see Pt. I, ch. 1).

It is unclear whether Philolaus himself called his book *On Nature* or if he gave it any title at all. *On Nature* is the standard title given to the works of almost all the Presocratics by writers of the Alexandrian period and later. Some scholars doubt that this title was possible for authors of the sixth century, such as Anaximander, because it presupposes a comprehensive sense of Nature that did not arise until later (Kirk 1954: 229). Kirk (1954: 37) is rightly skeptical about the use of passages such as *VM* 20 by Verdenius (1947/8) to prove that the title existed in the fifth century (Ἐμπεδοκλῆς ἢ ἄλλοι οἳ περὶ φύσεως γεγράφασιν). Such passages can just as easily be read as referring to a general subject matter as a title ("those who have written on nature" – see also Plato *Phlb.* 59a2, *Prt.* 315c5). On the other hand, some have felt that the title of Gorgias' book *On Nature or On What is Not* (Περὶ φύσεως ἢ περὶ τοῦ μὴ ὄντος) presupposes the existence of books entitled *On Nature* for the parody to work (Schofield, KRS 103

n. 1 and Guthrie 1962: 73). Similarly, Kahn (1960/85: 6 n. 2) takes Aristotle's remark at *GC* 333b18 to imply that he knew of Empedocles' book under the title *On Nature* ("[Empedocles] after all says nothing *On Nature*"). Thus, it appears possible that Philolaus, a contemporary of Gorgias, could have entitled his book *On Nature*, but it is also possible that it had no title and was later given the generic title for all Presocratic works.

Diogenes goes on to say that what follows is the ἀρχή of Philolaus' book. ἀρχή is used in similar phrases elsewhere in Diogenes and it seems clear that he means to indicate that what follow are the beginning words of the book. Scholars have generally accepted Diogenes' evidence for the beginnings of books elsewhere (e.g. 1.119 [Pherecydes]; 6.81 and 9.57 [Diogenes of Apollonia]; 8.83 [Alcmaeon]). It is somewhat disquieting that Diogenes seems to be in error about the beginning of Anaxagoras' book (2.6), providing a brief paraphrase of its first part rather than quoting the actual first words. In the latter case Diogenes does not use ἀρχή but rather ἀρξάμενος ['Αναξαγόρας] οὕτω τοῦ συγγράμματος..., but this clearly also refers to the beginning of a book. No doubt Diogenes is not as reliable as could be desired in such matters, but the words he assigns to the beginning of Philolaus' book do make a good beginning. The fragment presents the central insight of Philolaus' metaphysical system in a very compact fashion appropriate for the beginning of a book. In F2 Philolaus argues for the thesis which is stated dogmatically here. Anaxagoras' book also begins with a statement of his main theme, "All things were together"(ὁμοῦ χρήματα πάντα ἦν – see Schofield 1980: 39).

Modern scholarship has generally accepted the testimony of Diogenes. However, Boeckh (1819: 45–7) argued that there were strong internal reasons for rejecting the fragment as the beginning of the book. His first complaint was that the particle δέ could not occur in the first line of the book. It is now recognized that this is in fact the practice of several authors of the fifth century (Heraclitus F1, Ion F1, ps.-Xen. *Ath.* 1, etc.) and is thus even evidence for the authenticity of the fragment (Burkert 1972: 252 n. 68). It is likely that the δέ originally followed upon a title or some introductory phrase including the title (Verdenius 1947: 272 n. 7 and West 1971: 9). Burkert argues that the δέ accordingly "guarantees the title Περὶ φύσεως," but it at best only guarantees some sort of introductory sentence. Some scholars deny that any such introductory sentence needs to be supposed and point out that δέ is just a weaker form of δή (Kirk 1954: 36).

Boeckh also found the fragment's meaning to be confused. He argued that F2 would make a much better beginning and that F1 was a later summary of the main thought of F2. It is true that F1 is very close in wording to a part of F2 (... ἐκ περαινόντων τε καὶ ἀπείρων ὅ τε κόσμος καὶ τὰ ἐν αὐτῷ συναρμόχθη). However, the passage in F2 comes at the conclusion of an argument and can well be read as restating the thesis to be proved which was first set out in F1. Such repetition is frequently found in Empedocles. Burkert finds this sort of repetition to be "the typical style of the Presocratics" and thus strong evidence for the authenticity of the fragments (1972: 252). Thus, Boeckh's attempts to use internal evidence to show that F1 cannot be the beginning of the book are not successful and we should accept Diogenes' testimony.

φύσις: The meaning of this term in this context is "nature" or "real constitution," which is the typical meaning in early Greek thought (Kirk 1954: 42, Kahn 1960/85: 201 n. 2 and Holwerda 1955). Heraclitus' famous statement that "φύσις loves to hide" (F123) is a clear example of this meaning and a good parallel for Philolaus' usage. (Indeed, Kirk, who doubts the authenticity of the fragments, concedes that in Fragments 1–6 "the meaning of φύσις may be the same as for the Presocratics" and goes on "even though these fragments were probably not by Philolaus himself they show considerable knowledge of Presocratic modes of expression" [1954: 230 n. 1].) Thus Philolaus' use of φύσις as the first word in his book puts him squarely in the main line of the Presocratic tradition (Mourelatos 1970: 60–1 and Kahn 1960/85: 201–3). Philolaus' point is that the "nature" of whatever we choose to study in the cosmos is to be explained in terms of the fitting together of two basic types of components, limiters and unlimiteds. The last clause of the sentence then makes the point that the nature in question can be either the nature of the cosmos taken as a whole or the nature of any individual thing in it. The etymology of φύσις also suggests the meaning "growth," which can be activated in certain contexts (e.g. Empedocles F8). Since Philolaus clearly gave a cosmogony to explain the world ("was fitted together" here and even more explicitly in F7), it is probable that he also means that the genesis of anything in the cosmos has to involve limiters and unlimiteds. It is absolutely typical of the Presocratics to see no sharp distinction between φύσις in the sense of "genesis" and in the sense of "nature." Philolaus clearly subscribes to this view which says that something's nature is revealed by giving its genesis (Kahn 1960/85: 201 n. 1).

Burkert and Holwerda mistakenly understand φύσις in this fragment to be equivalent to πᾶν τὸ ὄν, "all that exists" (Holwerda 1955: 78, Burkert 1972: 250 n. 58, 274). Burkert, evidently following Holwerda's evidence, says that "the use of φύσις to mean the totality of ἐόντα is common in the time of Philolaus," and cites Euripides F910 as an example (ἀθανάτου φύσεως κόσμον). Holwerda lists twenty examples of the use from Plato, Euripides, Middle and New Comedy, and the Hippocratic corpus. However, what is common to all the instances mentioned, *except* Philolaus F1, is that φύσις is used without any dependent noun or phrase. This is just what one would expect if φύσις is being used to mean "all there is," but it is not what is found in Philolaus where ἐν τῷ κόσμῳ is added in a modifying phrase.

More importantly there are two internal reasons for ruling out the Burkert–Holwerda reading. First, if φύσις is "all there is," how does the phrase ἁ φύσις ἐν τῷ κόσμῳ differ from the last words of the fragment, τὰ ἐν αὐτῷ πάντα? The sentence becomes intolerably repetitious: "All there is in the cosmos was fitted together from unlimiteds and limiters, both the cosmos as a whole and all there is in the cosmos." If φύσις means "nature" or "real constitution," then the latter part of the sentence has a real function. It specifies the two areas in which "nature" is being considered, in the case of the cosmos as a whole and in the case of the individual things in it. Second, when φύσις appears again in F6, it is used with the intensive αὐτή ("nature itself") and is paired with ἁ ἐστὼ τῶν πραγμάτων ("the being of things") as being beyond human knowledge. It is hard to see how it can mean "all there is" in such a context, and a meaning such as "inner nature" or "real constitution" is called for. The point is not that we cannot know the totality of things, but rather that the ultimate nature of reality ("the being of things") is not accessible to us.

ἐν τῷ κόσμῳ . . . ὅλος ⟨ὁ⟩ κόσμος: κόσμος occurs six times in the relatively short compass of the genuine fragments (F1 [2]; F2 [1]; F6 [2]; F17 [1]). It is a central term in the Presocratic tradition (e.g. Heraclitus F30, Empedocles F26, Anaxagoras F8, Diogenes F2) and the emphasis that Philolaus puts on it, along with the emphasis on φύσις, ties him closely to that tradition. Its meaning is also perfectly in accord with what we would expect for the second half of the fifth century. The contrast that is set up here in F1, and repeated in F2, between the whole cosmos and all the things in it clearly suggests that it has the all-embracing sense of "world". Similarly in F17 the κόσμος that is said to be one and whose generation is described must be the "whole world." However, it is also the subject of verbs which emphasize that this world is an "organized system". Thus, here in F1 and in F2 the κόσμος is "fitted together" (ἁρμόχθη, συναρμόχθη), and in F6 it is "put together" or "composed" (συνέστα). The verb κοσμηθῆναι is used in F6 as part of the argument to show that the unlike first principles, limiters and unlimiteds, could not become part of an "organized system" if a harmony did not intervene to fit them together. Finally, κόσμος is used a few lines later in F6, without the article, in the simple sense of "order." Thus, while κόσμος is clearly being used to refer to the whole structure of reality and is in this sense close to the meaning "world," it is constantly used with verbs and in arguments that emphasize the earliest meaning of the term ("order"), so that to translate it as "world" is misleading and it is best rendered as "world-order."

Studies of the word κόσμος in Greek thought have shown that it develops from an early sense of "order," where the primary reference may be to the "disciplined array" of an army or to a moral–political order (on this and what follows see Kahn 1960/85: 219ff and 1979: 132ff, 312 n. 120; Kirk 1954: 311ff; Kerchensteiner 1962). It also has the sense of "beautiful order" and hence "ornament" or "adornment." In some Presocratic contexts it still has the simple meaning of "order" (Melissus F7; Parmenides F4), but comes to refer specifically to the all-embracing "ordered whole" (Anaxagoras F8; Diogenes F2 [τὰ ἐν τῷδε τῷ κόσμῳ ἐόντα]). Heraclitus F30 seems to mark the transition to this latter sense which is prominent in the fifth century. At Empedocles F134 it appears to be used for the first time as simply "world." Thus, the usage in Fragments 1, 2, 6, and 17 of Philolaus fits very well with the rest of the fifth-century uses where the sense of "ordered whole" is dominant, but where the sense of simply "world" is becoming possible. Kirk recognizes this (1954: 314) but, since he assumes that the fragments are spurious, he is driven to the tortured explanation that they were forged shortly after Aristotle, but "perhaps used known pronouncements of Philolaus as a model." Kahn (1960/85: 228) also notes that the use of κόσμος in these fragments of Philolaus is "at least as archaic as that of Empedocles and Diogenes."

It is interesting to note that in the doxographical tradition Pythagoras himself is credited with having given κόσμος its philosophical sense (Aetius 2.1.1 = DK 14.21: Π. πρῶτος ὠνόμασε τὴν τῶν ὅλων περιοχὴν κόσμον ἐκ τῆς ἐν αὐτῷ τάξεως, "Pythagoras first named that which surrounds the whole 'cosmos' on account of the order in it"). This does not fit with the gradual development of the term which is traceable completely independently of Pythagoras, but it does fit with the later Academic tradition which tends to assign all great discoveries to the master. Particularly relevant here is the similarly fanciful report of Heraclides Ponticus, a member of the early Academy, which ascribes the invention of the word "philosophy" to Pythagoras (Burkert 1972: 65, 77 nn. 152–3). It is possible that the story of Pythagoras' use of the term κόσμος is based on a reading of Philolaus' fragments in the Academy.

ἁ φύσις δ' ἐν τῷ κόσμῳ ἁρμόχθη . . . : As has been shown above, each of the components of this phrase, φύσις and κόσμος, is used in senses that fit well with Philolaus' date, the second half of the fifth century. However, this particular combination of the terms seems to be unique to Philolaus and is used to make an important point. What is unusual is the combination of φύσις and ἐν τῷ κόσμῳ. There are no precise parallels for this phrase. There are not even any parallels for the combination φύσις ἐν before the time of Aristotle (to judge from Holwerda's study) and it is rare then (Aristotle, *GA* 1.22, 730b19, ἡ φύσις ἡ ἐν τῷ ἄρρενι τῶν σπέρμα προϊεμένων; pseudo-Eurytus [Thesleff 1965: 88.11], ἐπεὶ γὰρ δύο φύσεις ἐν τῷ ὅλῳ τῷδε καὶ τῷ παντὶ ἐνυπάρχοντι). Burkert (1972: 250 n. 58) gives Anaxagoras F8, τὰ ἐν τῷ ἑνὶ κόσμῳ (see also Diogenes F2) as a parallel. However, this is not a parallel for ἁ φύσις ἐν τῷ κόσμῳ, but rather for the last words of the fragment, τὰ ἐν αὐτῷ πάντα (Nussbaum 1979: 94).

It would be possible to avoid the difficulties with the phrase if ἐν τῷ κόσμῳ were taken with the verb ἁρμόχθη ("Nature was harmonized in the world-order...") instead of ἁ φύσις. However, there are two problems with this suggestion. First, since φύσις is frequently found followed by a dependent noun or noun phrase (usually in the genitive), there is a natural tendency to associate ἐν τῷ κόσμῳ with ἁ φύσις. Indeed, this reading is so natural that most scholars assume it without argument. Second, if ἐν τῷ κόσμῳ is taken with the verb it is hard to see what force it has and how it relates to Philolaus' overall argument. There is no evidence that Philolaus was concerned to say *where* harmonization takes place, but F6 shows that he *is* concerned to define the scope of his discussion of "nature" (see below).

Heidel (1907: 79) suggested that the passage be emended to ἁ φύσις τῶ κόσμω. The Doric genitive would look identical to an Attic dative, since the iota subscript is often ignored in manuscripts. A scribe would then have inserted the ἐν to explain the dative, using the phrase τὰ ἐν αὐτῷ from the end of the sentence as a model. Although it is difficult to find an exact parallel for Heidel's emendation (Nussbaum 1979: 94 n. 77 cites the title περὶ φύσεως κόσμου reported for Democritus [A2, A31, F56]; see also the title of the *Timaeus Locrus* as given by Iamblichus, περὶ φύσιος κόσμω καὶ ψυχᾶς, Thesleff 1965: 203.7), the construction of φύσις with the genitive is very common. (Note especially the expression φύσις πάντων in the Δίσσοι λόγοι and Critias F19. See also Archytas F1, περὶ γὰρ τᾶς τῶν ὅλων φύσιος.) However, Burkert argues that ἁ φύσις τῶ κόσμω "would in itself be suspicious" and cites Euripides F910 where it seems the other way around, ἀθανάτου φύσεως κόσμον. But the Euripides passage is not sufficient to rule out Heidel's emendation. In Euripides κόσμος seems to be used in the common sense of "order." If it is used in the sense "world-order," as it is in F1 of Philolaus (see above), there is no reason why it could not have a different construction with φύσις. The general development of Greek usage is in accord with Heidel's suggestion. From expressions dealing with a particular existent such as ἡ φύσις τοῦ ἀνθρώπου ("the nature of man," Soph. *Aj.* 762, etc.) the use spread to phrases like ἡ φύσις πάντων ("the nature of all things," Critias F19, etc.). Why not ἁ φύσις τῶ κόσμω?

Nussbaum has accepted Heidel's emendation both because it is more typical Greek usage and because it is "what the sense of the passage very plainly requires" (1979: 94). The preceding discussion shows that she is surely right that Heidel's reading is more standard Greek. However, I think that the sense of this passage and its connection with F6 show that something different is required and that Philolaus is using a strange phrase to underline an important idea.

Philolaus discusses φύσις again in F6 and makes it clear there that he is talking about φύσις in a limited sense. Once again he uses a slightly strange collocation of words. He denies that mortals can know "nature itself" (αὐτὰ ἁ φύσις), which he seems to equate with the eternal being (ἐστὼ ἀΐδιος) of things. Philolaus thus seems to be rejecting anything like Parmenides' attempt to define "what is" in the basic sense and in effect to be limiting himself to an account of the world as we experience it. He limits himself to a discussion of the φύσις that must exist to explain the world we experience. Given that he is at such pains in F6 to limit the scope of his discussion of φύσις, it is reasonable that Philolaus would try to limit φύσις in a similar way when it is first introduced in his book. The problem with Heidel's emendation in F1 is that it suggests the type of discussion that Philolaus rules out in F6. The expression "the nature of the world-order" might well suggest that Philolaus is looking for the sort of eternal principle Parmenides had in mind. Philolaus chose the phrase ἐν τῷ κόσμῳ to avoid such a suggestion and to indicate that he wants to discuss φύσις as it is in the world-order which we know, not as an eternal principle that goes beyond our experience. On first reading ἐν τῷ κόσμῳ encourages the reader to ask what is meant by this odd restriction on φύσις. The answer is provided in F6.

ἁρμόχθη: For Philolaus' concept of harmony see below on F6.

ἀπείρων τε καὶ περαινόντων: See Pt. II, ch. 1.

. . . ὅλος ⟨ὁ⟩ κόσμος καὶ τὰ ἐν αὐτῷ πάντα: This phrase is awkward in that it is made the subject of the verb in apposition to ἁ φύσις ἐν τῷ κόσμῳ. But this initial awkwardness demonstrates Philolaus' main point. When he is talking about "nature in the world-order" he means precisely the nature of the world order viewed as a whole as well as the nature of each thing in it. With Heidel's reading the transition is very problematic. First it is the nature *of* the world-order that is at issue and then, in the second part of the sentence, the world-order itself and the things in it come to the fore. But the latter seem to be a different subject matter than the former, just as physics differs from metaphysics. Such distinctions of course do not literally apply at this point in the history of philosophy, but it should be remembered that Aristotle's puzzlement about the Pythagoreans is at least partly that they seem to use principles suited to metaphysics, but to "waste" them on the physical world (*Metaph.* 989b29ff). In F1 and F6 Philolaus shows just such a focus on the physical world and a conscious avoidance of consideration of being in itself.

Fragment 2

Stobaeus, *Eclogae* 1.21.7a (1.187.16 Wachsmuth) Ἐκ τοῦ Φιλολάου Περὶ κόσμου· (1) ἀνάγκα τὰ ἐόντα εἶμεν πάντα ἢ περαίνοντα ἢ ἄπειρα ἢ περαίνοντά τε καὶ ἄπειρα· (2) ἄπειρα δὲ μόνον οὐκ ἀεί. (3) ἐπεὶ τοίνυν φαίνεται οὔτ᾽ ἐκ περαινόντων
5 πάντων ἐόντα οὔτ᾽ ἐξ ἀπείρων πάντων, δῆλον τἆρα ὅτι ἐκ περαινόντων τε καὶ ἀπείρων ὅ τε κόσμος καὶ τὰ ἐν αὐτῷ συναρμόχθη. (4) δηλοῖ δὲ καὶ τὰ ἐν τοῖς ἔργοις. (5) τὰ μὲν γὰρ αὐτῶν ἐκ περαινόντων περαίνοντι, τὰ δ᾽ ἐκ περαινόντων τε καὶ ἀπείρων περαίνοντί τε καὶ οὐ περαίνοντι, τὰ δ᾽ ἐξ ἀπείρων
10 ἄπειρα φανέονται.

2–3 πάντα ἢ περαίνοντα: πάντα ἥπερ αἴνοντα M   ἢ ἄπειρα ἢ περαίνοντα: om. RY
3–4 ἄπειρα δὲ μόνον: καὶ μόνον V   4 post μόνον ⟨ἢ περαίνοντα μόνον⟩ Diels   οὐκ
ἀεί: οὐ κα εἴη Badham   οὔτ᾽ FGVME οὐχ PRYH   5 τ᾽ ἄρα FH τ᾽ ἄρα
GPVMERY corr. Meineke   6 τε καί: καὶ RY   8–9 ἐκ περαινόντων περαίνοντι
FGPVME ἐκ περαινόντων περαίνοντα RYH, Canter   9 περαίνοντί τε... ἐξ ἀπείρων
om. V περαίνοντά τε καὶ οὐ περαίνοντι P²RY περαίνοντά τε καὶ οὐ περαίνοντα Canter
10 φαινέονται FPGVMEH φαίνονται RY Friedlander φανέονται Heeren φαίνεται Usener

(1) It is necessary that the things that are be all either limiting, or unlimited, or both limiting and unlimited (2) but not in every case unlimited alone. (3) Well then, since it is manifest that they are neither from limiting things alone, nor from unlimited things alone, it is clear then that the world-order and the things in it were fitted together from both limiting and unlimited things. (4) Things in their actions also make this clear. (5) For, some of them from limiting (constituents) limit, others from both limiting and unlimited (constituents) both limit and do not limit, others from unlimited (constituents) will be manifestly unlimited.

AUTHENTICITY

This fragment is very likely to be authentic for two main reasons. First, it deals exclusively with the concepts that Aristotle assigns to fifth-century Pythagoreans: limiters, unlimiteds, and harmony. The emphasis on the plurals and hence on classes of things (limiters and unlimiteds), as opposed to Aristotle's and Plato's tendency to use the singular and thus to indicate an abstract principle (limit and unlimited), is just what we would expect of a Presocratic. Second, the fragment shows none of the characteristics of the

Pythagorean pseudepigrapha either in style or in terminology. There is nothing here that belongs to the conceptual world of Plato and Aristotle (e.g. no form–matter distinction, no demiurge, no world soul). The only parallel is with Plato's *Philebus* (not a prominent influence in the pseudepigrapha) and Plato explicitly tells us there that he is borrowing to some extent from his predecessors.

COMMENTARY

The structure of the argument: F2 is probably the most perplexing of all the Philolaus fragments. There are many difficulties in the details of the fragment, but before turning to these it is important to define the general structure of the argument. The consensus among scholars is that the argument proceeds in an Eleatic fashion giving "an exhaustive enumeration of possibilities and reaching the correct one by eliminating its rivals."[1] On this view the fragment is divided into five sentences (see the divisions given in the text above). The first sentence is understood as listing the three possibilities: things are either all limiting, or all unlimited, or all both limiting and unlimited. In the second sentence the first two possibilities are ruled out (ἄπειρα δὲ μόνον ⟨ἢ περαίνοντα μόνον⟩ οὔ κα εἴη – "But they would not be only unlimited or only limiting"). The third sentence then states as a conclusion the remaining possibility, the world and everything in it were harmonized out of *both* limiting things and unlimited things. Finally, the last two sentences offer another argument, in this case based on an appeal to facts or experience, for the same conclusion. This interpretation is attractive because the Eleatic style of argument ties the fragment to the Presocratic tradition. However, there are several very serious difficulties with it.

To begin with, the argument in sentences 4 and 5 which is supposed further to support the conclusion in the first three sentences has not been convincingly shown to do so.[2] In fact, it appears to contradict that conclusion. The first three sentences are supposed to conclude that all things are both limiting and unlimited. The argument in sentences 4 and 5 does recognize things that are composed out of both limiting and unlimited constituents, but it also recognizes things that are composed of limiting elements and others that are composed of unlimited elements. These latter two cases are clearly separated from the case where things are composed of

---

[1] Nussbaum (1979: 97). Boeckh (1819: 47–50), Burkert (1972: 259–60), and Barnes (1982: 386) all see the argument as following the same pattern, although there are some differences in detail.

[2] Nussbaum's paraphrase of the argument in sentences 4 and 5 conceals the contradiction with the first three sentences (1979: 99). On Barnes's account Philolaus' reference in sentences 4 and 5 to things that both limit and do not limit becomes unnecessary (1982: 387).

both types of elements and thus must be understood to mean that some things are composed of just limiting elements and others of just unlimited elements. Therefore, the fourth and fifth sentences clearly embrace the existence of three classes of things, those that limit, those that both limit and do not limit, and those that are unlimited. Yet, on the standard interpretation, the first part of the fragment ruled out two of these possibilities.

There are also problems with the standard interpretation in its account of the first three sentences, the core of the "Eleatic argument." First the second sentence as we have it in the manuscripts only rules out one possibility at best, that all things are unlimited. In order to rule out the possibility that all things are limiting most scholars resort to a textual supplement.[3] Next, if the second sentence does rule out two possibilities, it gives no argument for doing so, unless we resort to an even more extensive textual supplement.[4] Third, the first half of the third sentence is nothing more than a bald restatement of what was a bald assertion eliminating two possibilities in sentence 2. This is, at the least, an awkward redundancy. Finally, the standard interpretation does not account for the shift from talking about things *being* limiting, etc., to talking about the cosmos being *out of* limiting, etc., constituents. Thus the third possibility of the first sentence is not explicitly inferred in the third sentence. The third possibility was that *all things* (ἐόντα) *are* both limiting and unlimited. The conclusion in the third sentence is that *the cosmos* and *all the things in it* were fitted together harmoniously *out of* both limiting and unlimited things. It is not at all obvious that these statements are equivalent.

In light of these difficulties with the standard interpretation of F2, I want to offer an alternative. The first thing to recognize in addressing the problems with the standard interpretation is that, when Philolaus refers to "the things that are" (τὰ ἐόντα) in the first sentence, he has in mind a very restricted class of things, i.e. the basic elemental powers in the world, and he is not referring to the very general class of all the unique individual things in the world (e.g. this tree, that man, this rock, etc.). This restriction of meaning for "the things that are" (τὰ ἐόντα) is found in a number of places in the Presocratics, where the examples given are things like earth and water and air and fire (Diogenes F2) or air and aither (Anaxagoras F1 – see further Kahn 1965/80: 180), and not people or trees or horses. Thus, in the first sentence of F2, Philolaus is stating what he takes to be a logical

---

[3] Diels's ⟨ἢ περαίνοντα μόνον⟩ is accepted by Burkert and Barnes. Nussbaum (1979: 98) suggests that "Philolaus might well have taken it as self-evident that this possibility is ruled out: the *perainon* implies the existence of that which gets bounded." Boeckh (1819: 49) thinks there is a lacuna, but prudently refrains from giving a specific supplement since it is unclear how large the gap might be.

[4] Nussbaum (1979: 98) and Barnes (1982: 387) suggest that F3 would be a good candidate, but do not argue that it should literally be inserted into the text at this point.

truth about the elemental powers that make up the world. It is necessary that they be either all limiters or all unlimiteds or comprised of both limiters and unlimiteds.[5] The standard interpretation is right, then, in seeing that three possibilities are listed in the first sentence, but wrong to see those possibilities as ranging over all the things that are rather than just over the basic elemental powers.

As noted above, the next sentence ("but they are not just unlimited") is usually taken to eliminate one of these possibilities. However, I think that it should be taken closely with the last of the three possibilities listed, as a pointed remark by Philolaus directed against his predecessors. There is, in fact, a clear trend in Presocratic thought which regards the elemental powers as all unlimited. Anaxagoras' book begins with the assertion that all things (= all elemental powers) were together and were unlimited. Earlier Anaximander had made his primary being the unlimited and Anaximenes had argued that his air was unlimited. Philolaus then is saying that there are in fact three possibilities about the elemental powers. They might be all unlimited, or all limiting, or, and this is the case Philolaus will argue for, they might consist of both limiters and unlimiteds and "not just unlimiteds in every case" (as is commonly argued). The reason that Philolaus does not here make the parallel point, that things are not just limiting in every case, is that this is not a position that has been prominently held by his predecessors. Thus, the second sentence goes closely with the first and should be separated from it only by a high stop. So far Philolaus is just listing logical possibilities spiced with a jab at earlier views. In what follows he will argue for the thesis that the elemental powers consist of both limiters and unlimiteds and not just unlimiteds alone as earlier thinkers had assumed.

The next sentence begins the argument for this thesis. It is crucial to note that the subject of the sentence is no longer the elemental powers, but the world-order and the things in it. The latter presumably now include people and animals and trees, etc. The strategy will be to determine the nature of the elemental powers by examining the nature of the things that are made up out of those powers, i.e. the world-order and the whole range of unique individual things in it. Thus, instead of talking about things *being* unlimiteds, etc., Philolaus shifts to talking about things being *out of* unlimiteds, etc. This is the shift that is unexplained on the standard reading of the argument. Philolaus' argument is based on appeal to the way the world appears to us. Since the world and the things in it are manifestly (φαίνεται ... ἐόντα) not composed of only limiters or only unlimiteds it is clear (δῆλον) that only one of the three possibilities remains, that the basic elements from which the world-order and the things in it were fitted together were both limiters and unlimiteds. Philolaus' point seems perfectly reasonable. Things

---

[5] See Barnes (1982: 387) for the nature of the logical truth Philolaus is enunciating.

in the world around us, e.g. trees, clearly have both features that limit (e.g. their shapes) and features that are unlimited (e.g. the wood which is capable of unlimited division), so that we must suppose that they did not arise from limiting elements alone or from elements that are just unlimited; they must have been fitted together out of both elements that limit and elements that are unlimited.

In the fourth and fifth sentences Philolaus goes on to give a second, related but distinct, argument for this same conclusion. In this argument he appeals once again to the evidence of individual things in the world in order to argue about the nature of the elemental powers. This time he focuses on the way individual things in the world act (τὰ ἐν τοῖς ἔργοις). He identifies three basic types of things: things that limit, things that both limit and do not limit, and things that appear unlimited. No examples are given, but it is plausible to suppose that the things that limit might include shapes, the things that appear unlimited might be the air around us or a fire, while the things that both limit and do not limit would be things like an animal, which has a shape and structure that limit, but also has aspects such as its heat or its material constituents that do not themselves impose limits. Given that we observe these three types of things around us, we must suppose that there are two basic types of elements, those that limit and those that are unlimited. Things which limit are composed of just limiters, things that both limit and do not limit are composed of both limiters and unlimiteds, and, finally, things that appear unlimited will arise from elements that are unlimited. This argument in sentences 4 and 5 differs from the argument in sentence 3 by being more specific. In sentence 3 Philolaus just points out that it is obvious that there are both limiting and unlimited aspects of the world around us, so that both limiters and unlimiteds must be presupposed as basic elements. Sentences 4 and 5 are more specific in that they provide an exhaustive threefold classification of things in the world on the basis of the way they act, and conclude that, in order to explain these three classes of things, it is necessary to suppose two types of basic elemental powers, limiters and unlimiteds.

Thus, on this interpretation, as on the standard interpretation, the fragment does proceed by first listing three possibilites and then eliminating two. However, what the standard interpretation did not recognize is that this argument applies only to the basic elemental powers, i.e. the basic elemental powers must be both limiters and unlimiteds and not solely unlimiteds or solely limiters. On the other hand, the things that are composed out of these elemental powers fall into three classes, things that are composed of limiters alone, things that are composed of unlimiteds alone, and things that are composed of both. These are the cases that are clearly listed in the last sentence of the fragment but which had to be rejected on the standard interpretation which held that two of them had been eliminated.

This interpretation of F2 gains some support from Plato's presentation of the Pythagorean system in the *Philebus*. Plato does not mention either Philolaus or even the Pythagoreans explicitly, but he refers (16c5) to a gift from the gods brought to men by some Prometheus and handed down to the present day by "our forefathers" (οἱ παλαιοί) who lived closer to the gods. This gift is the recognition that the things that are said to be have both a limiting and an unlimited aspect in them by nature (πέρας δὲ καὶ ἀπειρίαν ἐν αὐτοῖς σύμφυτον ἐχόντων). It is not uncommon for Plato to introduce his own ideas under the guise of the wisdom of some unnamed sages and such a reading would be possible here if the only evidence we had was Plato's text.[6] However, since Aristotle tells us that the distinction between the limiting and the unlimited was central to the Pythagoreans of the fifth century, we have to take Plato at his word here and conclude that he really is reporting a doctrine held by his predecessors, the Pythagoreans. On the other hand, there is no reason to go to the extreme of the Neoplatonic interpretation which takes the passage to show that Plato thought the entire truth of reality was revealed to Pythagoras and saw himself simply as unfolding it. Plato is taking a Pythagorean distinction and applying it to problems in his philosophy. It is therefore impossible to be sure where the Pythagoreans end and Plato begins. But that the basic distinction between limiters and unlimiteds belonged to his predecessors is what the text of the *Philebus* suggests and this is supported by Aristotle. Socrates later (23c4) goes on to distinguish three classes of things, the limit, the unlimited, and a third class which is a combination of the two. He then laughs at himself for having to add as a fourth whatever is responsible for mixing the two. Marking the addition of the fourth type in this way suggests that it may be Plato's own addition and perhaps a reference to the demiurge. This is not the place to discuss all the possible relations between what Plato says in the *Philebus* and the Fragments of Philolaus, but it is tolerably clear that the identification of limit and unlimited as the two basic aspects of things which Plato assigns to his predecessors, and his further division of things into three classes (limit, unlimited, and the mixture), match very well with the interpretation of F2 which I have given above.[7]

---

[6] For examples of Plato's introduction of his own ideas under the guise of the wisdom of some unnamed sage see *Meno* 81a5–6, *Phaedo* 108c8.

[7] Opponents of authenticity argue that the theory of the *Philebus* is clearly the result of mature thought and hence is Plato's (Frank 1923: 304, Bywater 1868: 34). These critics oddly seem to assume that if Plato borrowed something from the Pythagoreans the whole *Philebus* becomes a "plagiarism." This is of course absurd. Assuming that Plato adopted the concepts of limiters and unlimiteds and the mixture of them from his predecessors, which is what he literally says, there is more than ample scope for Plato's originality in his reworking of these concepts for his own purposes.

There is one final advantage to the general structure of the argument in F2 as I have reconstructed it. In Diogenes Laertius (8.85) we are given the brief doxographical statement that Philolaus thought that all things came to be by necessity and harmony (πάντα ἀνάγκη καὶ ἁρμονίᾳ γίνεσθαι). Little attention has been paid to this statement and it indeed looks like a formula that is applied to many philosophers. To say that a philosopher thought that things came to be by necessity comes to mean that he explained things in terms of mechanical causation, i.e. matter in motion (e.g. the atomists, cf. D.L. 9.45).[8] Plato's distinction between the works of reason and the works of necessity in the *Timaeus* (47e33) is important in this regard. What I would like to suggest is that the doxography could make sense as applied to the doctrine developed in F2. The existence of limiters and unlimiteds as basic elemental powers is what is required by necessity, as is indicated by Philolaus' use of "necessity" (ἀνάγκα) at the beginning of F2. However, as is clear in F2 and will become clearer in F6, these two types of things are not adequate to explain the world. The world-order and most of the things in it are compounds of limiters and unlimiteds and such compounds cannot be explained by the simple existence of limiters and unlimiteds. We must also posit something that holds these limiters and unlimiteds together and holds them together in a pleasing way. This is the role of *harmonia* in Philolaus. Thus, F2, according to the interpretation given above, helps to make sense of the doxography on Philolaus which says that in his system things come to be both through the agency of necessity (limiters and unlimiteds) and through harmony.

ἀνάγκα τὰ ἐόντα . . . : This first sentence is an assertion of what Philolaus regarded as a logical truth. The elemental powers in the world must be either all limiters, all unlimiteds, or both limiters and unlimiteds. There are two possible interpretations of the last case. At first sight it seems most natural to read it to mean that "all the elemental powers are a compound of both limiters and unlimiteds." However, the last sentence of the fragment seems clearly to presuppose the existence of elemental powers that are just unlimited and others that just limit ("some out of limiting [constituents] limit..."). Thus, it is necessary to read the third possibility here in the first sentence as meaning "some of the elemental powers are limiting and some are unlimited." Close examination of the text in fact supports this latter reading, since Philolaus uses the verb ἁρμόζω ("fit together," see F1 and below in F2), when he wants to indicate that something is a compound of limiters and unlimiteds, while here limiters and unlimiteds are simply listed together without the verb. A further advantage to this reading is

---

[8] On the class of explanations "by necessity" see Furley 1987: 13.

that, as Barnes points out, "these disjuncts are indeed logically exhaustive" (1982: 387).

In the account of the general structure of the argument above I have argued that ἐόντα must be understood as "elemental powers" rather than as the collection of all the unique individual things in the world. This may seem initially implausible but Kahn (1965/80: 180) has argued convincingly that while the phrase is in itself quite general, it was common usage among the Presocratics to restrict it in this way. Thus, when Anaxagoras (F1) refers to all things being together at the beginning of the world (πάντων ὁμοῦ ἐόντων), the examples that we get are air and aither and not animals and trees. Likewise when he refers to "the things in the world-order" (τὰ ἐν τῷ κόσμῳ) the examples are the elemental powers hot and cold. In Diogenes F2, "the things that are now in this world-order" (τὰ ἐν τῷδε τῷ κόσμῳ ἐόντα νῦν) turn out to be earth, air, water, and fire. Similar examples can be found in Melissus F8 and On the Nature of Man 7. Thus in the Presocratic discussion of "the things that are" (τὰ ὄντα) what is usually at issue is the nature of the elemental powers of the world and not the class of all the unique individual things in the world.

This use of ἀνάγκα ("necessity") to convey a logical truth has a number of parallels in Presocratic authors. See for example Zeno F1.15, "If it exists, it is necessary that each thing have some magnitude" (εἰ δὲ ἔστιν, ἀνάγκη ἕκαστον μέγεθός τι ἔχειν), and line 21 of the same fragment, "thus if they are many, it is necessary that they are small..." (οὕτως εἰ πολλά ἐστιν, ἀνάγκη αὐτὰ μικρά...). In Philolaus the if-clause is suppressed, but clearly implied: "If things exist they must be either..." For similar uses see also Melissus F7. Anaximenes F3 is even closer to Philolaus in that it says that it is necessary that air is unlimited. This fragment is frequently rejected as spurious, but both West (1971: 100 n. 3) and Barnes (1982: 597 n. 27) have recently argued that, although some parts of it must be rejected, it may still represent Anaximenes' words in part: "It is necessary that it [air] be both unlimited and rich..." (ἀνάγκη αὐτὸν καὶ ἄπειρον εἶναι καὶ πλούσιον...).

πάντα: By itself the position of this word in the line leaves the meaning somewhat ambiguous. The structure of the argument shows that Philolaus must mean that "it is necessary that the things that are be either all limiting or all unlimited..." Philolaus could have made this meaning clearer by putting πάντα after ἤ (see περαινόντων πάντων in sentence 3). As it is, the position of πάντα before ἤ leaves the sentence ambiguous and it could be read to say that Philolaus is giving the three classes into which all things fall, i.e. that things are distributed over these three classes rather than that all things belong to just one of the classes.

ἄπειρα δὲ: This should be taken not as a separate sentence but as a pointed remark appended to the last of the three alternatives just listed and thus should be separated from the first part of the sentence only by a high stop. The supplement to the text proposed by Diels is unnecessary since it is based on the standard interpretation of the fragment which should not be accepted (see the account of the general structure of the argument above).

οὐκ ἀεί: Badham's οὔ κα εἴη has been commonly accepted (so DK) primarily because the force of ἀεί was not clearly understood and because the optative suggested that Philolaus was at least implying an argument against one of the three possibilities given just before ("but they would not be unlimited alone"). Thus Badham's conjecture fitted well with the standard interpretation of the argument which required elimination of two of the possibilities at this point (the second one being eliminated through Diels's supplement to the text). There are parallels for the emendation in the Presocratics, e.g. Melissus F7 οὐκ ἂν ἔτι ἓν εἴη (DK 1.270.18). However, in Melissus the phrase does have a supporting argument which is lacking in Philolaus.

The emendation is in fact unnecessary. The whole phrase goes closely with the first sentence and shares its tone of dogmatic assertion: "but they are not in every case just unlimited." As I have argued above, it is a remark directed at the tradition in Presocratic thought which regards the basic elements of things as all unlimited. The temporal idea introduced by ἀεί is not that of the ordinary sequence of temporal events in the world. Philolaus is not arguing that at some time things were all unlimited, but are not *always* unlimited. Instead the temporal idea is the sequence that is involved in considering to what class each of the elemental powers of the world belong. Philolaus is arguing that, as we mentally survey them, the elemental powers are "not in every case" (οὐκ ἀεί) just unlimited. This meaning of ἀεί is paralleled in a passage from Plato's *Parmenides* (165a7–b1), ὅτι ἀεί αὐτῶν ὅταν τίς τι λάβῃ τῇ διανοίᾳ ὥς τι τούτων ὄν, πρό τε τῆς ἀρχῆς ἄλλη ἀεὶ φαίνεται ἀρχή... – "Since whenever you grasp any part of them with your thought, as being one of these [beginning, middle, or end], *in every case* another beginning appears before the beginning..." The point of the Plato passage is that whenever we carry out a certain mental process, *in every case* we find that a certain result follows.

Since εἶμεν is still understood as the verb we might have expected μή as the negative with the infinitive, but here οὐχ goes closely with ἀεί (cf. Isoc. 15.117 δεῖ οὐχ ἁπλῶς εἰπεῖν where οὐχ is used because it belongs to ἁπλῶς and not the infinitive).

τοίνυν: The use of τοίνυν has been thought by some scholars to support the standard reading of the fragment which emends and supplements the text to show that Philolaus has just ruled out two of the three possibilities which are listed in the first sentence. Nussbaum (1979: 98) says "*toinun* surely indicates that some evidence has intervened." However, τοίνυν only rarely marks the conclusion of a formal syllogism (see Denniston 1954: 571), which it is made to do here on the standard interpretation (i.e. the standard view says that the argument proceeds as follows: A, B, or C, not A, not B, *therefore* [τοίνυν] C).

Denniston (1954: 568) says that "then," "well then," or "well now" rather than "therefore," are usually the best equivalents. Thus it quite frequently has more of a transitional than an inferential sense (574–5), and indicates the transition to another point which is related to what precedes but which in no way follows from it. In Philolaus F2 it marks the transition from the logical truth enunciated in the first sentence to an argument which is a particular application of that truth, and thus should be translated "well then" (i.e. "in light of this"). Denniston (1954: 576) gives parallels for just such a use and notes that in such cases it introduces what is virtually a minor premise. Thus the use of τοίνυν, rather than supporting what has been the standard interpretation of the fragment, in fact suggests that no argument has intervened and marks the introduction of the minor premise (i.e. the passage runs A, B, or C, well then (τοίνυν), since manifestly not A or B, it is clear that C).

Parallels for the combination ἐπεὶ τοίνυν also support this interpretation. There are six examples in Herodotus (1.112; 3.134; 5.50; 7.162; 9.42; 9.46). In all but one of these cases, the combination occurs at the beginning of a speech and τοίνυν indicates that what is to follow is spoken in the light of the preceding circumstances. The correct translation is clearly the transitional "well then, since . . . " and not "therefore."

φαίνεται . . . ἐόντα: From its position and the lack of an article, it is clear that ἐόντα is used predicatively rather than as the subject. The subject of φαίνεται is delayed and is finally supplied by ὅ τε κόσμος καὶ τὰ ἐν αὐτῷ ("both the world-order and the things in it"). On the other hand, if we were to supply the subject from the preceding sentence (τὰ ἐόντα, "the things that are"), several problems would arise. First, while τὰ ἐόντα ("the things that are") were originally said to *be* unlimited, etc., now they would inexplicably be described in terms of being *out of* unlimited, etc. This latter "out of" language is particularly difficult if "the things that are" are the elemental powers, as I have argued above, since as elements they should not be composed "out of" something else. Second, the argument in the third sentence would become incoherent: since τὰ ἐόντα ("the things that are") are manifestly not from only unlimited elements or only limiting elements, it is clear that *the world-order and the things in it* were fitted together from both. This is a *non sequitur* unless we assume that τὰ ἐόντα were equivalent to "the cosmos and the things in it," but for the reasons given in the account of the structure of the argument this is not possible.

φαίνεται has the meaning of "to be manifest" here, which is the common meaning of the verb when combined with a participle (cf. LSJ s.v. B 2). Thus, Philolaus is appealing quite generally to our experience of the world to show that it manifestly has both limiting and unlimited aspects. For the use of φαίνεται with ἐόντα as a predicate see Diogenes of Apollonia F2 (DK 2.59.20–1), γῆ καὶ ὕδωρ καὶ ἀὴρ καὶ πῦρ καὶ τὰ ἄλλα ὅσα φαίνεται ἐν τῷδε τῷ κόσμῳ ἐόντα... ("Earth and water and air and fire and as many others as are manifest in this world-order...").

ὅ τε κόσμος καὶ τὰ ἐν αὐτῷ... ("the world order and the things in it...): This is a near repetition of ὅλος ὁ κόσμος καὶ τὰ ἐν αὐτῷ πάντα ("the whole world-order and all the things in it") in F1. It seems that the repetition is intentional and is used to mark the end of at least one of the arguments for the assertion made in F1. This assertion (especially with the emphatic "all" in F1) might lead one to conclude that all *things* in the cosmos are combinations of limiters and unlimiteds (as opposed to elements which are either limiters or unlimiteds). However, as the end of F2 shows, Philolaus seems to recognize some things that just limit and others that are just unlimited. This unclarity results from fuzziness about what is meant by "things" in the cosmos. Unique individuals in the cosmos (horses, trees) will all be compounds of limiters and unlimiteds. However, there is also a clear sense in which a mass of air, or earth, or a shape taken by itself are part of the cosmos and yet are usually thought of as just unlimiteds or just limiters (even if in one sense they can been said to be part of the compound that is the cosmos as a whole). It is cases like this that Philolaus must mean when he talks of things that just limit or that are just unlimited.

δηλοῖ δὲ καὶ τὰ ἐν τοῖς ἔργοις: The expression τὰ ἐν τοῖς ἔργοις ("things... in their actions") has caused scholars as much difficulty as any other in Philolaus. Most attention has been given to determining the meaning of τοῖς ἔργοις (which I translate as "actions"). Some scholars have tried to give it a quite specific meaning, such as "buildings," "fields," or even "mountain meadows" (Burkert 1972: 254 n. 79). However, on the basis of what we have in the text, Burkert is right to conclude that it is "impossible to tell what specific sense ἔργα has." Recent interpreters have taken it to be a very general term, as did Heidel earlier: "things" (Heidel 1907: 80), "facts" (Barnes 1982: 386), "actual experience" (Nussbaum 1979: 97).

Such an interpretation is supported by the common use of the λόγος–ἔργον (word–deed) contrast in Philolaus' day (e.g. Th. 2.65, Eur. F360. 13). The contrast is often between what one says and what one does (S. *El.* 357–8), but can also be a more general contrast between theory and what in fact is the case (Th. 2.65). At *Phaedo* 100a1–3 where Socrates is discussing his philosophical method, he says, οὐ γὰρ πάνυ συγχωρῶ τὸν ἐν τοῖς λόγοις σκοπούμενον τὰ ὄντα ἐν εἰκόσι μᾶλλον σκοπεῖν ἢ τὸν ἐν τοῖς ἔργοις ("I do not at all admit that an inquiry by means of *theory* employs 'images' any more than one which confines itself to *facts*" [tr. Tredennick]) The expression τὸν ἐν τοῖς ἔργοις ("the one which confines itself to facts") here is very close to the wording in Philolaus and suggests that Philolaus too is referring broadly to what is revealed by the study of the empirical world.

However, the context in Philolaus also suggests that τὰ ἔργα still preserves some of its original sense of "deeds" and draws our attention not just to the empirical world but specifically to the actions of things in that world. What activates this sense of the word is Philolaus' emphasis on action in the next sentence where he spells out his meaning: "some of them from limiting (constituents) *limit*, others from both limiting and unlimited (constituents) both *limit and do not limit*... An interesting parallel for this use of ἐν τοῖς ἔργοις to mean "in actions" is found in a treatise in the Hippocratic corpus which probably was written around 400, *Off.* 15.2: φύσις δὲ ἐν μὲν ἔργοις, τοῦ ἔργου τῇ πρήξει, ὃ βούλεται τεκμαρτέον ("Now nature shows itself in actions, and one must judge what nature wants by the performance of actions" [tr. Withington]). The context is the proper bandaging of bones and the suggestion is that proper bandaging of the arm or the leg requires knowledge of the actions that it carries out (see also *Fractures* 2.24).

In light of these parallels and the context in Philolaus the whole phrase τὰ ἐν τοῖς ἔργοις must mean something like "things in their actions." It is apparently taken to be equivalent to τὰ ἔργα by most commentators but this leads to some very awkward translations in the next sentence. The τὰ at the beginning of the next sentence picks up the τὰ here, so that τὰ ἔργα becomes the subject of the last sentence. Thus, Barnes translates "and the facts too make this clear, for some of them ... limit ..." However, facts cannot be properly described as limiting or not limiting, whereas individual things can.

φανέονται: Most of the manuscripts give the impossible form φαινέονται, which is more likely to be the result of a copyist's mistaken use of the present stem φαιν-, when confronted by an unusual future form, than the mistaken introduction of a stray epsilon. So we should accept Heeren's emendation as the *lectio difficilior* rather than Usener's facile present.

The future is used in a prospective sense here to state what follows from a given set of circumstances, in this case, what follows when something is

composed of unlimited constituents. The use of the future puts emphasis on
the necessity of the connection between the circumstances and the result
(Schwyzer 1950: 291–2). By using the future only in the third of the three
cases given in this sentence, Philolaus lays special emphasis on the connection between constituents and resultant behavior where the constituents
are unlimited. This is part of his attack on earlier thinkers who made their
principles all unlimited (cf. lines 2 and 3 of this fragment and F3). These
thinkers assume a world of distinguishable things, but claim that it arises
from elements that are all unlimited. Philolaus is pointing out here that
if a thing is composed only of unlimited constituents, it will not appear
limited in any way, but rather unlimited. What is limited or distinguishable
cannot arise from what is just unlimited.

Fragment 3

Iamblichus, *In Nic.* 7.8 κυρίως δὲ τὸ μὲν συνεχὲς καὶ ἡνωμένον
καλοῖτ’ ἂν μέγεθος, τὸ δὲ παρακείμενον καὶ διῃρημένον πλῆθος....
ἀλλὰ τοῦ μὲν ἡνωμένου ἐπ’ ἄπειρον μὲν ἐκ παντός ἐστιν ἡ τομή,
ἡ δ’ αὔξησις ἐπὶ ὡρισμένον· τοῦ δὲ πλήθους κατὰ ἀντιπεπόνθησιν
5   ἐπ’ ἄπειρον μὲν ἡ αὔξησις, ἔμπαλιν δὲ ἡ τομὴ ἐπὶ ὡρισμένον,
φύσει δὴ κατ’ ἐπίνοιαν ἀμφοτέρων ἀπείρων ὄντων, καὶ διὰ τοῦτο
ἐπιστήμαις ἀπεριορίστων· **ἀρχὰν** γὰρ **οὐδὲ τὸ γνωσούμενον**
ἐσσεῖται πάντων ἀπείρων ἐόντων κατὰ τὸν Φιλόλαον.
ἀναγκαίου δὲ ὄντος ἐπιστήμης φύσιν ἐνορᾶσθαι τοῖς οὖσιν οὕτως
10   ὑπὸ θείας ἠκριβωμένοις προνοίας, ἀποτεμόμεναι ἑκατέρου καὶ
περατώσασαί τινες ἐπιστῆμαι τὸ περιληφθὲν αὐταῖς, ἀπὸ μὲν τοῦ
πλήθους ποσὸν ἐκάλεσαν, ὅπερ ἤδη γνώριμον, ἀπὸ δὲ τοῦ
μεγέθους κατὰ τὰ αὐτὰ πηλίκον· καὶ τὰ ἀμφότερα αὐτῶν γένη
ἐπιστήμαις ὑπήγαγον ταῖς ἑαυτῶν εἰδήσεσιν, ἀριθμητικῇ μὲν τὸ
15   ποσόν, γεωμετρίᾳ δὲ τὸ πηλίκον.

But, properly speaking, the continuous and unified should be called
magnitude, and the juxtaposed and discrete should be called multitude.... But, in the case of what is unified, division proceeds everywhere without limit, while increase is limited. In the case of multitude the reverse is true, increase is unlimited, and in turn division is
limited. Both [magnitude and multitude] then are by nature unlimited in conception, and on account of this undefinable by science.
For, **there will not be anything that is going to know at all, if**
everything is unlimited according to Philolaus. But since it is necessary that the nature of science be seen in the things that have been
so perfected by divine providence, certain sciences have cut off and

delimited a domain from each of them [e.g. magnitude and multitude]. They called what was cut off from multitude, quantity, which is already familiar, and what was set off, in the same way, from magnitude, size. And both of these classes were subsumed under their own kinds of science, quantity under arithmetic, and size under geometry.

AUTHENTICITY

In the case of fragments as short as this one, the problem of determining authenticity becomes particularly acute simply because of lack of enough evidence on the basis of which to make a decision. However, there are certainly no obviously Platonic or Aristotelian features that would lead us to doubt the fragment. More positively, the fact that F3 focuses on the concept of the unlimited, which figures prominently in Aristotle's accounts of the early Pythagoreans and in other fragments of Philolaus, which we have independent grounds for believing authentic (e.g. 1, 2, 6), makes it quite likely that it is genuine.

The only major argument which has been brought against the authenticity of F3 is that such epistemological concerns are not possible at this early stage of Greek philosophy (Frank 1923: 308). But this argument must be rejected, since much of recent scholarship on the Presocratics and early Greek thought in general has shown that epistemological concerns were prominent (Nussbaum 1979: 66). Opponents of authenticity go on to point out that Aristotle makes no mention of epistemology in his account of the Pythagoreans. However, such arguments from Aristotle's silence are dangerous, given the fact that his treatment of his predecessors is so heavily determined by his own purposes in a given passage. Just how unreliable such arguments are can in fact be shown in this case since, although it is true that Aristotle does not comment on Pythagorean epistemology in his accounts of Pythagoreanism in the *Metaphysics,* a recently identified passage of Aristotle's special treatise on the Pythagoreans shows him ascribing the following epistemological theme to Pythagoreanism:

> So that whoever wishes to comprehend the true nature of existing things should turn his attention to these things, that is to numbers...
> and proportions, because it is by them that everything is made clear.
> (ὥστε τῷ βουλομένῳ θεωρεῖν τὰ ὄντα πῶς ἔχει, εἰς ταῦτα βλεπτέον
> εἶναι, τοὺς ἀριθμοὺς...καὶ λόγους, διὰ τὸ δηλοῦσθαι πάντα διὰ
> τούτων.) (Iamblichus, *Comm. math.* 78.14–18; see Burkert 1972: 50 n. 112, 447ff)

Thus, Aristotle not only shows awareness of Pythagorean epistemology but specifically ties it to the concept of number, as Philolaus does in F4. This passage of Aristotle, then, gives us solid grounds for rejecting the arguments against the authenticity of both F3 and F4.

COMMENTARY

Context: This fragment is preserved as part of Iamblichus' commentary on Nicomachus' *Introduction to Arithmetic* (D'Ooge 1926: 127–32; O'Meara 1989: 51). The fragment is quoted in the discussion of multitude and magnitude, which are identified as the two primary types of being and therefore the primary objects of knowledge. Both Nicomachus and Iamblichus then point out that each of these two types of being has both a limited and an unlimited aspect. Multitude is unlimited in "increase," but limited in regard to division (i.e. an atomic unit is assumed), while magnitude can be divided without limit, but is limited in size. In so far as each of these is unlimited, they cannot be the object of knowledge or science. Iamblichus then quotes Philolaus to support this latter point and is obviously drawing on a source other than Nicomachus, since Nicomachus does not quote Philolaus on this point. Immediately after the quotation, Iamblichus, following Nicomachus, goes on to say that an aspect of both magnitude and multitude (i.e. their limited aspect) can be separated off and treated as the object of a science. Thus quantity can be separated from multitude and is the object of arithmetic, and size can be separated from magnitude and is the object of geometry.

For Iamblichus' purposes no very detailed reading of F3 of Philolaus is presupposed. He takes it simply to mean that what is unlimited cannot be the object of knowledge and does not go into further detail. We can be reasonably confident that γάρ is Iamblichus' connective but the rest of the words seem to belong to the quotation.

Nature of the argument: The structure of the argument in F3 is clear, although there are many controversial points in the details. Under certain conditions ("if everything is unlimited") we will not be able to recognize or know individual things in the world. Since we all admit that we do know individual things in the world, it follows that the supposed conditions do not exist: all things are not unlimited. Although the fragment does appeal to the nature of our thought processes, it primarily functions as an argument about the nature of the world rather than as an exposition of Philolaus' views on epistemology. The conclusion we are to draw is that the things that are are not exclusively unlimited. Thus the argument is more closely tied to the issues in F2 than those raised in F4 and F5. It is only in F4 and F5 that we find epistemology to be the main concern.

ἀρχάν: The adverbial use of ἀρχάν is particularly common with a negative such as we have here (LSJ s.v. 1.1.c). Nussbaum (1979: 84) gives the correct translation "not...at all [or, in the first place]."

οὐδέ: The use of οὐδέ could support Nussbaum's contention (see the note on γνωσούμενον below) that γιγνώσκειν does not indicate knowledge, but a less sophisticated level of cognitive activity (i.e. "There will not even be an object of apprehension [let alone an object of knowledge]"). However, there is another equally plausible way to explain οὐδέ on my reading. It emphasizes the fact that (putting aside the question about whether there are objects of knowledge) there will *not even* be anything that is going to know. When considering the conditions for knowledge, the existence of a knower is often assumed and attention is focused on the nature of the object of knowledge. Philolaus is taking the argument back a step further to consider the nature of the knower.

τὸ γνωσούμενον: The meaning of γιγνώσκειν here is an issue of particular importance, because Nussbaum has put forth a sophisticated new interpretation of Philolaus' philosophy which is founded on her view of the meaning of the verb. The usual meaning for γιγνώσκειν is "know" or "apprehend" and it is especially used in situations where a specific object is recognized or identified (von Fritz in Mourelatos 1974: 24). Snell (1924: 21) says that it shows that "the thing apprehended is grasped as a certain sort of object, in its What-it-is, e.g., I recognize an appearance as a tree." The more recent studies of Lesher (1981, 1983) have shown that von Fritz and Snell were overly schematic and that e.g. γιγνώσκειν sometimes indicates a more complicated realization of the significance of a situation and thus overlaps with νοεῖν. Moreover, Lesher has shown that γιγνώσκειν is not always the simple and almost automatic process of recognizing something once we have perceived it, as is suggested by Snell and von Fritz. There are cases already in Homer where it involves difficulty and effort and can be directed towards a general truth and not just an individual object in the world (Lesher 1983: 162–3).

In Heraclitus γιγνώσκειν comes to be used as the term for "cognition in the privileged sense, for the insight which men lack and which his own discourse attempts to communicate" (Kahn 1979: 103–4). While this use may be to some extent anticipated by the Homeric uses Lesher identifies and while the verb may also still be used for recognition of ordinary objects and not just cosmic insights (Lesher 1983: 160–1), Heraclitus does rather consistently use it to refer to the knowledge that he thinks men lack:

> F57 Hesiod...who did not know (οὐκ ἐγίνωσκεν) day and night, that they are one.

F17 For most men do not think of things in the way they are encountered, nor do they know them (γινώσκουσιν) when they have learned, although they think they do.   (The translations are Lesher's.)

Such uses are not limited to Heraclitus. The Delphic oracle's famous injunction to "know yourself" clearly implies some significant understanding of the self and not simple recognition (γνῶθι σαυτόν). Again when Anaxagoras says that "mind knew all things" (πάντα ἔγνω νοῦς) as they were separated off from the primordial mixture, it seems likely if not certain, that mind is doing more than just recognizing that things are distinct from each other.

Nussbaum, however, has argued that there is a sharp distinction between γιγνώσκειν and εἰδέναι (1979: 84–7). According to Nussbaum εἰδέναι is consistently used to mean "certain knowledge" which is denied to mortals by many early Greek thinkers including the Eleatics. On the other hand, γιγνώσκειν refers to an activity that can be accurate or inaccurate and does not mean "to know with certainty" or even "to know." In fact γιγνώσκειν does not imply a successful cognitive activity at all, it merely indicates that we are seeing individual things as something. Nussbaum says that Philolaus used γιγνώσκειν because he wanted to argue against Parmenides and Melissus, but from assumptions that they would admit. While denying that mortals have certain knowledge, the Eleatics would be willing to admit that mortals do have cognitive activity, however misguided it may be.

Nussbaum has given Philolaus a very sophisticated response to the Eleatics, but the basis for her reconstruction of the argument, the distinction between εἰδέναι as "certain knowledge" and γιγνώσκειν as mere "cognitive activity," does not seem to be sound. She cites the studies of Snell and von Fritz in support of her view, but they nowhere make any distinction between εἰδέναι and γιγνώσκειν on the grounds of certainty and uncertainty. Lesher's more recent work further undercuts Nussbaum's position in that he shows that Snell and von Fritz had overlooked a number of cases in which γιγνώσκειν clearly goes beyond mere identification of objects in the world to refer to knowledge of difficult-to-grasp general truths. Moreover the texts from Heraclitus quoted above clearly use γιγνώσκειν to refer to successful cognition.

Nussbaum also cites evidence from early Greek writers which shows that εἰδέναι is often used with "nothing" (οὐδέν) as an object (εἰδότες οὐδέν Parmenides F6.4), while γιγνώσκειν is not so used, but described as true or false, accurate or inaccurate. This is taken as evidence that γιγνώσκειν does not mean "certain knowledge" since if it did "true" or "false," "accurate" or "inaccurate" would not be used as modifiers. This is an interesting general observation about the two words (although later, in Plato, γιγνώσκειν does take οὐδέν as an object: *Prm.* 134e; *Plt.* 302b), but it is not to be explained in the way Nussbaum suggests. Rather, the crucial point to notice is that as a perfect εἰδέναι indicates a state while γιγνώσκειν can indicate an activity. A state either exists or it does not. We are either in a state of knowing or we are not. However, γιγνώσκειν in so far as it refers to an activity can in principle either proceed properly or go astray, and thus admits of adverbs indicating accuracy or inaccuracy. However, this does not show that without any modifiers there is any doubt about the success or certainty of the cognitive activity of γιγνώσκειν. When the Delphic Oracle says "know yourself" (γνῶθι σαυτόν) surely the knowledge or recognition involved is assumed to be certain or accurate.

Nussbaum's interpretation is also disproved from within the fragments of Philolaus themselves. In F6 Philolaus proclaims that "the essence of things and nature itself admit of divine and not human knowledge" (γνῶσις). The fact that γνῶσις is assigned to divinity and is of the essence of things suggests that it refers to certain knowledge or accurate recognition of reality. Nussbaum seems to contradict herself in dealing with γνῶσις in this passage. She states (1979: 101) that in F6 Philolaus does admit that we do know one thing certainly, that there is one "sure truth for mortals." But the word used for this certain knowledge is γνῶσις without any adjective. Thus, on her own reading of F6, γνῶσις used by itself indicates certain knowledge.

A second major problem deals not with the meaning of γιγνώσκειν, but with the particular form in which it occurs, γνωσούμενον. The context in Iamblichus is loose enough that it is impossible to be sure whether he took this to be passive or active in meaning. Modern scholars have almost unanimously declared that γνωσούμενον *must* be taken in a passive sense, "object of apprehension". Burkert agrees (1972: 260 n. 107), but is also aware that, while the future middle is often used in a passive sense, this is very rare in verbs with a deponent future such as γιγνώσκειν (Kühner and Gerth 1897: 2.1.114, 116). Kühner is himself skeptical about two of the parallels he offers, and the third (Aes. *Ch.* 305) is commonly understood in an active sense. Burkert does not mention Kühner's parallels, but offers his own from Antiphon (DK 87 F7). He says that "Antiphon the sophist used the expression τὸ ὀψόμενον along with ὄψις, ὀφθαλμοί, ὀπτήρ ... where it must mean 'the object of the act of seeing'. Thus the remarkable expression of Philolaus has its parallel in a 5th-century author, and only there." Unfortunately, I do not think that the passage in fact shows that Antiphon used τὸ ὀψόμενον in a passive sense. Antiphon F7 is drawn from Pollux's *Onomasticon* (2.57) which is in large part a collection of synonyms and a thesaurus of terms. The Antiphon fragment is from a section entitled "Vision as sensation and the eyes and vision as a dream" (ὄψις ἡ αἴσθησις καὶ τὰ ὄμματα, καὶ ὄψις ὁ ὄνειρος). Pollux then goes on to give forms of ὀπ- words which he has found in Greek writers. The first entry is ὄψομαι, ὀφθήσομαι, ὦμμαι ὡς Ἰσαῖος.

I take it that this simply indicates that these forms (or at least the last one) occur in Isaeus. The passage in Pollux continues Ἀντιφῶν δὲ καὶ τὸ ὀψόμενον εἶπε, καὶ τῇ ὄψει οἷον τοῖς ὀφθαλμοῖς, καὶ ὀπτήρ, καὶ ἄοπτα. Surely this is just a list of forms found in various places in Antiphon (Diels refers ὄψει to F1, ἄοπτα to F4, and ὀπτήρ to the speech on the *Murder of Herodes*) and there is no indication that τὸ ὀψόμενον occurred in one passage in Antiphon where it was contrasted with the other forms listed in a way that showed it was understood as passive. Burkert's point is probably that the way Pollux lists the forms suggests that he took it to be passive, but this is very questionable. Since "the eyes" and "someone who sees" follow, it might be supposed that τὸ ὀψόμενον which comes first must be a reference to what is seen. However, the last term in the sequence "what is unseen" is an odd addition if such a sequence is intended. These features suggest that it is just as likely that Pollux is just giving a catalogue of "sight words" he finds in an author without any strict logic in their presentation. Certainly such a passage is the weakest of grounds to adduce for the otherwise unparalleled use of γνωσούμενον as a passive.

In light of this it seems prudent to ask Wackernagel's question about the passage: "ist die Übersetzung '... ein Subjekt der Erkenntnis'... unmöglich?" ("Is the translation...'a subject who knows'...impossible?" [1970: 216]). Presumably scholars have concluded that γνωσούμενον must be passive because of the way they understand the argument to proceed in the fragment. *Prima facie* it seems more likely that Philolaus would say that "if all things are unlimited, there will not be anything that is going to be known" than "if all things are unlimited, there will not be anything that is going to know." Indeed in Aristotle there is a common argument that an unlimited object is unknowable. But given that we have no context for the fragment of Philolaus and that it is very brief, it is far from clear that this *prima facie* reading is right, and we must examine the consequences of accepting τὸ γνωσούμενον as meaning "one who is going to know," which is what the philological evidence overwhelmingly indicates is the correct meaning.

Burkert himself provides us with the correct parallel for Philolaus' usage, Plato, *Cratylus* 440b2–4. In that passage Socrates concludes that if all things are in flux, including the Form of Knowledge itself, there would neither be τὸ γνωσούμενον ("what is going to know") nor τὸ γνωσθησόμενον ("what is going to be known"). Here we can see that τὸ γνωσούμενον is active and a parallel is provided for Philolaus' use of the neuter. Indeed, the neuter gender has probably been another main reason that scholars have assumed the form to be passive. It is easier to conceive of a "thing known" than a "knowing thing." Yet, as the Plato passage shows, in cosmological contexts it might be quite reasonable to talk of the emergence of "things" that know rather than people who know. Burkert's point about the Plato passage is that the active translation of τὸ γνωσούμενον is guaranteed by the fact that it is paired with the passive which is not the case in Philolaus. The problem of course is that we do not know what the context in Philolaus might have been. It too might have made it crystal clear that the form had to be taken as an active. But, even apart from doubts about the context, the philological evidence discussed above shows that γνωσούμενον is always in itself to be taken as an active and the burden of proof must fall on anyone who treats it as passive to show something in the context that necessitates such a singular translation.

On this reading Philolaus will not be arguing about what something must be like to be known, but what something must be like to know. He would seem to be saying that if all things are unlimited, something that knows will not arise because the activity of knowing is itself a limiting thing. One might object, though, that even if the reference is to the activity of knowing the argument still turns out to depend on the nature of objects of knowledge and not on the nature of the knower or knowing. The argument would be that if all things are unlimited, there will be no objects of knowledge (following the Aristotelian dictum that the unlimited is unknowable) and *a fortiori* there will be nothing that is going to know. Still, if this were Philolaus' point, it seems much more likely that he would have limited himself just to objects of knowledge rather than introducing an odd expression like τὸ γνωσούμενον.

Interest in the nature of the activity of knowing can be seen already in Parmenides. In the "Doxa" section of his poem knowledge and perception are tied to the condition of the body and the relation of the opposites that compose it (Vlastos 1946: 66–77). Thus Philolaus' interest in the activity of knowledge and the knower rather than just the object of knowledge is not unique. We have no evidence as to how Philolaus would have employed the concept of limit in explaining the activity of knowing. However, a passage from Plato's *Sophist* suggests some lines along which such an argument may have proceeded.

At 261c6ff the stranger discusses speech and judgment with Theaetetus. The two are considered as parallel cases since judgment is regarded as inner speech. It is first shown that a list of nouns or a list of verbs does not constitute an assertion or thought. A verb and a noun must be combined. In speech and thought "one does not only name, but also limits (περαίνει) something, weaving together verbs with names" (262d3–4). There is no speech or thought unless a noun is limited by a verb or a verb by a noun. Thus, thought requires us to set limits. Of course there is no evidence that Philolaus used this particular argument. However, the passage shows that such issues were discussed in the generation following Philolaus and it suggests possible connections between the concept of limit and our thought processes.

Is the unlimited unknowable? Barnes has cited F3 as evidence that
Philolaus thought that what was unlimited is unknowable (1982: 390).
Nussbaum is more circumspect and makes the point that the fragment does
not say that what is unlimited is unknowable, but that an object of knowledge is not possible if *all* things are unlimited (1979: 88). However, she
thinks that F4 does show that what is known must be limited. Things that
are known are said to have number and she argues that having number is
closely related to having limit (92). On the other hand, given the interpretation of F3 which I have developed above, there are absolutely no grounds
for believing that Philolaus thought that what is unlimited is unknowable.
Indeed, a careful reading of F2 indicates that Philolaus did regard unlimiteds as knowable. At least he talks of things manifestly being composed of
unlimited elements and of things that appear unlimited because they are
composed of constituents that are unlimited. Such language both shows
that Philolaus regards unlimiteds as identifiable parts of the world and
makes little sense if he thought of them as unknowable. In F5 three classes
of number are introduced that seem to correspond to the three classes
of things in F2 (limiting, unlimited, and both limiting and unlimited).
This again suggests that the unlimited is knowable since it is tied to number which is the central concept in Philolaus' account of the objects of
knowledge (F4). Thus there seems to me to be very strong evidence in the
fragments that Philolaus thought that the unlimited has number and is
knowable. Likewise, Plato in the *Philebus* seems perfectly capable of talking
about and clearly designating a class of unlimiteds, which certainly suggests
once again that they are not completely unknowable.

Whom is Philolaus attacking? In F3 Philolaus is directing his argument
against a view which maintains that all things are unlimited. He could
have a specific thinker in mind or he may just be rejecting one of the set of
three logical possibilities given in F2. Nussbaum has put forth the view that
Philolaus is arguing against the Eleatics, especially Parmenides. For several
reasons I do not think that this can be right. This is, however, a difficult
point to argue because it requires an extensive analysis of the fragments of
Parmenides which would go beyond the confines of this study and still
remain controversial. Therefore, what I present here is not a fully developed argument against Nussbaum's view but some reasons for doubting it.

To begin with, if we go to the fragments of Parmenides to see what he has
to say about the principles which Philolaus posits, limiters and unlimiteds,
we find that the word ἄπειρον ('unlimited") never occurs in the fragments,
whereas "limit" not only occurs frequently (F8.42 πεῖρας; F8.49 πείρασι;
F8.3 πείρατος), but is in fact thematic (Mourelatos 1970: 115ff). For Aristotle the main contrast between Melissus and Parmenides was precisely

that the latter described the whole as limited rather than unlimited (*Physics* 3.6, 207a15ff). Thus *prima facie* it seems perverse to say that in his attack on someone who maintains that all things are unlimited, Philolaus has Parmenides in mind, or that any of his readers would have understood him in this way.

Nussbaum does rightly emphasize that both Parmenides and Philolaus rely on arguments about the conditions of thought in putting forth their view on the nature of reality. However, I do not think that she puts forth Parmenides' argument in a way that shows its true thrust. She emphasizes (1979: 86) F8.22–5 where Parmenides argues that an object of thought must be continuous (συνεχές) and not divisible (διαιρετόν). She takes this to be a denial of any internal boundaries or demarcations and hence as equivalent to an assertion that what is knowable must be ἄπειρον, which she translates as "undifferentiated." However, lines 22–5 need to be considered as part of Parmenides' overall argument in order to see their full significance.

Parmenides' main complaint with "what is not" as an object of thought is that it is incurably vague and incomplete: οὔτε γὰρ ἂν γνοίης τό γε μὴ ἐόν (οὐ γὰρ ἀνυστόν) ... ("For neither would you know that which is not [for it is incomplete] ... ," F2.7, Mourelatos 1970: 75–6). Correspondingly his account of what is an object of thought stresses that it is complete (F8.42 τετελεσμένον). It is in order to stress the notions of completeness, definiteness, and invariancy that Parmenides introduces the image of bounds or limits (Mourelatos 1970: 115ff and Owen in Furley and Allen 1975: 64–5). If we are looking for Parmenides' attitude toward the opposite of limit, i.e. what is unlimited, we should look not to his remarks on continuity at F8.22 but rather to his comments on incompleteness at F2.7. He rejects the unlimited in the sense of what is incomplete as insufficient to account for knowledge no less than does Philolaus.

Seen in the light of Parmenides' general argument the passage at F8.22–5 emphasizes that the object of knowledge is complete in the sense of having no discontinuity. In this sense the object of thought cannot be differentiated into objects of different natures (cf. μορφὰς ... δύo, "two forms," F8.53) and could therefore be described as "unlimited" in the sense of being "undifferentiated,"as Nussbaum argues. What should be stressed is that it is by no means a prominent theme in Parmenides that what is known is "unlimited." It is unlimited in a very special sense that is in fact a result of the rigorous application of the idea of limit. It seems very unlikely that Philolaus is directing his attack at such an out-of-the-way aspect of Parmenides' argument about the conditions of thought, especially since the main thrust of Parmenides' argument with its emphasis on limit is so congenial to Philolaus' point of view.

On the other hand Melissus does describe "what is" as unlimited and Nussbaum may be right in seeing Philolaus' remarks as a reaction to Melissus. However, Anaximander, Anaximenes, Anaxagoras, and Democritus all prominently describe the basic principles of their system as "unlimited." It is not clear that Melissus is any more likely to have been the object of Philolaus' attack than some of these other Presocratics. The interest in conditions of thought ties Philolaus to Parmenides, but not to Melissus. In Pt. II, ch. 1 I have argued that Philolaus is in fact attacking Anaxagoras.

Fragment 6

Stobaeus, *Eclogae* 1.21.7d (1.188.14 Wachsmuth)   περὶ δὲ φύσιος καὶ ἁρμονίας ὧδε ἔχει· ἁ μὲν ἐστὼ τῶν πραγμάτων ἀΐδιος ἔσσα καὶ αὐτὰ μὰν ἁ φύσις θείαν τε καὶ οὐκ ἀνθρωπίνην ἐνδέχεται γνῶσιν πλάν γα ἢ ὅτι οὐχ οἷόν τ' ἦν οὐθενὶ τῶν ἐόντων καὶ
5 γιγνωσκομένων ὑφ' ἁμῶν γεγενῆσθαι μὴ ὑπαρχούσας τᾶς ἐστοῦς τῶν πραγμάτων, ἐξ ὧν συνέστα ὁ κόσμος, καὶ τῶν περαινόντων καὶ τῶν ἀπείρων. ἐπεὶ δὲ ταὶ ἀρχαὶ ὑπᾶρχον οὐχ ὁμοῖαι οὐδ' ὁμόφυλοι ἔσσαι, ἤδη ἀδύνατον ἦς κα αὐταῖς κοσμηθῆναι, εἰ μὴ ἁρμονία ἐπεγένετο ᾡτινιῶν ἂν τρόπῳ ἐγένετο. τὰ μὲν ὦν
10 ὁμοῖα καὶ ὁμόφυλα ἁρμονίας οὐδὲν ἐπεδέοντο, τὰ δὲ ἀνόμοια μηδὲ ὁμόφυλα μηδὲ † ἰσοταχῆ, ἀνάγκα τὰ τοιαῦτα ἁρμονίᾳ συγκεκλεῖσθαι, εἰ μέλλοντι ἐν κόσμῳ κατέχεσθαι.

2 ὧδε Heeren οὐ ' δε F οὐδε GVM οὐ δέ E   ἐστὼ τῶν Boeckh ἐστώτων FGVE ἐστώτων M   3 αὐτὰ μὰν Usener αὐτὰ μὲν FGVME αὐτὰ μόνα Badham αὐτὰ ἁ vel ἀεὶ ἐσομένα Zeller   θείαν τε FV θεῖάν τε GME θείαν γα Diels θεία ἐντὶ Badham ἀνθρωπίναν Wachsmuth   4 πλάν γα ἢ Badham πλέον γα ἢ FGVM πλέοντα ἢ E πλήν γα ἢ Heeren   οἷόν τ' ἦν Diels οἷον τὴν FGVME οἷόν τ' ἦς Heeren   οὐθὲν Mullach οὐδὲν Wachsmuth   5 γιγνωσκόμενον Usener γεγενῆσθαι Burkert γεγνέσθαι FGVM γενέσθαι E, Usener γα γενέσθαι Diels γνωσθῆμεν Boeckh   ὑπαρχοίσας Meineke   τᾶς ἐστοῦς Badham τὰς ἐντοὺς FGVME αὐτᾶς ἐντὸς Boeckh   7 ταὶ ἀρχαὶ Badham τε ἀρχαὶ FGVME   ὑπάρχον FGVME   ὁμοιαι FGVME   8 ὁμόφιλοι V ἦς κα Badham ἦς καὶ FV ἦσαν καὶ GME   αὐτοῖς FGVME corr. Boeckh κοσμηθῆμεν Heeren   εἰ FGVME αἰ Wachsmuth   9 ᾡτινιῶν ἂν τρόπῳ scripsi ᾡτινι ὦν ἂν τρόπων FV ᾡτινι ὂν ἂν τρόπον GE ᾡτινι ὂν ἂν τρόποι M ᾡτινιῶν ἆδε τρόπῳ Diels ᾡτινι τρόπῳ Meineke ᾡτινι ἄρα τρόπῳ Badham   ὦν FGVME   10 ὁμοια FGVME   ὁμόφυλος V   11 ἰσοταχῆ FGVME ἰσοπαλῆ vel ἰσολαχῆ Meineke ἰσοταγῆ Heidel ἰσοτελῆ Heeren   τᾷ τοιαύτᾳ Badham   ἁρμονίᾳ Boeckh ἁρμονίαις FGVME   12 εἰ scripsi ἢ εἰ FGVME αἰ Meineke οἷα Diels

Concerning nature and harmony the situation is this: the being of things, which is eternal, and nature in itself admit of divine and not human knowledge, except that it was impossible for any of the things that are and are known by us to have come to be, if the being of the things from which the world-order came together, both the limiting things and the unlimited things, did not preexist. But since these beginnings preexisted and were neither alike nor even related, it would have been impossible for them to be ordered, if a harmony had not come upon them, in whatever way it came to be. Like things and related things did not in addition require any harmony, but things that are unlike and not even related nor of [? the same speed], it is necessary that such things be bonded together by harmony, if they are going to be held in an order. [The text of the fragment continues as F6a]

AUTHENTICITY

I regard this fragment as continuous with F6a, although there is a possibility of some gap between them. If it were certain that these two fragments were a continuous text, the strongest arguments for authenticity would be those developed in the commentary on F6a. However, since the connection between the two fragments is not totally secure, it is more prudent to discuss the authenticity of F6 separately.

The best reasons for regarding F6 as authentic are the obvious continuities with fragments (1–4, 7) which have already been shown to be authentic largely on the grounds of the connection with Aristotle's testimony about early Pythagoreanism. The concepts that are prominent in those other fragments are prominent here: limiters, unlimiteds, and a harmony that binds them. This fragment makes a logical addition to the others in that it focuses on the concept of *harmonia* ("fitting together") which has not been directly discussed in the other fragments. Furthermore, there are no obviously Platonic and Aristotelian ideas or terminology. There are some similarities at first sight to some of the pseudepigrapha, particularly in the use of the words ἐστώ and ἀρχή. However, as the discussion in the commentary will show, detailed examination of these apparent similarities tends, in the end, in fact to demonstrate the difference between F6 and the pseudepigrapha. Thus, because of its close connection to other genuine fragments and the testimony of Aristotle on early Pythagoreanism, it should be regarded as authentic.

COMMENTARY

Importance of the Fragment: As the first words of F6 show, its main concern is with two topics, "nature" (φύσις) and "fitting together" (ἀρμονία).

In F1 and F2 Philolaus has already argued that nature (φύσις) must be explained in terms of two types of constituents, limiting things and unlimited things. In F6 Philolaus further supports this thesis, but he also does something new. He provides a careful statement about the scope of our possible knowledge of nature. In F1 Philolaus' remarks on nature were not about nature *simpliciter*, but about "nature in the world-order" (φύσις ἐν τῷ κόσμῳ). F6 allows us to understand what Philolaus meant by the somewhat enigmatic restriction of his discussion of nature to "nature in the world-order." While nature as seen in the world-order is a legitimate object of knowledge (F1), here in F6 nature in itself (αὐτὰ ἁ φύσις) and "the eternal being of things" is said to admit of only divine and not of human knowledge. What exactly Philolaus means by this can be better understood if we look at the earlier Greek tradition which distinguishes between divine and human knowledge.

Philolaus had plenty of predecessors in Greek thought who recognized that there were limits to what human beings can know in comparison with divine knowledge, and Kahn sees F6 as just another example of this "epistemic modesty characteristic of Archaic thought" (1974: 173). The appeals to the Muses in the Homeric epics are the earliest examples of this theme. In the philosophical tradition it is represented most prominently by Xenophanes, Alcmaeon, and the Hippocratic treatise *On Ancient Medicine*. There is a considerable amount of debate about the nature of the skepticism involved in this tradition and I will only pick out a few important trends that seem relevant to Philolaus here. (For good discussions of the tradition of contrast between divine and human knowledge see Barnes 1982: 136ff and Snell 1953: 136ff.)

There are two themes in this tradition that seem particularly relevant to Philolaus. First, what is denied to human beings is not mere thought or opinions about certain topics, but rather the clear understanding or knowledge which only the gods have. Second, this clear understanding is only denied to humans in a specific domain; knowledge is possible for humans in other domains. The domain in which human knowledge is denied is often one which is beyond direct human experience. Both of these themes are already visible in one of the earliest texts in the tradition, the invocation of the Muses before the Catalogue of the Ships in Book 2 (484ff) of the *Iliad*. Homer emphasizes that the goddesses "know all things" while men only know by rumor, thus setting out the distinction between the clear understanding of the gods and human beliefs fostered by rumor. In this case divine knowledge is superior because the goddesses "are there," i.e. have direct experience of what Homer will relate. Thus, the domain in which humans lack knowledge is in this case those aspects of the empirical world which we do not have direct access to because of our mortality and human nature (i.e. things that occur before we are born or in far-off localities).

The goddesses know these things because of their immortality and omni-presence.

Turning to the philosophical tradition, we find that Alcmaeon argues that the gods have "a clear understanding that humans do not," but this time the domain of human incompetence is the realm of "things unseen" (F1). This, of course, does not deny that things unseen can be known; it just argues that clear knowledge about such things is beyond human power. Likewise, it does not deny clear understanding to human beings; it just limits that understanding to the visible world. A fragment of Xenophanes (F34) also seems to deny knowledge of the "clear truth" to men; this time the domain specified is "the gods and...everything of which I speak" which Barnes has plausibly interpreted to mean "theology and natural science" (1982: 140). The Hippocratic treatise *On Ancient Medicine* (1–2) also is skeptical about human knowledge of some aspects of the natural world when it criticizes natural scientists, those who study the things in the air and the things under ground, for dealing with a subject where "there is no test the application of which would give certainty" (tr. Jones), in contrast to medicine where knowledge has been obtained by long inquiry. The implied problem is that while in medicine we can have direct experience of most of the relevant phenomena, things in the heavens and under the earth are in important ways removed from our experience so that we are forced to rely on hypotheses.

The great contrast to this skepticism about human knowledge of what is beyond our direct experience is Parmenides. He presents his account of a reality which is very much beyond our ordinary experience of the world in the guise of the revelation of the goddess. For Parmenides it is precisely what the gods know, the unseen, that is the only thing that we can be said to truly know, so that the great contrast between divine and human knowledge is undercut. The domain in which authors like Alcmaeon and the author of *On Ancient Medicine* found secure human knowledge to reside, the phenomenal world, is singled out as not susceptible to knowledge but only to opinon.

The contrast between divine and human knowledge in F6 of Philolaus has clear ties to this tradition of "epistemic modesty" and just as clearly denies any attempt like Parmenides' to state the nature of eternal being. In light of this tradition and Philolaus' use of γνῶσις (for the meaning see the commentary on F4) in F6, it is clear that once again what is being denied to humans is clear understanding or knowledge. But what domain is it which Philolaus finds to be beyond human capabilities?

Philolaus does not say that humans cannot have knowledge of things or of nature and indeed F1 and F2 clearly suggest that we can have knowl-edge in these areas. What is denied to humans is knowledge of nature *itself* and the *being* (ἐστώ) of things. Both of these locutions emphasize that it is not things in the natural world themselves, but rather the ultimate reality or being that underlies the world-order, which is unknowable. This is further confirmed by Philolaus' description of the unknowable being of things as "eternal." He is talking about the eternal underlying reality as opposed to the generated cosmos. It is hard to see what this can be besides something like the changeless being of Parmenides and Melissus, especially since Melissus uses the same adjective as Philolaus (ἀίδιος – "eternal") to describe his one being (F4, F7). That Philolaus is rejecting the search for ultimate reality here in favor of studying the visible world-order is strikingly confirmed by Aristotle, who emphasizes that the Pythagoreans "carry out all their discussions and investigations with regard to the physical world" (διαλέγονται μέντοι καὶ πραγματεύονται περὶ φύσεως πάντα – *Metaph.* 989b33). He goes on to say that they acted as though they agree with the other natural scientists that "reality was limited to what was perceptible and contained within the heavens" (τό γε ὂν τοῦτ' ἐστὶν ὅσον αἰσθητόν ἐστι καὶ περιείληφεν ὁ καλούμενος οὐρανός – *Metaph.* 990a4).

Up to this point I have emphasized the extent to which Philolaus denies the possibility of any knowledge of an ultimate reality such as the Eleatics were searching for; however, F6, while arguing that generally speaking we have no knowledge of the being of things, does in fact make a couple of exceptions to this general ban and concedes to mortals a limited knowledge of ultimate reality. It is here that Philolaus develops a quite original argument that both distinguishes him from the earlier skeptical tradition and shows his connections to the pluralist philosophers who were his contemporaries. It is commonly recognized that the pluralists, in their reaction to Eleatic monism, simply start from the assumption that there is a plurality of distinct entities in the world, and it is just this assumption which Philolaus states in F6. However, starting from this assumption he develops a new interpretation of what we can know about ultimate reality.

What Philolaus says is that none of the things that are and are known by us, by which he means the things in the world-order, as the end of the sentence shows, would have come to be unless the being of those things from which the world-order came to be preexisted. In this formulation Philolaus makes the pluralist assumption and on this basis argues that we have the right to draw some conclusions about the nature of the ultimate reality that underlies the world, although we have no complete knowledge of it. In doing so he of course parts company with thinkers such as the author of *On Ancient Medicine*, and perhaps Alcmaeon, who would see this as making assertions about what is unseen and hence beyond our grasp. I take it that thinkers like Empedocles and Anaxagoras made a similar move to Philolaus' here and concluded, in one case, that ultimate reality must be the four elements (earth, air, fire, and water), and in the other case that it is an infinite variety of infinitely divisible distinct substances, as many substances as there are kinds of things in the world.

Philolaus is not so confident, in that he does not claim complete knowledge of these basic principles as Anaxagoras and Empedocles seem to. Instead, he says that in order to account for the world-order which we know, the most we can assume is that the being of the things from which the world-order came together must have preexisted. But the things from which the world-order came to be are limiters and unlimiteds, so that we know that the eternal and ultimate reality that underlies the world must have included limiters and unlimiteds. Seen in comparison to the other pluralists this is a very strange idea. Instead of something readily identifiable like earth or fire, Philolaus seizes on what he takes to be the essence of all such things, their unlimited nature, their innate lack of any unique quantity. Along with these unlimiteds he recognizes that there must also be limiting principles to produce a world-order, principles which thinkers like Empedocles and Anaxagoras clearly assumed, but which they did not isolate as constituents of the world-order on a par with unlimiteds. What is striking about Philolaus' conclusion is that he has in effect combined Parmenides and Melissus. Melissus argued that "what is" must be unlimited while Parmenides had just as clearly argued that it must be held "in the bonds of limit." Neither of these accounts can explain the origin of the world-order as we know it but, so Philolaus suggests, if we combine the two accounts and suppose that ultimate reality comprises both limiters and unlimiteds, then a world-order can arise. Although Philolaus would have identified Emepdocles' four elements as "unlimiteds," he does not feel that our knowledge of the world-order can justify the conclusion that just these four "unlimiteds" characterize ultimate reality, rather than any one of them alone or more than four. In this respect he is closer to Anaxagoras who refused to boil things down to a small group of elements and regarded everything as basic (Furley 1987: 48). But Philolaus is still more cautious than Anaxagoras in that he refuses to assert that everything is an element. His sense of rigor leads him to assert that the only sure conclusion we can draw about ultimate reality is that it must be constituted by both limiters and unlimiteds: any further conclusions about their nature or number is unwarranted.

However, in the last half of F6 Philolaus points out that there is one further conclusion we can draw about reality. The mere assumption of the preexistence of limiters and unlimiteds will not in fact explain the world-order we know. Limiters and unlimiteds are in their very nature unlike and if we simply assumed their existence there would be no explanation of how they could ever be combined to form the world-order instead of remaining unmixed with one another. Philolaus' answer is that some sort of harmony must supervene upon the limiters and unlimiteds in order to bind them together in the world-order. What first leaps to mind here is the love and strife postulated by Empedocles to explain combinations of things, or the rotary motion of Anaxagoras and the vortex of the atomists. However, once again Philolaus is resolutely non-committal about the further nature of this force which "fits together." He simply says that it supervened "in whatever way it came to be." Rather than seeing this as a laughable evasion on Philolaus' part, we should recognize that it is completely in accord with the cautious approach in discussing ultimate reality which we see in the beginning of F6. The point is simply that we have no good basis on which to conclude what kind of harmonizing force is active in the world; we have no grounds to conclude that it is love or strife or a vortex or any other particular type of force; we can only conclude that a "fitting together" has occurred, and thus that a *harmonia* of some sort must also be included among the characteristics of ultimate reality.

Thus, in the end, Philolaus is not quite as epistemologically modest as it appeared at first glance. While denying any direct knowledge of the being of things, he nonetheless argues that this ultimate reality must include limiters, unlimiteds, and *harmonia*. But, having made these limited points about what we can know about ultimate reality, Philolaus now turns to the kind of things we can know more about, individual examples of "fitting together" in the world around us, things that have number. Thus in F6a, which is probably continuous with F6, he introduces the audible concords and the ratios of whole numbers that correspond to them as specific examples of the fitting together of limiters and unlimiteds in the world-order, and the rest of his book presumably concentrated on just such things (see Fragments 7, 17, 13 and the testimonia on astronomy and music).

περὶ δὲ φύσιος καὶ ἁρμονίας ὧδε ἔχει: At first sight this phrase looks suspiciously like the sort of introductory words that an excerptor or compiler might have added (Boeckh 1819: 62 n. 1). However, there are good parallels for such a locution in fifth-century authors and it should therefore be accepted as part of Philolaus' text. Thus the Hippocratic treatise *On the Sacred Disease* begins περὶ τῆς ἱρῆς νούσου καλεομένης ὧδ' ἔχει ("Concerning the so-called sacred disease the situation is this"). See also Herodotus 2.65: νόμος δέ ἐστι περὶ τῶν θηρίων ὧδε ἔχων ("Their [the Egyptians'] custom regarding animals is the following").

The parallel from the Hippocratic corpus might lead us to wonder if F6 was the beginning of Philolaus' book. However, the ancient tradition makes F1 the beginning of the book, and it does function well as a beginning. F6 seems rather to introduce a new topic in Philolaus' discussion in a similar way to the Herodotus passage above. The rest of the fragment does fall into two parts. The first sentence discusses nature (φύσις) in the sense of "being" (ἐστώ), while the rest of the fragment focuses on both the need for and the nature of "fitting together" (ἁρμονία). But the combination of nature and "fitting together" here is not to be explained simply as a list of two separate topics. F6 agrees with F1 in that nature, at least as it appears in the world-order, turns out to require "fitting together" because it consists of disparate components.

ἁ μὲν ἐστώ: Except for this fragment ἐστώ is only found in the later Pythagorean tradition, although it is very rare even there (pseudo-Archytas, Thesleff 1965: 19.19ff; see also 166.3 and Iamblichus, *VP* 162). This might cast doubt on the authenticity of F6 but the situation is not as simple as it appears. First, although ἐστώ itself does not occur in the fifth century, a number of compounds of ἐστώ do occur, and thus suggest that ἐστώ itself is also a possibility for the fifth century. Democritus, Philolaus' contemporary, is said to have used εὐεστώ to refer to the tranquility of mind (εὐθυμία) which he regarded as the end of all human action (D.L. 9.45–6; see also DK F2c). Aeschylus uses the same compound several times where it seems to mean something like good fortune or well-being (*A.* 647, 929; *Th.* 187). Harpocration reports that Antiphon used the compound ἀειεστώ in the sense of "eternity" in the second book of his *Truth* (F22). Finally, Herodotus uses the compound ἀπεστώ to mean "being away" or "absence" (9.85).

In light of these parallels Burkert may be right to conclude that ἐστώ "is obviously an Ionic formation" (1972: 256 n. 87). As he points out, Plato's *Cratylus* (401c2–4) suggests that the Doric form for οὐσία is ὠσία or ἐσσία. ἐστώ is evidently formed from the root *ἐσ-(εἰμί), and this, along with the compounds discussed above, indicates that it has the general meaning of οὐσία, "being." As in other uses of forms of the verb "to be" in the Presocratics, it does not seem that it is used strictly to refer to either existence or essence, but rather represents a fused notion of existence and essence. Thus ἐστώ is paired with φύσις (nature) where the notion of essential nature seems dominant, but all that we are said to know of the ἐστώ is that it preexists (ὑπάρχειν), which stresses its existential sense. It does seem to refer to the φύσις or inner nature that was the focus of earlier Presocratic philosophy. This is confirmed by Philolaus' description of it as ἀΐδιον ("eternal") and his pairing of it with "nature in itself" (αὐτὰ ἁ φύσις). The adjective ἀΐδιος was used by Melissus to describe "what is" (τὸ ὄν – F4 and F7), and Diogenes of Apollonia, a contemporary of Philolaus, describes the element which he argued to be the essence of things, air, as ἀΐδιος (F7.8).

Thus, the language Philolaus uses to describe ἀ ἐστώ accords well with other Presocratic descriptions of "what is" in the most basic sense, and the use of compounds of ἐστώ in authors contemporaneous with Philolaus suggests that the use of ἐστώ itself by Philolaus is possible. What are we to make of its use in the later Pythagorean tradition? In pseudo-Archytas (Thesleff 1965: 19.19) ἐστώ is clearly used in the sense of Aristotelian matter and both scholars who question the authenticity of F6 (Bywater 1868: 34ff) and scholars who regard it as authentic (Scoon 1922: 354) have argued that this same sense is found in Philolaus, but there is little support for such a contention. (In Nicomachus [Thesleff 1965: 166.3] ἐστώ is equated with the dyad, which suggests the same sense of "matter" that we find in pseudo-Archytas. The meaning in Iamblichus, *VP* 162 is unclear.)

It is true that pseudo-Archytas uses ἐστώ in just the same phrase in which it is found in Philolaus, ἀ ἐστώ τῶν πραγμάτων ("the being of things," Thesleff 1965: 19.23,26; 20.7,11), but it is here that the similarity ends. In pseudo-Archytas ἐστώ is used interchangeably with ωσία and is described by the whole range of Aristotelian terminology. It is called τὸ ὑποκείμενον παραδεχόμενον τὰν μορφώ ("the substratum which receives the form") and grouped with god (ὁ θεός) and form (ἀ μορφώ) as one of the three basic principles. While god is the artistic (τεχνίταν) and moving (κινέοντα) cause, the ἐστώ is described as "matter" (ἀ ὕλα) and "what is moved" (τὸ κινούμενον). The ἐστώ is described as what is without form (ἄμορφος) and is identified with what is without order (ἀτάκτων) and undefined (ἀορίστων) in contrast to what is ordered and defined.

In Philolaus F6 all of the Aristotelian conceptual framework and terminology is missing. There is no mention of matter (ὕλη) or its opposite form (μορφή), nor is ἐστώ described as the substratum (τὸ ὑποκείμενον). It is true that ἐστώ is said to preexist (ὑπάρχειν) but this need not be an equivalent to the Aristotelian "underlying" principle. As Nussbaum has pointed out (1979: 101 n. 94) concerning ὑπάρχειν, "the verb, though not a technical term before the Stoics, is amply attested in fifth-century prose in the relevant senses. No suspicions of the fragment's authenticity can get their start from this word." Scoon argued that ἐστώ must be a material principle, since "the author speaks of the ἐστώ of things, out of which (things) the ordered universe arose" (1922: 354). Yet, the things "out of which" the universe arises need only be constituents in some sense, and there is no reason to suppose that they are constituents in the specific sense of Aristotelian matter. As Burkert (1972: 256) has pointed out, ἐστώ in Philolaus is not equated just with "unlimited things" (τὰ ἄπειρα), which in some contexts might plausibly be argued to be equivalent to "matter without quality" (ἄποιος ὕλη), but also to limiters (τὰ περαίνοντα) which must be associated with form in an Aristotelian system. Indeed, the whole force of the pseudo-Archytas passage is to associate ἐστώ τῶν πραγμάτων with the "unlimited" side of the table of opposites, while in F6 it clearly embraces both limit and the unlimited. Thus, comparison with pseudo-Archytas shows that the use of ἐστώ in Philolaus F6 is both conceptually and terminologically distinct from the pseudo-Pythagorean tradition and in fact has connections to the "ultimate being" or "essence" for which thinkers such as Parmenides, Melissus, and even Diogenes of Apollonia were searching.

τῶν πραγμάτων: πράγματα just seems to be used by Philolaus in the general sense of "things," but it is not very common among other Presocratics. They generally seem to use the neuter of adjectives like πάντα ("all things") to convey this meaning, although Anaxagoras uses χρήματα. Democritus does use πράγματα in this sense in F164. However, there are a number of uses of πράγματα in the general sense of "things" in other fifth-century authors (Aristophanes, *Clouds* 228, 250, 741). There are several texts where πράγματα as "things" are contrasted with ὀνόματα as the "names" of those things. See for example Δίσσοι λόγοι 1.11 and 3.13 as well as Plato, *Cratylus* 390e1. *Protagoras* 337d3–4 τὴν . . . φύσιν τῶν πραγμάτων εἰδέναι ("to know the nature of things") is a close parallel to Philolaus' own phrase ἁ ἐστώ τῶν πραγμάτων. It does not seem to me to be good to translate πράγματα as "objects," as Barnes does, simply because for Philolaus πράγματα might well include things that we would not normally call objects. F6a in connection with F6 suggests that musical pitches might well be πράγματα for Philolaus, but I doubt that we would call them objects.

καὶ . . . μάν: The manuscripts all read καὶ . . . μέν. Scoon defends this second μέν (ἁ μὲν ἐστώ is the first) as "resumptive and confirmative of the first" (1922: 354). However, a resumptive μέν usually occurs after considerable intervening material where there is need to resuscitate the first μέν (Denniston 1954: 384). But in this passage of Philolaus there is no long intervening passage and hence no need for resumptive μέν. Furthermore, while the combination καὶ μέν does occur elsewhere, nowhere else do we find καὶ . . . μέν. Thus, Denniston seems right to conclude that in Philolaus F6 "the second μέν seems impossible and Usener's μάν highly probable" (1954: 391). The use of καὶ . . . μάν is probably progressive here (Denniston 1954: 358): "the being of things which is eternal and indeed nature itself . . ."

αὐτά . . . ἁ φύσις: αὐτά is used here to indicate that what is at issue is not the nature of a specific kind of thing, but nature "in itself." It is also in contrast with things known "by us" (ὑφ' ἁμῶν) which will be discussed below. This meaning is also shown by pairing "nature in itself" with "the

132

being of things which is eternal". Philolaus is discussing the eternal, ultimate, inner nature of things, the inner nature that Heraclitus said loved to hide itself (F123), the eternal being that Parmenides and Melissus sought to define. Although Philolaus denied human knowledge of such an eternal nature, he is nonetheless interested in nature as it is displayed in the world-order.

θείαν τε καὶ οὐκ ἀνθρωπίνην ἐνδέχεται γνῶσιν: This is the manuscript reading. Diels read γα for τε and Badham followed by Wachsmuth read θεία ἐντί. Both of these readings were evidently motivated by doubts about the combination τε καὶ οὐκ. However, Denniston (1954: 513) cites several passages from tragedy to show that τε καὶ οὐκ is used in passages that couple opposites (e.g. Soph. *OT* 1275 πολλάκις τε κοὐχ ἅπαξ – "often and not once"; *OC* 935 βίᾳ τε κοὐχ ἑκών – "by force and not willingly"). But it is just such a coupling of opposites that is found in Philolaus, "divine and not human."

Philolaus does not say explicitly why the "being of things" does not admit of human knowledge. Nussbaum (1979: 100 n. 91), however, argues that to show "how human understanding is inferior to that of the gods is clearly the point of the fragment" and says that Philolaus' point is that human nature requires that there be an ordered plurality for cognition to occur (i.e. the ordered plurality that results from the combination of limiters and unlimiteds). However, this interpretation suggests that, while human knowledge does require an ordered plurality, divine knowledge does not. This seems to me very unlikely. Certainly in F4 Philolaus' points about knowledge seem to be about knowledge in general and not just human knowledge. In F6 Philolaus need only mean that human knowledge is limited in that our experience is less extensive than that of the gods. We cannot for example experience eternal entities and are not omnipresent as Xenophanes' god may be. That this is the type of difference between divine and human knowledge is supported by other Greek authors who contrast the two and seems more plausible than supposing Philolaus to mean that the gods have some special type of knowing that has radically different logical requirements than human knowledge.

γνῶσιν should be translated "knowledge" (not "apprehension," Nussbaum), as the contrast between divine and human suggests. For the interpretation of γνῶσις see my comments on γνωσούμενον in F3.

πλάν γα ἢ ὅτι: All the manuscripts have πλέον γα ἢ ὅτι and this is accepted by Boeckh, Diels, and Scoon. Here πλέον is taken as adverbial to ἐνδέχεται (Scoon 1922: 354 – not as modifying γνῶσιν, as Burkert thinks [1972: 250 n. 61]). The translation would be "nature itself admits of divine and not human knowledge, no more at any rate than the knowledge that..." Although such a use of πλέον seems plausible theoretically, in actual usage it is hard to find a case where it is used in a phrase with the sense of "no more than" = "except" which is required here and Scoon provides no parallels for it. On the other hand, as Burkert remarks, πλήν ἤ is a very common combination in this sense. Herodotus 4.189 preserves just the same combination as is proposed for Philolaus here (πλὴν ἤ ὅτι) with the sense "except that." Other texts have πλὴν ἤ (Aristophanes, *Clouds* 361 and Herodotus 2.111, 130) while still others have πλὴν ὅτι (Plato, *Phd.* 57b2 and *Tht.* 183a9). Until a good parallel for πλέον in this construction is forthcoming, it seems better to follow the parallels above except that the Doric πλάν should probably be read (Badham), since it is more plausible that this would come to be changed to πλέον than the very familiar πλήν. The difference in sense between the two readings is not large.

οὐχ οἷόν τ' ἦν οὐθενὶ τῶν ἐόντων καὶ γιγνωσκομένων ὑφ' ἀμῶν γεγενῆσθαι . . . : Scholars have spent a considerable amount of time rewriting this passage, but it is important to note that the only real problem raised by the manuscript text (except for the easy and necessary correction from the manuscripts' οἷον τὴν to οἷόν τ' ἦν) concerns the last word. Most of the mauscripts have the impossible γεγνέσθαι. E has γενέσθαι but, given the general nature of the readings in that manuscript, this seems more likely to be a scribe's correction or simplification than the preservation of the true reading. The issue of γεγνέσθαι can and should be separated from changes made to the manuscript readings οὐθενὶ and γιγνωσκομένων which I will discuss below.

The goal is to try to come up with a form of γίγνομαι that works in this context and still explain how the manuscript error came about (i.e. to explain how the initial γε- arose). Thus the emendation of Diels (γα γενέσθαι) assumes that an original γα came to be incorrectly combined with γενέσθαι. Both Burkert (1972: 251 n. 62) and Scoon (1922: 356) complain that γα produces an undesirable sense, but neither explains what this sense is. Given that Philolaus has set up a strong contrast between divine and human knowledge earlier in this sentence, it seems not at all inappropriate to have γα with ὑφ' ἀμῶν to emphasize that he is limiting himself to things known by *us*. On the other hand the text adopted by Scoon, Usener and Wachsmuth which simply has γενέσθαι without γα does produce reasonable sense and we could suppose that the manuscript reading arose by a sort of dittography of the first syllable. Burkert's emendation is the only one to keep the initial γεγ- and does so by supposing that the the original reading was the perfect infinitive γεγενῆσθαι.

In the end all of these proposals seem to explain the corruption equally well and to produce adequate sense. However, Burkert's proposal seems slightly preferable to me since the perfect infinitive stresses, in a way that the aorist infinitive does not, that the things that are and are known by us have in fact come to be, thus underlining the contrary-to-fact nature of the sentence (on the perfect infinitive as emphasizing finished action see Goodwin 1965: 34). The difference in English translation would be that between "it was not possible for any of the things ... to come to be" and "it was not possible for any of the things to have come to be [as they clearly have]." As Burkert points out, Philolaus does use the perfect infinitive συγκεκλεῖσθαι a few lines further on in the fragment. There it also seems to emphasize that the action involved is finished or complete. Antiphon uses γεγενῆσθαι in F58 similarly to emphasize the completeness of an action: ἐν μὲν τῷ γεγενῆσθαι οὐκ ἔνεστιν ("In the case of what has happened it is not possible" [to change one's mind]).

Usener and Diels, followed by Wachsmuth and Nussbaum, have altered the text further, replacing the manuscript readings οὐθενὶ and γιγνωσκομένων with οὐθέν and γιγνωσκόμενον respectively. γιγνωσκόμενον ... γενέσθαι is then understood as a periphrastic formation and the translation is "it would not be possible for any of the things that are also to come to be known by us if there were not ... " The passage would thus state conditions not for coming to be (as it does on the manuscript text), but for coming to be known or apprehended. The discussion of this emendation has been confused by the fact that both Burkert and Nussbaum combine it unnecessarily, in my opinion, with the textual problem surrounding γεγενῆσθαι which I have discussed above.

Looked at in itself the change appears largely indefensible. What solid basis is there for changing two readings found in all manuscripts and which give us a text that is perfectly grammatical and that makes good sense? The motive seems to be the desire to have a reference to the conditions for knowledge in the fragment. To be sure this is a perfectly possible topic for Philolaus and he addresses it directly in F4, but there is no reason to assume that this is what he is talking about in F6. Surely it is correct methodology to base our interpretation of Philolaus on the texts preserved in the manuscript tradition and only alter those texts when they are ungrammatical or when they give a sense that is seriously defective; otherwise we are in danger of rewriting Philolaus in our own image.

There are some further problems with the proposed emendation to οὐθέν ... γιγνωσκόμενον. Burkert objects to the periphrastic construction (γιγνωσκόμενον ... γενέσθαι) on the grounds that "the passive is never expressed elsewhere, I believe, by γίγνεσθαι and the present passive participle" (1972: 251 n. 62). Nussbaum (1979: 99 n. 91) doubts "Burkert's generalizations" although she cannot, on the basis of an incomplete survey, find exact parallels for the periphrasis. She does give evidence for the perfect passive participle in such periphrases. It may be that a parallel can be found, but it is at least clear that the periphrasis with the present passive participle is not a common one. This simply casts more doubt on the proposed emendation. We would seem to need very strong grounds indeed to introduce two emendations into a perfectly intelligible text when these emendations produce what is, at the least, an unusual periphrastic construction. Both Barnes (1982) and Schofield (KRS) keep the manuscript text.

Nussbaum goes on to suggest that the difference in meaning between the two readings is not as radical as Burkert (1972: 251 n. 2) suggests. She says that even on the manuscript text it does not follow "that the fragment is about the conditions of the origin of the world and *not* about the conditions of thought." She maintains that "for a writer concerned with Eleatic questions... the addition of γιγνωσκομένων to ἐόντων must surely be the conscious restriction of the argument to what becomes an object of thought for us" (1979: 100 n. 91). But in context the function of the reference to "the things known by us" (γιγνωσκομένων ὑφ' ἀμῶν) is clearly to contrast them with the things we cannot know, and which admit only of divine knowledge, that are mentioned in the first part of the sentence. Nussbaum is right, then, if she means that Philolaus is restricting himself to talking only about things which are in the domain of human knowledge. However, on the manuscript reading the fragment is not about how these things become *known*; it is about their coming *to be*. It is not at all obvious that the conditions necessary for their coming to be are the same as the conditions for their coming to be known.

It is important to notice that Philolaus refers to "coming to be" here (γεγενῆσθαι) and later in the fragment (ἐπεγένετο, ἐγένετο) without any Eleatic uneasiness. In fact the assumption of this first sentence is that there are things that are known by us which come to be. As the last words of the sentence make clear, it is the existence of this "world-order" which we perceive that is the controlling assumption in Philolaus' argument.

ὑπαρχούσας: Nussbaum has a good note on the meaning of ὑπάρχειν (1979: 101 n. 94). She discusses two possible meanings: (1) "to be present to" or "to belong to someone," (2) "to be already in existence." As she points out, both meanings are "amply represented in fifth-century authors" (see LSJ). However, the first meaning does not work very well in F6 because it usually involves at least an implied dative specifying the person to whom the thing in question "is present" and here it is awkward to supply a dative such as ἡμῖν ("to us") when the genitive "by us" has just been used. If this were the sense intended, "to us" really needed to be stated explicitly. Moreover, the point of Philolaus' remarks on the "being of things" is that it is never directly present to us (and hence not knowable), but that we must assume that the being of the limiting and the unlimited was already in existence for the cosmos to have arisen.

Beyond this there are other signs in the context that the meaning "be already in existence" or "preexist" is what is intended. Thus, ὑπάρχον is used to describe the beginnings (i.e. limiters and unlimiteds) at the start of the next sentence in clear contrast to ἐπεγένετο which describes the "fitting together" of the limiters and unlimiteds. What is needed as a contrast to the meaning "supervene" is precisely a word that means "preexist." For a good example of the meaning "preexist" see Herodotus 7.144 where a contrast is made between αὖται αἱ νέες τοῖσι Ἀθηναίοισι ὑπῆρχον (the ships which already existed for the Athenians) and those they were about to build.

ταί: This is Badham's correction for the τε of the manuscripts, which is impossible. The unusual form would easily be corrupted in transmission. It seems best to follow Burkert and give ταί a demonstrative force, "these beginnings." Such an interpretation gives better continuity between this sentence and what precedes.

ἀρχαί: Like ἐστώ this word has aroused considerable suspicion about the authenticity of the fragment (e.g. Bywater 1868: 51). ἀρχή is a common Aristotelian word for "first principle" and has a prominent role in his description of Presocratic thought. However, it is also used by the Presocratics and by writers in the Hippocratic corpus, so that the mere appearance of the word need not arouse suspicion. I have argued in some detail that Philolaus is consciously developing an explanatory method using ἀρχαί and that this method has closer connections to both the Hippocratic writings of the later fifth century and the mathematician Hippocrates of Chios (430) than it does to Aristotle (see Pt. II, ch. 3). It means "starting-point" and specifically a starting-point in explanation.

οὐχ ὁμοῖαι οὐδ' ὁμόφυλοι: Philolaus' description of "the beginnings" as "not alike" is in strong contrast to Parmenides who describes "what is" in F8.22 as follows: "it is not divided since it is all alike" (οὐδὲ διαίρετον ἐστιν, ἐπεὶ πᾶν ἐστιν ὁμοῖον). Melissus (F7) agrees and describes "what is" as "eternal ... and unlimited and one and all alike" (ἀΐδιον ... καὶ ἄπειρον καὶ ἓν καὶ ὅμοιον πᾶν). Philolaus' language is so close to this last passage from Melissus that it is tempting to see him as literally commenting on it. He is talking about the same "eternal being" as Melissus (both use ἀΐδιος), but he does not believe that the world-order which we perceive can have arisen from beginnings that were "all alike." Rather it arises from origins that are not alike. He agrees with Melissus that unlimiteds must be eternal, but argues that limiters too must be eternal. Empedocles also rejected the notion that the origin of the world could be found in one principle that is "all alike." He advocates four elements each of which, however, he describes as internally "alike" (ὁμοῖον – F17). Philolaus does not comment on the internal homogeneity of the limiters and unlimiteds here, but rather focuses on the problem of how to explain combinations of these unlike elements.

It is hard to determine what distinction, if any, there is between ὁμοῖαι and ὁμόφυλοι. In some contexts ὁμόφυλος refers to human relationships and seems to mean "of the same race" or "akin" ("Hippocrates", *Airs, Waters, Places* 12.31; Plato, *Lg.* 843a4; *Mx.* 244a2 and 242d2). In one Hippocratic text it refers to copulating partners as needing to be akin in the sense of the same species (*Nat. hom.* 3.3). On the other hand it is applied to inanimate objects as being of the same kind or akin. Thus Theophrastus, in his report of Democritus' account of perception, cites the general principle of "like knowing like" using ὁμόφυλα (DK 68A135.50 τὰ γὰρ ὁμόφυλα μάλιστα ἕκαστον γνωρίζειν). Plato also uses it of "like things associating with like" at *Ti.* 81a6 as does Aristotle at *De caelo* 307b1. The fact that Philolaus uses οὐδέ ("not even") between ὁμοῖαι and ὁμόφυλοι may suggest that the latter indicates a somewhat weaker connection than the former. In this case the contrast can be brought out best by translating "since the beginnings preexisted, not being alike or even related" (after Scoon).

... ἤδη ἀδύνατον ἧς κα αὐταῖς κοσμηθῆναι, εἰ μὴ ἁρμονία ἐπεγένετο ... : The manuscript reading ἧς καί suggests a misunderstanding by a copyist of the unfamiliar Doric form ἧς. Since καί seems to have no particular force here it seems reasonable to accept Badham's ἧς κα.

Philolaus is arguing that since the beginnings were unlike, it would have been impossible for them to be ordered, if a "fitting together" had not supervened. The notion that likes are naturally bound together and not in fact in need of any "harmonizing" factor is a commonplace in Greek thought (Democritus F164). No need is felt to explain why it is that water mixes with water or sand with sand. However, in the case of unlike things, if they are found together in some sort of combination, it seems necessary to look for some third factor to explain this breach of the rule of like to like.

Philolaus calls this principle ἁρμονία. The development of this term has been well discussed by others (Kirk 1954: 207ff; Kahn 1979: 196ff). The root meaning is "to join" or "to fit together". It is applied literally in shipbuilding where a ἁρμονία is a joint (*Od.* 5.248). The use in music is a figurative application of this meaning to the tuning of a musical instrument. A ἁρμονία is then a specific "fitting together" or "attunement" of an instrument and later in F6 (F6a) is used of an "attunement an octave long" (see Barker 1984: 163ff).

The concept of ἁρμονία plays a prominent role in Heraclitus' philosophy. It is a matter of debate whether it just has the sense of "connection" and "agreement" or whether it also has a musical sense (Kirk 1954: 207 and Kahn 1979: 196–7). However, most scholars would agree that in Heraclitus "*harmonie* as a unity composed of conflicting parts is... the model for an understanding of the world ordering as a unified whole" (Kahn 1979: 200). Thus, in Heraclitus just as in Philolaus, ἁρμονία is a principle that explains the connection between things that differ or are unlike (F51 "They do not understand how in differing it agrees with itself, a backturning *harmonia* like that of a bow or lyre" [οὐ ξυνιᾶσιν ὅκως διαφερόμενον ἑωυτῷ ὁμολογέει· παλίντροπος ἁρμονίη ὅκωσπερ τόξου καὶ λύρης]). The same holds true in Empedocles where ἁρμονία is invoked to explain how unlike elements (earth, water, fire) can be joined to form one substance, bone (F96 "... and these came to be white bones, marvelously held together by the gluing of Harmony" [tr. Wright] [τὰ δ' ὀστέα λευκὰ γένοντο, ἁρμονίης κόλλησιν ἀρηρότα θεσπεσίηθεν]). In Empedocles Harmonia is equated with Love which along with Strife are the two efficient causes of change in the world. That part of Empedocles' cycle in which Love/Harmony comes into complete dominance is characterized by the complete unification of the unlike elements into a sphere in which none of the differing parts can be distinguished (see F27 where Empedocles refers to the "close covering of harmony" [ἁρμονίης πυκινῷ κρυφῷ]).

A "fitting together" need not be good or harmonious. It is possible to have a bad craftsman. However, in passages such as Empedocles F96 it is clear that the "fitting together" does not proceed haphazardly, but involves specific proportions of constituents (two parts water, four parts fire, etc.). The fitting together is usually made with a certain use or function in mind. In *Odyssey* 5 Odysseus fits his raft together with the goal of reaching Ithaca. Musical *harmonia* is not just any "fitting together" of strings or pitches, but one that produces a certain attunement. For Philolaus it is clear that ἁρμονία has this sense of "harmonious fitting together," both because it is specifically tied to a musical attunement in F6a, and because it is explicitly used not just to explain any old combination of dissimilar elements but a combination of elements into an order (κόσμος).

Thus, it is clear that the main outlines of Philolaus' conception of ἁρμονία were already well developed in the Presocratic tradition by Heraclitus and Empedocles. What seems to be peculiar to Philolaus is both the emphasis on the musical sense of ἁρμονία and also the close connection between ἁρμονία and number. To be sure Heraclitus may be alluding to the musical idea of harmony in some places and Empedocles connects *harmonia* to numerical proportions of constituents in F96. However, Heraclitus does not use the structure of the diatonic scale as a model for the structure of the world as explicitly as Philolaus does in F6a (but see Shipton 1985), and Empedocles does not always associate the working of harmony with number as it appears that Philolaus does. Heraclitus famously says that "the hidden attunement is better than the obvious one" (F54 ἁρμονίη ἀφανὴς φανερῆς κρείττων). Recently, Shipton (1985: 129ff) has argued that this is an attack on the Pythagoreans for only paying attention to the "obvious harmony of numerical ratios" whereas Heraclitus himself is pointing to the hidden harmony of opposites. However, this will not work as an attack on Philolaus who clearly sees his harmony as tying together opposites as well. Moreover, it seems to be a real question as to how obvious the numerical ratios are that correspond to the audible concords. They certainly are only arrived at by investigation that goes beyond the obvious. Indeed, Philolaus seems to be clearly most interested in a hidden harmony that is very similar to Heraclitus. As F5 of Philolaus shows, we may well start with the obvious harmony displayed by given things in the world, but our goal is to come to know them by determining the number of which they give signs.

ἐπεγένετο is used of something "coming upon" something else, i.e. of something occurring in the context of a defined set of circumstances. Thus it is frequently used in the Hippocratic treatises of the coincidence of two meteorological phenomena. Thus "rain comes upon the rising of the dog star" (*Airs, Waters, Places* 10.19 ἐπὶ κυνὸς ἐπιτολῇ ὕδωρ ἐπιγένηται). It also can refer simply to changes in weather, but usually with reference to a person upon whom they come "whenever the cold comes upon a man and causes him some pain" (tr. Jones, *VM* 16.7 ὅταν τὸ ψυχρὸν ἐπιγένηται καί τι λυπήσῃ τὸν ἄνθρωπον). It is also used of symptoms that "come on" or "supervene" on other symptoms or at a certain stage in the disease or treatment (*Prog.* 15.15; 19.7; 23.24). Among the Presocratic writers it is used by Empedocles at F17.30 in his assertion that in addition to the six principles (the four elements, Love and Strife) "nothing will come to be later in addition to these" (tr. Wright, καὶ πρὸς τοῖς οὔτ' ἄρ τι ἐπιγίνεται ...).

Thus in his use of this word Philolaus is clearly emphasizing that *harmonia* is something that "comes upon" or "supervenes on" the two beginnings that he has just posited, limiters and unlimiteds. The contrast between limiters and unlimiteds preexisting and *harmonia* supervening on them is emphasized by the prefixes of the two Greek verbs (ἐπεγένετο, ὑπᾶρχον). This might suggest that Philolaus is not thinking of *harmonia* as an origin of things in the same way as he thinks of limiters and unlimiteds as origins. Indeed, F2 clearly indicates that there are some things in the world that just limit and others that are just unlimited. Thus harmony does not exist everywhere, but supervenes to produce certain combinations of limiters and unlimiteds. It remains unclear then whether *harmonia* belongs to "the eternal being of things" in the same sense as limiters and unlimiteds do, and indeed Philolaus seems to regard any further explanation of *harmonia* as beyond our knowledge.

ᾧτινιῶν ἂν τρόπῳ ἐγένετο: It is best to keep the ἂν indicated by the manuscripts rather than emending to something like Diels's ἆδε. It is true that Philolaus does not have any doubts that the *harmonia* did supervene and hence that the indicative might be expected. However, he is in doubt about the manner in which it occurred and that doubt is expressed here with ἂν and the aorist in a past potential construction. It is also true that κα is used above in the fragment so that we might want to restore it here, but as stated in the introduction my policy has generally been to try and reproduce what the manuscript tradition preserves rather than trying to guess what was actually Philolaus' usage.

Raven, as part of his attack on the authenticity of the fragments, complains that it is surprising "to find the author of the fragments expressing . . . perplexity about what seems to have been the most important constituent in his whole cosmology" (KR 310). But this is just to misunderstand Philolaus' skeptical stance towards our knowledge of ultimate reality. Philolaus' reticence on this point does not arise out of confusion, but out of a careful argument about what is within the bounds of human knowledge. The world as we know it shows that *harmonia* does hold together many things and we are perfectly capable of defining the nature of these "fittings together" as Philolaus shows in F6a in the exposition of the diatonic scale. What we are not in the position to know is the ultimate origin and nature of *harmonia* in itself, because this, like the eternal being of things, can only be known to us indirectly by its results in the world-order. Such a consistent denial of knowledge of ultimate principles is much more likely to arise from a reasoned philosophical point of view than from the ignorance of a forger. The latter, after all, is free to supply many answers to such problems.

τὰ μὲν ὦν ὁμοῖα . . . : The previous sentence argued that in the specific case of the unlike beginnings of the world-order, limiters and unlimiteds, there was need of a harmonious fitting together, if they were to be ordered. This sentence supports that point by making the same point about all things that are like or unlike. Like things naturally combine with like things and do not require anything to fit them together, while things that are unlike do require *harmonia* if they are going to be held together in an order.

ὦν seems to be used to emphasize the prospective μέν (Denniston 1954:

473). The manuscript reading (ὦν) is best explained as generated by a misunderstanding of the Doric form.

The text of the whole sentence presents some problems. The text found in the manuscripts, which I print, involves a somewhat awkward change in construction. The δέ clause starts out with the expectation that τὰ ἀνόμοια will be the subject of a finite verb similar to ἐπεδέοντο in the first part of the sentence, but after introducing τὰ δὲ ἀνόμοια μηδὲ ὁμόφυλα . . . Philolaus shifts into an impersonal construction that treats these forms as accusatives governed by ἀνάγκα. Although this is somewhat awkward, it gives a perfectly intelligible sense and does not seem impossible to me. Burkert's suggestion (1972: 251 n. 65) is to punctuate before ἀνάγκα, but this produces an asyndeton, as he recognizes, so that it does not seem much less awkward than following the manuscript punctuation. Diels emended to τᾷ τοιαύτᾳ ἁρμονίᾳ . . . οἵᾳ ("fastened together by such a harmony, through which they are destined to endure in the universe" tr. Freeman 1971: 74). However, this produces an awkward prospective sense of τοιοῦτος (looking forward to οἵᾳ). The meaning "by such a harmony" is also inappropriate since the kind of harmony does not seem to be at issue.

In the last clause the manuscripts' ἢ εἰ does not produce sense. The best solution seems to be to remove ἢ and read just εἰ. It is possible that in the transmission of the text some copyist misunderstood μέλλοντι as a participle and tried to join the two infinitives (συγκεκλεῖσθαι and κατέχεσθαι) together with an ἤ.

There is a noteworthy similarity between this passage and a passage in the treatise Περὶ ἀρχῶν among the pseudepigrapha ascribed to Archytas (Thesleff 1965: 20.3). This is the same treatise that also has the phrase ἁ ἐστὼ τῶν πραγμάτων in common with F6. The passage in pseudo-Archytas runs as follows:

ἀλλ' ἐπεὶ τὸ κινεόμενον ἐναντίας ἑαυτῷ δυνάμεις ἴσχει τὰς τῶν ἁπλῶν σωμάτων, τὰ δ' ἐναντία συναρμογᾶς τινος δεῖται καὶ ἑνώσιος, ἀνάγκη ἀριθμῶν δυνάμιας καὶ ἀναλογίας καὶ τὰ ἐν ἀριθμοῖς καὶ γεωμετρικοῖς δεικνύμενα παραλαμβάνειν, ἃ καὶ συναρμόσαι καὶ ἑνῶσαι τὰν ἐναντιότατα δυνασεῖται ἐν τᾷ ἐστοῖ τῶν πραγμάτων ποττὰν μορφώ.

But since that which is moved has opposing powers, the powers of the simple bodies, and opposites require some fitting together and unification, it is necessary that it also take up the powers of numbers and proportions and the things which are shown in numbers and geometrical figures, which are able both to fit together and also to unify the opposition in the being of things with regard to a form.

It is undeniable that the basic thought of this passage is close to Philolaus F6, but this thought, that unlike things require something to hold them together, is by no means unusual and is assumed by both Heraclitus and Empedocles. It is also a natural conclusion from the common notion that like naturally associates with like. It is true that some of the language in the pseudo-Archytas passage is similar to F6 (ἐστώ, συναρμογᾶς... δεῖται, ἀνάγκη). However, some of this similarity is rather superficial (ἀνάγκη, δεῖται) and can be explained by the similar thought, and the dissimilarity in language and conception between the two passages is in fact more striking than the similarity. As was pointed out above in the commentary, ἐστώ is not at all the same concept in the two passages. Moreover, the pseudo-Archytas passage is replete with Platonic, Aristotelian, and other late ideas and terminology which are not found in F6 (τὸ κινεόμενον, δυνάμεις, ἁπλῶν σωμάτων, ἕνωσις, μορφώ). Thus, once again, close examination of the passage shows F6 to have more dissimilarities than similarities to the tradition of Pythagorean pseudepigrapha.

† ἰσοταχῆ: This is the reading of the manuscripts, but a reference to "equal speed" has no clear sense in context and the text is generally regarded as corrupt. A great variety of possible corrections have been proposed, but many of them are unattested or poorly attested forms and it seems better to print the manuscript text with an obelus than make what seems a largely arbitrary decision between unlikely forms.

DK prints Heidel's emendation ἰσοταγῆ, "of the same rank" (1907: 78). Heidel argued that we wanted a word that suggested the Pythagorean συστοχίαι which are mentioned by Aristotle and "to which allusion is clearly made." This was his reason for rejecting Meineke's ἰσολαχῆ, "equally alloted," which was accepted in an earlier edition of DK and by Wachsmuth. But it is not in fact clear that Philolaus is referring to the συστοχίαι, but quite the reverse. Aristotle's account of the Pythagoreans presents the material that has most similarity to Philolaus as being distinct from the Pythagoreans who posited the συστοχίαι (thus *Metaph.* 985b24ff has close ties to Philolaus and is contrasted with the views of the Pythagoreans who posit the συστοχίαι at 986a23). Meineke's ἰσολαχῆ is not found elsewhere in Greek literature while ἰσοταγῆ is only found in late Pythagorean texts (*Theol. ar.* 51). Meineke also suggested ἰσοπαλῆ, "of equal strength," which would fit better with actual Presocratic vocabulary (see Parmenides F8.44 where "what is" is compared with a well-rounded sphere and said to be "equally poised in every direction from its center" [tr. Coxon, μεσσόθεν ἰσοπαλὲς πάντη]). The most recent suggestion is Mansfeld's ἰσοκρατῆ ("of equal power") which also has the advantage of being attested for the fifth century.

Although Heidel could remark that the manuscript reading, ἰσοταχῆ, was "so clearly inept that nobody has been found to defend it," it is not an orphan after all, since Burkert accepts the reading and argues that it "could be understood by comparison with Leucippus" (1972: 251 n. 64). It is not completely clear what Burkert means by this, but it is plausible that Leucippus talked of the equal speeds of atoms moving in the void and there are connections made between the atomists and Philolaus in the later tradition (Burkert 1972: 259 n. 101). It is also true that Epicurus uses ἰσοταχοί to describe the motion of atoms (*Letter to Herodotus* 61). But none of this is very convincing, since we have had no clear reference to anything like atoms whose motion we could refer to as "of equal speed." If we thought in terms of Philolaus' astronomical system in light of the reference to the harmony of the spheres in F6a, we might suppose that the reference might be to the motion of the planets which are not "of equal speed." Alternatively a musical interpretation might be given, also in light of F6a, in which it is vibrations of strings that are not "of equal speed" (I owe this last suggestion to Alex Mourelatos). But the problem with all these interpretations of "of equal speed" is that they seem too specific for the context which otherwise talks in the most extreme generality of things that are like or unlike.

ἁρμονίᾳ συγκεκλεῖσθαι: Since the rest of the fragment always talks of ἁρμονία in the singular, it is reasonable to accept this emendation of the plural found in the manuscripts. However, the plural does not seem to be completely impossible. Since Philolaus is talking about a plurality of things that are "unlike and not even related," it is not implausible for him to be thinking in terms of a plurality of "fittings together" as well. It may be that generally speaking Philolaus has in mind a *harmonia* that holds together the whole world-order but there must also be individual *harmoniai* that hold together each of the individual unities of limiters and unlimiteds in the world.

The most common meaning for συγκλείω is "shut," "shut up," or "enclose." Aristotle uses it of catching fish in a net (*HA* 533b26). In the Hippocratic corpus it is used of the mouth of the womb being closed by fat (*AWP* 21) or of the eyebrows meeting. But it also comes to refer to things that are closed together in an order of some sort. Thus Thucydides uses the word of troops that close their ranks (4.35). Perhaps the closest parallel to what we have in Philolaus is Euripides *Ba.* 1300 where Agave asks if the remains of the dismembered Pentheus have all been put together decently limb by limb (ἢ πᾶν ἐν ἄρθροις συγκεκλημένον καλῶς). Thus Philolaus conceives of the ranks of unlike things being closed together by a *harmonia* or put together in order like the parts of a skeleton.

εἰ μέλλοντι ἐν κόσμῳ κατέχεσθαι: The meaning of ἐν κόσμῳ must be "in an order" rather than "in the world-order" as the lack of an article suggests. In this sentence Philolaus is not talking specifically about the ordered world we know, but about the general requirements for something to be "held in order."

κατέχω: This is quite a strong word which has two basic meanings: (1) "to hold back" (someone by force *Il.* 15.186) or "check," "restrain" (one's anger, tears, tongue etc.); (2) "possess," "occupy," "master" (especially of rulers, but note night "covering" the heavens and the moon "being covered" by clouds *Od.* 9.145). It is the same word Anaxagoras uses in F1 to describe the mastery of all things at the beginning of the world by air and aither (πάντα γὰρ ἀήρ τε καὶ αἰθὴρ κατεῖχεν – it is controversial whether it means "cover" or "predominate" here: Sider 1981: 47ff). Philolaus' use seems closer to the typical usage than Anaxagoras' somewhat strained usage, in that the sense of physical restraint fits the context of F6. For Philolaus the idea seems to be that the limiters and unlimiteds are "mastered" by the *harmonia* so as to be "restrained" in an order which they would not otherwise form because of their dissimilar natures.

Fragment 6a

Nicomachus, *Harm.* 9 (252.4 Jan; see also 264.2) ὅτι δὲ τοῖς ὑφ᾽ ἡμῶν δηλωθεῖσιν ἀκόλουθα καὶ οἱ παλαιότατοι ἀπεφαίνοντο, ἁρμονίαν μὲν καλοῦντες τὴν διὰ πασῶν, συλλαβὰν δὲ τὴν διὰ τεσσάρων (πρώτη γὰρ σύλληψις φθόγγων συμφώνων), δι᾽ ὀξειᾶν
5 δὲ τὴν διὰ πέντε (συνεχὴς γὰρ τῇ πρωτογενεῖ συμφωνίᾳ τῇ διὰ τεσσάρων ἐστὶν ἡ διὰ πέντε ἐπὶ τὸ ὀξὺ προχωροῦσα), σύστημα δὲ ἀμφοτέρων συλλαβᾶς τε καὶ δι᾽ ὀξειᾶν ἡ διὰ πασῶν (ἐξ αὐτοῦ τούτου ἁρμονία κληθεῖσα, ὅτι πρωτίστη ἐκ συμφωνιῶν συμφωνία ἡρμόσθη) δῆλον ποιεῖ Φιλόλαος ὁ Πυθαγόρου διάδοχος οὕτω
10 πως ἐν τῷ πρώτῳ φυσικῷ λέγων. ἀρκεσθησόμεθα γὰρ ἑνὶ μάρτυρι διὰ τὴν ἔπειξιν, εἰ καὶ πολλοὶ περὶ τοῦ αὐτοῦ τὰ ὅμοια πολλαχῶς λέγουσιν. ἔχει δὲ οὕτως ἡ τοῦ Φιλολάου λέξις.
ἁρμονίας δὲ μέγεθός ἐστι συλλαβὰ καὶ δι᾽ ὀξειᾶν. τὸ δὲ δι᾽ ὀξειᾶν μεῖζον τᾶς συλλαβᾶς ἐπογδόῳ. ἔστι γὰρ ἀπὸ ὑπάτας ἐπὶ
15 μέσσαν συλλαβά, ἀπὸ δὲ μέσσας ἐπὶ νεάταν δι᾽ ὀξειᾶν, ἀπὸ δὲ νεάτας ἐς τρίταν συλλαβά, ἀπὸ δὲ τρίτας ἐς ὑπάταν δι᾽ ὀξειᾶν. τὸ δ᾽ ἐν μέσῳ μέσσας καὶ τρίτας ἐπόγδοον, ἁ δὲ συλλαβὰ ἐπίτριτον, τὸ δὲ δι᾽ ὀξειᾶν ἡμιόλιον, τὸ διὰ πασῶν δὲ διπλόον. οὕτως ἁρμονία πέντε ἐπόγδοα καὶ δύο διέσιες, δι᾽ ὀξειᾶν δὲ
20 τρία ἐπόγδοα καὶ δίεσις, συλλαβὰ δὲ δύ᾽ ἐπόγδοα καὶ δίεσις.
(Also preserved in Stobaeus, *Eclogae* 1.21.7d [1.189.7 Wachsmuth – missing in Stobaeus P] as a continuation of F6.)

μεμνῆσθαι δὲ δεῖ, ὅτι τρίτην νῦν καλεῖ τὴν ἐν τῇ ἑπταχόρδῳ
παραμέσην, πρὸ τῆς τοῦ διαζευγνύντος τόνου παρενθέσεως τῆς
25 ἐν ὀκταχόρδῳ. ἀπεῖχε γὰρ αὕτη τῆς παρανεάτης τριημιτόνιον
ἀσύνθετον, ἀφ' οὗ διαστήματος ἡ μὲν παρεντεθεῖσα χορδὴ
τόνον ἀπέλαβε, τὸ δὲ λοιπὸν ἡμιτόνιον μεταξὺ τρίτης καὶ
παραμέσης ἀπελείφθη ἐν τῇ διαζεύξει. εὐλόγως οὖν ἡ πάλαι
τρίτη διὰ τεσσάρων ἀπεῖχε τῆς νήτης, ὅπερ διάστημα νῦν
30 ἀπέλαβεν ἡ παραμέση ἀντ' ἐκείνης. οἱ δὲ τοῦτο μὴ συνιέντες
αἰτιῶνται ὡς οὐκ ὄντος δυνατοῦ ἐν ἐπιτρίτῳ λόγῳ εἶναι
τρίτην ἀπὸ νήτης. ἄλλοι δὲ οὐκ ἀπιθάνως τὸν παρεντεθέντα
φθόγγον οὐχὶ μεταξὺ μέσης καὶ τρίτης ἐντεθῆναί φασιν, ἀλλὰ
μεταξὺ τρίτης καὶ παρανεάτης· καὶ αὐτὸν μὲν τρίτην ἀντ' ἐκείνης
35 ἐπικληθῆναι, τὴν δὲ πάλαι τρίτην παραμέσην ἐν τῇ διαζεύξει
γενέσθαι. τὸν δὲ Φιλόλαον τῷ προτέρῳ ὀνόματι τὴν παραμέσην
τρίτην καλέσαι καίτοι διὰ τεσσάρων οὖσαν ἀπὸ τῆς νήτης.

13 ἐστι om. Nicom.   ἐντι Wachsmuth   ὀξεῖαν Stobaeus throughout   14 τῆς
συλλαβῆς Nicom. R   ἐντι Wachsmuth   14–15 ἐπί...ἐπί Stobaeus F εἰς...πότι
Nicom.   15 μέσαν...μέσας Nicom. (μέσας R)   συλλαβάν Stob. VME νέαταν
Stobaeus F   16 ἐς...ἐς Nicom. εἰς...ἐς Stobaeus F εἰς...εἰς Stob. VME
16 συλλαβή Nicom. R συλλαβάν Stob. GME   17 τὸ δ' μέσον Stob. GME   τρίτας
καὶ μέσας Nicom. ἐπ' ὀγδώῳ Stob. F   18 ἐπίτριτος Stob. F   ἀμιόλιον Nicom.
R   τὸ om. Stob. F   πᾶσαν Stob. F   19 ἐπόγδοα καὶ δύο διέσιες Nicom. 264.3–4
Jan and Boeckh ἐπ' ὀγδώῳ καὶ διέσιος Stob. F ἐπογδόων καὶ δυοῖν διέσεοιν Nicom.
δι' ὀξειᾶν...διέσις om. Nicom. RM add. M⁴   δέ om. Nicom.   20 ἐπ' ὀγδόα
Stob. F   συλλαβά...διέσις om. Stob. F συλλαβὰ δ' ἃ δύ' Nicom. R

The most ancient thinkers also proclaimed things that are consistent
with what I have set forth. They call the octave *harmonia*, the fourth
syllaba (for it is the first grasp [*syllēpsis*] of concordant notes), the fifth
dioxeion (for the fifth is continuous with the first concord to be
generated, the fourth, and advances to what is higher [*to oxy*]), and
the octave is the composite of both the *syllaba* [fourth] and *dioxeion*
[fifth] (for this very reason being called *harmonia*, because it was the
first concord fitted together [*harmosthē*] from concords). Philolaus,
the successor of Pythagoras, makes this clear when he says something
like the following in the first book of *On Nature*. For we will
be content with one witness in order to get on with things, even if
there are many who in many ways say similar things about this same
topic. The text of Philolaus is as follows:

'The magnitude of harmonia (fitting together) is the fourth
(*syllaba*) and the fifth (*di' oxeian*). The fifth is greater than the fourth

by the ratio 9:8 [a tone]. For from *hypatē* [lowest tone] to the middle string (*mesē*) is a fourth, and from the middle string to *neatē* [highest tone] is a fifth, but from *neatē* to the third string is a fourth, and from the third string to *hypatē* is a fifth. That which is in between the third string and the middle string is the ratio 9:8 [a tone], the fourth has the ratio 4:3, the fifth 3:2, and the octave (*dia pasōn*) 2:1. Thus the *harmonia* is five 9:8 ratios [tones] and two *dieses* [smaller semitones]. The fifth is three 9:8 ratios [tones] and a *diesis*, and the fourth two 9:8 ratios [tones] and a *diesis*.'

One should bear in mind that at this point he calls the string in the seven-string scale which is next to the middle string (*paramesē*), the third string, before the insertion of the disjunct tone in the eight-string scale. For this note [*tritē = paramesē*] used to be an undivided tone-and-a-half from the string that is next to *nētē* (*paranētē*), from which interval the inserted string took away a tone; the remaining half-tone was left between the third string and the one next to the middle (*paramesē*) in the disjunct scale. It makes sense then that the ancient third string was a fourth away from *nētē*, the very interval which the string next to the middle now marks off instead of it (i.e. *nētē*). But some who do not understand this find fault on the grounds that it is not possible for the third string to be at a ratio of 4:3 from *nētē*. Others, not unconvincingly, say that the inserted note was not inserted between the middle string and the third string, but between the third string and the string that is next to *nētē* (*paranētē*). They also say that it was called the third string in place of that one and that the ancient third string became the string next to the middle in the disjunct scale. And they say that Philolaus called the string next to the middle by the earlier name, third string, although it was a fourth from *nētē*.

AUTHENTICITY

Before discussing the specifics of this fragment of Philolaus it is important to give a brief overview of what other early Pythagoreans knew about music theory in order to see the context in which Philolaus was working. This overview will be extremely brief and avoid many points of controversy so that the reader should refer to Barker (1989: 28–52), Burkert (1972: 369–86), and van der Waerden (1943: 163–99) for more detailed discussion and references to other literature. The later tradition, beginning as early as Xenocrates (F9), ascribed the discovery of the ratios corresponding to the concordant intervals (2:1 = octave, 4:3 = fourth, 3:2 = fifth) to Pythagoras himself and also associated Hippasus with an experiment that confirmed the ratios (DK 18.12). However, the tradition also portrays Lausus of Hermione (sixth century), who is not a Pythagorean, as knowing the ratios. Accordingly, the first important point to recognize about early Pythagorean knowledge of music theory is that it was not exclusively Pythagorean, but was rather connected to the broader Greek musical tradition. The second crucial point is to recognize that the stories that the tradition tells about the discovery of the ratios for the most part describe observations that are impossible (e.g. the story that Pythagoras detected the concords in sounds he heard as he passed a smithy, which falsely presupposes that the pitch of sounds emitted from hammers as they strike the anvil is proportional to their weight). The only observation that is scientifically correct is the one assigned to Hippasus, that in the case of bronze disks of equal diameter the pitch emitted when struck will vary with their thickness. Thus we can have some confidence that Hippasus (early fifth century) had knowledge of the ratios, but it is uncertain whether they in fact go back to Pythagoras himself.

Van der Waerden argues that the ratios were discovered from everyday experience with musical instruments, on the basis of mention of musical instruments in some passages in the Aristotelian *Problems*. There are some problems with this explanation, since Greek musical instruments were not ideally suited to the discovery of the ratios corresponding to concords (e.g. most stringed instruments had strings of equal length and no finger board). Nonetheless, some harps did have strings with unequal lengths (Barker 1984: 197 n. 47) and the relevant observations are simple enough that they could result from casual experimentation with strings. The monochord or "canon" (a single string stretched across a board on which precise measurements can be made) is not explicitly attested before the *Sectio canonis* ascribed to Euclid (late fourth century and if it is not Euclidean even later). Thus, the only reasonably solid conclusion that can be drawn is that in the generation before Philolaus Hippasus, at least, knew of the ratios that corresponded to the concordant intervals of the octave, fourth, and fifth, but there is no evidence of knowledge of the ratios that correspond to the tone and the "remainder" (*diesis* or *leimma*) which are used to fill out the rest of the diatonic scale.

Scholars who have given detailed treatment to the fragments and testimonia which discuss Philolaus' views on music have generally regarded them as either all authentic (Boeckh and Burkert) or all spurious (Tannery, Frank, van der Waerden). The major exception to this is A26 which Boeckh found to be so confused that he supposed that the source, Boethius, must be blamed for an error. Tannery was hesitant to assign it even to a forger. The possibility that has not been given consideration and which I will argue for here is that some of the fragments come from the genuine work of Philolaus (F6a) while others are from a later spurious work (F6b, A26). Most of the arguments against authenticity have been directed against material contained in F6b and A26 which are both dervied from Boethius and which are discussed in the appendix below. Even opponents of authenticity such as Tannery and van der Waerden find the musical theory ascribed to Philolaus in F6a quite possible for someone of his date although Tannery suspects that Philolaus' *tritē* might be a case of "over archaising." Only Frank tries to develop a set of arguments specifically against F6a. However, close examination shows that these arguments are not well founded and that there are very strong reasons for regarding F6a as authentic.

There are three remarkable things about the musical scale which is attributed to Philolaus in F6a. First, the terminology is in several respects not typical (i.e. *syllaba* [grasp] instead of *diatessarōn* [through four] for the fourth, *dioxeion* [through the higher] instead of *diapente* [through five] for the fifth, *harmonia* instead of *diapasōn* [through all] for the octave, and *diesis* for *leimma*, the smaller semitone). Second, the use of *tritē* (third string) rather than *paramesē* as the name for the string that is a fourth from *nētē* (the highest string) is very unusual. Third, the scale is in most respects identical to that used by Plato in the *Timaeus*. This last point is what raises the most suspicion that what is assigned to Philolaus is a forgery arising out of the tradition of commentary on the *Timaeus*, a pattern that is repeated many times. However, the other two peculiarites of the fragment clearly suggest that it is in fact more likely to be genuinely early Pythagorean than a later forgery and that in this case Philolaus' work is the basis for the *Timaeus* rather than the other way around.

First, what are the connections with the *Timaeus*? At 34b10 Plato turns to the discussion of the construction of the world-soul. To begin with he describes it as composed of a certain compound of "the same," "the different," and being. He then portrays the demiurge as dividing this soul "stuff" in accord with certain ratios. These ratios are represented by the sequence 1, 2, 3, 4, 8, 9, 27 (a combination of the two sequences 1, 2, 4, 8 and 1, 3, 9, 27). Plato then has the demiurge put two means between each of the terms in this sequence, the arithmetic mean $(A-M = M-B)$ and the harmonic mean $(A-H:A = H-B:B)$. For the purposes of comparison with Philolaus we need only examine the means between 1 and 2. Here the arithmetic mean would be $\frac{3}{2}$ and the harmonic mean would be $\frac{4}{3}$. Plato then says that each of the intervals of 4:3 which are created in this way is to be filled in with two intervals of 9:8 and a remainder of 256:243. In this whole passage Plato never explains where he is deriving this sequence of numbers from, nor does he refer explictly to music, yet their origin is clearly in music theory. The ratio of 2:1 is the octave, and the two means to which

Plato refers mark off the intervals of the fifth (3:2) and the fourth (4:3). Further, the ratio of 9:8 is the interval between $\frac{4}{3}$ and $\frac{3}{2}$, a whole tone ($\frac{3}{2}:\frac{4}{3} = 9:8$). If two whole tones are subtracted from the interval 4:3 the difference is in fact 256:243 ($4:3-9:8 = 32:27-9:8 = 256:243$). Thus the division of the interval 2:1 would look like this:

$$1, \quad \tfrac{9}{8}, \quad \tfrac{81}{64}, \quad \tfrac{4}{3}, \quad \tfrac{3}{2}, \quad \tfrac{27}{16}, \quad \tfrac{243}{128}, \quad 2$$

And the ratios between the terms in this sequence would be:

$$9:8, \ 9:8, \ 256:243, \ 9:8, \ 9:8, \ 9:8, \ 256:243$$

Thus each fourth consists of two intervals of 9:8 with one remainder of 256:243, each fifth of three intervals of 9:8 and one remainder, and the whole interval between 1 and 2 consists of 5 intervals of 9:8 and two remainder intervals of 256:243. But this corresponds exactly to the structure of the scale (*harmonia*) that Philolaus gives in F6.

Plato's failure to make any mention of the musical origin of the sequence of numbers which he provides is probably purposeful. In the *Republic* Plato recognizes the Pythagoreans as the thinkers who "seek numbers in heard consonances," but he complains that "they do not ascend to problems to consider which numbers are concordant and which are not" (531c1–4). The sequence in the *Timaeus* represents just such a sequence of "concordant" numbers with no reference to any audible concords. It is striking then that Plato's numbers in the *Timaeus* do correspond to the scale of Philolaus F6 without any direct reference to music. This is precisely what we would expect, given Plato's comments in the *Republic*, if Plato were basing the sequence of concordant numbers in the *Timaeus* in part on Philolaus. (Of course, it is also possible that the scale found in Philolaus F6a was not unique to him but common knowledge at the time, and that Plato's actual source was neither Philolaus nor, for that matter, even a Pythagorean.) On the other hand if Philolaus F6a were a forgery based on the passage of the *Timaeus*, we would expect that there would be at least some hint of the context in the *Timaeus*, but apart from the structure of the scale nothing in the two passages is similar. None of the unusual musical terminology of the Philolaus fragment is derived from Plato, nor is there any mention of such Platonic concepts as the world-soul or the demiurge in Philolaus F6a. Thus, it is easier to see Plato as dependent on Philolaus than the reverse.

Frank (1923: 266ff), on the other hand, argues that the "scale" that Plato presents in the *Timaeus* is a purely *a priori* construction that has nothing to do with actual music. Further, since Plato expressly marks his *a priori* approach to music as new and as distinct from the Pythagorean approach (*Republic* 531a1ff) it follows that Philolaus F6a, which has exactly the same scale as Plato's, cannot be early Pythagorean, but must be dependent on

Plato. The problem here is that Frank took Plato's words too literally and did not pay enough attention to the evidence for the diatonic scale used in the *Timaeus* elsewhere in the ancient musical tradition. This evidence suggests that the scale was not an *a priori* construction, but was in fact in common use by practical musicians. Most notably Ptolemy in his *Harmonics* discusses the scale as one of four types of diatonic scales without any reference to Plato. Instead he presents the scale as one that is commonly used by musicians in tuning (οὕτω γὰρ ἁρμόζονται οἱ κιθαρῳδοί..., "The kithara-players tune in this way..." 44.1; see also 39.14ff; 80.16ff and van der Waerden 1943: 187–91 and Burkert 1972: 387ff). Plato's complaint in the *Republic* is not that the Pythagoreans *started* from the numbers found in heard consonances, but that they did not go on to "ascend to problems," but rather stayed at the level of phenomenal consonances (for an insightful evaluation of Plato's complaint see Barker 1989: 46–52). Both the astronomy and the harmonics of the *Timaeus* show that Plato himself was perfectly willing to start from motions of heavenly bodies and audible concords, but that he did not focus on the phenomena but rather on the abstract principles that govern them. Thus, it would appear that the similarity with the *Timaeus* in fact argues for the authenticity of Philolaus F6a. What about the unusual musical terminology of the Fragment?

Typical Greek terminology is very commonsensical. The fourth is called "through four," the fifth "through five," and the octave "through all" because they are produced by playing the first and fourth, first and fifth, and first and last note respectively. What then are we to make of Philolaus' terminology for these concords? Is it characteristic of later Greek thought or is it genuinely early Pythagorean? The testimonia make it clear that this terminology is in fact early. Thus Theophrastus says (Aelian, ap. Por. *In Ptol.* 96.21ff):

Οἱ μὲν Πυθαγόρειοι τὴν μὲν διὰ τεσσάρων συμφωνίαν συλλαβὴν ἐκάλουν, τὴν δὲ διὰ πέντε δι' ὀξειᾶν, τὴν δὲ διὰ πασῶν τῷ συστήματι, ὡς καὶ Θεόφραστος ἔφη, ἔθεντο ἁρμονίαν.

The Pythagoreans used to call the concord "through four" [i.e. the fourth] syllabe, the concord "through five" [i.e. the fifth] dioxeion, and the concord "through all" [i.e. the octave], which referred to the scale, they named harmonia, *as Theophrastus also said.*

It is possible that Theophrastus is only being quoted as a source for the last name, but it is at least as likely that he is the source for all three names, and all three are assigned to "the ancients" by Aristides Quintilianus 1 (15 W-I.) Hesychius also says that the expression *dioxeion* was Pythagorean (παρὰ τοῖς Πυθαγορικοῖς λέγεται). That *harmonia*, rather than *diapasōn*, should be the term for the octave for Pythagoreans of the fifth century is supported by the fact that *harmonia* was commonly used in the fifth and fourth century to refer to attunements which were commonly thought of as an octave long (Barker 1989: 14ff). Frank, arguing against authenticity, recognizes that Theophrastus is the *terminus ante quem* for the use of all three of these terms. However, Theophrastus does more than mention the terms, he explicitly assigns them to the Pythagoreans. We might suppose that Theophrastus is talking about the "Pythagoreans" of the Academy, but other evidence supports the conclusion that he is referring to fifth-century Pythagoreans.

Thus, two of the terms occur in the Hippocratic treatise *On Regimen* (1.8) which probably is to be dated somewhere around 400. The author is discussing the development of embryos and says:

χώρην δὲ ἀμείψαντα καὶ τυχόντα ἁρμονίης ὀρθῆς ἐχούσης συμφωνίας τρεῖς, συλλαβήν, δι᾽ ὀξειῶν, διὰ πασέων [Bernays and Delatte; συλλήβδην διεξιὸν διὰ πασέων MSS – see Burkert 1972: 262 n. 114], ζώει καὶ αὔξεται . . .

If, having changed position, they achieve a correct attunement, one which has the three concords, fourth [syllabē], fifth [dioxeiōn], octave [diapason], they live and grow . . .   (after Jones)

On Regimen is characterized by its use of Presocratic ideas borrowed from figures such as Heraclitus, Empedocles and Anaxagoras. In this passage it could well be that it is drawing on Philolaus.

In the face of the explicit testimony of Theophrastus that the terms are Pythagorean both Frank (1923: 273) and Levin (1975: 96), neither noticing the passage from *On Regimen*, quote Aristoxenus' remark at *Harm.* 1.22 that "the ancients" called the fourth *dia tessarōn* because it encompassed four notes and assume that "the ancients" must be the Pythagoreans. However, this rests on the assumption that the Pythagoreans were the dominant figures in music before Aristoxenus and thus the only possible referents for "the ancients," an assumption that even Levin rejects, and also that Aristoxenus saw himself as primarily arguing against the Pythagoreans. However, Barker has argued convincingly (1978) that Aristoxenus regarded the Pythagoreans as not even involved in the same sort of enterprise as himself and correspondingly almost never refers to them. References to his predecessors are almost always to those whom he calls οἱ ἁρμονικοί who are clearly distinct from the Pythagoreans. Thus, this passage from Aristoxenus carries virtually no weight in trying to determine early Pythagorean musical terminology.

It thus appears that the terminology for the octave, fourth, and fifth which is found in F6 is likely to be genuine early Pythagorean terminology.

What about the use of diesis to refer to the smaller semitone? The term usually used is *leimma* which literally means "left over" and refers to the fact that it is what is left over after two whole tones are subtracted from the fourth (Plato does not use *leimma*, although he uses the verb form to describe it as "left over" [*Timaeus* 36a–b]). Although we do not have as early a source as Theophrastus in this case, it is common in later authors to identify the use of *diesis* for the smaller semitone as belonging to the Pythagoreans or the ancients (Theo Sm. 55.11; 56.18, Chalcidius 45, Macrobius *Somn. Sc.* 2.1.23, Procl. *In Ti.* 2.168.28, Boeth. *Mus.* 2.28). On the other hand Aristotle uses *diesis* to refer to the smallest interval (*APo.* 84b39; *Metaph.* 1053a12 etc.), and Aristoxenus (*Harm.* 14.18–25; 25. 11–15) commonly uses it to refer to the quarter tone, although he also uses it, suitably qualified, to refer to other small intervals. Thus, here too, the usage in Philolaus F6 agrees with what is said to be early and not with later usage. The use of the musical term *tritē* makes this even clearer.

In order to understand Philolaus' use of the term *tritē* it is first necessary to discuss some fundamentals of standard Greek musical theory. The most basic Greek scale consisted of two fourths (tetrachords, literally "four strings") which were combined in one of two ways. One form was called *synēmmenōn* (joined) because the last note in one fourth was the beginning note of the next fourth. The other form was called *diezeugmenōn* (disjunct) because the two fourths are arranged so that they do not share a note, but so that there is a tone between the last note of one fourth and the first note of the next fourth. Thus the two scales look like this:

synēmmenōn: e f g a

a b-flat c d

diezeugmenōn: e f g a

b c d e

Thus the tetrachords joined *diezeugmenōn* comprise an octave while those joined *synēmmenōn* fall one tone short of an octave.

The Greeks assigned a name to each of the notes in these paired tetrachords. The highest note in pitch was called *nētē* (which, confusingly means "lowest," and refers not to pitch but to the position of the hand on the lyre). The lowest note in pitch was called *hypatē* (which means "highest," once again referring not to pitch but to the position of the hand holding the lyre). The upper note in the lower tetrachord (as in the example above, which is also the lower note of the upper tetrachord in the *synēmmenōn*) was called *mesē* (middle). In the case of the tetrachords joined *diezeugmenōn* the bottom note of the second tetrachord was called *paramesē* ("next to the middle"). Each of the two tetrachords is then filled in with two further notes whose pitch varies depending on whether the tetrachord is in the diatonic, enharmonic or chromatic genus, but whose names are the same despite the variation in pitch. In the lower tetrachord the lowest note is *parhypatē* ("next to the lowest") and the note above it is called *lichanos* ("forefinger"). In the upper tetrachord the upper note is called *paranētē* ("next to the highest") and the note below it is called *tritē* "third"). Thus the whole system of names looks like this in the diatonic genus:

diezeugmenōn	*synēmmenōn*
nētē – e	
paranētē – d	nētē – d
tritē – c	paranētē – c
paramesē – b	tritē – b flat
mesē – a	mesē – a
lichanos – g	lichanos – g
parhypatē – f	parhypatē – f
hypatē – e	hypatē – e

In the *synēmmenōn* pattern the highest note (*nētē*) is not a full octave above the lowest (*hypatē*). In the *diezeugmenōn* the intervals from *hypatē* to *mesē* and from *paramesē* to *nētē* are fourths.

What is odd about F6a of Philolaus is the position assigned to *tritē*. It is said to be a fourth from *nētē*, whereas in the usual Greek system outlined above it is *paramesē* that is a fourth from *nētē*. Nicomachus, when quoting F6a, notes this difficulty and gives two somewhat obscure explanations. The key to understanding these explanations has been recognized by Burkert (1972: 393). Nicomachus, in this passage, is clearly thinking of both the seven-note scale and the eight-note scale as comprising an octave, contrary to the usual assumption that the seven-note scale (the tetrachords joined *synēmmenōn*) falls one note short of an octave (Nicomachus himself refers to such a seven-note scale earlier, in chapters 3 and 5). If this is what Nicomachus is doing, it would follow that a scale consisting of seven notes but comprising an octave would be missing one of the traditional notes.

Nicomachus' first explanation is that Philolaus was working with such a scale and the missing note was in the upper tetrachord so that it consisted of only three notes. Thus *tritē* (the "third" note, counting the first note as the Greeks always did) would be an interval of a fourth from *nētē*. He says that the interval from *tritē* to *paranētē* was a tone and a half, which leaves a full tone between *paranētē* and *nētē* to fill out the fourth. Nicomachus then says that when the note was inserted into this heptachord to make the octochord it took a whole tone away from the tone and a half interval

154

between *tritē* and *paranētē* and left a half tone between itself and *tritē*. On first reading this surely suggests that the new note was inserted between the old *tritē* and *paranētē*, at an interval of a tone away from *paranētē*, since in this way it would obviously be cutting of a tone from the interval of a tone and a half. However, Barker (1989: 261 n. 72) has suggested that Nicomachus really means that the inserted note is conceived of as between *mesē* and *tritē* and bumps the old *tritē* up a half tone. Nicomachus certainly uses odd language to express this idea since the new note only very indirectly "cuts off" a tone from the tone-and-a-half interval. However, Barker's suggestion solves the problem which scholars have had of distinguishing between Nicomachus' solution and the solution of some others which he will present in a moment. Moreover, as Barker notes, the insertion of the new note between *mesē* and the old *tritē* seems to be paralleled by what Nicomachus says in an earlier passage (1989: 255 n. 39). In the new scale the old *tritē* is still *tritē* but moved up a half tone and the inserted note is *paramesē* but has *tritē*'s old position. The following diagram will make Nicomachus' explanation clear:

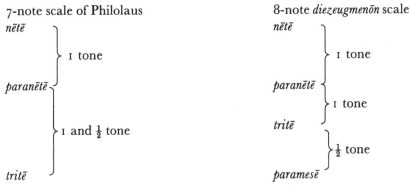

7-note scale of Philolaus   8-note *diezeugmenōn* scale

Nicomachus then remarks that some who do not understand this Philolaic usage of *tritē* find fault with him because it is impossible for *tritē* to be a fourth from *nētē*.

Nicomachus then turns to an explanation of some "others" which he describes as "not unpersuasive." These people say that the inserted note was not between *mesē* and *tritē* (as on Nicomachus' explanation given above), but between *tritē* and *paranētē* (all these notes being understood in terms of the traditional *diezeugmenōn* tetrachords). The inserted note then became known as *tritē* and the old *tritē* was called *paranētē*. Philolaus, however, was before all of this and called *paramesē* by its old name of *tritē*. In the end the explanations of Nicomachus and these others come to the same thing and only differ slightly in how they explain the transition from the heptachord to the octachord.

There are serious questions as to whether these explanations of Nico-machus in fact reflect the scale in existence in Philolaus' time or whether it is simply a construct of Nicomachus in order to explain Philolaus' puzzling use of *tritē* as Winnington-Ingram argued (1928: 87–8). However, there is a consensus among scholars that Nicomachus is right on the general point that Philolaus' use of *tritē* does reflect an early stage in Greek music where a full octave scale consisted of seven notes, and hence that one note was left out (Barker, Tannery, Winnington-Ingram, van der Waerden). If this is so, this use of *tritē* is one of the very strongest reasons for regarding the frag-ment as authentic, since it is almost inconceivable that a forger would introduce such a complicated idea. The pseudo-Pythagorean writings as a whole may use a coloring of Doric dialect to suggest authenticity, but the goal is not to construct historically accurate Presocratic documents by the use of correct Archaic terminology. Rather, the goal is to show that these early figures had already arrived at the concepts of mature Greek philoso-phy, terminology and all, and the use of *tritē* and other Archaic terminology in F6a is militantly in conflict with such a goal.

One final piece of evidence that is not conclusive, but which corroborates the conclusion that F6a is authentic, should be mentioned here. The scalar divisions which Archytas develops in the generation after Philolaus have been shown to presuppose the diatonic scale which is presented in F6a (Burkert 1972: 389 and Barker 1989: 46–52). This does not guarantee that Archytas was drawing on Philolaus (it might also have been Plato or more probably common musical practice in tuning instruments), but it shows that the scalar division found in F6a was prominent in the Pythagorean musical tradition when Archytas wrote and it is thus very plausible to connect it with Philolaus.

COMMENTARY

The context in Nicomachus and Stobaeus: Stobaeus presents F6a as a direct continuation of F6. Nicomachus quotes only F6a without any hint as to its context in Philolaus' book. Nicomachus' *Enchiridion* (handbook) is a brief treatise on some basic points of harmonics addressed to an unnamed lady (Barker 1989: 245ff).

One feature of the *Enchiridion* is that it focuses on the achievements of Pythagoras himself, although Levin (1975) goes too far in arguing that it is not a proper treatise in harmonics at all, but rather written just to glorify Pythagoras (Barker 1989: 245ff). In section five he is introduced as the person who added the eighth string to the seven-string lyre. In section six we are given the story of Pythagoras' discovery of the ratios of whole num-bers which correspond to the concordant intervals. Finally in section seven

Nicomachus presents the structure of the diatonic scale as Pythagoras' discovery (with the promise that his work with the enharmonic and chromatic scales will be discussed later). Chapter eight is then a digression on the interpretation of the passage in Plato's description of the construction of the world-soul in the *Timaeus* which deals with the harmonic and arithmetic mean. The digression is odd in that section seven, which dealt with Pythagoras' construction of the diatonic scale, did not refer explicitly to means, but the implicit connection that Nicomachus is making is that when Plato introduces these means he is thinking of the fifth and the fourth which are determined according to them (the fourth $= 4:3$ and the fifth $= 3:2$ are the intervals between 1 and the harmonic and arithmetic means [$\frac{4}{3}$ and $\frac{3}{2}$] between 1 and 2). Nicomachus gets wrapped up in demonstrating features of these two means that go beyond the immediate needs of the context, and one is tempted to see him as elaborating on this topic as worthy in its own right for the attention of the lady he is addressing. Certainly there are important sections on each of the means in Nicomachus' most famous work, the *Introduction to Arithmetic*. It may be this preoccupation with the means which Plato uses that leads Nicomachus to truncate his treatment of the rest of the *Timaeus* passage, and in particular to omit discussion of Plato's use of the tone and the *leimma* to fill in the intervals of the fourth and fifth. At any rate it is hard to see the purpose of this faulty representation of the Platonic material as an attempt to deny Plato's originality as Levin argues. It would in fact suggest that Plato was not even a good student of the Pythagoreans, since it would show that he could not even follow Pythagoras' and Philolaus' earlier articulation of the diatonic scale (Barker 1989: 259 n. 60).

The quotation from Philolaus comes in section nine immediately following on the digression on the *Timaeus*. Philolaus is introduced to show that the ancients "proclaimed things consistent with what I have set forth." What is quoted from Philolaus has to do with the structure of the diatonic scale and has nothing to say about means so that it seems clear that Nicomachus is using the quotation as support for what he said in section seven about Pythagoras' construction of the diatonic scale rather than as support for his analysis of the *Timaeus* passage in section eight (*pace* Levin [1975: 85], who takes section nine to refer to "the Timaeus material"). Nicomachus' account of Pythagoras' construction of the diatonic scale is supported by showing that one of his successors, Philolaus, used the same scale. Levin argues that Nicomachus' description of Philolaus as a διάδοχος of Pythagoras is an attempt to make him a direct pupil of Pythagoras and thus exaggerate the antiquity of the Philolaic material as part of the attempt to minimize Plato's contribution (1975: 13, 85–6). But the term need only mean that Philolaus is a follower of Pythagoras, and Nicomachus would gain very little by the supposed exaggeration of Philolaus' antiquity since, as a contemporary of Socrates, he was clearly working before Plato anyway. Nicomachus assures us that there are other authors he could quote to make the same point, but in the interests of time he limits himself to one example. That Nicomachus sees Philolaus' *harmonia* as a clear example of the early diatonic scale is revealed once again at the end of the *Enchiridion* where a sentence from F6a is quoted again to show that contrary to the views of later theorists (e.g. Aristoxenus, although he is not named by Nicomachus) the octave consists not of six whole tones but five whole tones and two so-called semitones which in reality do not add together to make a whole tone ("Philolaus agrees with us in the aforementioned text [i.e. F6a] saying 'harmony is five tones and two *dieses*,' that is to say two semitones: which would have made one tone if they were really semitones" [264.2 Jan]).

Given Nicomachus' purposes there is nothing surprising in the fact that he did not include the material in F6 which Stobaeus presents as continuous with F6a, since that material has nothing directly to do with the diatonic scale and is instead concerned to show the necessity of *harmonia* as a basic principle in Philolaus' system along with limiters and unlimiteds. But do F6 and F6a in fact constitute a continuous whole?

The connection between F6 and F6a: The manuscripts of Stobaeus give Fragments 2 and 4–7 of Philolaus continuously so that the manner in which they are to be broken up into separate fragments is determined largely by scholarly judgments of what goes with what. Traditionally F6 and F6a have been printed together, although DK prints a dash between them with a note in the apparatus suggesting that the two parts do not cohere. The reason that they have typically been taken to constitute a continuous text is presumably that in both texts *harmonia* is the central topic. However, most readers will feel at least some surprise when the *harmonia* that was a principle holding together limiters and unlimiteds in F6 suddenly turns into the diatonic scale in F6a. Boeckh (1819: 65) recognizes this as startling, but sees the continuity of F6 and F6a as articulating an important connection in Philolaus' thought. Tannery on the other hand felt that the meaning of *harmonia* in the two texts was radically different and that they must accordingly be distinct fragments (1904: 238). Certainty is impossible in this matter, but good sense can be made of the two fragments if they are taken as a continuous text.

In the first part of F6 *harmonia* simply refers to the third principle that "fits together" the limiters and unlimiteds. F6a begins by promising to say more about this third principle by specifying its magnitude, and suddenly we are in the midst of the whole-number ratios that govern the structure of

158

the diatonic scale. However, such a move is not all that surprising in light of what we know about early Pythagoreanism from our best single source on the topic, Aristotle.

In his account of early Pythagoreanism in the first book of the *Metaphysics* Aristotle makes precisely the connection between the Pythagorean recognition that harmonics was governed by number and their willingness to call the universe a *harmonia* which is found in F6 and F6a, if they are read as a continuous text (985b31ff: "...since, again, they saw that the attributes and ratios of the *harmonia* are found in numbers... they supposed that... the whole heaven is a *harmonia* and a number" [tr. Barker]). This same connection is also found in the doctrine of the harmony of the spheres, also attested by Aristotle (*De caelo* 290b12), which sees the universe as precisely a musical harmony. Seen in such a light the initially surprising transition between F6 and F6a in fact contains what was one of the central Pythagorean insights and shows us the theoretical basis for the doctrine of the harmony of the spheres, at least as it was found in Philolaus' system (Kahn 1974: 177). The limiters and unlimiteds that make up the world are held together in accordance with the whole-number ratios that make up the diatonic scale.

It is of course possible that there was intervening material that made the transition between F6 and F6a less startling, but it will not do to argue against their continuity on the grounds that the sense of *harmonia* changes between the two fragments, since precisely that change of meaning can be shown to be at the center of the Pythagorean view of the cosmos as reported by Aristotle. Thus F6a followed F6 either directly or with not much intervening material. It should be remembered that since the tradition suggests that Philolaus wrote only one book which appears to have been in the Presocratic tradition of books *On Nature* we are not to imagine him as having written a treatise on harmonic theory. We should in fact expect his comments on harmonics, such as they were, to be incorporated in his discussion of the nature of the cosmos, just as they are if we regard F6 and F6a as constituting a continuous text.

One final point to note is that there are not good grounds for the conclusion first drawn by Boeckh (1819: 65) and later adopted by Frank (1923: 268) that the connection of F6 and F6a shows that Philolaus equated the principle of limit with the one and the principle of the unlimited with the indefinite dyad, thus anticipating Plato on this point. Of course the later Pythagorean tradition is glad to assume that Pythagoras himself had anticipated Plato on this point, although Aristotle is emphatic that the conception of the unlimited as the dyad is Platonic and not Pythagorean (*Metaph.* 987b25 etc.). Clearly Boeckh thought that since the *harmonia* turned out to be the octave whose ratio is 2:1, Philolaus regarded the two numbers in this ratio as the two elements that are held together by the *harmonia* and thus equivalent to the limiters and the unlimiteds. However, besides the fact that Philolaus' consistent use of plurals for both limiters and unlimiteds comports very ill with identifying them with the one and the dyad (how can the one be a plural?), it is clear that the *harmonia* is identified with the ratios that Philolaus introduces and is not something different from the numbers that compose them. For he says that "the size *of the harmonia* is...," that is the quantities introduced are attached to the *harmonia* itself and are not the objects of the action of *harmonia* (i.e. limiters and unlimiteds). Indeed, in the Platonic system where the one and the dyad occur the one is usually conceived as an active principle acting on the dyad and there is no evidence for some third principle of harmony that brings together the one and the dyad. Furthermore, in Philolaus F6a *harmonia* seems primarily to mean an attunement covering an octave rather than octave, although the two senses do easily merge with each other. If this is so, then the *harmonia* is properly said to have "the size" of $2:1$ (the octave), but Philolaus is clearly thinking of it also in terms of the inner articulations which he goes on to specify and not just in terms of the numbers 1 and 2. In Philolaus number and ratio first appear with the introduction of the concept of *harmonia* and they are not to be read back into the limiters and unlimiteds upon which they act.

ἁρμονίας δὲ μέγεθος . . . : What is preserved by Nicomachus and Stobaeus gives the impression of being a complete section and not of breaking off in the middle. The *harmonia* is first said to consist of the fifth and the fourth, the whole tone is introduced as the distance between the fifth and the fourth, and then each of the major concords is measured by the whole tone with a remainder, the *diesis*, in each case, so that the fourth is two whole tones and a *diesis*, the fifth three whole tones and a *diesis*, and the whole octave therefore is five whole tones and two *dieseis*. The only thing missing is a definition of the *diesis*, although it may have been assumed. The important thing to note is that there is nothing here that requires Philolaus to go on to talk about smaller divisions than the *diesis*, such as Boethius has him do in introducing the *comma, schismata*, and *diaschismata* which might be useful in constructing an enharmonic scale, nor to talk about the *apotome* which is the "larger half" of the whole tone. I have argued on other grounds that the Boethius testimony is likely to be based on a spurious text, and the impression given by F6a is also that Philolaus is not going beyond the diatonic scale to consider either the enharmonic or chromatic genera, but is rather identifying that scale with the *harmonia* so that he need invoke no smaller interval than the *diesis*. At least it is hard to imagine him, after announcing programmatically that the *harmonia* has the structure of the diatonic scale, going on in the next sentence to say "the *harmonia* is also..."

and continue on to spell out a chromatic or enharmonic scale (Taylor 1928: 145 n. 3).

Finally, note that when Nicomachus quotes Philolaus to show that for the Pythagoreans the diatonic scale is not equal to six whole tones and that correspondingly the *diesis* is not a half-tone, he just quotes Philolaus' statement that the octave is five whole tones and two *dieses* (264.2 Jan). However, if Philolaus had introduced the *comma* as the difference between two *dieses* and a whole tone (as Boethius has him do), surely this would be just the evidence that Nicomachus should quote to show that Philolaus did not regard two *dieses* as equaling a whole tone. This suggests, but of course does not prove (especially since on other grounds it is likely that Nicomachus is the source for Boethius), that Nicomachus knows nothing of the musical material ascribed to Philolaus by Boethius.

ἁρμονίας: The major question about this term in a musical context is whether Philolaus thought of it as referring primarily to the octave as a concordant interval or to the whole series of intervals that make up the internal structure of the octave (Boeckh [1819: 65] took it to be the octave, but it is translated 'scale' by Tannery [1904: 238], van der Waerden [1943: 176.2], and Burkert [1972: 390]. Barker prefers "attunement over an octave" rather than "scale" as a translation, since the latter implies a linear progression which is more appropriate to the Aristoxenian system [1989: 37 n. 32]). It would appear that, as with the term octave in English, these two senses are often confused. In his introduction to F6a Nicomachus says that *harmonia* is the equivalent of the *dia pasōn* i.e. the octave as a concord. However, the internal structure of the fragment as well as external testimony about early uses of the term suggest that "attunement over an octave" is a better translation.

When he comes to specifying the mathematical ratios that correspond to the concords later in F6a (⅘ for the fourth, ⅔ for the fifth and ¾ for the octave) Philolaus in fact uses *dia pasōn* to refer to the octave and not *harmonia*. This surely suggests that *harmonia* refers not to the concordant interval, but to the octave conceived of as an attunement, while *dia pasōn* refers to the concord. This is confirmed by the connection between the musical and cosmological uses of *harmonia*. In F6 *harmonia* is introduced as necessary to hold together the limiters and unlimiteds that make up the world. This clearly implies some sort of structural articulation of the cosmos which has much more of an analogy with the structural articulation of sound by an attunement than with one interval, even if that interval is the octave.

From its general meaning of "fitting together" *harmonia* comes to have "a number of important and overlapping musical uses of which the primary one is probably that which designates the adjustment or tuning of the notes of an instrument. What is created by tuning is a 'fitting together' of notes, a structure of relations that can be used to form the basis of melodies" (Barker 1984: 163ff). This structure of relations would include scales, but is broader and includes also what are usually called modes, most notably the modes mentioned by Plato in the *Republic*. That *harmonia* in the sense of a structure of relations goes back before Plato is clear from *Philebus* 17d3. In that passage Socrates refers to predecessors (οἱ πρόσθεν) who taught their successors to call systems (συστήματα – a word used to mean scale in e.g. Aristoxenus 2.36) of intervals by the name *harmonia*. Now these predecessors are not necessarily Pythagoreans, although the main focus of the early part of the dialogue is the appropriation of the Pythagorean concepts of limiters and unlimiteds, but at the very least this indicates that *harmonia* in the sense of systems of intervals, which is the sense that works best in F6a, is possible for the fifth century. Aristoxenus 2.36 suggests the same thing and, although the predecessors there seem to be distinguished from Pythagoreans, the passage need not imply that the Pythagoreans did not use *harmonia* in the same sense. Aristotle refers in several passages to ancients (οἱ ἀρχαῖοι) who used "seven-string *harmonias*" (e.g. *Metaph.* 1093a14 and cf. pseudo-Arist. *Pr.* 919b21), and in a Pythagoreanizing passage of an early work (F47) he refers to the *harmonia* as quadripartite and interprets it in terms of the sequence of numbers 12, 9, 8, 6, which embody the ratios that correspond to the fifth, fourth, and octave. But the clearest testimony of all is that of Theophrastus, quoted above in the discussion of authenticity (Aelian, ap. Por. *In Ptol.* 96.21ff). He says not just that the Pythagoreans used the term *harmonia* for the octave (*dia pasōn*) but explicitly says that they used it for the octave in the sense of a "scale" (τῷ συστήματι). Thus the external evidence shows that *harmonia* in the sense of an attunement an octave long, the sense which is called for by Philolaus F6, was available in the fifth century and associated with the Pythagoreans.

συλλαβά: See the remarks above on the authenticity of the fragment for the argument that this is in fact an early Pythagorean term for the fourth, which is usually called *dia tessarōn* in Greek musical writings. The origin of the term was explained by Aelian in his lost commentary on the *Timaeus* (Por. *in Ptol.* 97.2) as coming from the practice of playing the lyre where the fourth was the first "grasp" (σύλληψις) of the hand of the lyre player. (This also seems to me to be what Nicomachus means when he glosses *syllabē* as the first "grasp" of concordant sounds, although Burkert [1972: 390 n. 21] implies that Nicomachus adopted Aelian's second explanation.) Levin (1975: 95) implies that since the origin of the term seems to be in the realm of practical music it cannot belong to Pythagoreans who were primarily interested in theory. But what is unnatural about a theorist using a term that originated in practice? It is true that Aelian also gives the alternative explanation that the term had its origin in a comparison between tone and letter, syllable and interval, and scale and word (Por. *In Ptol.* 96.30. See also Procl. *In R.* 1.213.1 and Olymp. *In Phd.* 169.16 Norvin). Frank (1923: 273) finds the origin of this analogy in Democritus and thus argues that it is too late to be ascribed to Philolaus. However, (1) the explanation of the origin of the term *syllabē* in terms of the pratice of lyre-playing is much more plausible; and (2) even if we were to accept that it was used by Democritus in the sense of syllable (and Frank's argument for this [1923: 167–72] is conjectural and not based on direct evidence from Democritus) it is not certain that he originated it, nor (3) if he did that it is impossible for Philolaus to have used it since he is only a slightly older contemporary than Democritus and hence could have been influenced by him.

δι' ὀξειᾶν: If the fourth is the "first grasp" in playing the lyre then it is reasonable to see the fifth, which is one tone larger, as progressing "through the higher" notes (Burkert 1972: 390 and Düring 1934: 179). This is the gloss that Nicomachus gives it in his introduction to the fragment. For the argument that this is an early Pythagorean term see the discussion on authenticity above. δι' ὀξειῶν (the Attic form) is used for the fifth in the pseudo-Aristotelian *Problems* at 19.34,41.

τὸ δὲ δι' ὀξειᾶν μεῖζον τᾶς συλλαβᾶς ἐπογδόῳ: After saying that the *harmonia* consists of the intervals of a fifth and a fourth, Philolaus goes on to introduce the interval $\frac{9}{8}$ (the whole tone) as the difference between the fifth and fourth. This is exactly the way the tone (τόνος) is defined in Aristoxenus (*Harm.* 21.21–2; 45.34–46), but it is interesting that Philolaus uses no other term for the tone than the mathematical ratio $\frac{9}{8}$.

ἔστι γὰρ ἀπὸ ὑπάτας . . . : This serves as the demonstration that the fifth is bigger than the fourth by a whole tone. Philolaus assumes the reader's familiarity with the standard structure of Greek stringed instruments and the names of the strings. He starts from the lowest string, *hypatē*, and goes up a fourth to the middle string, *mesē*, and then points out that from that string to the highest string, *nētē*, is a fifth. The process is then reversed so that he starts with the highest note and comes down a fourth to the string he calls *tritē* and from *tritē* down a fifth to the lowest string again (*hypatē*). Finally, he asserts that the difference between the middle string, *mesē*, and *tritē* is the interval $\frac{9}{8}$. This procedure does show us, if we know the structure of the seven strings that Philolaus is referring to, that the difference between the fourth and fifth will be the interval between *mesē* and *tritē*, since the distance up from *hypatē* to *mesē* was a fourth while the larger interval of *hypatē* up to *tritē* was the fifth.

Tannery (1904: 222) interprets Philolaus as following a process for finding the greatest common measure between two terms which is also used in arithmetic and geometry and which is quite plausible for the fifth century. The smaller of the two terms (in this case the fourth) is subtracted from the larger (the fifth) until the remainder is smaller than the term being subtracted. In this case after the fourth is subtracted from the fifth only once, the remainder is smaller than the fourth, i.e the whole tone. This remainder (the whole tone) is then subtracted from the fourth in the same way. After it is subtracted twice the remainder is smaller than the whole tone, i.e. the *diesis*. Now in the case of the ratios that govern the musical concords, this process will never reach a measure that goes into both the fourth and the fifth without a remainder. F6 of Philolaus suggests that he stopped at the *diesis* as sufficient for his purposes (as did Plato in the *Timaeus*). If the process were continued and the *diesis* subtracted from the whole tone, the next remainder would be what is called the *comma* in the later tradition (2 dieses + 1 comma = 1 whole tone). The comma is mentioned in Boethius' testimony about Philolaus' music (A26 and F6b) and thus could be argued to be a point of contact with the procedure in F6a. However, the other intervals mentioned in the Boethius testimony (*apotomē*, *schisma*, and *diaschisma*) would not result from the process of reciprocal subtraction used in F6a, and the *schisma* ($\frac{1}{2}$ of a *comma*) and *diaschisma* ($\frac{1}{2}$ of a *diesis*) are antithetical to that procedure, since they presuppose that the *diesis* and *comma* can be bisected, whereas the process of reciprocal subtraction shows that they cannot. Thus, the process of reciprocal subtraction which seems to be behind F6a shows the incompatibility of that fragment with Boethius' testimony on Philolaus, and thus casts further doubt on the authenticity of that testimony.

Frank (1923: 270) refers to Tannery's analysis and concludes that this shows that Philolaus conceived of musical intervals atomistically as sums of interval parts. He then argues that this is connected to the procedure described in Boethius (A26) where Philolaus is presented as thinking of intervals not as corresponding to whole-number ratios but to arithmetical differences. However, this is misguided. The process of reciprocal subtraction can be applied to ratios without implying that Philolaus confuses intervals as ratios with intervals as arithmetical differences (indeed Plato's description of the *diesis* as the left-over interval [*Timaeus* 36b2] suggests a similar process). The system of ratios described in F6a shows that Philolaus carried out the mathematics of the subtraction of ratios (i.e. it is actually division) in a manner that shows a correct understanding of the nature of ratios.

τρίτας: The problems associated with Philolaus' use of the term *tritē* and the implications of that usage for the question of authenticity have been discussed in some detail in the section on authenticity above. It should be noted that, while there seems to be agreement that Philolaus' use of *tritē* does reflect an early scale an octave long in which there were only seven notes, so that one note is missing, it remains controversial as to which seven notes Philolaus included. Nicomachus' proposal, which is discussed above, may be nothing more than his own educated guess and Winnington-Ingram (1928: 83–91), on the basis of other evidence about early defective scales, has proposed a scale that differs from Nicomachus'. While Nicomachus proposed the scale EFGAB DE with C missing, Winnington-Ingram on the basis of his study of the other evidence for early defective scales suggests that EFGABC E with D missing is more likely. The point is that other early scales showed similarity to the enharmonic scale in that they had a ditone, although in the early period the semitone that completed the fourth was not divided in half as it was later. Thus, Winnington-Ingram thinks it more likely that the gap in the scale was a ditone between C and E than the tone and a half Nicomachus proposes between B and D.

δίεσις: The evidence for this term as the early Pythagorean term for the *leimma* or "left-over" when two tones are subtracted from the fourth is provided above in the discussion of authenticity. It is noteworthy that Philolaus introduces the term without any definition of it nor any specification of the ratio that corresponds to it (256:243), although he provides the ratios for all the other intervals he introduces. Literally the term means a "sending through" or "letting through" (from διΐημι) and it is tempting to interpret its origin in the idea that it is the interval that you must let (e.g. your voice) go through to complete the fourth after you have progressed through two whole tones. However, the discussion of the term in Arist. Quint. (12.6–7) indicates that by that time at least any such etymological connection had been lost, since a fanciful etymology of the *diesis* as the "vanishing point of sound" (*dialysis*) is offered instead (Barker 1989: 412 n. 77).

Testimonium A9

Aetius 1.3.10 (283 Diels – under the heading Περὶ ἀρχῶν) Φιλόλαος ὁ Πυθαγόρειος τὸ πέρας καὶ τὸ ἄπειρον.

Proclus, *in Ti.* 1.176.28 ...καὶ εἷς ἀποτελεῖται κόσμος ἐξ ἐναντίων ἡρμοσμένος, ἐκ περαινόντων τε καὶ ἀπείρων ὑφεστηκὼς κατὰ τὸν Φιλόλαον.

Damascius, *De prin.* 1.101.3 ...τὸ ὂν ἐκ πέρατος καὶ ἀπείρου, ὡς ἔν τε Φιλήβῳ λέγει ὁ Πλάτων καὶ Φιλόλαος ἐν τοῖς Περὶ φύσεως ... 111.9 καὶ πῶς λέγεται μικτὸν ὑπὸ τοῦ Πλάτωνος καὶ τῶν ἄλλων φιλοσόφων τῶν Πλατωνικῶν, καὶ ἔτι πρότερον ὑπὸ
5 Φιλολάου καὶ τῶν ἄλλων Πυθαγορείων; οὐ μόνον ὅτι ἐκ περαινόντων καὶ ἀπείρων συμπέπηγεν οἷον τὸ ὂν φησιν ὁ Φιλόλαος, ἀλλ' ὅτι καὶ μετὰ τὴν μονάδα καὶ ἀόριστον δυάδα τίθενται τρίτην ἀρχὴν τὴν ἡνωμένην τριάδα.

(Under the heading On Principles) Philolaus the Pythagorean, limit and unlimited.

... and one cosmos is completed having been fitted together from opposites, constituted from limiters and unlimiteds according to Philolaus.

... being is from limit and unlimited as Plato says in the *Philebus* and Philolaus in *On Nature*... And why is it [the third class of being at *Philebus* 23c11–d1] called mixed by Plato and the Platonists, and still earlier by Philolaus and other Pythagoreans? Not only because being has been compounded out of limiters and unlimiteds as Philolaus says, but because they posit the unified triad as a third principle after the monad and the indefinite dyad.

AUTHENTICITY

There is no doubt that these testimonia are genuine and ultimately based on Philolaus' book. The Pythagorean pseudepigrapha largely shove aside limiters and unlimiteds and replace them with the one and the indefinite dyad which Aristotle explicitly labels as Platonic rather than Pythagorean. The section of Aetius immediately preceding this report on Philolaus is devoted to the theory of principles of Pythagoras himself and explicitly assigns the Platonic distinction between the one and the indefinite dyad to Pythagoras and is replete with vocabulary typical of the pseudepigrapha. The testimonium about Philolaus on the other hand is in accord with what Aristotle tells us is distinctive of the early Pythagoreans (limit and unlimited), and is clearly based on texts like Fragments 1,2, and 6 of Philolaus. Damascius' report likewise distinguishes between Philolaus' explanation of reality in terms of limiters and unlimiteds and the one and indefinite dyad as principles of the Platonists. A great deal of the doxography is dominated by the Platonizing interpretation of Pythagoreanism and testimonia like these in A9 show that "Philolaus appears as the sole representative of the original Pythagoreanism" (Burkert 1972: 230).

It is interesting to note that Aetius replaces Philolaus' limiters and unlimiteds with the more abstract limit and unlimited. This was the practice of both Plato and Aristotle, and Theophrastus, who is the ultimate source of the doxography, undoubtedly followed their lead. On the other hand it is surprising that Proclus does not use the more abstract expressions, but preserves Philolaus' original language. This suggests that he may have had access to at least excerpts from Philolaus' book. The same may be true of Damascius who also uses Philolaus' plurals in one place, although when he groups Plato and Philolaus together as employing the same principles he uses the more abstract singulars. In light of this it is tempting to suppose that Damascius is referring to an actual text when he suggests that Philolaus used the term "mixed" (see *Philebus* 23c11–d1) to refer to things that are a combination of limiters and unlimiteds. F2 of Philolaus clearly refers to this class of things that both limit and are unlimited, but the term "mixed" (μικτός) is not used there.

Testimonium A 24

Nicomachus, *Arithmetica introductio* 2.26.2 (135.10 Hoche) τινὲς δὲ αὐτὴν [τὴν μεσότητα] ἁρμονικὴν καλεῖσθαι νομίζουσιν ἀκολούθως Φιλολάῳ ἀπὸ τοῦ παρέπεσθαι πάσῃ γεωμετρικῇ ἁρμονίᾳ, γεωμετρικὴν δὲ ἁρμονίαν φασὶ τὸν κύβον ἀπὸ τοῦ κατὰ
5 τὰ τρία διαστήματα ἡρμόσθαι ἰσάκις ἴσα ἰσάκις· ἐν γὰρ παντὶ κύβῳ ἥδε ἡ μεσότης ἐνοπτρίζεται. πλευραὶ μὲν γὰρ παντὸς κύβου εἰσὶν ιβ, γωνίαι δὲ η, ἐπίπεδα δὲ ϛ· μεσότης ἄρα ὁ η τῶν ϛ καὶ τῶν ιβ κατὰ τὴν ἁρμονικήν. [cf. Boethius, *Arith.* 2.49]

Iamblichus, *in Nic.* 118.23 εὕρημα δ' αὐτήν [μουσικὴν ἀναλογίαν] φασιν εἶναι Βαβυλωνίων καὶ διὰ Πυθαγόρου πρώτου εἰς Ἕλληνας ἐλθεῖν. εὑρίσκονται γοῦν πολλοὶ τῶν Πυθαγορείων αὐτῇ κεχρημένοι ὥσπερ Ἀρισταῖος ὁ Κροτωνιάτης καὶ Τίμαιος ὁ
5 Λοκρὸς καὶ Φιλόλαος καὶ Ἀρχύτας οἱ Ταραντῖνοι καὶ ἄλλοι πλείους καὶ μετὰ ταῦτα Πλάτων ἐν τῷ Τιμαίῳ... [cf. Nicom. *Arith.* 29.1 (144.20 Hoche)]

Some, following Philolaus, believe that it [the mean] is called harmonic from its attendance on all geometric harmony, and they say geometric harmony is the cube from its having been harmonized in all three dimensions, equal times equal times equal [e.g. 3 × 3 × 3]. For this mean is reflected in every cube. For in every cube there are 12 sides, 8 angles, and 6 surfaces. Then, 8 is the mean of 6 and 12 in accordance with the harmonic proportion.

They say that it [musical proportion] is a discovery of the Babylonians and through Pythagoras first came to the Greeks. At least, many of the Pythagoreans are found to have used it, such as Aristaeus of Croton, Timaeus of Locri, Philolaus and Archytas of Tarentum, and many others, and after this Plato in the *Timaeus*.

AUTHENTICITY

Before discussing these testimonia it is necessary briefly to consider the early Greek theory of means. The later tradition is fairly consistent in presenting a coherent account of Greek knowledge of the means. The first three means are said to have been known by Pythagoras or his followers, Plato, and Aristotle. Plato's immediate successors, notably Eudoxus, are said to have developed the fourth, fifth, and sixth means, while certain Pythagoreans sometime after Eratosthenes found four more to round out a total of ten means (Nicom. *Arith.* 2.22 [122.11 Hoche]; Iambl. *in Nic.* 100.15). If we turn from the testimonia to primary sources we find this scheme basically confirmed. Already in Archytas (F2) and Plato (*Timaeus* 35b1ff) there is clear evidence for knowledge of three means. Archytas calls these the arithmetic (the second term exceeds the third by the same amount as the first exceeds the second, e.g. 12, 9, 6), geometric (as the first term is to the second so is the second to the third e.g. 8, 4, 2) and subcontrary (*hypenantia* – the part of the third by which the middle term exceeds the third is the same as the part of the first by which the first exceeds the second e.g. 12, 8, 6). However, he also uses the name harmonic instead of subcontrary, once saying that it is what "they" call the subcontrary and once saying that it is what "we" call the subcontrary. Indeed, the later tradition assigns the replacement of the name "subcontrary" with the name "harmonic" to Archytas and Hippasus (Iambl. *in Nic.* 100.22; 113.16; 116.1). The puzzling inconsistency between "we" and "they" in F2 of Archytas should perhaps be removed by emending the first "they" to "we", in which case this fragment of Archytas would very much support the idea that he introduced the name "harmonic" for the third mean. The juxtaposition of Hippasus and Archytas as both introducing the term is somewhat problematic in that Hippasus (first half of the fifth century) is likely to have been active a full hundred years before Archytas, so that it is hard to see how they can jointly be said to have been the first to use the name "harmonic." At any rate F2 makes clear that Archytas did use the name "harmonic" and moreover that he is evidently taking over a theory of three means from his predecessors in which the third mean was called subcontrary.

Thus, while the ascription of the knowledge of the three means to Pythagoras himself must remain uncertain, F2 of Archytas makes it likely that all three were known before Plato in the fifth century and not just assigned to earlier Pythagoreans on the basis of Plato's use of them in the *Timaeus*. Knowledge of these means in the fifth century is further corroborated by the fact that Theaetetus (414–369 BC) used the three means to classify different types of irrational lines. This testimony suggests that Theaetetus is using an already existing classification of means to help in dealing with irrational lines rather than that Theaetetus himself invented the classification of means (Eudemus, in Pappus *Comm. on Euclid 10* 1.1; 2.17 [63, 138 Junge and Thomson]). For more on early Pythagorean use of means see Burkert (1972: 440ff).

The testimonia in A24 make two claims about Philolaus and the theory of means. The first suggests that he gave the name "harmonic" to the harmonic mean because it is displayed in the cube which he called "geometric harmony." The second says that he used what is called "musical proportion," i.e. a proportion in four terms which combines arithmetic and harmonic proportion e.g. the series 12, 9, 8, 6. Thus these reports are not saying the same thing, although they are not unrelated in that the harmonic mean has a role in the "musical proportion" and the cube as "geometric harmony" is seen as embodying the harmonic proportion in the series 12, 8, 6 which is obviously part of the series 12, 9, 8, 6 which embodies the "musical proportion."

To start with the second passage, that Philolaus knew of and used the "musical proportion" (12, 9, 8, 6) is very probable in light of the musical theory found in F6a. In fact when Iamblichus says Philolaus is "found using" the musical proportion he may well be referring exactly to F6a. The "Pythagorean diatonic" scale which is presented there is very naturally derived from representing notes an octave apart by the progression 6, 12 and then filling in the arithmetic and harmonic means (6, 8, 9, 12). These mean terms in fact mark the boundaries of two fourths (8:6 and 12:9) which are joined by an interval of a whole tone (9:8 – see Barker 1989: 48). Furthermore, this "musical proportion" is just a combination of the harmonic with the arithmetic proportion, both of which have been shown to have probably been known when Philolaus was active (second half of the fifth century).

The first testimonium is a little more problematic. As we have seen, there is no particular problem with Philolaus knowing about the harmonic mean, but there are some difficulties with making him the originator of the name harmonic. First, as we have seen above, a clear tradition supported by F2 of Archytas suggests that Archytas (perhaps following Hippasus) was the first to use the name "harmonic." Second, the reason given for Archytas' (or Hippasus') coinage of the name harmonic (i.e. because the proportion was important in music theory – Iambl. *in Nic.* 100.24) is plausible, while the reason given for Philolaus' coinage is very tortured.

The first problem could be avoided by assuming that Nicomachus is not saying that Philolaus originated the term "harmonic" for the third mean, but rather that Philolaus gave a novel explanation of the term which was already in existence, having been first coined by Hippasus. The second problem is not so easy to deal with. Nicomachus says that "some... following Philolaus, thought that the harmonic mean got its name from the fact that it "attends upon all geometric harmony." So far this is not very helpful, since we do not know what could be meant by "geometric harmony." He then tells us that "geometric harmony" is the cube and that the harmonic mean is always found in a cube because it has 12 sides, 8 angles, and 6 surfaces. Thus, the harmonic mean gets its name because it occurs in every cube and the cube is called "geometric harmony." What is so unsatisfactory about this explanation is that lots of things can be called a harmony, just about anything in Philolaus' cosmos in fact. Therefore to seize upon the fact that the cube is called harmony is to seize upon something that is not very distinctive. One cannot help feeling that something is missing in this text or that there is something that we do not understand, for as it stands the explanation of the name harmonic is contrived and incredibly weak.

Burkert (1972: 268 n. 139) has tried to make a connection between the assertion here that the cube was called "geometric harmony" and an obscure passage in Anatolius (30 = *Theol. ar.* 6.11). Anatolius reports the Pythagoreans as saying that "a henadic fiery cube lies about the middle of the four elements, the central position of which Homer also knew, as he shows when he says '[Tartarus] is as far below Hades as heaven is from the earth.'" Burkert speculates that this fiery henadic cube might be equated with the central fire in the middle of Philolaus' cosmos which he also calls a unit (ἕν) and the first thing harmonized. This might in turn be connected with Philolaus' name of "geometric harmony" for the cube. However, as Burkert himself notes, the Anatolius passage with its reference to Homer clearly suggests a geocentric system which cannot be made to fit with Philolaus. Moreover, surely we would expect that the central fire would be circular or spherical in shape both because of being called "the hearth," which was traditionally thought of as circular, and because of considerations of symmetry, given that it is in the center of a sphere.

If we set aside this passage of Anatolius, we are left with no other reference to the cube or any other geometric shape except the sphere in Philolaus. Certainly Aristotle's reports emphasize the role of numbers for the early Pythagoreans and make little mention of geometrical figures, which seem more associated with Plato and the Academy. There is the lone report that Philolaus said that "Geometry is the starting-point and mother city of the sciences" (A7b), which could be used to support Philolaus' honorific name of "geometric harmony" for the cube. However, given the paucity of our evidence for Philolaus' views on geometry, I think that it is impossible to decide whether we should accept the explanation of the name "harmonic" which Nicomachus ascribes to Philolaus as being a genuine early Pythagorean idea.

2. EPISTEMOLOGY

Fragment 4

Stobaeus, *Eclogae* 1.21.7b (1.188.5 Wachsmuth)   καὶ πάντα γα μὰν τὰ γιγνωσκόμενα ἀριθμὸν ἔχοντι. οὐ γὰρ ὁτιῶν ⟨οἷόν⟩ τε οὐδὲν οὔτε νοηθῆμεν οὔτε γνωσθῆμεν ἄνευ τούτω.

2 ἀριθμεῖν Y   ὁτιῶν τε F ὅτι ὢν τε GVME ὁτιῶν ⟨οἷόν⟩ τε Boeckh οἷόν τε Meineke 2–3 οὐ γὰρ ... τούτω desunt PYR   3 οὔτ᾿ ἐνοήθημεν οὔτ᾿ ἐγνώσθημεν FGVME corr. Boeckh   τούτω FVE τούτῳ G τούτου M, Wachsmuth, DK

And indeed all the things that are known have number. For it is not possible that anything whatsoever be understood or known without this.

AUTHENTICITY

The brevity of this fragment makes it very difficult to be sure of its authenticity. It is preserved in Stobaeus between F2 and F5 both of which are authentic, but this does not guarantee anything about F4, since Stobaeus does preserve spurious fragments elsewhere. However, there is certainly nothing in F4 that arouses immediate suspicion. Nothing in the terminology or style is particularly Platonic or Aristotelian, nor are there strong connections to the pseudepigrapha. The expression "having number" does occur in Plato and Aristotle, but is not distinctively Platonic or Aristotelian and in one place where it occurs in Aristotle the reference is specifically to the Pythagoreans (*De caelo* 268a10), which rather speaks for it as a genuine Pythagorean locution. It also occurs in a couple of passages in the Hippocratic corpus which are likely to be contemporary with Philolaus (see below).

The only serious argument that has been advanced against its authenticity is based on the contention that Aristotle does not assign epistemological concerns to the Pythagoreans and that such concerns are foreign to the Presocratics. But it has been shown in the discussion of the authenticity of F3 that such arguments are flawed in several ways.

COMMENTARY

General nature of the argument: F3 argued about the nature of τὰ ὄντα ("the things that are") on the basis of what was required for there to be something that knows. In F4 attention is turned from "the things that are" to "the things that are known" (τὰ γιγνωσκόμενα). It is here that Philolaus begins his study of knowledge in its own right rather than just as a control for determining the nature of reality. All of the discussions of the "world-order" (κόσμος) and "the things that are" are based on the division of things into limiters and unlimiteds. The discussion of objects of knowledge in F4 makes use of a new concept, ἀριθμός ("number").

From Aristotle (*Metaph.* 1.5) onward scholars have regarded "number" as the basic principle of Pythagorean metaphysics. Zeller (1923: 446) says that "The most generally distinctive doctrine of the Pythagorean philosophy is contained in the proposition that number is the essence of all things, that everything, in its essence, is number." It is therefore striking that "number" is only invoked in epistemological and never in cosmological contexts in the surviving fragments of Philolaus. To be sure, limiters and unlimiteds are sometimes related to the even and the odd (F5). Nevertheless, the exclusive use of limiters and unlimiteds with regard to "the things that are" suggests that these concepts are derived independently of considerations about the nature of number.

καὶ πάντα γα μάν: For the use of γα μάν see Denniston (1954: 347ff). He points out that the γε usually goes closely with the preceding word. Therefore, in this case it puts special emphasis on πάντα (*all* the things known). The combination of γε μήν with other particles, such as καί here, is very rare (1954: 350). The combination usually has an adversative or progressive force. Without a broader context it is impossible to be sure which is the case here, but the use of καί suggests that it is progressive. The combination γα μάν occurs again in F5 where it seems progressive.

τὰ γιγνωσκόμενα: See the commentary on γνωσούμενον in F3.

ἀριθμὸν ἔχοντι: Before addressing the meaning of this phrase as a whole it is important to elucidate the distinctive Greek conception of number (ἀριθμός – on what follows see the helpful discussions of Burkert 1972: 260–6 and Nussbaum 1979: 88–93). Since the fundamental studies of Stenzel (1933: 25ff) and Becker (1957: 21ff) it has been recognized that "number' for the Greeks is not usually an entity separate from ordinary things, but rather "an ordered plurality" of things of some sort. When Aristotle (*Physics* 219b6–7) distinguishes between "number with which we count" (ἀριθμὸς ᾧ ἀριθμοῦμεν) and "number as that which is being counted" (ἀριθμὸς ἀριθμούμενος), the former corresponds more closely to our usual understanding of number as something we use to count things, while the latter is the notion, more common in Greek authors, of number as the ordered plurality which is counted. Becker suggests (1957: 21) that these latter "numbers" are best rendered by expressions such as "couple" or "dozen," since such terms are always tied to the objects counted. We do not usually think of "a dozen" abstracted from any particulars, but always of a dozen eggs or doughnuts, etc. Since the Greek concept of ἀριθμός usually refers to a concrete ordered plurality, it naturally follows that it usually refers to whole numbers and not to zero or to fractions or to irrational numbers. Thus, the notion of the average family having $2\frac{1}{2}$ children produces ludicrous results on this conception of number since one pictures a concrete ordered plurality and wonders what the $\frac{1}{2}$ child looks like (the top half? the bottom?). It should be noted, however, that, on such a conception of number, ratios (as distinct from fractions) could be referred to as "numbers" (ἀριθμοί), since they just state a relationship between two ordered pluralities of things (e.g. the ratio 4:3 might express the relationship of two ordered pluralities such as the number of times two different strings vibrate in a given time). In a passage in Plato's *Republic* "number" does in fact seem to be used in this way. At 531c1–2 Plato describes the Pythagoreans as searching for "numbers" (ἀριθμούς) in heard harmonies, where he can only be referring to the Pythagorean connection of whole-number ratios to musical concords (2:1 is the octave, 4:3 is the fourth, etc.). Thus the usual meaning of ἀριθμός is "an ordered plurality," but it can also be used of the relations between different ordered pluralities, as the *Republic* passage shows.

With this as background it is necessary to explicate what Philolaus means by the expression "having number" (ἀριθμὸν ἔχοντι). The natural assumption would be that it meant "having an ordered plurality" in the sense of being constituted by an ordered plurality in some sense. The simplest example of something having an ordered plurality would be just a collection of a certain number of things, such as eight apples. This sense would seem to be represented in Plato's *Theaetetus* (198c1–2), where the arithmetician is described as counting "either the numbers themselves in his own head or some set of external things *that have a number*" (tr. Cornford – αὐτὸς πρὸς αὑτὸν αὐτὰ ἢ ἄλλο τι τῶν ἔξω ὅσα ἔχει ἀριθμόν).

But in many cases "having a number" is more complex than just being a set of things with count. At *De caelo* 268a10–13 Aristotle says that the Pythagoreans thought that the whole world was summed up in the number 3 and then continues "for end, middle, and beginning have the number of the whole, and they have the number of the triad'" (τελευτὴ γὰρ καὶ μέσον καὶ ἀρχὴ τὸν ἀριθμὸν ἔχει τὸν τοῦ παντός, ταῦτα δὲ τὸν τῆς τριάδος). Here having the number of the whole is not just being three distinct things, but constituting a specific type of ordered plurality such that we say that it is a whole, i.e. something with a beginning, middle, and end, although this plurality is also triadic. Similar uses which refer to complex ordered pluralities which are not just groups of countable objects can be found in the Hippocratic corpus. Thus in *On Fleshes* (8.612L) seven-month and nine-month babies are said to survive because they "have a number that divides evenly into sevens" (ἔχει τὸν ἀριθμὸν ἀτρεκέα ἐς τὰς ἑβδομάδας). Having a number in this case seems to mean that they are governed in some essential way by ordered pluralities. A similar passage is found in *On Generation* (7.484L) where the author explains that lame parents can still produce healthy offspring, because "the lame part has the same number as the healthy part" (ἔχει γὰρ τὸν ἀριθμὸν πάντα τὸ πεπηρωμένον τῷ ὑγιεῖ). In this case "number" has almost the sense "constitution" where the reference is to the proper constitution of the body by the four humours. In light of all these passages it seems justifiable to conclude that things "have number" in so far as they are constituted in some fashion by ordered pluralities or relations between ordered pluralities. Thus, in the last passage the human body has number in so far as it is constituted by the properly ordered plurality of four humours and in the penultimate example infants have number in so far as their birth was governed by pluralities that are divisible by seven. Burkert seems to endorse this view of what it means to "have number" when he says that to say that something has number is to say that it is involved in certain numerical relationships (1972: 267).

Nussbaum makes the important point that in light of all these parallels there is no reason to assume that when Philolaus talks of things "having number" he is referring to some "mysterious abstract entity" (1979: 92) mixed up in things that makes them knowable. However, Nussbaum's own interpretation of "having number" is interestingly different from the one that I have developed so far. She lays particular emphasis on the connection between counting and number and concludes that what has number "has whatever makes something countable" which is roughly equivalent to "has *peras*"or limit (1979: 92). This interpretation lays emphasis on the minimum conditions for something to be countable, i.e. that it must be a limited thing, marked off from other things. Such an interpretation goes closely with Nussbaum's understanding of γιγνώσκειν as the simplest type of cognitive activity. Philolaus, according to Nussbaum, is giving the minimum conditions for the minimal type of cognitive activity to occur.

However, this interpretation simply does not accord with the Greek uses of "number" and "having number" which have been discussed above and which Nussbaum herself uses. The difficulty is in Nussbaum's paraphrase of "number" as "what makes something countable" and thus as roughly equivalent to "limit." The examples given above show that "number" (ἀριθμός) *is* the ordered plurality which is counted, it is not what *makes* that plurality *countable*. The number is the four humours in proper balance, it is not the conditions which make us able to distinguish the four humours.

If number is not "what makes something countable," then it is much less plausible to identify it with limit as Nussbaum does. Moreover, the fragments of Philolaus appear to keep the two concepts quite separate from each other. F6, for example, in agreement with F1 and F2, treats limiters and unlimiteds as the two basic "starting-points" (ἀρχαί) from which the cosmos arises. Number is not mentioned until a third concept is introduced in order to hold the limiters and unlimiteds together, *harmonia*. Once *harmonia* is introduced suddenly number appears on the scene in the guise of the whole-number ratios that govern the concordant musical intervals. Indeed, if number and limit were equivalent in the way Nussbaum suggests one would wonder why Philolaus introduces the concept of number at all since the concept of limit alone would do.

Finally, F5, which Nussbaum does not discuss, points to an elaborate theory of number. The final clause says that each thing in the world "gives signs" of one of the "many forms of number." This surely suggests that each thing in the world is associated with a specific number or specific numerical relationships. We would then know each thing in so far as we grasped the distinctive numerical relationships associated particularly with it. In light of this, when Philolaus says that things are known in so far as they have number, it certainly looks as if he is not arguing simply that to grasp them at all they have to have what makes things countable, i.e. limit, but rather that we gain correct understanding of things in so far as we recognize the specific numerical relationships of which they give signs. In conclusion then, the phrase "having number" (ἀριθμὸν ἔχοντι) signifies much more than that something is countable. Things that "have number" are constituted by systems of numerical relationships, the simplest of which is the series of natural numbers.

ὁτιῶν ⟨οἷόν⟩ τε: This is Boeckh's emendation for the ὁτιῶν τε of the manuscripts which does not produce sense. Meineke's οἷόν τε would also work, but keeping ὁτιῶν makes the more emphatic statement that nothing *whatsoever* is known without number. This emphasis accords very well with the use of γα μάν in the first part of the fragment which emphasizes that *all* things that are known have number.

οὔτε νοηθῆμεν οὔτε γνωσθῆμεν: The pairing of νοεῖν with γιγνώσκειν admits of a variety of explanations. Without a larger context it is difficult to feel secure about their respective meanings. However, a few points can be made about their relation. First, since the beginning of the fragment makes its point only in terms of γιγνώσκειν (τὰ γιγνωσκόμενα), if νοεῖν introduced a significantly more sophisticated cognitive process, we would expect some special emphasis to be put on it. Such emphasis could have been achieved by putting νοηθῆμεν after γνωσθῆμεν in sequence ("nothing can be either γνωσθῆμεν [as I just said] or νοηθῆμεν [new point]), or by using an emphatic conjunction such as οὐδέ ("not even"). As it is, νοηθῆμεν and γνωσθῆμεν are put on an equal basis by the οὔτε … οὔτε construction. Further, since νοηθῆμεν comes before γνωσθῆμεν it seems awkward to take it as introducing a new phase of the argument. Thus the structure of the argument casts doubt on Nussbaum's view (1979: 88) that F4 extends Philolaus' argument from γιγνώσκειν (which she takes to be the most basic cognitive activity) to νοεῖν (knowledge in a Parmenidean sense). Instead, the structure indicates that νοηθῆμεν is very similar in meaning to γνωσθῆμεν, and that no significant distinction is being made between them. They seem to be paired simply for emphasis without any significant distinction being made between them. (Thus in my translation, "nothing is understood or known without this," the distinction between "understood" and "known" is not important; they simply reinforce each other.) We should thus accept "understand" as the meaning of νοεῖν here, which is in fact its commonest meaning in early Greek thought.

Number as a condition for knowledge: The second sentence of F4 indicates that having number is considered to be necessary for something to be an object of knowledge: "For it is not possible that anything at all be understood or known without this." Barnes goes further to say that the fragment "suggests that 'having a number' is a sufficient condition for knowability" (1982: 390). It does seem quite plausible that Philolaus believes that our knowledge of a thing simply consists in our knowledge of its "number." Certainly, there is no hint as to other conditions which objects of knowledge must meet besides having a number. However, given the state of the evidence we cannot conclude with certainty that for Philolaus number is not only a necessary but also a sufficient condition for knowability.

Fragment 5

Stobaeus, *Eclogae* 1.21.7c (1.188.9 Wachsmuth) ὅ γα μὰν ἀριθμὸς ἔχει δύο μὲν ἴδια εἴδη, περισσὸν καὶ ἄρτιον, τρίτον δὲ ἀπ' ἀμφοτέρων μιχθέντων ἀρτιοπέριττον. ἑκατέρω δὲ τῶ εἴδεος πολλαὶ μορφαί, ἃς ἕκαστον αὐτὸ σημαίνει.

2 ἔχη μὲν δύο GME   3 ἑκατέρῳ M   τῷ GM   4 ἅς MSS ὡς Usener   αὐτὸ
scripsi αὐτ᾽ αὐτὸ FGVME αὐταυτό Gaisford αὖ ταὐτό Heeren   σημαίνει Heeren
δημαίνει FGVME

Number, indeed, has two proper kinds, odd and even, and a third
from both mixed together, the even-odd. Of each of the two kinds
there are many forms, of which each thing itself gives signs.

AUTHENTICITY

The authenticity of this fragment is supported most strongly by its close
correspondence to what Aristotle tells us about fifth-century Pythagoreanism. At *Metaphysics* 986a17–20 Aristotle reports that the Pythagoreans
thought that the even and the odd were the elements of number and that
the one was from both of these and was thus both even and odd (τὸ δ᾽ ἓν
ἐξ ἀμφοτέρων εἶναι τούτων [καὶ γὰρ ἄρτιον εἶναι καὶ περιττόν]). Theon
(22.5–9) reports that Aristotle (F199) said the same thing about the one in
his special treatise on the Pythagoreans and here the Pythagoreans are said
to have called the one "even-odd" (διὸ καὶ ἀρτιοπέριττον καλεῖσθαι τὸ ἕν).
It is obvious that this is exactly the account of the number 1 given in F5 of
Philolaus. Moreover, this account of the one is central to neither Plato nor
Aristotle, nor is it ever found in the Pythagorean pseudepigrapha collected
by Thesleff. Thus, it seems overwhelmingly likely that F5 should be regarded as genuine and as the probable source for Aristotle's report.

COMMENTARY

Importance of the fragment: F5 is the only fragment that focuses on
number itself and subdivides it into two primary kinds, the even and the
odd. To these is added a third kind, the "even-odd," which is a mixture of
the first two. The two primary kinds are then divided into many forms "of
which each thing in the world gives signs." This last point is exceptionally
important because it is a clear attempt by Philolaus to try to characterize
the relation between numbers and things, and this relation has been one
of the central puzzles in interpreting Pythagoreanism since the time of
Aristotle.

Thus, one of the central questions is what exactly Philolaus meant by
saying that individual things "give signs of numbers." A second related
problem raised by the fragment is to determine what relation, if any, there
is between the threefold division of number here in F5 and F2's threefold
division of things into limiters, unlimiteds, and things that both limit
and are unlimited. This second question is particularly pressing because

Aristotle's presentation of the Pythagoreans seems to simply equate the even with the unlimited and the odd with the limiting.

The relation between odd and even and limiters and unlimiteds:
Aristotle's initial presentation of the Pythagoreans in the *Metaphysics* (1.5, 985b23ff) focuses almost entirely on number. It is clear that he is not just presenting a list of Pythagorean doctrines, but rather "telling a story" that attempts to make sense of the Pythagorean outlook as a whole. This story is necessarily selective and leaves out important points in order to preserve coherence. Aristotle sees the origin of Pythagorean philosophy in their work with the μαθήματα, which, in Aristotle's mind, included straightforward mathematical subjects such as arithmetic and geometry, but probably also astronomy and harmonics. Because of their work in these areas, so Aristotle's story goes, they came to believe that the principles of numbers, which were the primary elements in the μαθήματα, were the principles of all things. I have shown elsewhere that Aristotle's repeated statements that for the Pythagoreans "all things are numbers" or are "from numbers" can be shown, on the basis of the text of Aristotle himself, to be Aristotle's own statements of what Pythagorean philosophy amounted to rather than anything that the Pythagoreans literally said (Huffman 1981). In addition to this it is clear, once again from Aristotle's own testimonies, that this account of the Pythagoreans in terms of mathematics also distorts by omission. Based on what is said in *Metaphysics* 1.5 we would conclude that the principles of all things were the principles of numbers and that these were identified as the even and the odd. Limiters and unlimiteds are only mentioned once (986a19 – they are also mentioned in the table of opposites) and then only as adjectives to describe the even as unlimited and the odd as limited.

When Aristotle returns to the Pythagoreans later in the same chapter (987a14), in his summary of the first principles which had been proposed by his predecessors, he says that the Pythagoreans had in a similar manner to others proposed two first principles. Based on what we have read so far we would naturally suppose that these two principles would be the odd and the even. What we get instead is the assertion that the unlimited and the limit are the two Pythagorean principles. The passage is confusing, because Aristotle also mentions the one and seems to treat it as equivalent to limit, but, leaving that problem aside, it is striking that only the unlimited and the limit are mentioned and not the odd and even. However, Aristotle emphasizes that the Pythagoreans do not treat the unlimited and the limit as attributes of other entities such as fire or water, but rather as the essence of those things of which they are predicated. Aristotle concludes from this that the essence of all things will be number, which clearly shows that he is thinking of the limit and the unlimited as somehow equivalent to numbers. In light of the earlier passage in the *Metaphysics*, the connection probably is simply that Aristotle is thinking of the unlimited as the even and the limit as the odd. In his commentary on the passage Alexander explicitly says that the even and the odd are being treated as the substrate of things, and that when Aristotle talks of the unlimited as the essence of that of which it is predicated he is thinking of it as predicated of the even. While it is clear that Aristotle is still thinking of the principles of numbers as the principles of things in this passage, what is striking is how naturally it came to him to use the limit and the unlimited as the two basic Pythagorean principles, when they are really peripheral in his "story" of Pythagoreanism. This clearly indicates that the limit and the unlimited must have been prominent and well known principles for the Pythagoreans so that Aristotle could assume his readers knew of those principles independently of his own explanation. Of course this is exactly what is suggested by Plato's *Philebus* and most importantly by the fragments of Philolaus.

Thus it is clear, from what we have seen so far, that Aristotle virtually equates the even and the odd with the unlimited and the limit, and in fact treats the first pair as primary in so far as it accords with his story of the origin of Pythagoreanism in mathematics. A few chapters later in the *Metaphysics* (1.8) he is still telling the same story. Pythagorean principles are abstruser than those of others who have written on nature and in fact ill suited to explain the natural world and particularly inappropriate to explain motion. Once again this is seen as the result of the origin of those principles in mathematics. It is interesting in this passage, however, that when he lists the basic principles of the Pythagoreans he lists limit and unlimited side by side with odd and even. This suggests that Aristotle found both sets of principles in the Pythagoreans, but here at least he does not identify them, suggesting that the identification may not have been quite so clear in the Pythagoreans themselves.

One final passage continues Aristotle's presentation of the close connection between the unlimited and the even. At *Physics* 3.4 Aristotle discusses the Pythagorean view of the unlimited as part of his general review of his predecessors' accounts of that concept. He concludes by asserting that for the Pythagoreans the unlimited is even, and goes on to assert that the even, entrapped by the odd, gives things their unlimitedness. Thus, Aristotle once again shifts to the even as the most basic principle which is used to explain the unlimited aspect of things.

What can we conclude from these accounts of Aristotle? The story Aristotle is telling about the Pythagoreans is likely to have led to a considerable over-emphasis on the role of number and on the role of the even and odd as the principles of all things, at the expense of the role of limiters and unlimiteds which Aristotle's own text shows to have been commonly accepted Pythagorean first principles. The question that must be answered then is the extent to which the identification of the unlimited with the even and the limit with the odd was explicitly made by the Pythagoreans, as opposed to being made by Aristotle himself in his attempt to give a persuasive account of Pythagoreanism. This brings us back to the fragments of Philolaus.

There is a *prima facie* case for supposing that there is a connection between the two triadic divisions made in the fragments, although it is not necessary to regard them as identical. It is not merely that both F2 and F5 present a division into three kinds. The parallels are more extensive. In both cases two of the classes are made up of constituents that are opposed to each other (limiters–unlimiteds, odd–even). But even more importantly the third kind in each case is not a proper kind at all, in that it is derived from the other two and is in fact a combination of the elements in the two opposed classes. In F2 the third class comprises things that result from the fitting together of limiters and unlimiteds. In F5 the third kind is composed of the even and the odd "mixed together" (ἀμφοτέρων μιχθέντων) and is called the "even-odd." Such similarities suggest that the two triadic systems might be related.

On the other hand there are clear indications that there was a sharp distinction made between limiters and unlimiteds and the even and the odd. Most obviously, in the three fragments (1, 2, 6) which focus on the exposition of the basic principles of the cosmos only limiters and unlimiteds are mentioned and never the even or odd or number. Number is only explicitly introduced in connection with the problem of knowledge (F4) and in F5 even and odd are first introduced as kinds of number, not as principles of all things.

Thus, the fragments of Philolaus make it tolerably clear that for him the even and the odd were not equated with unlimiteds and limiters, but at the same time F5 does construct the triad of two basic classes of number (even and odd) and one derived class (even-odd) in a way that is parallel to the triad of limiters, unlimiteds, and things that are both limiting and unlimited. What is suggested is a parallelism between two sets of concepts which are in fact used in separate domains. Limiters and unlimiteds are used when discussing the basic principles of the cosmos and all the things in it, and in cosmology, while the even and the odd come in as part of the discussion of the role of number in explaining how things can be known. F5 gives strong support for this view since it asserts that individual things in the world "give signs" of the forms of numbers, which certainly suggests that we first grasp things as simple appearances and then on further examination see that they are only completely understood when we see the "forms

of number" to which they point. Thus, we first perceive the audible concords of the octave, fifth, and fourth and only after further examination
see the numbers to which they point (i.e. the ratios $1:2$, $3:2$, and $4:3$).
Aristotle's interpretation seems to be that if we gain true knowledge of
things by learning the numbers of which the phenomena give signs, then
these numbers have a strong claim to being what things really are. However, the fragments of Philolaus give no indication that he in fact came to
this conclusion, and instead indicate that he kept limiters and unlimiteds
distinct from numbers.

What then is the nature of the connection between unlimiteds and
limiters and even and odd for Philolaus? F5 is simply not explicit enough
to provide firm evidence. However, it is tempting to see Philolaus as supposing that if numbers are going to give us secure knowledge of what is
presented in the phenomena, then there ought to be some connection
between numbers and phenomena. Thus, if we see phenomena primarily as
limiters and unlimiteds and their combinations, then it would be natural
to try to connect these three types of things with similar divisions in the
numbers by which we come to have secure knowledge of them. Thus it
might be tempting to say that the main divisions of number, i.e. the even
and odd, correspond in some sense to the basic phenomenological concepts
of unlimiteds and limiters. The thought may be that we come to know
unlimiteds and limiters in so far as we identify the even and odd numbers that correspond to them. Things give signs of numbers which give us
knowledge of those things, but things are not therefore said to be numbers,
nor are unlimiteds said to be even numbers or the limiters said to be odd
numbers, although we may come to know them through seeing the even
and odd numbers to which they point.

Barnes has denied that there is any connection between the even and the
odd and the unlimited and the limit, and argues that since Aristotle emphasizes the connection "this is the chief reason for doubting that Philolaus
was the main source for Aristotle's account of fifth-century Pythagoreanism"
(1982: 390). His main reason for doubting any tie between the two pairs of
concepts is that "it does not...lead to any clear overall understanding of
Philolaus' theory of principles." Given the scanty nature of the evidence it
is impossible to arrive at any absolutely clear account, but I believe that the
sketch which I have given above of how the limiters and unlimiteds might
have been thought to be connected with odd and even is at least plausible.
This is a far cry from Aristotle's identification of the two pairs of terms, and
Barnes is right to reject such an identification. Aristotle may have come to
an unjustified conclusion in this regard, but it is still obvious that the
Pythagoreans whom he discusses are working with all the same concepts

that Philolaus did (limiters, unlimiteds, number, even, odd). It seems pretty implausible to me to suppose that Aristotle is basing his account of Pythagoreanism on a book by a different Pythagorean, of whom we have no knowledge, and who used all the same concepts as Philolaus, but who differed by explicitly equating the even and odd with limiters and unlimiteds. Certainly, it is more reasonable to explain Aristotle's difference from what is found in the fragments of Philolaus as the result of his interpretation of what is going on there, especially since we have ample evidence that Aristotle typically presents the views of others under a heavy interpretation.

Barnes cites two subsidiary arguments against any connection between limiters and unlimiteds and odd and even. First, he points out that since F4 suggests that "having number" is a sufficient condition for knowability, if unlimiteds "have" numbers they will be knowable. This, he argues, contradicts F3 which says that the unlimited is unknowable. However, there is in fact no contradiction since I have shown above that F3 in no way implies that the unlimited is unknowable. Furthermore this doctrine is in fact contradicted by what we find in other fragments. Thus, after ascribing the view that the unlimited is unknowable to Philolaus, Barnes himself (1982: 392) recognizes that this is a "baseless prejudice" which is "implicitly contradicted the third type of fact to which the end of Fragment 2 appeals." Once we see that F3 does not say that the unlimited is unknowable, we can agree with Barnes that it is a baseless prejudice, but also confidently reject it as a prejudice that Philolaus held.

Barnes's second point is that the use of μορφαί in F5 ties having a number with having a shape. However, since unlimiteds have no shape they cannot have a number. It is of course true that μορφαί often has the meaning "shape"; however, it is not true that it always carries that connotation. Indeed, in the most prominent use of the word in Presocratic philosophy it clearly does not have any connection to shape. When Parmenides (F8.53) chides mortals for positing two forms (μορφάς), these two forms turn out to be fire and night, which I would suppose to be two things which would be least likely to be thought to have a shape. In fact fire and night are good examples of what Philolaus meant by unlimiteds, so that Parmenides' use of μορφάς here shows that it need not have the connotations of shape and can very well be applied to Philolaus' unlimiteds.

Thus, I do not think that Barnes has shown that there is any basis in the fragments we have for denying a connection between unlimiteds and even numbers, and limiters and odd numbers. Moreover, while Aristotle's simple indentification of the two pairs must be rejected, the parallelism between F2 and F5 and the natural assumption that there would be some

183

connection between Philolaus' ontological principles and his epistemological principles supports the idea that the two sets of principles were intended to be parallel along the lines I have sketched above.

γα μάν: See the note on F4. This is probably a progressive use, as Denniston suggests (1954: 349). F5 might well have followed on a general discussion of number's role in knowledge, such as is suggested by F4. In that case γα μάν would indicate the transition to the detailed discussion of the divisions within number itself. In fact, the manuscripts run Fragments 2 and 4–7 together without any divisions. It seems to me quite possible that what are usually designated F4 and F5 should be regarded as one fragment. Boeckh (1819: 58–9) prints them as one fragment.

ἴδια εἴδη: ἴδια has a double significance in this fragment. First, it indicates that the two classes belong properly to number and to no other domain (e.g. animals). Second, and more importantly, it marks off the first two as the "proper"classes of number as opposed to the third derived class which is introduced next.

The standard rendering of εἴδη here as "kinds " or "types" (Burkert 1972: 264, Barnes 1982: 389, etc.) is clearly right. Burkert cites Democritus F11 as another pre-Platonic instance of this meaning of εἴδος (γνώμης δὲ δύο εἰσὶν ἰδέαι, ἡ μὲν γνησίη, ἡ δὲ σκοτίη – "of knowledge there are two kinds, legitimate and bastard"). This classificatory use is also common in the Hippocratic Corpus and is particularly used, as it is here in Philolaus, with numbers. See for example *Surgery* 3 (αὐγῆς μὲν οὖν δύο εἴδεα – "There are two kinds of light [i.e. ordinary and artificial]"), and *Nature of Man* 15.1 (οἱ πλεῖστοι τῶν πυρετῶν γίνονται ἀπὸ χολῆς· εἴδεα δὲ σφέων ἐστὶ τέσσαρα – "Most fevers come from bile. There are four kinds of them"). For further discussion of this use and more examples see Gillespie (1912: 183ff).

In a famous article Taylor (1911) argued that εἴδος has a meaning that almost always has some overtones of structure or shape and never really has a pure classificatory sense of "kind," "class," or "species." Gillespie's careful study has shown that this is false and that that there are many cases in which it has a virtually pure classificatory sense. Taylor also argued that for the Pythagoreans εἴδη referred to "patterns of numbers" and that the Pythagorean use had significant influence on the technical use of the term elsewhere in Greek. But Gillespie shows that the use of the word in the Hippocratic Corpus can be explained very well without any reference to the Pythagoreans. He finds two basic senses. First, it is used in a mainly physical sense to refer to the form of a bodily object where sometimes the outer visible form is emphasized (see the frequent sense "physique" in *Airs, Waters, and Places*), and sometimes the inner form or structure. Second, it

184

has a semi-logical classificatory sense which is often found with numbers, e.g. "there are two kinds of..."

Taylor's claim that the term was used to refer to "patterns of numbers" by the Pythagoreans might lead us to suppose that when Philolaus uses the term here he is making some sort of reference to the so-called Pythagorean pebble arithmetic (see Burnet 1948: 99–105). In such arithmetic numbers are viewed as a group of pebbles set out in a given shape. The evidence for such a practice is not extensive. We are told (Theophr. *Metaph.* 11.19 Ross-Fobes) that Philolaus' pupil Eurytus used to equate a given number with a given thing in the world (e.g. a man), and then take that number of pebbles and arrange them in the shape of a man. Aristotle (*Metaph.* 1092b11–12) relates this practice to certain unnamed people who arrange numbers in figures (σχήματα) like the triangle and the square. Again at *Physics* 203a10ff Aristotle explains the connection between even and the unlimited and odd and the limit by comparing the figures obtained by placing odd numbers of pebbles in the form of gnomons around the one with the figures obtained by a series of even numbers of pebbles placed around the two:

In the former case just one figure results, a square, whereas in the latter case an infinite variety of rectangles result (Burnet 1948: 103). Thus the odd numbers of the first figure are associated with one limited shape (the square) while the even numbers of the second figure are associated with an unlimited number of rectangles (for further ancient discussions of this text see Burkert 1972: 33 n. 27).

It was on the basis of setting out numbers as patterns of pebbles that the later Greek commentators also explained the association of the unlimited with even numbers and the limited with odd numbers. Even numbers (= unlimited) do not set a limit to division into equal halves whereas odd numbers (limit) do and can only be divided into unequal parts (e.g. 4, .. | .. ; 5, .. | ... – see Burnet 1948: 288–9 for references). The idea is not that even numbers can be halved indefinitely, which is the false explanation given by some ancient commentators, but rather that an equal division can take place in the case of even numbers since it would fall between the points, while in the case of odd numbers it "meets with an indivisible unit" and "is at once arrested" (Burnet 1948: 289).

Much of the testimony about this Pythagorean pebble arithmetic is late, but the testimony of Aristotle makes it likely that some Pythagoreans, for some purposes, thought of numbers as arrangements of pebbles, and Theophrastus' report on Eurytus brings this practice closer to Philolaus in so far as Eurytus was Philolaus' pupil. However, it would be very rash to conclude that the mere use of the term εἴδη in F5 is a reference to such arithmetical procedures. No one in the ancient tradition ever directly assigns the pebble arithmetic to Philolaus. Furthermore, nothing in F5 directly suggests such a conception of numbers nor does such a conception occur elsewhere in the fragments of Philolaus. As has been shown above, the use of εἴδη here is clearly paralleled by its use meaning "kind" both in the Presocratics and in the Hippocratic corpus. In light of this evidence it would be a tremendous overreading of the term to find in it a reference to Pythagorean pebble arithmetic.

ἀρτιοπέριττον: The first thing that should be noticed about this third kind of number is that it is carefully distinguished from the two "proper" kinds of number, even and odd. The third kind is not one of the basic elements of number, but rather the result of the combination of these elements.

Given that the third kind is derived from the two proper kinds, odd and even, there is still difficulty in determining what numbers might fall into this class. What numbers can properly be described as even-odd? Nothing in F5 itself gives an answer to this question, but two answers are given by the ancient tradition: (1) "the one" or (2) even numbers whose halves are odd (e.g. 6 or 10). The best evidence is that "the one" was the "even-odd" number for the early Pythagoreans. In two passages where he refers specifically to Pythagorean doctrine (*Metaph.* 986a20 and F199) Aristotle identifies the one as a combination of the even and odd, and in the latter case he explicitly uses the same word we find in F5, ἀρτιοπέριττον.

The explanation given for this identification is that since when added to even numbers it produces an odd number, but when added to odd numbers it produces an even, the one must participate in both the nature of the odd and of the even (F199). This is not a very satisfying explanation since all odd numbers produce the same result, and it is not clear whether it was the Pythagorean explanation or that of someone else trying to make sense of things. Other passages suggest that Aristotle saw the one as a sort of intermediate stage between the basic principles of even and odd, and numbers (e.g. *Metaph.* 986a17–21 and Alex. *in Metaph.* 41.9). Even and odd first come together to produce the one (the "even-odd"), and then the one generates the rest of the series of even and odd numbers. But this looks like Aristotelian interpretation since, although F5 does present the "even-odd" as derived from the even and the odd, it certainly does not suggest that this "even-odd" generated the rest of the numbers. The even and odd are not in fact presented as "principles" of number in F5, but rather as simply "kinds" of number. Still, the identification of the "even-odd" with the one suggested by Aristotle will work in F5, and appears to be strongly supported by F7. In F7 the first thing "fitted together" is called "the one in the center of the sphere." As I will argue below, this is not a reference to the number 1, as Aristotle takes it to be, but it is an assertion that unities arise from the "fitting together" of dissimilar elements (limiters and unlimiteds). Thus, it would make sense that the number which symbolizes unity, the one, should be regarded by Philolaus as also a combination of dissimilar elements, even and odd.

The other tradition which maintains that the class of the even-odd consists of even numbers whose halves are odd is neither so closely tied with early Pythagoreanism in the tradition, nor supported by the fragments of Philolaus. The earliest reference to this notion of even-odd is in Aristotle F47, which is drawn from pseudo-Plutarch, *De musica*. Parts of the fragment contain what are explicitly labeled as Aristotle's own views and these portions are usually taken to be from an early work of Aristotle. In section twenty-four the *harmonia* is said to consist of the unlimited, the limiting and the even-odd. In what follows it is just assumed that the unlimited is the even and the limit is the odd. The numbers 12, 9, 8, and 6 which can be put in ratios that correspond to the basic musical concords are said to embody the even, the odd, and the even-odd. 12 is said to be even as is 8, 9 is odd, and 6 is called even-odd. Barker (1984: 231 n. 164) argues that this account is purely Pythagorean and should not be assigned to Aristotle. I would agree that it is unlikely to represent Aristotle's own views, but it might have been found in Aristotle's work in the mouth of a character of a dialogue, as it does bear some of the marks of Aristotelian interpretation of Pythagoreanism. At any rate this passage of Aristotle does not assign this view of the even-odd to any Pythagoreans, while the view that the one is the even-odd is unambiguously assigned to fifth-century Pythagoreans in the texts discussed above. Other texts that present the understanding of the even-odd as even numbers with odd halves are late (e.g. Iambl. *In Nic.* 22.8ff).

While the even-odd understood as the one will work in F5 and is even supported by F7, taking the even-odd as even numbers whose halves are odd only produces confusion in Philolaus. If the even-odd is equated with even numbers whose halves are odd, then it becomes merely a subdivison of the even and Philolaus' "neat classification is spoiled" (Burkert 1972: 264 n. 124).

Barnes regards the clause in F5 which refers to the even-odd as an interpolation (1982: 632 n. 31), but his argument is not convincing. His first point is that the third type of number plays no obvious role in Philolaus' system. If we were dealing with an author whose work survived intact, this type of argument might be forceful, but it is very slippery in the case of Philolaus where we have such fragmentary remains. To excise a passage in this case we would need evidence not just that there was no clear role for the even-odd, but that it was inconsistent with what Philolaus says elsewhere. I hope that my discussion of the fragment as a whole at least suggests that there are plausible ways to connect the one as even-odd both with the unity that is fitted together out of dissimilar elements in F7 at the beginning of Philolaus' cosmogony and also with the general class of things that both limit and are unlimited. It is of course also important that Aristotle clearly shows that some fifth-century Pythagoreans accepted such a threefold division of number.

Close inspection of the language of F5 also goes against Barnes's proposal. He argues that if three kinds of number are listed in the first part of the fragment, it is very odd that the second part of the fragment goes on to talk of "each of the *two* kinds" (ἑκατέρω δὲ τῶ εἴδεος). But this is not the great difficulty Barnes supposes it to be, since in the first part of the fragment it is emphatically asserted that there are two "proper" kinds of number and that the third kind is thus not a proper kind of number, but a derivative kind. It is not at all unnnatural for Philolaus to go on to talk of the two kinds of number when it is easy for us to understand them in this context as the two "proper" kinds. Furthermore, there are some difficulties, which Barnes does not recognize, with regarding the reference to the third kind of number as an interpolation. First, how would it come about? The answer might seem easy. A later commentator reading the fragment notices that only two kinds of number are mentioned but remembering Aristotle's testimony inserts in the margin or in the text a reference to the third kind. The big problem here is that the later tradition is not very interested in Aristotle's account of the Pythagoreans, as Burkert has shown, and the later tradition as seen both in the pseudepigrapha and in writers like Nicomachus makes virtually no reference to Aristotle's brand of Pythagoreanism. It is still possible of course that the interpolator was relying on the interpretation of the even-odd as numbers that are even with odd halves, an interpretation which is found in Nicomachus, etc.

But the biggest problem is that if we regard the interpolation as τρίτον δὲ ἀπ' ἀμφοτέρων μιχθέντων ἀρτιοπέριττον ("and a third from both mixed together, the even-odd"), other changes will have had to be made in the first part of the fragment as well. The position of μέν ("on the one hand") right after δύο ("two") in the first part of the fragment clearly corresponds to the position of δέ ("on the other hand") immediately after τρίτον ("a third") in the supposed interpolation. This problem might be avoided by arguing that it is not implausible to suppose that the μέν was inserted by the interpolator in the first part of the fragment in order to integrate the interpolation into the fragment. This is starting to stretch things, but even bigger problems arise when we realize that the use of ἴδια ("proper") to describe the first two kinds of number loses most of its force if a reference to the third derived (and hence "improper") kind of number does not follow. Thus, both the μέν and the ἴδια in the first part of the sentence are preparing us for the third kind of number, and it is quite implausible to suppose that both were inserted by the interpolator, especially when the only reason to think there was an interpolation in the first place, i.e. that the role of the third class of number in Philolaus' philosophy is unclear, is so shaky. Barnes's suggestion that the reference to the even-odd is an interpolation must thus be rejected and we should regard the even-odd as referring to the one.

One problem does remain for associating the one with the even-odd. As Zeller points out (1923: 455 n. 1), "we should scarcely expect the one to be described as a separate species." Indeed, if we accept that the third class of number has only one member, the one, this does not correspond well to the third mixed class of things in F2, which surely has more than one member. Of course, this difficulty could be taken to show that there is no connection between the threefold division of numbers in F5 and the threefold division of things elsewhere, but we should not jump to this conclusion too soon.

As was suggested in the introductory remarks on this fragment, Philolaus' idea seems to be that limiting things are associated with and known through odd numbers, while unlimiteds are tied to even numbers. What about the third class of things, that was "fitted together" out of limiters and unlimiteds? This class of things in fact seems to be the focus of Philolaus' interest and to be the class of things that show the order of the world. In so far as things are ordered they are combinations of limiters and unlimiteds held together by harmony (F6). But how are we to gain secure knowledge of such things? In answering this question it is important to notice first that it is appropriate that this class, which consists of things unified through harmony, should be related to the number which is the symbol of unity, the one. By treating the one as itself a unity of diverse components, the even and the odd, Philolaus has heightened this symbolism. However, granted that the one as even-odd is an excellent symbol for the whole mixed class of things, it cannot serve to give us knowledge of the great variety of things in the mixed class; they cannot all be known through the same number one or they would all be the same. If even and odd numbers are already in use for knowing individual limiters and unlimiteds, what numbers can be left to give us knowledge of the compounds of limiters and unlimiteds around us?

If we look at the concrete examples of harmony or "fitting together" which Philolaus gives us in F6, an answer suggests itself. The examples of harmony given there are the concordant musical intervals which are said to correspond to the numerical ratios $2:1$, $3:2$, $4:3$. It is crucial to note that in each of these ratios an even and an odd number are mixed (the octave [$2:1$] is a problem since 1 is not simply an odd number, but it does contain the principle of the odd in it according to Philolaus). Thus,

189

I suggest, Philolaus thought that things that were fitted together out of limiters and unlimiteds were known by grasping the ratio consisting of an even and an odd number which uniquely determined them. So that the audible concord of the fourth comes to be known securely when we see the ratio 4 : 3 to which it "points." Properly speaking, "numbers" (ἀριθμοί) for the Greeks were only whole numbers and would not include ratios. But when Plato (*R.* 531c2) describes the Pythagoreans as looking for numbers (ἀριθμούς) in "heard harmonies," it is surely *ratios* of numbers to which he is referring. This suggests that it would not be impossible for Philolaus to think of ratios of whole numbers as a class of numbers (ἀριθμοί), especially when he goes out of his way to note that this is in fact not a "proper kind" (ἴδια εἴδη).

In summary, I believe that the even-odd is a derived class of numbers whose first member is, as the ancient tradition indicates, the one, but which also includes numbers that consist of even and odd numbers combined in ratios (e.g. 2 : 1, 4 : 3, and 3 : 2). This class of numbers corresponds to the third class of things in F2, which consists of members that are harmonized from both limiting and unlimited constituents. The even-odd numbers are the numbers by which these harmonized things are known. This connection of course remains conjectural, but I believe that it is a plausible way to make sense of both F2 and F5 of Philolaus and Aristotle's testimony that there was a connection between the even – odd dichotomy and the unlimited – limiter dichotomy, although my suggestion does not identify the two as Aristotle does.

ἑκατέρω δὲ τῶ εἴδεος: The word ἑκατέρω ("each of two") clearly picks out just the two proper kinds of number, even and odd. Burkert makes the suggestion that, since this sentence goes on to say that each of these two kinds of number has "many forms," the implication may be that the third kind of number does not have many forms. This would be further evidence that the third kind of number, the even-odd, is simply "the one" and thus does not have many forms (1972: 264 n. 124). My account of the third class of numbers suggested that Philolaus may also have included in it ratios of even and odd numbers. If this is so, my reading of this sentence is simply that Philolaus is focusing on the two proper kinds of number, even and odd, and pointing out that they have many forms. It would also be true that the derived class has many forms, but this variety is the direct result of the fact that there are a variety of forms of the primary classes and hence Philolaus makes no special mention of it.

πολλαὶ μορφαί: Like εἶδος, μορφή can mean simply "kind" or "form" in a classificatory sense (πολλαί γε πολλοῖς εἰσι συμφοραὶ βροτῶν, / μορφαὶ δὲ διαφέρουσιν – "The misfortunes of mortals are many and widespread, and they differ in kind" Eur. *Ion* 382; see also Plato *R*. 397c5), and that is the most likely meaning here. It is also similar to εἶδος in that it more often refers to the "form," "shape," or "appearance" of a thing and is often a synonym of εἶδος, although it is a much less common word. When a distinction is made between the two terms it seems that "εἶδος denotes the appearance of the kind, what is common to the individuals, while μορφή is the individual form of appearance" (J. Behm in Kittel 1965). Although this is a judgment made on later Greek it seems to have some validity in earlier texts as well. Thus in the Hippocratic corpus a passage from *On the Sacred Disease* (16.21) reports that clay jars stored under ground or in the house are said to διαλλάσσει τὴν μορφὴν ἐς ἕτερον εἶδος. Since μορφή is the direct object of the verb "change" it would seem to refer to the actual appearance of the jug while εἶδος is the new "form" in the sense of a "kind" of shape. This distinction between εἶδος as the more general term and μορφή as the more particular works well here with the classificatory senses in F5, since εἶδος is in fact used to refer to the two most general kinds of number, whereas μορφή is used in reference to the specific forms of those two general kinds. As in the case of εἶδος, there is no reason to assume that the simple use of the word μορφή implies that Philolaus is referring to the representation of numbers by shapes in the Pythagorean pebble arithmetic. Parmenides F8.53 shows that for a Presocratic the use of μορφή need have no reference to physical shape.

What then are the "many forms" of the two basic kinds of number? The most obvious answer is that they are the even and odd natural numbers. Thus the individual odd numbers (3, 5, 7, 9...) would be the "many forms" of the odd that limiting things point to, while the individual even numbers (2, 4, 6, 8...) would be the "many forms" of even to which unlimited things point. Things which both limit and are unlimited will "give signs of" both even and odd numbers, i.e. they will be best understood in terms of ratios of even and odd numbers.

There are of course many problems in working out the details of the correspondence between limiters and unlimiteds and even and odd numbers. Undoubtedly this is just another of the many Presocratic "bluffs" where a bold theoretical structure is proposed without much empirical grounding. The impulse behind the correlation between numbers and things is presumably the belief that all phenomena will turn out to be numerically determined in the same way that the concordant musical intervals were discovered to be. However, there is one particular problem with this correlation of numbers and things that requires comment here. It has seemed very awkward to a number of commentators that things which are unlimited turn out to have number, whereas anything that has number would appear *ipso facto* to be limited and definite. However, most of the difficulty here comes from mistaken applications of later conceptions of what it means to be unlimited to Philolaus' unlimiteds.

To begin with, it is clear that Philolaus' unlimiteds are not unlimited in the radical sense that many scholars assume, i.e. totally without limits in any respect. If there were such an entity, there could only be one, since there would be no way to distinguish one totally unlimited entity from another. That this is not what Philolaus is talking about is clear first of all from the fact that he always talks about unlimiteds in the plural. This surely suggests that there are a plurality of unlimiteds that can be distinguished from one another and which therefore have some recognizable characteristics. Moreover, F2 freely talks about unlimiteds as if they were readily observable and distinguishable in the phenomenal world. In the introduction I have argued that unlimiteds include aspects of the world which have readily identifiable characteristics, but which are not defined by any particular amount. Examples would be breath, fire, earth, etc. If this is what Philolaus has in mind, I think that it is not at all implausible for him to think that the qualitative characteristics of such things are determined by number in some way. Thus, in Philolaus' system all the stuffs ("unlimiteds") in the world, all the structural principles ("limiters") in the world, and all combinations of stuffs and structural principles have number and become known when we grasp that number.

ἃς ἕκαστον αὐτὸ σημαίνει: There are several difficulties with the text here. σημαίνει is Heeren's conjecture for δημαίνει which occurs in all the manuscripts, but which is an impossible word. The change is easy and makes good sense and has accordingly been accepted by most editors.

αὐτό is my emendation of the manuscripts αὐτ' αὐτό. The commonly accepted reading is αὐταυτό, the Doric equivalent to ἑαυτό. Such a reading simply will not work syntactically. Scholars translate as if it were the nominative intensive agreeing with ἕκαστον ("each thing itself"), yet, as Burkert notes (1972: 264 n. 121), in all other instances αὐταυτό is used as a reflexive. My emendation produces the sense given in the usual translation. The manuscript reading can be explained as arising through dittography rather than as preserving a Doric form.

ἕκαστον is also confusing at first sight. The only antecedents immediately available are the two "kinds" of number. However, these were picked out by ἑκατέρω ("each of the two") at the beginning of this sentence and it would be odd now to use ἕκαστον. Further, if ἕκαστον did refer to the "two kinds," the relative clause would merely repeat the thought of the main clause ("of each of the two kinds there are many forms which each [of the two kinds] gives signs of"). There are two other possibilities for the reference of ἕκαστον. It could mean "each thing" and thus provide a general reference to the sensible world (Burkert 1972: 264, Barnes 1982: 389). Or, if this fragment is in fact to be joined with F4, it might reasonably be taken to mean "each thing that is known." This last possibility need not differ greatly from the former ("each thing"), since the things that are known may be coextensive with the individual things in the world.

Thus the individual things that are known in the world stand in the relation of σημαίνειν to the many forms of each kind of number. What sort of relation is indicated by σημαίνει? In Heraclitus F93 the lord at Delphi is said "neither to speak plainly (λέγει) nor conceal (κρύπτει) but to give a sign (σημαίνει)." When someone or something "gives a sign," they do not display the meaning on the surface, but rather give indications that point to a meaning that is not immediately obvious. Thus in Democritus F212 sleep in the daytime is said to *indicate* some bodily trouble, etc. In Plato the verb is often used of what an argument *shows* (e.g. *Gorg.* 511b7). What is shown is not obvious at first glance, but the result of reasoning.

The use of σημαίνει in F5 suggests that the individual things that are known do not directly manifest one of the many forms of each of the kinds of number. Each thing, rather, gives indications of or points to one of these forms. Thus, when we hear the musical interval of an octave, the ratio of 1:2 is not given to us on the surface, but is pointed to by further study of the phenomenon. This relation of "pointing to" remains somewhat vague, as did Plato's notion of "participation" in a form. However, as Aristotle emphasizes, the Pythagoreans have less difficulty in that they do not think of the numbers that are pointed to as separate from the things which do the pointing, but rather as in some way part of them.

Testimonium A7a

Plutarch, *Quaest. conv.* 8.2.1, 718e γεωμετρία κατὰ τὸν Φιλόλαον ἀρχὴ καὶ μητρόπολις οὖσα τῶν ἄλλων (μαθημάτων)...

1 Φιλόλαον Hubert Φίλωνα earlier edd. φίλαον T

Geometry being, as Philolaus says, **the source and the mother-city** of the rest (of the mathematical sciences)...

AUTHENTICITY

The difficulty of determining the authenticity of such a short text is compounded in this case by the fact that the name Philolaus (Φιλόλαον) is introduced by emendation for the nonsensical φίλαον of the manuscripts.

However, the suggested textual emendation of Φιλόλαον for φίλαον in fact presupposes a very plausible error of transmission, the loss of a syllable by *homeoteleuton*. This is much more likely than the error that would produce the Φίλωνα suggested by earlier editors. Moreover, the content of the fragment gives no strong reason for doubting its authenticity and both its divergence from the typical characteristics of the Pythagorean pseudepigrapha and its connections with other, genuine, fragments of Philolaus allow us to comfortably regard it as representing Philolaus' actual views (Burkert accepts it [1972: 249]). However, its form suggests that it could just as well be an apophthegm passed down orally (as F16 probably was), as a sentence from Philolaus' book.

Consideration of the context of the fragment shows strikingly how it diverges from the later Platonizing tradition of the Pythagorean pseudepigrapha. It is cited in the second question of Book 8 of Plutarch's *Table Talk*. The question under discussion is "What Plato meant by saying that God is always doing geometry." The first speaker, Tyndareus, addresses the question by appealing to Book 7 of the *Republic* where geometry, along with four other mathematical sciences (μαθήματα – arithmetic, stereometry, astronomy, and harmonics), is praised because the true study of it draws us away from the world of the sensible and directs us towards the intelligible realm. Now the problem is that, although Plato does assign this value to geometry, he does not anywhere in the dialogues single out geometry as having a unique value in relation to the other mathematical sciences. In *Republic* 7 it is simply the second of five sciences listed. Thus, Plutarch has to turn to another source which suggests that geometry has some sort of primacy among the mathematical sciences, and this source is Philolaus. Immediately after bringing in the idea of geometry as "the source and mother-city" of the other sciences, the text continues along Platonic lines, pointing out the power of geometry to lead the understanding upward and turn it in a new direction. What is striking about the fragment from Philolaus is that it stands out in a heavily Platonic context as something not derived from Platonic doctrine. This is in direct contrast to the Pythagorean pseudepigrapha which both in content and terminology follow Plato and Aristotle very closely. None of the pseudepigrapha collected by Thesleff, nor the later Pythagorean theorizing found in Nicomachus, assigns geometry the focal role in the mathematical sciences. The implication is in fact usually that arithmetic is the science with the best claim to being a starting-point (ἀρχή). The Platonic derivation scheme makes number primary, and Aristotle refers to arithmetic as more exact than geometry (*Metaph.* 982a26ff – ἀκριβεστέρα γεωμετρίας). It is only much later than Plutarch that the Neoplatonist Proclus (fifth century AD) comes to replace the Pythagoreanizing emphasis on arithmetic (Nicomachus and Iamblichus) with geometry as the primary mathematical science (O'Meara 1989: 166ff). It seems very likely that a forgery would stick to the standard view which assigns arithmetic the first place among the sciences. Thus the idiosyncrasy of the assertion of the primacy of geometry at this early date speaks for the authenticity of the fragment.

Its authenticity is also supported by its accurate reflection of the development of mathematical science in Greece during Philolaus' time and by connections to important themes elsewhere in Philolaus such as the method of positing "starting-points" for each field of inquiry. Particularly important is the strong similarity between the centrifocal image of the mother-city here and two other centrifocal images elsewhere in Philolaus, the central fire and the navel (ὀμφαλος) as the center of the human being. These points will be developed in the commentary.

COMMENTARY

Extent of the fragment: It seems natural to call it a fragment rather than a testimonium, since it is likely that at least three of the words are Philolaus', even if the full wording of the sentence cannot be recovered. "Geometry" and "mother-city" must surely come from Philolaus, since they provide the central image of the fragment. On the other hand "source" (ἀρχή) could be Plutarch's word introduced to elucidate "mother-city." However, given that Philolaus uses ἀρχή prominently in the genuine fragments (F6, F13, A27), it seems reasonable to suppose that this word too belongs to Philolaus. Finally, it is uncertain what word Philolaus used to refer to the other mathematical sciences. It might have been μαθήματα, which does occur in Archytas F1, or he might have referred to individual sciences, either with an abstract term (music, astronomy) or with a description of their subject matter, without using a general term.

μητρόπολις: What is most noteworthy about the fragment is, of course, the splendid image of geometry as the "mother-city" of the other sciences. Somewhat surprisingly, μητρόπολις is not a very common word in what survives of ancient Greek literature. Herodotus uses it four times, Thucydides seven, and Plato once (*Critias* 115c5). It appears in none of the genuine writings of Aristotle (although it does appear at *Rh. Al.* 1420b22 and *Oec.* 1348a12). In its literal sense it primarily refers to the "mother-state" which sends out colonies (e.g. Corinth is called the μητρόπολις of Corcyra at Thuc. 1.24), although it is also used of more general relationships such as that of Athens to the Ionians (Hdt. 7.51). It is important to note that the mother-city was viewed as the origin of the colony in more than just a spatio-temporal sense. The colonists also looked upon the mother-city as the source of their institutions, and represented this ritually by taking fire from the sacred hearth of the mother-city to kindle the sacred hearth of the colony (Graham 1964: 25).

Philolaus appears to be the first author to have applied the word metaphorically. But the same metaphorical use is found not much later than Philolaus in the Hippocratic treatise *On Fleshes* (late fifth or early fourth century BC). Later examples come from the pseudo-Aristotelian *Rhetoric to Alexander* (1420b2), Chrysippus (apud Athen. 104b – the *Gastrologia* of Archestratus is called the mother-city of the philosophy of Epicurus), and Diodorus Siculus (1.2 – history is called the mother-city of philosophy). In the amusing example in Chrysippus the point is that the *Gastrologia* is the mother-city not only as the starting-point of Epicurean philosophy, but also as its central continuing motivation. Diodorus' use is similar in that, in context, his point seems to be that history by preserving the memory of noble deeds provides the continuing motivation for the virtuous action which is the goal of philosophy. (It might also be that Diodorus means that history provides the general experience from which we draw the generalizations of philosophy.) Thus, these two examples portray the mother-city both as the necessary starting-point and also as providing continuing support for the "colony."

In *On Fleshes* 4 the usage of the mother-city image is very similar. It is important to note that this use occurs in a medical writing which is probably only a generation later than Philolaus' book, which itself contained medical speculations. Accordingly it is not impossible that there are some connections between the passages. Here the brain is said to be the mother-city of the cold and glutinous, while the hot is called the mother-city of the oily. In support of the second statement the author of the *On Fleshes* points out that when things are heated and melt they first become oily. Thus, the hot is the mother-city not in the sense that it is itself oily, but in so far as its action leads to the production of the oily. The case of the brain and the cold and glutinous appears to be different. However, the statement is not explained in the text and we must inevitably resort to some sort of conjecture. The image would be most parallel with the example of the hot, if the brain served the function of producing the cold and glutinous in some way. Regrettably, there is no statement of such a doctrine in the *On Fleshes*. There are suggestions later in chapter 4 that there is perhaps a greater quantity of the cold and glutinous in the brain, and it may be called the mother-city because it contains the most of the cold and glutinous and makes them available to the rest of the body.

This analysis of the literal and metaphorical uses of μητρόπολις indicates that to say that something is the "mother-city" of something else is to suggest not only that it is the origin or starting-point of that other thing, but also that it has a continuing relationship with its "colony" which accounts for the essential characteristics of that "colony." If we apply this understanding of μητρόπολις to Philolaus, a coherent and interesting picture emerges. The suggestion would be that geometry is the origin from which the rest of the mathematical sciences (μαθήματα) developed. This can be interpreted as what is in fact a correct historical claim, i.e. that geometry was the first of the μαθήματα to be developed in Greece. Certainly, Philolaus' contemporary Hippocrates of Chios is reputed to have been the first to develop some sort of a system of elements of geometry. However, it is probably also a point about the structure of the mathematical sciences as a whole, i.e. that problem areas in other sciences could be illuminated by appeal to geometry (see Burkert 1972: 221 n. 14). Thus, Philolaus' claim of some sort of primacy for geometry in fact makes very good sense in the context of the general development of Greek mathematics and in particular in terms of the development of geometry at the hands of Hippocrates of Chios in the middle of the second half of the fifth century.

It is also interesting to note that the image of the "mother-city" has important connections to two other images of centrality found in the testimonia and fragments of Philolaus. As mentioned above, the colonists look to the mother-city as the source of their institutions and represent this ritually by taking fire from the sacred hearth of the mother-city in order to kindle their own hearth. The image of the hearth is also one of the most striking features of Philolaus' astronomy, where the heavenly bodies circle around an invisible central fire, which is called the hearth. Furthermore, in Philolaus' cosmogony the cosmos develops from this central fire as a starting-point (F7 and F17), just as the other sciences develop from geometry as a starting-point or mother-city. Moreover, when we turn to biology we find this same image of growth from the center. In the center of the human body is the navel (ὄμφαλος) which is viewed as the starting-point of growth by Philolaus (F13). However, we also know that Philolaus associated heat with the first growth of the human being, since he argues that human beings are constituted out of the hot (A27), so that there is a clear analogy with the central fire. There is also evidence that the Greeks in fact associated the sacred hearth with the navel (ὄμφαλος), particularly in that the hearth can be seen as rooted in the earth, just as the umbilical cord (another meaning of ὄμφαλος) roots the embryo in the womb (see Vernant 1969: 121–2, 157). Thus, the centrifocal image of the mother-city is used to construct a parallel between the structure of the sciences and the structure of the cosmos and the human being.

ἀρχή: As I have argued above (Pt. II, ch. 3), Philolaus follows a general methodology according to which he tries to determine a minimum set of starting-points (ἀρχαί) required for explanation in each area which he investigates. The use of ἀρχή in this fragment fits perfectly into this sense of indispensable "starting-point" of explanation. Thus, Philolaus is developing a hierarchy of mathematical sciences in which geometry occupies the ground floor as that science without which the others cannot develop. But is it possible to believe that, already in the second half of the fifth century, Philolaus had clearly envisioned a canonical group of mathematical sciences (μαθήματα) with such a structure? Certainly F1 of Archytas suggests that some sort of special group of mathematical sciences existed before his time, because he refers to τοὶ περὶ τὰ μαθήματα ("those concerned with the mathematical sciences") as if they had been active for some time (for the authenticity of F1 see Huffman 1985). Archytas gives four sciences (astronomy, geometry, arithmetic, and music) to which Plato will add stereometry in *Republic* 7 to make five. Archytas does not really seem to be giving any sort of hierarchy in his presentation of the sciences (astronomy comes first according to the correct text [Huffman 1985], followed by geometry). Plato already has arithmetic first, followed by geometry, and the *Republic* passage clearly shows an interest in treating the sciences in their proper order. At any rate, Archytas' reference to already existing mathematical sciences in the first part of the fourth century makes it not at all implausible that a roughly defined group of four sciences (μαθήματα) was recognized by Philolaus in the second half of the fifth century, although we have no way of knowing exactly how he would have described each of these sciences.

However, there is one lingering puzzle. It is in fact the opposite side of one of the arguments for authenticity. Despite the fact that A7a does correctly reflect the fact that geometry was the first of the mathematical sciences to develop a rigorous structure, it remains true that it is number which has the dominant role both in the genuine fragments of Philolaus and in Aristotle's reports on the early Pythagoreans, and that geometry is scarcely mentioned. In the face of this, how is it possible that Philolaus should assert that geometry and not number or arithmetic should be regarded as the mother-city of the mathematical sciences?

There is too much that is unknown to give any firm answer, but the following conjecture can be made. For Philolaus numbers consitute the sort of objects of knowledge which Parmenides demanded. Geometrical figures cannot play this role since they have no determinate value of themselves (if you say something is composed of a triangle it is reasonable to ask what size of triangle). However, the geometry of Philolaus' time, although still in its infancy, is likely to have a much more developed structure of basic principles and proofs than any other mathematical science (e.g. the work of Hippocrates of Chios). Moreover, the fragments of Philolaus show that he was interested in the basic principles of explanation in a wide range of fields. Thus, it may be that he saw geometry with its relatively developed set of first principles and method of proof as a model for an even wider range of "sciences" than the four Archytas mentions, possibly including a science such as medicine. The point would be that, while it is numbers that ultimately allow us to know things, it is the model of geometry that we should follow in organizing our knowledge and not the relatively undeveloped science of arithmetic. Number may be the mother-city of human knowledge, but it is geometry that is the mother-city of science.

Testimonium A29

Sextus Empiricus, *Adversus mathematicos* 7.92 ὥστε ὁ μὲν Ἀναξαγόρας κοινῶς τὸν λόγον ἔφη κριτήριον εἶναι· οἱ δὲ Πυθαγορικοὶ τὸν **λόγον** μέν φασιν, οὐ κοινῶς δέ, **τὸν δὲ ἀπὸ τῶν μαθημάτων περιγινόμενον, καθάπερ ἔλεγε καὶ ὁ Φιλόλαος,**
5 θεωρητικόν τε ὄντα τῆς τῶν ὅλων φύσεως ἔχειν τινὰ συγγένειαν πρὸς ταύτην, ἐπείπερ ὑπὸ τοῦ ὁμοίου τὸ ὅμοιον καταλαμβάνεσθαι πέφυκεν· [F109 of Empedocles is then quoted].

As a result Anaxagoras said that reason in general was the criterion. The Pythagoreans said that **reason was the criterion**, but not reason in general, but rather **the reason that arises from the mathematical sciences, just as Philolaus also said**, and since it is concerned with the nature of wholes [they said that] it has a certain kinship to that nature, since it is the nature of like to be apprehended by like: [F109 of Empedocles is then quoted].

AUTHENTICITY

It is crucial to recognize that the only thing which is ascribed to Philolaus here is the belief that the criterion is the reason which arises from the mathematical sciences (Burkert 1972: 249 n. 55). Boeckh (1819: 191), DK, and Bury in his translation of Sextus mistakenly assign the following statement also to Philolaus (i.e. that since like is known by like, the reason which knows the nature of the whole must be related to the nature of the whole). Close scrutiny of the structure of the passage in Sextus shows that the latter interpretation is very unlikely. Sextus first asserts that the Pythagoreans thought that the reason which arises from the sciences is the criterion. In support of this assertion he adds the remark "just as Philolaus also says."

He then goes on to make a further point about the Pythagorean view. This point is added by the connective τε and is still in indirect statement dependent on "the Pythagoreans say." If the clause joined by τε is taken as depending on "just as Philolaus says," the sentence becomes very awkward, since it would start out to be a general assertion about the Pythagoreans and then be hijacked by a parenthetical reference to Philolaus which takes over the rest of the sentence. Indeed the τε makes little sense if the passage is supposed to depend on the immediately preceding "Philolaus said." The further point added by Sextus is that the Pythagoreans thought that the reason that arises from the sciences must be akin to the nature of the whole which it studies, since like is known by like. Sextus then supports this assertion by a quotation from Empedocles whom he clearly regards as a Pythagorean. Thus, Sextus makes two assertions about the Pythagorean account of the criterion and supports each by a reference to something actually said by the Pythagoreans, in the first case by a reference to Philolaus and in the second by a quotation from Empedocles. To suppose that the second assertion belongs to Philolaus, as Boeckh, DK, and Bury do, ignores this structure of the passage and awkwardly supposes that a quotation from Empedocles is introduced to support a point of view ascribed to Philolaus.

Once we have identified what Sextus is ascribing to Philolaus, it is important to recognize that what is ascribed is under a heavy interpretation. This passage is part of Sextus' attempt to determine what the Presocratics had to say about the criterion. However, the whole concept of a criterion is a Hellenistic creation and to ask this question of the Presocratics is to ask a question which they themselves never raised. Thus, Sextus is really reporting on what each of the Presocratics *in effect* uses as the criterion.

Just before turning to the Pythagoreans he discusses Anaxagoras and concludes that he like most of the Presocratics came to distrust the senses and therefore made λόγος the criterion of truth. Of course λόγος has a wide range of meanings (saying, discourse, statement, account, explanation, reason, measure, ratio, formula, law of the universe – see e.g. Kirk 1954: 37ff). In determining the meaning here it is important to recognize that it is very likely to be Sextus' word rather than anything he found in the fragments of Anaxagoras or Philolaus. The context in Sextus emphasizes the contrast with the senses as the criterion so that it is most likely that λόγος is used loosely to refer to the whole realm of reasoning and discourse in contrast to the realm of sensory experience. There is evidence that Anaxagoras distrusted the senses and of course that "intelligence" played a crucial role in his system. Sextus' assertion that reason was the criterion for Anaxagoras is thus not unreasonable as interpretation, but we must be clear that it probably relies on no specific text.

If we turn to Philolaus, then, we must recognize that this testimonium certainly does not show that Philolaus said anything like "the reason that arises from the senses is the criterion." It is doubtful that any of the language, including "reason" (λόγος), should be ascribed to Philolaus. What the testimonium tells us is that Philolaus gave a prominent role to the mathematical sciences in his account of the world. This is of course not very informative, since this is obvious from the fragments and from Aristotle's early accounts of Pythagoreanism. However, it is also clear that the testimonium could well be based on Philolaus' genuine book and nothing in it suggests that it is based on a forged text. Frank (1923: 312 n. 1) pointed out that the word περιγίγνεσθαι occurs both here in the testimonium about Philolaus and in Sextus' account of Speusippus at *M.* 7.146. But far from suggesting that the Philolaus passage reflects Academic ideas this simply reflects Sextus' own usage.

COMMENTARY

Importance of the testimonium: While this testimonium need only be based on the obvious interest in the mathematical sciences in the fragments of Philolaus, it might be connected with A7a where geometry is said to be the mother-city of the sciences. If we in turn take this in connection with F4, where Philolaus asserts that nothing is known without number, it is tempting to think that there was a section of his book where he directly addressed epistemological questions. In response to Parmenides he argued that knowledge of the world is possible in so far as the world is governed by number, which because of its completely determinant character is a suitable object of knowledge (F4). He may then have gone on to stress the importance of the mathematical sciences and described a hierarchy among them with geometry claiming the most prominent place, because of its developed state relative to the other mathematical sciences in his day (A7a). If this is the case, then Sextus' testimony would be based on more than Philolaus' use of the mathematical sciences. It would be based on an explicit assertion of the value of such a group of sciences in understanding the cosmos. Philolaus would thus anticipate Plato's assertion of the value of the study of the μαθήματα (mathematical sciences) in the *Republic*, although Plato's reason for pursuing them, their ability to direct us to intelligible reality, is completely different from that of Philolaus who saw them as the key to secure knowledge of sensible reality, the only reality which he recognized.

3. COSMOGONY

Philolaus' cosmogony

The primary sources for Philolaus' cosmogony are seemingly very meagre indeed (F7 and F17 – about six lines in total), but they are absolutely crucial both for understanding Philolaus' philosophy and for evaluating Aristotle's accounts of Pythagoreanism. One of the central features of Aristotle's description of the Pythagoreans is his claim that they confused the arithmetical unit with a spatial magnitude and that they "generated" the one and then generated the whole cosmos from this one by means of the one breathing in the unlimited. At first sight F7 of Philolaus seems to accord so well with Aristotle's reports about the generation of the one that scholars have generally accepted Aristotle's account of Pythagoreanism and concluded that "... there is no distinction between the arithmetic and geometric unit, nor between mathematical points and physical or sensible bodies" (Kahn 1974: 173). However, I believe that close consideration of the fragment will show that, while Philolaus was interested in the parallels between the generation of the cosmos and the generation of the number series, he did not identify the two in the puerile way that Aristotle suggests. Furthermore, I will want to argue that scholars including Aristotle have misunderstood what is meant by "the one" in F7 and that the fragment is not concerned with the generation of a "monad with position" at the center of the cosmos, but rather with the generation of the famous central fire as a paradigm case of the unity of limiter and unlimited. This interpretation will show Philolaus' cosmogony to share many features of the Presocratic cosmogonical tradition begun by the Ionians, and to be tied particularly to the strand of that tradition, developed by Anaximander and Parmenides, which emphasizes the structural features of the cosmos.

To begin with we need to examine Aristotle's testimony on Pythagorean cosmogony with some care. Most of the passages come from the *Metaphysics*, but Pythagoreans are discussed in two passages in the *Physics* (3.4, 203a1 dealing with the unlimited; 4.6, 213b22 dealing with the void), and the famous Pythagorean astronomical system that includes the central fire and the counter-earth is discussed in the *De caelo* (2.13). One of the most striking features about Aristotle's testimonia is that the discussion of the Pythagoreans is almost always either embedded in a larger discussion of Platonic and Academic views or explicitly compared with Plato's views. In the *Metaphysics* Plato and the Pythagoreans are often said to agree in treating "the one" as a substance and as an element and principle. They are contrasted with Empedocles who is said to have reduced "the one" to a more basic principle, love (*Metaph.* 996a5, 1001a9, 1053b9). Similarly, in the *Physics* Plato and the Pythagoreans are said to agree in regarding the unlimited as a principle and a substance. On the other hand, Aristotle always distinguishes Plato from the Pythagoreans by pointing out that Plato separated numbers from things and regarded the unlimited as a duality composed of the great and the small, whereas in Aristotle's view the Pythagoreans identified things with numbers and treated the unlimited as a single principle. There are indications that this constant comparison with Plato distorts Aristotle's account of the Pythagoreans, although it should be clear that on a number of points Aristotle is careful to distinguish the Pythagoreans from Plato.

In the *Metaphysics* Aristotle has two related criticisms of the Pythagoreans. First, he complains that they confuse the arithmetical unit with a material magnitude. Second, he objects to their view that the one is generated or constructed and taunts them for not being able to say out of what it is constructed. He is emphatic that they explicitly say that it is constructed and that after it was constructed it started to draw in the unlimited (1091a15):

φανερῶς γὰρ λέγουσιν ὡς τοῦ ἑνὸς συσταθέντος, εἴτ' ἐξ ἐπιπέδων εἴτ' ἐκ χροιᾶς εἴτ' ἐκ σπέρματος εἴτ' ἐξ ὧν ἀποροῦσιν εἰπεῖν, εὐθὺς τὸ ἔγγιστα τοῦ ἀπείρου ὅτι εἵλκετο καὶ ἐπεραίνετο ὑπὸ τοῦ πέρατος.

For they clearly say that after the one was constructed, whether out of planes, or surfaces, or a seed, or out of they know not what, immediately the closest part of the unlimited began to be drawn in and limited by the limit.

Aristotle almost always refers to the Pythagoreans as a group and seldom to individual Pythagoreans, but what he says here seems to be commentary on F7 of Philolaus. In that fragment there does indeed seem to be a generation of "the one," although the fragment breaks off before any description of the breathing in of the unlimited.

τὸ πρᾶτον ἁρμοσθέν, τὸ ἕν ἐν τῷ μέσῳ τᾶς σφαίρας, ἑστία καλεῖται.

The first thing fitted together, the one in the center of the sphere, is called the hearth.

It may be that Philolaus gave a further account of how the one was fitted together either before or after this fragment, but it also may be that he said no more than what we have in F7. In that case, it would make sense as a target for Aristotle's attack, since it in fact provides no explicit account of the components from which the one is fitted together.

The apparent congruence of the Aristotelian account with F7 has led to what may be said to be the standard account of Pythagorean cosmogony. This account is well represented by Charles Kahn and maintains, following Aristotle, that:

> ... the primitive One was conceived not as an abstract unit or number but as a unit with position or "a monad with magnitude" (*Met.* 1080b20). Thus there is no distinction between the arithmetic and geometric unit, nor between mathematical points and physical and sensible bodies: The same process that generates the numbers will generate geometrical solids and the visible heavens. (1974: 173)

This process is then explained by appeal to Aristotle who says both that the unlimited was breathed in and limited by the limit and that the *void* was breathed in and was thought to be a distinguishing and separation of things (*Ph.* 213b22). Kahn suggests that this is best understood by thinking in terms of the Pythagorean pebble arithmetic. There the numbers are generated by the reproduction of units (pebbles) with space in between. The dots are analogous to "the unit or limiting principle; the space between them represents the unlimited void or breath that has been 'drawn in and limited.'" On this view, then, the one that is fitted together in F7 is equated with the limiting principle and is conceived of as a "monad with position" devoid of any other characteristics. However, a close reading both of F7 and of Aristotle's testimony raises serious problems for this view.

The first thing to recognize is that F7 is a cosmological fragment and not a fragment dealing with the generation of the number series. This is clear from the fact that the subject of the sentence, "the first thing harmonized," is called "the hearth" and is said to be located in "the center of the sphere." Now the testimonia about Philolaus and Aristotle's own reports about the Pythagoreans make perfectly clear that what was located in the center of their spherical cosmos was the central fire. It seems certain then that when Philolaus talks about something coming to be in the center of the sphere and calls that something "the hearth" he must be referring to the central fire. But, as soon as we recognize this, the traditional Aristotelian interpretation of the fragment goes up in flames, so to speak. For, however bemused by number speculation we might want to suppose Philolaus to be, it is impossible to imagine that he confused the arithmetical unit with the central fire. For if he did, his arithmetical unit is more than a bare monad with position; it is also fiery and orbited by ten bodies.

The standard view also presupposes the identification of the one in F7 with the principle of limit which limits the void that is breathed in. But this assumption too is simply not in accord with F7 or indeed with the most reasonable reading of Aristotle's evidence. Philolaus' central thesis about the cosmos is that "Nature in the world-order was fitted together out of limiters and unlimiteds, both the world-order as a whole and everything in it" (F1). In F6 he makes clear that the role of "fitting together" (ἀρμονία) in his system is to hold together the unlike elements, limiters and unlimiteds. Thus, when the one is said to be fitted together in F7, this clearly means that the one in question (i.e. the central fire) is a compound of limiters and unlimiteds and cannot be identified with the limiting principle alone. Further, as Burkert (1972: 36 n. 38) and Stokes (1971: 245, 338 n. 27) have already argued, there is no explicit testimony in Aristotle to support the view that the one is to be identified with the principle of limit, whereas he supplies unambiguous evidence that it was regarded as a compound of limiter and unlimited and that the numerical one was regarded as a compound of even and odd (*Metaph.* 986a17–20 and F199). The passages that some have thought to *imply* the equation of the one with limit are in fact best explained as Aristotle thinking in Platonic terms, since they fly in the face of direct testimony to the contrary in Aristotle and in F5 and F7 of Philolaus.

The passage at *Metaph.* 987a16 is particularly revealing of Aristotle's treatment of the relationship between the one, limiters, and unlimiteds.

> The Pythagoreans while they likewise spoke of two principles, made this further addition, which is peculiar to them; they believed not that the Limited and Unlimited and the One are separate entities, like fire or water or some other such thing, but that the Unlimited itself and the One itself are the essence of those things of which they are predicated, and hence that number is the essence of all things. (tr. Tredennick)

Since Aristotle introduces the passage by talking about two principles, it may seem odd that he goes on to list three, the limited, the unlimited, and the one. Because of this and since only one of the major manuscripts (A^b) includes "and the one" (καὶ τὸ ἕν) some scholars have excluded it from the text (e.g. Ross). If "and the one" is excluded, then the passage would first mention the pair limited–unlimited and in the next sentence refer to them as one–unlimited which would clearly equate the one with the principle of limit. However, as Burkert emphasizes, Alexander (*Met.* 47.11) read "and the one" (καὶ τὸ ἕν) even though it would be natural for a later Platonist to equate the one with limit. This tells strongly in favor of keeping it in the text. Furthermore, it is possible to read the passage as an instance of Aristotle listing the primary pair of principles used by the Pythagoreans (limit and unlimited) to fit them into his characterization of the Presocratics as having developed just two principles, but also going on to list other principles that they used, such as the one and numbers. Aristotle's testimony here does accord in a way with what we find in the fragments since Philolaus there posits an ultimate pair of principles, limiters and unlimiteds, but also goes on to specify a third principle, *harmonia*, and to emphasize the role of number in making things intelligible. The Pythagoreans simply do not fit into Aristotle's scheme that assigns the discovery of only two principles to the Presocratics and the awkwardness of this passage is an indication of the misfit.

However, Aristotle's report on the Pythagoreans here is not only distorted by his over-generalization about the Presocratics' treatment of causes, it is also influenced by the comparison with Plato. In Plato there are two primary principles, the one and the indefinite dyad. Aristotle consistently tries to equate these with the Pythagoreans' limiters and unlimiteds. He recognizes that Plato's unlimited is distinct from the Pythagoreans' unlimited in that for Plato it consists of a dyad, the great and the small, whereas the Pythagoreans mention no such duality. However, he does not equally recognize that Plato's one cannot be equated with Pythagorean limiters and often, consciously or unconsciously, slides from talking about the Pythagorean principle of limit to talking about the one. That is what seems to be happening in this passage of the *Metaphysics*, where he first of all correctly lists the one as distinct from limiters and unlimiteds, but then goes on a few lines later to mention only the one and the unlimited on the clear assumption that for the Pythagoreans as for Plato the one and limit are equivalent. However, Aristotle's own constant assertion that the Pythagoreans constructed the one, an assertion that is borne out by F7 of Philolaus, shows that this assumption is wrong, since if the one is a compound it cannot be identified with an ultimate principle such as the limit.

It should be clear then that both the assumptions of the standard account of Pythagorean cosmogony, first that what comes to be in the center of the sphere is a bare "monad with position" and second that this monad is to be equated with the principle of limit, are incompatible with the cosmogony described in Philolaus. We might assume then that Aristotle is talking about some other Pythagoreans but, since there are such clear similarities between Philolaus and Aristotle's account, it is more likely that he is interpreting Philolaus under Platonic influence, as outlined above. My view is that what is being described in F7 is not the generation of the arithmetical unit, but a cosmogony beginning with the central fire which, like everything else that comes to be, is a compound of limiters and unlimiteds. There are, however, several things that need to be explained before this view can be accepted. The first problem concerns

Philolaus' calling the central fire "the one." I have argued that this one cannot be equated with a Platonic one (= limit) but have not given any explanation of what Philolaus in fact means by the one. This is an important problem because it is surely the mention of the one here that is the basis for the standard, Aristotelian, interpretation. Furthermore, it is still necessary to explain what connection there is between the generation of the cosmos and the generation of numbers. If Philolaus is not equating (or confusing, as Aristotle would say) the generation of the arithmetical unit with a material magnitude, how are numbers tied to cosmogony, for Aristotle's testimony and the fragments of Philolaus clearly suggest a connection?

In analyzing Philolaus' use of "the one" in F7, the first point to remember is that the Presocratics frequently talked about things as being one and Melissus even refers to *the* one. It is surely better to interpret Philolaus' usage in light of this Presocratic background than in light of the theory of the one in Plato's Academy. Plato may have been influenced by Philolaus, but Philolaus' own roots are in the Presocratic tradition. It is impossible to give any sort of complete account of Presocratic usage of "one" here (see Stokes 1971). In the commentary on F7 I have examined some of the passages in Heraclitus, Empedocles, and Melissus that provide the background for Philolaus' usage here. Those passages show that both Empedocles and Heraclitus describe a one that is the result of a fitting together (ἁρμονία) of disparate elements in a very similar way to F7 of Philolaus. Accordingly the most natural interpretation of the one in Philolaus is simply as referring to a concrete unity of disparate elements (i.e. the central fire) with no reference at all to an arithmetical unit. Many scholars have seen the atomists as responding to Melissus' assertion that if reality consisted of a plurality of entities "it is necessary that they be exactly such as I say the one (τὸ ἕν) to be" (F8). Philolaus can likewise be seen as writing in light of Melissus' assertion, although we can hardly be confident of his chronological relationship to Melissus and hence of whether he knew of Melissus' work. Clearly for Melissus "the one" is the only reality, the only thing that satisfies the conditions for intelligible existence. The atomists replaced "the one" with a plurality of entities, but each of these satisfies crucial criteria for existence (they are full, admit of no internal distinctions, do not change internally, etc.). In the same way Philolaus postulates a plurality of existents but his basic unit is the unity of limiter and unlimited held together by a *harmonia* that is completely intelligible in so far as it can be expressed by a mathematical relationship. The crucial requirement for existence is intelligibility and this for the Eleatics is based on invariability. Philolaus proposes that each combination of limiters and unlimiteds is fully intelligible in so far as that combination is a *harmonia* that can be expressed by mathematical relationships which have the requisite invariability. Thus, when Philolaus calls the central fire, the first thing put together by *harmonia*, the one, he is saying that it is the paradigm case of something that truly exists, a paradigm that will be embodied again and again in the further generation of the cosmos from limiters and unlimiteds.

It may well seem to those who are used to understanding Pythagorean cosmology in terms of Aristotle's account that my interpretation of "the one" in Philolaus twists the obvious reference to the arithmetical unit. But the point is that it is only after Plato and Aristotle that reference to "the one" naturally suggests the arithmetical unit. In the Presocratic tradition in which Philolaus must be read, reference to "the one" would have no such connotations, and if Philolaus intended his readers to understand that he was talking about a mathematical unit he would have had to be much more explicit. But how then could Aristotle be so mistaken? I would want to argue that Aristotle had very little specific interest in the Pythagoreans (at least in treatises such as the *Metaphysics* – the special treatises devoted to the Pythagoreans, of which we have only fragments, are another matter) and thus mentions them primarily in their connection to Plato. He is careful to distinguish some differences between Plato and the Pythagoreans, but is still susceptible to treating some of their views as identical. Thus, while correctly observing the important role of mathematics for the Pythagoreans, and recognizing that they did not separate mathematicals from things as Plato did, he still overinterpreted the role of "the one" in Pythagoreanism in light of its importance in Plato. But what then is the connection between "the One" in Pythagorean cosmogony and "the One" in mathematics, if Philolaus does not equate them?

In order to answer this question it may be helpful to look at the range of possibilities that Aristotle considers for the relation between things and mathematicals at *Metaphysics* 1076a32ff (see Annas 1976; Burnyeat 1987). He identifies four basic possibilities: (1)

mathematicals do not exist; (2) mathematicals exist in sensibles, but are distinct from them; (3) mathematicals exist separately from sensibles; (4) mathematicals exist in another manner. It is clear that the Pythagoreans rejected the first possibility, and Aristotle makes plain that they did not follow Plato in adopting the third. Aristotle justifiably regards the second possibility as quite confused and himself argues for a version of (4). It would appear that on Aristotle's view the Pythagoreans adopted still a fifth possibility, that things and mathematicals were identical, and he may see this as involving some of the confusions of (2) above.

The problem is that the Pythagoreans are unlikely to have sorted out the question of the metaphysical status of mathematicals in anything like the clear way suggested by Aristotle's schema. However, Aristotle's testimony in another place may help bring some clarity. He says that the Pythagoreans noticed "similarities" between numbers and things (ὁμοιώματα – *Metaph.* 985b27). Moreover, the fragments do suggest that Philolaus saw a parallelism between the basic principles of numbers and the basic principles of the world. Since he was impressed with the cognitive reliability of numerical and mathematical relationships, he took advantage of this parallelism by suggesting that understanding mathematical relationships can provide us with secure knowledge of the world that they parallel. The fragments show that Philolaus then saw things as somehow "giving signs of" or "pointing to" numbers (σημαίνει – F5), but the fragments do not at all support the further step that Aristotle took of arguing that the Pythagoreans identified numbers and things. It seems likely that Philolaus simply was not clear on the relationship between things and numbers, but that he did reject the separate existence of numbers and rather found them to be in some sense directly tied to things. Aristotle took this unclarity in the worst possible fashion and concluded that the Pythagoreans identified numbers and things, but it is just as plausible to conclude that Philolaus was taking the first steps towards a view closer to Aristotle's, in which numbers are seen as telling us something important about things and as existing in a way, but not as having independent existence.

F7, then, describes the first step in the generation of the cosmos. This coming to be is a combination of limiter and unlimited as is all coming to be in Philolaus. In this case the unlimited fire is combined with the limiting notions inherent in the structure of the sphere, especially the notion of a center, and the result is the central fire. The central fire is called the one in so far as it is the primeval unity, the paradigm case of unity in the cosmos. There is, of course, no real account of what brings this combination about; it is simply asserted. Then the primeval ball of fire attracts breath and other unlimiteds (e.g. time and void) from the surrounding unlimited and these are combined with limiters to produce the famous Pythagorean cosmos described in the *De caelo*. However, these combinations do not occur in a haphazard way but they are fitted together ("harmonized") according to mathematical proportions, and accordingly the cosmos is intelligible in terms of mathematics. If the cosmos is to be explained in terms of number there must be correspondences between numbers and things, such as the equation of even with unlimited and odd with limiters, as well as the unification of these opposing principles in an even-odd (the unit and proportions). To be sure the relationship of correspondences and similarities remains vague, but there is no good support for Aristotle's assertion that the Pythagoreans *identified* the creation of the material world with the generation of numbers and thought of the first step in the generation of the cosmos as identical with the generation of the arithmetical unit.

Up to this point I have concentrated on the interpretation of F7 and its relationship to Aristotle's accounts of Pythagorean cosmogony. In what follows I will conclude by providing an overview of Philolaus' cosmogony that takes into account F17 and looks forward to his famous astronomical system. It seems most reasonable to assume that F17 in fact came before F7 in Philolaus' book, in so far as it describes the general pattern or framework of the cosmogony while F7 actually describes the first thing generated. F17 begins by asserting that the cosmos is a unity and the next clause, by saying that it began to come to be at the *center*, shows that Philolaus conceived of that unity as the unity of a sphere. The fragment in effect introduces a set of basic limiting notions that will be combined with unlimiteds to produce the cosmos. It emphasizes the notion of a center and the symmetry of the sphere around that center such that the cosmos will be generated symmetrically around the center.

Although the fragment talks about the cosmos coming to be "upwards in the same way as downwards," the point is not that there is an absolute above and below in the cosmos, but rather that above and below "have the same relationship to the middle except that their positions are reversed." Philolaus would therefore seem to be saying that the terms above and below are adopted by convention and that whichever part of the sphere we label "above" will have the exact same relationship to the center as "below" but will be set opposite to what is "below." This point of view is closer to Plato than to Aristotle, although the context in which we find it in Philolaus is much different than the context of the discussion of above and below in Plato's *Timaeus* (see the commentary on F17).

F7 might have followed directly on F17 (a connective having dropped out in the transmission of the text). It describes the creation of the first individual unity, the central fire, as the first step in the generation of the overall unity that is the cosmos. This follows the pattern of F1 where we are told that both the cosmos as a whole and also everything in it are harmonious unities of limiters and unlimiteds. We would then expect that the rest of the cosmogony would describe the generation of the Pythagorean astronomical system, which we know from the *De caelo*, in terms of the combination of limiters and unlimiteds. Indeed, as has been mentioned above, Aristotle says that after the generation of the first unity more unlimiteds were "breathed in."

The most straightforward account of this part of the cosmogony is found in a fragment from the first book of Aristotle's special treatise devoted to the Pythagoreans (F201):

ἐν δὲ τῷ περὶ τῆς Πυθαγόρου φιλοσοφίας πρώτῳ γράφει [sc. Aristotle] τὸν μὲν οὐρανὸν εἶναι ἕνα, ἐπεισάγεσθαι δ᾽ ἐκ τοῦ ἀπείρου χρόνον τε καὶ πνοὴν καὶ τὸ κενὸν ὃ διορίζει ἑκάστων τὰς χώρας ἀεί.

In the first book of On the Philosophy of Pythagoras *he [sc. Aristotle] writes "the world is one, and from the unlimited time and breath were brought in, as well as the void which distinguishes the place of each thing in each case."*

The significance of this passage is that it shows that what was breathed in was not "the unlimited" but rather a series of unlimiteds. The realm of the unlimited is conceived of as being outside the heaven. As Aristotle says at *Ph.* 203a6 the Pythagoreans say that the unlimited "is in sensible things and that what exists outside the heaven is unlimited." It appears that what is outside the world is viewed as a sort of reservoir from which unlimiteds can be drawn.

Each of the three unlimiteds brought in has its own significance. The generation of the cosmos is seen as analogous to the birth of an animal. The basic mechanism is respiration and accordingly breath is one of the things that is brought in from the unlimited. The testimonia about Philolaus' embryology (A27) show clearly that there is a parallelism between the birth of human beings and the birth of the cosmos. Philolaus maintains that our bodies are composed solely of the hot when they are in the womb, but after birth the animal immediately draws in the cold breath outside and then pays it back like a debt (i.e. breathes out), thus starting the process of respiration. Just so the cosmos begins just from the hot, the central fire, which then draws in breath. This of course also introduces the basic element, air, and probably, judging by the analogy with the child, the element, cold.

Time is naturally brought in at this point since it will be involved in the measurement of the movement of the heavenly bodies. Void is portrayed as essential to produce plurality. In F201 it is said to distinguish the place of things and this seems to be the best interpretation of what Aristotle means at *Ph.* 213b24–5 when he says that void distinguishes (διορίζειν as in F201) the natures (φύσεις), especially since he glosses this statement by saying that void is a separation (χωρισμοῦ) and division (διορίσεως) of the continuous. It may well be that the void is seen as separating off bits of the central fire to produce the fires that constitute the fixed stars, planets and sun.

In both passages of the *Physics*, although not in F201, Aristotle goes on to tie this phase of the cosmogony to a mathematical parallel. At *Ph.* 203a10 he asserts that the unlimited is the even and that when this is taken up and limited by the odd it provides the unlimited for things. He then gives a somewhat obscure mathematical example of the even's power to produce the unlimited in terms of gnomons placed around the one. At *Ph.* 213b26–7 Aristotle says that void is also primary in numbers in that it distinguishes their nature. Here it is legitimate to think of the pebble arithmetic. Again these parallels are important for Philolaus in so far as he wants mathematics to *correspond* to the sensible world, but we must be wary of following Aristotle's lead in identifying the unlimited with the odd.

Once we have cleared away the distortions introduced by the Aristotelian interpretation, we can see more clearly both the connections with Ionian cosmogony and also what is so revolutionary about Philolaus. Even on the old interpretation of Pythagorean cosmogony scholars have pointed out that the image of the breathing in of unlimiteds clearly suggests that the cosmos was thought to be alive, as it was by the Milesians. There is clear evidence that the Milesians used the image of the seed and the growth of a plant to describe the generation of the cosmos, but Kahn suggests that the notion of cosmic respiration may also be Milesian in light of Anaximenes' comparison of cosmic breath with the human soul (1960/85: 97). However, when we recognize that the first step in Philolaus' cosmogony was the coming to be of the central fire and that the next stage involves interaction between fire and breath, the Milesian connection becomes clearer. The Milesians also had a central role for fire acting on air. This is particualry clear with Anaximander for whom fire grew around the air like bark (A10). Kahn also notes that the Milesian conception of a surrounding *apeiron* is adopted by the Pythagorean cosmogony, although it should be pointed out that in Philolaus there seems to be a plurality of unlimiteds that are drawn into the world. Thus, when it comes to a discussion of the material elements of the world – what Philolaus would call unlimiteds – and the mechanism of generation, he appears to be a good Ionian.

However, there is also something quite new about the Philolaic cosmogony. Philolaus takes another strain of earlier Greek thought, begun by Anaximander but neglected by some of his successors, that gave the world a pleasing geometric structure, and makes that emphasis on structure thematic. The extent to which Anaximander viewed the cosmos as spherical is controversial and some would argue that Parmenides is the first thinker to do so (Furley 1987: 23, 54). But while we have no clear picture of Parmenides' cosmos, in the Philolaic system we have a clearly articulated spherical and centrifocal cosmos. Philolaus takes the emphasis on pleasing structure found in Anaximander and Parmenides and brings it up to date by explicitly including the five planets in that structure for the first time (Simpl. *Cael.* 471.1). Even more importantly, he is the first thinker self-consciously to examine the role of structure in cosmology. Thus, in F17 he explores the consequences of the spherical shape for the traditional notions of up and down. But the best evidence of the revolution that Philolaus is starting is the fact that for the first time structural elements (limiters) are posited as first principles along with the traditional material elements like air and the hot (unlimiteds). The fact that the central fire is in the center of a spherical cosmos is just as important as that it is fiery. There is some insight in the ancient slander directed against Plato which said that he cribbed the *Timaeus* from Philolaus (DK 44A1).

Fragment 17

Stobaeus, *Eclogae* 1.15.7 (1.148.4 Wachsmuth) Φιλολάου Βάκχαι· ὁ κόσμος εἷς ἐστιν, ἤρξατο δὲ γίγνεσθαι ἄχρι τοῦ μέσου καὶ ἀπὸ τοῦ μέσου εἰς τὸ ἄνω διὰ τῶν αὐτῶν τοῖς κάτω, ⟨καὶ⟩ ἔστι τὰ ἄνω τοῦ μέσου ὑπεναντίως κείμενα τοῖς κάτω. τοῖς γὰρ
5 κάτω τὸ κατωτάτω μέρος ἐστὶν ὥσπερ τὸ ἀνωτάτω καὶ τὰ ἄλλα ὡσαύτως. πρὸς γὰρ τὸ μέσον κατὰ ταὐτά ἐστιν ἑκάτερα, ὅσα μὴ μετενήνεκται.

2 ἄχρι MSS ἀπὸ Meineke   3 ⟨καὶ⟩ Wachsmuth   4 ἔστι ⟨γὰρ⟩ Diels   5 μέρος Wachsmuth μέγα MSS τοῖς γὰρ κατωτάτω τὰ μέσα (Canter) ἐστὶν Diels   τὸ ἀνωτάτω P τῷ ἀνωτάτω F τὰ ἀνωτάτω Diels

From the *Bacchae* of Philolaus: The world-order is one. It began to come to be right up at the middle and from the middle ⟨came to be⟩ upwards in the same way as downwards and the things above the middle are symmetrical with those below. For, in the lower ⟨regions⟩ the lowest part ⟨for the upper regions⟩ is like the highest and similarly for the rest. For both ⟨the higher and the lower⟩ have the same relationship to the middle, except that their positions are reversed.

AUTHENTICITY

There are two difficulties that can be raised about the authenticity of this fragment. First, it is written in Ionic dialect rather than the Doric in which the rest of the authentic fragments are composed. Second, it has some similarities to the discussion of up and down in the *Timaeus*, which might lead us to think it was a post-Platonic forgery. Neither difficulty is conclusive, however, and the comparison with Plato in fact gives strong indications that the fragment is authentic.

The lack of the Doric features is bothersome, but given that there are no serious grounds for doubt in the contents of the fragment, it is not too implausible to suppose that the Doric features were leached out in the transmission. This is especially plausible since, given the particular forms in the fragment (note especially the predominance of neuter forms), there would be little difference between a Doric and Ionic version. (Note that genitives in -ου are found in a number of the other fragments [F13, F4], either representing what Philolaus wrote or the effects of transmission, so that they are no grounds for suspicion here in F17.) Boeckh (1819: 90ff) solved the problem by supposing that the fragment was in fact an epitome of a passage of Philolaus made by a later excerptor writing in Ionic. He also tries to explain some of the obscurity of the fragment as arising through the shortening of the passage and its recasting by the excerptor. However, the awkwardness of the fragment seems to be sufficiently explained by the fact that it is a first attempt to express a difficult concept.

The content of the passage is paralleled by a section of the *Timaeus*. Bywater (1868: 52) sets the two passages side by side and simply asserts that whole sentences echo Plato, without doing any analysis. But when the two passages are examined carefully, while there is some general agreement in doctrine, it is clear that the Philolaus passage does not fit the mold of the Platonizing forgeries in the Pythagorean tradition. In fact, apart from the use of some of the same single words, such as "up," "down," and "center," which was inevitable given a similarity in subject matter, there is not a single example of a phrase even two words long that is common to the two passages. If F17 is supposed to be composed on the basis of the *Timaeus*, it is particularly odd that it makes no mention of the "extremities" of the cosmos (ἔσχατα) or the "circumference" (πέριξ), which are central to Plato's account. Similarly, Plato's frequently used words for "to be distant from" (ἀφίστημι) and "opposite" (καταντικρύ) are found nowhere in Philolaus F17.

Even more important than these differences in detail is a radical difference in the means of presentation of the basic idea that the notions of up and down in the cosmos are relative. The Platonic passage (*Ti.* 62c3ff) discusses up and down in relation to light and heavy, and this pairing of the two opposites is picked up again in the Aristotelian discussion of the *Timaeus* passage at *De caelo* 4.1, 308a15. The later pseudo-Pythagorean tradition keeps this connection, as can be seen in *Timaeus Locrus* 53–4:

βαρὺ δὲ καὶ κοῦφον ἀφὰ μὲν προκρίνει, λόγος δ' ὁρίζει τᾷ ποτὶ τὸ μέσον καὶ ἀπὸ τῶ μέσω νεύσει. κάτω δὲ καὶ μέσον ταὐτόν φαντι. τὸ γὰρ κέντρον τᾶς σφαίρας τοῦτό ἐντι τὸ κάτω, τὸ δ' ὑπὲρ τούτω ἄχρι τᾶς περιφερείας ἄνω.

Touch distinguishes the heavy and the light, and reason defines them by inclination to and from the center. They say that down and the middle are the same. For this center of the sphere is down and that ⟨region⟩ which is above this, reaching to the circumference, is up.

Furthermore, note that this passage of *Timaeus Locrus* agrees with Aristotle in the *De caelo*, against Plato, that the center and down are the same whereas the periphery is up. Plato argues that "up" and "down" are strictly relative concepts and that no part of the cosmos is to be properly called "up" any more than "down."

On the other hand, F17 discusses the notion of the relativity of up and down with no mention of light and heavy, and does not make the equations of down and center and up and periphery that are found in Aristotle and *Timaeus Locrus*. Burkert found the closest parallel to Philolaus in a passage from the pseudo-Hippocratic treatise *On Sevens* which says that "The earth lying at the center of the cosmos... rides on air so that for those below up is down and down is up" (κατὰ μέσον δὲ τὸν κόσμον ἡ γῆ κειμένη ... ἐν τῷ ἠέρι ὀχέεται, ὥστε τοῖσι κάτω τὰ δὲ μέντοι ἄνω κάτω εἶναι, τὰ δὲ κάτω ἄνω. See Mansfeld [1971: 62] for a defense of this text). Since Burkert regarded *On Sevens* as a fifth-century document (1972: 269), he saw this correspondence as strong support for the fifth-century date of F17 and hence its authenticity. However, Mansfeld (1971) has shown very convincingly that *On Sevens* in fact is a late document which probably originated in the first century BC. What then are we to make of the similarity between the passage in *On Sevens* and Philolaus F17?

Mansfeld solved this problem by arguing that F17 is spurious and thus of a late origin like *On Sevens* (1971: 62–3). He suggests that it could be connected with the spurious second half of Philolaus A16 where a geocentric system is ascribed to Philolaus. However, Mansfeld's arguments against the authenticity of F17 are not in the end convincing. Besides mentioning the dialect problem which I have discussed above, Mansfeld makes two points. The first point is that in Philolaus' system it is very unlikely that the opposite side of the earth is inhabited, since that side is turned towards the counter-earth (and central fire), and inhabitants of our earth are said never to see the counter-earth or central fire. The second point is that the fragment apparently speaks in terms of a central earth because it puts great emphasis on the middle of the universe.

The problem here is that Mansfeld is assuming that F17 is adopting a doctrine of antipodes, i.e. that the opposite side of the earth is inhabited and that accordingly people there walk upside down from our point of view, with their feet placed opposite to ours. Of course such a doctrine does lend itself to the idea of the relativity of up and down. Anaximander (A11) seems to be the earliest to discuss the idea of the antipodes, although in his case, where the earth is drum-shaped, the point may simply be that there are two flat surfaces on the earth which are opposed to each other, without implying that the side opposite to ours is inhabited. Likewise there is no direct evidence that Anaximander made a point about the relativity of up and down (Mansfeld 1971: 62 and see Kahn 1960/85: 84ff). Plato alludes to the idea of someone walking around the earth and makes the earliest clear reference to the idea of someone standing with feet opposed to ours (*Ti.* 63a2), and later the pseudo-Pythagorean *Hypomnemata* of Alexander Polyhistor adopts a doctrine of antipodes and adds the point about the relativity of up and down (D.L. 8.25ff, εἶναι δὲ καὶ ἀντίποδας καὶ τὰ ἡμῖν κάτω ἐκείνοις ἄνω).

The problem is that nothing in F17 indicates that Philolaus is talking about the antipodes or, indeed, that he is talking about the earth at all. F17 focuses on the cosmos as a whole, which it asserts to be a unity, and in particular on the generation of the cosmos. It asserts that this generation began at the center and proceded in a symmetrical fashion outwards from the center. There is no reason at all to assume that what is in the center is the earth rather than Philolaus' famous central fire. Indeed, the emphasis on the center of the sphere as the starting-point for the generation of the cosmos here in F17 exactly accords with what we find in F7 of Philolaus, where the "first thing fitted together" is specifically said to be in the center of the sphere and to be called the hearth (a clear reference to the central fire). The points that Philolaus makes about the relativity of up and down are made in terms of the cosmos as a whole, and used to support the idea that the universe came to be in a symmetrical fashion around the center rather than just growing "up" or "down." The notion seems to be that, if no region is any more up or down than any other, then there is no good reason for it to develop differently in one direction than another.

It may be that Mansfeld interpreted the datives in the second sentence of F17 as referring to the inhabitants of the earth ("For to those ⟨people⟩ below the lowest part is like the highest and similarly for the rest," τοῖς γὰρ κάτω ...). Indeed, the datives which occur in *On Sevens* (τοῖσι κάτω – note the following reference to right and left) and in Alexander Polyhistor (τὰ ἡμῖν κάτω ἐκείνοις ἄνω) and which are the main point of parallelism with Philolaus F17 clearly do refer to the people who inhabit the opposite side of the earth. However, F17 uses the same dative phrase (τοῖς κάτω) twice in the first sentence of the fragment, where it is clear that it simply means "the things below" (notice the contrast between "the things above," τὰ ἄνω and "the things below," τοῖς κάτω). The phrase has this same sense in the second sentence of the fragment, where the point is that, taking a viewpoint in the lower regions (τοῖς κάτω), the region that was the lowest from the perspective of the upper regions is the highest and *vice versa*.

The upshot of this discussion is to make clear that F17 does not make the point of the relativity of up and down in terms of the doctrine of the antipodes, and hence Mansfeld's objections to its authenticity, which assume that doctrine to be in the fragment, have no force. The discussion also shows that the passage in *On Sevens* and the passage in Alexander Polyhistor which bear some similarity to F17 are not in fact as similar as they first appeared. They do share the use of the expression τοῖς κάτω with Philolaus, but this is not a striking usage and is just a typical way for a Greek to refer to "those below" or "the regions below." More importantly they both differ from F17 in that they make the point about the relativity of up and down in terms of the antipodes idea and thus would seem to be ultimately dependent on Plato who is apparently the first to use the antipodes idea in relation to up and down.

The points made above seem to me to respond to all the major doubts raised about the authenticity of the fragment. On the more positive side, the discussion above also indicates that F17 fits in very well with the other genuine fragments of Philolaus. It is particularly noteworthy that it lays the same emphasis on the fact that the cosmos is generated as the other fragments (and contra some of the pseudepigrapha such as Ocellus and Philolaus 21, which assert the eternity of the world), and specifically that the cosmos starts to come to be at the center as is emphasized in F7. It is also important to note that in a fragment from Aristotle's special treatise on the Pythagoreans he reports that for the Pythagoreans "the heaven is one" (τὸν μὲν οὐρανὸν εἶναι ἕνα..., F201) which is very plausibly to be taken as based on the first line of F17, "the world-order is one" (ὁ κόσμος εἷς ἐστιν), and which would thus guarantee that F17 is from Philolaus' genuine book.

COMMENTARY

ὁ κόσμος εἷς ἐστιν: κόσμος here is used to refer to the entire world-order. This is the same use as we find in F1 where there is a contrast between ὅλος ⟨ὁ⟩ κόσμος and τὰ ἐν αὐτῷ πάντα. What sort of a statement is Philolaus making about the world-order when he says that it is "one"? Clearly he is not advocating a holistic monism, i.e. asserting that the world is just one thing with no parts or structure, in the way that Melissus does (F5, 6, 9, etc.), since none of the other fragments even hint at such a monism but rather seem gladly to embrace a plurality of entities. He is asserting that the world is a unity, i.e. there is a coherent structure that embraces it all, and that there is just one such unity. This is similar to what Heraclitus means when he says that "all things are one" (F50), i.e. that "all things...are united in a coherent complex" (KRS 187). Empedocles also talks of the four elements coming into "one order" (εἰς ἕνα κόσμον) through love, which once again does not suggest monism but a plurality of elements held in an order. The rest of F17 clearly envisages the world as a sphere and as there-fore having the uniform nature of a sphere. This uniformity is in fact the theme of the fragment, which stresses that it came to be in the same way above as it did below and that any side of the sphere can be viewed as top or bottom.

ἤρξατο δὲ γίγνεσθαι ἄχρι τοῦ μέσου καὶ ἀπὸ τοῦ μέσου εἰς τὸ ἄνω διὰ τῶν αὐτῶν τοῖς κάτω: The first problem here is ἄχρι. In itself the word is not problematic since, although it is rare in the Presocratics, it is fairly common in the Hippocratic writings of the late fifth century. However, most com-mentators have felt uneasy with the construction in which it is used here, probably because one usually expects reference to an extension of space with a starting-point from which one moves "as far as" (ἄχρι) something else. So in Aristotle's *History of Animals* he talks of the cleft in the foot of the camel reaching "as far as" the first joint of the toes (499a26). But here in Philolaus the sense seems to be that the cosmos started to come to be *at* the center with no reference to any extension in space until the next clause, so that ἄχρι appears to be used of the starting-point rather than the end "as far as" which the generation goes. Accordingly Diels followed Meineke in reading ἀπὸ for ἄχρι. However, Burkert is clearly right that this produces a very awkward repetition with the ἀπό in the next clause and it is very hard to account for the ἄχρι of the manuscripts.

Burkert seems to want to take ἄχρι in a temporal sense and suggests that "Perhaps ἄχρι could be understood in relation to a primary phase of cosmic development, 'as far as the middle,' i.e. until the middle is formed (τὸ πρᾶτον ἁρμοσθέν)" (1972: 268 n. 142). Boeckh's translation (1819: 91) may be on the same lines – "bis zur vollendeten Mitte" – but this does not make sense to me. What does it mean to say that "the cosmos began to come to be until the middle was formed"? The passage is difficult but it seems best to take ἄχρι spatially and translate "the cosmos began to come to be *right up at* the middle." Philolaus is viewing the spherical cosmos from the outside and is stressing that it started to come to be at the very center. Such a point of view is perhaps appropriate for someone like Philolaus who does not regard the earth as in the center of the world-order and who therefore thinks of the center as removed from us. This sense of ἄχρι used by itself is not easy to parallel elsewhere in Greek, but some uses suggest that, although it is commonly used to mean simply "as far as" and is equivalent to μέχρι, it sometimes emphasizes going to the extreme or to the limit more than μέχρι. Thus at *HA* 499a26 Aristotle describes the cloven feet of the camel. The back feet are said to have a small cleft reaching as far as (μέχρι) the second joint of the toe, while the front feet are said to have a long cleft and this is emphasized by saying that it reaches "right along as far as" (ὅσον ἄχρι, tr. Peck) the first joint of the toes (see also Thphr. *Char.* 19.3 and *Reg. in Act.* 3.12). This connotation of the word can also be seen in its adverbial usage "to the uttermost" (see LSJ s.v.). The translation I have given above ("right up at the middle") might in fact work more easily if we emended the text so that ἄχρι was used adverbially with a preposition as it is in many places in Greek (see LSJ). Thus, we might suppose that the text was originally ἄχρι ἐπὶ τῷ μέσῳ, which would give the sense which I have translated above. It is not at all implausible to suppose that either ἐπί fell out in transmission or that a scribe was bothered by what appeared to be two prepositions in a row. In either case, after the loss of ἐπί, it would be natural for τῷ μέσῳ to be changed to a genitive so as to go with ἄχρι.

διὰ τῶν αὐτῶν: This phrase must be taken adverbially. The world comes to be upwards "in the same way as" downwards. This is a typical use of διά with a noun in the genitive to indicate manner, see LSJ s.v. A.3c and Epicharmus F1. Boeckh has the implausible "aus denselben Dingen" ("from the same things") while DK has "in denselben Abständen" ("in the same intervals") which is better, but Philolaus says nothing about "intervals".

⟨καὶ⟩ ἔστι τὰ ἄνω τοῦ μέσου ὑπεναντίως κείμενα τοῖς κάτω: Wachsmuth's suggestion ⟨καὶ⟩, which Burkert reads, seems slightly preferable to Diels's ἔστι ⟨γάρ⟩. Some conjunction is needed, but this clause seems rather to expand on and further explain the previous clause than to provide evidence for it.

The major difficulty in understanding this passage is determining the construction of the genitive τοῦ μέσου. Does it depend on τὰ ἄνω, as the translation in DK suggests ("was oben liegt von der Mitte aus" – "the parts above from the center...," Freeman 1971) or does it go with ὑπεναντίως, as Burkert argues ("What is above is that which is over against the middle...," [1972: 269 n. 145]). Neither of these constructions is very common and the passage could be construed in either way. Burkert gives parallels for ὑπεναντίως with the genitive from Herodotus (3.80; 7.153), but it is much more common for it to take the dative (see LSJ and Bonitz's index to Aristotle). Since ἄνω is used as a preposition with the genitive it seems very possible Greek to have τὰ ἄνω τοῦ μέσου meaning "the things above the middle." However, there are not many precise parallels for such a use (Hdt. 1.142).

Since the preceding passage as a whole seems to presuppose a viewpoint outside the spherical cosmos, it is slightly preferable to take the genitive as dependent on τὰ ἄνω, since this makes the point about the symmetry of the cosmos from the point of view of a neutral observer. If the genitive depends on ὑπεναντίως the point is made from the point of view of "those below," and such a switch in perspective does not seem justified.

τοῖς γὰρ κάτω τὸ κατωτάτω μέρος ἐστὶν ὥσπερ τὸ ἀνωτάτω καὶ τὰ ἄλλα ὡσαύτως: There are serious difficulties about the text here, but the text defended by Burkert (1972: 268 n. 144) makes most sense of the passage with the least change in the manuscript reading. The μέγα of the manuscripts produces nonsense, but Wachsmuth's μέρος, which Burkert follows, produces a good sense. Diels read μέσα (following Canter) which also calls for changes in the earlier part of the sentence and, as Burkert points out, does away with the reversal in direction presupposed by the last sentence of the fragment (μετενήνεκται). On Diels's reading the middle will turn out to be "the highest" for anyone on the circumference. Burkert's view is that from the point of view of "the bottom" of the sphere the region that is lowest (from the point of view of the top of the sphere) i.e. the bottom, is the highest and *vice versa*.

Boeckh (1819: 93) regards καὶ τὰ ἄλλα ὡσαύτως not as Philolaus' own words, but as introduced by an excerptor who is presenting this passage in a compressed form. However, there is no reason for Philolaus to go on to give further examples of his main point, and we may confidently assign these words to Philolaus.

κατὰ ταὐτά: This is a common adverbial phrase. See Powell (1966).

ἑκάτερα: sc. τὰ ἄνω καὶ τὰ κάτω

ὅσα μή: Boeckh (1819: 93) correctly glosses this as πλὴν ὅτι.

APPENDIX
Above and below, right and left in Aristotle's reports on the Pythagoreans

De caelo 2.2, 284b6   ἐπειδὴ δέ τινές εἰσιν οἳ φασιν εἶναί τι δεξιὸν καὶ ἀριστερὸν τοῦ οὐρανοῦ, καθάπερ οἱ καλούμενοι Πυθαγόρειοι (ἐκείνων γὰρ οὗτος ὁ λόγος ἐστίν) σκεπτέον...

Since there are some who say that there is a right and left to the heaven, just as the so-called Pythagoreans do (for this contention belongs to them), we must examine...

285a11   διὸ καὶ τῶν Πυθαγορείων ἄν τις θαυμάσειεν ὅτι δύο μόνας ταύτας ἀρχὰς ἔλεγον, τὸ δεξιὸν καὶ τὸ ἀριστερόν, τὰς δὲ τέτταρας παρέλιπον οὐθὲν ἧττον κυρίας οὔσας.

Wherefore someone might be surprised that the Pythagoreans mentioned these two principles alone, i.e. the right and the left, and omitted the other four [i.e. front, back, top, bottom], although they are no less important.

285a26   διά τε δὴ τὸ παραλείπειν τὰς κυριωτέρας ἀρχὰς δίκαιον αὐτοῖς ἐπιτιμᾶν, καὶ διότι ταύτας ἐν ἅπασιν ὁμοίως ἐνόμιζον ὑπάρχειν.

It is right to criticize them both because they left out the more important principles and because they thought that the principles which they did use belonged to all things alike.

285b25   ...ἐναντίως ἢ ὡς οἱ Πυθαγόρειοι λέγουσιν· ἐκεῖνοι γὰρ ἡμᾶς ἄνω τε ποιοῦσι καὶ ἐν τῷ δεξιῷ μέρει, τοὺς δ’ ἐκεῖ κάτω καὶ ἐν τῷ ἀριστερῷ. συμβαίνει δὲ τοὐναντίον.

...contrary to what the Pythagoreans say. For they put us above and in the right part, and put those down below also in the left. But the opposite is the case.

Aristotle, F200 (= Simplicius, in De caelo 386.9)   οἱ μὲν οὖν Πυθαγόρειοι εἰς δύο συστοιχίας πάσας τὰς ἀντιθέσεις ἀναγαγόντες...ἑκάστην ἀντίθεσιν τῶν δέκα οὕτω παρέλαβον ὡς πάσας τὰς ἑαυτῆς συγγενείας συνεμφαίνουσαν. καὶ τῶν τοπικῶν οὖν σχέσεων τὸ δεξιὸν καὶ
5   τὸ ἀριστερὸν παρέλαβον...(19) ἐκ τούτων καὶ τὰς ἄλλας τοπικὰς ἀντιθέσεις ἐδήλωσαν. τὸ οὖν δεξιὸν καὶ ἄνω καὶ ἔμπροσθεν ἀγαθὸν ἐκάλουν, τὸ δὲ ἀριστερὸν καὶ κάτω καὶ ὄπισθεν κακὸν ἔλεγον, ὡς αὐτὸς Ἀριστοτέλης ἱστόρησεν ἐν τῇ τῶν Πυθαγορείοις ἀρεσκόντων συναγωγῇ.

The Pythagoreans, having brought together all the oppositions into two paired columns... took each of the ten oppositions as also indicating all the oppositions related to it. And regarding spatial relations they used right and left... From these [right and left] they revealed all the other spatial relations. They called right, above, and in front good, but they said left, below, and behind were bad, as Aristotle himself reports in his collection of the doctrines of the Pythagoreans.

Aristotle F205 (= Simplicius, in De caelo 392.16–32)   πῶς δὲ τοὺς Πυθαγορείους ἡμᾶς ἄνω ποιεῖν φησι καὶ ἐν τῷ δεξιῷ, τοὺς δὲ ἐκεῖ κάτω καὶ ἐν τῷ ἀριστερῷ, εἴπερ, ὡς αὐτὸς ἐν τῷ δευτέρῳ τῆς συναγωγῆς τῶν Πυθαγορικῶν ἱστορεῖ, τοῦ ὅλου οὐρανοῦ τὸ μὲν ἄνω λέγουσιν
5   εἶναι τὸ δὲ κάτω, καὶ τὸ μὲν κάτω τοῦ οὐρανοῦ δεξιὸν εἶναι τὸ δὲ ἄνω ἀριστερόν, καὶ ἡμᾶς ἐν τῷ κάτω εἶναι; ἢ τὸ μὲν ἄνω καὶ πρὸς τοῖς

δεξιοῖς ἐνταῦθα λεγόμενον οὐ κατὰ τὸ ἑαυτῷ ἀρέσκον εἶπεν ἀλλὰ κατὰ
τοὺς Πυθαγορείους· ἐκεῖνοι γὰρ τῷ δεξιῷ τὸ ἄνω καὶ τὸ ἔμπροσθεν
συνέταττον, τῷ δὲ ἀριστερῷ τὸ κάτω καὶ τὸ ὄπισθεν. τὰ δὲ ἐν τῇ
10 τῶν Πυθαγορικῶν συναγωγῇ μεταγεγράφθαι μᾶλλον ὑπό τινος ὁ
Ἀλέξανδρος οἴεται ὀφείλοντα ἔχειν οὕτω, τὸ μὲν ἄνω τοῦ οὐρανοῦ
δεξιὸν εἶναι τὸ δὲ κάτω ἀριστερὸν καὶ ἡμᾶς ἐν τῷ ἄνω εἶναι, οὐχὶ ἐν τῷ
κάτω ὡς γέγραπται· οὕτω γὰρ ἂν συνάδοι τοῖς ἐνταῦθα λεγομένοις, ὅτι
ἡμεῖς κάτω λέγοντες οἰκεῖν καὶ διὰ τοῦτο καὶ ἐν τοῖς ἀριστεροῖς, εἴπερ τῷ
15 ἀριστερῷ τὸ κάτω συντέτακται, ἐναντίως λέγομεν ἢ ὡς οἱ Πυθαγόρειοι
λέγουσιν ἄνω καὶ ἐν τοῖς δεξιοῖς. καὶ τάχα ἔχει λόγον τὸ μεταγεγράφθαι,
εἴπερ οἶδεν ὁ Ἀριστοτέλης τῷ μὲν δεξιῷ τὸ ἄνω τῷ δὲ ἀριστερῷ τὸ
κάτω συντάττοντας.

Why does he say that the Pythagoreans put us above and on the right, and
those down below also on the left, if indeed, as he himself reports in the
second book of the collection of Pythagorean doctrines, they say that there
is an above and below of the whole heaven, and what is below in the
heaven is to the right, while what is above is to the left, and we are in
the region below? Or is the above and to the right spoken of here [in
the *De caelo*] not in accordance with his own theory but with that of the
Pythagoreans? For those people ranked together above and in front with
right, and below and behind with left. Alexander thinks that the text in
the collection of Pythagorean doctrines has instead been changed by someone and that it should be as follows, what is above in the heavens is right
and what is below is left and we are in what is above, and not in what is
below as has been written. For in this way it would fit with what is said
here [in the *De caelo*], i.e. in saying that we dwell below and on account
of this to the left, if indeed what is below has been ranked together with
left, we say the opposite of the Pythagoreans who say we are above and to
the right. And perhaps the argument that the text is corrupt is sound,
if indeed Aristotle knows that they ranked above with right and below with
left.

As can be seen from the texts above, Aristotle, at *De caelo* 2.2, 284b6ff,
says that the Pythagoreans distinguished a right and a left in the cosmos
and at the end of the chapter says that they thought that we live in the
upper and right part. Since F17 presents Philolaus' views on above and
below in the cosmos, this seems the natural place to discuss the relationship
of Aristotle's testimony to Philolaus. We do not have all of the cosmological
section of Philolaus' book and it is therefore impossible to be sure whether
he said anything about a right and a left side of the world or not. However,
the main thrust of F17 is that there really is no absolute above or below in
the heavens. What we conventionally call above and below in the heavens

in reality bear the same relation to the middle except that they have been reversed. If Philolaus has recognized the relativity of the notions of above and below in a spherical cosmos, it seems overwhelmingly likely that he would also regard right and left as relative. Thus, while Philolaus may use the conventional terms up and down in the fragment, it seems unlikely that he would in his book make any strong points about there being an (absolute) right, left, above, or below of the cosmos.

We might then begin to worry that Aristotle's treatment of the Pythagoreans as recognizing a right and a left and an up and a down in the cosmos casts suspicion on the authenticity of F17 which is clearly in conflict with this view. However, if we examine Aristotle's comments closely they make most sense if they are directed against the Pythagoreans who adopted the famous table of opposites. Moreover, Aristotle seems to distinguish these Pythagoreans from Philolaus. For at *Metaphysics* 986a23 he clearly indicates that the Pythagoreans who posited the table of opposites are different from the Pythagoreans whom he has been discussing up to that point. Philolaus must have been included among these Pythagoreans which Aristotle discussed first, and in fact he was probably the main person Aristotle had in mind, since their system included the concepts of limiters, unlimiteds, *harmonia*, and the astronomical system with the central fire, all of which are Philolaic ideas.

The first link between Aristotle's comments and the table of opposites appears when he complains that the Pythagoreans posited only the two opposites, right and left, without positing two other pairs of opposites that Aristotle considers to be prior to or just as important as right and left, namely above and below and front and back (285a11). Indeed, if we look at the table of opposites we find that only the pair right and left are included and that no mention of above and below or front and back is made.

The second connection is that Aristotle complains at 285a26ff that the pair of opposites, right and left, is applied to all things alike (and not just to living things which, in Aristotle's theory, are the only things admitting of right and left); and this seems to be precisely the force of the table of opposites, i.e. that the list of ten primary opposites is thought to apply to all parts of reality alike. For these reasons it seems to me that in this chapter of the *De caelo* Aristotle is primarily thinking of the Pythagoreans who made the table of opposites the center of their philosophy, but there are still some difficulties.

First, it is difficult to suppose that this chapter of the *De caelo* is based only on the Pythagorean assumption of the ten categories and their universal application. Aristotle must know of some oral or written assertion by the Pythagoreans that the cosmos as a whole has a right and a left; he cannot be deducing it himself from the universal application of the categories. Indeed, the later part of the *De caelo* says that in what the Pythagoreans *say* they put us above and in the right part (285b25). But this just introduces further difficulties because here the Pythagoreans are said to introduce the notion of "above" in their description of the cosmos, while Aristotle has just a few pages earlier said that they did not apply the opposition, above–below, to the cosmos.

Simplicius' commentary on the *De caelo* provides information from Aristotle's special treatise on the Pythagoreans (F200 and F205) which solves some of these problems. It is important to note first of all that Simplicius talks of two distinct passages from Aristotle's book on the Pythagoreans: (1) A passage in which Aristotle asserted that the Pythagoreans called right, above, and in front all good, and left, down, and behind all bad (F200). Simplicius' introduction to this passage and indeed the passage itself show that this is clearly a reference to the table of opposites. (2) A passage in which Aristotle reports that the Pythagoreans said that there was an above and below in the heavens, and that what was below was to the right and what was above was to the left, and that we are in the lower region. This latter passage clearly conflicts with what Aristotle says at the end of the *De caelo* (that the Pythageoreans put us above and to the right), and Simplicius is inclined to follow Alexander who supposed that the text of this second passage in Aristotle's treatise had been changed in transmission.

These two passages from Aristotle's treatise on the Pythagoreans to which Simplicius refers make it all but certain that the Pythagoreans who Aristotle says (in the *De caelo*) posited a right and a left of the heavens are in fact the Pythagoreans who developed the table of opposites, and not Philolaus. Certainly Simplicius interprets the passage in that way since he uses the passage about the table of opposites (F200) in order to support a reading of the passage about above, below, right, and left in the cosmos (F205). Moreover, Simplicius' testimony shows what I suggested above, that Aristotle is not just extrapolating from the table of opposites when he says that the Pythagoreans applied right and left to the heavens, but in F205 seems to be referring to some explicit statement to that effect in the Pythagoreans. It remains a puzzle as to why Aristotle in the *De caelo* first seems to chastise the Pythagoreans for only mentioning right and left and not above, below, in front, and behind, but then, at the end of the passage, asserts that the Pythagoreans did mention above in so far as they put us above and to the right in the cosmos.

Fragment 7

Stobaeus, *Eclogae* 1.21.8 (1.189.17 Wachsmuth) τὸ πρᾶτον ἁρμοσθέν, τὸ ἓν ἐν τῷ μέσῳ τᾶς σφαίρας, ἑστία καλεῖται.

The first thing fitted together, the one in the center of the sphere, is called the hearth.

AUTHENTICITY

The authenticity of the fragment seems secure for two reasons. First, it flies in the face of the Platonic postulation of the one and the indefinite dyad as basic principles in so far as the one mentioned here is not a basic principle, but something that is generated out of basic principles, something that is fitted together out of limiters and unlimiteds. Second, it coheres very well with Aristotle's reports on Pythagorean cosmology and in fact seems to be the text Aristotle is interpreting (incorrectly on my view) at *Metaphysics* 1091a13ff where he complains of the Pythagoreans for talking about the generation of an eternal body such as the one (see Pt. III, ch. 3).

COMMENTARY

Context in Stobaeus: This is the last in a string of five fragments (2, 4, 5, 6, and 7) preserved in chapter 21 of Stobaeus under the heading "On the cosmos and whether it is animate and arranged by providence and where it has its controlling factor and whence it is nourished." Testimonia A18 and A17b (spurious) are also found under this heading. There are no breaks in the text of the string of five fragments and it is possible that F7 followed immediately upon F6. Certainly the connection between the two fragments is very close. F6 argues for the necessity of a "fitting together" of limiters and unlimiteds in order for the world we know to come to be and F7 describes the first "fitting together" in Philolaus' actual cosmogony. However, F17 is best understood as coming before F7, since it gives the general framework within which the cosmogony takes place. It would then seem most natural to place F17 between F6 and F7.

τὸ πρᾶτον ἁρμοσθέν: As πρᾶτον shows, this fragment must be the first line of the account of the actual generation of the world. Given the basic principles that Philolaus outlines in the first part of his book, any generation would have to be a fitting together of a limiter and an unlimited, and that is just what is indicated here by ἁρμοσθέν, although Philolaus does not specify what the limiter and unlimited are in this case. Since the final product of the fitting together is the central fire, it is natural to see the fire as the unlimited component and the center of the sphere as the limiter.

τὸ ἓν ἐν τῷ μέσῳ : It is possible to see ἕν as dittography with the following ἐν and thus remove all reference to "the one" from the fragment (Burkert 1972: 255 n. 83). However, Aristotle's account of Pythagorean cosmogony (*Metaph.* 1091a13) clearly refers to the generation of a one (even if he misrepresents what is meant by this) and makes it very probable that we should keep the manuscript reading.

Aristotle's reading of the text clearly takes "the one" (τὸ ἕν) to refer to the arithmetical unit. However, this is likely to be a misreading influenced by his knowledge of the Platonic one and indefinite dyad (see Pt. III, ch. 3). Certainly we would never be tempted to read "the one" here as the arithmetical unit, just taking into consideration the Presocratic parallels. In the Presocratic context "the one" is more likely to refer to a unified whole of some sort. Thus, when Heraclitus tells us that "Listening not to me but to the Logos it is wise to agree that all things are one (F50 – ἓν πάντα εἶναι), his point is that the plurality of diverse things that we experience is in fact held together by a structure or coherence that gives them unity. It is striking that Heraclitus like Philolaus also associates this structure and unification with *harmonia* (F51 and F54). Empedocles likewise connects *harmonia* (= Love) with unity and describes the world as in constant oscillation between a unification in a sphere under the influence of Love (εἰς ἕνα κόσμον – F26) and complete separation of the elements under Strife (F17 and F31).

One might object that these parallels do not apply to Philolaus' use in F7 where the definite article is used ("the one"); however, there is also a Presocratic parallel for the use of "the one" to refer to a unified reality without reference to the arithmetical unit. Melissus asserts that if reality consisted of a plurality of entities "it is necessary that they be exactly such as I say the one (τὸ ἕν) to be" (F8). Of course Melissus is arguing for monism here and Philolaus is not, but Melissus' usage coheres with the other Presocratic uses given above in that his one is a unified reality, but of course in his case it is unified by the expulsion of all difference. Philolaus is writing in the tradition of Heraclitus and Empedocles where unity is achieved by a fitting together of differing components. In light of the close connection between Philolaus' usage here and the usage in Heraclitus and Empedocles, it seems much more plausible to see Philolaus' reference to a unity that results from a fitting together of disparate components as a reference to a unified whole of some sort rather than to an arithmetical unit. Of course, once these parallels are before us, it becomes clear that "the unity in the center of the sphere" which Philolaus is referring to is the central fire, as the first part of the cosmos to be put together out of limiters and unlimiteds.

The Presocratic parallels also suggest a different punctuation of the fragment. As long as it was assumed that Philolaus was referring to the arithmetical unit, it seemed natural to punctuate after "the one," so that "the one" (i.e. the arithmetical unit) was identified as the first thing fitted together. However, if Philolaus is primarily talking about the central fire as the first unity of limiter and unlimited, it seems better to take "the one" with what follows ("in the center of the sphere") as identifying this unity of limiter and unlimited as "the unity in the center of the sphere" as opposed to other unities that will be generated later.

On this reading one might expect that the article would be repeated (i.e. τὸ ἓν τὸ ἐν τῷ μέσῳ). It would be possible to argue that, if this was the original text, the second article could easily drop out in transmission and hence that the text should be emended. However, it is common for prepositional phrases used attributively to follow their noun without a repeated article, when the noun is a verbal substantive expressing a state or action, and this also occurs occasionally with other types of substantives as well (Kühner–Gerth 1897: 1.464.1). Thus, it is possible Greek for the article not to be repeated in this case and there is a motive for the omission of the second article in the fact that its inclusion would make the sentence even more difficult to pronounce than it already is.

Indeed, this punctuation of the text has fewer problems than the traditional one. On the traditional reading "the one" is put in apposition to "the first thing fitted together," but then "in the center of the sphere" is left hanging. If we take the sense to be "the first thing fitted together in the center of the sphere, the one, ..." there are two problems. First, it surely would have been more natural to put "in the center of the sphere" immediately after "the first thing fitted together." Second, this reading in fact has the unwanted consequence of suggesting that there might be a second thing fitted together in the center of the sphere. I suspect, however, that the sense that most scholars have been at least tacitly assuming is "the first thing fitted together, the one, which is in the center of the sphere, is called the hearth" (Freeman 1971: 74). But this interpretation really goes quite a way beyond the Greek by constructing a subordinate clause out of a prepositional phrase ("in the center of the sphere"). In the end then I would argue that the most natural interpretation of the Greek is in fact "the first thing fitted together, the unity in the center of the sphere, ..." a meaning which also fits with what is likely to have been the meaning of τὸ ἓν given the Presocratic context.

σφαίρας: The reference to the spherical shape of the cosmos of course leads us to think of Parmenides' famous lines describing what is as "like the mass of a well-rounded sphere" (F8.43) and Empedocles' reference to the sphere under the sway of Love (F28 and F29).

ἑστία: On the significance of calling the central fire the hearth see Pt. III, ch.4.

4. ASTRONOMY

Texts relevant to the astronomical system of Philolaus
(including Testimonia A16, A17, and A21)

1 Aristotle, *De caelo* 2.13, 293a18ff   Περὶ μὲν οὖν τῆς θέσεως
[sc. τῆς γῆς] οὐ τὴν αὐτὴν ἅπαντες ἔχουσι δόξαν, ἀλλὰ τῶν
πλείστων ἐπὶ τοῦ μέσου κεῖσθαι λεγόντων, ὅσοι τὸν ὅλον
οὐρανὸν πεπερασμένον εἶναί φασιν, ἐναντίως οἱ περὶ τὴν Ἰταλίαν,
5 καλούμενοι δὲ Πυθαγόρειοι λέγουσιν· ἐπὶ μὲν γὰρ τοῦ μέσου πῦρ
εἶναί φασι, τὴν δὲ γῆν, ἓν τῶν ἄστρων οὖσαν, κύκλῳ φερομένην
περὶ τὸ μέσον νύκτα τε καὶ ἡμέραν ποιεῖν. ἔτι δ' ἐναντίαν ἄλλην
ταύτῃ κατασκευάζουσι γῆν, ἣν ἀντίχθονα ὄνομα καλοῦσιν, οὐ
πρὸς τὰ φαινόμενα τοὺς λόγους καὶ τὰς αἰτίας ζητοῦντες, ἀλλὰ
10 πρός τινας λόγους καὶ δόξας αὐτῶν τὰ φαινόμενα προσέλκοντες
καὶ πειρώμενοι συγκοσμεῖν. πολλοῖς δ' ἂν καὶ ἑτέροις συνδόξειε μὴ
δεῖν τῇ γῇ τὴν τοῦ μέσου χώραν ἀποδιδόναι, τὸ πιστὸν οὐκ ἐκ
τῶν φαινομένων ἀθροῦσιν ἀλλὰ μᾶλλον ἐκ τῶν λόγων. τῷ γὰρ
τιμιωτάτῳ οἴονται προσήκειν τὴν τιμιωτάτην ὑπάρχειν χώραν,
15 εἶναι δὲ πῦρ μὲν γῆς τιμιώτερον, τὸ δὲ πέρας τῶν μεταξύ, τὸ δ'
ἔσχατον καὶ τὸ μέσον πέρας· ὥστ' ἐκ τούτων ἀναλογιζόμενοι οὐκ
οἴονται ἐπὶ τοῦ μέσου κεῖσθαι τῆς σφαίρας αὐτήν, ἀλλὰ μᾶλλον
τὸ πῦρ.

Ἔτι δ' οἵ γε Πυθαγόρειοι καὶ διὰ τὸ μάλιστα προσήκειν
20 φυλάττεσθαι τὸ κυριώτατον τοῦ παντὸς – τὸ δὲ μέσον εἶναι
τοιοῦτον – [ὃ] Διὸς φυλακὴν ὀνομάζουσι τὸ ταύτην ἔχον τὴν
χώραν πῦρ, ὥσπερ τὸ μέσον ἁπλῶς λεγόμενον, καὶ τὸ τοῦ
μεγέθους μέσον καὶ τοῦ πράγματος ὂν μέσον καὶ τῆς φύσεως.
καίτοι καθάπερ ἐν τοῖς ζῴοις οὐ ταὐτὸν τοῦ ζῴου καὶ τοῦ
25 σώματος μέσον, οὕτως ὑποληπτέον μᾶλλον καὶ περὶ τὸν ὅλον
οὐρανόν. διὰ μὲν οὖν ταύτην τὴν αἰτίαν οὐθὲν αὐτοὺς δεῖ
θορυβεῖσθαι περὶ τὸ πᾶν οὐδ' εἰσάγειν φυλακὴν ἐπὶ τὸ κέντρον,

ἀλλ’ ἐκεῖνο ζητεῖν τὸ μέσον, ποῖόν τι καὶ ποῦ πέφυκεν. ἐκεῖνο μὲν
γὰρ ἀρχὴ τὸ μέσον καὶ τίμιον, τὸ δὲ τοῦ τόπου μέσον ἔοικε
30 τελευτῇ μᾶλλον ἢ ἀρχῇ· τὸ μὲν γὰρ ὁριζόμενον τὸ μέσον, τὸ δ’
ὁρίζον τὸ πέρας. τιμιώτερον δὲ τὸ περιέχον καὶ τὸ πέρας ἢ τὸ
περαινόμενον· τὸ μὲν γὰρ ὕλη τὸ δ’ οὐσία τῆς συστάσεως ἐστίν.

Περὶ μὲν οὖν τοῦ τόπου τῆς γῆς ταύτην ἔχουσί τινες τὴν
δόξαν, ὁμοίως δὲ καὶ περὶ μονῆς καὶ κινήσεως· οὐ γὰρ τὸν αὐτὸν
35 τρόπον ἅπαντες ὑπολαμβάνουσιν, ἀλλ’ ὅσοι μὲν μηδ’ ἐπὶ τοῦ
μέσου κεῖσθαί φασιν αὐτήν, κινεῖσθαι κύκλῳ περὶ τὸ μέσον, οὐ
μόνον δὲ ταύτην, ἀλλὰ καὶ τὴν ἀντίχθονα, καθάπερ εἴπομεν
πρότερον. ἐνίοις δὲ δοκεῖ καὶ πλείω σώματα τοιαῦτα ἐνδέχεσθαι
φέρεσθαι περὶ τὸ μέσον, ἡμῖν δὲ ἄδηλα διὰ τὴν ἐπιπρόσθησιν τῆς
40 γῆς. διὸ καὶ τὰς τῆς σελήνης ἐκλείψεις πλείους ἢ τὰς τοῦ ἡλίου
γίγνεσθαί φασιν· τῶν γὰρ φερομένων ἕκαστον ἀντιφράττειν
αὐτήν, ἀλλ’ οὐ μόνον τὴν γῆν. ἐπεὶ γὰρ οὐκ ἔστιν ἡ γῆ κέντρον,
ἀλλ’ ἀπέχει τὸ ἡμισφαίριον αὐτῆς ὅλον, οὐθὲν κωλύειν οἴονται
τὰ φαινόμενα συμβαίνειν ὁμοίως μὴ κατοικοῦσιν ἡμῖν ἐπὶ τοῦ
45 κέντρου, ὥσπερ κἂν εἰ ἐπὶ τοῦ μέσου ἦν ἡ γῆ· οὐθὲν γὰρ οὐδὲ νῦν
ποιεῖν ἐπίδηλον τὴν ἡμίσειαν ἀπέχοντας ἡμᾶς διάμετρον.

21 δ secl. Allen   28 τι Prantl and Allen τε Bekker based solely on L

1 Concerning its [sc . the earth's] position there is some divergence
of opinion. Most of those who hold that the whole universe is finite
say that it lies at the centre, but this is contradicted by the Italian
school called Pythagoreans. These affirm that the centre is occupied
by fire, and that the earth is one of the stars, and creates night and
day as it travels in a circle about the centre. In addition they invent
another earth, lying opposite our own, which they call by the name
of "counter-earth," not seeking accounts and explanations in conformity with the appearances, but trying by violence to bring the
appearances into line with accounts and opinions of their own.
There are many others too who might agree that it is wrong to
assign the central position to the earth, men who see proof not in the
appearances but rather in abstract theory. These reason that the
most honourable body ought to occupy the most honourable place,
that fire is more honourable than earth, that a limit is a more
honourable place than what lies between limits, and that the centre

and outer boundary are the limits, Arguing from these premises, they say it must be not the earth, but rather fire, that is situated at the centre of the sphere.

The Pythagoreans make a further point. Because the most important part of the universe – which is the centre – ought more than any to be guarded, they call the fire which occupies this place the Watch-tower of Zeus, as if it were the centre in an unambiguous sense, being at the same time the geometrical centre and the natural centre of the thing itself. But we should rather suppose the same to be true of the whole world as is true of animals, namely that the centre of the animal and the centre of its body are not the same thing. For this reason there is no need for them to be alarmed about the Universe, nor to call in a guard for its mathematical centre; they ought rather to consider what sort of thing the true centre is, and what is its natural place. For it is that centre which should be held in honour as a starting-point; the local centre would seem to be rather an end than a starting-point, for that which is defined is the local centre, that which defines is the boundary; but that which encompasses and sets bounds is of more worth than that which is bounded, for the one is matter, the other the substance of the structure.

This then is the opinion of some about the position of the earth, and on the question of its rest or motion there are conformable views. Here again all do not think alike. Those who deny that it lies at the centre suppose that it moves in a circle about the centre, and not the earth alone, but also the counter-earth, as we have already explained. Some even think it possible that there are a number of such bodies carried around the centre, invisible to us owing to the interposition of the earth. This serves them too as a reason why eclipses of the moon are more frequent than those of the sun, namely that it is blocked by each of these moving bodies, not only by the earth. Since the earth's surface is not in any case the centre, but distant the whole hemisphere from the centre, they do not feel any difficulty in supposing that the phenomena are the same although we do not occupy the centre as they would be if the earth were in the middle. For even on the current view there is nothing to show that we are distant from the centre by half the earth's diameter.

(tr. Guthrie)

2 Aristotle, *Metaphysics* 986a2 ... τὰ τῶν ἀριθμῶν στοιχεῖα τῶν ὄντων στοιχεῖα πάντων ὑπέλαβον εἶναι, καὶ τὸν ὅλον οὐρανὸν ἁρμονίαν εἶναι καὶ ἀριθμόν. καὶ ὅσα εἶχον ὁμολογούμενα δεικνύναι ἔν τε τοῖς ἀριθμοῖς καὶ ταῖς ἁρμονίαις πρὸς τὰ τοῦ
5 οὐρανοῦ πάθη καὶ μέρη καὶ πρὸς τὴν ὅλην διακόσμησιν, ταῦτα συνάγοντες ἐφήρμοττον. κἂν εἴ τί που διέλειπε, προσεγλίχοντο τοῦ συνειρομένην πᾶσαν αὐτοῖς εἶναι τὴν πραγματείαν. λέγω δ' οἷον, ἐπειδὴ τέλειον ἡ δεκὰς εἶναι δοκεῖ καὶ πᾶσαν περιειληφέναι τὴν τῶν ἀριθμῶν φύσιν, καὶ τὰ φερόμενα κατὰ τὸν οὐρανὸν δέκα
10 μὲν εἶναί φασιν, ὄντων δὲ ἐννέα μόνον τῶν φανερῶν διὰ τοῦτο δεκάτην τὴν ἀντίχθονα ποιοῦσιν. διώρισται δὲ περὶ τούτων ἐν ἑτέροις ἡμῖν ἀκριβέστερον.

2 ... they assumed the elements of numbers to be the elements of everything, and the whole universe to be an attunement or number. Whatever analogues to the characteristics and parts of the heavens and to the whole order of the universe they could exhibit in numbers and attunements, these they collected and harmonized; and if there was any deficiency anywhere they were eager to supply it so that their system would be a connected whole. For example, since the number ten is considered to be perfect and to comprise the whole nature of numbers, they also assert that the bodies which revolve in the heavens are ten; and there being only nine that are visible, they make the counter-earth the tenth. We have treated this subject in greater detail elsewhere. (tr. after Tredennick)

3 Aristotle, F203 (= Alex. Aphr. *in Metaph.* 38.20) καὶ τὸν ἥλιον δέ, ἐπεὶ αὐτὸς αἴτιος εἶναι τῶν καιρῶν, φησί, δοκεῖ, ἐνταῦθά φασιν ἱδρῦσθαι καθ' ὃ ὁ ἕβδομος ἀριθμός ἐστιν, ὃν καιρὸν λέγουσιν· ἑβδόμην γὰρ αὐτὸν τάξιν ἔχειν τῶν περὶ τὸ μέσον καὶ τὴν ἑστίαν
5 κινουμένων δέκα σωμάτων· κινεῖσθαι γὰρ μετὰ τὴν τῶν ἀπλανῶν σφαῖραν καὶ τὰς πέντε τὰς τῶν πλανήτων· μεθ' ὃν ὀγδόην τὴν σελήνην, καὶ τὴν γῆν ἐννάτην, μεθ' ἣν τὴν ἀντίχθονα... (40, 26) αὐτίκα γοῦν τέλειον ἀριθμὸν ἡγούμενοι τὴν δεκάδα, ὁρῶντες δὲ ἐν τοῖς φαινομένοις ἐννέα τὰς κινουμένας σφαίρας, ἑπτὰ μὲν τὰς τῶν
10 πλανωμένων, ὀγδόην δὲ τὴν τῶν ἀπλανῶν, ἐννάτην δὲ τὴν γῆν (καὶ γὰρ καὶ ταύτην ἡγοῦντο κινεῖσθαι κύκλῳ περὶ μένουσαν τὴν ἑστίαν, ὃ πῦρ ἐστι κατ' αὐτούς), αὐτοὶ προσέθεσαν ἐν τοῖς δόγμασι καὶ τὴν ἀντίχθονά τινα, ἣν ἀντικινεῖσθαι ὑπέθεντο τῇ γῇ

καὶ διὰ τοῦτο τοῖς ἐπὶ τῆς γῆς ἀόρατον εἶναι. λέγει δὲ περὶ
15 τούτων καὶ ἐν τοῖς Περὶ οὐρανοῦ καὶ ἐν ταῖς τῶν Πυθαγορικῶν
δόξαις ἀκριβέστερον.

3 The sun too, since it is itself thought to be (he [sc. Aristotle] says)
the cause of the seasons, they say is situated [in the place] where the
number seven is, which they call "due season"; for they say that the
sun occupies the seventh place [from the periphery] among the ten
bodies that move around the centre, or hearth. For the sun, they say,
moves after the sphere of the fixed stars and after the five spheres of
the planets; after it is the moon, eighth, and earth, ninth, and after
earth the counter-earth....

From the outset, at any rate, they considered ten the perfect number, but seeing that, in what appears to the eye, the moving spheres
are nine in number – seven spheres of the planets, an eighth that of
the fixed stars, ninth the earth (for they thought, in fact, that the
earth too moves in a circle around the stationary hearth, which,
according to them, is fire) – they themselves added in their theory a
counter-earth as well, which they assumed to move opposite the
earth, and for this reason to be invisible to those on earth. Aristotle
discusses these matters both in his treatise *On the Heaven* and with
greater precision in *The Doctrines of the Pythagoreans*.

4 Aristotle, F204 (= Simplicius, *in De Caelo* 511.25) ἀντιφάσκουσι
δὲ οἱ Πυθαγόρειοι, τοῦτο γὰρ σημαίνει τὸ "ἐναντίως," οὐ περὶ τὸ
μέσον λέγοντες αὐτήν, ἀλλ᾽ ἐν μὲν τῷ μέσῳ τοῦ παντὸς πῦρ εἶναί
φασι, περὶ δὲ τὸ μέσον τὴν ἀντίχθονα φέρεσθαί φασι, γῆν οὖσαν
5 καὶ αὐτήν, ἀντίχθονα δὲ καλουμένην διὰ τὸ ἐξ ἐναντίας τῇδε τῇ
γῇ εἶναι. "μετὰ δὲ τὴν ἀντίχθονα ἡ γῆ ἥδε φερομένη καὶ αὐτὴ
περὶ τὸ μέσον, μετὰ δὲ τὴν γῆν ἡ σελήνη·" οὕτω γὰρ αὐτὸς ἐν τῷ
περὶ τῶν Πυθαγορικῶν ἱστορεῖ· τὴν δὲ γῆν ὡς ἓν τῶν ἄστρων
οὖσαν κινουμένην περὶ τὸ μέσον κατὰ τὴν πρὸς τὸν ἥλιον σχέσιν
10 νύκτα καὶ ἡμέραν ποιεῖν· ἡ δὲ ἀντίχθων κινουμένη περὶ τὸ μέσον
καὶ ἑπομένη τῇ γῇ ταύτῃ οὐχ ὁρᾶται ὑφ᾽ ἡμῶν διὰ τὸ ἐπιπροσθεῖν
ἡμῖν ἀεὶ τὸ τῆς γῆς σῶμα.... (512.9) καὶ οὕτω μὲν αὐτὸς τὰ τῶν
Πυθαγορείων ἀπεδέξατο· οἱ δὲ γνησιώτερον αὐτῶν μετασχόντες
πῦρ μὲν ἐν τῷ μέσῳ λέγουσι τὴν δημιουργικὴν δύναμιν τὴν ἐκ
15 μέσου πᾶσαν τὴν γῆν ζωογονοῦσαν καὶ τὸ ἀπεψυγμένον αὐτῆς
ἀναθάλπουσαν· διὸ οἱ μὲν Ζανὸς πύργον αὐτὸ καλοῦσιν, ὡς

αὐτὸς ἐν τοῖς Πυθαγορικοῖς ἱστόρησεν, οἱ δὲ Διὸς φυλακήν, ὡς ἐν
τούτοις, οἱ δὲ Διὸς θρόνον, ὡς ἄλλοι φασίν. ἄστρον δὲ τὴν γῆν
ἔλεγον ὡς ὄργανον καὶ αὐτὴν χρόνου· ἡμερῶν γάρ ἐστιν αὕτη καὶ
20 νυκτῶν αἰτία· ἡμέραν μὲν γὰρ ποιεῖ τὸ πρὸς τῷ ἡλίῳ μέρος
καταλαμπομένη, νύκτα δὲ κατὰ τὸν κῶνον τῆς γινομένης ἀπ'
αὐτῆς σκιᾶς. ἀντίχθονα δὲ τὴν σελήνην ἐκάλουν οἱ Πυθαγόρειοι,
ὥσπερ καὶ " αἰθερίαν γῆν," καὶ ὡς ἀντιφράττουσαν τῷ ἡλιακῷ
φωτί, ὅπερ ἴδιον γῆς, καὶ ὡς ἀποπερατοῦσαν τὰ οὐράνια,
25 καθάπερ ἡ γῆ τὸ ὑπὸ σελήνην.

4 But the Pythagoreans contradict them [sc. the ones who put the
earth in the center], for this is what "oppositely" means [sc. in the
De caelo], saying that it [sc. the earth] is not around the center, but
they say that in the center of everything is fire, and they say that the
counter-earth moves around the middle, being itself also an earth,
and being called counter-earth because it is opposite to this earth.
"After the counter-earth this earth itself also moves around the middle, and after the earth the moon," for this is what he himself reports
in the treatise on Pythagoreanism. But the earth, since it is one of the
stars moving around the middle, makes day and night according to
its position relative to the sun. But the counter-earth, moving about
the middle and following on this earth, is not seen by us because the
body of the earth is always in our way . . .

And he himself understands the views of the Pythagoreans in this
way. But those who partake of these views more genuinely say that
the fire in the middle is the demiurgic force which, from the middle,
generates life on the whole earth and warms the parts of it that have
become cool. Wherefore some call it the tower of Zeus, as he himself
reported in the treatise on Pythagoreanism, but others the guard-
house of Zeus, as here in the *De caelo*, but others the throne of Zeus,
as others say. They said that the earth was a star in so far as it was
also an instrument of time. For it is the cause of night and day. It
makes day when it is illumined on the part towards the sun, and
night by the cone of the shadow which it produces. And the Pythagoreans called the moon the counter-earth, in so far as it is also an
"earth in the aither," and since it blocks the light of the sun, which
is a peculiar characteristic of the earth, and since it marks the end of
the heavens just as the earth marks the end of the region under the
moon.

5 DK 58B36 (= Aetius 2.29.4) τῶν Πυθαγορείων τινὲς κατὰ τὴν Ἀριστοτέλειον ἱστορίαν καὶ τὴν Φιλίππου τοῦ Ὀπουντίου ἀπόφασιν ἀνταυγείᾳ καὶ ἀντιφράξει τοτὲ μὲν τῆς γῆς, τοτὲ δὲ τῆς ἀντίχθονος [sc. ἐκλείπειν τὴν σελήνην]. τῶν δὲ νεωτέρων εἰσί
5 τινες οἷς ἔδοξε κατ' ἐπινέμησιν φλογὸς κατὰ μικρὸν ἐξαπτομένης τεταγμένως ἕως ἂν τὴν τελείαν πανσέληνον ἀποδῷ, καὶ πάλιν ἀναλόγως μειουμένης μέχρι τῆς συνόδου, καθ' ἣν τελείως σβέννυται.

5 Some of the Pythagoreans, according to the research of Aristotle and the assertion of Philip of Opus, [say that the moon is eclipsed] by the interposition sometimes of the earth and sometimes of the counter-earth which reflects [the sun's light]. There are some of the more recent [Pythagoreans] who thought that [the phases of the moon?] were in accord with the spreading of fire which was kindled little by little in an orderly fashion until it produced the complete full moon, and again analogously became smaller until the new moon, when it is completely extinguished.

6 Simplicius, *in Ph.* 1354.2 ...καὶ οἵ γε Πυθαγόρειοι ἐν τῷ μέσῳ λέγειν ἐδόκουν αὐτό [sc. τὸ κινοῦν τὸν οὐρανόν] ...

6 ... and the Pythagoreans seemed to say that it [sc. what moves the cosmos] was in the centre...

7 DK A16 (= Aetius 2.7.7) Φιλόλαος πῦρ ἐν μέσῳ περὶ τὸ κέντρον ὅπερ ἑστίαν τοῦ παντὸς καλεῖ καὶ Διὸς οἶκον... [see A16b]. καὶ πάλιν πῦρ ἕτερον ἀνωτάτω τὸ περιέχον. πρῶτον δ' εἶναι φύσει τὸ μέσον, περὶ δὲ τοῦτο δέκα σώματα θεῖα χορεύειν,
5 οὐρανόν, πλανήτας, μεθ' οὓς ἥλιον, ὑφ' ᾧ σελήνην, ὑφ' ᾗ τὴν γῆν, ὑφ' ᾗ τὴν ἀντίχθονα, μεθ' ἃ σύμπαντα τὸ πῦρ ἑστίας περὶ τὰ κέντρα τάξιν ἐπέχον. [For the rest of this testimonium see the commentary on A16b.]

5 οὐρανόν τε πλανήτας F [οὐρανόν] ⟨μετὰ τὴν τῶν ἀπλανῶν σφαῖραν⟩ τοὺς ε̄ πλανήτας Diels   6 περὶ Meineke ἐπὶ FP

7 Philolaus [says] that there is fire in the middle around the center which he calls the hearth of the whole and house of Zeus... [see A16b]. And again another fire at the uppermost place, surrounding

[the whole]. [He says] that the middle is first by nature, and around this ten divine bodies dance: heaven, planets, after them the sun, under it the moon, under it the earth, under it the counter-earth, after all of which the fire which has the position of a hearth about the center.

8 DK A17 (= Aetius 3.11.3) [Περὶ θέσεως γῆς] Φιλόλαος ὁ Πυθαγόρειος τὸ μὲν πῦρ μέσον (τοῦτο γὰρ εἶναι τοῦ παντὸς ἑστίαν), δευτέραν δὲ τὴν ἀντίχθονα, τρίτην δὲ τὴν οἰκουμένην γῆν ἐξ ἐναντίας κειμένην τε καὶ περιφερομένην τῇ ἀντίχθονι· παρ' 5 ὃ καὶ μὴ ὁρᾶσθαι ὑπὸ τῶν ἐν τῇδε τοὺς ἐν ἐκείνῃ.

8 [On the Position of the Earth] Philolaus the Pythagorean [says] that fire is in the middle (for this is the hearth of all), and that the counter-earth is second, the inhabited earth is third and lies opposite to and moves around with the counter-earth. Accordingly, those on the counter-earth cannot be seen by those on this earth.

9 DK A21 (= Aetius 3.13.2) [Περὶ κινήσεως γῆς] οἱ μὲν ἄλλοι μένειν τὴν γῆν. Φιλόλαος δὲ ὁ Πυθαγόρειος κύκλῳ περιφέρεσθαι περὶ τὸ πῦρ (κατὰ κύκλον λοξὸν) ὁμοιοτρόπως ἡλίῳ καὶ σελήνῃ.

3 κύκλου λοξοῦ Plut. corr, Reiske

9 [On the Motion of the Earth] Others [say] that the earth is stationary. But Philolaus the Pythagorean that it moves in a circle around the fire according to an inclined circle in the same way as the sun and moon.

10 Eudemus, F146 (= Simplicius, *in de Caelo* 471.4 = DK 12A19) ...Ἀναξιμάνδρου πρώτου τὸν περὶ μεγεθῶν καὶ ἀποστημάτων [sc. τῶν πλανωμένων] λόγον εὑρηκότος, ὡς Εὔδημος ἱστορεῖ τὴν τῆς θέσεως τάξιν εἰς τοὺς Πυθαγορείους πρώτους ἀναφέρων.

10 ...Anaximander having been the first to find an account of the sizes and distances [sc. of the planets], as Eudemus reports while referring to the Pythagoreans as the first [to assign] the [sc. correct] order of their positions.

11 Aristotle, *Mete.* 342b30   τῶν δ᾽ Ἰταλικῶν τινες καλουμένων Πυθαγορείων ἕνα λέγουσιν αὐτὸν [sc. τὸν κομήτην] εἶναι τῶν πλανήτων ἀστέρων, ἀλλὰ διὰ πολλοῦ τε χρόνου τὴν φαντασίαν αὐτοῦ εἶναι καὶ τὴν ὑπερβολὴν ἐπὶ μικρόν . . .

11 Of the Italian schools some of the so-called Pythagoreans say that it [sc. a comet] is one of the planets, but that it appears only at long intervals and does not rise far above the horizon.   (tr. Lee)

12 Aristotle, *Mete.* 345a14   τῶν μὲν οὖν καλουμένων Πυθαγορείων φασί τινες ὁδὸν εἶναι ταύτην οἱ μὲν τῶν ἐκπεσόντων τινὸς ἀστέρων, κατὰ τὴν λεγομένην ἐπὶ Φαέθοντος φθοράν, οἱ δὲ τὸν ἥλιον τοῦτον τὸν κύκλον φέρεσθαί ποτέ φασιν· οἷον οὖν
5   διακεκαῦσθαι τὸν τόπον τοῦτον ἤ τι τοιοῦτον ἄλλο πεπονθέναι πάθος ὑπὸ τῆς φορᾶς αὐτῶν.

12 Of the so-called Pythagoreans some say that it [the milky way] is a path. Some say that it is the path of one of the stars that fell at the time of the legendary fall of Phaethon, others that the sun once moved in this circle. And the region is supposed to have been scorched or affected in some other such way as a result of the passage of these bodies.   (tr. after Lee)

A note on the texts: In the texts presented above, all of which rest ultimately on the authority of Aristotle or his pupils Theophrastus and Eudemus, there is clearly only one Pythagorean system presented, the system with ten bodies around a central fire which the doxography (Texts 7–9) shows to belong to Philolaus. This system did undergo a considerable variety of interpretations in the later tradition (see Simplicius' "more genuine Pythagoreans" discussed below and Plutarch, *De gen. an.* 1028b), and was even contaminated by other later systems (A16b), but remains the only complete system that can be assigned to the early Pythagoreans. However, the texts above also show that there was considerable divergence among Pythagoreans in the explanation of individual astronomical phenomena. In fact this is one of the areas of Pythagorean thought where we have clearest evidence of divisions among Pythagoreans. I will comment briefly on some of these divergences here before giving a detailed explication of Philolaus' system.

Some of these explanations clearly violate crucial principles of the Philolaic system. Thus, in Text 1 above some Pythagoreans are said to have supposed that even more bodies than the counter-earth could exist, invisible to us, and hence explain the greater frequency of lunar than solar eclipses. This is impossible in Philolaus' scheme which emphasizes that exactly ten bodies are around the central fire. Others (Text 5) are said to have explained the phases of the moon according to a theory in which the moon's fire is gradually kindled until it is fully lit at full moon and then gradually dies out until it disappears at new moon, but Philolaus' view of the moon is somewhat different and he does not seem to see it as a fire (see A20).

The last two texts given above refer to Pythagorean explanations of comets and the milky way. The explanation of a comet as a planet that only appears at long intervals does not seem to fit Philolaus' system, since none of his ten orbiting bodies would fit this description of appearing only at long intervals, and the system rules out any eleventh planet. Two divergent Pythagorean theories of the milky way are given in Text 12. The second says that it is the previous path of the sun which was scorched by its passage. It is not impossible that Philolaus thought that the sun had once had a different path, but his system rather suggests that the current order is the one that arose at the beginning (he probably did not believe in periodic destructions of the whole cosmos; see A18). Moreover, his sun is a glassy body that focuses heat elsewhere, such as on the earth, without necessarily heating its immediate vicinity (see A19). The first explanation says that the milky way is the path of a star that fell at the time of the legendary fall of Phaethon. Since Philolaus did think that parts of the earth were visited by periodic conflagrations (A18), it is possible that he mentioned Phaethon, but once again it would appear that such conflagrations in his system were connected to the sun focusing heat on the earth, and not tied to the fall of other stars.

The astronomical system of Philolaus

The astronomical system of Philolaus has been subject to the widest range of assessments imaginable, but the true nature of its contribution to the development of Presocratic thought has seldom been appreciated. Scholars such as Frank and van der Waerden, dazzled by the fact that Philolaus was the first to move the earth from the center of the cosmos and under the influence of the false analogy with Copernicus, supposed the system to be so sophisticated that it could not be the work of Philolaus writing in the latter part of the fifth century, but must rather belong to an author of the fourth century.[1] However, Burkert (1972) and Dicks (1970) have success-fully shown that the system is not so advanced as Frank and van der Waerden supposed and that it in fact has close ties to the thought of other fifth-century authors such as Empedocles and Anaxagoras.[2] Yet, Burkert has gone to the opposite extreme from Frank and van der Waerden and argues that the Philolaic system is simply "mythology in scientific clothing" (1972: 342). He suggests that the best analogy for Philolaus' account of the cosmos is found in the writings of the fifth-century interpreter of myths, Herodorus of Heraclea, author of *The Story of Heracles*. Similarly, the most recent work on Presocratic cosmology concludes that "the system [of Philolaus] makes very little astronomical sense, and it is hard to be-lieve that it was intended to do so," and asserts that with Philolaus' account of the inhabitants of the moon (A20) "the whole scheme lapses into fantasy."[3] My own thesis is that this attempt to turn the Philolaic system into myth or fantasy is misguided. To be sure, the system is not a mathematically sophisticated account of planetary motion either, but it is clearly a product of the tradition of Presocratic thought on the cosmos. Despite its peculiarities (central fire, counter-earth), it can account for all the phenomena that the systems of Anaxagoras, Empedocles, and Democritus can and is in fact more sophisticated in that it recognizes just the five canonical planets rather than an indefinite number. It is in fact the most impressive example of Presocratic speculative astronomy and establishes Phi-lolaus as an important precursor of Plato.[4]

The only fragments which are relevant to the astronomical system

[1] Frank 1923: 35ff, 207ff; van der Waerden 1951: 49ff, 54. See Burkert 1972: 337 n.3 for other followers of the Frank and van der Waerden approach. Other important early accounts of Philolaus' system are to be found in Martin 1872 and Schiaparelli 1876.

[2] Dicks 1970: 65ff, 70, 72; Burkert 1972: 337–50.

[3] Furley 1987: 58. His main interest is not in the Pythagoreans, and he in fact spends less than a page on the Philolaic system. His judgment on its nature seems to be largely based on Burkert.

[4] Some would argue that none of the work of the Presocratic philosophers really qualifies as astronomy, since it was not concerned with precise measurement and does not give a mathematical account of planetary motion; and I have no real quarrel with this. See e.g. Neugebauer's great work (1975) and Goldstein and Bowen 1983. However, Philolaus and other Presocratics were clearly interested in assigning places in the world-order to the vari-ous heavenly bodies in conformity with general observations, and in that basic etymological sense of the word the Presocratics can be said to be concerned with astronomy.

are F7 and F17 which I have already discussed in relation to Philolaus' cosmogony. They show that the cosmos as a whole is conceived of as a sphere and that there is a fire in the center. On the other hand, the details of the astronomical system are all derived from the secondary sources, which are of two main types. First there are Aristotle (Texts 1, 2 and 5; see also F16 Walzer = Aet. 2.29.4) and the commentators on Aristotle who had access to Aristotle's treatise on the Pythagoreans (Texts 3 and 4). This tradition knows of only one Pythagorean astronomical system, the one that includes the central fire, and that system is always ascribed to the Pythagoreans in general with no mention of any individual Pythagoreans. Some have thought that Simplicius gives evidence for an earlier Pythagorean system in which the earth is at the center. However, Burkert has conclusively shown that the views of the "more genuine Pythagoreans" to which Simplicius refers at *in de Caelo* 512.9ff are not derived from Aristotle's book on the Pythagoreans and are thus not representative of early Pythagoreanism, but are in fact clearly constructed as an attempt to show that Aristotle had misunderstood the Pythagoreans in assigning to them the outrageous (to the ancients) doctrine of a moving earth.[5] The source that Simplicius is using for these "more genuine Pythagoreans" thus belongs to the post-Aristotelian tradition of Pythagorean pseudepigrapha whose goal is to show that early Pythagorean beliefs anticipated the achievements of Platonic and Aristotelian philosophy.

The second source for early Pythagorean astronomy is the doxographical tradition represented in Aetius, which ultimately goes back to Aristotle's pupil Theophrastus (Texts 7–9). Here we find the same astronomical system mentioned in Aristotle, but this time it is ascribed to Philolaus. There is no reason to doubt this ascription, since it probably goes back to Aristotle's pupil Theophrastus. Aristotle's failure to assign it to Philolaus is just part of his usual practice of talking of the Pythagoreans as a group rather than naming

---

[5] See Burkert 1972: 232–3. Burkert's points are enough to establish clearly that the interpretation of "those more genuinely partaking in Pythagorean views" belongs to someone in the post-Aristotelian period who is in fact responding to Aristotle and not to someone dating before Philolaus. However, it is also interesting to note that the idea of the distinction between the supra- and sub-lunary sphere which comes in the last line of Simplicius' report is Aristotelian and totally incompatible with a fifth-century date, while the description of the earth as an "instrument of time" seems to be clearly derived from the *Timaeus* (41e5).

individuals. In this case it could be the result of the fact that many Pythagoreans adopted the system after Philolaus or even that he was not the first to propose it. But Theophrastus' ascription of it to Philolaus strongly implies that Philolaus' book was the text where the theory was set out. Of course we can never be certain that no one before Philolaus put forth this astronomical system, but what we have of the rest of Philolaus' book shows that this system was carefully integrated with the rest of his views. Thus in F7 Philolaus clearly refers to the central fire, which is the hallmark of the system, as the first thing to be created in his cosmogony. Moreover, the doctrine of the central fire is mirrored in Philolaus' biology, the details of which are securely assigned to Philolaus on the authority of the history of medicine by Aristotle's pupil Meno. The human body is seen as originating from the hot, just like the universe, which then draws in cooling breath.[6]

However, the doxographical tradition cannot be accepted in its entirety, since it in fact describes two systems whose terminologies contradict one another (see Burkert 1972: 243ff and my commentary on A16b and A17b). Thus, only the first half of A16 is based on the genuine book of Philolaus while the second half is based on a later book forged in Philolaus' name. Likewise, the second half of A17 must be rejected. Indeed, Simplicius' more genuine Pythagoreans and the modified Philolaic system reported in Plutarch (*De an. proc.* 1028b) show that the system was worked over in the later tradition. But once these passages have been removed, the rest of A16, 17, and 21 are clearly describing the system which Aristotle knows and supplement his reports in interesting ways.

At first sight the system described in the testimonia is impressive for its symmetry and audacity. The earth is removed from its traditional place in the center of the cosmos and moves in a circular orbit like the other planets. However, the center of the cosmos is not the sun but a mysterious central fire which is called the hearth. A16 (Text 7) emphasizes that the center is "first by nature," which

---

[6] Burnet argued that the geocentric system described in Plato's *Phaedo* must be ascribed to Philolaus, since Simmias, who is said earlier in the dialogue to have heard Philolaus, agrees with Socrates' description of the earth in the center (1948: 297). But we have no grounds upon which to determine the extent of the historical Simmias' allegiance to Philolaus' views. Such an indirect argument has little force against the direct ascription of the central-fire system to Philolaus in the doxography.

accords with the statement in F7 that the hearth was "the first thing harmonized." Ten bodies circle around the central fire. Starting from the outside there are first the fixed stars, followed by the five planets (no specified order), the sun, the moon, the earth, and finally the counter-earth (Text 7, and for the sun as seventh from the outside see Text 3).

Aristotle focuses his attention on the moving earth and the introduction of the central fire and counter-earth. The notion of the earth moving is of course more familiar to us than it was to Aristotle and we have a tendency to assume that anyone who put forth such an idea was attempting to give a better account of actual phenomena than someone who has the earth motionless in the center of the cosmos. However, there is not the slightest bit of evidence that Philolaus removed the earth from the center of the cosmos and made it revolve around the center with the goal of giving a better explanation of phenomena. Indeed a motionless central earth could explain the astronomical phenomena known to fifth-century Greeks just as well as a moving earth. The moving earth appears not to have been introduced for its own sake, but is rather a consequence of the introduction of the central fire. If the earth is not in the center it must move around the center like other heavenly bodies.

Why, then, was the central fire introduced? We do not have any explicit statement on this point from Philolaus, but Aristotle's account in the *De caelo* (Text 1), although from a critic of the system, makes it tolerably clear that it had nothing to do with astronomical phenomena, but arose out of *a priori* notions of order and fitness. At 293b2 Aristotle explicitly says that the Pythagoreans regarded the center as the most important (κυριώτατον) part of the whole and this is supported by F7 and F17 of Philolaus which clearly show that his cosmogony began in the center. Just before this comment Aristotle had reported that many other people might agree that the central position should not be assigned to earth, but rather to fire, since fire is more honorable than earth and since the limit is more honorable than what lies between the limits – the center and the outer boundary being the limits of the sphere. It is hard to know whether Aristotle means that the doctrine that fire is more honorable than earth is a Pythagorean doctrine which these unspecified others are agreeing with or whether the only point of agreement is the location of the fire in the center, while the supporting argument

based on the priority of fire belongs to "the others." But the embryology assigned to Philolaus in A27 supports the notion that fire is
primary in some sense, since Philolaus argues that human bodies
originate from "the hot." It may then be that there was an argument from analogy to the effect that, since heat and fire are prior to
earth in biology, so in the generation of the world fire must be
primary and located at the starting-point for the generation of the
cosmos, the center of the cosmic sphere.

Such a view in fact makes sense in the context of Presocratic
thought of the late fifth century. Philolaus can be seen as adopting
the spherical shape for the cosmos which was probably first clearly
set out by Parmenides (Furley 1987: 54). However, reflection on this
shape shows that any given circle is determined by its center and
circumference, which as Aristotle himself points out are its limits. It
might well seem odd, then, to Philolaus that Presocratic thinkers
had usually placed earth at the center, when almost none of them
(Xenophanes?) regarded earth as the primary element from which
all things come. Accordingly, he postulated that the element that is
the origin of the world, fire, should be located at the center, which is
one of the origins of the sphere. Most of the rest of his astronomical
system can be seen as trying to square the obvious phenomena with
this initial postulate.[7]

The doxographical tradition (A16 = Text 7) maintains that there
was fire at the periphery of the cosmos as well as at the center, and
this might follow from the argument that Aristotle reports to the
effect that fire, as the most honored element, is associated with the
limits of the cosmos. However, Philolaus does not in the fragments
glorify limit *per se* (although the Pythagoreans of the table of opposites seem to) and the analogy with embryology would just suggest
that the starting-point of generation should be hot and suggests
nothing about the nature of the periphery of the cosmos. It could be

---

[7] The description of the fire at the center of the world-order as the "hearth" is very natural,
given that the Greek household was identified with the fire that was kept burning on the
hearth at its center (Burkert 1985: 170, 255). There is some evidence that in the later part
of the fifth century the earth was also called the hearth of the cosmos (Soph. F558N.; Eur.
F944; Anaxagoras A20b; see also Plato, *Phdr.* 247a1-6 and Plut. *De fac.* 923a). This evidence
has sometimes been used to support the ill-founded view that the early Pythagoreans had a
geocentric system with a fire located in the center of the earth (Richardson 1926 and
Guthrie 1962: 289ff). This view was largely based on a passage in Simplicius (*De caelo* 512.9)
which Burkert has shown not to be evidence for early Pythagorean views (see n. 5 above).

that the doxographical report is in fact a conclusion derived from Aristotle's report of the argument in the *De caelo* passage rather than an independent testimony about the nature of the Philolaic system. However, the testimonium on Philolaus' account of the sun (A19) also supports the idea that there was fire at the periphery of the cosmos as well, since the sun seems to get its light from that source and pass it on to the earth. Thus, it is probable that Philolaus thought of there being a fire both at the center and at the periphery of the spherical cosmos.

A similar emphasis on *a priori* notions is found in the reasons for introducing the counter-earth. Aristotle complains vigorously that here the Pythagoreans are not seeking theories (λόγους) and causes that accord with phenomena but dragging the phenomena into accord with certain theories and opinions that they hold (*De caelo* 293a25). In *Metaphysics* 986a8 (Text 2) Aristotle makes clear that it was because of the Pythagorean idea that the number ten was complete that they introduced the counter-earth to bring the bodies orbiting the central fire up to ten. There seems to be no good reason to reject Aristotle's explanation here, although it might not be the whole story. Some have thought that the counter-earth was introduced to explain phenomena, namely eclipses of the moon, and that Aristotle is slandering the Pythagoreans (e.g. Burnet 1948: 305; Cherniss 1935: 199; Heath 1913: 99, 119). Indeed, the *De caelo* passage on the Pythagoreans (Text 1) mentions that "some" (most likely Pythagoreans, in context) thought that there could be a number of bodies like the counter-earth which move around the center but are invisible to us due to the interposition of the earth. These bodies are then said to account for the fact that lunar eclipses are more frequent than solar. In Text 5 (Aet. 2.29.4), which cites Aristotle and Philip of Opus as sources, it is explicitly said that some Pythagoreans thought that lunar eclipses resulted sometimes from the interposition of the counter-earth as well as from the interposition of the earth. This text loses some of its power since it seems that the reference to Aristotle, at least, could well just be derived from a mistaken reading of the *De caelo* passage. It is clear, at any rate, that Philolaus is not likely to have been one of those who postulated numerous bodies invisible to us, since the doxography is so insistent on exactly ten orbiting bodies in his system. Moreover, what makes it unlikely even that he used the counter-earth to explain eclipses is that since the counter-earth is inside the orbit of the earth and the moon is outside the orbit of the earth there is no way that it could serve such a function.[8] He could, of course, have mistakenly thought that the counter-earth served such a purpose, but without more unambiguous evidence that he did so it seems best to suppose that Aristotle was right after all. Philolaus postulated the existence of the counter-earth in somewhat the same way as modern astronomers postulate the existence of planets beyond Pluto based on gravitational evidence; his understanding of the cosmos, that it is structured according to significant numerical relationships, suggests that there should not be just nine orbiting bodies, and, as Aristotle says, he is willing to try to make the phenomena fit what he takes to be the basic structure of reality even when they are recalcitrant.[9]

The emphasis on *a priori* principles of order, which we have seen so far in Philolaus, is paralleled by other fruitful theses about the physical world based on such principles put forward by the Presocratics. As Furley suggests, the beginning of what he calls the centrifocal theory of the cosmos, a theory that dominated ancient thought from Plato onwards, is in fact to be found in *a priori* metaphysical speculations by Parmenides (1987: 56). However, this emphasis on *a priori* principles without concern for the phenomena is only half the story of Philolaus' astronomy. Aristotle reports a number of cases where the Pythagorean system specifically responded to possible attacks alleging that it did not accord with phenomena. It is significant that Philolaus did not shrug such objections off ("what would one expect from the phenomena?"), nor ignore them as irrelevant to what his astronomy was about, but instead devised rather clever arguments to show that the system did in fact conform to appearances. It is this fact that undercuts Burkert's thesis that Philolaus' system is just myth in scientific clothing and that it is most akin to the writings of mythographers like Herodorus of Heraclea. Aristotle does complain

---

[8] Dicks 1970: 67 n. 78. The counter-earth could explain lunar eclipses if the moon received its light not from the sun but from the central fire. This is possible but not likely (see A20). The idea that lunar eclipses are caused by invisible bodies is also ascribed to Anaxagoras (A42.6, 9).

[9] Burkert, in accordance with his general interpretation of Philolaus' astronomy as closely tied to myth, treats the counter-earth as having its "real meaning in the world of myth" and as tied to "the tradition of shamanistic narrative" (1972: 347ff). But these connections are only striking if we accept his overall view of Philolaus' system to begin with, and are not in themselves compelling.

that the Pythagoreans had a tendency to adapt phenomena to their theories rather than the reverse, but this comment is made in the context of Aristotle's broader recognition that the Pythagoreans are part of the general tradition of Presocratic thought. Aristotle's remark puts the Pythagoreans at one end of the spectrum in Presocratic thought, the end that emphasizes *a priori* principles rather than phenomena, but his remark in no way shows that Philolaus' system is to be regarded as part of the mythical tradition of explanation of the cosmos which is largely unconcerned with empirical constraints.

I doubt that anyone would have thought to raise problems about the phenomena to Herodorus, because it was very clear that he was not concerned with them, but with the realm of stories. Burkert is impressed by the fact that Herodorus thought of the moon as inhabited by creatures fifteen times larger than those on earth (as Philolaus is said to have thought in A20) and that he appears to talk of a counter-earth when he says that vultures come from "another earth" not visible to us (*Fr. Gr. Hist.* 31, F21 and F22). He is also impressed with the extent to which the Pythagorean *acusmata*, which presumably date before Philolaus, betray a mythical world view (e.g. the *acusmata* that call the planets "the hounds of Persephone" [Por. *VP* 41 = DK 58C2] or the sun and moon "the isles of the blest" [Iambl. *VP* 82 = DK 58C4]). But we need to do more than just look for similarities on points of doctrine (as Burkert himself notes, Anaxagoras also thought of the moon as inhabited and is reported as thinking that the Nemean lion came from the moon [A77], as did Herodorus, yet no one would classify Anaxagoras with Herodorus); we need to look at the context in which those doctrines are presented. In Herodorus' case there is absolutely no evidence that he even attempted to present a coherent astronomical system. The other testimonia show that he was the author of three books on mythological topics (*The Story of Heracles*, an *Argonautica* and a *Pelopeia*) and was to be consulted for information about the Nemean lion, Helen's birth from an egg, and the number of nights Heracles took to deflower the fifty daughters of Thestius (F19), with no mention whatsoever of any attempt to explain even basic astronomical phenomena such as day and night. Aristotle certainly never mentions Herodorus as an astronomical thinker (although he knows of him since he mentions him three times in the biological treatises

[*HA* 563a7, 615a9; *GA* 757a4] – primarily for odd opinions about animals, such as the fact that vultures come from another world and that some animals have both male and female sex organs and mate with themselves). I have argued elsewhere (1988) that Aristotle does misrepresent Pythagorean ideas under the influence of his own system, but it is quite another thing to say that he completely misclassified the Pythagoreans as part of the Presocratic tradition, rather than as working in the realm of myth like Herodorus and Hesiod. But Burkert's thesis would require us to suppose that Aristotle made just such a mistake.

Furthermore, if challenged, I doubt that someone like Herodorus would have felt at all inclined to make his thoughts about the cosmos into a system that corresponded to phenomena. Certainly there is nothing in the tradition to suggest that he did so. But, as I have said, the Pythagoreans that Aristotle mentions did feel constrained to make their system compatible with the phenomena. It is this recognition that the system must at some level accord with the phenomena that clearly puts Philolaus' system in the Presocratic tradition of rational speculation about the cosmos rather than in the tradition of mythography. There is a clear attempt to explain phenomena such as night and day, the basic movement of the planets (not taking into account retrograde motion), and the motion of the fixed stars. They were also concerned with the problem of parallax and tried to explain how the introduction of bodies such as the central fire and the counter-earth could be squared with what we see. It may be that Pythagoras himself was primarily a shaman figure, as Burkert argues, and that the *acusmata* represent the dominant strain in pre-Philolaic Pythagoreanism, but we know too little about ancient Pythagoreanism to assume that Philolaus' thought must have these characteristics as well, particularly in the face of Aristotle's testimony and the majority of the fragments themselves, which show us someone working very much in the tradition of Empedocles and Anaxagoras. But let us turn to the ways in which the Philolaic system tries to address the phenomena.

The most obvious problem raised by moving the earth from the center is the explanation of night and day. In theories with a central earth day and night are easily explained in accord with phenomena as the result of the sun's revolving once around the earth in a twenty-four-hour period. The Pythagorean solution to the problem is quite clever. Aristotle tells us that they argued that the earth made night and day by its circular motion around the center (Text 1). As interpreters have seen, this must mean that the earth orbits the central fire once every twenty-four hours while the sun takes a year to complete the circuit (see Text 4). This means that as the earth completes its revolution the sun remains almost stationary, so that as the earth moves around to the other side of the central fire our side of the earth is turned away from the sun, thus producing night. As the earth completes its circuit our side is turned more and more towards the sun and day is the result. The sun will appear to have moved slightly against the background of the stars as the result of its much slower orbit around the central fire, and in a year it will complete a full circle through the zodiac.

In order for this explanation to work it is also necessary that the earth rotate once on its axis during each revolution around the central fire. If it did not, one side of the earth would always be turned to the sun. We know that the Pythagoreans in fact posited this axial rotation, because it is also the explanation of the fact that we do not see the central fire or the counter-earth. The rotation keeps our side of the earth always turned away from the center as it completes its circuit of the hearth. At *De caelo* 293b22 (Text 1) Aristotle talks of the invisibility of the counter-earth and possibly other bodies because of the "interposition of the earth" (ἐπιπρόσθησις τῆς γῆς) and Simplicius gives the same explanation (Text 4). Although the basic assumptions of Pythagorean astronomy are largely *a priori* (that fire is primary and hence in the center and that there are ten bodies) and not derived from the phenomena, the system developed from those assumptions is still, given the state of astronomical knowledge in the later fifth century, a remarkable attempt to "save the phenomena" and is in fact "a triumph of thought over mere appearance."[10]

Another problem with the theory is the need for some explanation for the fact that the axis of revolution for the sun, moon, and fixed stars is at an angle to that of the earth. Traditionally this is explained in Greek astronomy by the theory of the ecliptic. On this theory the revolution of the sun, moon, and planets around the central earth is

---

[10] See Burkert (1972: 339) in his description of how one "might see" Philolaus' system were it not for the problem of the motion of the fixed stars. I answer this problem below.

in a plane inclined to the plane of the earth's equator. This explains the fact that the sun is not always at the same height above the horizon, and thus is also the explanation for the seasons. In the Philolaic system, if the earth circles the central fire in the same plane as the sun, moon, and planets, there will be no explanation for these phenomena. The "discovery" of the ecliptic is often tied to Oenopides of Chios in the later part of the fifth century, so that there would be nothing anachronistic in Philolaus being aware of the ecliptic (Eudemus, F145 = DK 41A7).

Aetius (A21 = Text 9) does in fact ascribe to Philolaus the view that the earth "moves in a circle around the [central] fire according to an inclined circle in the same manner as the sun and moon." If this means that the earth, sun, and moon all move in the same plane inclined to that of the equator of the cosmic sphere (as Dicks argues that we must read the Greek [1970: 70–1]), the phenomena will not be accounted for, since the sun will be moving in the same plane as the earth and ought therefore always to move at the same height in the sky and not rise higher in the sky with the seasons. Burkert takes "in the same manner" (ὁμοιοτρόπως) to mean "in the same direction," which would solve the problem, since the earth would then be seen as moving in the same direction, but in a plane inclined to the plane of the orbit of the sun and moon (so also Heath 1913: 100). While Dicks is right about the literal meaning of the Greek, surely it is more charitable and reasonable to suppose that Philolaus understood why he introduced an inclined plane for the earth's motion and that Aetius is sloppy in describing the system. The doxographical tradition was probably most impressed by the fact that the earth moved "just like the sun and moon," and is emphasizing that fact without noticing the ambiguity about the plane of movement (if the phrase "according to an inclined circle" had been put at the end of the sentence the ambiguity would be considerably less). Alternatively the point might be that the earth moves in an oblique circle just as the sun and moon do (in traditional Greek astronomy).

Because Aetius uses language to describe the ecliptic which is typical of later Greek astronomy, and because the ecliptic is not mentioned elsewhere in reports about Philolaus, Dicks doubts that it can be assigned to Philolaus and thinks the later tradition assigned it to Philolaus "to make the latter's views sound more plausible" (1970: 71). But the doxographers were primarily interested in what was

251

new in Philolaus' system (the moving earth, central fire, etc.) rather than in features that accorded with traditional astronomy, and it is not at all surprising to me that the inclination of the earth's orbit is not mentioned in Aristotle or the commentators on Aristotle. He is not trying to give a complete account of the Pythagorean system but rather the noteworthy Pythagorean views on questions such as the position of the earth. The doxographical tradition represented in Aetius does not show a tendency to try to make Philolaus' system more reasonable; it rather adds material from the later tradition of Pythagorean pseudepigrapha (e.g. A16b and A17b), as Burkert has shown. Thus, while it is not impossible, it does not seem likely that the inclination of the earth's orbit was introduced by that tradition. Since there is no anachronism in Philolaus' having known about the ecliptic in the late fifth century, we should accept the doxographical tradition on this point.

Another problem faced by the system is the effect of the parallax, caused by the earth's movement, on the apparent movement of the planets. In the Copernican system it is precisely this that accounts for the apparent retrograde movement of the planets. The difference of the earth's period of revolution around the sun from the periods of the planets produces configurations of the heavenly bodies that make the planets appear to stop and move backward against the background of the fixed stars. But the planets in fact continue to move with their same motion and the appearance is just the result of the earth's own motion. There is no hint whatsoever that Philolaus likewise used parallax to explain retrograde motion, and in fact the Pythagoreans seem to have tried to discount the effect of parallax. In the *De caelo* (Text 1) Aristotle says that they did not feel any difficulty in supposing that the phenomena remained the same with a moving eccentric earth as they would be with a motionless central earth. The argument given is that even on the assumption of a central earth we are not in the center since, being on the earth's surface, we are a radius away from the actual center, but the phenomena still appear the same as if we were at the center. Presumably the point is that in the Pythagorean system the extra distance from the actual center would likewise not be significant enough to produce any noticeable changes in phenomena. However, this argument is clearly defective. The problem is not that the earth is not at the center but rather that the earth moves around the center so that it moves from one side of the center to another, relative to the position of the planets, sun, and moon, and thus would make them appear to move in ways that they would not appear to move if the earth had a fixed position. If we wanted to be very charitable, we might argue that the Pythagoreans understood this, but maintained that the diameter of the earth's orbit was so small relative to the distance to the planets that the effects of parallax would be negligible. Whether the Pythagorean explanation is satisfactory or not, the significant fact is that once again the Pythagoreans felt the force of possible or actual objections based on phenomena and tried to respond to them so as to show that the system conformed to appearances.

Let me then give an overview of the system as I have discussed it so far, and raise one last difficulty. Ten bodies are arranged around a central fire (see fig. 1). The earth is the second body out from the center after the counter-earth. However, we never see either the central fire nor the counter-earth, because the earth rotates once on its axis as it orbits around the central fire, thus keeping our side of the earth always turned away from the center. All of the bodies moving around the central fire have one circular motion from west to east. The earth's motion is far faster than the moon, sun, and five planets, since it completes its circuit around the central fire in twenty-four hours. Its motion thus accounts for the apparent movement of the sun across the sky (and hence for night and day) as well as the apparent nightly movement of the moon, stars, and planets from east to west. The earth's orbit is inclined to that of the sun, moon, and planets and this inclination accounts for the apparent movement of the sun higher and lower in the sky and hence accounts for the seasons. The movement of the counter-earth is not made clear, but presumably, since its name suggests that it is paired with the earth, it moves at a similar velocity and at the same angle to the plane of the motion of the sun and other planets.

The sun, moon, and planets then each have one circular motion from west to east which is much slower (in angular velocity at least) than that of the earth and which explains their observed motion from west to east through the zodiac. The moon completes its circuit in about a month, the sun in a year and each of the planets progressively slower. The idea would then seem to be that the farther away from the center the body is the slower it moves. The system is thus

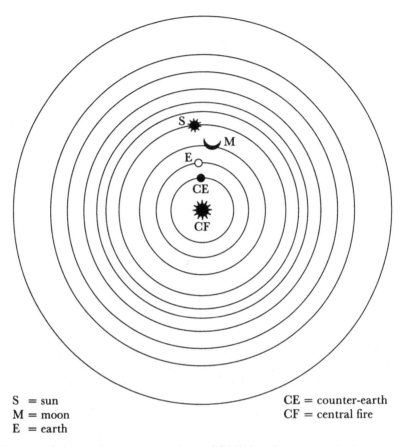

S = sun   CE = counter-earth
M = moon   CF = central fire
E = earth

Fig. 1. Schematic representation of Philolaus' astronomical system.
(After D. R. Dicks, *Early Greek Astronomy to Aristotle*, Ithaca, 1970.)

very simple and elegant, postulating just one motion for each body
with all the motions being in the same direction, although that of
the earth is in a plane inclined to that of the rest. Such a system
will explain the astronomical phenomena that are most commonly
known, but notably fails to account for the fact that the planets'
movement against the background of the zodiac does not progress
uniformly from west to east; i.e. it ignores the fact there are stationary points and points where the planets move from east to west for a
while (retrograde motion – a phenomenon not explained by any
Presocratic theory).

Burkert has raised what he regards as a fatal objection to this reconstruction of the system, an objection which he thinks reveals the true nature of Philolaus' astronomy as "mythology in scientific clothing." The description of Philolaus' cosmos that I have given above rests on the assumption that the fixed stars can be regarded as an essentially stationary background against which the heavenly bodies move. In traditional Greek astronomy the sphere of the fixed stars has the fastest movement, since its motion accounts for the stars' progress across the heavens each night, and by carrying the sun along in its motion accounts for day and night. But Philolaus accounts for these phenomena by the motion of the earth, thus obviating the need for motion of the fixed stars. Burkert's objection is that the testimonia about the Philolaic system talk of ten bodies moving around the central fire, which must mean that the fixed stars move. But even more disastrous is a report of Alexander which Burkert argues stems from Aristotle's book and which assigns the fastest movement to the sphere of the fixed stars. If this were so, the system would collapse into a whirl of motions with no point of reference, and Burkert argues that accordingly we must regard the Philolaic system as at its core mythic, rather than philosophical or scientific (1972: 340). However, I think that while there is a real inconcinnity in the Philolaic system here, the report of Alexander on which Burkert relies is in fact part of Alexander's speculative reconstruction of the harmony of the spheres doctrine, and thus is not based on Aristotle's book on the Pythagoreans and in fact provides no evidence about the Philolaic system.

The passage in question is embedded in Alexander's commentary on Aristotle's *Metaphysics* 985b26ff, which discusses the primacy of number in Pythagoreanism. In his commentary Alexander gives many examples of the role of number in Pythagoreanism and at 39.25 turns to the doctrine of the harmony of the spheres, which Aristotle does not discuss in the *Metaphysics* passage, but which he does discuss in the *De caelo* and in his lost books on the Pythagoreans. Alexander begins by saying, as does Aristotle in the *De caelo*, that the heavenly bodies move at speeds which are in proportion to their distances (from the center), with the slower-moving bodies giving out a low tone while the faster-moving give a high tone. The sound that is produced by the combination of these tones produces a harmony. Alexander goes on to say that the Pythagoreans thought that the number of this harmony was the first principle of the universe. Then, in order to illustrate the role of number in the harmony of the spheres, he starts to give examples of the relative distances of the heavenly bodies from each other, but he introduces these examples with the words φέρε εἰπεῖν (40.3: "supposing" or "say, for example"). As Burkert himself argues (1972: 354), these words show that "the figures given belong to a hypothetical case, cited for clarity's sake, and do not belong to a traditional account" and hence are not drawn from Aristotle's account of the Pythagoreans. But Alexander's statement that the bodies that are farthest away (i.e. the fixed stars) have the fastest movement comes in the immediately following sentence (40.7: κινεῖσθαι δὲ τάχιστα μὲν τὰ τὸ μέγιστον διάστημα κινούμενα, βραδύτατα δὲ τὰ τὸ ἐλάχιστον...) There is nothing to indicate that Alexander has now shifted back to reporting a traditional account which relies on Aristotle's book on the Pythagoreans, rather than continuing his own speculative account. That it is likely to be Alexander's own account is bolstered by the fact that for Aristotelians the motion of the fixed stars was the fastest (*De caelo* 291a34-b1). Alexander has just taken the basic idea of the harmony of the spheres and, lacking any specifics of the Pythagorean system, illustrated it in terms of Aristotelian astronomy.

Burkert argues that we cannot suppose that Alexander made a mistake, because he repeats the statement a page later (41.5) with the comment ὡς προείρηκε ("as he [Aristotle] said before"). But what Alexander repeats at 41.5 is not the statement that the bodies that are farthest away move fastest but the statement (also found in the *De caelo*) that for the Pythagoreans the bodies move in proportion to their distance (κινεῖσθαί τε κατὰ ἀναλογίαν τῶν διαστημάτων, ὡς προείρηκε). But this doctrine is perfectly in accord with the Philolaic system as I have reconstructed it. The bodies move slower the farther they are from the center.

Once it is shown that there is no reason to assign to Philolaus the view that the fixed stars have the *fastest* movement, the greatest challenge to the coherence of his system is removed, but there is still a difficulty as to whether or not the fixed stars do have any movement at all. As suggested above, Philolaus' astronomy would make most sense if the fixed stars had no movement and were just a stationary background for the movements of the sun, moon, and planets. However, both at *Metaphysics* 986a10 (Text 2) and in F203 (Text 3) Aristotle talks of ten bodies (thus including the fixed stars) *moving* (φερόμενα, κινούμενα) around the central fire. A16 (Text 7) also suggests that the sphere of the fixed stars moves when it says that ten bodies "dance" (χορεύειν) around the central fire. Now, to begin with, it seems to me at least a possibility that Philolaus originally said that there were ten bodies "arranged" around the central fire and focused on those that move, such as the earth. If he made no special point about the lack of movement of the fixed stars, the later tradition could very easily come to over-generalize and speak as if all ten bodies actually moved. If the fixed stars do move they would have the very slowest of all motions since they are farthest from the center. A second explanation would be that, for the sake of uniformity, Philolaus supposed that the sphere of the fixed stars did have an extremely slow movement, but regarded it as for practical purposes negligible. Some scholars have supposed that its slow movement was meant to explain the precession of the equinoxes, but there is no evidence that this phenomenon had been observed in the late fifth century. But even if the fixed stars do have a slow movement, it does not vitiate Philolaus' astronomy or show that he belongs in the tradition of Herodorus; rather it shows that he belongs to the early stages of Greek speculations on astronomy; that he belongs in the company of Anaxagoras rather than Eudoxus. To conclude my discussion of Philolaus' astronomy, I will examine his views in light of other Presocratic astronomy of the fifth century and argue both that he has very close ties to that astronomy and that he also makes an important advance beyond it in a way that makes him the true precursor of Platonic astronomy.

   Philolaus' speculations on astronomy are tied to those of other Presocratics of the fifth century such as Empedocles, Anaxagoras, and Democritus, both by similarities on specific points of doctrine and by a basic uniformity in the types of questions that were addressed. (This uniformity may, of course, be to some extent imposed by the form of the doxography.) First, Philolaus' account of the sun as not having light of its own (A19) is very similar to Empedocles' views. Likewise his belief that the moon is like the earth and inhabited (A20) is shared by Anaxagoras and Democritus. The types of phenomena that he takes into account are also in accord with the other fifth-century thinkers. He takes over a basic view of the cosmos as a sphere focused on a center from Parmenides (Furley 1987: 53) and is interested in what is at the center of that sphere and in the position of the earth, as are the other thinkers. We have seen that he tries to account for the phenomena traditionally associated with the obliquity of the ecliptic, and we have clear evidence that it was just at this period that others first started wrestling with this problem (e.g. Oenopides). He is also concerned with the basic ordering of the orbits of the moon, sun, planets, and fixed stars, as Democritus clearly was (A40, A86) and Anaxagoras may have been (A81). Indeed, there is no astronomical phenomenon that Philolaus deals with which is not also known to other fifth-century thinkers (except possibly the relative periods of the planets – see below). Thus, the phenomena on which he focuses, as well as some of his explanations of them, place Philolaus in the fifth century, but his approach to the phenomena shows some basic differences from other Presocratics in ways that look forward to Plato.

Empedocles, Anaxagoras, and Democritus are all concerned to give an account of how the cosmos came to be and how it works now in terms of physical causes. They all use the same basic mechanism, the vortex. The basic material elements are caught up in the whirl of a vortex and through that motion come to be separated out with the earth taking up its place in the lower central part of the vortex in virtue of its being the heaviest element. The sun, moon, planets, and stars are also carried by this vortex so that those at the periphery move fastest with those close to the earth moving slowest. There is interest in what the heavenly bodies are made of and how they come to be on fire. Again, the "turnings" of the sun are explained physically as the result of the air pressing on it. The earth itself is supported by air. There is considerable emphasis on explanations of meteorological phenomena such as lightning, thunder, hail, as well as earthquakes and comets. The system of Democritus (but probably not that of Anaxagoras – see Furley 1987: 71) is open-ended in the sense that it envisages an unlimited number of worlds with an unlimited variety of configurations. Even in our own world Anaxagoras and Democritus seem unwilling to posit a set number of planets and leave open the possibility of more than the canonical five (Anaxagoras A81; Democritus A92; see West 1980: 208).

Philolaus, on the other hand, shows little interest in providing physical causes and much more interest in giving a clear schematic model of the cosmos that is constructed according to principles of number and order. The closest he comes to a physical cause is in the analogy between the breathing of the new-born infant and the breathing in of unlimiteds by the central fire. There is no vortex. He gives no account of why the sun, moon, and planets move (unless the central fire has a motive force, as suggested in Simplicius [Text 6]). He says that the earth moves, but gives no cause of the motion. There is a fire located in the center of the cosmos, but he evidently did not feel compelled to say why it stayed there or how it came to be there. Nowhere in the testimonia do we hear of Philolaus' accounts of meteorological phenomena. In general the lack of interest in physical causation is borne out by the lack of a system of physical elements. Philolaus' basic principles are not atoms or earth, air, fire, and water but limiters and unlimiteds (unlimiteds do include material elements but are not limited to them). A further difference is that Philolaus presents us with a closed system. The system is complete and has no room for new planets.

However, because Philolaus is not interested in physical causation, he presents us with a much more coherent model of the cosmos than any other fifth-century thinker. His model accounts for all the phenomena that other fifth-century systems do. He assigns each heavenly body one circular motion with the speeds (angular velocity) being in proportion to the distance from the center and decreasing with distance from the center. He was in no position to assign specific numbers to those speeds, but expresses the basic belief that they have an intelligible mathematical relationship. Such a model is crude and in the next century the phenomena of retrogradations will call forth much more sophisticated models, but it is a model that is articulated enough to elicit criticisms based on the phenomena and to encourage the production of more sophisticated models. On the other hand there is no way of modifying the Anaxagorean or Democritean system in light of the phenomena, since they are not articulated enough to create expectations of what the phenomena should be that can then be tested by observation. Furthermore, the vortex works in some ways as a *deus ex machina* to explain any and all phenomena, whereas the Philolaic system says that heavenly motions have to be explained in terms of a single circular motion for each body, and supposes that these motions have a uniform relation to each other based on their distance from the center. It is in providing an elegant astronomical model, rather than a physical theory of the cosmos combined with a loosely connected group of speculations on specific phenomena, that Philolaus marks an advance over other Presocratic thinkers in the direction of the model which Plato provides in his *Timaeus*.

Up to this point I have been arguing that Philolaus is very much on a par with the rest of Presocratic astronomy in accounting for phenomena. However there is also some evidence that Philolaus was working with a slightly more sophisticated appreciation of the phenomena regarding the planets than his contemporaries. In Simplicius' commentary on the *De caelo* (471.5ff) he quotes Eudemus (F146 – Text 10) as saying that Anaximander first instituted the discussion of sizes and distances of the heavenly bodies, while assigning the first discovery of the order of their positions to the Pythagoreans. Eudemus is an excellent source and his report evidently means that the Pythagoreans first posited the correct order of the planets starting from the earth (i.e. moon, sun, five planets in the order Mercury, Venus, Mars, Jupiter, Saturn and finally the fixed stars). This is what we find in the reports about Philolaus, except that the order of the five planets is not specified. On the other hand none of the testimonia about other Presocratics of the fifth century suggests that they gave this order. Democritus is supposed to have written a book on the planets (DK 68B5b), but the order of planets assigned to him in the doxography puts Venus between the moon and the sun (A86, A40.4, A88), and a report in Seneca (A92) may suggest that he thought that there could be more than five planets. It seems most plausible to assume that Philolaus is the Pythagorean that Eudemus is talking about, and thus that Philolaus was the first to posit the correct ordering of the planets. Here we see that Philolaus was *au courant* with some of the best astronomical data available. This is yet another indication that he is to be placed in the domain of Presocratic speculation about the cosmos rather than in the tradition of mythography. It is also interesting that Censorinus assigns a theory of a Great Year of fifty-nine years to Philolaus, which is an attempt mathematically to relate the lunar and solar year. If this tradition is correct, it would show Philolaus as connected to figures like Meton and Oenopides (DK 41.9), who were interested in the mathematics of the solar and lunar year (see the commentary on A22).

Philolaus then would seem to have handed on several important astronomical doctrines: (1) the correct ordering of the planets; (2) the idea that the bodies closest to the center move fastest; (3) the general conception of the harmony of the spheres (see p. 279 below). But more than these specific points, Philolaus handed on the conception of an astronomical model of the cosmos which combined *a priori* postulates of order with an attempt to explain the major astronomical phenomena. He in fact seems to have taken over the "centrifocal" universe first put forth by Parmenides and developed it considerably towards what we find later in Plato. We have no reliable evidence that Plato ever accepted the postulate that 10 was the perfect number and that there must accordingly be ten heavenly bodies, or that he accepted the primacy of fire so that the earth was moved from the center (*pace* Plutarch, *Numa* 11). However, he seems very attracted by the attempt to explain planetary phenomena in terms of one regular motion for each body. In so far as Philolaus makes principles of order prior to mechanical causation (e.g. a vortex) and envisions the cosmos as held together by mathematical proportion of some sort (even if the proportions cannot be specified), he is the clear precursor of Plato.

Testimonium A18 – destructions of the world

Aetius 2.5.3 (333 Diels) Φιλόλαος διττὴν εἶναι τὴν φθοράν, τὸ μὲν ἐξ οὐρανοῦ πυρὸς ῥυέντος, τὸ δὲ ἐξ ὕδατος σεληνιακοῦ, περιστροφῇ τοῦ ἀέρος ἀποχυθέντος· καὶ τούτων εἶναι τὰς ἀναθυμιάσεις τροφὰς τοῦ κόσμου. (See also Stobaeus, *Eclogae*
5   1.20.1g; 1.21.6d.)

1 διττὴν... φθοράν Plut. φθορὰν τοῦ κόσμου Stob. 20 διττὴν... φθοράν om. et add. ἔφησε Stob. 21 τροφήν Galen   2 τὸ μὲν... τὸ δὲ Galen Stob. 21 τοτὲ μὲν... τοτὲ δέ Plut. Stob. 20   ἐξ οὐρανοῦ Stob. 21 Plut. ἐξ ὑγροῦ Stob. 20 ἐξ ante ὕδατος del. Usener   3 [τοῦ ἀέρος] Gomperz ἀέρος ἀποχυθέντος Stob. 21 Plut. ἀστέρος ῥυέντος Stob. 20 ἀστέρος ἀποχυθέντος Plut. B   3–4 καὶ... κόσμου om. Stob. 20 καὶ τούτων om. Stob. 21   τούτου Capelle

Philolaus [says] that destruction is twofold, on the one hand when fire rushes in from the heaven, and on the other from lunar water when it is poured out by the revolution of the air. And the exhalations of these are nourishment for the cosmos.

AUTHENTICITY

Doubts about the testimonium could arise if we thought it was too closely tied to Stoic accounts of the destruction of the world, but once it is seen that at most Philolaus is talking about localized catastrophes on the earth, it becomes clear that his doctrine would fit very well into the background that seems to be assumed by Plato's mention of destructions by fire and flood in the *Timaeus*. Heraclitus' account of destructions on the earth by fire and water shows that we need not assume that the Philolaus passage is in fact derived from Plato. On the other hand there is a fairly significant amount of evidence that, even before Aristotle's doctrine of two exhalations from the earth, Presocratic thinkers made use of the notion of exhalations to explain astronomical phenomena, so that once again Philolaus' reference to exhalations that nourish the cosmos can be plausibly seen to fit into a Presocratic context and need not be assumed to be late.

COMMENTARY

The text: The textual tradition for this testimonium is particularly confusing both because there are significant differences between the versions preserved in Plutarch and Stobaeus and because Stobaeus in fact presents the testimonium under two different headings with different texts. The testimonium occurs first in Stobaeus under the heading "Generation and destruction" (1.20.1g), and here the last sentence, which refers to the nourishing of the heaven through exhalations, is omitted. The testimonium's second occurrence is under the heading which addresses the question of the source of the nourishment of the cosmos. Here all mention of destruction is removed from the first sentence, leaving it ungrammatical (see Boeckh 1819: 111). It is thus clear that the testimonium was tailored differently for two different contexts. Plutarch's testimony allows us to see that the testimonium originally connected Philolaus' account of the destruction of the world with its nourishment.

Starting from Plutarch's complete text, then, we are faced with a series of smaller but important problems. First, the text in Plutarch says that Philolaus thought there was simply a twofold destruction or passing away (φθορά), but the version in Stobaeus 20 specifies that the destruction is "of the cosmos." If we accept the text which says that the destruction is of the cosmos, we must conclude, in light of Philolaus' use of cosmos to refer to all of reality in Fragments 1–6, that he has in mind some sort of universal cataclysm. On the other hand, if we accept the text which simply refers to destruction or passing away, Philolaus could be referring simply to the passing away of parts of the world through the action of heat and water. There is no way to decide the question on the grounds of the textual tradition alone. Plutarch is as likely to be right as Stobaeus, so that the decision must be made on the sense of the passage. The theory produced by the text in Plutarch is much more coherent, and should thus be accepted. If Philolaus were talking about the destruction of the whole cosmos (the Stobaeus text), at least two difficulties would arise. First, immediately after describing the destruction of the whole cosmos he talks about the same process as nourishing the now destroyed cosmos. It is not impossible to suppose that he means that one cosmos perishes and that a new cosmos arises nourished by the exhalations from the old one, but if this is what is meant it is stated in a very obscure fashion with no distinction made between the old and new cosmos. Second, it might be plausible to see the whole cosmos as being destroyed by a fire that rushes in from outside, especially since Philolaus seems to have thought that there was a fire at the periphery. However, it is hard to see how lunar water would have such a far-reaching effect on the cosmos as a whole. Water collected around the moon might be thought to have significant influence on the earth but not on the whole cosmos. Thus we should follow Boeckh (1819: 111) and Zeller (1923: 549) rather than DK and regard τοῦ κόσμου ("of the cosmos") as a careless insertion by someone in the transmission, probably influenced by the appearance of τοῦ κόσμου ("of the cosmos") at the end of the testimonium.

It is less clear whether we should read τὸ μὲν ... τὸ δέ or τοτὲ μὲν ... τοτὲ δέ. If Philolaus is thinking of a process of passing away that is going on continuously, it might be slightly more appropriate to use "on the one hand ... on the other." However, if he is thinking of more isolated incidents of radical scorchings of the earth or deluges by water, it would make better sense to read "at one time ... at another." Boeckh is probably right that τὸ μὲν ... τὸ δὲ is the *lectio difficilior* (1819: 111 n. 1).

The twofold destruction: Three different scenarios come to mind when thinking of the twofold destruction ascribed to Philolaus. The first would be a destruction of the whole cosmos later followed by a new cosmogony. This would correspond to the doctrine of ecpyrosis which Heraclitus probably accepted (Kahn 1979: 134ff). In the discussion of the text above I have argued that this scenario does not fit very well the text of Philolaus A18 which seems to focus on the region of the earth. A second scenario has been developed by Boeckh (1819: 111ff) and Zeller (1923: 549ff). According to them Philolaus is not talking about a major cataclysm at all but an ongoing process of corruption on the earth. Under the influence of heat and moisture parts of the earth are dissolved, giving off exhalations which in turn nourish the rest of the cosmos. Thus we can think of the evaporation of water and the wearing away of the earth through the action of rain.

A third interpretation might accept this latter view of the gradual wasting of the earth, but also maintain that in emphasizing a twofold destruction Philolaus is also thinking of major cataclysms on the earth, one by fire and one by water, which certainly do not destroy it, but affect large inhabited parts and wipe them out. In the *Timaeus* (22c1–3) Plato has the Egyptian priest talk of many destructions of the earth, the greatest of which come through fire and water at great intervals of time. Aristotle also speaks of a great winter which occurs at great intervals of time, in which excess of rain leads to widespread destruction (*Mete.* 1.14, 352a31). If we look back before Plato and Aristotle, we find that testimonia also associate Heraclitus (A13, A5) with a great year of 10,800 years, which would certainly include a great summer of cosmic fire and perhaps a winter of cosmic floods. There is controversy as to whether this testimonium is reliable, but Kahn has argued convincingly for accepting it (1979: 156ff). Indeed, Kahn feels that Plato's remarks at *Timaeus* 22c1–3 show that some Presocratic theorist must have put forth the view of periodic cataclysms by fire and water (1979: 159, 318 n. 184). He clearly is inclined to think that this theorist was Heraclitus, although he recognizes that the support for a doctrine of destruction through flood in Heraclitus is not strong. It would appear, in fact, that Philolaus would have a better claim to being this theorist upon whom Plato is drawing, since precisely a twofold destruction, one through fire and one through water, is ascribed to him here in A18.

The details of the mechanisms of these two destructions are very obscure. Philolaus evidently thought that there was a fire surrounding the cosmos as well as a fire at the center, and this surrounding fire might be seen as what rushes in. Alternatively, Philolaus could just be thinking of the fire manifested in the heavenly bodies and in particular the sun. Indeed, there is a possible connection that can be made between Philolaus' theory of the sun and the destruction by fire. The most plausible interpretation of his theory of the sun is that he saw it as a lens that functioned like a burning glass which passed on heat and light to the earth from the fire in the heaven. But this suggests that at some times the sun might collect too much light from the heavens and focus too much heat on the earth, thus producing the widespread conflagration which seems to be referred to here in A18; but this is very speculative.

Things are even less clear in the case of the destruction through lunar water. It is unclear both how this water comes to be around or on the moon and also how it is "poured out by the revolution of air." Some of the manuscripts read "star" (ἀστέρος) rather than "air" (ἀέρος) here, and in this case the reference to "the revolution of the star" would presumably be to the revolution of the moon which is often included with the stars. Gomperz tried for the same result by simply removing "air" from the text leaving the translation "poured out by the revolution," where it is easy to supply "of the moon" from the context. These corrections are attractive, but in the end we simply do not know enough of Philolaus' views on the moon or the position of air in the cosmos to be sure that it might not be air which he was referring to after all.

It is hard to see any direct connection between the comments on the moon in A20 and the role of lunar water in destruction here in A18. There is abundant evidence in the later tradition which connects the moon with moisture (e.g. Plutarch, *On the Face on the Moon* 940b; Aristotle, *HA* 582a34–b3). We simply do not know enough to say whether Philolaus thought of the moisture as collecting on or around the moon, or whether he thought of the moon as concentrating the moisture on and around the earth in some way so as to produce a deluge. The mention of the "revolution of air" might suggest action on the earth, but there is also evidence that some Presocratics associated air or mist with the moon. Thus Xenophanes (DK A43) is reported to have thought that the moon was "felted cloud," and Empedocles said that the moon was cloud-like and composed of air that is "twisted up" (συνεστραμμένον) and solidified by fire (DK A60, A30).

The exhalations: The second part of the testimonium says that the exhalations of "these" are nourishment of the cosmos. It seems that "these" here must refer to the fire that rushes in from the heaven and the lunar water. The exhalations need not be directly from heavenly fire and lunar water, but more probably arise from the earth as a result of their destructive effect. The basic phenomenon that inspired the idea of an exhalation in Greek thought is evaporation, and it is clearly seen as a vapor of sorts (see Kahn 1979: 259 and Kirk 1954: 272). Aristotle presents a developed theory of two exhalations from the earth, one moist and one dry, which account for rain and winds among other things (*Mete.* 341b6; 354b34, etc.). In Aristotle's theory the exhalations only explain phenomena in the sublunary sphere, and he is particularly scornful of earlier thinkers who have thought that a moist exhalation from the earth reached all the way to the sun and nourished it (*Mete.* 354b34). This would appear to be exactly the sort of theory that is ascribed to Philolaus in A18 where the cosmos is nourished by exhalations. There is evidence that even before Philolaus exhalation theories were developed, particularly by Heraclitus (D.L. 9.9), but scholars are divided about the exact nature of his theory and whether it included one or two exhalations (Kirk 1954: 270ff; Kahn 1979: 293). Xenophanes is said to have thought that the sun came from a moist exhalation (ὑγρᾶς ἀναθυμιάσεως – DK A40). Turning to figures closer to Philolaus' date, his contemporary Hippocrates of Chios appears to have explained the tail of comets and perhaps the milky way as a reflection from an exhalation (DK42 A6).

The notion that a moist exhalation should in some way nourish fire may seem strange to us, but it is clear that the notion of water nourishing fire was widespread in the Presocratic period (see e.g. *On Regimen* 1.3. This treatise seems to gather together Presocratic ideas from a number of sources). Thus, that Philolaus, writing in the latter part of the fifth century, should have had a theory which stated that the cosmos was nourished by exhalations from the effects of fire and water on the earth is very plausible. The details of this theory remain problematic, however. In particular it is unclear whether we should conclude from the assertion that destruction is twofold that Philolaus also advocated a theory of two exhalations (moist and dry).

Testimonium A19 – the sun

Aetius 2.20.12 (349 Diels)   Φιλόλαος ὁ Πυθαγόρειος ὑαλοειδῆ τὸν ἥλιον, δεχόμενον μὲν τοῦ ἐν τῷ κόσμῳ πυρὸς τὴν ἀνταύγειαν, διηθοῦντα δὲ πρὸς ἡμᾶς τό τε φῶς καὶ τὴν ἀλέαν, ὥστε τρόπον τινὰ διττοὺς ἡλίους γίγνεσθαι, τό τε ἐν τῷ οὐρανῷ πυρῶδες καὶ
5   τὸ ἀπ' αὐτοῦ πυροειδὲς κατὰ τὸ ἐσοπτροειδές, εἰ μή τις καὶ τρίτον λέξει τὴν ἀπὸ τοῦ ἐνόπτρου κατ' ἀνάκλασιν διασπειρομένην πρὸς ἡμᾶς αὐγήν. καὶ γὰρ ταύτην προσονομάζομεν ἥλιον οἱονεὶ εἴδωλον εἰδώλου. (See Stobaeus, *Eclogae* 1.25.3d.)

2 τὸν ἥλιον om. Plut.   πυρὸς Plut. πρὸς Stob. A   3 καὶ τὴν ἀλέαν om. Plut.
3–4 τρόπον... ἡλίους Stob. προσεοικέναι ἡλίῳ Plut.   5 κατὰ τὸ ἐσοπτροειδές Stob.
καὶ ἐσοπτροειδές Plut.   5–6 εἰ μή τις καὶ... λέξει om. Plut   7–8 καὶ... εἰδώλου om.
Stob.

Philolaus the Pythagorean says that the sun is like glass, receiving the reflection of the fire in the cosmos, straining the light and heat through to us, so that in a way there turn out to be two suns, both the fiery one in the heaven and that which is from it and fiery in reflection; unless someone will also say that there is a third, the light that is spread from the mirror to us by reflection. For we call this latter the sun which is, as it were, the image of an image.

Achilles, *Isagoga excerpta* 19 (46.13 Maass)   Φιλόλαος δὲ [sc. τὸν ἥλιον] τὸ πυρῶδες καὶ διαυγὲς λαμβάνοντα ἄνωθεν ἀπὸ τοῦ αἰθερίου πυρὸς πρὸς ἡμᾶς πέμπειν τὴν αὐγὴν διά τινων ἀραιωμάτων. ὥστε κατ᾽ αὐτὸν τρισσὸν εἶναι τὸν ἥλιον, τὸ μὲν
5   ἀπὸ τοῦ αἰθερίου πυρός, τὸ δὲ ἀπ᾽ ἐκείνου πεμπόμενον ἐπὶ τὸν ὑαλοειδῆ ὑπ᾽ αὐτοῦ λεγόμενον ἥλιον, τὸ δὲ ἀπὸ τοῦ τοιούτου ἡλίου πρὸς ἡμᾶς πεμπόμενον.

Philolaus (says) that (the sun), receiving what is fiery and translucent from the aithereal fire above, sends it to us through certain pores. The result is that according to him the sun is threefold, one (sun) is from the aithereal fire, another is sent from that to what is called by him the glassy sun, and another sent from that sort of sun to us.

AUTHENTICITY

The testimonium from Achilles given above is not included in DK because Diels initially judged that it was dependent upon pseudo-Plutarch. However, as Burkert points out, what Achilles reports is in fact superior to what we find in pseudo-Plutarch and based on independent testimony. Diels himself later accepted this view (Burkert 1972; 342 n. 23). The doctrine of the sun put forth in this testimonium is very likely to belong to the genuine book of Philolaus because of its very strong connections to other accounts of the sun and astronomical phenomena which were current in the late fifth century. Of course the testimonium also has been contaminated by later ideas and we cannot suppose that all the vocabulary belonged to Philolaus. It seems particularly clear that the idea of the sun we see being "the image of an image" must be later interpretation since it matches so well Platonic descriptions of the relation between forms and their copies (*R.* 10, 600e5). Indeed, it is tempting to see the whole idea of there being not just one but three suns as the result of later interpretation, rather than an explicit assertion of Philolaus. He proposed the idea of the glassy sun and later commentators, influenced by Platonic ideas of a series of copies of an original, drew out the implication that there were in fact three suns in his system.

However, under these later interpretive comments the core of Philolaus' theory is that the sun does not have its own light, but derives it from elsewhere and passes on light and heat like a magnifying glass (or possibly a mirror – see below) to the earth. A number of scholars have argued that this idea was presumably inspired by the knowledge that the moon has borrowed light and noted that theories that try to extend this idea to the sun and to other astronomical phenomena are very common in the late fifth century (Burkert 1972: 342ff). Directly after the testimonium on Philolaus

in Aetius a report is given about Empedocles' theory of the sun (A56 –
see also A30) according to which the sun does not have its own light, is
the result of some sort of reflection (ἀνάκλασις), and is described as like
crystal (κρυσταλοειδῆ). There are some difficulties in interpreting these reports (see Burnet 1948: 238 for a plausible interpretation), but they clearly
show strong similarities to Philolaus. Wright (1981: 201ff) has argued that
these testimonia must be mistaken, but her arguments are not convincing (note particularly "it is at variance with the main lines of Presocratic
cosmology") since she ignores the parallels with Philolaus and the other
fifth-century figures mentioned below. This is not the place to argue about
Empedocles' theory in detail, but even on Wright's account which is based
on F44 there are striking similarities with Philolaus. Once again the sun,
which is lentiform, is seen as having no light of its own but as gathering it
from the heaven and then transmitting it to the earth like a lens.

Diogenes of Apollonia also saw the sun as borrowing light from elsewhere. In this case it is supposed to be like a pumice stone (notice the
implication of "pores," as in Philolaus) on which the rays from the aither
concentrate (A13 – see also A12 and A14). The notion of light and heat
passing through pores in glass, which is assigned to Philolaus by Achilles,
is also found in Gorgias at about the same time in his description of a
burning-glass (F5, ἀπιέναι τὸ πῦρ διὰ τῶν πόρων – see also Aristophanes,
Clouds 767–9 for another late fifth-century reference to burning-glasses).
Thus, it is clear that Philolaus' view of the sun as not having its own light,
but as being glass-like and drawing fire and heat from another source and
sending it to the earth like a magnifying glass, is very much of a piece
with late fifth-century thought. It seems very unlikely to have been forged
after the time of Plato and Aristotle, whose theories of the sun bear no
resemblance to this, and it should therefore be accepted as from Philolaus'
genuine book.

COMMENTARY

τοῦ ἐν τῷ κόσμῳ πυρὸς . . . τό τε ἐν τῷ οὐρανῷ πυρῶδες: The first difficulty is determining what is meant by the expression "the fire in the cosmos
or heaven," from which Philolaus' sun is said to receive a reflection. Burnet
(1948: 298 n.1) and Guthrie (1962: 285 n.2) assume that both phrases must
refer to the central fire. Burnet's point is that the first phrase ("the fire in
the cosmos") was presumably Theophrastus' wording, since he is the source
of the doxographical tradition, and that in his mouth it would have to be
a reference to the central fire. But, if Theophrastus wanted to refer to the
central fire, it was perfectly possible to do so, as can be seen in Testimonia

A16 and A17, which are also derived ultimately from Theophrastus ("fire in the middle" – πῦρ ἐν μέσῳ, A16; "central fire" – τὸ πῦρ μέσον, A17). Again Burnet argues that "the fire in the heavens" must refer to the technical Pythagorean sense of "heavens" as the sublunary region, and hence be the central fire. But this "Pythagorean" sense of heavens is clearly part of the later tradition of the pseudepigrapha and does not belong to Philolaus (see the commentary on A16). Indeed, if we look at the testimonia on Philolaus' theory of the sun without preconceptions, it is clear that there is simply no reference to a central fire at all. Achilles' text could not be clearer that the fire is "from above." In fact the reports make much more sense if we assume that "the fire in the cosmos or heaven" refers to a fire which surrounds the cosmos, a view which is clearly ascribed to Philolaus in A16.

Is the sun a magnifying glass or a mirror?: The testimony of Achilles treats the sun unambiguously as if it were a lens or magnifying glass of some sort (notice the reference to the fire coming from above and the reference to "pores" [ἀραιωμάτων] through which the light comes). Aetius' report on the other hand seems to mix the ideas of a mirror and a magnifying glass or lens in a confusing way. The reference to the sun as filtering (διηθοῦντα) light and heat through to us has close connections to Achilles' reference to "pores," and views the sun as a lens. On the other hand there is explicit reference to "reflection" (κατὰ τὸ ἐσοπτροειδές), and the sun is even referred to directly as a mirror (τοῦ ἐνόπτρου κατ' ἀνάκλασιν). Since both the accounts make reference to the sun as a lens, it is tempting to see the reference to reflection in Aetius' account as a misunderstanding. Indeed, there is an easy explanation for this misunderstanding. An ancient scholar who knew of the central fire theory of Philolaus assumed that it must be present here, and accordingly interpreted the sun as reflecting light from the central fire back to the earth rather than as passing light on from the fire surrounding the cosmos. Guthrie does exactly this, partially because he does not pay enough attention to Achilles (1962: 285 n. 2).

It seems to be just possible that the reference to the sun as a mirror reflecting light is in fact compatible with the view of the sun as a lens. If we are to explain the appearance of the sun as a fiery ball in the sky, it cannot merely pass light through itself but must in some sense "reflect" the light that it gathers from the fire at the periphery. It may be that the references to reflection just explain this phenomenal sun without at the same time implying that the sun is a mirror rather than a lens. At any rate the best evidence seems to indicate that Philolaus viewed the sun as a glass-like body that served as a lens, which gathered and then transmitted to us both light and heat.

One point about the vocabulary of the testimonia on the sun is worth noting. Much of the language is of course derived from the doxographers. However, on my reading of Achilles, Philolaus is explicitly cited as having used the word "glassy" (ὑαλοειδής) to describe the sun, and the word interestingly also occurs in Aetius. Elsewhere the word is very rare, although it does occur in Theophrastus (*Lap.* 30), so that it does not seem impossible that it was used by Philolaus.

Fragment 18

Stobaeus, *Eclogae* 1.25.8 (1.214.21 Wachsmuth)   Φιλολάου ἐκ Βακχῶν

From the *Bacchae* of Philolaus

COMMENTARY

Nothing other than this heading is preserved in Stobaeus. It falls under chapter 25 of Stobaeus, which is devoted to a series of excerpts on the sun, so that we know the subject matter of the lost fragment or testimonium. Could it be that the heading has become misplaced and belongs with the testimony about the sun assigned to Philolaus by Stobaeus earlier in the chapter (1.25.3d = A19)?

Testimonium A20 – the moon

Aetius 2.30.1 (361 Diels)   τῶν Πυθαγορείων τινὲς μέν, ὧν ἐστι Φιλόλαος, γεώδη φαίνεσθαι τὴν σελήνην διὰ τὸ περιοικεῖσθαι αὐτὴν καθάπερ τὴν παρ' ἡμῖν γῆν ζῴοις καὶ φυτοῖς μείζοσι καὶ καλλίοσιν· εἶναι γὰρ πεντεκαιδεκαπλάσια τὰ ἐπ' αὐτῆς ζῷα τῇ
5   δυνάμει μηδὲν περιττωματικὸν ἀποκρίνοντα, καὶ τὴν ἡμέραν τοσαύτην τῷ μήκει. (See Stobaeus, *Eclogae* 1.26.4.)

1–2 τῶν... Φιλόλαος Stob. οἱ Πυθαγόρειοι Plut.   2–3 γεώδη... αὐτὴν Plut. τὸ γεωφανὲς αὐτῆς εἶναι διὰ τὸ περιοικεῖσθαι τὴν σελήνην Stob.   3 μείζοσι ⟨δὲ⟩ Kranz μείζοσι ζῴοις καὶ φυτοῖς καλλίοσι Plut.   5 ἡμέραν Plut. ἡμετέραν FP(Stob.)

Some of the Pythagoreans, including Philolaus, say that the moon appears earth-like because it is inhabited, just like our earth, with animals and plants which are greater and finer. For [he says] that the animals on it are fifteen-fold in power and give off no excrement, and that the day is this same length [i.e. fifteen times an earth day].

270

AUTHENTICITY

This is, at least at first sight, one of the more bizarre testimonia regarding Philolaus' views. In itself, this is no reason for questioning its authenticity, and it is accepted by Burkert as deriving from Philolaus' genuine book. The main reason for concluding that the testimonium is trustworthy is the same reason which supported the authenticity of the testimonia about Philolaus' explanation of the sun (A19). Namely, Philolaus' views about inhabitants on the moon find striking parallels in the mid and late fifth century. There are similar reports from the fourth century, and some testimonia suggest a tie to the later Platonizing tradition, but, although there is some room for doubt, the parallels with the fifth-century authors seem strong enough to allow us to accept this testimonium as deriving from Philolaus' book of the late fifth century.

The report on Philolaus' account of the moon comes from the section in the doxography devoted to the appearance or face (περὶ ἐμφάσεως) of the moon. In Plutarch this heading is expanded by the words "why it appears earthlike" (διὰ τί γεώδης φαίνεται). It is, of course, risky to conclude from such a title that it was exactly this question which was being asked in the fifth century, but the answers given certainly seem appropriate as answers to questions about the uneven appearance of the moon's surface.

Anaxagoras, who was a generation earlier than Philolaus, and Democritus, who was his contemporary, are both reported by Aetius (2.25.9) as having thought that the moon was a fiery solid body and that it had plains, mountains, and ravines. Anaxagoras is also said to have believed that the moon had high, low, and hollow places (2.30.2). Democritus (2.30.3) believed that shadows were cast by high parts on the moon and that it had glens and valleys. There may well have been some tendency to argue on the basis of these topographical similarities to the earth that the moon was also similar in being inhabited. At any rate we are told that Anaxagoras did regard it as inhabited (A77 and D.L. 2.8 where hills and ravines are men-' tioned again – there seems no reason to assume that this derives from F4 as Cherniss [1957: 156 n.b] suggests, since there is nothing in the fragment to suggest the moon). It is possible that Ach. *Is.* 21 (in Anaxagoras A77) also ascribes the idea that the moon is inhabited to Democritus, since the theory of the moon mentioned first, that it is a fiery solid body, is one that is ascribed to both Anaxagoras and Democritus elsewhere in the doxography. We are told that Anaxagoras went even further and said that the Nemean lion originally came from the moon (A77), a view which is also assigned to the mythographer Herodorus of Heraclea (5th–4th century – Athenaeus 2.57ff). If we can believe Cicero, Xenophanes may have been the first Presocratic to assert that the moon was inhabited (A47), but it is commonly supposed that the reference is to Anaxagoras or Xenocrates (Cherniss [1957] 156 n.b).

It should be clear from these parallels that the idea that the moon was inhabited was in circulation in the fifth century and even held by such staunch "rationalists" as Anaxagoras and perhaps Democritus. Moreover, Anaxagoras' story of the Nemean lion shows that he supposed its inhabitants to be different from those on earth. Even Aristotle considered the possibility that a type of life different from ours might be on the moon (*GA* 761b21–3). Herodorus of Heraclea, who was primarily interested in myth, also parallels Philolaus in holding that the creatures on the moon are fifteen times larger than those on earth (*Fr. Gr. Hist.* 31F4), but it is hard to be sure who influenced whom. Later in the fourth century Heraclides of Pontus retailed the story that a man fell from the moon (D.L. 8.72), and Hecataeus of Abdera draws connections between the moon and the Hyperboreans (*Fr. Gr. Hist.* 264F7 = DK 73B5).

But perhaps the most striking parallel with A20 of Philolaus is found in Philoponus' commentary (160.16–21) on the passage in Aristotle's *Generation of Animals* mentioned above. Philoponus first explicates Aristotle's argument for supposing that there must be an animal corresponding to the fourth element, fire, and that this animal would be found not on the earth but on the moon. He then baldly asserts that "there are and come to be special intellectual animals in the aither." He goes on to describe them in some detail, asserting that, although not immortal, they live 3,000 years and that they spend their time in theoretical pursuits, having a home in aer and aither (he has said above [15] that they are in the sphere of the moon). This matches A20 of Philolaus in general terms in that these moon creatures are clearly superior to earthly ones, although none of the details mentioned so far matches exactly. However, Philoponus makes one further assertion that is very relevant to Philolaus' account. He asserts that these creatures neither eat nor drink (μήτε ἐσθίοντα μήτε πίνοντα). But, of course, this would inevitably mean that they would also be creatures such as Philolaus describes, i.e. they would produce no excrement. Indeed, in light of Philoponus' testimony, it is very tempting to suppose that Philolaus ascribed all three features to the creatures, i.e. that they neither ate, nor drank, nor produced excrement. In the transmission the first two could easily have been left out in favor of the more bizarre description of creatures which produce no excrement.

Philoponus concludes his account by asserting that the reason Aristotle puts off further discussion of these moon animals is that he does not in fact agree with such a doctrine which, Philoponus says, is Platonic. Nothing which we have of Plato corresponds very closely with this account of moon creatures, although Aristophanes' story in the *Symposium* (190b2–3) has it that some humans originated on the moon. The *Epinomis* (981b2ff), which may rather represent the ideas of the Academy than those of Plato himself, does present a doctrine of five kinds of creatures in which one kind is identified with fire and the stars, and the *Phaedo* (109b4ff) talks about the regions above what we consider to be the earth as being purer and its inhabitants as having no bodies. However, there is no explicit mention of the moon's inhabitants in either the *Epinomis* or the *Phaedo*. Thus, if Philoponus is not just asserting that the idea "sounds Platonic," it must have been developed explicitly by Plato's successors in the Academy. We do know that Xenocrates had a developed demonology (Heinze 1965: 78). At any rate what is significant is that on the basis of Aristotle, Philoponus' commentary, and the passage of Heraclides of Pontus mentioned above, we have some indication of interest in the Academy in speculations about the inhabitants of the moon, speculations which show moon creatures to be far different but also clearly "better" or "higher" than those on earth (more intellectual and less dependent on the body).

Since many of the forged documents in the collection of Pythagorean pseudepigrapha show such strong ties to the early Academy, parallels from the Academy for Philolaus' views on the moon are disquieting. Particularly worrisome is the common emphasis on the superiority of the moon creatures (more powerful, not eating or drinking). This makes sense in a Platonic or Aristotelian universe where the earth is at the center and the upper regions are viewed as more divine. It is less clear how it fits into the Philolaic universe where the center of the universe is just as divine as the periphery with the result that it is uncertain what status the moon would have in comparison with the earth. However, the connections to the fifth-century authors are also close in detail (Anaxagoras' view that the moon is inhabited and Herodorus' view that the creatures on the moon are fifteen times larger than those on earth), and we must conclude that it is as likely as not that the account of the moon ascribed to Philolaus is really his, and was developed in the same sort of intellectual environment as Anaxagoras' account of the moon and perhaps influenced by it.

COMMENTARY

General character of the testimonium: The parallels with other Presocratic authors as well as fourth-century authors show that we need not conclude with Burkert (1972: 347) that Philolaus' knowledge of the moon is based on a shamanistic journey unless we want to suppose that Anaxagoras, Aristotle, and other members of the Academy were shamans who journeyed to the moon as well. Similarly, the testimonium should not be used to discount Philolaus' whole cosmology as fantasy (Furley 1987: 58) unless we want to do the same for Anaxagoras and Democritus.

The nature of the moon: It is interesting to note that while this testimonium appears in Aetius under the heading "On the appearance of the moon," there is no view ascribed to Philolaus in the earlier heading "On the nature of the moon." However, under this latter heading we are told that Ion of Chios thought that the moon was glass-like (ὑελοειδές – 2.25.11 [356 Diels]), which is exactly how Philolaus described the sun; and more significantly "Pythagoras" is said to have thought that the moon was like a mirror (κατοπτροειδές – 2.25.14 [357 Diels]). In light of these testimonia it is not too implausible to suppose that Philolaus regarded the moon, as well as the sun (A19), as being glass-like and explained its light on the analogy of a mirror, although this must remain speculation. Empedocles also seems to have regarded the moon as like a lens, at least in shape (A60; see Wright 1981: 201). The question of where the moon gets its light is left open. It is possible that it could reflect light from the fire at the periphery of the cosmos, as the sun does for Philolaus (or even light from the central fire, which would fit with the idea that the counter-earth causes eclipses [Aet. 2.29.4], although the parallel with the sun argues against this); but it seems more likely that Philolaus would adhere to the standard view that the moon gets its light from the sun. Some Pythagoreans may have thought that the moon was fiery and thus had its own light (Aet. 2.29.4 = DK 58B36).

Inhabitants of the moon: As presented in the doxography Philolaus' point about the moon is that it appears to be like the earth (mountains, valleys, etc.) because it is inhabited just like the earth. This would most reasonably seem to mean that the moon appears to be like the earth because it is like the earth, i.e. it has the same topography, and accordingly might be supposed to be inhabited as the earth is. However, Philolaus then goes on to list three ways in which plants and animals on the moon differ from those on earth: (1) they are bigger and finer; (2) they are fifteen times more powerful; (3) they produce no excrement. The second of these points is clearly related to the last line of the testimonium where the lunar day is said to be "so great" (i.e. fifteen times that of earth). It is not clear why a longer day should make the inhabitants of the moon more powerful, unless it is somehow thought to be related to exposure to longer sustained periods of sunlight and/or darkness. There seems to be little hint in the passage as to why lunar creatures should be bigger, finer, and not produce excrement (and presumably not eat or drink). However, some light can be shed on each of these questions by Plutarch's treatise *The Face on the Moon*. It is risky

274

to use such a source to explicate Philolaus since, while it does seem to refer to fifth-century ideas, it also clearly draws on Plato and the Stoics, among others. Thus, we can draw ideas from Plutarch as to what might have been some of the ideas behind Philolaus' theory, while at the same time recognizing that we are largely in the realm of speculation.

The argument at 938aff suggests that Philolaus' idea of creatures on the moon (and Philolaus actually only mentions "creatures," and not specifically people) not eating, drinking, or excreting might have arisen from reflection on the much different meteorological conditions which appear to apply on the moon, where the heat would seem to be more intense than on earth and where there is no sign of clouds or other atmosphere. Aristotle (*Sens.* 445a16 = DK 58B43) in fact reports that some Pythagoreans thought that some animals were nourished by smells, and as Burkert points out (1972: 347 n. 51) this could be a reference to moon creatures. Plutarch does mention the stories of people on earth who are supposed to live just on smells in connection with his discussion of the moon people (938c).

The passage in Plutarch goes on to say that, from the point of view of those on the moon, it might be very surprising that there is life on the earth which would appear to be "the sediment and dregs of the universe" (ὑποστάθμην καὶ ἰλύν, 940e). This clearly suggests a point of view from which moon creatures would be seen as "finer" and "more powerful" than those on earth, which is what we find in Philolaus. However, this passage in Plutarch seems to be closely tied both to the Stoics (Zeno called the earth sediment and dregs – *SVF* 1.104–5) and to Plato's *Phaedo* (109c2), where the water and mist around the earth are called the sediment (ὑποστάθμη) of aither. Moreover, Plato describes those who ascend to the real surface of the earth as living without any bodies (114c2), and thus presumably without eating or drinking. These parallels between Philolaus' view on the perfections of the moon and Plato and the Stoics once again raise doubts about the authenticity of A20 of Philolaus. Of course, others might be tempted to see Philolaus' views as background for the *Phaedo's* account of the earth, since this is the one dialogue of Plato in which Philolaus is mentioned by name, and since it has been fashionable to find Philolaic ideas lurking behind much of what Plato says in the dialogue. It is striking that A20 of Philolaus does not follow the specifics of the *Phaedo* passage, as might be expected from a later forger, and introduces its own peculiarities such as the fifteen-fold strength of those on the moon.

It is interesting to note that the phrase used to describe the moon creatures as not producing excrement (περιττωματικὸν ἀποκρίνοντα) is paralleled in Aristotle. In *Parts of Animals* 665b24 he seems to use the phrase to refer to excrement, but at *HA* 511b9 the word translated as "excrement" in fact seems to refer to any sort of residue and is said to include phlegm, yellow and black bile, as well as dung. Indeed, περιττώματα is the standard word for "residues" for the Peripatetics, as can be seen in Meno's division of theories of disease into two types, those which say diseases are caused by the elements and those which say they are caused by residues (*Anon. Lond.* 4.26). The context in Philolaus does not rule out the possibility that he is talking about residues in a medical sense. His point could be that moon creatures do not produce residues like bile and phlegm and thus are not subject to disease (see A29). However, the parallels from Plutarch's treatise suggest that there was more discussion about whether moon creatures ate or not than about their medical condition (but note at *Phaedo* 111b2 Plato says that the inhabitants of the "upper" earth are free from disease); and it is thus somewhat more likely that Philolaus is denying that moon creatures produce excrement than that they produce harmful residues such as bile and phlegm.

Length of the lunar day: Most scholars have seen the assertion that the moon's day is fifteen times longer than that on earth as a mistake in computation. Since the moon takes thirty days (i.e. twenty-four-hour periods) to circle the central fire, as opposed to the earth's one day, if we assume that the moon rotates once on its axis during its orbit around the central fire as the earth does, it would seem that its period of daylight would last about half the time of its orbit around the central fire, or fifteen twenty-four-hour periods. This would mean, however, that this period of daylight would in fact be thirty times an average period of daylight on the earth. It is not clear whether this confusion between the two types of day (twenty-four-hour period or a period of daylight) is introduced by the doxographical tradition through a misunderstanding (Heath 1913: 119) or whether Philolaus made the mistake. If the fifteen-fold increase in size and beauty of moon creatures is tied to a longer period of daylight, which seems plausible, then the mistake would seem to apply to Philolaus. Martin (1872: 16) tried to get around this by supposing that the moon rotated on its axis twice during its revolution around the central fire so that the moon's daylight periods would turn out to be fifteen times those of earth, but this goes quite a bit beyond the evidence. The state of the evidence simply does not allow us to be sure what lies behind the assertion of the doxography that Philolaus regarded the lunar day as fifteen times an earth day.

Testimonium A22 – the great year

Censorinus 18.8   est et Philolai Pythagorici annus ex annis LIX, in quo sunt menses intercalares XXI ... (19.2) Philolaus annum naturalem dies habere prodidit CCCLXIIII et dimidiatum.

18.8 There is also a (great) year of Philolaus the Pythagorean consisting of fifty-nine years, in which there are twenty-one intercalary months... Philolaus proposed that the natural [i.e. solar] year has $364\frac{1}{2}$ days.

AUTHENTICITY

The concept of the great year for Philolaus is likely to be the smallest number of solar years into which a whole number of lunar months goes evenly. In other words it is an attempt to harmonize two important ways of measuring time, the lunar month and the solar year (on such cycles see Neugebauer 1975: 2.615ff). Some scholars have wanted to make Philolaus' great year also refer to the periods of the planets, but this is unlikely. In the *Timaeus* (39d) Plato remarks that people are familiar with the periods of the sun and moon but largely ignorant of the periods of the planets, which he describes as vast in number and admirable for their variety. Nonetheless, he says that there is a period of time, which he calls a "perfect year" (τέλεον ἐνιαυτόν), in which all the planets, sun, and moon return to the same position relative to one another (i.e. a period in which the solar year coincides not only with the end of a lunar cycle but also with the end of the period of each of the other planets). Plato gives no hint that anyone has ever successfully computed the length of such a perfect year, and the language he uses emphasizes the complexity of the problem and suggests that he is posing it as a problem to be solved rather than referring to something that has been accomplished (see Taylor's commentary ad. loc.). When Censorinus (18.8) refers to the great year of Philolaus and other fifth-century figures, he seems only to mean spans of time that reconcile the lunar and solar periods, and there is no mention of planetary periods. Thus, it is all but certain that Philolaus could only have been concerned with the lunar and solar cycles and we must reject the figures arrived at by Schiaparelli for the supposed Philolaic periods of the planets (see Heath 1913: 102 n. 2; Dicks 1970: 76).

A number of scholars have recognized that there is a coherence between the figure reported for Philolaus' great year and his figure for the natural year. If we multiply fifty-nine years by twelve to convert to months, and add the twenty-one intercalary months, the total is 729 months in the great year ($59 \times 12 + 21 = 729$). If this number of months is multiplied by 29.5, which was the commonly accepted round value for the lunar month (Neugebauer 1975: 2.619, 624), the result is 21,505.5 as the number of days in Philolaus' great year. If this number is then divided by 59, the result will be the number of days in a solar year, and this result is 364.5, which is exactly the value Censorinus gives us for Philolaus' natural year. Thus, assuming the value of 29.5 days for the length of the lunar month, the numbers assigned for Philolaus' great year and his natural year are consistent.

The crucial question is how did Philolaus arrive at this set of numbers?

Where did the number 59 for his great year come from? The most plausible explanation is that it is the result of trying to reconcile two commonly accepted round numbers for the lunar month and the solar year (29.5 days and 365 days respectively). In order to find the number of solar years in which a whole number of lunar months fits exactly, one might begin by doubling the period of the lunar month in order to obtain a whole number, which is 59. Then, since 59 is a prime number, it follows that there will be no common factors with 365 except 1 and 59 itself. Accordingly 59 is the lowest number of years in which the lunar cycle of 29.5 days will occur a whole number of times. If we multiply the 59 years by the 365 days in each year ($= 21,535$ days) and divide the 29.5 days in a lunar month into this figure, we see that there are 730 lunar months in the 59-year period. Testimony about Oenopides of Chios, a slightly older contemporary of Philolaus, suggests that he in fact had 730 months in his great year (so Tannery, reported in Heath 1913: 132). There are problems in connecting this procedure with Oenopides' figure of $365\frac{22}{59}$ days for the solar year (Neugebauer 1975: 2.619) but nonetheless the procedure outlined above seems a very plausible explanation of the origin of the 59-year cycle. But if the figures of 29.5 days for the lunar month and 365 days for the solar year point to a great year of 730 months, how do we explain Philolaus' use of 729? For it is clear that he accepted 729 as the number of months in the great year and then recomputed the length of the solar year as 364.5 days (multiplying $729 \times 19.5 = 21,505.5$ and then dividing by the 59 years). Neugebauer argues that 729 is introduced solely because of its connection to the sun in the "Pythagorean" system described by Plutarch (*De an. proc.* 1028b). In that system the heavenly bodies are assigned numbers according to the powers of the number three, starting from the central fire. Thus the counter-earth is 3, the earth 9, the moon 27, Mercury 81, Venus 243, and the sun 729. However, this system cannot possibly be Philolaus', despite the mention of the central fire, since Aristotle's testimony clearly shows that in Philolaus' system the sun came after the moon and, if identified with any number, was identifed with the number 7 as being the seventh orbit counting from the fixed stars inward (Philolaus A16, Alexander *In Metaph.* 38.20–39; see Burkert 1972: 313 n. 75; 318 n. 98 and Cherniss 1976 ad loc.). Thus if Neugebauer's explanation of the use of 729 were correct, we would have to suppose that Censorinus' testimony about the great year is not based on the authentic work of Philolaus but is rather based on a later reinterpretation of the central fire system..

However, there is another explanation at hand (see Tannery as reported in Heath 1913: 102). If Oenopides had already developed his great year consisting of 730 months, or if Philolaus had reached this figure on his own, based on the commonly accepted figures for the lunar month and solar year (see above), it might have been tempting for him to replace the relatively insignificant number 730 with 729, which is a more significant number in that it is a power of three and both a cube and a square (cube of 9 and square of 27). If one assumes, as Philolaus did, that the cosmos is put together according to a mathematical order, it is not at all unreasonable to hypothesize that the figure of 730 months for the great year is inaccurate, based as it is on rough and ready measurements, and to assume that closer observations will eventually confirm that the much more pleasing number of 729 in fact governs the great year. This may seem to be a rather arbitrary change, but it displays precisely the type of thinking that underlies the much cited passage in Aristotle where he complains that the Pythagoreans introduced the counter-earth as a tenth body, contrary to all observational evidence, simply because of the assumption that the cosmos must be constructed according to the perfect number 10. Philolaus' attitude in these two cases is very similar to Plato's. He puts more confidence in his theory that the cosmos is constructed according to pleasing mathematical principles than in the observational data, and is more willing to suppose that the data are defective than that the theory is. If we assume this explanation for the use of the number 729, there is no reason to doubt the authenticity of Censorinus' report, since there is nothing in it that contradicts the Philolaic astronomical system described by Aristotle. In fact the parallel between the report on Philolaus and the report on his contemporary Oenopides in other sources further supports the authenticity of Censorinus' report. However, this explanation of the use of 729 is quite speculative, and it may be that Neugebauer's account should be accepted and the testimonium be regarded as spurious.

It is important not to assume that because Philolaus and Plato were willing to prefer *a priori* theoretical constructions to the data available in some cases, their astronomical theories should be relegated to the realm of myth. Clearly Philolaus' 59-year cycle was derived from observation of the actual periods of the moon and sun, just as the astronomy of Plato's *Timaeus* is also based on the data of his day.

The harmony of the spheres

The doctrine of the harmony of the spheres may have had more influence on the western intellectual tradition than any other aspect of Pythagoreanism. However, the doctrine has long been misunderstood as a scientific system worked out in detail. This mistaken view has now been put to rest by Burkert, who has shown that the earliest testimonia about the doctrine indicate that it was not tied to any sophisticated astronomical system and indeed "we need not suppose that any detailed system formed its basis" (1972: 355). On the other hand Burkert goes too far when he maintains that the Pythagorean harmony of the spheres "has *nothing* to do with mathematical or musical theory" (my emphasis). The harmony of the spheres is in fact a typically bold Presocratic conjecture about the nature of reality, that is based on some "scientific" observations (the discovery of the relationship of whole-number ratios to musical intervals, and certain very basic astronomical observations), but which, given the scientific capabilities of the late fifth century, remained a daring hypothesis which could not be embodied in a system articulated in detail. Like many other Presocratic and Hippocratic theories it promises more than it can deliver, but this is no reason to suppose that it, any more than a number of other Presocratic theories, has nothing to do with mathematical or empirical science. This is not the place to discuss the full history of the doctrine and all its permutations. I will briefly present what we can say about the form of the doctrine known to Aristotle and then go on to argue, largely in agreement with Burkert, that, while we cannot be sure that Philolaus accepted the doctrine (let alone originated it), the evidence of both the testimonia and the fragments makes it probable that it was a part of his system.

It is striking that in their discussion of the harmony of the spheres neither Aristotle (*De caelo* 290b12ff) nor Alexander in his commentary on Aristotle's *Metaphysics* (where he also refers to Aristotle's special works on the Pythagoreans) makes any reference to a Pythagorean scheme in which the musical intervals are tied to an astronomical system in a systematic way (and neither does Simplicius in his commentary on the *De caelo*). At *De caelo* 290b12ff Aristotle says that for the Pythagoreans the speeds of the heavenly bodies judged by their distances (from the center) had the ratios of the musical consonances, but he gives no example of precisely what the relative distances or speeds were nor of how they were correlated with the planets. What is even more striking is that Alexander evidently found no such information in Aristotle's special works on the Pythagoreans, for when he needs an example of what is meant he makes one up (*in Metaph.* 40.3 – φέρε εἰπεῖν, "let us say"). In his imaginary example he also reverts to the Aristotelian geocentric universe, because he is clearly starting from the earth when he gives the example of the sun being twice as far away as the moon. It seems very hard to believe that, if there were a detailed account of the system in Philolaus' book or any other written source, Aristotle would have ignored it in his special treatise on the Pythagoreans, or that Alexander would make up his own example if Aristotle had given the Pythagorean system (Burkert 1972: 353–4).

Of course in the later tradition a number of ways to fill out the system were proposed and were sometimes ascribed to Pythagoras himself (Heath 1913: 107ff). The first detailed account based on something like the Philolaic system is found in Plutarch who describes the distances of the heavenly bodies from the central fire as increasing by powers of three, but the system he is describing is clearly a later elaboration of Philolaus' cosmos, since the sun is assigned the sixth position out from the center after the counter-earth, earth, moon, Mercury and Venus, whereas testimony going back to Aristotle makes clear that the sun came after the counter-earth, earth, and moon for Philolaus (Plut. *De an. proc.* 1028b). Other detailed accounts of the harmony of the spheres not tied to the Philolaic astronomy begin with Plato (the myth of Er in the *Republic*), and scholars have tended to assume that there must have been a Pythagorean astronomy before Philolaus that was geocentric and had seven moving bodies to correspond to the heptachord (Heath 1913: 107). However, such an assumption simply has no basis in the early evidence. Neither Aristotle in his extant treatises nor Alexander who had access to Aristotle's lost book on the Pythagoreans knows of any other Pythagorean astronomical system than that of Philolaus.

What then does the Pythagorean doctrine of the harmony of spheres seem to have included according to Aristotle's account? The basic point is that the heavenly bodies produce music by their movements in that the sounds which they produce by their rapid movement through the heavens form a *harmonia* or scale (Barker 1989: 33 n. 22). Thus the Pythagoreans are said to have assumed that the speeds of the heavenly bodies, judged by their distances, are in the ratios of the concordant musical intervals. It is noteworthy that Aristotle says not that they *argued* that the speeds were in the whole-number ratios but that they assumed it (ὑποθέμενοι – 290b21). The Pythagoreans had no way to obtain precise enough measurements in order to show that the speeds were in fact in such ratios. That the speeds had such ratios was an assertion of faith in the order of the cosmos. Aristotle spends most of his time disputing the idea that the heavenly bodies make any sound at all. Evidently the Pythagoreans had argued by analogy with what happens on earth. Since large bodies in motion on earth make noise, it is reasonable to assume that bodies as large as the sun, moon, etc., moving as fast as they do, should make a sound. The Pythagoreans had responded to the obvious objection that we hear no sound by suggesting that we are accustomed to it from birth and have no experience of silence to compare it with. This response is very much of a piece with the testimony about Philolaus' astronomy. It is clear that the Pythagoreans were concerned to make their doctrines consistent with the phenomena although they often used tortured reasoning.

One last point about Aristotle's and Alexander's testimony. Since Aristotle does not discuss the details of the ordering of the heavenly bodies in the *De caelo*, it is unclear whether he connected the harmony of the spheres doctrine with the Pythagorean (Philolaic) astronomical system which he discusses elsewhere. However, he never mentions any other astronomical system. Moreover, Alexander, in his commentary on the *Metaphysics*, not only does not mention any other astronomical system, but he also explicitly ties the harmony of the spheres doctrine to the astronomy of Philolaus, which uniquely has ten orbiting bodies rather than the eight that were typical in Greek astronomy:

καθ᾽ ἁρμονίαν δὲ τὴν τούτων τάξιν ἐποίουν λαβόντες τὸ τὰ δέκα τὰ κινούμενα σώματα, ἐξ ὧν ὁ κόσμος, διεστάναι ἀπ᾽ ἀλλήλων κατὰ τὰς ἁρμονικὰς ἀποστάσεις... (*in Metaph.* 41.2ff)

...they made the arrangement of the celestial bodies harmonious by supposing that the ten *moving bodies which make up the universe are separated from each other by concordant intervals.*

(tr. Dooley – my emphasis)

How then does this Aristotelian testimony compare with what we find in the fragments of Philolaus? What evidence is there for or against the thesis that Philolaus accepted the doctrine of the harmony of the spheres? As many scholars have noted, there is no direct mention of the doctrine in the fragments, but there is strong implicit evidence that the harmony of the spheres had an important role in Philolaus' system. First, it is obvious that harmony was a central concept in Philolaus' system and that he thought it had to be invoked in order to explain the cosmos. Thus, it would be natural to suppose that he went beyond saying that harmony was a principle necessary to tie together the unlike principles, limiters and un-limiteds (F6), to say that it tied them together in the cosmos according to the whole-number ratios that would generate a musical harmony. As Kahn has noted (1974: 177) this is precisely what happens in the second part of F6. The fragment starts by talking about the necessity of harmony in a broad sense, but abruptly switches to talking about harmony in terms of the octave and the whole-number ratios. Thus, while we cannot be sure that Philolaus originated the doctrine, it appears to be a natural consequence of his broader philosophical outlook, according to which everything in the cosmos is a numeri-cally determined *harmonia* of limiters and unlimiteds.

Numbers and concepts in the cosmos

Aristotle, *Metaphysics* 1.8, 990a18ff ἔτι δὲ πῶς δεῖ λαβεῖν αἴτια μὲν εἶναι τὰ τοῦ ἀριθμοῦ πάθη καὶ τὸν ἀριθμὸν τῶν κατὰ τὸν οὐρανὸν ὄντων καὶ γιγνομένων καὶ ἐξ ἀρχῆς καὶ νῦν, ἀριθμὸν δ' ἄλλον μηθένα εἶναι παρὰ τὸν ἀριθμὸν τοῦτον ἐξ οὗ συνέστηκεν ὁ
5 κόσμος; ὅταν γὰρ ἐν τῳδὶ μὲν τῷ μέρει δόξα καὶ καιρὸς αὐτοῖς ᾖ, μικρὸν δὲ ἄνωθεν ἢ κάτωθεν ἀδικία καὶ κρίσις ἢ μῖξις, ἀπόδειξιν δὲ λέγωσιν ὅτι τούτων μὲν ἕκαστον ἀριθμός ἐστι, συμβαίνει δὲ κατὰ τὸν τόπον τοῦτον ἤδη πλῆθος εἶναι τῶν συνισταμένων μεγεθῶν διὰ τὸ τὰ πάθη ταῦτα ἀκολουθεῖν τοῖς τόποις ἑκάστοις, πότερον
10 οὗτος ὁ αὐτός ἐστιν ἀριθμὸς ὁ ἐν τῷ οὐρανῷ, ὃν δεῖ λαβεῖν ὅτι τούτων ἕκαστόν ἐστιν, ἢ παρὰ τοῦτον ἄλλος; ὁ μὲν γὰρ Πλάτων ἕτερον εἶναί φησιν.

7 μὲν Alexander μὲν ἐν E ἐν Aᵇr Bonitz   συμβαίνη Bonitz

But yet how must we understand that number and the character-istics of numbers are the causes of the things that are and come to be in the heavens, both from the beginning and now, but that there is no other [kind of] number besides the number from which the world-order is constituted? For whenever opinion or due season are in such and such a region in their view, and a little above or below injustice and separation and mixture, and they state as proof that each of these is a number, and that there are already a multitude of composite magnitudes in this place because these characteristics [of number] correspond to these several regions, is it this same number, the number in the heavens, which we must understand each of these [concepts] to be, or is it another kind of number besides this? Plato, at least, says that it is another. (after Tredennick)

Alexander, *in Metaph.* 74.6 ἔλεγον γὰρ ἐν τινὶ μὲν μέρει τοῦ κόσμου δόξαν συνίστασθαι, ἐν ἄλλῳ δὲ καιρόν, πάλιν δ' αὖ ἐν ἄλλῳ ἢ κάτωθεν τούτων ἢ ἄνωθεν ἢ ἀδικίαν ἢ κρίσιν ἢ μῖξιν ἢ ἄλλο τι τῶν ἐν τῷ οὐρανῷ. τῆς δὲ τούτων κατὰ τὴν τάξιν τὴν
5 τοιαύτην συστάσεως ἀπόδειξιν ἔφερον ὅτι τούτων μὲν ἕκαστον τοῦ ἀριθμοῦ ἐστιν, ἑκάστῳ δὲ τόπῳ ἐν τῷ κόσμῳ οἰκεῖός τίς ἐστιν ἀριθμός. τῷ μὲν γὰρ μέσῳ τὸ ἕν (πρῶτον γάρ ἐστιν ἐνταῦθα), μετὰ δὲ τὸ μέσον τὰ δύο, ἃ δόξαν τε ἔλεγον καὶ τόλμαν· καὶ οὕτως ἀεὶ ἀφισταμένων ἀπὸ τοῦ μέσου πλείονα τὸν ἀριθμὸν γίγνεσθαι
10 τῶν συνισταμένων διὰ τὸ καὶ τοὺς ἀριθμοὺς ἐξ ὧν συνίστανται, μᾶλλον δὲ οἷς ἐστι ταὐτά, τοιούτους εἶναι· τὰ γὰρ τῶν ἀριθμῶν πάθη καὶ τοὺς ἀριθμοὺς τοῖς τόποις ἀκολουθεῖν τοῖς ἐν τῷ οὐρανῷ καὶ οἰκείους αὐτοῖς εἶναι· διὸ καὶ τὰ μεγέθη ἐκ τούτων ἐπισυμβαίνειν... (75.15) τῆς δὲ τάξεως τῆς ἐν τῷ οὐρανῷ, ἣν
15 ἐποιοῦντο τῶν ἀριθμῶν οἱ Πυθαγόρειοι, μνημονεύει ἐν τῷ δευτέρῳ περὶ τῆς Πυθαγορικῶν δόξης.

11 ταὐτά Dooley cf. Alex. 75.15 ταῦτα MSS

For they said that opinion is established in a particular part of the universe, and due season in another, and in yet another in turn, whether below or above these, either injustice or separation or mixture or some other of the things in the heavens. The proof they offered that these things are established according to an arrangement such as this is that each of them belongs to a number, and there is a particular number proper to each place in the universe. For at the center is 1 (for the center is the first place in the universe); after the center is 2, which they called both "opinion" and "daring"; and in this way the number of things being constituted becomes greater as they keep moving away from the center, because the numbers too from which they are constituted, or rather with which they are identical, are of this kind. For they said that numbers and their characteristics follow the places in the heavens, and are

284

proper to them; and that for this reason spatial magnitudes too come into existence at a later stage out of these numbers... In the second book of his treatise on the doctrine of the Pythagoreans, Aristotle mentions the arrangement of the numbers in the heavens which the Pythagoreans devised. (tr. Dooley with changes)

Alexander, *in Metaph.* 75.21 οἷον ἦν ᾤοντο τάξιν ἔχειν τὴν δυάδα, ταύτην ἔλεγον ἔχειν τὴν τάξιν ἐν τῷ κόσμῳ τὴν δόξαν, ἐπειδὴ δυὰς δόξα ἦν αὐτοῖς. πάλιν ἦν τάξιν ἡ ἑπτάς, ταύτην ἀπεδίδοσαν ἐν τῷ κόσμῳ τῷ καιρῷ, ἐπεὶ καὶ τὸν ἑπτὰ ἀριθμὸν
5 [καὶ] καιρὸν ἡγοῦντο εἶναι. μικρὸν δὲ ἄνωθεν τοῦ καιροῦ ἢ κάτωθεν ἐποίουν, εἰ ἔτυχεν, ἀδικίαν ἢ κρίσιν, ὅτι καὶ ἡ τῶν αὐτῶν τούτοις ἀριθμῶν τάξις ἡ αὐτὴ ἦν. γράφεται δὲ ἔν τισιν ἀντιγράφοις ἀντὶ τοῦ ἀδικίαν "ἀνικίαν·" ἀνικίαν δέ φασιν ὑπὸ τῶν Πυθαγορείων λέγεσθαι τὴν πεντάδα...

They said, for instance, that opinion occupies that place in the universe which, they believed, 2 occupies, since for them 2 was opinion. To due season they gave in turn that place in the universe which 7 occupies, since they also thought that the number 7 is due season. And a little above or below due season they located injustice or separation, whichever it happened to be, because the arrangement of the numbers which are the same as these was also the same. Certain transcriptions of the text have the reading *anikia* (non-victory) instead of *adikia* (injustice). For they say that the Pythagoreans called the number 5 *anikia*. (tr. Dooley with changes)

COMMENTARY

These texts present a seldom commented upon aspect of early Pythagorean cosmology according to which abstract concepts such as opinion, injustice, due season, mixture, and separation are assigned specific places in the cosmos. There are many puzzling features about these reports, but for present purposes two main problems need to be addressed: (1) What can be made of the theory which Aristotle is assigning to the Pythagoreans? (2) Is that theory likely to have been held by Philolaus or is it the work of other Pythagoreans?

The general outlines of the theory are tolerably clear from Aristotle's words and Alexander's commentary on them, but our information is so limited that much must remain uncertain. Aristotle assigns an argument to the Pythagoreans that runs as follows: (1) concepts such as due season, opinion, separation, etc. are numbers; (2) every number has its own particular region in the cosmos; (3) therefore, each of these concepts is also found in a particular region of the cosmos. Thus, to use Alexander's example, the number 2 is found in a specific region of the universe and therefore opinion, which is identified with the number 2, is to be found in that region as well. The first premise above is clearly supported as Pythagorean by testimony elsewhere in Aristotle, although it is not clear that Aristotle is right to say that the Pythagoreans literally identified concepts and numbers. Thus, at *Metaphysics* 985b29 we are told that certain characteristics of number are associated with justice and others with mind, soul, and due season respectively, and Alexander expands on this in his commentary. At *Metaphysics* 987a21 Aristotle says that the Pythagoreans first began the attempt to define "the what" of things, and this would seem to be connected to the attempt to tie certain concepts to certain numbers.

The second premise, that each number (presumably just numbers 1–10) belongs to a specific region of the cosmos, is not stated as explicitly elsewhere in Aristotle. To be sure, he says that the Pythagoreans thought that the world-order was a harmony and a number (986a3) and searched for analogues between things and numbers, but up to this point in the *Metaphysics* he has made no assertion that they assigned specific numbers to specific places in the cosmic order. Alexander says that Aristotle mentioned the arrangement of numbers in the heavens in the second book of his work on the Pythagoreans. It is hard to know whether this means that Aristotle dealt with the topic in some detail or whether he just literally "mentioned" the basic idea. Certainly Alexander does not provide much more detail on this topic. He only tells us that the number 1 was associated with the center and that the numbers went in order out from the center. However, he never explicitly ties any other number with any other specific region in the cosmos in his commentary on this passage of Aristotle. Earlier in his commentary (38.22) he mentioned that the number seven was associated with the sun, but this does not square very well with the system that counts outward from the middle, at least if we are counting heavenly bodies, since the sun would be 5 on such a count.

It is also interesting to note that in Alexander's commentary on *Metaphysics* 990a22ff, with the single exception of "daring," he only discusses the concepts that Aristotle has introduced (opinion, due season, mixture, separation, and injustice [with the variant non-victory]). Aristotle gave none of the specific numbers with which these concepts were connected, and Alexander fills in some but not all of the holes (2 = opinion and daring, 7 = opportunity). Still, it is somewhat surprising that, if Alexander had Aristotle's special treatises on the Pythagoreans, he does not fill in more or mention other concepts. One gets the suspicion that Aristotle may not have said much more about the position of concepts in the cosmos than we find in the *Metaphysics*. Indeed, Alexander reports that Aristotle, in his special treatises on the Pythagoreans, mentioned the arrangement of *numbers* in the cosmos, not the arrangement of *concepts*.

It is possible that the Pythagoreans did present a fully worked out theory of the positions of numbers in the cosmos and assigned a well defined set of abstract concepts to each of these regions. However, to judge from Alexander's and Aristotle's testimony (which is admittedly risky especially given that we lack Aristotle's works on the Pythagoreans), it would appear more likely that the system was more analogous to the theory of the harmony of the spheres, in that the general argument according to which numbers and concepts were assigned to regions of the cosmos was articulated and some examples were given, but the details were not filled in, or admitted of widely different interpretations among the Pythagoreans themselves.

Given the state of the evidence it is impossible to determine exactly what the purpose of this system was. It is noteworthy that the concepts which are assigned positions in the cosmos are not a haphazard group but have certain features in common. Almost all of them are in fact paralleled by earlier Presocratic thinkers. Thus, Empedocles is famous for having mixed the concepts of love and strife in with his four material elements. But the functions of love and strife are to mix and separate the elements, so that we would seem to have here the precursor of the Pythagorean idea that "mixture" and "separation" have a place in the cosmos. Much earlier, Anaximander is famous for invoking the idea of the injustice of the elements to each other (F1) and the necessary retribution. So that the role of injustice in the Pythagorean cosmos (as well as justice) also has a precedent. It should also be remembered that Anaxagoras puts mind in the cosmos as well (mind is mentioned in Aristotle's account of the Pythagoreans at *Metaph.* 985b30). Given the scarcity of the sources, it is probably not profitable to speculate further about the nature of the Pythagorean theory, and I will now turn to the second question: Did Philolaus espouse anything like this theory?

It appears that in general terms the theory could very plausibly be assigned to Philolaus, but that some of the details of Alexander's account of it conflict with Philolaus' system, so that it must remain in doubt whether it should be assigned to him. The assumption that certain concepts are tied to specific numbers is very plausible for Philolaus, who maintains that all things are known through number (F4). Moreover, Alexander in his commentary on Aristotle's account of Pythagoreanism at *Metaphysics* 985b26ff does associate the concept of due season with the number 7 and with the sun, where the sun is clearly the sun in Philolaus' astronomical system, since the central fire is mentioned (38.22). This would suggest that Philolaus identified the concept due season with 7 and gave it a specific place in the cosmos, the region around the sun. Some cosmological sense lies behind this, in that the sun is clearly the cause of seasons. Likewise, when Alexander says in his commentary on *Metaphysics* 990a18ff (74.13) that the number 1 is associated with the center, it is possible to see this as based on F7 of Philolaus, where "the first thing harmonized" is called "the one in the center of the sphere." As I have argued above in the account of Philolaus' cosmogony, Aristotle seems to have read this fragment as saying that the number 1 was constructed. This is probably a misunderstanding of Philolaus, but nonetheless it can be taken as evidence that Philolaus' book is behind Alexander's assertion (based on Aristotle) that the number 1 is at the center.

However, what will not work in Philolaus' system is Alexander's assertion that the number 2 came after the center and that the numbers increased with the distance from the center. The problem is that Alexander's other testimony that the sun was tied to the number 7, which must refer to Philolaus' astronomical system since it mentions the central fire (38.22), clearly counts from the fixed stars inwards, so that the sun is seventh after the fixed stars and the five planets.

It is worth noting that Alexander's account of the system that starts in the center and counts outward is nowhere explicitly tied to the central fire system, and we might therefore suppose that he and his source Aristotle are describing a different Pythagorean system. The problem is that it simply is not tied to any specific astronomical details that would allow us to be sure that the reference was not to Philolaus either. Even if it could be determined that it was the central fire system, it still could be a reinterpretation of Philolaus' system by his successors, since there are parallels for such reinterpretations (Plutarch, *De an. proc.* 1028b). There is also the possibility that here as elsewhere Alexander is not giving an account based on actual texts of the Pythagoreans but just an example of his own creation. However, the language he uses in no way indicates that he is using his own example and rather implies that it is the Pythagoreans'.

It is worth noting that none of the accounts of Philolaus' astronomical system, either in Aristotle or in the later doxography, mentions anything about specific positions of numbers or concepts in the cosmos. However, such arguments from silence, given the state of our sources for Philolaus, carry almost no weight. Thus, it seems best to conclude that it is impossible to be certain whether Philolaus is to be connected with the Pythagorean theory that assigned concepts to places in the cosmos.

5. EMBRYOLOGY AND MEDICINE

Testimonia A27 and A28

The text below follows that of Diels with the following conventions:

⌊ααα⌋ Letters added in the margin or above the line by scribe.

α̣α̣α̣ Letters that are ambiguous or that can not be read clearly.

[ααα] Letters added by the editor (Diels unless otherwise noted) for obliterated or mistaken letters.

⟨ααα⟩ Letters added by the editor (Diels unless otherwise noted).

⟦ααα⟧ Letters deleted by the editor (Diels unless otherwise noted).

A27 Meno Anonymi Londinensis 18.8 (suppl. Arist. 3.1.31 ed. Diels) Φιλόλαος δὲ ὁ Κρ[ο]τωνιάτης συνεστάναι φησὶν τὰ ἡμέτερα σώμ[ατα ἐκ] θερμοῦ. ἀμέτ̣⟨οχ⟩α γὰρ αὐτὰ εἶναι ψυχροῦ [, ὑπομι]μνήσκων ἀπό τινων τοιούτων· τὸ σπέρμ[α εἶναι θερ]μόν,
5   κατασκευαστικὸν δὲ τοῦτο τ̣[οῦ ζῴο]υ· καὶ ὁ τόπος δέ, εἰς ὃν ἡ καταβολ[ή – μήτρα] δὲ αὕτη – ἐστὶν θερμοτέρα καὶ ἐοι[κυιᾶ ἐκ]είνῳ· ⌊τὸ δὲ ἐοικός τινι τἀτὸ δύναται, ᾧ ἔοικεν⌋· ἐπεὶ δὲ τὸ κατασκευάζ[ον ἀμέ]τ̣οχ̣ό̣ι̣ν ἐστιν ψυχροῦ καὶ ὁ τόπο̣ι̣ς̣ι δέ, ἐν ᾧ[ι ἡ καταβολ]ή, ἀμέτοχός ἐστιν ψυχροῦ, δῆλον [ὅτι καὶ
10   τὸ] κατασκευαζόμενον ζῷον τοιοῦτο[ν γίνε]ται. εἰς δὲ τούτου τὴν κατασκ[ευὴν ὑ]πομνήσει προσχρῆται τοιαύτῃ· με̣[τὰ γὰρ] τὴν ἔκτεξιν εὐθέως ⟦το⟧ τὸ ζῷον ἐπισπᾶται τὸ ἐκτὸς πνεῦμα ψυχρὸν ὄν· εἶτα πάλιν καθαπερεὶ χρέος ἐκπέμπει αὐτό. διὰ τοῦτο δὴ καὶ ὄρεξις τοῦ ἐκτὸς πνεύματος, ἵνα τῇ[ι] ἐπ⟨ε⟩ισάκτῳ τοῦ πνεύματος
15   ὁλκῇ θερμ[ό]τερα ὑπάρχοντα τὰ ἡμέτερα σώματα πρὸς αὐτοῦ καταψύχηται. καὶ τὴν μὲν σύστασιν τῶν ἡμετέρων σωμάτων ἐν τουτοῖς φησίν. λέγει δὲ γίνεσθαι τὰς νόσους διά τε χολὴν καὶ αἷμα καὶ φλέγμα, ἀρχὴν δὲ γίνεσθαι τῶν νόσων ταῦτα· ἀποτελεῖσθαι δέ φησιν τὸ μὲν αἷμα παχὺ μὲν ἔ⌊σω⌋ παραθλιβομένης τῆς σαρκός,

20 λεπτὸν δὲ γίνεσθαι διαιρουμένων τῶν ἐν τῇ σαρκὶ ἀγγείων· τὸ δὲ
φλέγμα συνίστασθαι ἀπὸ τῶν ὄμβρων φησίν. λέγει δὲ τὴν χολὴν
ἰχῶρα εἶναι τῆς σαρκός. παράδοξόν τε α⌊ύ⌋τὸς ἀνὴρ ἐπὶ τούτου
κεινεῖ· λέγει γὰρ μηδὲ τετάχθα[ι] ἐ̣π̣ὶ τ[ῷ] ἥπατι χολήν, ἰχῶρα
μέντοι τῆς σαρκὸς εἶναι τὴν χολήν. τό τ᾽ αὖ φλέγμα τῶν
25 πλείστων ⌊ψυχ⟨ρ⟩ὸν⌋ 〚θερμον〛 εἶναι λεγόντων αὐτὸς θερμὸν τῇ
φύσει ὑπ[ο]τίθεται· ἀπὸ γὰρ τοῦ φλέγειν φλέγμα εἰρῆσθαι· ταύτηι
δὲ καὶ τὰ φλεγμαίνον[τα] μετοχῇ τοῦ φλέγματος φλεγμ[α]ίνει.
καὶ ταῦτα μὲν δὴ ἀρχὰς τῶν νό[σ]ων ὑπ[ο]τ̣ίθεται, [σ]υνεργὰ δὲ
ὑπερβολ[άς] ⌊τε⌋ θερμασίας, τροφῆς, καταψύ[ξ]εω[ς καὶ ἐ]νδείας
30 ⟨τούτων ἢ⟩ τῶν τού[το]ι̣[ς παραπλησίων.]

2 κρωτωνιατης P: Suppl. Kenyon   3 ἀμέτοχα Diels αμετα vel αμεγα P ἀμιγῆ Kenyon
4–5 suppl. Blass   6 suppl. Kenyon   6–7 suppl. Kenyon   8 ἀμέτοχον altera o ex
η corr. P   ψυχρον P   9 suppl. Kenyon ω ex η P   9–10 suppl. Kenyon
10 τοιουτο[ν ἐσ]ται suppl. Kenyon   11 suppl. Kenyon   19 μεϲϙν, addito εν
compendio et superscriptis σω (vel σωι), denique deletis ϲον in μεν εσω corr. P.
22 ατος P   25 ψυχον deletis θερμον superscr. P   26 suppl. Kenyon   27–8 suppl.
Kenyon   29 vel υπερβαλ, sed ὑπερβαλλούσαϲ propter spatium suppleri nequit τε
pallidiore atramento ante versum supplevit P

A28 Meno Anonymi Londinensis 20.21 (*Suppl. Arist.* 3.1.36 ed.
Diels) καὶ σχεδὸν [οὗτος [Petron] ὤ]ς ὁ Φιλόλαος οἴεται μὴ
εἶναι ἐν ἡμῖν χολὴ[ν ἢ] ἀ[χρ]είαν. καὶ κατὰ μὲν ταῦτα
συνηγόρευσεν τῷ Φιλολάῳ, κατὰ δὲ τἆλλα †αὐ̣τ̣ονει†.

3 ἀχρείαν Diels α...ειαν vel α...αιον P   4 ταλλααυτονει vel τααλλαηγνει P
αὐτο⟨γνωμο⟩νει vel αὐτον⟨ο⟩εῖ Diels

A27 Philolaus of Croton says that our bodies are constituted out of
hot. For he says that they have no share of cold on the basis of
something like the following considerations: Sperm is hot and this is
what constructs the animal. Also the place into which it is sown, the
womb itself, is even hotter and like to the seed. But what is like
something has the same power as that to which it is like. Since that
which constructs has no share of cold, and the place in which the
sowing occurs has no share of the cold, it is clear that the animal
that is constructed turns out to have the same character. He also
mentions the following sort of consideration regarding the construction of the animal: Immediately after birth the animal breathes in
the external air which is cold. Then it sends it out again like a debt.
Indeed, it is for this reason that there is a desire for external air, so

that our bodies, which were too hot before, by the drawing in of breath from outside are cooled thereby. He says, then, that the constitution of our body depends on these things.

He says that diseases arise through bile and blood and phlegm, and that these are the origin of diseases. He says that the blood is made thick when the flesh is squeezed inwards, but that it becomes thin when the vessels in the flesh are broken up. He says that phlegm is constituted from rains. Bile, he says, is a serum of the flesh. And the same man stirs up a paradox on this topic. For he says that bile is not even assigned to the liver, but rather that bile is a serum of the flesh. And again, while most people say that phlegm is cold, he himself postulates that it is hot by nature. For he says that "phlegm" gets its name from *phlegein* ("to burn"). In this way also things that are inflamed are inflamed by taking part in phlegm. It is these then that he postulates as the origins of diseases. He says that excesses of heat, nutriment, and cooling as well as deficiencies of these or things like these also have a role.

A28 This one [Petron] also, pretty much like Philolaus, thinks that bile does not exist in us or is useless. In this respect he agreed with Philolaus, but in other respects he †has views of his own†.

AUTHENTICITY

Both of these testimonia are preserved in the papyrus known as the *Anonymus Londinensis* which dates from the second century AD. The papyrus deals solely with medical matters and falls into three distinct parts which ultimately derive from quite different sources (Diels 1893a and Jones 1947). The first part presents some medical definitions that show Stoic influence, while the third part is a history of physiology from after 300 BC. down to Alexander Philatheles. Sandwiched in between these two is a section devoted to the aetiology of disease in which the opinions of twenty thinkers are given. All of these figures of whom we have knowledge (seven were unknown before the discovery of the papyrus) can be dated before Aristotle. Moreover, in the course of this section the text of the papyrus cites Aristotle in several places as the source for the views it is reporting. Although there are some indications that Aristotle may himself have written on diseases (Lloyd 1979: 97 n. 204) it seems most likely that the "Aristotle" that the papyrus cites as its source is in fact the history of medicine by Aristotle's pupil Meno. Galen (*In Hipp. de nat. hom.* 15.25 K) reports that a "medical collection" was in circulation under the name of

Aristotle, but that it was agreed to be by his pupil Meno and was therefore called by some the *Menoneia*.

The testimonia on Philolaus are found in this middle section and thus rest on the authority of Meno. The accounts of Philolaus' medical views are quite detailed and it seems very likely that Meno, working at the end of the fourth century, had access to Philolaus' book and is thus our earliest direct evidence for its existence. To doubt this would be to suppose that a work was forged in Philolaus' name before the end of the fourth century and that Meno was taken in by it. Moreover, the medical views assigned to Philolaus by Meno, although containing some idiosyncrasies, accord very well with what we know of Hippocratic medicine around 400 BC, as will be seen in the commentary below. Furthermore, while there are some connections with Plato's comments on diseases in the *Timaeus*, there are also radical differences that preclude supposing that what are presented as Philolaus' medical views are in fact from a spurious work forged after the *Timaeus*. Thus, the testimonia about Philolaus' medical views are some of our most reliable evidence for his thought. It is a good reminder of the inadequacy of our sources to point out that if not for the discovery of the *Anonymus Londinensis* we would never have known that Philolaus dealt with medical topics at all.

COMMENTARY

Context of the testimonia: Although the *Anonymus Londinensis* is a very important source for Philolaus there are a number of difficulties inherent in using it. It is crucial to realize that while the views ascribed to Philolaus and the other thinkers on the aetiology of diseases are likely ultimately to go back to Meno, the papyrus is not likely to be a direct copy of Meno's text. There are several places where the papyrus text in fact states disagreement with "Aristotle" (6.42ff), and other places where it inserts much later material into the earlier account (e.g. at the beginning of the account of Plato's views a definition of blending is introduced that is not Plato's but shows Stoic influence [14.16ff]). The papyrus in fact has many corrections and passages marked out which suggest that it is more likely to be someone's private notes than a text meant for circulation. Perhaps the likeliest scenario is that the papyrus is the notes of a medical student, based on lectures by a teacher who primarily used Meno for the section on diseases, but who also introduced other material. The section on Philolaus does not have any material that is obviously from a different source and is thus likely to rest almost exclusively on the authority of Meno. However, there are serious questions as to the extent to which the account of Philolaus is distorted both by Meno's arrangement of materials and terminology and also by the influence of the anonymous "lecturer" who is presenting Meno's views (Jones 1947: 4–5).

At the beginning of the section on diseases (4.26ff) the theories of disease are divided into two classes: (1) those which find the origin of disease in residues of nutriment; (2) those which hold that diseases arise from the elements that constitute the body. The presentation of the opinions on diseases is then divided in half along these lines. However, several of the medical writers in the first section in fact have nothing to say about residues and explain diseases in terms of other principles (e.g. Hippo of Croton and Thrasymachus of Sardis). In the second section it is likewise not clear that all the thinkers mentioned explained disease through the basic elements of the body, and it is clear that in many cases, even when the elements do have a role in causing disease, other causes are adduced as well. However, there is at least a structural uniformity in the case of the second section. In every case a given author's theory of the basic constitution of the body is presented first and then followed by his account of disease. In the case of Plato other aspects of his medical views are discussed, such as the role of the various organs in the body and the structure of the soul. The section on Philolaus conforms to this general pattern: first we are given his account of the constitution of the human body and then his theory of diseases. It is possible that this structure of the account of opinions on diseases does not go back to Meno but is imposed by an intermediary source (e.g. the "lecturer'). However, the word "residues" (περισσώματα), which is used to label one of the two main types of disease theory, is a word heavily used in Aristotle and this perhaps suggests that the structure of the whole section should be assigned to Meno.

Whoever is responsible for the structure, it undoubtedly distorts the doctrines of Philolaus and others in that it orders them according to the questions of later thinkers rather than presenting them in their original sequence. Since we have Plato's *Timaeus* we can compare what Plato actually says with the report in Meno. Such a comparison shows that a basically accurate summary is given, but the sequence of ideas is quite a bit different than in Plato, and what purports to be a quotation is in fact a loose paraphrase (Jones 1947: 3). Thus great caution is needed in evaluating the report on Philolaus. Certainly we should not assume that the structure of the report reflects the structure of Philolaus' book very much, and it is impossible to assume that the language used in every case reflects Philolaus' actual words, although some expressions seem likely to be his.

The constitution of the human body: Philolaus is unique among the theorists discussed in this section of the *Anonymus Londinensis* in that he appears to explain the body in terms of just one constituent – "the hot."

Plato and Philistion say that the body is composed of the four elements, Menecrates has two hot elements (blood and bile) and two cold (breath and phlegm), while Polybus and Petron appeal to just the hot and the cold. However, that there were other monistic theories of the body's composition in fifth-century Greek medicine is clear from the Hippocratic treatise *On the Nature of Man*. In the first chapter of that treatise the author rejects theories that explain the body in terms of just one of the four elements (earth, air, fire, and water). In this case he complains not only about the monism, but also because these elements are not evident constituents of the body. In the second chapter he goes on to object to other monistic theories which are this time put forward by doctors and based on one of the "obvious" constituents of the body such as blood, bile, or phlegm. Thus, it is clear that monistic theories were much mooted at a date sometime before the writing of *On the Nature of Man* (*c.* 400), although there is no reference to any theory based just on "the hot," so that there does not seem to be any specific reference to Philolaus.

None of the extant Hippocratic works are quite as thoroughly monistic as Philolaus is presented as being. *Breaths* tries to make breath the only cause of disease (ch. 5), but only argues that breath is the most important and controlling element in the body, not that it is the only one. Similarly *On Fleshes* regards the hot as immortal, as thinking all things, and as crucial in the formation of the body, but not as the only constituent. Thus, Philolaus' theory is not exactly paralleled in any of the works in the Hippocratic corpus, but it fits very well into the types of theory that were common at the end of the fifth century, and specifically those attacked in *On the Nature of Man*.

But what exactly is the nature of Philolaus' claim about the constitution of the human body? Does he mean the same kind of thing as Anaximenes presumably meant when he said that all things are air, i.e. that everything in the world is wholly constituted out of some form of air? If so, Philolaus would be arguing that the body is wholly constituted by fire in some form, so that e.g. bones would be one form of fire, and flesh another. This is the usual interpretation and is what the text of the *Anonymus Londinensis* seems to mean at first sight. However, there are problems which suggest that this view needs to be modified slightly. Before speculating further, though, it is necessary to go on and examine the arguments which Philolaus presents to support the thesis that the body is constituted of the hot.

It is characteristic of both arguments that they are, in form at least, only adequate to show that the body is originally hot and has no share of cold, without proving anything about whatever other constituents it may have. The first argument begins by asserting that both the sperm which constructs the animal and also the place in which the sperm is sown (i.e. the womb) are hot. Philolaus then draws the conclusion that since the components have no share in the cold, what is constructed out of them must have the same quality, and hence that our body has no share in the cold. This involves a common Presocratic principle, that the product cannot have anything in it that cannot be explained in terms of the constituents, i.e. it recognizes Parmenides' ban on absolute coming-to-be. It is interesting that the conclusion is stated only in the negative form, i.e. it asserts that the body has no innate cold rather than that it is hot. It would seem to be an open question as to whether it has other qualities besides heat. We might object that Philolaus' own reasoning suggests that it must. Surely he would admit that sperm is moist as well as hot, and by the argument just described it would follow that our bodies have the moist in them.

The second argument similarly tries to show that our bodies are hot by showing that they have no innate cold and must bring it in from outside. Philolaus points out that after birth the organism draws in breath from outside, breath which is cold. This cold breath is then sent back out again like a debt. What is striking about the language here is the emphasis on showing that cold is something foreign to the body, that it is brought in from outside (τὸ ἐκτὸς πνεῦμα) and then sent back as something not properly belonging to the body, but only borrowed. Philolaus then concludes the argument by asserting that our desire for breath in fact demonstrates the central thesis that our bodies are, in their own nature, hot. It is in order to cool down our bodies which are in themselves too hot (θερμότερα ὑπάρχοντα τὰ ἡμέτερα σώματα) that we draw in breath from *outside* (ἐπεισάκτῳ πνεύματος ὁλκῇ). Thus once again the whole point of the argument is to show that the body is hot and not cold, and it does nothing to show that the body might not have other constituents besides the hot. But there is one further noteworthy point about this last argument, that may perhaps suggest another way of understanding what Philolaus means.

This second argument in fact concedes that after birth the cold and air do have a role in our body. They play a crucial role in cooling down the body which is too hot. Thus, if Philolaus' position is that our bodies after birth and during our life are composed just of the hot, there seem to be problems. It might be possible to maintain that the cold and air are always to be viewed as external to our true nature, and thus still argue that humans are only composed of the hot, but surely this position is at least made weaker by the admission that we take these external substances into ourselves and cannot in fact live without them. What this suggests is that Philolaus' point may be not about our adult bodies, but about the embryo. The thesis is that the human body is *in origin* hot with no share of the cold, which would not deny that we come to share in the cold when we are born.

This interpretation can be made more plausible if we notice a similarity between the arguments given here and Philolaus' methodology elsewhere. In each area of inquiry Philolaus seems to have tried to identify the starting-points necessary to account for the origin of things, without going beyond the limits of our knowledge (see pt. II, ch. 3). It may be that this methodology is at work in the account of the human body as well. In order to explain the first origin of our bodies we are justified in supposing that they are constituted by the hot since the factors that lead to their development are hot (sperm and the womb), and since upon birth our bodies act, in the process of respiration, as if they lacked the cold and as if it were foreign to them. Philolaus' point is that we can account for the origin of our bodies pretty well by just appealing to the hot. However, once we get beyond the stage of embryology, he may be willing to concede that other principles are required to explain the functioning of the living human being. Certainly F13 will suggest that other starting-points are required in order to explain different kinds of living organisms.

Further support for the thesis that Philolaus is doing embryology when he says that we are constituted of the hot can be found in the often noticed analogy between Philolaus' description of the breathing of the new-born infant here and the description of the first stages of Pythagorean cosmogony both in F7 of Philolaus and in Aristotle's reports on the Pythagoreans. F7 clearly states that "the first thing fitted together" was in the center of the world and was called the hearth. This is a clear reference to the famous central fire. Aristotle (F202) tells us that in the next stage of the cosmogony time and breath and void were "breathed in" (ἐπεισάγεσθαι – similar to ἐπεισάκτῳ in Meno's account) from the unlimited. The analogy is clear and does suggest that, as the fitting together of the central fire is just the first stage in the coming to be of the cosmos, so the constitution of our body by hot occurs in just the first stages of our life, i.e. when we are embryos. Both the world and our bodies then become considerably more complex at the next stages, and other principles must be invoked, such as the cold and breath in the case of our body, and breath, time, and void in the case of the world.

Thus, I would suggest, Philolaus is arguing about the initial constitution of our bodies in the womb, and seems to be directing his remarks primarily against the dualistic views of other medical thinkers such as Polybus and Petron who had maintained that the body was constituted out of both hot and cold. His point is that while we do need to appeal to the hot to do embryology there is no need to appeal to the cold. We might still wonder whether Philolaus made mention of other constituents, such as the moist. Given the emphasis on monism in Meno's report, it seems most likely that Philolaus only mentioned hot in his account of embryology, and it is unclear whether he would have recognized that other constituents, such as the moist, were involved in the embryo or not. The parallel with the origin of the world starting with the central fire does suggest that he may have focused just on heat.

Philolaus' theory of diseases: The second half of Meno's report on Philolaus focuses on his theory of the origin of disease. The basic outline of Philolaus' view is clear: diseases arise from three factors, bile and blood and phlegm. However, difficulties appear almost immediately. How is this aetiology of disease related to Philolaus' account of the origin of the body? In the case of the other theorists in this section of the *Anonymus Londinensis* there is at least some connection drawn between their theory of the constituents of the body and their theory of disease. This is what was promised at the beginning of the whole account of diseases in the papyrus, where theorists were put into two groups, the first of which explained diseases in terms of residues and the second in terms of the elements of the body. However, in Philolaus' case there is no direct mention of the hot, his one element, as a cause of disease. One very much suspects that the hypothetical lecturer or the student who made the papyrus is at fault here, and that the connection may have been clearer in Meno. However, Lloyd (1963: 120) has made an appealing suggestion to fill in the gap between the two halves of the account of Philolaus' medical views. He suggests that Philolaus thought that the three humors which he cites as the origin of diseases were all hot. In fact the striking thing about Philolaus' account of these humors is that he argues that phlegm is hot, whereas it is almost universally regarded as cold elsewhere. Since bile and blood were regularly considered hot, this peculiarity with regard to phlegm is well explained if we see it as an attempt by Philolaus to make all the origins of disease partake in the prime constituent of our bodies, the hot.

On this reading of Philolaus, his views become a likely target for the famous attack by the author of *On Ancient Medicine* on those medical writers who base their theory of disease, not on the manifold constituents of the body revealed by direct experience with the body and what regimen best suits it, but on one or two postulates such as the hot or cold, in terms of which they explain all disease (Lloyd 1963). It is true that a treatise like *Breaths* is more explicit in stating that all diseases have just one cause than Philolaus is, but breath is not as much in the forefront of the attack in *On Ancient Medicine* as hot is (Kühn [1956: 46ff] argues that *Breaths* is in fact the object of attack). Moreover, Philolaus appears to have consciously developed a methodology which proceeds by postulating a set of "starting-points" (ἀρχαί) necessary to explain the phenomena in each domain of inquiry, and which seems to be exactly the sort of procedure attacked in *VM* (see Pt. II, ch. 3).

I have given a detailed account of how Philolaus' theory of disease fits into his general method of ἀρχαί in my chapter on that method. In that chapter I have also addressed the other major problem presented by the account of Philolaus' theory of disease in the *Anonymus Londinensis*, namely how we are to understand the claim in the last sentence that excess and deficiency of heat, cold, and nutriment are also causes of disease when bile, blood, and phlegm seemed to be identified as the sole causes of disease earlier. It is not necessary to repeat all of that argument here. However, a brief overview of what emerges as Philolaus' medical theory is perhaps appropriate before discussing the details of that theory in the commentary.

Philolaus' goal in developing a medical theory is to identify the starting-points that must be postulated in each branch of the inquiry in order to explain the phenomena. In order to explain the intial development of the human body as an embryo, heat alone seems to be a sufficient postulate. After birth heat alone is inadequate to explain the organism, and breath sets a limitation to our heat, so that the healthy body consists of heat, which is in itself unlimited, limited by the cooling process of breathing. There may be other unlimiteds and limiters involved in the account of the healthy body, but the evidence does not allow us to posit them. As long as our heat is limited in the appropriate way we remain healthy, but excesses in heating or cooling as well as in nutriment (which produces excess in heating or cooling?) lead to disease. However, in order to account for the diseases we commonly observe we must postulate three new starting-points, bile, blood, and phlegm, in terms of which we can explain the development of all commonly observed diseases. Thus at each level of explanation different starting-points or postulates are required: the hot for embryology; the hot and a limitation of hot by breathing for the healthy body; bile, phlegm, and blood that is too thick or too thin for diseases.

συνεστάναι: This is the same word that Philolaus uses in F6 when the world-order is said to have come together (συνέστα) from limiters and unlimiteds. However, it is a common enough word that its use here cannot be surely asigned to Philolaus rather than Meno.

τὸ σπέρμα . . . κατασκευαστικὸν . . . τοῦ ζῴου . . . ὁ τόπος δὲ . . . μήτρα: Since the sperm is here said to "construct" the organism and since the womb is described as the place in which the sperm is sown, it seems clear that Philolaus is adopting a common view according to which the womb is viewed as simply the soil in which the seed is planted, and not as contributing any substance to the child which is derived solely from the father. There is evidence that there was some debate among Presocratic philosophers of the fifth century as to whether the female also contributed seed, but the sources are confused, often assigning opposite views to the same figure. For a full discussion see Lloyd (1983: 86ff).

καταβολή: This word is also used in F13 of Philolaus, where the genitals are described as the origin of "the sowing of seed" (αἰδοῖον δὲ σπέρματος καταβολᾶς...). Since this is a somewhat unusual expression and is not found in Aristotle or Plato, it is tempting to think that Meno drew it from Philolaus. (It also never occurs in the Hippocratic corpus. καταβολή itself is used once at *De off.* 9.20 L, but in a much different sense). If so this connection between Meno's report on Philolaus' book and F13 is good evidence for the authenticity of the latter. Aetius also uses καταβολή in his description of the account of conception assigned to Parmenides and Anaxagoras (DK 28A53), and it appears in this sense in a few texts in later Greek.

μήτρα ... θερμοτέρα: The force of the comparative here is unclear. When it is used later in the testimonium it seems to mean "too hot," and is part of the explanation of why we breathe (i.e. to cool our bodies which are too hot). However, here it is not clear what it would mean to say that the womb is "too hot." Perhaps it is best to take it as a straight comparative. In that case the point would be that the sperm is hot but the place in which it is sown, the mother, is (even) hotter.

... ἐοικυῖα ἐκείνῳ· τὸ δὲ ἐοικός τινι τὰτὸ δύναται, ᾧ ἔοικεν: The exact train of thought here is not very clear. Philolaus has just asserted that the womb is even hotter than the sperm and now goes on to say that "it is like to that [i.e. the sperm]. But what is like something has the same power as that to which it is like." Now this really seems to be belaboring the obvious and adds nothing to the observation that the womb was hot in the first place. Since the phrase beginning with τὸ δὲ ἐοικός was evidently added in the margin or above the line by the scribe it is tempting to regard it as a gloss of some sort on the passage rather than reflecting anything in Meno, but it would still be hard to make sense of.

... τὸ ζῷον ἐπισπᾶται τὸ ἐκτὸς πνεῦμα ψυχρὸν ὄν: The idea of the new-born infant, which is said to be constituted of the hot, breathing in cold air from outside is clearly paralleled by the Pythagorean account of the generation of the universe. F7 of Philolaus says that the first thing fitted together was in the center of the sphere and called the hearth, which is a clear reference to the central fire. Aristotle refers to the next stage in cosmogony when he talks of the cosmos breathing in time, breath, and the void from the unlimited (F201).

The presupposition here that the hot naturally attracts breath is found in a number of places in the Hippocratic corpus. See *The Nature of the Child* 12 and *Regimen* 2.40 (here of hot attracting cold). *Fleshes* 6 (8. 592.11 L) refers to the related idea of the cold as the nourishment of the hot.

καθαπερεὶ χρέος: The image of the infant sending back its first breath "just like a debt" seems almost certain to go back to Philolaus himself. It is hard to explain why Meno would introduce it if it were not in Philolaus in the first place. Of course the image is very reminiscent of the only words that survive of an earlier Presocratic, Anaximander: "And the source of coming-to-be for existing things is that into which destruction, too, happens *according to necessity* (κατὰ τὸ χρεών); *for they pay penalty and retribution to each other for their injustice according to the assessment of time*" (F1 tr. KRS). The translation "necessity" masks the fact that χρεών, which Anaximander uses, is closely related to χρέος = "debt," which is found in Philolaus, and it is probable that Anaximander was making a secondary allusion to cosmic retribution as paying a debt (Kahn 1960/85: 180). What is important is that Philolaus' use of "debt" here suggests a view of the coming to be of a human being and also, by analogy, of the world, that is based on the notion of a cosmic paying of debts which is very close to Anaximander's conception of the world arising in accord with cosmic justice. χρέος is also used by Parmenides in F8.9 (see Mourelatos 1970: 152).

In terms of Philolaus' general philosophical system the description of breathing as paying back a "debt" suggests the sort of balance implied in the notion of the "fitting together" (ἁρμονία) of limiters and unlimiteds. The human body itself is recognized as being constituted by unlimiteds (such as hot and cold) and limiters (such as the process of breathing) which are "fitted together" in a balanced way. Our breathing limits the heat of the body by introducing the cold, but the cold itself cannot be allowed to come to dominate the body and accordingly the "justice" or "attunement" that governs the healthy body must be maintained by paying back the debt of cold to the external air.

...ἐπεισάκτῳ...ὑπάρχοντα...: The contrast in the prefixes of these two verbs emphasizes the fact that at birth our bodies were already (ὑπάρχοντα) hot and that cooling breath had to be "brought in besides" (ἐπεισάκτῳ). It is striking that the verb form which corresponds to the adjective used here is employed by Aristotle in his description of the Pythagorean cosmogony in which the cosmos "brings in besides" time and breath and void from the unlimited (F201: τὸν μὲν οὐρανὸν...ἐπεισάγεσθαι δ' ἐκ τοῦ ἀπείρου χρόνον τε καὶ πνοὴν καὶ τὸ κενόν...). This might lead us to suppose that Philolaus himself used ἐπείσακτος or ἐπεισάγω. However, at *Parts of Animals* 659b19 Aristotle uses just the contrast between ὑπάρχω and ἐπείσακτος which appears in Meno's account of Philolaus, and the latter adjective is found in several other places in Aristotle. The verb ἐπεισάγω, on the other hand, occurs in no other place in Aristotle than in his account of the Pythagorean cosmos. Neither the adjective nor the verb is found in any of the texts of the Presocratics, although it is used in a report in Stobaeus describing Pythagorean views on luck (DK 1.478.33). Plato uses the verb twice and the adjective once. Thus, since neither the verb nor the adjective is very common and yet both appear twice in relation to Philolaus, it remains tempting to see their appearance as reflecting Philolaus' actual usage, but it is possible that it is a Peripatetic term common to Aristotle and Meno.

λέγει δὲ γίνεσθαι τὰς νόσους διά τε χολὴν καὶ αἷμα καὶ φλέγμα . . . : At this point the discussion of Philolaus' medical views leaves his account of the constitution of the body and turns to consider the theory of diseases. The structure of the passage on diseases is as follows: (1) a statement of Philolaus' general thesis that diseases arise from bile, blood, and phlegm; (2) an account of the thickening and thinning of blood as well as the origin of bile and phlegm; (3) a discussion of Philolaus' paradoxical views on bile and phlegm; (4) a restatement of the initial thesis along with mention of other factors that help in producing disease.

At first sight it is not very clear what section 2 has to do with the main thesis stated in section 1. However, the connection becomes intelligible when we realize that bile and phlegm are not natural parts of the body, but purely noxious substances. An account of how these substances arise is then central to Philolaus' aetiology of disease. In the case of blood, since it is a naturally occurring substance in the body, Philolaus gives an explanation of how it is corrupted through thickening and thinning and hence becomes a cause of disease.

Although bile, blood, and phlegm are all mentioned prominently in Hippocratic and philosophical accounts of disease it is hard to find just this trio singled out as the cause of disease. In fact there is very considerable variety in the Hippocratic corpus in the type of humors which are chosen to explain health and disease. *On the Nature of Man* 5 (*CMG* 1.1.3.174.11ff) mentions the three humors emphasized by Philolaus, but divides bile into two types to arrive at four (blood, phlegm, yellow bile, and black bile). *On the Seed* 3 (7.474.7–9 L) also mentions four humors, but this time they are Philolaus' three plus water (*Diseases* 4, which is probably by the same author, also has these four [7.542.6–9 L]. *Affections* 1 (6.208.7–8 L) and *Diseases* 1.2 (6.142.13–14 L) say that all human diseases arise from just bile and phlegm. *Internal Affections* does not state a list, but in the accounts of diseases it appeals to three: blood, dark bile, and phlegm (7.294.4–5 L). Thrasymachus of Sardis in the *Anonymus Londinensis* (9.42) is said to have explained diseases in terms of blood. If we turn away from humors to consider elements such as earth, air, fire, and water and opposites such as hot, cold, dry, and wet the variety of theories of diseases rises even more sharply. Moreover, it is misleading to just cite the humors or other elements that an author uses in his theory of disease, since these humors can be used in radically different ways between various authors. What is important to note here is that several authors are close to Philolaus in their list of disease-causing humors and thus Philolaus appears to fit in very well with late fifth-century medicine. However, none exactly parallels Philolaus, and when we turn to consider the way in which those humors work the differences become even larger. These differences will be explored more fully in the notes below. As a final comment, it is worth noting that despite the reputed Pythagorean reverence for the number 4, the primary *tetraktys*, and despite the fact that four-humor theories abounded in Greek medicine, Philolaus only appeals to three.

ἀρχὴν δὲ γίνεσθαι τῶν νόσων ταῦτα: "[He says] that these are the origin of diseases." At first sight this appears to be an odd repetition of the immediately preceding clause ("he says that diseases arise through blood, bile, and phlegm"). It may in fact just be a repetition, but it seems more likely to make a new point, namely that Philolaus called phlegm, bile, and blood the ἀρχή ("origin") of diseases. This is supported by the fact that virtually the same statement is repeated at the end of Meno's account of Philolaus: "And these [i.e. phlegm, etc.] indeed he postulates as the origins of diseases" (καὶ ταῦτα μὲν δὴ ἀρχὰς τῶν νόσων ὑποτίθεται). We might suppose that this is just Peripatetic terminology used by Meno to describe Philolaus. It is true that ἀρχή is used at the beginning of Meno's account of the theories of disease as part of his description of one of the two main branches of theorists, those who cite residues as the cause of disease (4.28ff: "Those postulating residues as origin and matter of diseases...," καὶ οἱ μὲν ἀρχὴν καὶ ὕλην ὑποθέμενοι τὰ περισσώματα...). However, it is striking that this is the only place in which ἀρχή occurs in Meno's account other than the two uses in the section on Philolaus. If this was Meno's standard language for discussing the various theories of disease, we would expect that it would have appeared in the accounts of at least some of the other theorists (αἰτία is in fact the preferred word: see e.g. 4.41; 5.35; 9.40). Moreover, that Philolaus explicitly used ἀρχή in his medical theory is strongly supported by the fact that we also find it used in a similar way both in F6 and F13.

ἀποτελεῖσθαι ... τὸ μὲν αἷμα παχὺ μὲν ... λεπτὸν δὲ γίνεσθαι ...: It seems most reasonable to assume that the thinning and thickening of blood described here are meant to explain the way in which blood causes disease, although this is not explicitly stated. Healthy blood is neither too thick nor too thin. Thrasymachus of Sardis (*Anon. Lond.* 9.42) advances an account of disease that at first sight seems very similar to this. He says that blood is the cause of disease, and more specifically that changes in blood produce disease. However, Thrasymachus does not explain the changes in blood in the same way (he refers to excess heating and cooling of blood), and in his account blood is changed into bile, phelgm, and pus which in turn cause disease. Philolaus' later account makes clear that for him bile and phlegm do not arise from the corruption of blood. Plato also talks of the blood becoming corrupted (*Ti.* 82e1–83a5), but there is no emphasis on the thickening and thinning of blood as in Philolaus and blood seems not to be corrupted *into* bile, phlegm, and pus as in Thrasymachus, but corrupted *by* these things which are produced through the wasting of flesh. *Internal Affections* explains disease in terms of blood in several cases but lays more emphasis on there being too much in the wrong place rather than on any corruption of blood (e.g. chapters 5, 7, and 32).

Some of the vocabulary used to describe the changes of blood in Philolaus' account is unusual. παραθλιβομένης ("being squeezed," literally "being pressed from the side") does not occur in the Hippocratic corpus or other early writers, although it does appear in Galen and later medical writers. This might make us suspect that it is the terminology of later medicine and that it was perhaps used by the "lecturer" who is reporting Meno's views in the second century AD. On the other hand the simple verb θλίβω is used in scientific contexts in the fifth and fourth century (*Timaeus* 60c4; *Nature of Man* 14 [6.63 L]) so that it is just possible that Philolaus might have used the compound. The idea seems to be that, if the flesh is compressed inward, this will also compress the veins which carry the blood and thus thicken it.

The difficulty in determining how Philolaus thought blood was thinned is connected with the meaning of ἀγγείων. What are the "vessels" which when "broken open" lead to the thinning of blood? Since blood is involved we might naturally think of blood vessels. However, the normal meaning of this word is "vessel" in the sense of a jar or a sack, and it is used elsewhere of cavities in the body such as the head (*Timaeus* 73d2). Aristotle uses it to refer to the lungs (*GA* 787b3) and compares the way the blood leaves the veins at death to liquid being poured out of a vessel (*HA* 511b17), without actually using ἀγγεῖον as a term for "blood vessel" (for which he uses the usual φλέβες). In light of this usage it may well be that Philolaus was thinking of the blood being thinned when certain organs in the body were broken open, thus losing blood. However, the modification "in the flesh" which is applied to the vessels in the report on Philolaus may be a way of picking out blood vessels rather than other organs.

τὸ δὲ φλέγμα συνίστασθαι ἀπὸ τῶν ὄμβρων: The major question here is what is meant by ὄμβρων. Clearly it at least shows the typical connection of phlegm with the moist. The most natural meaning of ὄμβρων is "rains," and in *Nature of Man* 7 blood is said to be increased "by the rains and by hot days" (ὑπὸ τῶν ὄμβρων καὶ ὑπὸ τῶν θερμημεριῶν). However, in Meno's account of Philolaus both bile and blood have been discussed independently of environmental considerations and it would be odd if only phlegm were discussed in such terms. Further, "rains" does not fit well with the verb "constituted" (συνίστασθαι) which suggests that ὄμβροι must refer to actual constituents rather than external factors that have an influence on phlegm. A passage in Aristotle may be some help in resolving the difficulty. At *Parts of Animals* 653a2 he describes phlegm as being produced when warm exhalations are carried upward and cooled by the brain. He then comments that this process can be compared to the one which produces rain. Although the word used here is ὑετῶν rather than ὄμβρων, the comparison is suggestive and it may be that Philolaus too thought of phlegm as produced by a process analogous to rain. In that case, though, it would remain a puzzle as to how Philolaus reconciled phlegm's association with the production of rain through cooling with his contention stated below that phlegm is hot.

DK (3.308) interprets ὄμβρων as urine, but this is not a meaning of ὄμβρος by itself (but cf. ἀναγκαῖοι ὄμβροι at Oppian, *Cynegetica* 4.443).

λέγει δὲ τὴν χολὴν ἰχῶρα εἶναι τῆς σαρκός ...: This means that Philolaus thought that bile was a watery fluid (ἰχώρ) produced by corruption of the flesh. Thus, he probably saw no connection between the liver and bile, and Meno in fact goes on in the next sentence to cite as one of the absurdities of Philolaus' medical views the fact that he did not assign bile to the liver. Moreover, Philolaus did not regard bile as a natural constituent of the healthy body in balance with other humors, but rather as purely noxious and a sign of disease. Thus, in A28 Petron and Philolaus are said to agree that bile either does not exist in us or that it is useless. Philolaus differs from Petron, however, in that bile is a cause of disease in his system while for Petron it is said to be a mere by-product of disease. Plato's views seem to bear some similarity to Philolaus on this point, in that he seems to regard bile, ichor, and phlegm as all produced by corruption of the flesh and thus as all being causes of disease by entering the blood-stream. Thus, as in Philolaus, bile is not a natural substance in the body and is produced by decomposing flesh. But Plato does not call bile an ἰχώρ as does Philolaus, but rather seems to regard bile and ἰχώρ as two separate types of fluid along with phlegm.

It is not clear whether ἰχώρ was in fact used by Philolaus or whether it is

Meno's word. ἰχώρ is used in the Hippocratic corpus to refer to a noxious fluid produced by the corruption of flesh (*Nature of Man* 12; Duminil 1977: 65–76), although it also has the meaning of just a watery fluid in the body. In Aristotle as in the Hippocratics it often refers to the serum or watery part of blood. Aristotle thought blood was produced from it by concoction (*HA* 521a18). However, ἰχώρ besides being the raw material for blood appears in some passages to be produced by corruption (*PA* 651a17). The fact that in Philolaus' system bile is a purely harmful substance makes it appropriate for him to refer to it as an ἰχώρ in the typical Hippocratic sense, and I am inclined to think that ἰχώρ is his word.

Since Philolaus is said not to associate bile with the liver it is possible that he denied the existence of the gall bladder (the usual name for which is also χολή), but it appears that all reference to χολή in the accounts of Philolaus and Petron in the *Anonymus Londinensis* must be to bile itself rather than to the organ. Lonie (1981: 285) says that Philolaus and Petron both denied the existence of the gall bladder, but it is not clear whether this is his reading of the text or whether he assumes that they denied the existence of the gall bladder since they did not associate bile with the liver.

χεινεῖ: = κινεῖ. This is the consistent spelling in the papyrus.

τὸ τ' αὖ φλέγμα ... μετοχῇ τοῦ φλέγματος φλεγμαίνει: For a good general discussion of the meaning of φλέγμα and its role in Hippocratic medicine see Lonie (1981: 277–9) and Friedrich (1899: 36–43). What Meno finds παράδοξον ("incredible," "contrary to expectation") about Philolaus' view on phlegm is that he makes it hot rather than cold as was usually assumed (e.g. *Diseases* 1.24; *Sacred Disease* 9). The argument which Meno attributes to Philolaus appears to be etymological. Since φλέγμα comes from φλέγειν, "to burn," it must be hot. Prodicus (F4) is also said to have made the same etymological point and suggested that, since etymologically φλέγμα should refer to something hot, we should pick a new name for the cold moist substance in the head and he suggests βλέννα.

Diels thought that Philolaus must be dependent on Prodicus and therefore wanted to date Philolaus slightly later than is traditional. However, it is by no means certain that Philolaus is dependent on Prodicus. There are a number of passages in the Hippocratic corpus in which φλέγμα is associated with φλεγμαίνειν ("to inflame") and with heat (Friedrich 1899: 38–9). Democritus evidently also made the connection (A159). While it is possible that all this originated with Prodicus, there is no statement that he was the first to suggest a connection between φλέγμα and φλέγειν or φλεγμαίνειν. The point of the report about Prodicus, which is preserved in Galen, is that having noticed this supposed connection Prodicus corrected the names accordingly. In the end we simply do not know enough to say who first emphasized the connection, but it could just as easily have been Philolaus, Democritus, or one of the medical writers as Prodicus.

On first reading, Meno's report seems to suggest that the etymological argument was the only basis for Philolaus' view, and that carried away by "philological enthusiasm" (Diels 1893a: 419) he simply postulated (ὑποτίθεται) that the fluid in the head, traditionally called phlegm, was hot and not cold, whatever our senses might tell us. His view would thus be much more radical than Prodicus' in that the latter devised names to suit the facts, while Philolaus is changing facts to suit a name. However, a closer reading of Meno's report suggests that Philolaus might have had more than just an etymological argument. After mentioning the etymological point, Meno goes on to say that the parts of the body that are inflamed (τὰ φλεγμαίνοντα) are inflamed (φλεγμαίνει) by participation in phlegm (μετοχῇ τοῦ φλέγματος). Now this reads very much like an example of Philolaus' principle that the products have no features that are not already found in the ingredients. He would naturally argue that whatever causes something to be inflamed must be hot itself. It is then possible that he was aware of phlegm causing inflammations either from experience or from reading medical writers, and that this was the real basis of his argument that phlegm was hot. The etymology may have been used as a subsidiary argument which merely showed words mirroring reality. As a hot product must be derived from hot elements so the word φλεγμαίνω must be derived from a word of similar form (φλέγμα).

συνεργά . . . : The idea that excess or defect of certain powers or substances (and especially of the hot, the cold, and nutriment) causes disease goes back at least to Alcmaeon and is very common in the Hippocratic corpus. Meno does not give very much prominence to these ideas in Philolaus, but given the role of number and attunement (ἁρμονία) in Philolaus' philosophy as a whole it may be that excess and defect were quite important for Philolaus and that Meno's account is misleading. Certainly, συνεργός in itself does not suggest that this type of cause is any less important than bile, blood, and phlegm. Rather the idea is that excess and defect work along with them in some way.

Testimonium A28: For commentary on this testimonium see the commentary on λέγει δὲ τὴν χολὴν . . . above.

6. SOUL AND PSYCHIC FACULTIES

Fragment 13

Theologumena arithmeticae 25.17 καὶ τέσσαρες ἀρχαὶ τοῦ ζῴου
τοῦ λογικοῦ, ὥσπερ καὶ Φιλόλαος ἐν τῷ Περὶ φύσεως λέγει,
ἐγκέφαλος, καρδία, ὀμφαλός, αἰδοῖον. κεφαλὰ μὲν νόου, καρδία
δὲ ψυχᾶς καὶ αἰσθήσιος, ὀμφαλὸς δὲ ῥιζώσιος καὶ ἀναφύσιος
5 τοῦ πρώτου, αἰδοῖον δὲ σπέρματος [καὶ] καταβολᾶς τε καὶ
γεννήσιος. ἐγκέφαλος δὲ ⟨ἔχει⟩ τὰν ἀνθρώπω ἀρχάν, καρδία
δὲ τὰν ζώου, ὀμφαλὸς δὲ τὰν φυτοῦ, αἰδοῖον δὲ τὰν
ξυναπάντων. πάντα γὰρ ἀπὸ σπέρματος καὶ θάλλοντι καὶ
βλαστάνοντι.

3 κεφαλὰ MSS ἐγκέφαλος Diels   5 [καὶ] Boeckh   6 ⟨ἔχει⟩ scripsi ⟨σαμαίνει⟩ Boeckh
ἀνθρώπω Boeckh ἀνθρώπων MSS   8 ἀπὸ σπέρματος E om. cet.   8-9 θάλλοντι
καὶ βλαστάνοντι E θάλλουσι καὶ βλαστάνουσι cet.

And there are four principles of the rational animal, just as Philolaus
says in *On Nature*: brain, heart, navel, genitals. **The head [is the
seat] of intellect, the heart of life and sensation, the navel of
rooting and first growth, the genitals of the sowing of seed
and generation. The brain [contains] the origin of man, the
heart the origin of animals, the navel the origin of plants,
the genitals the origin of all (living things). For all things
both flourish and grow from seed.**

AUTHENTICITY

Since this fragment has a substantially different subject matter than F1-7
whose authenticity is secure, and since its genuineness has been doubted
despite Burkert's arguments in its favor, it is appropriate to discuss its
claim to authenticity in some detail. First, Bywater (1868: 44), Frank
(1923: 320), and most recently Kahn (1985: 20 n. 45) have felt that the

division of the human body into regions associated with a hierarchy of psychic faculties is too sophisticated for someone of Philolaus' date and shows such strong affinities to Platonic and Aristotelian doctrines that the fragment must be the work of a post-Aristotelian forger. Secondly, von Fritz has argued both that the use of ἀρχή in the fragment is impossible for someone of Philolaus' date and also that what is said about soul (ψυχή) is in conflict with the view of soul that we should regard as Philolaus' on the evidence of Plato's *Phaedo* (1973: 480).

The first area of doubt is the most important, since the forgeries in the Pythagorean tradition were motivated by a desire to assign the sophisticated views of Plato and Aristotle back to the master and his early followers. However, it is not sufficient to point out a few similarities to Plato and Aristotle and therefore conclude that a given fragment is a forgery. The forgeries in the Pythagorean tradition are characterized not by a subtle or general similarity to Platonic or Aristotelian views but rather by slavish copying both at the level of content and of terminology. Thus it is first necessary to compare in some detail the doctrine of F13 with the relevant Platonic and Aristotelian views in order to see what type of similarities there are and then examine the Pythagorean pseudepigrapha to see if F13 fits the pattern of the forgeries.

The one great similarity between F13 and Plato (*Timaeus*) is that both assign human psychic faculties to specific regions of the body. Philolaus also agrees with Plato (and other Presocratics) in locating the intellectual faculty in the head. However, beyond these two points the similarities cease and the rest of F13 is quite different from Plato. Most obviously, Philolaus has a fourfold division of faculties rather than the famous Platonic tripartite soul. Next, there is no trace of Plato's characteristic doctrine of the spirited part of the soul (θυμός) in Philolaus. The heart, which Plato associates with θυμός, is said in Philolaus to be the seat of life and sensation (ψυχή καὶ αἴσθησις) and Burkert's point is well taken when he asks "Can anyone equate ψυχή καὶ αἴσθησις with θυμός?" (1972: 270 n. 50). Next, there is no clear reference to Plato's appetitive (ἐπιθυμητικόν) element, although since the navel (ὀμφαλός) in Philolaus has some nutritive function one might see a vague similarity. However, the "rooting" associated with the ὀμφαλός in Philolaus presumably refers to nutrition in the womb and is not a permanent faculty. Moreover, there is nothing in Plato that corresponds to Philolaus' focus on the navel (ὀμφαλός) and its connection with plants, nor are the genitals placed in a hierarchy with other parts of the body in the *Timaeus* as they are in Philolaus. Further, the clear hierarchy of plant, animal, and man and the association of the origin (ἀρχή) of each with a specific organ of the body, while prominent in Philolaus, is hardly found in

Plato. Plato does mention the soul of plants (77b1–6), but says it has sensation, which plants are denied in Philolaus, and does not specifically locate it at the navel or associate it with rooting. On the other hand, the important Platonic emphasis on the liver as helping to control the appetitive part finds no parallel in Philolaus, where the liver is not even mentioned. As a whole the differences from Plato are much more striking than the similarities, and the latter may be best explained by similarity of interests and background rather than as any borrowing from Plato by the author of F13.

The affinities between Aristotle's psychology and F13 are stronger. It is possible to suggest that Philolaus' hierarchy of plant, animal, and man matches up in general terms with the Aristotelian division of faculties into nutrition and reproduction (θρεπτικόν-γεννητικόν), sensation (αἰσθητικόν), and reasoning (διανοητικόν – De an. 414a31–2). Thus the genitals (αἰδοῖον) and their association with reproduction (γέννησις), along with the navel and its association with nutrition through rooting, correspond to Aristotle's nutritive and reproductive faculty. The heart as the seat of sensation (αἴσθησις) in Philolaus and intellect (νόος) located in the brain can be related to the faculties of sensation and reasoning in Aristotle. There is also one interesting similarity in detail. Aristotle like F13 treats the umbilical cord as a root (GA 745b25). However, there are again important differences between Philolaus and Aristotle. First, F13 does not make explicit use of the Aristotelian terms for the parts of the soul. Second, the only organ which Aristotle emphasizes in his psychology is the heart (Juv. 469a5ff) and he certainly does not systematically assign the particular parts of the soul to specific parts of the body. In particular he of course does not put intellect in the head, as does Philolaus, but rather follows Empedocles in associating thinking with the heart. The generative and nutritive faculty is not specifically tied to genitals and navel. Thirdly, for Aristotle generation and nutrition are combined in one faculty whereas in Philolaus they are clearly distinct (De an. 416a19–20).

In summary, F13 (1) does not use the technical language of either Plato's or Aristotle's psychology; (2) is similar to Plato in relating faculties to organs, but differs in almost all other respects both at the level of general structure and at the level of detail; (3) does have a hierarchy of faculties that is similar to Aristotle's; (4) nonetheless does differ significantly in detail from Aristotle, especially in assigning intellect to the head and in general by associating faculties with specific organs. In light of these points of comparison, if F13 is a forgery, we would have to conceive of a forger who borrowed general ideas from both Plato and Aristotle while leaving out prominent points of each system, combined these ideas with some original points of his own and scrupulously avoided Platonic and Aristotelian technical vocabulary. Does such a forger fit the pattern of the forgeries to be found in the tradition of Pythagorean pseudepigrapha?

Several of the pseudepigrapha collected by Thesleff in *Pythagorean Texts of the Hellenistic Period* deal with psychology. It is characteristic of these texts that they reproduce Plato's tripartite soul with little deviation from the master. In the case of "Aresas" (Thesleff 1965: 48–50) we find the soul divided into the clearly Platonic understanding, appetite, and spirit (νόος, ἐπιθυμία, and θύμωσις). "Diotogenes" (73) discusses the spirited part and the appetitive part (τὸ θυμοειδές and τὸ ἐπιθυμητικόν). Again "Hippodamos" (103) talks of the three divisions of the soul: the part which is reasoning, the part which is spirit and the part which is desire (ὁ μέν τί ἐστι λογισμός, ὁ δὲ θυμός, ὁ δὲ ἐπιθυμία). "Metopos" (118) divides the soul into the rational and irrational part (τὸ λογιστικόν and τὸ ἄλογον) and further divides the latter into the spirited (τὸ θυμοειδές) and the appetitive (τὸ ἐπιθυμητικόν). Theages (190) says that the arrangement (διάκοσμος) of the soul is as follows: one part of it is reasoning, one spirit, one appetite (τὸ μὲν γάρ τι αὐτᾶς ἐντι λογισμὸς τὸ δὲ θυμός τὸ δ' ἐπιθυμία). The most famous of the pseudepigrapha, the *Timaeus Locrus*, toes the Platonic line in great detail (217ff). The soul is first divided into the rational and the irrational (τὸ λογικόν and τὸ ἄλογον) and the former is said to come from the nature of "the same" and the latter from the nature of "the different." The rational (τὸ λογικόν) is located in the head while the irrational (τὸ ἄλογον) is divided into the spirited part (τὸ θυμοειδές) which is located around the heart and the appetitive part (τὸ ἐπιθυμητικόν) which is located near the liver, details which exactly correspond to the *Timaeus* (69d6ff). The only texts in Thesleff's collection that deviate from this monotonous adherence to Platonic doctrine are the *Hypomnemata* excerpted by Alexander Polyhistor and preserved in D.L. (8.24–33 – see Festugière 1945), but its threefold division into φρένες, νοῦς, and θυμός has no connection with F13 either.

It should be clear that these writings not only reproduce the basic structure of Plato's psychology, but that they also use language that is closely modeled on Plato's. F13 of Philolaus simply does not fit this pattern. Characteristic Platonic and Aristotelian psychological terminology is almost completely lacking and the fragment does not produce a clear version of either Platonic or Aristotelian psychology. This of course does not prove that F13 is a genuine fragment of Philolaus, but since it does not fit the pattern of the Pythagorean pseudepigrapha it is much less suspect and anyone who argues that it is a forgery will have to explain with some probability why someone should produce such a forgry.

It is now necessary to return to the similarities between F13 on the one hand and Plato and Aristotle on the other and to try to determine which way the influence went. Is F13 part of the problematic of Presocratic psychology by which both Plato and Aristotle were influenced, or must we suppose that it is post-Aristotelian even if it does not fit the pattern of the pseudo-Pythagorean writings? The strongest similarity to Plato was in the attempt to set up a correspondence between psychic faculties and parts of the body, but is there anything peculiarly Platonic about such a procedure? It appears that one of the central questions in Presocratic psychology concerned the location of the seat of the intellect (Empedocles F105, Alcmaeon A5 and 8, Anaxagoras A108: see p. 318).

F13 does admittedly go beyond this Presocratic problematic in so far as it distinguishes between a number of psychic faculties and tries to relate each of them to specific seats in the body. Charles Kahn has recently argued that Democritus was the first to distinguish clearly between sense perception and rational thought and noted that in thinkers such as Empedocles, Anaxagoras, and Diogenes sensation and cognition seem to be identified. He is then sceptical that Philolaus can have made such a distinction prior to Democritus and with even greater terminological precision than Democritus (1985: 20 n. 45). It should be pointed out first that in all probability Philolaus is at most ten or twenty years older than Democritus and that he belongs to the generation after Anaxagoras and Empedocles just as Democritus does. If Democritus could have developed the distinction at this point, surely it is plausible that the intellectual environment was such as to allow Philolaus to make a similar distinction. Such a development is in fact what one would expect from a thinker such as Philolaus who is particularly interested in articulating the structure of the cosmos. If there were other strong grounds for doubting the authenticity of the fragment, this development of terminology might arouse more suspicion, but as has just been shown the fragment does not fit the pattern of Pythagorean forgeries. There is a tradition that makes Democritus a pupil of Philolaus but their relative chronology is so close that it is difficult to say who influenced whom

Again, the strongest similarity with Aristotle was in the notion of a hierarchy of man, animal, and plant with the higher levels containing the principles of the lower levels plus their own distinctive principle. However, as Burkert has pointed out Alcmaeon had already distinguished between man and animal (F1a) and Diogenes of Apollonia (A19) had an implied hierarchy of plant, animal, and man. Indeed, such hierarchies originate long before the Presocratics (Burkert 1972: 270 n. 157).

It is true that the best parallel for Philolaus' view of the navel (ὀμφαλός) as a root is found in Aristotle, but Philolaus' view is not identical with Aristotle's and he goes further in making it the principle of plants. Furthermore, plant–embryo analogies were well developed in Philolaus' time as can be seen in the Hippocratic corpus and in Democritus (Lloyd 1966: 347–8). The author of *De nat. pueri* goes so far as to say that one "will find that the whole nature of things produced in the earth and that of things produced in human beings is similar" (7.528.22ff L). Democritus even describes the navel with a plant metaphor (F148). Thus, as in the case of Plato, the similarities with Aristotle do not necessitate a post-Aristotelian date. Although Philolaus does show development beyond other Presocratics, his system is clearly recognizable as a development of Presocratic ideas in a way appropriate for a thinker who emphasized limit, number, and harmony. Is there any other evidence that can be used to show that the fragment is in fact a Presocratic product?

Examination of the terminology of the fragment provides just such evidence. ψυχή is not used in F13 in the comprehensive Aristotelian and Platonic sense in which it encompasses all human psychic faculties, but is presented as a single faculty shared by animals and men, but not plants. It does not include understanding (νοῦς), which is characteristic of human beings alone, and is located in the heart with perception (αἴσθησις). This evidence suggests that it means "life" or "animal vitality," including the ability to move, breathe, and receive external stimuli, but specifically excludes intellect. Now this sort of conception of ψυχή is very common in the later fifth century before the idea of a comprehensive personal soul becomes dominant in the thought of Socrates and Plato (Burnet 1915; Dodds 1951: 139; Claus [1981] rightly argues that Burnet's view overemphasizes Socrates' originality, but even in his view the meaning "life" is still dominant in the late fifth century. Claus [118] agrees that the use of ψυχή in F13 is in a "physiological mode"). Most importantly, it is hard to see how anyone writing in a philosophical context after Plato and Aristotle could use ψυχή in this way unless he were consciously trying to write in a Presocratic fashion, but there is no parallel for such a "clever" forger. Similarly, αἴσθησις appears to be used "not as sense perception through the various specialized sense organs, but as the apprehension of stimuli, the faculty of being influenced and reacting" (Burkert 1972: 270).

Given that the usage of ψυχή and αἴσθησις points clearly to a Presocratic context for the fragment, is there anything in the language that clearly points to a post-Aristotelian date? Von Fritz has argued against the authenticity of the fragment on the grounds that the use of ἀρχή in the fragment is not paralleled in the texts of the Presocratics (1973: 480). However, while Philolaus does play an important part in developing a sense of ἀρχή that will turn into the Aristotelian usage as "principle," his usage in fact has strong connections to the Hippocratic corpus and Hippocrates of Chios, and thus makes much better sense as a late fifth-century development than as part of a post-Aristotelian forgery (for the arguments see Pt. II, ch. 3).

Von Fritz has raised one further doubt, this time based on the supposed inconsistency between the use of ψυχή in F13 and what we know about Philolaus' views on the soul from the *Phaedo*. It might be possible to reconcile the view of soul as a harmony (if such a view can be ascribed to Philolaus) with what is said in F13, but how could Philolaus use ψυχή in a physiological mode to mean just "life" in F13 and yet also believe in the soul existing apart from the body after death as is suggested by his prohibition against suicide attested in the *Phaedo*? The problem with this objection is that in the end we know too little about Philolaus' views on the soul to be sure if a contradiction does arise. Further, such a contradiction, if it exists, would have a good Presocratic parallel. Empedocles clearly believes in transmigration of souls yet he locates ψυχή as a mortal center of thought and feeling in the heart. It is identified with the blood around the heart and presumably perishes with that blood (F138; Wright 1981: 288). When Empedocles talks about rebirth it appears that he used the word *daimon* (Wright 1981: 69ff and F59, 115). Thus in Philolaus' case too it is possible that he discussed the part of us that survives without reference to the word ψυχή.

Detailed consideration of F13 has thus shown that much of the content and terminology points clearly to a late fifth-century date, while nothing requires a post-Aristotelian date of composition. The similarities with Plato and Aristotle are best regarded as due to the fact that F13 is part of the Presocratic discussion of psychology that formed the soil from which Plato's and Aristotle's views grew. Philolaus should be regarded as an important precursor to Plato and Aristotle in articulating the structure of the soul. Yet this raises another troubling question, one common in the study of early Pythagoreanism. Why does Aristotle make no reference to Philolaus' views on psychology, if they were important background for his own? The fact that Aristotle does not commonly refer to Philolaus by name elsewhere makes it unsurprising that he does not do so in this case, but it is surprising that he does not at least present Philolaus' views as those of the "Pythagoreans." There are a number of possible answers to this question (Aristotle does not discuss all aspects of his predecessors, e.g. Democritus' ethics), but in the end, given the nature of our sources, it is unanswerable. However, there is at least one point that should be made. There is nothing in the fragments or testimonia about Philolaus that suggests that he tried to give any detailed accounts of the sense organs or of any of the "psychic" faculties mentioned in F13. It is possible that he had little more to say on psychology than what we see in F13, and thus contented himself with presenting a schematic view of the structure of human psychic capabilities in order to suggest how number, limiters, and unlimiteds were involved. Accordingly, Aristotle may have been more interested in thinkers like Empedocles and Democritus who attempted to give much more detailed accounts of sensation and thinking.

The significance of Philolaus' psychology: Given that F13 is authentic what sort of a contribution to Presocratic psychology does it make? Does Philolaus make any advances in the area or is his system merely eclectic or eccentric? On some points, such as the location of intellect in the head, he seems to be merely taking sides on preexisting Presocratic debates without presenting any argument for the view, although in other areas, such as the association of sensation (αἴσθησις) with the heart, the analogy between the umbilical cord and a root, and the recognition of the hierarchy of human, animal, and plant it may be that he is showing some originality. What is clearly striking and new is that Philolaus distinguishes sharply between a number of psychic faculties and then arranges all of these faculties in a coherent system. Such systematization is just what we would expect from someone who emphasized the role of limit and harmony in the cosmos. It is hard to appreciate the significance of this step because such systematization becomes commonplace in Plato and Aristotle, but it is precisely this emphasis on structure and system in psychology that Philolaus bequeathed to the giants that followed him.

Particularly noteworthy is the distinction he makes between rational thought (νόος) and sensation (αἴσθησις). Democritus makes the same distinction in a more colorful way with his famous contrast between genuine (γνησίη) and spurious (σκοτίη) cognition, where the latter refers to the five senses (F11). However, Democritus does not use the terminological precision of Philolaus; both rational thought and sensation are regarded as kinds of cognition (γνώμη), and αἴσθησις is not used as a general term for sensation in the surviving fragments (Kahn 1985: 20 n. 45).

In other areas his psychology would seem to be at much the same stage of development as Democritus'. Neither author presents a unified conception of the soul. Philolaus does not use any term to refer to the combination of all the faculties he has distinguished, and it is hard to know what term he would use since ψυχή has been used for one of the individual faculties. (It is thus slightly odd to refer to "psychic" faculties in Philolaus but I have used the term for lack of a better one.) Like Democritus Philolaus makes no distinction between the rational and emotional aspects of the soul. In fact there is no mention of emotions at all in the surviving fragments of Philolaus, while Democritus refers to them extensively. F13 is primarily in a physiological mode and may well come from the same context where Philolaus put forth his medical views (A27). As a result the fragment provides no real moral psychology except in so far as it begins to make distinctions in psychic faculties. It will remain for Socrates and Plato to develop the notion of a comprehensive soul and to make the clear distinction between rational and emotional aspects.

In addition to the distinction between rational thought and sensation Philolaus would appear to be the first to distinguish the faculty that provides for nutrition and growth and the faculty that provides for generation, both from each other and from the faculties that govern sensation and intellect respectively. But what is even more striking is the way in which he combines the hierarchy of psychic faculties which he has distinguished with a hierarchy of regions of the body (head, heart, navel, and genitals) and the hierarchy of living things (human, animal, and plant). As Burkert has noted, it is the discovery of such correspondences that helped the Pythagoreans view the world as a harmony. In the *Timaeus* Plato will go further in the search for such "works of reason," but he is following a path already cleared by Philolaus.

Context of the fragment: F13 is preserved in the strange work known as the *Theologumena arithmeticae* which, although preserved anonymously in the manuscripts, has often been ascribed to Iamblichus. Indeed, Iamblichus indicates that he planned to write such a work at *In Nic.* 125.15ff. Burkert thinks that what we have is in fact this work of Iamblichus, which is a compilation of extracts from Nicomachus' *Theologumena* and Anatolius' *On the Decad*. In that case anything not labeled as from Anatolius is likely to be from Nicomachus, including the passage in which F13 occurs (1972: 98). However, O'Meara (1989: 15) has shown that recently discovered information about Iamblichus' *Theologumena* indicates that it had a more developed metaphysics than anything we find in the *Theologumena* which is preserved, and that the latter must therefore be a compilation by someone other than Iamblichus. Dillon (1973) thinks it may be the work of a later compiler drawing on (1) a work of the same name by Nicomachus, (2) Anatolius' *On The Decad and the Numbers Comprised By It*, (3) the *Theologumena* of Iamblichus. Whichever view we take on Iamblichus' role, it remains most likely that the passage on Philolaus came originally from Nicomachus' *Theologumena*, since Anatolius' work survives and since we know that much of the rest of the *Theologumena* came from Nicomachus.

The work discusses the marvelous characteristics of the numbers 1–10 and the ways in which their influence is manifested in the world. F13 is quoted in the middle of the section on the tetrad. The immediately preceding passage has pointed out, among others, the following manifestations of the number 4: (1) the four "seasons" of man (child, youth, man, and old man); (2) four types of plants (δένδρα, θάμνοι, λάχανα, πόα); (3) the four

315

most elemental characteristics (στοιχειωδέστατα ίδιώματα) in number (the same in the monad, the different in the dyad, surface [χροία] in the triad, and body in the tetrad). Although the section on the tetrad as a whole seems to develop from more general observations about the cosmos and our knowledge of it to more specific discussions of the parts of the cosmos such as plants and human beings, there is no tight structure and there is some repetition. Accordingly, F13 is just one in a long line of examples of the prominence of the number 4 in the world and is not cited as part of a sustained argument of any sort.

Given that this is the use made of the fragment of Philolaus in the *Theologumena*, it still remains unclear to what extent this interest in the number 4 was also to be found in Philolaus. In the actual quotation from Philolaus there is no direct mention of the number 4. Given that the rest of the evidence for Philolaus' book shows that it covered a range of topics typical of Presocratic accounts of the world, it is not likely that the book was structured like the *Theologumena*, which treats the marvelous properties of the numbers 1–10 in order. Thus, it seems likely that there was no explicit mention of the number 4 in Philolaus' book and that the passage was excerpted by someone like Nicomachus because he saw that a fourfold distinction was being made.

Philolaus is mentioned elsewhere in the *Theologumena* for his views on the numbers 4–8 (74.10 = DK A12), but this material can be shown to be derived from a later forgery and not from Philolaus' book. This need not cast any doubt on the authenticity of F13, since it is overwhelmingly likely that, by the date of Nicomachus' *Theologumena* (*c.* 100 AD) and later writings of that sort, both spurious and genuine works of Philolaus were in circulation. It is not at all surprising that fragments from both the genuine book of Philolaus and also spurious works of Philolaus should be preserved in a compilation like the *Theologumena*.

Grammar of the fragment: Both sentences of the fragment are missing a main verb. In the case of the first sentence the verb may well have been supplied by the preceding sentence in Philolaus' book. Since the fragment is quoted in the *Theologumena Arithmeticae* to show that there are "four principles of the rational animal" (τέσσαρες άρχαì τοῦ ζῴου τοῦ λογικοῦ) it is tempting to suppose that the construction of the first sentence should be "the head is the origin of understanding..." (κεφαλὰ μὲν νόου ⟨άρχή⟩ ἐστι⟩...). Thus DK supplies "ist das Prinzip" in the translation. However, the use of head (κεφαλά) rather than brain (ἐγκέφαλος) suggests that the primary purpose of the sentence is to identify the *location* in the body of various psychic and physical faculties. In light of this it is best to understand something like "the head is the seat of understanding" (κεφαλὰ μὲν

316

νόου ⟨ἕδρα ἐστί⟩ ...) with "seat" (ἕδρα) perhaps to be understood from the preceding sentence (so Boeckh translated "Sitz" and Freeman "seat"). For ἕδρα in a similar sense see Plato, *Ti.* 67b5, 72c2, etc.

The second sentence goes on to identify the four ἀρχαί and relate them to the hierarchical structure of living things (human, animal, plant). However, here again a main verb is missing. Diels's σαμαίνει is the only suggestion that has been made, but it is not totally satisfactory. What does it mean to say that the brain "indicates" or "gives signs of" the origin of man? It seems to make much better sense to suppose the sentence to mean that the brain "contains" (ἔχει) or perhaps "provides" (παρέχεται) the origin of man, in so far as, for example, it is the thought that arises in the brain which distinguishes human beings from other living beings and is thus the origin of what is uniquely human in humanity.

κεφαλὰ μὲν νόου: This is the reading of all the manuscripts and is kept by DK[6] although earlier Diels read ἐγκέφαλος to preserve consistency with the use of ἐγκέφαλος at the beginning of the next sentence. De Falco followed this earlier view of Diels in his edition of the *Theologumena arithmeticae*. DK[6] cites Frank (1923: 322) in support of keeping κεφαλά. Frank's argument was that in places Plato and Aristotle seem to use κεφαλή in a sense equivalent to ἐγκέφαλος. *Timaeus* 69e2 which Frank cites is not in fact very helpful, because there κεφαλή in contrast with θώραξ clearly must mean simply "head." However, in some passages κεφαλή is clearly used to indicate the head as specifically including the brain (e.g. *Ti.* 76c7 where κεφαλή is called εὐαισθητοτέρα and φρονιμωτέρα). A difficulty still remains, however, in that in F13 κεφαλά and ἐγκέφαλος are used in very close proximity and it seems questionable whether they can be used as virtual synonyms in such a context. When they are mentioned together at *Timaeus* 73d1ff Plato makes a sharp distinction between the κεφαλή which is called the "vessel" (ἀγγεῖον) and the "marrow brain" (μυελοῦ ἐγκεφάλου) located inside it.

There seem to be two ways, then, of keeping the manuscript reading κεφαλά. First, we can follow Frank and regard it as having virtually the same sense as ἐγκέφαλος, and cite passages like *Timaeus* 76c7 for support, while recognizing that there is not good evidence for the use of the two words in equivalent senses when they are in such close proximity. The second alternative is to keep κεφαλά but recognize that it has a different meaning than ἐγκέφαλος (head rather than brain) and that the use of the two different words is purposeful. In the first sentence I suggest that Philolaus is discussing the human body as a whole and identifying the parts of it where certain faculties have their origin or location. In such a context there is nothing unreasonable in saying that the head is the place where νόος arises. In the second sentence, however, Philolaus is trying to identify that from which as a distinctive ἀρχή men, animals, and plants develop. He cannot very well say that the head is the ἀρχή in this sense since he can hardly deny that animals have heads as well. Accordingly, he refers not to the head but to the brain (ἐγκέφαλος) as the ἀρχή, presumably in the belief that animals do not have a brain in the same sense as men do.

But if the view that I am suggesting is true, then would we not expect the terms καρδία, ὀμφαλός, and αἰδοῖον to change between the two sentences for similar reasons? No, κεφαλή was a special case. It is perfectly possible for Philolaus to call καρδία the specific ἀρχή of animals because animals (and humans) have hearts while plants do not. With ὀμφαλός and αἰδοῖον there is no problem because they do not distinguish ἀρχαί that are denied to classes of being below them. It is only in the case of the head where Philolaus had to be more specific and mention the brain as the ἀρχή of humans, because animals also happen to have heads.

In regarding the head as the seat of intellect Philolaus is taking sides in a prominent controversy in Presocratic thought: is it the head or the heart with which we think? Socrates refers to this controversy as current in the days of his youth in the "autobiographical" section of the *Phaedo* (96a6ff). Among Presocratics Empedocles championed the view that it is the blood around the heart with which we think (F105), and some Hippocratic treatises localize thinking in the heart (*The Heart* 10 [9.88.7 L] mentions the left ventricle, but this treatise is late) or blood (*Diseases* 1.30 [6.200.11 L]). It may be that the heat of the blood is associated with thinking in these two theories. On the other hand Alcmaeon (A5, A8) regards the brain as the center of sensation and thinking and he was followed by Anaxagoras (A108). Diogenes of Apollonia evidently regarded the air in the brain as the seat of thought (A19) and a similar view is found in the Hippocratic treatise *The Sacred Disease* (Grenseman 1968a: 14.1–3; 16.1–3). Plato agreed that the intellect was situated in the head, but from Aristotle onwards the view that the heart is the central organ of intelligence is dominant (so the Stoics and Epicureans), although Galen will argue for the primacy of the head (*The Doctrines of Hippocrates and Plato*). See Taylor (1928: 518–21) for a discussion of the controversy.

καρδία δὲ ψυχᾶς καὶ αἰσθήσιος: The most striking thing here is the use of ψυχή. It is clearly not being used in the broad sense found in Plato and Aristotle where it is responsible for all life functions and is divided into parts or types. Instead it is a faculty that humans and animals have but plants do not, and is associated with perception (αἴσθησις) but not understanding (νόος). Burkert (1972: 271) sees the closest parallels with Critias (A23), who said that "perception is most proper to the soul" (τὸ αἰσθάνεσθαι ψυχῆς οἰκειότατον) while identifying the soul with blood, and Diogenes of

Apollonia (F4) who says that air "is both life-principle and intelligence" (καὶ ψυχή ἐστι καὶ νόησις) for men and other animals (ζῷα). The context makes clear that ψυχή is the life that leaves us at death and is distinct from intelligence. This seems to be the right context in which to place Philolaus' words. For Philolaus ψυχή refers to life as visible in the processes of breathing and perception, both of which are common to humans and animals.

The use of αἴσθησις raises more complicated issues. Two central points need to be made at the beginning. First, the fragment clearly indicates that Philolaus had both a conceptual and a terminological distinction between perception and intellect. On the other hand, and this is the second point, it is not at all clear how sophisticated a conception of αἴσθησις is presupposed by the fragment. There is no mention of the five senses either in F13 or elsewhere in the evidence for Philolaus' philosophy. Further, since αἴσθησις is joined with ψυχή ("animal vitality") and located in the heart, it is more likely that it refers to the simple ability to apprehend external stimuli that animals and human beings obviously share than that it is used as a general term to refer to perception through the five senses (Burkert 1972: 270; Langerbeck 1935: 44).

Philolaus F13 represents, for us, the first terminologically precise expression of the distinction between perception and intellect which becomes important in Plato and Aristotle. As Charles Kahn has shown, Democritus, who is perhaps slightly later than Philolaus, clearly has made the conceptual distinction (F11, F125) although he does not, in the surviving fragments, display the clear terminological distinction found in Philolaus (in Democritus αἰσθάνεσθαι is used of touch but not as a general term in opposition to intellect – Kahn 1985: 19ff). However, Democritus does seem to have a clear idea of a canonical group of five senses, treats them as a type of "knowing" (γνώμη), and considers their value relative to rational thought, all of which goes beyond anything found in Philolaus. It would appear that Philolaus and Democritus, as near contemporaries, were working independently of each other, each making a distinct contribution to the development of Presocratic psychology.

Philolaus' association of the heart with αἴσθησις is paralleled in the Hippocratic treatise *On the Sacred Disease* 17, where the heart and diaphragm "perceive most of all" (αἰσθάνονται μάλιστα) but have no role in thinking (see also the connection between blood and αἴσθησις in Critias [DK A23] discussed above).

ὀμφαλὸς δὲ ῥιζώσιος καὶ ἀναφύσιος τοῦ πρώτου: ὀμφαλός can mean either "umbilical cord" when talking of the foetus or "navel" when describing the mature animal. It can be likened to a root in two ways: (1) as the means by which food is brought from the mother (earth) to the embryo (plant); (2) as what anchors the embryo (plant) in the womb (earth). Philolaus may have had both senses in mind. Aristotle provides the clearest parallel for the first notion:

> ... The nutritive power of the soul immediately sends forth the umbilical cord, like a root, into the womb (... ἡ θρεπτικὴ δύναμις τῆς ψυχῆς ἀφίησιν εὐθὺς οἷον ῥίζαν τὸν ὀμφαλὸν εἰς τὴν ὑστέραν.
>
> (*GA* 745b25. See also the fuller description at 740a25)

At 740b9 he makes explicit the comparison between both the embryo (κύημα) and plant and also the ὀμφαλός and roots. However, Aristotle was not the first to describe the ὀμφαλός in terms of a botanical metaphor. Democritus used such a metaphor, but in a context that stresses the stabilizing or anchoring aspect of the umbilical cord. According to Democritus it is the first thing to come to be after fertilization, and serves both as an anchor and also as a "cable and a branch for the fruit that has come to be and is going to be" (πεῖσμα καὶ κλῆμα τῷ γεννωμένῳ καρπῷ καὶ μέλλοντι, F148). The main metaphor is nautical, but κλῆμα suggests the stalk or twig of a plant. It is worth noting that Plutarch (*De amore prolis* 495e) cites this fragment of Democritus immediately after mentioning the "rooting" (ῥιζώσεως γενομένης) of the embryo. Plutarch assigns the "rooting" (ῥίζωσις) to the time immediately after conception, and is thus primarily appealing to Democritus for the idea that the ὀμφαλός is the first thing to come to be in the womb, but he may well see a parallel between his notion of "rooting" and Democritus' view of the ὀμφαλός as a "cable and a branch."

The comparison of embryo to plant is well developed in the Hippocratic treatises as well. See especially *De nat. pueri* 22ff (7.514ff L – esp. 528.22ff) and see further Lloyd (1966: 347–8) and Heidel (1941: 83–4).

Although this is not stated explicitly here, it is not unlikely that Philolaus regarded the navel as the center of the human body. The association of the navel and the center is common in Greek thought as is shown by the ὀμφαλός or navel stone at Delphi which marked it as the center of the world. The navel with its connotations of a center and a root has strong connections with another important image in Philolaus, that of the central hearth of the universe. As his account of the generation of the universe as breathing is parallel to that of a child's first breath, so here Philolaus seems to be continuing the analogy between the microcosm and macrocosm. The household hearth not only is round like the navel and similarly associated with the center, but is also conceived of as rooted in the earth. Thus the goddess of the hearth Hestia is sometimes portrayed as sitting on a navel stone. For Philolaus, just as the world begins to come to be with the hearth at the center of the universe, so the navel at the center of the human body is the site of first growth. On the connections between the navel and the hearth see further Vernant (1969: 121–2, 157). For another centrifocal image in Philolaus see geometry as the mother-city of the sciences in A7a.

ῥιζώσιος: This is not a common word but it occurs several times in Theophrastus (CP 2.12.5, 4.1 etc; HP 8.1.3), as well as in Hippoc. Alim. 31 (which shows Stoic influence and is to be dated late – see Lloyd 1983: 153 n. 117), and several times in Plutarch including the passage from which the Democritus fragment cited above is drawn (De amore prolis 495e).

ἀναφύσιος: The only other use of this word which I have found is that listed in LSJ, Aelian, NA 12.18. There it is used of the "growing again" of horns on deer. The verb ἀναφύομαι has both the meanings "grow again" and "grow up" (or just "grow"). It is this later sense of "growing up" that is relevant here in Philolaus. It may well suggest that the ὀμφαλός is the first part of the embryo to appear and that the foetus literally grows up from it. If this is so Philolaus' view would be similar to Democritus' (F148).

τοῦ πρώτου: As the gender shows this cannot modify "growing up" (ἀναφύσιος) but is a genitive dependent on ἀναφύσιος. Diels translates it as "embryo", but there do not seem to be any parallels for that meaning and such a sense is probably too precise. τοῦ πρώτου probably refers to the "first part" of the growth of any living thing and would thus include the sprouting of a plant as well as the first stages of the growth of animal and human embryos. Philolaus refers to "the first thing fitted together" (τὸ πρᾶτον ἁρμοσθέν) in F7 when describing the coming into being of the cosmos, which once again points to the analogy between the coming to be of the cosmos and the coming to be of living beings.

αἰδοῖον δὲ σπέρματος [καὶ] καταβολᾶς τε καὶ γεννήσιος: Boeckh was surely right to exclude καὶ here. It was probably inserted by a scribe who failed to realize that σπέρματος depended not on αἰδοῖον but rather on καταβολᾶς.

καταβολᾶς: The use of καταβολή here is paralleled in the report on Philolaus' medical views preserved in the Anonymus Londinensis (see the commentary on A27). This is a slight further indication of the authenticity of F13 since the report in the Anonymus is surely based on an authentic work of Philolaus.

ἐγκέφαλος: See the note on κεφαλά above.

⟨ἔχει⟩: See the note above on the grammar of the fragment.

ἀρχάν: The best method for determining the sense of ἀρχή is to start with what evidence can be gleaned from the context here in F13 and then turn to the use of ἀρχή elsewhere in Philolaus. To begin with it is worth noticing that the context is physiological, that is bodily organs are said to ⟨have?⟩ or ⟨provide?⟩ the ἀρχή of man. However, the best clue to the meaning of ἀρχή here is provided by the last sentence of the fragment, which is an attempt to explain (γάρ) why the genitals are said to provide the ἀρχή for all (living) things. The answer is that all things "flourish and grow" *from* seed (ἀπὸ σπέρματος). This strongly suggests that ἀρχή is here being used in the sense of "starting-point," "origin," or "originating cause." The genitals provide the ἀρχή of all things in that they produce the seed from which, as a starting-point, all things develop. Some translators have taken ἀρχή to mean "ruler" or "ruling factor" (Freeman 1971: 76; Claus 1981: 118), but the last sentence as I have interpreted it is strong evidence against such an interpretation. Further, it is at least slightly odd to say that the brain is ruler in man, the heart in animals, navel in plants, and then turn around and say that there is another ruler (the genitals) in all. It makes better sense to think of a number of originating causes in human beings rather than to suppose there are a number of different rulers.

   Given that the context strongly suggests that the appropriate meaning of ἀρχή is "origin" or "starting-point," is it possible to specify with any more precision what sort of an "origin" Philolaus is talking about? Is it simply a temporal or spatial origin that is at question or something more? It is hard to see how the brain could be said to be the spatio-temporal origin of a human being, the original stuff out of which human beings developed. Rather, the human brain and its capabilities are what distinguish humans from other living creatures. The brain is or provides the "origin" of humanity in that it is what must be present in order for a human being, rather than any other living creature, to develop. This usage connects neatly with the usage of ἀρχή elsewhere in Philolaus, and is in fact just one manifestation of his general method of explanation (see Pt. II, ch. 3).

καρδία δὲ τὰν ζώου: In Galen (see *The Doctrines of Hippocrates and Plato*) there is a distinction between "animal spirit" (πνεῦμα ζωτικόν) located in the heart and "psychic spirit" (πνεῦμα ψυχικόν) located in the brain. The association of "animal spirit" (πνεῦμα ζωτικόν) with the heart might suggest some connection with Philolaus' system where the heart is associated with the "origin" (ἀρχή) of animals and thus cast some suspicion on the authenticity of F13. However, the resemblance is in fact insignificant in light of the more general differences. Galen's pneumatology involves only a twofold division (although he divides the soul into three parts and it has occasionally been argued that there is a third "natural spirit" [πνεῦμα φυσικόν], but see Temkin cited below) in contrast to Philolaus' fourfold division. Further, the "psychic spirit" (πνεῦμα ψυχικόν) is centered in the brain for Galen while "psyche" (ψυχή) is associated with the heart in Philolaus. For Galen's pneumatology see Temkin (1951) and Siegel (1968: 183ff).

αἰδοῖον δὲ τὰν ξυναπάντων: ξυναπάντων clearly must refer to the three classes of living beings (man, animal, plant) already listed. Bywater (1868: 46) thought that it meant "the perfect whole in which vegetative, animal, and rational elements are combined," but this hardly seems possible given the plural ξυναπάντων and the context. Bywater went on to argue that the doctrine embedded in this passage is that of the Stoics that *in semine omnis futuri hominis ratio comprehensa est* (Seneca, *Nat. quaest.* 3.29), but this depends completely on his misreading of ξυναπάντων. Philolaus' point is that the faculty of sending forth seed is common to all living beings.

πάντα γὰρ ἀπὸ σπέρματος καὶ θάλλοντι καὶ βλαστάνοντι: Boeckh (1819: 159) thought that this sentence might be the explanation of the author of the *Theologumena* rather than Philolaus' own, but such explanations are not common in the *Theologumena* and there is nothing in the explanation to make us doubt that it is Philolaus. The next sentence in the *Theologumena* clearly begins a new topic. The Doric forms preserved only in E would show that this sentence must be ascribed to Philolaus, if we could be sure that they are not the work of a later scribe "correcting" non-Doric forms.

Both θάλλω ("flourish") and βλαστάνω ("grow") are most common in poetry, and seem to have special reference to plants, but are also commonly used of other things. βλαστάνω is already used by Empedocles to apply to both plants and men (F21, F10). For the order "flourish and grow" see Plato, *Smp.* 203e2 where love is said to flourish and live (θάλλει καὶ ζῆ). *Cra.* 414a draws out the sense of rapid luxuriant gowth implied in θάλλω: "The word θάλλειν itself seems to model the growth of the young, which is swift and sudden" (αὐτό γε τὸ θάλλειν τὴν αὔξην μοι δοκεῖ ἀπεικάζειν τὴν τῶν νέων, ὅτι ταχεῖα καὶ ἐξαιφνιδία γίγνεται).

Testimonium A23

Macrobius, *Somnium Scipionis* 1.14.19   Pythagoras et Philolaus harmoniam [animam esse dixerunt].

Pythagoras and Philolaus [said that the soul was] a harmony.

Related texts:

1 Plato, *Phaedo* 86b5 καὶ γὰρ οὖν, ὦ Σώκρατες, οἶμαι ἔγωγε καὶ αὐτόν σε τοῦτο ἐντεθυμῆσθαι, ὅτι τοιοῦτόν τι μάλιστα ὑπολαμβάνομεν τὴν ψυχὴν εἶναι, ὥσπερ ἐντεταμένου τοῦ σώματος ἡμῶν καὶ συνεχομένου ὑπὸ θερμοῦ καὶ ψυχροῦ καὶ ξηροῦ καὶ
5 ὑγροῦ καὶ τοιούτων τινῶν, κρᾶσιν εἶναι καὶ ἁρμονίαν αὐτῶν τούτων τὴν ψυχὴν ἡμῶν, ἐπειδὰν ταῦτα καλῶς καὶ μετρίως κραθῇ πρὸς ἄλληλα – εἰ οὖν τυγχάνει ἡ ψυχὴ οὖσα ἁρμονία τις, δῆλον ὅτι, ὅταν χαλασθῇ τὸ σῶμα ἡμῶν ἀμέτρως ἢ ἐπιταθῇ ὑπὸ νόσων καὶ ἄλλων κακῶν, τὴν μὲν ψυχὴν ἀνάγκη εὐθὺς
10 ὑπάρχει ἀπολωλέναι, καίπερ οὖσαν θειοτάτην, ὥσπερ καὶ αἱ ἄλλαι ἁρμονίαι αἵ τ' ἐν τοῖς φθόγγοις καὶ ἐν τοῖς τῶν δημιουργῶν ἔργοις πᾶσι . . .

1 [Simmias speaking:] For I think Socrates, that you have realized yourself that we believe the soul to be something much like this: our body is as it were tensioned and held together by hot and cold and dry and wet and other things of this sort, and our soul is a blending and *harmonia* of these same things, when they have been finely and proportionately blended with one another. So if the soul turns out to be some sort of *harmonia*, it is clear that when our body is excessively slackened or tautened by diseases and other evils, it is inevitable that the soul must perish at once, most divine though it be, just like other *harmoniai*, those in the notes and in all the things craftsmen make . . .

(tr. Barker)

2 Plato, *Phaedo* 88d3 θαυμαστῶς γάρ μου ὁ λόγος οὗτος ἀντιλαμβάνεται καὶ νῦν καὶ ἀεί, τὸ ἁρμονίαν τινὰ ἡμῶν εἶναι τὴν ψυχήν, καὶ ὥσπερ ὑπέμνησέν με ῥηθεὶς ὅτι καὶ αὐτῷ μοι ταῦτα προυδέδοκτο.

2 [Echecrates speaking.] This theory that our soul is a kind of attunement [*harmonia*] has a strange hold on me, now as it always has done, so your statement of it has served to remind me that I'd formerly held this view myself. (tr. Gallop)

3 Plato, *Phaedo* 92c11 ὅδε μὲν γάρ μοι γέγονεν ἄνευ ἀποδείξεως μετὰ εἰκότος τινὸς καὶ εὐπρεπείας, ὅθεν καὶ τοῖς πολλοῖς δοκεῖ ἀνθρώποις.

3 [Simmias speaking:] Because I acquired the latter [the view that the soul is a *harmonia*] without any proof, but from a certain likelihood and plausibility about it, whence its appeal for most people...

(tr. Gallop)

4 Aristotle, *De anima* 1.4, 407b27 καὶ ἄλλη δέ τις δόξα παραδέδοται περὶ ψυχῆς, πιθανὴ μὲν πολλοῖς οὐδεμιᾶς ἧττον τῶν λεγομένων... ἁρμονίαν γάρ τινα αὐτὴν λέγουσι· καὶ γὰρ τὴν ἁρμονίαν κρᾶσιν καὶ σύνθεσιν ἐναντίων εἶναι καὶ τὸ σῶμα συγκεῖσθαι ἐξ ἐναντίων.

4 Another view has also been handed down about the soul which many find as convincing as any view put forward... for they say that the soul is a kind of *harmonia*. Indeed [they say] also that *harmonia* is a blending and combination of opposites and the body is composed of opposites.

5 Aristotle, *Politics* 8.5, 1340b18 διὸ πολλοί φασι τῶν σοφῶν οἱ μὲν ἁρμονίαν εἶναι τὴν ψυχήν, οἱ δ' ἔχειν ἁρμονίαν.

5 Therefore many of the wise say, some of them that the soul is a *harmonia* and others that it has a *harmonia*.

6 Aristotle, *De anima* 1.2, 404a16 ἔοικε δὲ καὶ τὸ παρὰ τῶν Πυθαγορείων λεγόμενον τὴν αὐτὴν ἔχειν διάνοιαν· ἔφασαν γάρ τινες αὐτῶν ψυχὴν εἶναι τὰ ἐν τῷ ἀέρι ξύσματα, οἱ δὲ τὸ ταῦτα κινοῦν. περὶ δὲ τούτων εἴρηται διότι συνεχῶς φαίνεται κινούμενα, κἂν ᾖ νηνεμία παντελής.

6 That which is said by the Pythagoreans seems to be based on the same thought [as that of the atomists]. For some of them said that the soul was the motes in the air, and others that it was what moved the motes. These motes are said to manifestly move continuously, even if the the air is completely calm.

7 Aristotle, *De anima* 1.3, 407b 21 ... ὥσπερ ἐνδεχόμενον κατὰ τοὺς Πυθαγορικοὺς μύθους τὴν τυχοῦσαν ψυχὴν εἰς τὸ τυχὸν ἐνδύεσθαι σῶμα.

7 ...just as if it were possible, in accordance with the Pythagorean stories, that any soul be clothed in any body.

AUTHENTICITY

It is not impossible that Macrobius' assertion that Philolaus thought the soul was a harmony is ultimately based on something in Philolaus' book or an oral report of Philolaus' views. Many of Philolaus' views are not explicitly ascribed to him except in the later doxographical tradition (e.g. his astronomical system). However, the problems in the case of the doctrine of soul as harmony are: (1) only one isolated text in the doxography ascribes the view to Philolaus; (2) Aristotle made it his practice only to assign views to the Pythagoreans as a group and not to individuals, so that it is not surprising that views he ascribes to Pythagoreans in general are ascribed to Philolaus in particular in the later tradition (e.g. the astronomical system). However, in the case of the doctrine of soul as harmony, Aristotle (Texts 4–5) does not even assign it to the Pythagoreans (although he does mention different Pythagorean views on soul – Texts 6–7), labeling it simply as a view that "many" or "many of the wise" hold; (3) The statement in Macrobius could well be based simply on Plato's *Phaedo*. Certainly modern scholars have been very willing to ascribe any view that Simmias puts forth to Philolaus, on the grounds that Simmias "heard" Philolaus at Thebes. It would not be surprising that some ancient interpreters should do the same thing. Indeed, there is good reason to believe that the spurious F22 and F15 are derived from just such a later tendency to ascribe views found in the *Phaedo* to Philolaus.

Of course it might be argued that we should follow this ancient line of interpretation. Simmias and Cebes are clearly said to have heard Philolaus at Thebes (61e6-9), so that, when Simmias says (Text 1) that "we" believe that the soul is a harmony, the "we" in question must be the Pythagoreans and especially his teacher Philolaus. This is supported by the fact that Echecrates, also known as a Pythagorean in the later tradition, says that he too is strongly attracted to the view that the soul is a harmony, although he rather implies that he does not hold that view at the present (Text 2). The problem with this whole line of interpretation is that it is in fact based on some very tenuous assumptions as to how close a follower of Philolaus Simmias is, as opposed to being an independent thinker, and how accurately Plato is portraying either his or Philolaus' views. Those who derive Philolaus' philosophy from the *Phaedo* are clearly assuming that there was a great deal of solidarity in thinking among the Pythagoreans and that Plato is representing it accurately. Unfortunately, the name Pythagorean is never mentioned in the *Phaedo*, nor is there any sort of reference that would suggest such a monolithic group. Philolaus is only mentioned in one early passage (61d3ff) in which Cebes reports that he and Simmias were not clear on Philolaus' account of the prohibition on suicide, which can hardly make us confident that either of them is presented as a mouthpiece for Philolaus' views. Finally, all the "Pythagoreans" in this dialogue (Simmias, Cebes, Echecrates) show an amazing open-mindedness about their views, which indicates that they cannot be relied on to present the "Philolaic doctrine." All of these characteristics of the *Phaedo* clearly suggest that it is folly to use it as a basis for ascribing any view to Philolaus other than what is explicitly ascribed to him at 61dff, i.e. a belief that suicide should be prohibited. When Simmias says (Text 1) that "we" believe that the soul is a harmony, we should take his reference in the most natural way given the context: "we" has a narrow reference to those with whom Socrates is talking, Simmias and Cebes, and not to an otherwise unmentioned Pythagorean orthodoxy lurking in the shadows or to "people in general" for whom Simmias is no more a spokesman than for Philolaus. (See Gallop 1975 ad loc. for a different view. Although Simmias does [Text 3] mention the appeal of the doctrine to many people, this need hardly be a reference to the man in the street.)

In the end then it is clear that we should not conclude that Philolaus believed that the soul was a harmony on the basis of the *Phaedo*. Moreover, the ascription of that view to Philolaus by Macrobius, isolated as it is in the doxographical tradition and unsupported by an ascription of that view to the Pythagoreans by Aristotle, is more likely to be based on an overreading of the *Phaedo* than to be derived from Philolaus' book. Accordingly, we have no reliable external evidence that Philolaus thought that the soul was a harmony.

COMMENTARY

Context in Macrobius: Not much is to be gleaned from the context of this testimonium in Macrobius, because it occurs as simply part of a list of views on soul. Macrobius gives the list to show that the discussion of soul in the *Somnium Scipionis* embraces the views of everyone who has given an opinion on the nature of the soul. The grouping of Philolaus with Pythagoras is somewhat disturbing since the genuine tradition has a tendency to distinguish Philolaus' views from those of Pythagoras, as Burkert has shown. However, it may be that, as Burkert suggests, the ascription to Pythagoras and Philolaus is simply a rendering of the standard doxographical formula "some of the Pythagoreans one of which was Philolaus" (1972: 272 n. 165).

Did Philolaus think that the soul was a harmony?: These texts involve a tangle of problems and I will not attempt to deal with them all here, nor will I deal with the later history of the theory of the soul as a harmony in Greek thought. Good accounts of the problems can be found in Guthrie (1962: 306-19) and Gottschalk (1971). The following remarks will address one main question: Given the general principles of Philolaus' philosophical system and his remarks on soul (ψυχή) in F13, is he likely to have held that the soul is a *harmonia* and if so is he likely to have thought that the soul was mortal or immortal?

Having argued that the external evidence does not show that Philolaus thought that the soul was a harmony, it may now seem perverse for me to consider whether Philolaus might not have held that view after all on the basis of the surviving fragments. However, it is often as important to know the grounds for ascribing a given view to Philolaus as it is to know what view he held. If we look at the surviving fragments, it might appear that Philolaus was almost trivially committed to the view that the soul is a *harmonia* or attunement. For Philolaus' basic thesis is that the world-order and everything in it is a *harmonia* or attunement of limiters and unlimiteds (F1). Thus, if the soul is something in the world-order, it would seem to need to be an attunement of limiters and unlimiteds. Against this view we might argue that the soul is a special case, and that instead of being composed of limiters and unlimiteds it is simply the attunement that orders the limiters and unlimiteds in the body. It would then be identified with the *harmonia* that "supervenes" on limiters and unlimiteds as described in F6. Indeed, Aristotle already recognized that the doctrine that the soul is a *harmonia* could admit of these two interpretations: either it is identified with the harmonious arrangement of elements or it is the formula governing that arrangement (*De anima* 408a5-9). However, F1 rather suggests that attunements are always attunements of something and not to be regarded as independent entities, as does the vague description of a *harmonia* supervening "in whatever way it does" in F6.

Some more light can be shed on the problem if we turn from consideration of the implications of the general principles of Philolaus' system to his specific mention of soul (ψυχή) in F13. What is striking about that fragment is that soul (ψυχή) does not refer to a comprehensive soul including all psychic faculties. Instead, it is just one faculty of what Aristotle would call soul and is associated with the basic phenomena of animal life. It is shared by animals and man and is grouped along with sensation as located in the heart, but distinguished from reason which is peculiar to man and is located in the head. It is most likely then to refer to the breathing and locomotion that distinguish animals from plants. This connection is further supported by Aristotle's report that the Pythagoreans thought that soul was the motes in the air or what moves them (Text 6). The context in Aristotle makes clear that the main concern of this theory, as of the atomist theory to which he compares it, is to explain the ability of animals to move. Aristotle's reports on the Pythagoreans do not always refer to Philolaus, but much of what he says about them is paralleled in the fragments. Thus, in this case, it would be consistent with what we find in Philolaus F13 and Aristotle to suppose that he thought of soul as the source of motion in the animal and located it in the heart. This would in turn suggest that the soul was some attunement of very fine material elements which were always in motion and located in the heart, whence motion was transmitted to the rest of the body.

Following this line of suppositions we would then arrive at a view of soul which is not too dissimilar to what Simmias describes in the *Phaedo*, although Simmias talks of a harmony of the whole body with no mention of the heart and specifically mentions the hot, cold, dry, and wet which we do not see in Philolaus F13. However, Philolaus' medical views suggest that he may have adhered to the very common idea that health depended on a balance of elements such as these and his views on soul may have been influenced by this medical background (A27 and Alcmaeon F4). Thus, if we focus on the most reliable evidence we have for Philolaus' view on soul, F13 and Aristotle's report about Pythagorean views on soul, it appears very likely that Philolaus thought of the soul in largely material terms as a group of constantly moving elements in attunement located in the heart. Such a materialisitic view of soul might well make sense for someone with the medical interests which Philolaus had. This soul did not include all human psychic capabilities (notably excluding intelligence), but was rather limited to accounting for the ability to move and breathe that humans and animals have in common.

There is one text in Aristotle that might seem to cause problems for this interpretation of Philolaus. At *Metaphysics* 985bff Aristotle reports that the Pythagoreans saw more similarities between things and numbers than between things and the traditional material elements. Accordingly, Aristotle says, they maintained that such and such a characteristic (πάθος) of number was justice and such and such soul or mind, etc. Guthrie (1962: 316) takes "characteristic" (πάθος) as "disposition" and concludes that Aristotle is saying that soul was equated with a certain disposition of numbers and hence that soul is a harmony of its own parts and not of bodily parts. But this is not a legitimate reading of Aristotle. It may well be that the Pythagoreans thought of soul as defined in some way by a particular number or characteristic of number, but Aristotle is emphatic throughout his treatment of them that the Pythagoreans did not separate numbers from things, so that he cannot mean that the Pythagoreans thought of soul as just an arrangement of numbers.

But if Philolaus did put forth such a materialistic account of soul (ψυχή), how are we to reconcile this with a Pythagorean belief in the immortality of soul as is presupposed in the doctrine of transmigration? Philolaus might well seem to be open to Socrates' criticism of Simmias' view of soul in the *Phaedo* (Text 1). Socrates points out that if the soul is an attunement of material parts it only exists as long as the given arrangement of material elements exists, and hence that the soul must perish along with the body. Some have thought that Philolaus in fact might not have believed in immortality (Wilamowitz 1920: 2.90). This seems to me a real possibility. Certainly, it will not do simply to assert that since he was a Pythagorean he must think that the soul was immortal unless the tradition explicitly says otherwise (Cameron 1938: 45). We do not know how much latitude in belief was allowed in order for the later tradition to call someone a Pythagorean (and note that Philolaus is not called a Pythagorean in the *Phaedo*). There is some more force to the argument that Philolaus must have believed in the immortality of the soul since he is explicitly said to have forbidden suicide. But even here we cannot be sure that he did not argue, for instance, that committing suicide would be abandoning a post given by the gods, without also implying that there is any afterlife. The role of the gods could just as easily be equated with bringing it about that such and such an attunement of elements arises in such and such a place at such and such a time (i.e. as accounting for the mysterious appearance of a *harmonia* – cf. F6), as with the idea of the gods putting an immortal soul in a series of bodies, as traditional Pythagoreans believed (Text 7).

On the other hand we might speculate that Philolaus did believe that the soul was immortal, but had a different name for this soul than ψυχή. The ψυχή would be a specific attunement of material principles responsible for giving a particular animal body the ability to move and breathe, and would hence perish when those material principles became disordered. However, there might still be a different "soul" in the body which does survive and is immortal. This idea might be supported by the fact that Philolaus separates "intelligence" from ψυχή in F13. Moreover, we have almost a precise parallel for this in Empedocles, who clearly believed in transmigration, but seems to call the transmigrating soul not ψυχή, which for him too is a certain mortal combination of elements in the heart, but rather *daimōn* (F115; see Dodds 1951: 174ff and Guthrie 1962: 319). Furley has argued that the Pythagoreans almost uniquely among the Presocratics were hostile to the notion of a material soul, and in fact thought of the ψυχή as being a comprehensive soul that included all psychic functions

(Furley 1956). However, the basis for this conclusion is one fragment of Xenophanes which raises more questions than it answers. In F7 Xenophanes is satirizing the Pythagorean belief in transmigration when he reports that Pythagoras once heard a puppy squealing as its master hit it, and said: "Stop, do not beat it; for it is the soul of a friend (φίλου ἀνέρος ἐστὶν ψυχή), which I recognized when I heard it giving tongue" (tr. Schofield). Clearly it would be very rash to assume that Xenophanes' language here is a faithful representation of Pythagorean usage. The use of ψυχή with its common overtone of "shade" or "ghost" might have a comic purpose. Also, Burkert (1972: 134 n.77), following Frankel, has noted that, as stated, the Xenophanes fragment rather suggests that the soul is identified with a given state of the body than that it is seen as an immortal entity in the body and distinct from it. Thus, the puppy is said to be the ψυχή, not to have the ψυχή in it, and it is the soul that is said to give voice, not the puppy. Thus, when Empedocles, whose beliefs on transmigration seem close to the Pythagoreans', does not use ψυχή to refer to the immortal soul but only to a mortal life-principle, and when Philolaus, whose fragments represent the only actual words of the early Pythagoreans which we possess, uses ψυχή just as Empedocles did to refer to animal life, with the strong implication that it is tied to material elements in the heart, it seems perverse to seize upon the second-hand satirical remark of Xenophanes and use it as the basis on which to reconstruct the Pythagorean doctrine of ψυχή. Admittedly what we have of Empedocles and Philolaus is skimpy, but it surely suggests that it is unwarranted to conclude that "...the Pythagorean tradition throughout its history seems to have been hostile to the notion of a material soul..." (Furley 1956: 16–17).

If Empedocles and Philolaus distinguished between ψυχή as material life-principle and some other word (δαίμων) which referred to the soul that was reborn, it would remove the formal contradiction between their view of ψυχή and their belief in transmigration, but there still seems to be a serious weakness in a view that argues for our immortality, but does not identify what is immortal with what accounts for our life here and now, but rather with some occult soul that seems to have no function other than to account for transmigration. Thus, the *Phaedo* can be seen as Plato's attempt to expose this weakness.

It is typically assumed that, since the Pythagoreans put forth a doctrine of transmigration of souls, they had a coherent philosophical account of soul, but this is hardly necessary. The fragments of Philolaus combined with Aristotle's reports on the Pythagoreans rather suggest that Philolaus, who certainly presents us with the most detailed Pythagorean philosophical system we know of, only gave an account of ψυχή as an attunement of limiters and unlimiteds which was located in the heart, and which neither included all psychic faculties nor was immortal. He may have believed in another "occult" soul that was immortal, but we have no evidence for this, and if he did it is hard to see how he can have given a coherent account of it without making a distinction between different kinds of reality which is precisely the distinction Aristotle denies to the Pythagoreans. It would appear that so far as a philosophical account of the immortal soul goes Plato is the more original thinker, and that he owes little to the Pythagoreans.

7. MISCELLANEOUS GENUINE FRAGMENTS AND TESTIMONIA

Fragment 16

Aristotle, *Eudemian Ethics* 2.8, 1225a30   ὥστε καὶ διάνοιαί τινες καὶ πάθη οὐκ ἐφ' ἡμῖν εἰσιν, ἢ πράξεις αἱ κατὰ τὰς τοιαύτας διανοίας καὶ λογισμούς, ἀλλ' ὥσπερ Φιλόλαος ἔφη **εἶναί τινας λόγους κρείττους ἡμῶν**.

So that certain thoughts and affections are not in our control, nor are the actions which are in accord with such thoughts and calculations, but as Philolaus said **some motives are stronger than we are**.

AUTHENTICITY

Everyone would accept that this passage reflects the words of Philolaus. Scholars who reject the authenticity of the fragments as a whole are quick to point out that the citation in no way requires that Aristotle had a book by Philolaus (Bywater 1868: 22, Burnet 1948: 284). It is certainly true that it has the form of an apophthegm which is easily passed down orally, although it is not impossible that it is based on something in Philolaus' book.

COMMENTARY

Context in Aristotle: We are largely at the mercy of Aristotle's interpretation of the fragment, which has to be derived from close consideration of the context in the *Eudemian Ethics*. The general context is a discussion of the voluntary, the involuntary, and what is under compulsion. At 1225a20 Aristotle mentions that many consider love and anger as being involuntary in that they are too strong for human nature. This is also the case when someone acts to avoid severe pain. "For what is in one's power, on which the whole issue turns, is what one's nature is able to withstand" (1225a25–6). Aristotle then mentions the example of prophets, who do produce a work of thought, but yet are not thought to act under their own control. The sentence which mentions the apophthegm of Philolaus then follows and seems to serve to wrap up the whole section. "Certain thoughts and affections are not in our control, nor are the actions which are in accord with such thoughts and calculations." The affections (πάθη) mentioned would refer back to actions undertaken out of fear of pain that is too great to bear (see 1225a8 for this use of πάθος), or out of love or anger, while the thoughts (διάνοιαι) refer back to the inspired utterings of the prophet (1225a28 talks of the prophets' utterances as διανοίας ἔργον). If we translate Philolaus' λόγοι as "motives" (following Diels – see Wilamowitz 1920: 2.88), this captures the fact that both rational and irrational forces are at work on the soul, as is suggested by the Aristotelian passage. The saying of Philolaus would then seem to mean that certain "motives" are too strong for our natures and make our actions under the influence of those motives "not up to us." Thus, contrary to the Socratic thesis, it is not always possible to exercise self-control.

What is meant by λόγοι?: A wider range of possible meanings for Philolaus' apophthegm arises if we leave the Aristotelian context aside and survey the possible meanings of λόγος. However, the lack of a controlling context makes it pointless to speculate extensively. λόγος can range from word, speech or discourse to the reasoning or reckoning that lies behind the discourse, to the measure, proportion, or law of nature in the world that our reasoning discovers (see e.g. Kirk 1954: 37ff). Burkert (1972: 185) thinks the apophthegm refers to "daemonic" forces and suggests that it implies that humans are surrounded by "stronger powers." He connects it with the Pythagorean view mentioned by Aristotle that souls are like motes in a beam of light. Thus he appears to take the reference to be to "reasonings" which are known to the daemonic powers but not us. Given Philolaus' interest in number and music we might suppose that "ratio" or "proportion" was a possible meaning. Some proportions or numerical formulas might be "stronger than us" in that we are not able to grasp all the ways in which they govern our world, or the implication might be that they control the world independent of our wishes. Such epistemic modesty would be in accord with Philolaus' tone elsewhere (F6).

Fragment 20

Lydus, *De mensibus* 2.12 (33 Wünsch)   οἵ γε μὴν Πυθαγόρειοι τῷ ἡγεμόνι τοῦ παντὸς τὴν ἑβδόμην ἀνατίθενται, τουτέστι τῷ ἑνί, καὶ μάρτυς Ὀρφεὺς λέγων οὕτως·

ἑβδόμη, ἣν ἐφίλησεν ἄναξ ἑκάεργος Ἀπόλλων

5 Ἀπόλλωνα δὲ μυστικῶς τὸν ἕνα λέγεσθαι προειρήκαμεν διὰ τὸ
ἄπωθεν εἶναι τῶν πολλῶν, τουτέστι μόνον. ὀρθῶς οὖν **ἀμήτορα**
τὸν ἑπτὰ ἀριθμὸν ὁ Φιλόλαος προσηγόρευσε· μόνος γὰρ οὔτε
γεννᾶν οὔτε γεννᾶσθαι πέφυκε· τὸ δὲ μήτε γεννῶν μήτε γεννώμενον
ἀκίνητον· ἐν κινήσει γὰρ ἡ γέννησις ἐπειδὴ καὶ τὸ γεννῶν καὶ τὸ
10 γεννώμενον οὐκ ἄνευ κινήσεώς ἐστι, τὸ μὲν ἵνα γεννήσῃ, τὸ δὲ ἵνα
γεννηθῇ· τοιοῦτος δὲ ὁ θεός, φησὶ γοῦν καὶ Ὀνήτωρ ὁ Ταραντῖνος
οὕτως·

ἔστι γὰρ ἡγεμὼν καὶ ἄρχων ἁπάντων εἷς ἀεὶ ὢν θεός, μόνιμος,
ἀκίνητος, αὐτὸς ἑαυτῷ ὅμοιος.

9–11 ἀκίνητον πέφυκε· τοιοῦτος δὲ ὁ θεός...S   10–14 τὸ μὲν...ὅμοιος desunt Y
11–12 φησὶ... οὕτως S ὡς καὶ αὐτὸς ὁ ῥήτωρ ὁ Ταραντῖνος· φησὶ δὲ οὕτως BA (ὁ ῥήτωρ
ὁ in corr. A)

The Pythagoreans dedicate the hebdomad [the number 7] to the
leader of the universe, that is the one, and Orpheus is a witness (to
this) when he says:

Hebdomad, which the lord who works from afar, Apollo,
loved...

But we have said before that the one is mystically called Apollo, because he (Ἀπόλλων) is apart from the many (ἄπωθεν τῶν πολλῶν),
that is alone. So then, Philolaus rightly called **the number 7
motherless**. For it alone neither has the nature to generate nor to
be generated. But what is neither generating nor being generated is
unmoved. For generation involves motion since both what generates
and what is being generated is not without motion, the one in order
to generate, the other in order to be generated. But god is like this,
at least Onetor the Tarentine says the following:

For there is a leader and Ruler of all, one, eternal, god, abiding,
unmoved himself like to himself.

Additional texts:

Philo, *De opificio mundi* 100   δι' ἣν αἰτίαν οἱ μὲν ἄλλοι φιλόσοφοι
τὸν ἀριθμὸν τοῦτον ἐξομοιοῦσι τῇ ἀμήτορι Νίκῃ καὶ παρθένῳ,
ἣν ἐκ τῆς τοῦ Διὸς κεφαλῆς ἀναφανῆναι λόγος ἔχει, οἱ δὲ
Πυθαγόρειοι τῷ ἡγεμόνι τῶν συμπάντων· τὸ γὰρ μήτε γεννῶν
5 μήτε γεννώμενον ἀκίνητον μένει· ἐν κινήσει γὰρ ἡ γένεσις, ἐπεὶ

⟨καὶ τὸ γεννῶν⟩ καὶ τὸ γεννώμενον οὐκ ἄνευ κινήσεως, τὸ μὲν ἵνα γεννήσῃ, τὸ δὲ ἵνα γεννηθῇ· μόνον δ' οὔτε κινοῦν οὔτε κινούμενον ὁ πρεσβύτερος ἄρχων καὶ ἡγεμών, οὗ λέγοιτ' ἂν προσηκόντως εἰκὼν ἑβδομάς. μαρτυρεῖ δέ μου τῷ λόγῳ καὶ Φιλόλαος ἐν τούτοις·

10 **ἔστι γάρ, φησίν, ἡγεμὼν καὶ ἄρχων ἁπάντων, θεὸς εἷς ἀεὶ ὤν, μόνιμος, ἀκίνητος, αὐτὸς ἑαυτῷ ὅμοιος, ἕτερος τῶν ἄλλων.**

For this reason the other philosophers liken this number to the motherless and virgin Victory, who legend says appeared from the head of Zeus, but the Pythagoreans liken it to the ruler of all. For what neither begets nor is begotten remains unmoved. For generation involves motion, since both what generates and what is being generated are not without motion, the one in order to generate, the other in order to be generated. But the highest ruler and leader alone is neither moving nor being moved. The hebdomad is fittingly called the image of this. Philolaus also gives witness to what I say in these words:

There is, he says, **a ruler and leader of all, god, one, eternal, abiding, without motion, himself like to himself, different from all others.**

Anatolius, *De decade* 35 Heiberg   ἑβδομὰς μόνη τῶν ἐντὸς δεκάδος οὐ γεννᾷ οὔτε γεννᾶται ὑπ' ἄλλου ἀριθμοῦ πλὴν ὑπὸ μονάδος· διὸ καὶ καλεῖται ὑπὸ τῶν Πυθαγορείων παρθένος ἀμήτωρ.

The hebdomad alone of the numbers in the decad does not generate nor is generated by another number except the monad. Therefore, it is called motherless virgin by the Pythagoreans.

Aristotle, F203 = Alexander, *in Metaph.* 39.3ff   ἐπεὶ δὲ οὔτε γεννᾷ τινα τῶν ἐν τῇ δεκάδι ἀριθμῶν ὁ ἑπτὰ οὔτε γεννᾶται ὑπό τινος αὐτῶν, διὰ τοῦτο καὶ Ἀθηνᾶν ἔλεγον [οἱ Πυθαγόρειοι] αὐτόν...ὁ δὲ ἑπτὰ οὔτε τινὰ γεννᾷ οὔτε ἔκ τινος γεννᾶται· τοιαύτη δὲ καὶ ἡ Ἀθηνᾶ ἀμήτωρ καὶ ἀεὶ παρθένος.

Since 7 neither generates any of the numbers in the decad nor is generated by any of them, they [the Pythagoreans] called it Athena...7 neither generates any nor is generated from any. But such is the character of Athena who is mother and always virgin.

See also Theon 103 where the number 7 is also said to be called Athena by the Pythagoreans.

AUTHENTICITY

It seems almost certain that Lydus' statement that Philolaus called the number 7 motherless is genuine, since this view is assigned to the Pythagoreans by Aristotle in the fragment quoted above which is in all probability ultimately derived from his special treatise on the Pythagoreans. The only other possibilities are either that (1) it is an early Pythagorean view but is falsely ascribed to Philolaus by Lydus or his source, or (2) the passage about Athena quoted by Alexander is an insertion into information he derived from Aristotle, in which case it could have its origin in the later Pythagorean tradition. However, on the whole we should reject these possibilities. If Philolaus called 7 motherless it is then likely that he also regarded it as virgin and accepted the equation with Athena which is also attested for the early Pythagoreans by Aristotle. (Szymanski [1981: 115–17] argues that an equation of 7 with Athena could not be ascribed to Philolaus since it would conflict with the system of correlations between numbers and concepts/deities found in Philolaus A12, 13 and 14. I don't see what the conflict would be, but at any rate A12, 13 and 14 are not likely to be based on authentic material.)

It has often been thought that both Lydus and Philo go on to cite another fragment of Philolaus which describes the hebdomad (or in some interpretations, the one) as the unmoved, abiding, etc., ruler of all. However, Thesleff has brought attention to an alternate reading in the manuscript tradition of Lydus which is clearly preferable to the traditional reading. The text accepted by Wünsch in his edition and by DK is ὡς καὶ αὐτὸς ὁ ῥήτωρ ὁ Ταραντῖνος· φησὶ δὲ οὕτως· (...as also the Tarentine rhetor himself. He says the following:...). Since Philolaus was referred to a few lines above in Lydus, scholars have read this as a reference back to him. However, it is a very odd and awkward reference. Philolaus is said to be from Tarentum by a number of authors so that that is no problem but it is unparalleled to call him a rhetor (public speaker? rhetorician?). The manuscript S however reads ὀνήτωρ (Wünsch–Thesleff reports ὁ νήτωρ for S) instead of ὁ ῥήτωρ and this is clearly preferable as the *lectio difficilior*. The strange name Onetor has been replaced through a one-letter change with the easily recognizable word rhetor and the whole passage then understood as a reference back to Philolaus. Thesleff (1965: 138–40) prefers to read 'Ονήτας presumably because other fragments of pseudo-Pythagorean writings ascribed to Onatas have been preserved. However, an Onetor, as Thesleff notes, is mentioned in the scholia to Proclus' commentary on the *Republic* (2.378 Kroll) as having written a work *On Arithmetical Proportion*

(Περὶ ἀριθμητικῆς ἀναλογίας), in which he discussed the successful births of seven- and nine-month babies and the abnormalities of eight-month babies. Such a book seems a very plausible source for the fragment quoted in Lydus, and we should therefore read Ὀνήτωρ (so Burkert 1972: 249 n. 51). Philo's ascription of the fragment to Philolaus suggests that the alternate readings may have already existed in the source for Pythagorean arithmology common to Philo and Lydus, or that Philo himself made the misreading which was then used by later scholars to "correct" Lydus.

Having clarified the text of Lydus, it is possible to make sense of the very confused passage in Philo. He straightforwardly assigns to Philolaus the fragment Lydus quotes from Onetor. Since Lydus (6th century AD) is so much later than Philo (1st century AD), we may be tempted to assume that Philo is more reliable, and since there are great similarities between Philo and Lydus in many passages discussing the characteristics of number, we might assume that Philo is the source for Lydus. However, it has been shown that Lydus is independent of Philo in most passages, and the similarities in content are to be explained by the fact that Philo and Lydus are using the same source (Robbins 1921: 97–123 and Boyance 1963: 91–5). In fact careful comparison of the Lydus and Philo passages shows that Philo has misunderstood the source in several ways, including the mistaken ascription of the Onetor fragment to Philolaus.

The passage in Lydus makes the following points: (1) The Pythagoreans *dedicate* (ἀνατίθενται) the hebdomad to the leader of the universe. In support of this Lydus quotes the Orphic saying that Apollo (equated with the one) loved the hebdomad. It is important to note that nothing here suggests the identification of the leader of the universe and the hebdomad. (2) Philolaus rightly called 7 motherless. For it alone neither generates [any number in the decad] nor is generated [by any number in the decad] and is therefore unmoved. (3) But this is what [the highest] god is like, as Onetor says: "There is a ruler and leader of all, one, eternal, god, abiding, *unmoved*..." [Thus 7 is naturally associated with the highest god.]

In contrast the passage in Philo asserts that "other philosophers," who are contrasted with the Pythagoreans, likened seven to motherless and virgin Athena. This contradicts point (2) in Lydus. Next, Philo does not say with Lydus that the Pythagoreans *dedicated* the number 7 to the leader of the universe but that they *likened* (ἐξομοιοῦσι) it to the leader of the universe rather than to Athena. Philo takes this to mean that they identified seven and the leader of the universe. He then quotes the Onetor fragment (as Philolaus') in order to support this point. The passage in Philo is just loose enough that it is impossible to be certain whether or not he is citing the "Philolaus" fragment as a description of the hebdomad (so DK and Frank 1923: 324) or of the one (Boeckh 1819: 151, Boyance 1963: 93 and Thesleff 1961: 104 n. 1).

The tradition starting with the fragment of Aristotle quoted above shows that Philo is wrong to imply that the Pythagoreans did not liken the number 7 to Athena (Szymanski [1981] overlooks the testimony of Aristotle and thus mistakenly accepts Philo's account). Why should Philo go astray on this point? One explanation would be that his text of the source for Pythagorean numerology, which he shares with Lydus, had the mistaken reading "the Tarentine rhetor," leading Philo to assume that the Onetor fragment belonged to Philolaus. If he then took this as Philolaus' description of the hebdomad, he may well have concluded that Philolaus and the Pythagoreans cannot also have equated it with Athena, who cannot be considered the leader of the universe. Therefore he concluded that the equation of 7 with Athena must belong to "other philosphers." However we explain the origin of the confusion, it is clear from Aristotle's testimony about the Pythagoreans that Philo is confused, and we should reject his ascription of the Onetor fragment to Philolaus.

Testimonium A10

Theo Sm. 20.19 Ἀρχύτας δὲ καὶ Φιλόλαος ἀδιαφόρως τὸ ἓν καὶ μονάδα καλοῦσι καὶ τὴν μονάδα ἕν.

Archytas and Philolaus without making a distinction call the one also monad and the monad one.

AUTHENTICITY

Theon presents a series of views on the relationship between the monad and the one. He first asserts that the monad is distinguished from the one in the same way as number is distinguished from the numerable (19.14). Thus the monad is intelligible, indivisible, and the principle of numbers whereas the one is perceptible, infinitely divisible, and the principle of things that can be numbered (e.g. one horse). He then talks of "those later" who make the monad and the dyad principles of numbers, in contrast to "those from Pythagoras" who make the sequence of even and odd numbers the principles of things numbered in the sensible world, e.g. the triad is the principle of threes in the world of sense. He then talks of still others (οἱ δέ – 20.12) who posit as principle of these same things (the sequence of numbers) the monad and the one, understood as separated from all difference, the one itself rather than a particular one (e.g. one horse). It is after this that he asserts that Archytas and Philolaus use the terms one and monad interchangeably. Theon then immediately goes on to talk of "most" (οἱ δὲ πλεῖστοι) who use

339

the expression "the first monad itself" to designate the primary intelligible substance of the one by participation in which things are called one. Finally he turns to yet another distinction between the monad and the one which he finds in the *Philebus*. The whole context is thus a complicated discussion of the different relationships that various thinkers have seen between the one and the monad, with an emphasis on the distinction between the two terms. The comment on Philolaus and Archytas is in contrast to the main development of the passage, and clear testimony that Theon or his source could find no basis for such a distinction in the writings of Philolaus and Archytas.

The standard presentation of Pythagoreanism elsewhere in the later tradition includes a sharp distinction between the monad as belonging to the intelligible realm and the one in numbers and the realm of sense (Anon. Phot. in Thesleff 1965: 237.17, but see Burkert 1972: 58 n. 30; Sextus, *M.* 10.276; Lydus, *Mens.* 2.6; Philo, *Qu. in Gen.* 4.110). Burkert argues convincingly that Theon's evidence is not only in conflict with this tradition but in fact agrees with Aristotle's presentation of the early Pythagoreans as making no distinction of grades of being, unlike Plato and later Academics. Further, Aristotle, in his special treatise on the Pythagoreans (F203), says that they called intelligence (νοῦς) both monad and one. This indicates that Aristotle saw them as making no distinction between the two terms, which is just the import of Theon's testimony.

There are several different things that Theon's testimony could mean. It is possible, but unlikely, that Philolaus or Archytas explicitly said that they would use the terms monad and one interchangeably. Such an assertion would seem to assume an already existing distinction between the two which is unlikely at a date before Philolaus. It is more likely that Theon is simply observing that Archytas and Philolaus never draw a distinction between the two terms. This could mean that Theon found both terms used, but interchangeably, or that he found only one of them used even where, on the basis of the later tradition, he would have expected the other term to be used. The term monad does not in fact occur in the fragments of Philolaus that are likely to be genuine, although "the one in the center of the sphere" is referred to in the cosmogony that starts with F7. Although it is hard to be confident, it seems best to conclude that Theon is preserving a tradition that is genuine and which represents the early Pythagoreans as not making the distinction in grades of being that is assumed in the contrast between the monad and the one.

Part IV
SPURIOUS OR DOUBTFUL FRAGMENTS AND TESTIMONIA

1. THE WORLD SOUL

Fragment 21

Stobaeus, *Eclogae* 1.20.2 (1.172.9 Wachsmuth) Φιλολάου Πυθαγορείου ἐκ τοῦ Περὶ ψυχῆς. Φιλόλαος ἄφθαρτον τὸν κόσμον εἶναι. λέγει γοῦν οὕτως ἐν τῷ Περὶ ψυχῆς·

παρὸ καὶ ἄφθαρτος καὶ ἀκαταπόνατος διαμένει τὸν ἄπειρον
5 αἰῶνα· οὔτε γὰρ ἔντοσθεν ἄλλα τις αἰτία δυναμικωτέρα αὐτᾶς
εὑρεθήσεται οὔτ' ἔκτοσθεν φθεῖραι αὐτὸν δυναμένα· ἀλλ' ἦν ὅδε ὁ
κόσμος ἐξ αἰῶνος καὶ εἰς αἰῶνα διαμενεῖ, εἷς ὑπὸ ἑνὸς τῶ συγγενέος
καὶ κρατίστω καὶ ἀνυπερθέτω κυβερνώμενος. ἔχει δὲ καὶ τὰν
ἀρχὰν τᾶς κινήσιός τε καὶ μεταβολᾶς ὁ κόσμος εἷς ἐὼν καὶ συνεχὴς
10 καὶ φύσει διαπνεόμενος καὶ περιαγεόμενος ἐξαρχίδιον· καὶ τὸ
μὲν ἀμετάβλατον αὐτοῦ, τὸ δὲ μεταβάλλον ἐστί· καὶ τὸ μὲν
ἀμετάβολον ἀπὸ τᾶς τὸ ὅλον περιεχούσας ψυχᾶς μέχρι σελήνας
περαιοῦται, τὸ δὲ μεταβάλλον ἀπὸ τᾶς σελήνας μέχρι τᾶς γᾶς.
ἐπεὶ δέ γε καὶ τὸ κινέον ἐξ αἰῶνος ἐς αἰῶνα περιπολεῖ, τὸ δὲ
15 κινεόμενον, ὡς τὸ κινέον ἄγει, οὕτως διατίθεται, ἀνάγκη τὸ μὲν
ἀεικίνατον τὸ δὲ ἀειπαθὲς εἶμεν· καὶ τὸ μὲν νῶ καὶ ψυχᾶς
† ἀνάκωμα πᾶν, τὸ δὲ γενέσιος καὶ μεταβολᾶς· καὶ τὸ μὲν πρᾶτόν
τε δυνάμει καὶ ὑπερέχον, τὸ δ' ὕστερον καὶ καθυπερεχόμενον· τὸ
δὲ ἐξ ἀμφοτέρων τούτων, τοῦ μὲν ἀεὶ θέοντος θείου τοῦ δὲ ἀεὶ
20 μεταβάλλοντος γενατοῦ, κόσμος.

διὸ καὶ καλῶς ἔχει λέγεν, κόσμον ἦμεν ἐνέργειαν ἀΐδιον θεῶ τε
καὶ γενέσιος κατὰ συνακολουθίαν τᾶς μεταβλατικᾶς φύσιος. καὶ ὁ
μὲν ⟨εἷς⟩ ἐς ἀεὶ διαμένει κατὰ τὸ αὐτὸ καὶ ὡσαύτως ἔχων, τὰ δὲ
καὶ γινόμενα καὶ φθειρόμενα πολλά. καὶ τὰ μὲν ⟨ἐν⟩ φθορᾷ ὄντα
25 καὶ φύσεις καὶ μορφὰς σῴζοντι καὶ γονῇ πάλιν τὰν αὐτὰν μορφὰν
ἀποκαθιστάντι τῷ γεννήσαντι πατέρι καὶ δημιουργῷ . . .

4 ἀκατοπόνατος P οὐκ ἀταπείνωτος F   6 δυναμένου PF δυναμένα Canter   7 διαμενεῖ Kranz: διαμένειν P διαμένων F διαμένει Heeren   7 συγγενέω PF συγγενέος Boeckh   10 ἐξ ἀρχιδίου PF ἐξ ἀρχ⟨ᾶς ἀ⟩ιδίω Rose ἐξαρχίδιον Diels cf. *CIG* 5235.2   15 διατίθεσθαι PF διατίθεται Heeren   20 κόσμου PF κόσμος Heeren   21 ἔχειν ἔλεγε PF ἔχει λέγεν Badham   23 ⟨εἷς⟩ Diels   24 μὲν ⟨ἐν⟩ φθορᾷ Meineke μὲν φθορὰ PF   25 φύσει MSS φύσεις Heeren   σώζοντι Diels σώζεται MSS   26 ἀποκαθιστάντι Diels ἀποκαθίσταντα PF

From *On the Soul* by Philolaus the Pythagorean. Philolaus (says) that the cosmos is indestructible. At least he says the following in *On the Soul*:

Therefore it [the cosmos] endures for endless time both indestructible and inexhaustible. For there will not be found either within it or outside of it any other cause more powerful than it is and able to destroy it. But this cosmos existed from eternity and it will endure for eternity, one, governed by one which is akin to it, most powerful, and incomparable. The cosmos, being one, continuous, inspired by the breath of nature, and rotating from the beginning (?) holds also the first principle of activity and change. Part of the cosmos is unchanging and part is changing. The unchanging part reaches from the soul that embraces the whole to the moon and the changing part from the moon to the earth. Since the part that is active goes around from eternity to eternity, and the part that is moved is disposed as the part that is active directs, it is necessary that one-part is always active while the other is always passive. The one is wholly the dwelling (?) of mind and soul and the other of generation and change. The one is first in power and exceeds while the other is second and exceeded by much. But that which is composed of both of them, on the one hand the always running divine and on the other the always changing mortal, is the cosmos.

Therefore it is well to say that the cosmos is the everlasting activity of god and generation in accordance with the attendance of changeable nature [on god]. The one endures forever constant and unvarying, but the many are both coming to be and being destroyed. And these, although they are subject to destruction, preserve both their nature and form, and by generation reestablish the same form as the father and craftsman who gave them birth...

AUTHENTICITY

This is the fragment whose authenticity has been questioned most widely and for the longest time. See especially Burkert (1972: 242–3) and Zeller (1923: 1.476 n. 1). Its spuriousness is certain for the following reasons:

(1) Platonic and Aristotelian doctrines: F21 clearly adopts the doctrines of the world soul (τὰς τὸ ὅλον περιεχούσας ψυχᾶς) and demiurge which are first developed by Plato in the *Timaeus*. It also asserts the eternity of the world (ὁ κόσμος ἐξ αἰῶνος εἰς αἰῶνα διαμενεῖ), which might be paralleled among the Presocratics by Heraclitus F30, but is a theme first developed by Aristotle (see e.g. *De caelo* 1. 10–12). On the other hand Fragments 1–7 and 17 of Philolaus, whose authenticity is supported by agreement with Aristotle's accounts of Pythagoreanism, clearly discuss the generation of the world, and do not even assert its endless duration let alone its eternity.

(2) Platonic and Aristotelian terminology: the Aristotelian technical term ἐνέργεια is used. The description of the universe as ἐς ἀεὶ διαμένει κατὰ τὸ αὐτὸ καὶ ὡσαύτως ἔχων is very similar to the standard phrasing that Plato uses to describe the immutability of the forms (*Phd.* 78c6-8, *R.* 484b4, *Ti.* 29a1). Further, the fragment also describes the demiurge as the "father who gave them birth" (τῷ γεννήσαντι πατέρι), which exactly matches the description of him at *Ti.* 37c7 (ὁ γεννήσας πατήρ).

(3) The fragment shows extensive and close connections to other pseudo-Pythagorean writings and especially to Ocellus. Particularly important here is the division of the cosmos into two parts, one part described as unchanging but always active (ἀεικίνατον) and the other as changing and always passive (ἀειπαθές). The first part extends from the fixed stars to the moon and the second part extends from the moon to the earth. In Macrobius (*Somn. Scip.* 1.11.5) just this division is ascribed to a group of Platonists. The pseudo-Pythagorean writing by Ocellus uses exactly the same terms to describe the division (15.19, 21.17, 26.12; see also Damippus 68.22; Metopos 119.15; Anon. Alex. 235.1) and in two places gives extended passages that match F21 word for word (26.13, 20.9–11). The argument for the indestructibility of the cosmos given in F21, that there is nothing more powerful than it either within it or outside of it, is also closely paralleled at Ocellus 13.24ff.

(4) The expression φύσει διαπνεόμενος ("inspired by the breath of nature," Freeman 1971) certainly looks Stoic.

(5) The style of the fragment is very exalted and piles adjectives on top of each other ("indestructible and inexhaustible," "akin to it and most powerful and incomparable," "one and continuous and inspired by the breath of nature and turning round") in a fashion that begins with the

343

"cosmic piety" of the *Timaeus*. See for example *Ti.* 33a7, where the cosmos is described as "complete, ageless and without disease" (τέλεον καὶ ἀγήρων καὶ ἄνοσον). This sort of piety is missing from the genuine fragments of Philolaus.

2. FRAGMENTS AND TESTIMONIA ON NUMBER

Fragment 8

Iamblichus, *in Nic.* 77.8   εἴτε κατὰ τὸν αὐτὸν δίαυλον οἱ ἐφεξῆς ἀριθμοὶ συνσωρεύοιντο, ἡ μὲν μονὰς ὡς ἂν ἀρχὴ οὖσα πάντων κατὰ τὸν Φιλόλαον (οὐ γὰρ **ἕν** φησιν **ἀρχὰ πάντων**;) καὶ τοῖς ἑτερομήκεσιν εἰς γένεσιν ὕσπληγα ὁμοίως ἑαυτὴν παρέξει,
5   οὐκέτι δὲ καὶ *νύσσα* ἔσται τῆς καθ᾿ ὑποστροφὴν παλινδρομίας καὶ ἐπανόδου, ἀλλὰ τὸ τοιοῦτον ἡ δύας ἀντ᾿ αὐτῆς ὑποστήσεται.

If the numbers in succession are put together according to the same racecourse [pattern], the monad, in so far as it is the first principle of all things according to Philolaus (for does he not say that **[the] one is the first principle [starting-point] of all things**?), will serve to start the genesis of oblong numbers as well [i.e. as square ones], but it will no longer also serve as the finish line of the race back after the turn, but the dyad will substitute for it in this role.

AUTHENTICITY

The context of the fragment is somewhat complicated. However, it is clear that it is only the statement that the one is the principle of all things that is assigned to Philolaus, and not the surrounding mathematics of the racecourse. (For the interpretation of the racecourse see Heath 1921: 1.113–14. Boeckh [1819: 147] gives a good discussion of the fragment, including the suggestion of punctuating with a question mark in the parenthesis.)

What makes the fragment suspect is the fact that the doctrine of a unity that stands above all opposition is a characteristic of Neoplatonism. Frank (1923: 309, 316) and Boeckh (1819: 147) were glad to assign this view to Philolaus. However, Aristotle's account of Pythagoreanism and Fragments

345

1–7 of Philolaus discuss no such view. The basic principles there are the limiters and unlimiteds, with no hint of any principle above them. Syrianus (*in Metaph.* 165.33 = F8b) has it that Philolaus had god establish the basic opposition of limit and unlimited, and Zeller (1923: 1.480 n. 1) cites *Philebus* 23c as evidence to support this view, but Proclus (*Theol. Plat.* 3.7, p. 132) asserts that the doctrine of god as the highest principle is Platonic, and only the opposition of limiters and unlimiteds goes back to Philolaus.

Burkert (1972: 257 n. 90) briefly notes that the assertion that "Unity is the first principle of all things " could refer to the unity that is the first thing harmonized in F7 of Philolaus, and hence that F8 might be authentic. However, since the one in F7 is something that is fitted together (ἁρμοσθέν), it is hard to see how Philolaus could call it the first principle of *all* things, especially since he calls the elements from which it is put together, limiters and unlimiteds, first principles (ἀρχαί) in F6. Since F8 is thus inconsistent with F7 and since it has such clear affinities with Neoplatonism, it should be regarded as spurious.

Fragment 8a

Syrianus, *in Metaph.* 165.33   ὅλως δὲ οὐδὲ ἀπὸ τῶν ὡσανεὶ ἀντικειμένων οἱ ἄνδρες ἤρχοντο, ἀλλὰ καὶ τῶν δύο συστοιχιῶν τὸ ἐπέκεινα ᾔδεσαν, ὡς μαρτυρεῖ Φιλόλαος **τὸν θεὸν** λέγων **πέρας καὶ ἀπειρίαν ὑποστῆσαι**, διὰ μὲν τοῦ πέρατος τὴν τῷ
5   ἑνὶ συγγενεστέραν ἐνδεικνύμενος πᾶσαν συστοιχίαν, διὰ δὲ τῆς ἀπειρίας τὴν ταύτης ὑφειμένην, καὶ ἔτι πρὸ τῶν δύο ἀρχῶν τὴν ἑνιαίαν αἰτίαν καὶ πάντων ἐξῃρμένην προέταττον, ἣν Ἀρχαίνετος μὲν αἰτίαν πρὸ αἰτίας εἶναί φησι, Φιλόλαος δὲ **τῶν πάντων ἀρχὰν** εἶναι διϊσχυρίζεται . . .

As a whole these men did not begin from opposites, but recognized what is beyond the two orders of opposites. Witness Philolaus who says that **god established limit and unlimited**. He indicated the whole order that is most related to the one by the [term] limit, and the order opposite to this by the [term] unlimited, and still ranked the cause that is unitary and transcends all things before these two principles. Archainetos calls it the cause before cause, but Philolaus maintains that **it is the first principle [starting-point] of all things** . . .

AUTHENTICITY

This fragment is not included in DK and, even though it is not really presented as a literal quotation, I have chosen to include it here rather than in the testimonia because of its close connection to F8. The second reference to Philolaus in the text from Syrianus which says that Philolaus referred to the transcendent cause as "the first principle of all things" is identical in content to F8 (Iamb. *in Nic.* 77.8). The other view assigned to Philolaus in Syrianus, that god produced limit and unlimited, is in perfect concord with this idea that Philolaus posited the one (= god) as a transcendent cause beyond the limit and unlimited. It is quite possible that Syrianus (5th century AD) is in fact dependent on Iamblichus for this account of Philolaus (O'Meara 1989: 128).

It is almost certain that F8a is spurious. All the same objections that are raised against F8 can be raised against it. The notion of a transcendent one = god from which limit and unlimited emerge clearly belongs in the later Platonic tradition. Philolaus F6 explicitly rejects discussion of any more basic principles of the world than limiters and unlimiteds and Aristotle's testimony about the early Pythagoreans agrees.

Fragment 11

Theo Sm., 106.10   περὶ ἧς [the decad] καὶ Ἀρχύτας ἐν τῷ Περὶ τῆς δεκάδος καὶ Φιλόλαος ἐν τῷ Περὶ φύσιος πολλὰ διεξίασιν.

Concerning which [the decad] both Archytas in *On the Decad* and also Philolaus in *On Nature* expound many things.

Stobaeus, *Eclogae* 1. proem 3 (1.16.20 Wachsmuth)   Φιλολάου·
θεωρεῖν δεῖ τὰ ἔργα καὶ τὴν οὐσίαν τῶ ἀριθμῶ καττὰν δύναμιν ἅτις ἐστὶν ἐν τᾷ δεκάδι· μεγάλα γὰρ καὶ παντελὴς καὶ παντοεργὸς καὶ θείω καὶ οὐρανίω βίω καὶ ἀνθρωπίνω ἀρχὰ καὶ ἀγεμὼν
5 κοινωνοῦσα *** δύναμις καὶ τᾶς δεκάδος. ἄνευ δὲ τούτας πάντ' ἄπειρα καὶ ἄδηλα καὶ ἀφανῆ.
γνωμικὰ γὰρ ἁ φύσις ἁ τῶ ἀριθμῶ καὶ ἡγεμονικὰ καὶ διδασκαλικὰ τῶ ἀπορουμένω παντὸς καὶ ἀγνοουμένω παντί· οὐ γὰρ ἧς δῆλον οὐδενὶ οὐδὲν τῶν πραγμάτων οὔτε αὐτῶν ποθ' αὐτὰ οὔτε ἄλλω
10 πρὸς ἄλλο, εἰ μὴ ἧς ἀριθμὸς καὶ ἁ τούτω οὐσία. νῦν δὲ οὗτος καττὰν ψυχὰν ἁρμόζων αἰσθήσει πάντα γνωστὰ καὶ ποτάγορα

ἀλλάλοις κατὰ γνώμονος φύσιν ἀπεργάζεται συνάπτων καὶ
σχίζων τοὺς λόγους χωρὶς ἑκάστους τῶν πραγμάτων τῶν τε
ἀπείρων καὶ τῶν περαινόντων.

15 ἴδοις δέ κα οὐ μόνον ἐν τοῖς δαιμονίοις καὶ θείοις πράγμασι
τὰν τῶ ἀριθμῶ φύσιν καὶ τὰν δύναμιν ἰσχύουσαν, ἀλλὰ καὶ ἐν
τοῖς ἀνθρωπικοῖς ἔργοις καὶ λόγοις πᾶσι παντᾶ καὶ κατὰ τὰς
δημιουργίας τὰς τεχνικὰς πάσας καὶ κατὰ τὰν μουσικάν.

ψεῦδος δὲ οὐδὲν δέχεται ἁ τῶ ἀριθμῶ φύσις οὐδὲ ἁρμονία· οὐ
20 γὰρ οἰκεῖον αὐτοῖς ἐστι. τᾶς τῶ ἀπείρω καὶ ἀνοήτω καὶ ἀλόγω
φύσιος τὸ ψεῦδος καὶ ὁ φθόνος ἐστί. ψεῦδος δὲ οὐδαμῶς ἐς ἀριθμὸν
ἐπιπνεῖ· πολέμιον γὰρ καὶ ἐχθρὸν τᾷ φύσει τὸ ψεῦδος, ἁ δ'
ἀλήθεια οἰκεῖον καὶ σύμφυτον τᾷ τῶ ἀριθμῶ γενεᾷ.

2 τῶ ἀριθμῶ Boeckh τῶν ἀριθμῶν F   καττὰν Boeckh κατὰ F   5 lacuna of 12
letters in F   8 ἧς Koen εἰς F   9 αὐτῶν Heeren αὐτοῖς F αὐτά Heeren αὐτὰ F
10 ἧς Koen εἰς F   τούτω Heeren τούτοις F   11 καττὰν Boeckh κατὰν F
12 συνάπτων Newbold σωματῶν Boeckh σωμάτων F   15 κα Meineke καὶ F
17 παντᾶ Boeckh πάντα F   19 ἁ Jacobs αἱ F   20 τῶ F γὰρ Heeren τοι Diels

One must consider the works and the essence of number according to the power which is in the decad. For it is great, all-complete, and all-accomplishing, the first principle of both divine and heavenly life and also of human life. Taking part *** power also of the decad. Without this all things are unlimited, unclear, and uncertain.

For the nature of number is knowledge-giving, authoritative, and instructive for everyone in every case in which they are perplexed or ignorant. For none of the existing things would be clear to anyone either in relation to themselves or in relation to one another, if number and its essence did not exist. But as it is, number in the soul, fitting together all things with perception, makes them known and agreeable with one another according to the nature of the gnomon, fixing and loosing the proportions of things, each separately, both of unlimited things and of limiting things.

It is not only in supernatural and divine matters that you can see the nature of number and its power prevailing, but also everywhere in all human deeds and words, both in all the arts of the craftsman and in music.

The nature of number and harmony do not admit of anything false. For it is not akin to them. Falsehood and envy belong to what is unlimited, unintelligible, and irrational. Falsehood in no way breathes upon [or "falls upon"?] number. For falsehood is inimical and hostile to its nature, but truth is of the same family and naturally tied to the race of number.

AUTHENTICITY

The best discussions of the fragment are those of Burkert (1972: 273–5) and Frank (1923: 313 n. 1). See also Newbold (1906: 176–83) and Heidel (1907: 78–9). There is a great deal both in the style and content of the fragment that links it to the philosophy of the early Academy and the later tradition of Platonism, while virtually nothing that accords with what one would expect from a Presocratic author or with Fragments 1–7 of Philolaus. It must be regarded as almost certainly spurious. The main points are the following.

(1) The most suspect feature of this fragment is the poetic and highly-wrought rhetorical style that hymns the power of number by heaping adjectives on top of each other. This is the "cosmic piety" that is so much the mark of F21 and the other pseudo-Pythagorean writings, and which originates in Plato's *Timaeus*, but that is generally foreign to Presocratic texts. The author of Fragment 11 is particularly fond of triads of adjectives of similar form (μεγάλα... καὶ παντελὴς καὶ παντοεργὸς [3], ἄπειρα καὶ ἄδηλα καὶ ἀφανῆ [6], γνωμικά... καὶ ἡγεμονικὰ καὶ διδασκαλικὰ [7], ἀπείρῳ καὶ ἀνοήτῳ καὶ ἀλόγῳ [20]). This use of adjectives is closely paralleled in F21 (see p. 343) and in the pseudo-Pythagorean writings. Eurytus (88.11) distinguishes two natures and then goes on to describe them with a string of adjectival phrases for each (ῥητὰ καὶ τεταγμένα καὶ λόγον ἔχουσα ποτὶ πάντα, ἄρρητος καὶ ἄτακτος καὶ ἄλογος καὶ οὐδεμίαν σύνταξιν ἔχουσα). Similar strings of adjectives can be seen in Brotinus (55.20), Aristaios (52.12), Kleinias (108.27), and Butheros (59.5).

(2) There are other parallels with the pseudo-Pythagorean writings. The expression ἁ οὐσία τῶ ἀριθμῶ, used twice in the fragment, is paralleled in pseudo-Pythagoras 164. 9–12, which also has phrasing similar to that of Fragment 11. The role of number in making things knowable in harmony with sense perception has parallels in pseudo-Archytas 36.22. The expression καττὰν ψυχάν is also paralleled at pseudo-Archytas 38.19.

(3) While the agreements with Plato and Aristotle both in doctrine and expression are not as striking as with F21, the idea of number being in the soul cannot fail to remind us of the Platonic connection between the soul and mathematicals which was so important in the later Neoplatonic tradition (see e.g. Merlan 1968: 11ff).

There are also some other suspect similarities. F11 describes number as making "all things knowable and agreeable with one another" (πάντα γνωστὰ καὶ ποτάγορα ἀλλάλοις [11–12]), which is very close to the passage in the *Republic* (546b7) about the nuptial number which renders "all things agreeable and commensurable with one another" (πάντα προσήγορα καὶ ῥητὰ πρὸς ἄλληλα). The distinction between the absolute and the relative (οὔτε αὐτῶν ποθ' αὐτὰ οὔτε ἄλλω πρὸς ἄλλο [9–10]) is conceptually and verbally similar to passages making the same distinction in Plato (*Sph.* 255c12–13: τῶν ὄντων τὰ μὲν αὐτὰ καθ' αὑτά, τὰ δὲ πρὸς ἄλλα). The distinction is common in the pseudo-Pythagorean writings (Ocellus, 12.24; Aristaios, 52.17; Butheros, 59.7).

Finally, while it is clear from Aristotle's testimony that the number 10 was important to the early Pythagoreans, the decad was also a prime topic of discussion in the early Academy. A report about Speusippus' book *On Pythagorean Numbers* indicates that he spent half of the book on the decad (see Philolaus A13). That same report suggests that Speusippus relied heavily on Philolaus, and the same tradition may be represented in Theon's comment about Philolaus having many things to say about the decad in his *On Nature* (the text is given with B11 above, p. 347). But Speusippus is not alone in his interest in the decad; Plato himself appears to have emphasized the decad in his latest philosophy (see Dillon 1977: 4). In the end it will be hard to decide how much of the Academic work on the decad already existed in early Pythagoreanism and how much was original with the Academy. Assertions in the later tradition such as that by Theon of Academic dependence on Philolaus do not carry much weight, however, since there was such a strong strand in later Platonism that viewed Plato's work as simply Pythagoreanism in a different guise.

(4) There are several aspects of the content that conflict with what is found in Fragments 1–7 and what we would expect of Presocratic Pythagoreanism based on Aristotle. First, this fragment clearly ties number to limit and opposes it to the unlimited, whereas both limiters and unlimiteds are associated with number in Fragments 1–7. Second, ψυχά is clearly used to refer to an all-embracing concept of soul, which would be surprising for the date and conflicts with the use of ψυχή in the genuine F13, where it means something close to "life." It is true that the phrase τῶν πραγμάτων τῶν τε ἀπείρων καὶ τῶν περαινόντων in this fragment (13–14) is very similar to F6, τῶν πραγμάτων... καὶ τῶν περαινόντων καὶ τῶν ἀπείρων, but this one parallel is not enough to overcome the massive similarities both in expression and content with the pseudo-Pythagorean tradition.

Fragment 20a

Lydus, *De mensibus* 4.64 (114.20 Wünsch) ὀρθῶς οὖν ὁ Φιλόλαος **τὴν δυάδα Κρόνου σύνευνον** εἶναι λέγει, ὃν κατὰ τὸ προφανὲς

Χρόνον ἄν τις εἴποι. συνάπτεται δὲ τῷ χρόνῳ ἡ δυὰς ὡς τῆς φθορᾶς αἰτίῳ· μήτηρ δὲ αὐτὴ τυγχάνει τῆς ρευστῆς οὐσίας.

Then Philolaus correctly says that **the dyad is the consort of Cronos**, whom one could obviously call Chronos [time]. It is to time as the cause of destruction that the dyad is joined. It [the dyad] is the mother of flowing being.

AUTHENTICITY

The strongest argument for the authenticity of this fragment is its similarity to F20, whose authenticity was supported by the testimony of Aristotle. The similarity is simply in the project of identifying each of the numbers in the decad with a divinity. However, a similar project was also carried out in the Academy and, although it can be difficult to distinguish genuine early Pythagorean ideas from later Academic ideas, there are serious reasons for doubting the authenticity of this fragment. Whereas both the identification of seven with Athena in F20 and also the argument for that identification are shown to be early Pythagorean by the Aristotelian testimony, we have no such corroborating testimony for the identification of the dyad with Rhea. Even more disturbing is the fact that the argument for the identification given in Lydus clearly has its origin in the Academy and is particularly connected with Xenocrates. In F15 Xenocrates identifies the dyad with the mother of the gods (the monad is identified with Zeus), where Rhea is probably meant. It is likely that there is an etymological play on the connection between Rhea and ρέω = to flow. In F28 Xenocrates identifies the two basic principles as the one and "the ever-flowing" (ἀενάου), which is clearly identified with matter. This is very close to the description of the dyad as the mother of "flowing being" (for which see also Plutarch, *Quaest. Rom.* 268d), which Lydus gives in the explanation of Philolaus' identification of the dyad with Rhea.

The idea of matter as flowing in Xenocrates may ultimately go back to the *Timaeus*. In the doxographical tradition we find the idea ascribed to Thales, Pythagoras, and the Stoics (Aet. 1.9.2), and the adjective ρευστός is used again. The most intriguing reference to the doctrine is found in a controversial fragment of Aristotle (F207). Aristotle is reported by Damascius to have said in his books on Archytas that Pythagoras called matter "other" because it is flowing (ρευστήν) and always becoming other. The ascription to Pythagoras is very suspect since Aristotle does not assign any doctrines of this sophistication to Pythagoras elsewhere. But the most problematic feature is that the concept of ὕλη originates in Plato and Aristotle, and Burkert (1972: 80 n. 164) is probably right that the comment is exegesis of Plato. Aristotle seems to ascribe the doctrine of the equation of matter with "the other" to Platonists at *Metaphysics* 1087b27.

The equation of Rhea with the dyad also appears in the *Theologumena arithmeticae* (14.6ff) and it is again based on the connection with ῥύσις (flowing). It is tempting to connect this with the Academic idea that the line is produced by the flowing (ῥύσις) of the point, an idea which probably goes back to Speusippus (see Taran 1981: 291, 362–3 and Burkert 1972: 66ff and n. 95), and is found in the famous passage of Sextus (*M.* 10.248ff) which is connected in some fashion to Plato's lecture on the good.

It thus appears tolerably clear that the grounds given by Lydus for Philolaus' connection of Rhea with the dyad have their origin in the Academy. Given the tendency in the pseudo-Pythagorean tradition to assign Academic ideas to early Pythagoreans there are thus grounds for having grave doubts about the authenticity of this fragment. Of course it is possible that Philolaus had different reasons for identifying the dyad with Rhea and that Lydus is giving a later Platonizing interpretation. Burkert (1972: 249 n. 53, 171 n. 32) points out that we also meet Rhea in the Pythagorean *acusmata*. However, she is not connected with numbers there. More important is the testimony of Aristotle (F203), who says that the Pythagoreans called the dyad opinion (δόξα) because it can move in both directions (ἐπ' ἄμφω μεταβλητήν – towards both truth and falsehood?). He also reports that they called it movement (κίνησιν) and addition (ἐπίθεσιν). Thus it appears that the connection of two with motion goes back beyond the Academy to the Pythagoreans. However, the expansion of this idea of motion to the flowing nature of matter and Rhea as the mother of the gods by an etymological play seems firmly grounded in Academic ideas associated with Xenocrates, so that Fragment 20a appears to be a good example of the type of reworking of Pythagorean ideas that went on in the Academy, and should not be regarded as from Philolaus' genuine book.

Fragment 20b

Lydus, *De mensibus* 1.15 (9.4 Wünsch) ὀρθῶς οὖν αὐτὴν ὁ Φιλόλαος **δεχάδα** προσηγόρευσεν, ὡς **δεκτικὴν τοῦ ἀπείρου** . . .

2 δεκάδα MSS Wünsch δεχάδα scripsi

Philolaus rightly called it [the decad] **dechad** (receiver), as it is **receptive of the unlimited** . . .

AUTHENTICITY

This is the third case in which Lydus quotes an appellation which Philolaus gives to a certain number (cf. F20 and F20a). This etymology for δέκας is repeated many times in the tradition of Greek arithmology. In these other cases δεχάς, "receiver," is consistently used as a term coined to describe the decad in a way that brings out the supposed etymology. For example Philo, *De dec.* 23 says παρό μοι δοκοῦσι καὶ οἱ πρῶτοι τὰ ὀνόματα τοῖς πράγμασι θέμενοι... εἰκότως αὐτὴν προσαγορεῦσαι δεκάδα, ὡσανεὶ δεχάδα οὖσαν, παρὰ τὸ δέχεσθαι καὶ κεχωρηκέναι τὰ γένη πάντα τῶν ἀριθμῶν... ("Therefore, those who first established names seem to me to reasonably call it the decad, as being the dechad (receiver), in so far as it receives and makes room for all of the numbers..."). It may be reasonable to refer to "those who first gave names" as calling it the decad, as in the passage from Philo, but the Lydus passage according to the text of Wünsch surely suggests that Philolaus first coined the term decad, which is absurd. Surely what lies behind the Lydus text is that Philolaus first called the decad by the name "dechad," for the reasons given. This is of course just the sort of thing that gets confused in the transmission of manuscripts. In the case both of *Theologumena arithmeticae* 59 (80.8 De Falco) and Asclepius 38.31, where δεχάς is used, some manuscripts mistakenly read δέκας instead.

Despite the fact that this explanation of the decad by an etymology which makes it "the receiver" is found in many places, it is only ascribed to Philolaus in Lydus, and the explanation of what it receives varies from source to source. Lydus has Philolaus say that it receives the unlimited, Philo has it receive every kind of number, proportion, progression, concord, and harmony, Asclepius says it contains all numbers, the *Theologumena arithmeticae* equates it with the universe as containing all things. The idea that the decad receives the unlimited does fit the best of any of the explanations with the genuine fragments of Philolaus and speaks for the authenticity of the fragment. Certainly it is hard to reconcile this fragment with what is said in the spurious F11 about number not receiving falsehood, which is there also closely related to the unlimited. However, etymological plays of the same sort as in this fragment are well documented for the Academy, as is seen from Plato's *Cratylus* and from Xenocrates (see the commentary on F20a, p. 351). It must therefore remain uncertain whether F20b represents something from Philolaus' book or Academic work inspired by the Pythagoreans.

Fragment 20c

Theologumena arithmeticae 81.15 πίστις γε μὴν καλεῖται [sc. ἡ δεκάς], ὅτι κατὰ τὸν Φιλόλαον **δεκάδι καὶ τοῖς αὐτῆς μορίοις**

περὶ τῶν ὄντων οὐ παρέργως καταλαμβανομένων πίστιν
βεβαίαν ἔχομεν. διόπερ καὶ Μνήμη λέγοιτ' ἂν ἐκ τῶν αὐτῶν,
5   ἀφ' ὧν καὶ μονὰς Μνημοσύνη ὠνομάσθη.

3 καταλαμβανόμενοι MSS καταλαμβανομένοις Ast, De Falco, DK καταλαμβανομένων Burkert

Nevertheless, it [the decad] is called **conviction** because, according
to Philolaus, **by means of the decad and its parts we have
secure conviction concerning the things that are when they
are not grasped in a cursory way.** Wherefore it could also be
called Remembrance on the same grounds on which the monad was
also called Memory.

AUTHENTICITY

In DK this fragment is included at the end of Testimonium A13, which
describes Speusippus' comments on the decad and which is also derived
from the *Theologumena arithmeticae*. However, it clearly belongs with the
citations about Philolaus' number theory found in Lydus, so that I have
numbered it F20c to follow on those three fragments. The reference to
Philolaus is embedded in the explanation for calling the decad "conviction,"
so that it is clear that both the use of the term πίστις and the explanation
of that usage are being assigned to him. On the other hand, there is no
compelling reason to assign the concluding remark, which equates the
decad with Remembrance, to Philolaus. The use of the optative suggests an
afterthought by the author of the *Theologumena arithmeticae*.

This equation of the decad with πίστις is not found elsewhere in the
arithmological tradition nor in Aristotle's remarks about the Pythagoreans,
so that there is no good external means of determining its authenticity.
The point of view of the fragment is reminiscent of the supurious F11 of
Philolaus in its emphasis on the epistemological function of the decad. On
the other hand Aristotle (F203) tells us that the Pythagoreans called one
"mind" and two "opinion" so that the equation given between "conviction" and ten in F20c could be seen as part of this sequence of identifications
of numbers with epistemological concepts. Once again it is unclear whether
we are dealing with original ideas of Philolaus or later Academic reworkings.

Fragment 23

Iamblichus, *in Nic.* 10.22 = Syrianus, *in Metaph.* 123.6 and
142.21   Φιλόλαος δέ φησιν ἀριθμὸν εἶναι τῆς τῶν κοσμικῶν
αἰωνίας διαμονῆς τὴν κρατιστεύουσαν καὶ αὐτογενῆ συνοχήν.

3 κρατιστεύοισαν Syrianus 123.6–7

Philolaus says that number is the controlling and self-generated bond of the eternal continuance of the things in the cosmos.

AUTHENTICITY

The fragment is quoted by Iamblichus in a string of definitions of number that includes definitions supposed to be by Thales, Pythagoras, Eudoxus, and Hippasus. Syrianus also gives the same fragment in two places with minor changes in word order. Philolaus' definition is paired with a spurious definition of Hippasus. It is very likely that the fragment of Philolaus is also spurious for the following reasons:

(1) Almost all of the vocabulary of the fragment has no parallel before Plato and Aristotle, and most of the parallels are even later. Moreover, the vocabulary and content are clearly similar not only to other spurious fragments of Philolaus (especially F11 and F21), but also to other writings in the pseudo-Pythagorean tradition, notably Ocellus. The notion of "the eternal continuance of the things in the cosmos" (αἰωνίας διαμονῆς) mentioned in F23 plays a large role in the spurious F21, where the cosmos is said to endure from eternity to eternity (ἐξ αἰῶνος καὶ εἰς αἰῶνα διαμενεῖ). As was pointed out in the commentary on F21, this emphasis on the eternity of the world is foreign to the genuine fragments of Philolaus, which freely talk of generation. The word "continuance" (διαμονή) is late and is found three times in the pseudo-Pythagorean writings of Ocellus (13.11, 17; 22.2), and also in the spurious report of Pythagorean doctrines by Alexander Polyhistor which is preserved in Diogenes Laertius (8.34). The adjective αἰώνιος first appears in Plato (*Ti.* 37d3, etc.). Again the word κοσμικός is post-Aristotelian (it is a variant reading at Aristotle, *Ph.* 196a25). The description of Speusippus' book *On Pythagorean Numbers* which is given in the *Theologumena arithmeticae* describes the decad (83.2) as the creative form (εἶδος τεχνικόν) for the things created in the cosmos (τοῖς κοσμικοῖς ἀποτελέσμασι). It might be that this reflects Speusippus' own language, but it is much more likely that this is a description given in Neopythagorean terms, since a quotation from Speusippus is clearly marked a few lines later. Such formations in -ικος start their prominence in Aristotle and they are common in the pseudo-Pythagorean writings. The spurious F11 of Philolaus abounds in such formations. αὐτογενής ("self-generated") is post-Aristotelian, and συνοχή in a philosophical sense is first found in the *Topics* of Aristotle (122b26). συνοχή is also found in another spurious testimonium about Philolaus (A16b).

Testimonium A11

Lucian, *Laps.* 5 εἰσὶ δὲ οἳ καὶ τὴν τετρακτύν, τὸν μέγιστον ὅρκον αὐτῶν [the Pythagoreans], ἢ τὸν ἐντελῆ αὐτοῖς ἀριθμὸν ἀποτελεῖ, ἤδη καὶ **ὑγιείας ἀρχὴν** ἐκάλεσαν· ὧν καὶ Φιλόλαός ἐστι.

3 ἀποτελεῖν οἱ δὲ καὶ MSS ἀποτελεῖ ἤδη καὶ Marcilius ἀποτελεῖν οἴονται τὸν δέκα Diels ἀποτελεῖ, νὴ Δία Macleod

There are those who also called the *tetraktys*, which is their [the Pythagoreans'] greatest oath, and which completes the perfect number for them, **the first principle of health**. Among whom is Philolaus.

AUTHENTICITY

This testimonium comes from Lucian's amusing treatise concerning a slip he made in greeting someone by wishing him health (ὑγιαίνειν) rather than joy (χαίρειν). Lucian defends himself by pointing out that early philosophers in fact preferred other greetings to "joy." After noting that Pythagoras himself left no writings, he refers to the practice of Ocellus and Archytas in letter-writing as showing that the master commanded disciples to begin with "health" as a salutation. (Lucian probably has seen some of the spurious letters. See Thesleff 1965: 45–6). The identification of health and the *tetraktys* which Lucian then assigns to Philolaus is not paralleled in the arithmological tradition or in the main tradition about the *tetraktys* (e.g. Sextus). The spurious A12 of Philolaus identifies health with 7, Iamblichus (*in Nic.* 34.22) with 6.

In passing judgment on the authenticity of this testimonium there are two conflicting lines of interpretation. One would emphasize the questionable nature of most of the rest of the arithmology ascribed to Philolaus. Certainly Lucian's reference to forged letters of Archytas and Ocellus immediately before discussing Philolaus does not inspire confidence. On the other hand, most would accept the *tetraktys* as representing early doctrine. Since there is nothing *prima facie* impossible about a fifth-century Pythagorean calling the *tetraktys* "the first principle of health," it is rash to reject it as spurious. The notion of a "first principle" or "starting-point" in a field of inquiry is paralleled in genuine fragments of Philolaus (B6 and 13, A7a). On the other hand there is nothing in Philolaus' medical views (A27–8) that supports the idea that he saw health as based on the *tetraktys*. In the end the testimonium must remain of uncertain authenticity.

Testimonium A12

Theologumena arithmeticae 74.10   Φιλόλαος δὲ μετὰ τὸ μαθηματικὸν μέγεθος τριχῇ διαστὰν ⟨ἐν⟩ τετράδι, ποιότητα καὶ χρῶσιν

ἐπιδειξαμένης τῆς φύσεως ἐν πεντάδι, ψύχωσιν δὲ ἐν ἑξάδι, νοῦν
δὲ καὶ ὑγείαν καὶ τὸ ὑπ' αὐτοῦ λεγόμενον φῶς ἐν ἑβδομάδι, μετὰ
5 ταῦτά φησιν ἔρωτα καὶ φιλίαν καὶ μῆτιν καὶ ἐπίνοιαν ἐπ' ὀγδοάδι
συμβῆναι τοῖς οὖσιν.

Philolaus [says] that after nature revealed three-dimensional mathematical magnitude in the tetrad, quality and color in the pentad,
animation in the hexad, intelligence and health and what he calls
light in the hebdomad, after these eros, love, wisdom, and thought
befall things in the ogdoad.

AUTHENTICITY

This derivation sequence is alluded to several times in the *Theologumena
arithmeticae*, but is only ascribed to Philolaus in this passage, which occurs as
part of the discussion of the number 8 (the ogdoad). Since most of the
Theol. ar. is a stitching together of sections from Anatolius' *De decade* and
Nicomachus' *Theol. ar.*, and since this section does not come from Anatolius
(whose treatise survives), it is likely that Nicomachus is the author of this
passage about Philolaus. The other passages in the *Theol. ar.* that mention
the sequence also seem to come from Nicomachus, but show some variations (44.1; 52.5; 63.25).

Proclus in his commentary on the *Timaeus* also refers to the sequence in
several places. He gives it most completely at 223e (2.270.5), and calls it a
doctrine of the Pythagoreans. Plutarch refers to the first five parts of the
derivation sequence at *Quaest. Plat.* 3.1, which is a discussion of the divided
line in the *Republic*. Even though only the first five numbers are mentioned,
the fact that the fifth is tied to "qualities" (ποιότητας) of bodies shows
that it is the same sequence as that ascribed to Philolaus in the *Theol.
ar.* However, Plutarch does not assign the sequence to Philolaus or the
Pythagoreans. He acts as if it is Platonic and explicitly ties it to the Platonic
doctrines of the forms and the one and the indefinite dyad.

Thus, the sources show that this derivation sequence was prominent in
later Platonism and is ascribed to Philolaus, the Pythagoreans in general,
Platonists, and sometimes asserted without any attribution. It is tempting
to see it as first assigned to the Pythagoreans by the later tradition and then
specifically assigned to Philolaus because of his reputed work on numbers.
Certainly, there are a series of good reasons for believing that it arose as
part of the tradition of *Timaeus* interpretation which begins in the Academy, and should not be assigned to Philolaus or any early Pythagoreans:

(1) This derivation sequence includes the connection of the first four

numbers with the point–line–solid sequence which the testimony of Aristotle shows to belong to the Academy and not to the Pythagoreans (see the commentary on A13).

(2) Plutarch associates it with the one and the indefinite dyad, which Aristotle clearly labels Platonic, but which are so often mistakenly regarded as Pythagorean in the later tradition.

(3) Aristotle says explicitly that the Pythagoreans used the word "color" to mean "surface" because it was hard to see what the distinction between the two could be (*Sens.* 439a30). Yet this derivation sequence clearly distinguishes surface as associated with 3 from color and quality as associated with 5 (see Burkert 1972: 247).

(4) Specific features of the sequence appear to be grounded in specific passages of the *Timaeus* and *Republic*. Thus, the association of ensouled body with the number 6 is tied to the soul as source of the six motions possible for the body as described in the *Timaeus* (43b2–5), as Proclus makes clear in his commentary (168c = 2.95.7; 223e = 2.270.5; 340a = 3.328.13). The strange notion of light's connection to 7 and to intellect has to do with the Platonic connection between the sun in the visible world and the good in the intelligible world. The Neoplatonic doctrine of light probably also has similar roots (see Wallis 1972: 61). Proclus uses the phrase "light in accord with intelligence" (τὸ κατὰ νοῦν φῶς) several times (168c = 2.95.2 and 224b = 2.271.18) in connection with 7 and in contrast to "intelligence" which is associated with the monad. This idea is clarified at 219d (= 2.257.19) where Proclus compares the way the circle of the same encompasses the circle of the other to intelligence which "surrounds the soul shining its light into it." Thus, the light in question is intelligible light. The specific connection with 7 may have to do with the fact that the sun is the seventh heavenly body after the fixed stars and the five planets in the *Timaeus*.

(5) Despite Frank's attempt (1923: 315) to show connections between this sequence and F13 of Philolaus there are in fact no good connections with the genuine fragments. In F13 soul is associated with the heart and if it can be attached to any number at all it would have to be 3, since it is the third of four psychic faculties mentioned. This clearly has nothing to do with 6 as connected to ensouled body in the derivation sequence. Furthermore, F13 of course only applies the word for soul (ψυχή) to one of the psychic faculties, and thus shows itself to be pre-Platonic, whereas the derivation sequence has a comprehensive notion of the soul.

(6) Finally, no intelligible connection can be established between the derivation sequence given in A12 and the associations between numbers and concepts assigned to the Pythagoreans by Aristotle (F203). In Aristotle

intelligence (νοῦς) and soul are associated with 1, whereas in A12 they are tied to 7 and 6 respectively. According to Aristotle the Pythagoreans associated 2 with opinion, movement, and addition and 4 with justice, whereas in A12 it appears that the first four numbers just have to do with producing three-dimensional magnitude. It is true that the tie between light and the number 7 reported in A12 could be connected with Aristotle's report that the Pythagoreans tied 7 to the sun, but on the whole the Pythagoreans according to Aristotle seem to have little to do with the derivation sequence in A12, and we must conclude that it does not represent early Pythagorean thought and cannot be assigned to Philolaus.

Testimonium A13

Theologumena arithmeticae 82.10 (= Speusippus F28 Tarán)   ὅτι
καὶ Σπεύσιππος ὁ Πωτώνης μὲν υἱὸς τῆς τοῦ Πλάτωνος ἀδελφῆς,
διάδοχος δὲ Ἀκαδημίας πρὸ Ξενοκράτου, ἐκ τῶν ἐξαιρέτως
σπουδασθεισῶν ἀεὶ Πυθαγορικῶν ἀκροάσεων, μάλιστα δὲ τῶν
5 Φιλολάου συγγραμμάτων, βιβλίδιόν τι συντάξας γλαφυρὸν
ἐπέγραψε μὲν αὐτὸ Περὶ Πυθαγορικῶν ἀριθμῶν, ἀπ᾽ ἀρχῆς
δὲ μέχρι ἡμίσους περὶ τῶν ἐν αὐτοῖς γραμμικῶν ἐμμελέστατα
διεξελθὼν πολυγωνίων τε καὶ παντοίων τῶν ἐν ἀριθμοῖς ἐπιπέδων
ἅμα καὶ στερεῶν περί τε τῶν πέντε σχημάτων, ἃ τοῖς κοσμικοῖς
10 ἀποδίδοται στοιχείοις, ἰδιότητος αὐτῶν καὶ πρὸς ἄλληλα
κοινότητος, ἀναλογίας τε καὶ ἀντακολουθίας, μετὰ ταῦτα λοιπὸν
θάτερον τὸ τοῦ βιβλίου ἥμισυ περὶ δεκάδος ἄντικρυς ποιεῖται
φυσικωτάτην αὐτὴν ἀποφαίνων καὶ τελεστικωτάτην τῶν ὄντων,
οἷον εἶδός τι τοῖς κοσμικοῖς ἀποτελέσμασι τεχνικόν, ἐφ᾽ ἑαυτῆς
15 ἀλλ᾽ οὐχ ἡμῶν νομισάντων ἢ ὡς ἔτυχε θεμένων ὑπάρχουσαν
καὶ παράδειγμα παντελέστατον τῷ τοῦ παντὸς ποιητῇ θεῷ
προεκκειμένην. λέγει δὲ τὸν τρόπον τοῦτον περὶ αὐτῆς· [For a
full apparatus and for the Greek text of the following fragment
20 of Speusippus see Tarán. An English translation of parts of the
fragment is given below.]

Speusippus the son of Potone, sister of Plato, and head of the Academy before Xenocrates, on the basis of Pythagorean lectures, which he always pursued especially zealously, and particularly on the basis of the writings of Philolaus, composed an elegant little book and entitled it *On Pythagorean Numbers*. In the first half of the book he most suitably discourses about the linear numbers, both the polygonal and also all sorts of plane and solid numbers, and about the five figures which are assigned to the elements in the cosmos, dealing both with what is peculiar to each and what they share with one another, and with similarities and correspondences. After this, he goes on to devote the second half of the book to the decad, showing that it is most in accord with nature and is what most brings to fulfilment the things that are. It is like a designing form for the things that happen in the cosmos, preexisting of its own accord and not on the basis of our beliefs or arbitrary conventions, and lying before the god who is maker of all as a complete model. He speaks in this way about it:

10 is the perfect number and it is right and in accord with nature that we arrive at it in all sorts of ways when we count, both Greeks and all human beings, without any deliberate purpose on our part. For it has many characteristics peculiar to it, which it is fitting that something so perfect have, and there are other characteristics which, although not peculiar to it, something perfect must have.

First of all it is necessary that it be even so that the evens and the odds in it be equal and not one-sided. For since the odd is always prior to the even, if the concluding number were not even, the other would gain the advantage.

Then it is necessary that it have prime and incomposite numbers that are equal to the secondary and composite. But 10 has an equal number and no other number less than 10 has this characteristic...

Since it has this characteristic it again has an equal number of multiples and submultiples (of which they are the multiples)...

These are primary both in planes and in solids: point, line, triangle, pyramid. These also have the number 10 and possess perfection...

Indeed, also in the case of figures, when one examines them in accord with number, 10 occurs...

And in the case of solids, going on in such a way, you would discover up to four, so that in this way also one reaches the decad...

The same is true also in generation. For the first starting-point of magnitude is the point, the second the line, third the surface, and fourth the solid.

AUTHENTICITY

This testimonium has sometimes been regarded as giving us valuable evidence about Philolaus based on an indisputably early source, Speusippus. However, careful examination reveals that it is closely tied to Academic interpretation of the *Timaeus* and gives no reliable information about Philolaus' thought. The testimonium comes from the *Theologumena arithmeticae* whose authorship is disputed. Some regard it as the work of Iamblichus (Burkert 1972: 98) while others take it as the work of a late author who in part draws on Iamblichus (a Byzantine excerptor – Tarán 1981: 296). O'Meara has recently argued that it does not in fact seem to be similar to the bits of Iamblichus' *Theologumena arithmeticae* which are preserved in Psellus (1989: 15 n. 24). The work consists in large part of extracts from Anatolius' work *On the Decad*, which has survived, and from Nicomachus' treatise, also called *Theologumena arithmeticae*, which has been lost, although we have a summary of it by Photius. The testimonium about Speusippus is not derived from Anatolius and thus is most likely to be the work of Nicomachus, although it could be derived from another unknown source. However, whoever the author is, the language of the passage is late and points to an author of Nicomachus' time or later (Burkert 1972: 246 n. 40).

It falls into two parts. The first part gives a general description of a small work of Speusippus entitled *On Pythagorean Numbers*. Speusippus' book is said to fall into two halves. The first half is described as dealing with certain types of numbers (linear, plane, and solid) as well as the five regular solids which are assigned to the elements in the cosmos. The second half is said to have discussed the decad as the paradigm used by god in fashioning the universe. In the second part of the testimonium a long section from this latter half of the book on the decad is then quoted.

The first thing to note is that nothing is said about either Philolaus or the Pythagoreans in the actual quotation from Speusippus. It is the later excerptor who says that Speusippus composed it on the basis of Pythagorean lectures and the writings of Philolaus. Does the excerptor have reliable evidence for this statement, or is it just an inference from the exalted notion of Pythagoreanism common in the later tradition? The language is clearly that of later Greek and cannot reflect Speusippus' own words very closely. Moreover, it is hard to believe that Speusippus himself said that he got his book "from Pythagorean lectures and especially the works of Philolaus." Such a claim would be unparalleled in philosophical writing at his time.

Both the description of Speusippus' book and the quotation from it show very close connections to the *Timaeus* and only very general ties to early Pythagoreanism. There is reference to the five regular solids and their connection to the elements as well as to a god who created all according to a preexisting model (clearly the Platonic demiurge). In the actual quotation from Speusippus the three types of triangles he mentions in showing the importance of the decad are the same as those that are prominent at *Timaeus* 54a1ff (see Tarán 1981: 285). It is possible that Speusippus never mentioned any Pythagorean and that even the title was given to the book at a later date. Given the later tradition's willingness to see Platonic doctrines as Pythagorean, its content alone would be enough for it to be given such a title and for someone steeped in Pythagoreanism to describe it as all derived from Philolaus. The doctrine of the decad which is prominent in the Speusippus passage was regarded as the core of Pythagoreanism in the tradition represented most notably in Sextus Empiricus. This would make it all the easier to label Speusippus' whole book as derived from the Pythagoreans. Certainly nothing in the fragment of Speusippus, beyond a general veneration for the number 10, can be tied specifically to Philolaus or early Pythagoreanism.

It is often thought that the association of the first four numbers with the sequence of point–line–plane surface–solid is early Pythagorean, and its prominence here in Speusippus is seen as confirming that Philolaus had this view; but this doctrine in fact appears to belong to the Academy. Scholars have thought that Aristotle ascribes the point–line–plane surface–solid sequence to the Pythagoreans, but the evidence for this is very meagre and, as Burkert has shown, close reading of Aristotle rather suggests that he distinguished it from Pythagorean views. Certainly when Aristotle explicitly sets out the Pythagorean system in the first book of the *Metaphysics*, and when he refers to them by name elsewhere, he makes no mention of this derivation sequence, although it would seem to be an important doctrine to overlook. Moreover, in the *De caelo* (299a2ff) Aristotle discusses the view that all bodies are generated out of planes, a view which is clearly tied to the derivation sequence of point–line–plane surface–solid (Aristotle himself makes the connection at 299a6). In the course of his criticism of this view Aristotle refers to the *Timaeus* at one point, which shows that Plato is one of the people he is thinking of. But, most significantly, after he has finished the discussion, he goes on to say: "The same thing happens to those who construct the world out of numbers. For some construct nature out of numbers, as do some of the Pythagoreans." Thus, Aristotle clearly distinguishes between those who construct bodies out of planes (thus advocating the derivation sequence) and the Pythagoreans who construct nature out of numbers. This description of the Pythagoreans matches what Aristotle says about their emphasis on numbers in the *Metaphysics* and, as has been shown above, Philolaus seems to be Aristotle's main source for this Pythagoreanism. Accordingly, it is very likely that Philolaus did not put forth the derivation sequence and that this doctrine is in fact Platonic or at least Academic.

In the face of the *De caelo* passage the text in Aristotle that some scholars have used to show that the derivation sequence is Pythagorean is very weak indeed. At *Metaphysics* 1036b12 Aristotle refers to people who are said to "reduce all things to numbers, and say that the formula of the line is the formula of 2." The connection of 2 with the line clearly suggests the derivation sequence, but whom is Aristotle referring to? There is no direct reference to the Pythagoreans. In the next sentence Aristotle goes on to say that of the exponents of the forms some say that the dyad is the ideal line while others say that the form of the line is the ideal line. Now since "the exponents of the forms" seems to refer to the Academy, scholars have assumed that those who are said to "reduce all things to numbers and say that the formula of the line is the formula of 2" must be the Pythagoreans (see e.g. Guthrie 1962: 256–7. Alexander also made this mistake, 512.20). In light of the fact that Aristotle never explicitly assigns such an important doctrine to the Pythagoreans elsewhere, and in light of the *De caelo* passage which pretty clearly denies it to them, this passage is a very slender reed. Moreover, scholars have in fact misinterpreted the passage in the *Metaphysics*. Not everyone in the Academy adopted the forms. Speusippus notably rejected them, so that Aristotle is distinguishing between different points of view in the Academy, and there need be no reference to the Pythagoreans (Burkert 1972: 67 n. 90, and on Speusippus see Tarán 1981: 12). Thus nothing in this *Metaphysics* passage contradicts the clear implication of the *De caelo* passage that the Pythagoreans did not adopt the derivation sequence, and the correct conclusion seems to be that it was Academic and of particular importance to Speusippus, especially since he uses it so prominently in the fragment preserved in the *Theologumena arithmeticae*.

That Philolaus is singled out as a source of Speusippus' book may indicate that there was a work (or works) of Philolaus circulating which discussed the properties of number. The citations of Philolaus' views on number which are found in Lydus and F11 also show this. Since F11 is surely spurious and the citations in Lydus are very suspect, it is tempting to assign all references to Philolaus' number theory to this spurious work, which then is seen by the later tradition as the source of Speusippus' book.

3. FRAGMENTS AND TESTIMONIA ON MUSIC

Fragment 6b

Boethius, *De institutione musica* 3.8 (278.11 Friedlein)   Philolaus igitur haec atque his minora spatia talibus definitionibus includit: **diesis**, inquit, **est spatium quo maior est sesquitertia proportio duobus tonis. comma vero est spatium, quo maior est sesquioctava proportio duabus diesibus**, 5   id est duobus semitoniis minoribus. **schisma est dimidium commatis, diaschisma vero dimidium dieseos**, id est semitonii minoris.

Philolaus, then, defined these intervals and intervals smaller than these in the following way: **diesis**, he says, **is the interval by which the ratio 4:3 is greater than two tones. The comma is the interval by which the ratio 9:8 is greater than two dieses**, that is than two smaller semitones. **Schisma is half of a comma, diaschisma half of a diesis**, that is a smaller semitone.

AUTHENTICITY

The difficulty with assessing this fragment, which purports to deal with Philolaus' musical theory, is that the terms which it introduces, *schisma* and *diaschisma*, are simply unparalleled elsewhere. Thus it is hard to make a convincing case connecting it either to the genuine book of Philolaus or the pseudo-Pythagorean tradition. In the end its authenticity must remain uncertain but it shows closer connections to the spurious tradition represented in testimonium A26 than to the genuine F6a.

To begin with it is important to consider the context of this fragment in Boethius. It follows Testimonium A26 of Philolaus, with seventeen lines of Boethius' text intervening. In those seventeen lines Boethius demonstrates, at least in part on the basis of the system ascribed to Philolaus in A26, that the tone consists of two smaller semitones and a comma. The beginning of F6b, with its reference to "these intervals" (i.e. *diesis* and *comma*) which Philolaus defined, clearly refers back to the earlier discussion of Philolaus (A26). It is thus tempting to suppose that, since Boethius (and thus probably his source Nicomachus) treats A26 and F6b as parts of the same system, and since A26 has been shown to be spurious, F6b is also spurious. However, so little is known about the way that knowledge of Philolaus' system was preserved at the time of Nicomachus that we cannot rule out the possibility that he was working with a collection of extracts of Philolaus that simply put these two passages next to each other, as Stobaeus does with other passages (e.g. Fragments 2, 3, 5, 6, 7), or that Nicomachus himself drew them from two different sources and uncritically set them together. Once again it is necessary to judge the fragment primarily on internal grounds.

After he quotes the fragment Boethius goes on to comment on it for half a page before turning to a new topic. In his commentary Boethius clearly indicates what he takes to be the purpose of Philolaus' division of the *diesis* and the *comma*. It is seen as a way to produce an integral half-tone. If a tone consists of two *dieseis* and a *comma* and the *comma* can be cut in half, then clearly the integral half-tone is one *diesis* plus half a *comma* (a *schisma*). If this is what is going on in Philolaus F6b, then it is clearly a piece of sophistry, because it tries to get around the fact that the tone cannot be bisected (as long as intervals are regarded as ratios). The *comma* was introduced as the amount that was left over when two smaller semitones are taken away from a tone, that is, it arises precisely because it is impossible to divide the tone in half. If the *comma* itself could be divided in half then the tone would have been divisible all along. Boethius' explanation also does not really give any reason for coming up with a term for half of a *diesis (diaschisma* – also an impossibility), since the supposed integral half-tone is said to be one *diesis* and a *comma*.

As long ago as Tannery it was recognized that the splitting of the *diesis* and *comma* is most likely to have to do with the structure of the tetrachord in the enharmonic and chromatic genera rather than the diatonic (1904: 224–5). Thus, F6b would seem to presuppose work not just in the diatonic genus (as in Philolaus F6a), but in the other two genera as well. This need not be impossible for someone of Philolaus' date. Archytas in the next generation of Pythagoreans put forth a theory of the structure of the tetrachord in all three genera (A16). However, what is problematic is that the emphasis on "halving" intervals in F6b does not accord with the Pythagorean tradition which sees intervals as superparticular ratios (i.e. ratios of the form $n + 1 : 1$) which cannot be divided in half. The impossibility of halving superparticular ratios is identified as a Pythagorean principle by Ptolemy and a proof for this principle is attested for Archytas in the fourth century (A19). F6b seems to take the rival Aristoxenian approach in that it regards intervals not as ratios, but as distances that can be divided in half. Tannery therefore concludes that F6b cannot belong to a Pythagorean and hence not to Philolaus (1904: 233). Burkert (1972: 398–9) on the other hand suggests that before Archytas' proof the indivisibility of superparticular ratios may well not have been a Pythagorean principle, and that F6b could therefore still be assigned to Philolaus.

Burkert's position is somewhat attractive in that the unique features of F6b are more reasonably explained as arising in the beginnings of Pythagorean music theory, before certain principles were fixed, than in the pseudo-Pythagorean tradition which tends to assign well-known and important doctrines back to the Pythagoreans, rather than the obscure and idiosyncratic. However, our ignorance of what went on in the "Pythagoreanizing" early Academy is considerable, and it is quite possible that what we find in F6b had its origin there, but was never developed in the later tradition. The best that can be done in the situation is to decide how F6b fits in with the other evidence for Philolaus' music theory. Is it closer to F6a, which we have independent grounds for regarding as authentic, or to A26, which we have independent grounds for regarding as spurious? As noted above, the context in Boethius/Nicomachus ties it closely if not conclusively to A26. However, DK printed F6b not with A26 but following F6a. The reason for this is clearly that the definition of the *diesis* (the interval by which the fourth is greater than two tones) with which F6b begins accords with the use of *diesis* in F6a (i.e. the fourth is said to consist of two tones and a *diesis*). However, that definition is also not incompatible with what is said in A26, although the connection is less obvious. A26 identifies the *diesis* with the number 13, but this in turn depends on associating the ratio 256:243 with the *diesis* (since the number 13 is arrived at by subtracting 243 from 256), and this ratio is arrived at precisely by regarding the *diesis* as what is left over after two tones are subtracted from the fourth $(4:3 - 9:8 - 9:8 = 256:243)$, which is the definition given in F6b.

If we turn from the definition of *diesis* to the rest of F6b the connections are much closer with A26. First, the *comma* is mentioned in A26 and its use there is perfectly consistent with the definition given in F6b, whereas F6a never mentions the *comma*. More importantly, the whole notion of dividing intervals in half which is found in F6b fits much better with the approach in A26 than in F6a. In A26 intervals are identified with differences between numbers, with magnitudes, even if there is also a recognition that they are also tied to ratios. Such a view of intervals makes their bisection unproblematic (as it does in the system of Aristoxenus). Finally, F6b has none of the archaic terminology that is found in F6a. This could be the result of chance or the process of translation into Latin. However, it is striking that in F6a the term tone is never used, the ratio 9:8 always being used instead, while in F6b tone is used on one occasion and the proportion 9:8 on another.

None of these arguments is conclusive and the authenticity of F6b must therefore be left as uncertain. However, it has more affinities with the spurious report in A26 than it does with the genuine F6a.

Testimonium A26

Boethius, *De institutione musica* 3.5 (276.15 Friedlein) Philolaus vero Pythagoricus alio modo tonum dividere temptavit, statuens scilicet primordium toni ab eo numero, qui primus cybum a primo impari, quod maxime apud Pythagoricos honorabile fuit,
5 efficeret. nam cum ternarius numerus primus sit impar, tres tertio atque id ter si duxeris XXVII necessario exsurgent, qui ad XXIIII numerum tono distat, eandem ternarii differentiam servans. ternarius enim XXIIII summae octava pars est, quae eisdem addita primum a ternario cybum XX ac VII reddit. ex
10 hoc igitur duas Philolaus efficit partes, unam quae dimidio sit maior, eamque apotomen vocat, reliquam, quae dimidio sit minor, eamque rursus diesin dicit, quam posteri semitonium minus appellavere; harum vero differentiam comma. ac primum
15 diesin in XIII unitatibus constare arbitratur eo, quod haec inter CCLVI et CCXLIII pervisa sit differentia, quodque idem numerus, id est XIII ex novenario, ternario atque unitate consistat, quae unitas puncti obtineat locum, ternarius vero primae inparis lineae, novenarius primi inparis quadrati. ex
20 his igitur causis cum XIII diesin ponat, quod semitonium nuncupatur, reliquam XXVII numeri partem, quae XIIII unitatibus continetur, apotomen esse constituit. sed quoniam inter XIII et XIIII unitas differentiam facit, unitatem loco commatis censet esse ponendam. totum vero tonum in XXVII
25 unitatibus locat eo, quod inter CCXVI ab CCXLIII, qui inter se distant tono, XXVII sit differentia.

Indeed Philolaus the Pythagorean tried to divide the tone in another manner, determining the first principle of the tone from that number which first produces a cube from the first odd number, because it was especially honored by the Pythagoreans. For, since the number 3 is the first odd, if you take 3 three times and this number three times, 27 necessarily results, which is a tone away from the number 24, preserving the same difference of 3. For the number 3 is the eighth part of 24, which added to it gives the first cube from 3, 27. Out of this then Philolaus makes two parts, one which is greater than half he calls *apotome*, the remainder which is less than half he in turn calls *diesis*, which later thinkers called the smaller semitone; and the difference between them [he calls] *comma*. And, first, he thinks that *diesis* consists in thirteen units, because this was clearly seen as the difference between 256 and 243, and because the same number, that is 13, consists of 9, 3, and 1, where 1 has the place of the point, 3 of the first odd line, and 9 of the first odd square. Therefore, since he makes *diesis* (which is called the semitone) 13 for these reasons, the remaining part of the number 27, which consists of 14 units, he determined to be the *apotome*. But since the difference between 13 and 14 is 1, he judges that 1 must be put in the place of the *comma*. But the whole tone he locates in twenty-seven units, 27 being the difference between 216 and 243 which are a tone apart.

AUTHENTICITY

This is surely one of the oddest of the testimonia about Philolaus that have been preserved. Boeckh, who is famous for the contention that the fragments are either all genuine or all spurious, could not in fact accept this testimonium as referring to any genuine doctrines of Philolaus and concludes that it must be the result of confusion on Boethius' part (1819: 79–80). Tannery, who rejects the musical fragments as genuine work of Philolaus, nonetheless refuses to assign the musical theory reported in this testimonium even to a forger, and suggests that Boethius has confused doctrines assigned to Philolaus with Neopythagorean commentary on them (1904: 223–4). What is it that elicits such a response from scholars? The testimonium treats musical intervals as if they corresponded not to ratios such as 2:1, 4:3, or 3:2, but rather to the arithmetical difference between the two terms of the ratio. Thus the tone is said to correspond not to the ratio 9:8, as in Philolaus F6a, but to the number 27. A number of reasons are given for this equation, but the clear origin of the idea is stated in the last line of the testimonium, where the tone is said to be 27 because this is the difference between 243 and 216, whose ratio constitutes the tone (243:216 = 9:8). Theon (86.15ff) preserves a calculation of the ratios in the tetrachord that uses these numbers (256:243, 243:216, 216:192 – where the first is the smaller semitone and the latter two are full tones), and they also appear in Plutarch (*De an. proc.* 1021e). But it is mathematical nonsense to regard the tone as constituted by the arithmetical difference between the two terms in a ratio. The absurd results of such a practice would seem to be obvious. The tone can be represented by the ratios 243:216 and 216:192 as well as the ratio 9:8 precisely because they are all the same ratio, with 9:8 being the ratio in its lowest terms. However, according to the principles of the testimonium about Philolaus the tone would be constituted by a different number in each case (27, 24, 1).

Nonetheless, the testimonium is not a confused or garbled report. As Burkert points out, there is method in the madness. In order to understand that method it must be recognized that what we have is not an attempt at typical Greek harmonic theory, but rather a search for significant numbers that starts from ratios that were standard in Greek harmonic theory. 27 is selected over 24 (or 1) as the "first principle of the tone" because it was honored by the Pythagoreans (according to Boethius) as the cube of 3, the first odd number. Moreover, this number 27 is a tone away from 24 (27:24 = 9:8) and their difference is the important number 3. Thus 27 is cavalierly treated in three mathematically distinct ways, as (1) the difference between 243 and 216, (2) the cube of 3, and (3) the first term in the ratio 27:24. The testimonium goes on to divide the tone further, but still preserves the basic assumptions that it corresponds not to a ratio but to a whole number and that its parts are arithmetical differences rather than differences between ratios. If we divide 27 into its two largest unequal parts (since it cannot be halved in whole numbers), we arrive at 14 and 13. 13 which is less than half is then called *diesis*, the smaller semitone. But here we have a striking coincidence in that 13 is also the difference between the two terms of the ratio that corresponds to the *diesis* in Greek musical theory (and Philolaus F6a), namely 256:243. The larger part of the tone, 14, is called *apotome*, and finally the difference between the *apotome* and the *diesis*, 1, is called *comma*. It is such a series of miraculous correspondences of numbers, irrespective of any mathematical sense, that is behind Philolaus A26.

Since there are solid reasons for regarding F6a and its music theory as genuine (see the commentary ad loc.), and since that fragment clearly shows knowledge that the concords correspond to ratios and that subtraction of musical intervals from one another means division of ratios (e.g. the difference between the fifth 3:2 and fourth 4:3 is said to be 9:8), it seems very natural to wonder whether A26, with its completely different understanding of the tone, can also be based on the work of Philolaus. Burkert (1972: 394) argues that since Boethius is virtually translating Nicomachus' lost *Harmonics*, and since Nicomachus preserves two genuine fragments (F6a in his summary of harmonic theory, the *Enchiridion*, and also part of F2 in the *Introduction to Arithmetic*), "one must suppose that the long word-for-word quotation, fragment 6, and the details reported by Boethius [A26] come from the same line of tradition and stand or fall together." But this is not at all convincing, especially in light of Burkert's own brilliant reconstruction of the ancient tradition. That reconstruction makes it clear that the practice of assigning Academic doctrines back to Philolaus and other early Pythagoreans began already in the early Academy, so that by the time of Nicomachus there were undoubtedly in circulation a variety of spurious works of Philolaus along with his genuine book. In this situation it is not at all clear why we should suppose that Nicomachus was in the position to make clear distinctions between the genuine and the spurious. While it is true that in some authors, such as Sextus Empiricus, the Platonizing tradition comes almost completely to replace any reference to the actual book of Philolaus, it is far from clear that it is impossible for a later author to combine elements from the Platonizing tradition with those from the tradition that rests on Philolaus' book. Certainly, Burkert accepts that Stobaeus preserves both genuine and spurious fragments of Philolaus (e.g. 2, 6, 7 genuine and 21 spurious). Thus, as in the case with other fragments and testimonia, we must rely on the internal evidence of the fragments to determine the authenticity and not the tradition.

On internal grounds it is conceivable that F6a and A26 derive from the same author. We might suppose that Philolaus did understand the mathematics of the scale in F6a, but saw nothing strange in using the ratios in that scale as the basis for a totally different type of exploration of the wonders of numbers. He was impressed by all sorts of miraculous properties of number, both those that are in concord with proper mathematical manipulation of ratios and those that appear to us as nothing more than number play. Burkert (1972: 400) seems to have something like the latter view in mind when he concludes that "the earliest Pythagorean musical theory is not founded on mathematics ... but on 'reverence' for certain numbers in their roles in music and cosmology" and that "Philolaus in his effort to express Pythagorean lore in the form of Ionian φυσιολογία, made individual statements about the numerical structure of ordinary music, showing a truly remarkable mixture of calculation and numerical symbolism, in which its 'sense' is more important than its accuracy." This last statement in fact encapsulates Burkert's overall thesis about the nature of Philolaus' work, and the acceptance of both F6a and A26 as based on authentic work of Philolaus is one of the prime pieces of evidence for that thesis.

It is important to note that there is clear evidence in the later philosophical tradition for a controversy as to whether or not it was legitimate to treat the numbers in the ratios developed in harmonic theory as having importance in their own right apart from the ratio of which they were part. Indeed, both Plutarch (*De an. proc.* 1027d) and Theo (69.3), who understand the proper mathematical manipulation of ratios, are attracted by number speculation such as we find in A26. Moreover, even Ptolemy seems to treat intervals as equal to the arithmetical difference between the terms of a ratio in one passage (*Harmonics* 2.13–14; see Barker 1989: 344). Thus, Philolaus would be in good company if he mixed proper understanding of ratios in F6a with number speculation in A26. However, examination of the specific parallels between the tradition of the *Timaeus* commentaries and what Boethius assigns to Philolaus in A26 shows that the latter has such close ties to doctrines that surely originated in the early Academy or later that it cannot be regarded as deriving from the genuine book of Philolaus.

The number games found in A26 are paralleled in striking detail in the tradition of commentaries on the *Timaeus*. In the *Timaeus* itself, when Plato is describing the construction of the world soul, he combines two sequences of numbers (1, 2, 4, 8 and 1, 3, 9, 27), where 27, which is the central number in Philolaus A26, is the last term of the sequence and where the sequence of the powers of 3 is crucial as it is in A26. Plutarch in his commentary on this passage of the *Timaeus* mentions two other points that are central in A26. At *De an. proc.* 1018e he says that the Pythagoreans assigned the number 27 to the tone and the number 13 to the *leimma* (= *diesis* in Philolaus; see also 1017f). The same view is assigned to "the mathematicians" at 1019a. At 1021e Plutarch, in discussing the *leimma*, uses exactly the numbers for the ratio of the fourth that are presupposed in Philolaus A26, namely 256:192, and, after identifying the ratio of 256:243 as the *leimma*, points out that the difference between these numbers is 13 and that this is why "they" called *leimma* 13. These correspondences between what Plutarch assigns to the Pythagoreans and what Boethius assigns to Philolaus in A26 are so close that some connection must be assumed. Tannery (1904: 240) adopts the view that Philolaus' book was forged on the basis of the *Timaeus* commentaries while Burkert (1972: 397) argues that the *Timaeus* commentators are drawing on the genuine book of Philolaus, written before Plato and upon which Plato probably drew.

Burkert's sole reason for regarding A26 as independent of the *Timaeus* commentators and hence as part of a genuine book of Philolaus upon which they drew is that a passage a few pages later in Boethius, which discusses Philolaus' further division of intervals (F6b – see commentary ad loc. for further discussion), countenances the bisection of the whole tone, which is something that the *Timaeus* commentators consistently reject (Burkert 1972: 398). This argument has some force, but note that on this point the

Philolaus of F6b stands quite alone in the Pythagorean tradition as well, so that we could just as easily follow Tannery and conclude that F6b cannot be by a Pythagorean; i.e. it is just as easy to assume that the author of F6b is someone writing in the Academic tradition who is unorthodox on the division of the tone as it is to assume that F6b is by Philolaus who is departing from Pythagorean orthodoxy on this point. The former is somewhat more likely in that if the author is from the time of the early Academy or later, there could be some influence from the rival Aristoxenian school of music (late 4th century) which of course accepted the bisection of the tone. Fortunately, there is more decisive evidence than this which shows that A26 has close connections to specifically Academic doctrines.

First, it should be noted that the fascination with the powers of the number 3 which is so prominent in A26 is paralleled in a striking way in the testimonia we have about Xenocrates, the head of the Academy after Speusippus. As Dillon points out (1977: 30), "a feature which seems to be peculiar to Xenocrates' philosophy is his preoccupation with triadic distinctions." He posits three forms of existence, the sensible, the intelligible, and a composite of the two, the opinable (Sextus, *M.* 7.147). Each of these realms is then connected with one of the three fates. Xenocrates also seems to have had a theory of three different densities of matter and a three-layer universe with the stars and sun in the top layer, the moon next, and the earth in the center (Plutarch, *De fac.* 943f–944a). But the most striking testimonium is found in Lydus (*Mens.* 48.18 = F58 Heinze), where Xenocrates is quoted in support of the idea that the number 9 is to be associated with the moon. The progression up to nine (3^2) is said to be indefinite and tied to multitude (ἀόριστος . . . καὶ πλήθει σύνοικος), and is seen as the end of the first series of numbers with 10 as a new beginning (this is obscurely tied to the growth of the moon from new to full). Some scholars will want to see all this fascination with the number 3 as just Pythagorean influence and as in fact going back to the Pythagoreans. However, nothing in Aristotle's reports about the early Pythagoreans supports such a thorough-going application of triadic divisions. It is true that in the later tradition (Gell. 1.20.6) Pythagoras himself is reported to have said that the cube of 3 controls the course of the moon (its orbit being taken as twenty-seven days), but Burkert has shown that what comes to be assigned to Pythagoras himself in the later tradition is almost always of Academic origin (most notably the one and indefinite dyad as first principles – see Burkert 1972: 65, 82). Thus this report about Pythagoras is just further evidence for the preoccupation with triads in the Academy and especially in Xenocrates. But there is further evidence that this fascination with triads led to a reworking, in the Academy, of the tradition about Philolaus' system.

Towards the end of Plutarch's *On the Generation of the Soul in the Timaeus,* the same treatise in which the parallels to the music theory of A26 are found, he describes an astronomical system which is clearly derived from Philolaus' astronomy in that it makes the central fire the focus of the universe and makes the earth orbit around it. However, as both Burkert and Cherniss have observed, this must in fact be a later reinterpretation of the Philolaic system, since it diverges on important points from Aristotle's description of the early Pythagorean system. First, it puts the orbit of the sun sixth from the center rather than fourth as it is in Aristotle's description. Second, it associates the sun with the number 729 while Aristotle's testimony suggests that the number 7 was tied to the sun. The grounds for associating the sun with 729 are crucial. It is a result of assigning each heavenly body, from the center out, a number that corresponds to the sequence of the powers of 3. The counter-earth is 3, the earth is 9, the moon 27 and the sun is 3^6 or 729. Now it is just such an infatuation with the powers of 3 that characterizes the "music theory" of A26 and is given as one of the bases for equating 27 (3^3) with the tone. Thus A26 has close connections to an astronomical system that has been shown to be a reinterpretation of Philolaus' system by the later tradition under the influence of the *Timaeus*, and certainly looks to be a similar reinterpretation of the genuine Philolaic music theory as represented in F6a.

This conclusion is further supported by a much neglected aspect of Boethius' report in A26. One of the reasons given for regarding the *diesis* as 13 is that it is the sum of the first three numbers in the sequence of powers of 3, if we include 1 in that sequence (i.e. $1 + 3 + 9 = 13$). The emphasis on the powers of 3 once again points to the *Timaeus* and commentaries on it, but even more important are the words which follow in Boethius: "1 has the place of the point, 3 of the first odd line, and 9 of the first odd square." This is reminiscent of nothing so much as of the famous derivation sequence, referred to by Aristotle, in which 1 is equated with the point, 2 with the line, 3 with a surface and 4 with a solid. This has often been regarded as genuine early Pythagorean doctrine, but Burkert has shown that the texts in Aristotle cannot refer to the Pythagoreans and are more closely tied to Speusippus (see the commentary on A13). In addition the whole project of deriving this world from principles that are "more real" is Platonic in origin and is contrary to what we are told of early Pythagoreanism by Aristotle, who emphasizes that the Pythagoreans were distinct from Plato in not separating numbers from things. Now it is true that the derivation sequence reported by Boethius in A26 is not the same as that reported by Aristotle and notably only reaches to surfaces rather than solids, since it is based on the number 3 rather than 4. It is tempting, though, to suppose that the important number 27 completed the system and corresponded to solid figures, since Boethius emphasized earlier that it was the first cube of an odd number. Moreover, the derivation system in Boethius can be seen as a conscious reaction to the system that is based on the first four numbers. The emphasis on the fact that 3 is the first *odd* line suggests awareness of a system in which the first line is 2. In his translation of the passage Burkert has 3 referring to the first "odd-number line" and 9 to the first "odd square number," which seems to try to make the passage as arithmetical as possible, but the mention of the point and the line makes clear that what we have is an attempt to relate numbers to geometrical figures as in the other derivation sequence. If this is so it is hard to see how A26 can be pre-Platonic, for the very reasons Burkert gives against regarding the other derivation sequence as early Pythagorean. Thus, here again A26 shows close connections to the speculations of the early Academy in contrast to Aristotle's reports about the early Pythagoreans, and we can reasonably reject the claim that it reflects anything in Philolaus' genuine book.

Testimonium A26a

Proclus, *in Timaeum* 2.190.7   δέδεικται μὲν οὖν ἐκ τῶν Φιλολάου τὸ πλῆθος τῶν παρὰ τῷ Τιμαίῳ γραφέντων ὅρων, τοῖς δὲ Πλάτωνος τὸ διάγραμμα προβαίνει καὶ ἄνευ τοῦ λόγου τῆς ἀποτομῆς.

To be sure, the number of terms produced in the *Timaeus* has been demonstrated [i.e. by other commentators] on the basis of the writings of Philolaus, but in Plato the series proceeds even without the ratio of the *apotome*.

AUTHENTICITY

This testimonium is not listed separately in DK and is only mentioned in the apparatus to A26. However, it is really a rather important piece of evidence in trying to reconstruct the ancient tradition about Philolaus' music theory. Just as in the cases of A25 and A26, it shows close ties to the tradition of *Timaeus* interpretation which began in the early Academy, and seems to be drawn from a book forged in Philolaus' name that sought to "explain" the *Timaeus* by demonstrating the true teaching of Plato's Pythagorean precursor. To this extent the book must have resembled the more famous book, known as the *Timaeus Locrus*, which sets out important points of the *Timaeus*, with some modifications, under the guise of the original book by the Timaeus whom Plato makes the principal speaker in the dialogue.

The context of the testimonium is important, but long and involved, so that I have chosen to summarize it rather than reproduce all of it here. In this section of his commentary Proclus is discussing the construction of the world soul and in particular the numerical structure that Plato gives it (*Ti.* 35b1ff). Plato first sets out two series of numbers (1, 2, 4, 8 and 1, 3, 9, 27), and then says that these series are to be "filled in" with two kinds of means (35c2-36a5). The upshot is that the series is "filled in" with the ratios of 9:8 (the whole tone) and 256:243 (the *leimma* – what is "left over" when two whole tones are subtracted from a fourth: $4:3 - 9:8 - 9:8 = 256:243$). Although Plato does not make this explicit, he is constructing a diatonic scale each octave of which consists of five whole-tones (9:8) and two *leimmata* (256:243). Plato's series, which stretches from 1 to 27, comprises four octaves and a sixth (27:1 = 16:1 [four octaves] + 3:2 [a fifth] + 9:8 [a tone]). Thus, if we fill in the whole sequence from 1 to 27 with the ratios 9:8 and 256:243 we will end up with thirty-four terms (the first term, seven terms in each of the four octaves, and five terms in the sixth).

Proclus mentions (188.9) that Timaeus the Pythagorean (i.e. Timaeus of Locri) said that there were thirty-six and not thirty-four terms in the sequence, and that since he accepted Plato's extreme terms (1 and 27) he had to insert two extra terms in the series. Accordingly, Timaeus in two places introduced another ratio into the series besides 9:8 and 256:243 (see *Timaeus Locrus* 96bff). This is the *apotome* (2,187:2,048 – a ratio only a mother could love), which is the interval left if the *leimma* is subtracted from the whole tone (9:8 – 256:243 = 2,187:2,048). Proclus protests loudly that this cannot be right, both because Plato never mentioned such a ratio and because such a ratio is not needed in the diatonic scale where the whole tone is not divided. He then concludes that Plato intended there to be thirty-four terms in the series. Nevertheless, Proclus goes on to illustrate the calculation according to which the *apotome* was inserted into the series in two places (189.7 – 190.7). It is immediately after these calculations that the sentence mentioning Philolaus occurs.

The sentence completes the section by making the additional remarks that some scholars have used Philolaus to clarify the number of terms in the *Timaeus* series (see Burkert 1972: 396 n. 46). Coming right after the calculations that established thirty-six terms, it seems most reasonable to take this to mean that some scholars supported their contention that there were thirty-six terms in the *Timaeus* on the basis of Philolaus. This is further supported by the second half of the sentence, which is set in contrast with

375

the first half and asserts that Plato did not use the *apotome*, with the clear implication that the system envisaged in the first half of the sentence did use it, and hence was the system of thirty-six terms.

Whether the passage in Proclus is adducing Philolaus as support for the system of thirty-four or thirty-six terms, this attempt is in fact inconsistent with Philolaus' genuine music theory as represented in F6a (I owe this point to a suggestion by Barker). Although the same diatonic attunement lies behind both Philolaus and Plato's *Timaeus*, Philolaus' use of the term *trite* (see the commentary on F6a) shows that he was working with a hepta-chord (spanning an octave) while Plato was working with an octachord. This means that there will be one less term in some of Philolaus' tetrachords (the upper one in each octave) than in Plato's. Accordingly, over the span of four octaves and a sixth which is found in the *Timaeus* Philolaus' attune-ment would give four fewer terms than Plato's (one in each octave = total of 30), if the span starts at the lowest number. If it starts at the highest number the tetrachord in the extra sixth will also be defective, so that Philolaus' system would have five fewer terms (i.e. 29). This makes it very clear that the use that is made of Philolaus here in A26a is inconsistent with his actual music theory represented in the genuine F6a, and casts further doubt on the rest of the tradition which connects Philolaus to the *Timaeus* (esp. A26). It looks very much as if this later tradition just assumed that Philolaus was behind all aspects of the musical theory in the *Timaeus* except where the *Timaeus* needs to be corrected in light of Philolaus' "superior" wisdom (e.g. that there were thirty-six and not thirty-four terms and the introduction of the *apotome*). This discrepancy between the genuine F6a and A26a strongly suggests that the latter is spurious, but there is further argument to support this same point, which also suggests that A26a and A26 belong to the same spurious tradition.

There is a connection to be made between the significant numbers of A26 and the tradition that Philolaus could be used to support the thesis that there were thirty-six terms in the *Timaeus* series (A26a). This connection becomes clear when we consider why anyone would want to argue that there were thirty-six rather than thirty-four terms in the first place. The answer is pretty clearly that 36 is a more significant number in terms of the other numbers of the *Timaeus* than 34 is. In fact Plutarch's discussion of the *Timaeus* passage makes clear that 36 was an important number for the early interpreters of the *Timaeus*. 36 particularly arises in Plutarch's discussion of those who arrange the two number series of the Timaeus (1, 2, 4, 8 and 1, 3, 9, 27), not in a single series, but so that the plane numbers are paired with plane numbers, squares with squares, and cubes with cubes, giving the following:

This arrangement is specifically assigned to Crantor (a pupil of Xenocrates) and his followers (1022d), and Plutarch discusses in some detail the remarkable numbers that arise from the addition and multiplication of the paired terms (1017e ff). In that discussion 36 is significant as the product of the first two square numbers in each series (4 × 9 = 36), and Plutarch mentions several other features that make it remarkable (1018c ff). Thus it seems likely that commenators on the *Timaeus* like Crantor, who were concerned to show the significant numbers embodied in it, were unimpressed with the idea that there should only be thirty-four terms in the series of numbers in the *Timaeus*, because 34 has no particular significance in terms of the powers of 2 and powers of 3, and therefore argued that Plato must have meant there to be thirty-six terms, which could be achieved by including the *apotome*.

What is important here is that the grounds for introducing thirty-six terms are found in the same sort of number speculation, and in particular the number speculation that emphasizes the powers of the number 3, that we find in the musical theory ascribed to Philolaus in A26 by Boethius. However, as is argued in the commentary on A26, that type of number speculation is specifically tied to the early Academy and is very unlikely to be the genuine work of Philolaus. Thus the work of Philolaus cited by commentators to support the doctrine of thirty-six terms is in all probability a spurious work, which may well have been generated precisely to support a certain early Academic interpretation of the *Timaeus*. This work is also the origin of A26 and probably of A25 and F6b as well.

Testimonium A25

Porphyry, *in Ptolemaei Tetrabiblon* 5 (91 Düring) Ἐρατοσθένης μὲν οὖν φησιν ἕτερον εἶναι διάστημα λόγου· ἐν γὰρ ἑνὶ διαστήματι δύο λόγοι γίνονται. ὁ δὲ λόγος δὶς φέρεται, ὅ τε τοῦ μείζονος πρὸς τὸ ἔλαττον καὶ τοῦ ἐλάττονος πρὸς τὸ μεῖζον καὶ κοινὴ διαφορὰ
5 ὑπεροχῆς καὶ ἐλλείψεως ὡς τῆς διαφορᾶς δηλονότι τὸ διάστημα ποιούσης. διπλασίου τε γάρ φησι πρὸς ἥμισυ καὶ ἡμίσεος πρὸς διπλάσιον ὁ μὲν λόγος ἕτερος, τὸ αὐτὸ δὲ διάστημα. ἐκ δὴ τοιούτων οὔτε τί καλεῖται διάστημα, οὔτε καθ᾽ ὃ διαφέρει τοῦ λόγου παρέστησεν.

10 ἀπὸ δὴ τούτου κινηθέντες τινὲς τῶν μετ' αὐτὸν διάστημα
ἐκάλεσαν εἶναι ὑπεροχήν, ὡς Αἰλιανὸς ὁ Πλατωνικὸς καὶ Φιλόλαος
δ' ἐπὶ πάντων τῶν διαστημάτων προσηγορίαν, ἀλλὰ καὶ
Θράσυλλος ἐν τῷ Περὶ τοῦ ἑπταχόρδου ἐπὶ τῆς διαφορᾶς εἶναι
τῶν φθόγγων τάττει τὸ διάστημα, γράφων οὕτως...

10 μετ' αὐτῶν p   12 ante προσηγορίαν scripsit ⟨ταύτην εἴληφε τὴν⟩ Boeckh (84)
13 τοῦ ἑπταχόρδου Düring (96.16) τῶν ἑπτὰ μόνον MSS

However, Eratosthenes says that the interval is different from the
ratio. For in one interval two ratios occur. Ratio is involved twice,
both the ratio of the greater to the lesser and of the lesser to the
greater, and the difference (an excess [in one case] and a deficiency
[in the other]) is common, while it is clear that it is the difference
that constitutes the interval. For, he says, the ratio of the double to
the half is different from the ratio of the half to the double, but the
interval is the same. From such arguments he neither made clear
why it is called "interval" nor in what respect it differs from the
ratio.

Moved by this, then, some of those after him called the interval
"excess," as Aelian the Platonist and Philolaus assign [this] name to
all intervals, but Thrasyllus also in *On the Heptachord* assigns [the
name] interval to the difference of sounds, writing as follows...

AUTHENTICITY

The most startling thing about this passage is that, read in the most natural
way, it seems to group Philolaus with Aelian the Platonist and Thrasyllus
as philosophers living after the time of Eratosthenes (3rd century BC).
Düring (1934: 177) concluded from this that Porphyry must be referring
to an otherwise unknown Philolaus who is distinct from Philolaus the
Presocratic. Positing another Philolaus may seem to be an extreme measure, but it must be granted that the passage is very odd if it is meant to
refer to the Presocratic. It is not simply that Porphyry lists Philolaus with
Aelian and Thrasyllus. He explicitly identifies these thinkers as coming after
Eratosthenes. Furthermore it is noteworthy that Philolaus is not further
identified as "the Pythagorean," nor is any Philolaus mentioned elsewhere
in Porphyry's commentary on Ptolemy or in Ptolemy himself. The Aelian
that Porphyry mentions, author of a commentary on the *Timaeus*, is virtually unknown to us, although he is mentioned in several other places by

Porphyry and by Proclus in his commentary on the *Timaeus* (Düring 1934: 158).

Boeckh and Diels tried to evade the difficulty by putting a full stop after Aelian the Platonist, so that he alone is identified as belonging to the time after Eratosthenes. The reference to Philolaus then comes in an independent sentence, and the text has to be supplemented to give the sense: "And Philolaus adopted this name for all intervals." But this really does not help very much, because Porphyry is still bringing Philolaus out of the blue into a discussion of Eratosthenes and his successors. Furthermore, Porphyry will go on to show that Plato conceived of intervals as ratios, and Porphyry asserts that most of the canonists and Pythagoreans did the same (92). He supports this latter claim by quoting from the *Sectio canonis* and from Archytas (B2). Now it is true that Porphyry only says that "most of the Pythagoreans" used interval and ratio in the same sense, so that he might have Philolaus in mind as the exception, but the structure of Porphyry's discussion as a whole (see especially 94–5) suggests that he regarded all of the ancients up to Eratosthenes (with the exception of the followers of Aristoxenus, who adopted yet a third view) as using "interval" and "ratio" as interchangeable. If Porphyry intended to single out Philolaus the Presocratic as the exception to this trend, he certainly did it in an awkward and unclear manner.

Regarding an interval as an "excess" need not in itself be in conflict with conceiving of intervals as ratios. It is perfectly possible to see the whole-tone as the excess of the fifth over the fourth while still regarding them as ratios (the difference between the ratios $3:2$ and $4:3$ is $9:8$). Something like this may be going on in the genuine F6a (see the commentary ad loc.), but it is striking that the term "excess" is not found in that fragment. However, the idea that an interval is an "excess" also fits very nicely with the attitude found in the musical theory falsely ascribed to Philolaus by Boethius (A26), and the Latin term *differentia* in Boethius is probably a translation of ὑπεροχή. Here intervals are identified with the *arithmetical* differences between the terms of the ratios that were traditionally equated with the concordant intervals. Burkert, who accepts A26 as genuine, takes A25 as further support for that view. However, once the spuriousness of A26 is recognized, the peculiarities of A25 become striking. In particular it is significant that the Philolaus whom Porphyry mentions is associated with an author of a commentary on the *Timaeus* (Aelian). Since A26 also has numerous connections to the tradition of the *Timaeus* commentaries, it is not unreasonable to assume that the Philolaus Porphyry has in mind is the Philolaus created in that tradition and not the Presocratic Philolaus. Thus, while the view that an interval is an excess can be squared with the genuine

379

F6a of Philolaus, the peculiarities of the context of this testimonium in Porphyry cast serious doubts about its authenticity and suggest that it is more closely tied to the spurious tradition about Philolaus' music which is found in Boethius.

4. GODS AND ANGLES

Testimonium A14

A Proclus, *in Euc.* 130.8 καὶ γὰρ παρὰ τοῖς Πυθαγορείοις εὑρήσομεν ἄλλας γωνίας ἄλλοις θεοῖς ἀνακειμένας ὥσπερ καὶ ὁ Φιλόλαος πεποίηκε τοῖς μὲν τὴν τριγωνικὴν γωνίαν τοῖς δὲ τὴν τετραγωνικὴν ἀφιερώσας καὶ ἄλλας ἄλλοις καὶ τὴν αὐτὴν πλείοσι
5 θεοῖς καὶ τῷ αὐτῷ πλείους κατὰ τὰς διαφόρους ἐν αὐτῷ δυνάμεις ἀνείς.

A For we will find among the Pythagoreans different angles dedicated to different gods, just as Philolaus also has done, consecrating the angle of the triangle to some (gods) and the angle of the square to others, and assigning other angles to other gods and the same angle to many gods and many angles to the same god according to the various powers in him.

B Proclus, *in Euc.* 166.25 εἰκότως ἄρα καὶ ὁ Φιλόλαος τὴν τοῦ τριγώνου γωνίαν τέτταρσιν ἀνέθηκεν θεοῖς, Κρόνῳ καὶ Ἅιδῃ καὶ Ἄρεϊ καὶ Διονύσῳ, πᾶσαν τὴν τετραμερῆ τῶν στοιχείων διακόσμησιν τὴν ἄνωθεν ἀπὸ τοῦ οὐρανοῦ καθήκουσαν εἴτε ἀπὸ
5 τῶν τεττάρων τοῦ ζῳδιακοῦ τμημάτων ἐν τούτοις περιλαβών. ὁ μὲν γὰρ Κρόνος πᾶσαν ὑφίστησι τὴν ὑγρὰν καὶ ψυχρὰν οὐσίαν, ὁ δὲ Ἄρης πᾶσαν τὴν ἔμπυρον φύσιν, καὶ ὁ μὲν Ἅιδης τὴν χθονίαν ὅλην συνέχει ζωήν, ὁ δὲ Διόνυσος τὴν ὑγρὰν καὶ θερμὴν ἐπιτροπεύει γένεσιν, ἧς καὶ ὁ οἶνος σύμβολον ὑγρὸς ὢν καὶ
10 θερμός. πάντες δὲ οὗτοι κατὰ μὲν τὰς εἰς τὰ δεύτερα ποιήσεις διεστήκασι, ἥνωνται δὲ ἀλλήλοις. διὸ καὶ κατὰ μίαν αὐτῶν γωνίαν συνάγει τὴν ἕνωσιν ὁ Φιλόλαος.

B It is reasonable then that Philolaus dedicated the angle of the triangle to four gods, Kronos, Hades, Ares, and Dionysus, having comprehended in them the whole four-part order of the elements which derives from the heaven above or from the four divisions of the zodiac. For Kronos gives substance to the whole of wet and cold being, but Ares the whole of fiery nature, and Hades embraces the whole of earthly life, but Dionysus oversees wet and hot generation, of which wine is a symbol being wet and hot. All these differ according to their effects on secondary things, but are unified with one another. Therefore, Philolaus also brings about their unification according to one angle.

C Proclus, *in Euc.* 173.11   καὶ πρὸς τούτοις ὁ Φιλόλαος κατ' ἄλλην ἐπιβολὴν τὴν τοῦ τετραγώνου γωνίαν 'Ρέας καὶ Δήμητρος καὶ 'Εστίας ἀποκαλεῖ. διότι γὰρ τὴν γῆν τὸ τετράγωνον ὑφίστησι καὶ στοιχεῖόν ἐστιν αὐτῆς προσεχές, ὡς παρὰ τοῦ Τιμαίου
5 μεμαθήκαμεν, ἀπὸ δὲ πασῶν τούτων τῶν θεαινῶν ἀπορροίας ἡ γῆ δέχεται καὶ γονίμους δυνάμεις, εἰκότως τὴν τοῦ τετραγώνου γωνίαν ἀνῆκεν ταύταις ταῖς ζωογόνοις θεαῖς. καὶ γὰρ 'Εστίαν καλοῦσι τὴν γῆν καὶ Δήμητρά τινες, καὶ τῆς ὅλης 'Ρέας αὐτὴν μετέχειν φασί, καὶ πάντα ἐστὶν ἐν αὐτῇ τὰ γεννητικὰ αἴτια
10 χθονίως. τὴν τοίνυν μίαν ἕνωσιν τῶν θείων τούτων γενῶν τὴν τετραγωνικὴν φησι γωνίαν περιέχειν.

C Philolaus, moreover, in accordance with another conception calls the angle of the square the angle of Rhea, Demeter, and Hestia. For since the square gives substance to the earth and is the element suited to it, as we have learned from the *Timaeus* [55d8ff], and since the earth receives effluences and generative powers from all these goddesses, he has reasonably dedicated the angle of the square to these life-generating goddesses. For some call the earth Hestia and Demeter, and say that it participates in the whole of Rhea, and all the generative causes are in it in earthly fashion. So then, he says that the angle of the square encompasses the sole unification of these species of the divine.

D Proclus, *in Euc.* 174.2   δεῖ δὲ μὴ λανθάνειν, ὅπως τὴν μὲν τριγωνικὴν γωνίαν ὁ Φιλόλαος τέτταρσιν ἀνῆκεν θεοῖς, τὴν δὲ τετραγωνικὴν τρισίν, ἐνδεικνύμενος αὐτῶν τὴν δι' ἀλλήλων χώρησιν καὶ τὴν ἐν πᾶσι πάντων κοινωνίαν τῶν τε περισσῶν ἐν
5 τοῖς ἀρτίοις καὶ τῶν ἀρτίων ἐν τοῖς περισσοῖς. τριὰς οὖν τετραδικὴ

καὶ τετρὰς τριαδικὴ τῶν τε γονίμων μετέχουσαι καὶ ποιητικῶν
ἀγαθῶν τὴν ὅλην συνέχουσι τῶν γενητῶν διακόσμησιν. ἀφ᾿ ὧν
ἡ δυωδεκὰς εἰς μίαν μονάδα τὴν τοῦ Διὸς ἀρχὴν ἀνατείνεται. τὴν
γὰρ τοῦ δωδεκαγώνου γωνίαν Διὸς εἶναί φησιν ὁ Φιλόλαος, ὡς
10 κατὰ μίαν ἕνωσιν τοῦ Διὸς ὅλον συνέχοντος τὸν τῆς δυωδεκάδος
ἀριθμόν. ἡγεῖται γὰρ καὶ παρὰ τῷ Πλάτωνι δυωδεκάδος ὁ Ζεὺς
καὶ ἀπολύτως ἐπιτροπεύει τὸ πᾶν.

D It is necessary not to overlook the fact that Philolaus dedicated
the angle of the triangle to four gods, but the angle of the square
to three, indicating their progression through one another and the
sharing of all in all, both of the odd in the even and the even in the
odd. A triad consisting of 4 and a tetrad consisting of 3, sharing in
the generative and productive goods, they hold together the whole
order of generated things. The number 12, which is their product,
reaches up to the one monad, the sovereignty of Zeus. For Philolaus
says that the angle of the dodecagon belongs to Zeus, since Zeus
holds together in a single unity the whole number 12. In Plato
also, Zeus leads the 12 and has absolute dominion over all things
[*Phaedrus* 246e4–247a1].

> **E** Proclus, *Theol. Plat.* 1.4 (1.20 Saffrey and Westerink) ὁ δὲ
> διὰ τῶν εἰκόνων Πυθαγόρειος, ἐπεὶ καὶ τοῖς Πυθαγορείοις τὰ
> μαθήματα πρὸς τὴν τῶν θείων ἀνάμνησιν ἐξηύρητο καὶ διὰ
> τούτων ὡς εἰκόνων ἐπ᾿ ἐκεῖνα διαβαίνειν ἐπεχείρουν· καὶ γὰρ τοὺς
> 5 ἀριθμοὺς ἀνεῖσαν τοῖς θεοῖς καὶ τὰ σχήματα, καθάπερ λέγουσιν οἱ
> τὰ ἐκείνων ἱστορεῖν σπουδάζοντες.

E The [mode of teaching theology] through images is Pythagorean,
since the mathematical sciences had been discovered by the Pythagoreans for the recollection of divine matters, at which they tried to
arrive through these as images. For they dedicated both numbers
and shapes to the gods, just as those who are zealous in reporting
their doctrines say.

> **F** Damascius, *De principiis* 2.127.7 διὰ τί γὰρ τῷ μὲν τὸν κύκλον
> ἀνιέρουν οἱ Πυθαγόρειοι, τῷ δὲ τρίγωνον, τῷ δὲ τετράγωνον, τῷ
> δὲ ἄλλο καὶ ἄλλο τῶν εὐθυγράμμων [τῶν] σχημάτων, ὡς δὲ καὶ
> μικτῶν, ὡς τὰ ἡμικύκλια τοῖς Διοσκούροις; πολλάκις δὲ τῷ αὐτῷ

5 ἄλλο καὶ ἄλλο ἀπονέμων κατ' ἄλλην ἰδιότητα καὶ ἄλλην, ὁ
Φιλόλαος ἐν τούτοις σοφός. καὶ μήποτε, ὡς καθόλου εἰπεῖν, τὸ μὲν
περιφερὲς κοινὸν σχῆμά ἐστιν πάντων τῶν νοερῶν θεῶν ᾖ νοεροί,
τὰ δὲ εὐθύγραμμα ἴδια ἑκάστων ἄλλα ἄλλων κατὰ τὰς τῶν
ἀριθμῶν, τῶν γωνιῶν καὶ τῶν πλευρῶν ἰδιότητας· οἷον Ἀθηνᾶς
10 μὲν τὸ τρίγωνον, Ἑρμοῦ δὲ τὸ τετράγωνον· ἤδη δέ φησιν ὁ
Φιλόλαος· καὶ τοῦ τετραγώνου ἥδε μὲν ἡ γωνία τῆς Ῥέας, ἥδε δὲ
τῆς Ἥρας, ἄλλη δὲ ἄλλης θεοῦ· καὶ ὅλως ἐστὶν θεολογικὸς ὁ περὶ
τῶν σχημάτων ἀφορισμός.

3 [τῶν] Diels   12 ὅλος . . . ὁ θεολογικὸς περὶ MSS corr. H. Schone

F For why did the Pythagoreans consecrate the circle to one [god],
the triangle to another, the square to another, and various others of
the rectilinear shapes to another, as also of the mixed [shapes], e.g.
the semicircle to the Dioscuri? Often assigning different shapes to the
same [god] in accord with [his] various characteristics, Philolaus
was wise in these matters. And perhaps, to speak generally, the circular shape is common to all the intelligible gods in so far as they are
intelligible, and the various rectilinear shapes are peculiarly tied to
each of the various gods in accord with the characteristics of the
numbers, angles, and sides. For example, the triangle belongs to
Athena and the square to Hermes. Indeed, Philolaus says "this angle of the square belongs to Rhea, and this angle to Hera, and other
angles to other goddesses." And in general the delimitation of shapes
is theological.

G Plutarch, *De Is. et Osir.* 30, 363a φαίνονται δὲ καὶ οἱ
Πυθαγορικοὶ τὸν Τυφῶνα δαιμονικὴν ἡγούμενοι δύναμιν. λέγουσι
γὰρ ἐν ἀρτίῳ μέτρῳ ἕκτῳ καὶ πεντηκοστῷ γεγονέναι Τυφῶνα·
καὶ πάλιν τὴν μὲν τοῦ τριγώνου ⟨γωνίαν⟩ Ἅιδου καὶ Διονύσου
5 καὶ Ἄρεος εἶναι· τὴν δὲ τοῦ τετραγώνου Ῥέας καὶ Ἀφροδίτης καὶ
Δήμητρος καὶ Ἑστίας καὶ Ἥρας· τὴν δὲ τοῦ δωδεκαγώνου Διός·
τὴν δ' ἐκκαιπεντηκονταγωνίου Τυφῶνος, ὡς Εὔδοξος ἱστόρηκεν.

4 ⟨ ⟩ Kranz   7 ὀκτωκαιπεντηκονταγωνίου MSS ἐκκαιπεντηκονταγωνίου Xylander

The Pythagoreans also plainly consider Typhon to be a daemonic
power. For they say that Typhon was born in the even measure
fifty-six. And again that the ⟨angle⟩ of the triangle belongs to

Hades, Dionysus, and Ares, that of the square to Rhea, Aphrodite, Demeter, Hestia and Hera, that of the dodecagon to Zeus, and that of the fifty-six-sided polygon to Typhon, as Eudoxus has reported.

AUTHENTICITY

This is undoubtedly the most obscure and difficult set of testimonia about Philolaus' philosophy, and there is a natural tendency for the scholar to want to find a convenient rug to sweep it under. There are difficulties both in interpreting the relationship between the various sources and also in determining what sense can be made of the idea of "dedicating" angles of triangles, squares, etc., to various gods. Scholars have generally come to accept the view first presented by Tannery, that the dedication of the angles of triangles and squares has something to do with astrological practice. Astrology is usually thought to have been developed in Greece, with perhaps some Babylonian influence, in the third century BC (Bouché-Leclerq 1899: 37; Neugebauer 1957: 170–1, 187–8; 1975: 608, 613). This, combined with the fact that most of the testimonia for this doctrine in Philolaus are very late, suggests that it originates in a late forgery in Philolaus' name, but Plutarch cites Eudoxus, the great astronomer who was a contemporary of Speusippus, as his authority for assigning the view to the Pythagoreans; and this has led Burkert to accept the attribution to Philolaus and thus to find "the first traces of astrology" in Greece in Philolaus' book (1972: 350). In what follows I will argue both that Eudoxus' testimony probably does not indicate that the dedication of angles goes back to Philolaus and that, despite the acuity of scholars who have argued for a connection with astrology, the doctrine is likely to have nothing to do with astrology and in fact to have its origin in commentary on the *Timaeus* which began in the early Academy.

The text of Plutarch allows us to be sure that Eudoxus reported that the angle of the fifty-six-sided polygon was associated with Typhon by the Pythagoreans. It is less sure, but likely, that Eudoxus is also the source for the connections between the triangle, square, and dodecagon and various gods attributed by Plutarch to the Pythagoreans. But two aspects of Eudoxus' testimony must especially be emphasized. First, as far as we can tell from Plutarch, he referred to Pythagoreans in general in contrast to Proclus and Damascius, 800 years later, who single out Philolaus as principal author of the doctrine in question. Second, Eudoxus' testimony conflicts with the testimony of Proclus in important ways, notably in mentioning three gods in connection with the triangle and five goddesses in connection with the square, while Proclus emphasizes the surprising connection of four gods with the triangle and three goddesses with the square.

Whom did Eudoxus have in mind when he said these views were Pytha-gorean? Burkert oddly assumes that he must have meant pre-Platonic Pythagoreans, thus confirming Proclus' ascription to Philolaus. I say oddly, because Burkert has made a convincing case elsewhere in his book that already in the early Academy two conflicting traditions about the Pytha-goreans had arisen (1972: 53–96), but assumes here that Eudoxus, who was associated with the early Academy, can only belong to one of them. One of these is the Aristotelian view which, while recognizing important connec-tions between Plato and the Pythagoreans, makes important distinctions between them as well, emphasizing that the doctrines of the indefinite dyad and the independent existence of numbers are peculiarly Platonic. The other tradition begins with Speusippus and Xenocrates (and perhaps with Plato himself), and sees Plato and the early Academy as developing certain basic Pythagorean ideas, and is accordingly willing to call mature Platonic and Academic doctrines Pythagorean. It is this tradition that leads to most of the later testimonia about the Pythagoreans (e.g. the reports in Sextus Empiricus) which assign to them the doctrines of the one and the indefinite dyad and the derivation sequence of point–line–surface–solid. Burkert's conclusion that Eudoxus must be referring to early Pythagoreanism puts Eudoxus in the camp with Aristotle as maintaining a clear distinction between Pythagoreanism and Platonism, but why should this be so? Eudoxus is the contemporary of Speusippus, whom Burkert has shown to be a cen-tral figure in describing Academic doctrines as Pythagorean (1972: 64). Is it not just as likely that when Eudoxus talks of Pythagoreans he means what Speusippus apparently meant, i.e. Academic philosophers doing philoso-phy in the Pythagorean tradition? Thus, while it is possible that Eudoxus has early Pythagoreanism, and in particular Philolaus, in mind, this cannot be taken as given. It is just as likely that Eudoxus is referring to "Pytha-goreans" of his own day, including Speusippus. The crucial point is that Eudoxus' testimony does not allow us *prima facie* to decide between these two possibilities, and the question has to be decided on the basis of the content of the doctrines assigned to the Pythagoreans, to which I now turn.

Following the explicit distinction made by Zeller (1923: 499 n. 1) and Tannery (1889: 379) between the doctrines Proclus assigns to the Pytha-goreans and his Neoplatonic interpretation of them, most scholars implic-itly assume that Proclus' interpretation is useless for determining what the true meaning of the dedication of angles to divinities is. Nonetheless, it may be that Proclus' interpretation is in certain ways more accurate than the suggestions of modern scholars. Proclus' interpretation is closely tied to Plato's *Timaeus*, and interpretation of the *Timaeus* is closely tied to the pseudo-Pythagorean tradition (the most notable example being *Timaeus Locrus*.) Therefore, if we can make some sense of the dedication of angles to

386

gods in terms of the *Timaeus* there will be strong grounds both for regarding this doctrine as not possible for Philolaus, and also for accepting Proclus' interpretation as a legitimate reading of a "Pythagorean" text written in the Platonizing tradition. However, before turning to Proclus' interpretation and the connections with the *Timaeus* it is first necessary to examine the basis of the standard, astrological, interpretation of the doctrine.

The connections with astrology are not immediately apparent. There is no direct reference to the signs of the zodiac, or to the planets, or to the heavens at all. But two peculiarities of the testimonia have led scholars to see astrology as the underlying motive for the connection of gods to angles. The first peculiarity is the emphasis on the angle of the triangle, square, etc. Why should a god be tied to the angle rather than to the shape as a whole? Newbold (1906: 198) notes that in the anonymous commentary on Ptolemy's *Tetrabiblos* the angle of the triangle is said to be 120 degrees, which is exactly the arc subtended by the side of an equilateral triangle when it is inscribed in a circle (i.e. it divides the circle's 360 degrees into three parts). Second, scholars noticed Proclus' emphasis on the fact that Philolaus paradoxically associated four gods with a three-angled figure (the triangle), and three goddesses with a four-angled figure (the square). Tannery and Newbold were the first to relate these features of the testimonia to astrological practice, and in a striking way. In mature Greek astrological texts there is reference to the practice of inscribing triangles and squares in the circle of the Zodiac (e.g. Manilius, 2.270ff). Four triangles can be inscribed so that the vertex of each of the three angles of each triangle touches the circle of the Zodiac at a different astrological sign. Four triangles, with three angles each, thus exactly cover the twelve signs of the zodiac. Similarly, three squares, with four angles each, can be inscribed in the zodiac to cover the twelve signs. Here then we have just the connection between 4 and the triangle and 3 and the square which we find in the Philolaus testimony. Further, the dodecagon mentioned as belonging to Zeus can be accounted for as the single figure whose vertices each indicate one of the twelve signs of the zodiac when inscribed in the circle of the zodiac. There are some problems here – the four gods associated with the *angle* of the triangle become instead identified with each of the four triangles as a whole, as the patron deity of that triangle – but the connection is striking.

Tannery also points out that each of the four triangles in astrology was associated with one of the four elements, which connects with Proclus' suggestion that the four gods associated with the triangle in fact represent four elements. Newbold, Olivieri, and most recently Hübner have tried to make the theory work out in detail; i.e. they have tried to explain why just the specific gods and goddesses mentioned are connected with the specific triangles and squares mentioned. These attempts all involve considerable ingenuity, but it is fair to say that all leave many things unexplained. The mention of Typhon and his connection with a fifty-six-sided figure in particular seems unconnected with astrological practice, and Tannery saw it as a bit of Egyptian mythology that must have been an accretion to Philolaus' system at a later date (1889: 385 n. 6). The fact that the details of the system have not been able to be worked out in astrological terms is bothersome, but could well be explained in terms of our massive ignorance of the astrology of early times. More bothersome is the fact that the foundation upon which the theory is constructed is shaky.

First, it is only Proclus that mentions the key equation of precisely four gods with the triangle and three goddesses with the square. Our earliest source for the system, Eudoxus as reported by Plutarch, mentions three gods with the triangle and five goddesses with the square. If we accept these numbers the astrological connection is destroyed. Second, Proclus mentions that the same god is assigned to many angles and the same angle to many gods. If a god or goddess is assigned to each of the signs of the zodiac, then when we inscribe the squares and triangles it will turn out that each deity is part of one triangle and one square, so that it could well be said that the same deity is assigned to more than one figure. However, it will not work to say that the same angle has many gods assigned to it unless each sign of the zodiac has several gods connected with it, which seems to make a hopeless confusion of the system.

Besides these problems both in the details and in the basic principles of the system, the ascription of this sort of astrological practice to Philolaus, writing in the later part of the fifth century, goes contrary to the best evidence we have for the adoption of astrological practices by the Greeks. As mentioned above, the most authoritative work on ancient astrology (Bouché-Leclerq 1889: 37 and Neugebauer 1957: 170–1, 187–8; 1975: 608, 613) dates its development in Greece only in the third century BC. There are a few references in earlier authors that show some contact with Babylonian astrology, but for the most part they treat it as a foreign phenomenon to be rejected, and only the most general of influences can be seen. Capelle's interesting article (1925) showed similarities between the interpretation of dreams about the sun and moon in the Hippocratic *Regimen* (400 BC?) and Babylonian use of omens about the sun and moon for predicting the fortunes of the country as a whole. Similarly, Ctesias of Cnidos at the beginning of the fourth century, in his history of Babylon, describes in general terms some Babylonian "astrological" practices; and an isolated testimony assigns to Democritus a planetary order also found in Babylonia, but while this is evidence for some Greek connections to Babylon none of it is evidence for horoscopic astrology. Even the supposedly clear reference to astrology in the *Timaeus* (40c9), emphasized by Burnet (1948: 24 n. 1), has no real tie to astrology and can just as easily refer to more general omens derived from observation of the sky.

As Neugebauer emphasizes, mention of predictions based on "the day of birth" does not necessarily indicate that astrology is meant. Thus, the passage in Herodotus (2.82.1) that some (e.g. Dodds 1951: 261 n. 51) have seen as evidence of Greek knowledge of astrology, in fact refers to another practice attested by the evidence from Egypt which has nothing to do with a horoscope, but is connected with systems of lucky and unlucky days. Thus, when Cicero (*De div.* 2.42.87) tells us that Eudoxus rejected the Chaldaean practice of prediction from the date of birth, it is not certain that astrology is meant. On the other hand Proclus' assertion (*in Ti.* 3.151.1–9) that Theophrastus was amazed at Chaldaean predictions "from the heavens" may well refer to Babylonian astrology; but it is still treated as a foreign phenomenon, and at any rate Theophrastus may have written this at a date approaching 300 BC, almost a century and a half after Philolaus. Moreover, the developed form of ancient astrology, as it appears for example in Manilius, is in fact a Greek and not a Babylonian creation (Neugebauer 1975: 613). Thus, the evidence for the development of astrology, and especially horoscopic astrology (i.e. astrology that predicts the fate of an individual as opposed to a country as a whole, and is based on the sign of the zodiac at the horizon on the birth date of the individual), makes it all but impossible that Philolaus can have been involved with anything like the four triangles and three squares used in developed horoscopic astrology.

Indeed, even the idea of the zodiac consisting of a canonical twelve signs of thirty degrees each, which is assumed in the astrological practices being ascribed to Philolaus, is attested for the fifth century only by the most meagre and suspect evidence. Burkert points to a passage in Pliny (*NH* 2.31) where Cleostratus of Tenedos, pupil of Anaximander, is supposed to have introduced the signs of the zodiac to Greece, which would thus place their introduction by the end of the sixth century. But there is no trace of the impact of such a striking idea as the twelve signs of the zodiac in fifth-century literature except a fragment from Euripides' play *Hypsipyle*, quoted in a scholium to the *Frogs*. Indeed, it is far from clear that even this fragment refers to the twelve signs of the zodiac. Aristophanes refers to τὸ δωδεκαμήχανον (twelve-variety system – 1327) of Cyrene, who the scholiast tells us was a notorious and versatile prostitute. The scholiast also tells us that this is a parody of a line from Euripides' *Hypsipyle* (F755), which referred to τὸ δωδεκαμήχανον ἄστρον (the star with twelve devices), which might be interpreted as referring to the sun. However, it need not refer to the twelve signs of the zodiac. It could just as easily refer to the solar year as embracing twelve months. At any rate it is a slender reed indeed to use to support the idea that the twelve signs of the zodiac were fixed in the late fifth century after their introduction by Cleostratus at the beginning of the century. The earliest reference to the zodiac in Babylonia is from the first half of the fifth century, which leads Neugebauer to date its adoption in Babylonia to around 500 (1975: 593). If this is so, then Cleostratus would have gotten it almost immediately upon its introduction into Babylonia, and his introduction of it into Greece has left only the possible trace in Euripides during the fifth century. The zodiac does not appear as a well-known concept until around 300 BC in Autolycus and Euclid.

Thus there are difficulties with the astrological interpretation, both as possible for someone of Philolaus' date and, even if we doubted the connection with Philolaus, thus removing the chronological difficulties, also as a satisfying reading of the doctrine Proclus reports. It is worthwhile, therefore, to turn back to Proclus. Proclus himself was familiar with astrological practices, but does not try to explain the doctrine in this way. In text B above he does refer to the four divisions of the zodiac in relation to the four elements, but this reference is not significantly connected to the interpretation of "Philolaus" which Proclus gives. Proclus' interpretation is based on the *Timaeus*, and does just as good a job of explaining the connections of gods and goddesses with triangles and squares as does the astrological view. However, if this is the correct way of interpreting "Philolaus" we will have to conclude that the doctrine in question cannot belong to the historical Philolaus.

Proclus reports that the Pythagoreans regarded the triangle as the ultimate source of generation, and sees the use of the triangle as the basic structural unit of the four elements in the *Timaeus* as following in this tradition (*in Euc.* 166). Proclus interprets the four gods Philolaus mentions in connection with the triangle as equivalent to the four elements, and thus sees it as reasonable that Philolaus should dedicate the angle of the triangle, as the basic structural principle of matter, to the four gods who represent the four elements.

Again, when discussing the connection of three goddesses with the square, Proclus bases his interpretation on the fact that in the *Timaeus* Plato ties the element earth to the cube, which in turn is based on the square. The goddesses are all seen as having to do with the fertility of the earth, and thus Proclus sees it as natural that the basic element of earth, the square, should be dedicated to them. Now this is, of course, very fanciful, but it is the sort of fancy that is well attested in the later Pythagorean tradition which is closely tied to the *Timaeus*. It accordingly seems quite possible that Proclus' approach is in fact right, i.e. that the doctrine of the dedication of angles to gods is based on interpretation of the *Timaeus*. This of course means that the doctrine is part of the pseudo-Pythagorean tradition and cannot be ascribed to Philolaus himself. Moreover, since Eudoxus seems to have known of the doctrine, it must be assigned to the founders of that branch of the Pythagorean tradition which sees mature Platonic doctrines as Pythagorean, that is, to the early Academy. This conclusion is supported by the fact that Aristotle provides evidence that early Pythagoreans associated numbers with abstract conceptions, and in one case with a deity (7 with Athena; see Philolaus F20), but never hints that they used geometrical figures in the same way. It is with Xenocrates in the Academy that we have the first mention of a connection between gods and geometrical figures (F23).

5. FRAGMENTS AND TESTIMONIA ON COSMOLOGY

Fragment 12

Stobaeus, *Eclogae* 1 proem (1.18.5 Wachsmuth – immediately after F11) καὶ τὰ ἐν τᾶ σφαίρᾳ σώματα πέντε ἐντί, τὰ ἐν τᾶ σφαίρᾳ, πῦρ ⟨καὶ⟩ ὕδωρ καὶ γᾶ καὶ ἀήρ, καὶ ὃ τᾶς σφαίρας ὁλκόν, πέμπτον.

2 καὶ τὰ μὲν τᾶς σφαίρας Diels   3 ⟨καὶ⟩ Diels   ὁ τᾶς σφαίρας ὁλκός Wilamowitz 1920: 2.91 ὁλκόν Burkert ὁλκάς F

And there are five bodies in the sphere, the bodies in the sphere, fire, water, earth, and air and that which draws the sphere is the fifth.

AUTHENTICITY

This is a much discussed fragment. See especially Burkert (1972: 276), Frank (1923: 318 n. 2), and Wilamowitz (1920: 2.91). It is very difficult to make a confident judgment about its authenticity, because it is so short and because the meaning of the last clause is obscure. However, what evidence there is suggests that it is spurious:

(1) It is now commonly recognized that the "bodies" (σώματα) mentioned need have no reference to the five regular solids mentioned by Plato and probably first treated as a group by Theaetetus (see Sachs 1917: 41ff), and hence that there is no cause for suspicion on these grounds. This is true even if we do not accept Diels's emendation "the bodies of the sphere" for the manuscripts' "the bodies in the sphere." Some scholars have taken the latter expression to imply that the bodies meant are inscribed in a mathematical sphere and hence must be the regular solids of mathematics. However, as Sachs points out "bodies" (σώματα) clearly refer to the elements in the second half of the sentence, so that it would be strange if the word meant regular solids in the first part. A similar shift in meaning would need to be supposed for "sphere." The "bodies," then, simply refer to the ele-

ments, and there is nothing problematic in Philolaus adopting the four elements of his predecessor Empedocles.

The main reason for suspecting that the fragment is not authentic is the introduction of a fifth element. Mention of a fifth element immediately makes us think of Aristotle's aither (also in the *Epinomis*, see below), even though it is not expressly named, and it is hard to think what else the fifth element could be. It is significant that Sextus Empiricus (*M.* 10.316) joins Ocellus, to whom an important pseudo-Pythagorean writing is ascribed, with Aristotle as believing that everything comes to be from five elements. Sextus goes on to say that along with the four elements these two thinkers adopted a fifth body which revolves in a circle (πέμπτον καὶ κυκλοφορητικὸν σῶμα). The language here is very reminiscent of F12 of Philoaus, and it is hard not to see a connection (see further below). On the other hand, Sachs, following Diels, suggests that the fifth element is not aither or any particular stuff, but simply what gives shape to the world. However, in doing so she fails to answer her own question as to why Philolaus should label something of this sort a "body" and group it with earth, air, fire, and water.

Guthrie (1962: 269ff) argues for the authenticity of the fragment by suggesting that the fifth element actually goes back to the Presocratics. He argues that the fifth element is implicit in the Presocratic world view that sees four elements in the world, but also envisages something else that surrounds the world. He admits that it is unlikely that any Presocratic actually called this a fifth element, probably just referring to "the surrounding" or "the sphere." However, F12 of Philolaus does not fit Guthrie's picture because, while identifying the fifth with the sphere of the whole in some way, it also explicitly treats it on a par with the other four elements. It is treated as one of *the* five bodies and not a vague "something else" beyond the four elements, and it is just such schematism that shows, even on Guthrie's own evidence, that F12 cannot be Presocratic.

(2) As mentioned above, careful reading of the fragment shows that it does not deal with the five regular solids made famous by Plato. However, it has been commonly argued that there is in fact a connection, so that it is necessary to go into this issue in more detail. In the testimonia for Philolaus DK cites a report from Aetius (2.6.5 = A15) which assigns to Pythagoras the doctrine that the five solids were tied to the four elements and the sphere of the whole (the dodecahedron being connected to the latter). DK clearly view this testimonium as relevant to F12 of Philolaus, but there is no necessary connection. Most obviously the testimonium refers to Pythagoras and not Philolaus, and as Burkert has shown mention of Pythagoras himself often ties the report to the later Platonizing tradition. It is also noteworthy that the testimonium talks of shapes (σχημάτων) while Philolaus

F12 refers to bodies (σώματα), and that the testimonium explicitly mentions each of the five regular solids by name (cube, pyramid, octahedron, icosahedron, dodecahedron). Thus, the testimonium presupposes the proof that there are only five regular solids, which first became known in the fourth century (Schol. Eucl. 654.3ff – see Sachs 1917: 76ff), and thus shows that this is part of the pseudo-Pythagorean tradition that assigns Plato's views back to the Pythagoreans.

Guthrie (1962: 266) argues that the testimonium in Aetius must go back to Theophrastus, that we must accordingly accept it as clear evidence that the Pythagoreans had already correlated the five regular solids with the five elements, and that Philolaus F12 thus presupposes that doctrine. He treats the evidence for Theaetetus as the source for two of the regular solids (octahedron and icosahedron) and the Pythagoreans only as the source for the other three (Schol. Eucl. 654.3, used by Sachs and by Burnet 1948: 284 n. 1, where he argues against the authenticity of F12) as meaning only that Theaetetus was involved in the mathematical construction of the two figures which were probably still known in a less formal way by the Pythagoreans. However, Guthrie's certainty that the Aetius report must go back to Theophrastus is misplaced. Aetius clearly reports mainly the tradition on the Pythagoreans that goes back to Theophrastus and Aristotle, but there is other clear evidence that his reports are contaminated by the Platonizing interpretation of the Pythagoreans (see the commentary on A16). Even Guthrie notes that Theophrastus cannot have really ascribed the testimonium to Pythagoras himself, which would be contrary to the regular Peripatetic practice of referring to Pythagoreans rather than Pythagoras. Thus, the Aetius report has no special authority against the report in the scholia to Euclid, and the latter report is in fact much more believable, since the tendency in the later tradition is to magnify the accomplishments of the Pythagoreans, not to delimit them.

(3) Much of the discussion of the fragment has focused on the manuscript reading which describes the fifth element as the "cargo ship" (ὁλκάς) of the sphere. Many scholars have wanted to see the comparison of the cosmos to a ship as coming from the Pythagorean tradition, and have tried to find parallels for it, mostly in Plato (see Cherniss 1935: 186 n. 177; Richardson 1926: 116; Burnet 1948: 294 n. 1). However, none of these attempts is convincing in showing such a Pythagorean tradition. Wilamowitz recognized that the "verteufeltes Lastschiff" ("damned cargo ship") would not do, and removed any reference to a ship by suggesting an emendation, ὁλκός, which he wanted to interpret as the covering of the sphere; but, as others have pointed out (Burkert 1972: 276), the word does not really mean this and is best translated as " coils." Still, it does seem most likely that ὁλκάς is a corruption, both because of the troubles of making sense of

the ship image outlined above and because it refers not just to any ship, but is a technical term in shipping that refers to a merchant ship which has sails rather than oars, and thus has to be towed into and out of harbors (Casson 1971: 169 n. 2). Burkert follows Frank and Mullach in accepting Wilamowitz's emendation, but takes it as an adjective, so that the phrase ὃ τᾶς σφαιρᾶς ὁλκόν, πέμπτον would mean "and that thing which draws the sphere is the fifth." (For this meaning of ὁλκός see *Republic* 521d3, where Plato talks of studies that "draw" the soul.) Aristotle (*Mete.* 341a2) uses similar language when he talks of the earth and its atmosphere as drawn round (συνεφέλκεσθαι) by the motion of the heavens and the aither. The fragment thus becomes very close in meaning and language to the view ascribed by Sextus to Ocellus and Aristotle, where aither is πέμπτον καὶ κυκλοφορητικὸν σῶμα. Indeed, if this reading is accepted, and it is the best candidate to date, the fifth body is almost certainly aither, and accordingly the fragment must be a post-Aristotelian forgery.

(4) None of Aristotle's reports on the Pythagoreans describes a theory of elements (except the idea of numbers as the elements of things), and there is no trace of one in Fragments 1–7 of Philolaus. F7 does talk about the one coming to be in the center of the sphere, and there are close ties to Aristotle's reports here, but there is no necessary connection between the sphere in F7 and the sphere mentioned here in F12.

Testimonium A16b

Aetius, 2.7.7 (336 Diels = Stobaeus, *Eclogae* 22.1d, 1.196 Wachsmuth) Φιλόλαος πῦρ ἐν μέσῳ περὶ τὸ κέντρον ὅπερ ἑστίαν τοῦ παντὸς καλεῖ καὶ Διὸς οἶκον **καὶ μητέρα θεῶν βωμόν τε καὶ συνοχὴν καὶ μέτρον φύσεως**. καὶ πάλιν πῦρ ἕτερον
5 ἀνωτάτω τὸ περιέχον. πρῶτον δ' εἶναι φύσει τὸ μέσον, περὶ δὲ τοῦτο δέκα σώματα θεῖα χορεύειν, οὐρανόν, πλανήτας, μεθ' οὓς ἥλιον, ὑφ' ᾧ σελήνην, ὑφ' ᾗ τὴν γῆν, ὑφ' ᾗ τὴν ἀντίχθονα, μεθ' ἃ σύμπαντα τὸ πῦρ ἑστίας περὶ τὰ κέντρα τάξιν ἐπέχον. **τὸ μὲν οὖν ἀνωτάτω μέρος τοῦ περιέχοντος, ἐν ᾧ τὴν εἰλικρίνειαν εἶναι**
10 **τῶν στοιχείων, ὄλυμπον καλεῖ, τὰ δὲ ὑπὸ τὴν τοῦ ὀλύμπου φοράν, ἐν ᾧ τοὺς πέντε πλανήτας μεθ' ἡλίου καὶ σελήνης τετάχθαι, κόσμον, τὸ δ' ὑπὸ τούτοις ὑποσέληνόν τε καὶ περίγειον μέρος, ἐν ᾧ τὰ τῆς φιλομεταβόλου γενέσεως, οὐρανόν**. καὶ περὶ μὲν τὰ τεταγμένα τῶν μετεώρων γίνεσθαι
15 τὴν σοφίαν, περὶ δὲ τῶν γινομένων τὴν ἀταξίαν τὴν ἀρετήν, τελείαν μὲν ἐκείνην ἀτελῆ δὲ ταύτην.

6 οὐρανόν τε πλανήτας F [οὐρανόν] ⟨μετὰ τὴν τῶν ἀπλανῶν σφαῖραν τοὺς ε⟩ πλανήτας
Diels   8 περὶ Meineke ἐπὶ FP   15 τῶν γινωμένων τὴν ἀταξίαν Usener τὰ γενόμενα
τῆς ἀταξίας (τὴν ἀταξίαν F) FP

Philolaus [says] that there is fire in the middle around the center which he calls the hearth of the whole and house of Zeus **and
mother of gods, altar, continuity, and measure of nature**.
And again another fire, the surrounding [fire] at the uppermost
[part of the cosmos]. The middle is first by nature, and around this
ten divine bodies dance: heaven, the planets, after them the sun,
under it the moon, under it the earth, under it the counter-earth,
after all of which the fire of the hearth holds its place about the
center. **Moreover, he calls the uppermost part of the surrounding, in which [he says] is the purity of the elements,
Olympus; the things under the orbit of Olympus, in which
the five planets with the sun and moon are ordered, cosmos;
the sublunar and earthly regions under these, in which are
the things of change-loving generation, heaven. He also says
that wisdom arises concerning the things ordered in the
heavens, and virtue concerning the disorder of coming to be.
The former is complete, but the latter incomplete.**

AUTHENTICITY

This testimonium is interesting for the way in which it combines elements
from the tradition which goes back to Philolaus' book with other elements
which derive from the pseudo-Philolaic works. Burkert (1972: 243–6) gives
clear and convincing arguments to show that the second half of the passage
envisages a cosmic order which is contradictory to the system described in
the first half. Further, since the first half is in agreement with Aristotle's
reports of early Pythagoreanism and therefore genuine, it is the second half
that must be rejected. However, even in the first half of the report elements
of the later tradition have been introduced in the enumeration of the names
assigned to the central fire.

(1) Aetius' list of the names is far more extensive than is found in any
other ancient source. The earliest testimonia show that only the first two
names on Aetius' list (hearth, house of Zeus) can with any probability be
referred back to Philolaus. F7 of Philolaus, which has been shown to be
genuine, refers to a hearth in the center of the sphere of the cosmos.
Aristotle reports that the Pythagoreans thought that the center, as the most
important part of the universe, ought to be guarded, and hence called it

396

"the guard-post of Zeus" (*De caelo* 293b2). Aristotle is amused by this fancy and says that the Pythagoreans need not be alarmed about the universe or call in a guard, at least not for the mathematical center of the universe which is not its true center. Simplicius in his commentary on this passage (511.26) reports that Aristotle in his special treatise on the Pythagoreans said that some people called the central fire the tower of Zeus and some the guard-post of Zeus. But Simplicius goes on to mention that a different source than Aristotle gave the name as the throne of Zeus. Elsewhere Simplicus says the Pythagoreans called the central fire hearth and tower of Zeus (*in Ph.* 1355. 8–9). Proclus gives the name as both tower of Zeus and guard-post of Zeus in several places (*in Euc.* 90.17–18; *in Ti.* 1.199.3 and 2.106.22). Thus, it is clear that early Pythagoreans associated the central fire with Zeus, although the exact name seems to have varied somewhat. Oddly enough Aetius' "house of Zeus" is not mentioned elsewhere, and it would appear to be a later trivialization of the more specific "guard-post of Zeus" (similarly Boeckh 1819: 96).

It is not possible to be sure, but the likeliest explanation of this connection between Zeus and the central fire is the one provided by the later tradition (Simpl. *in Ph.* 1355.8ff; Procl. *in Euc.* 90.14ff), i.e. that the center of the circle is, along with the circumference, what determines its structure and is thus the natural place to put the god who holds together the structure of the cosmos. At *Physics* 267b7 Aristotle himself identifies the center and the circumference as the "principles" of the circle, and argues that that which is continuously moved in the cosmos must be located at one of these points. Aristotle argues that the circumference is the place to locate the origin of the motion that governs the cosmos, but he implicitly recognizes the train of reasoning that would lead the Pythagoreans to place the controlling deity in the center.

The rest of the titles given to the central fire by Aetius are not paralleled elsewhere in the tradition, and there is good reason to regard them as later accretions. It is hard to see how the fire can be called mother of gods (Rhea) at the same time as it is tied to Zeus. But Proclus may be referring to a similar tradition when he reports that the Pythagoreans called the pole (of the cosmos) the seat of Rhea (*in Euc.* 90.14). It has been shown elsewhere that Rhea played an important role in Xenocrates' system and was identified with the dyad (see F20a). Thus it is tempting to see the reference to Rhea as indicating an alternative interpretation of the central fire that sprang up in the early Academy.

The last three titles in Aetius, "altar, continuity, and measure of nature," seem to be connected. Clearly Philolaus or other early Pythagoreans could have used the terms altar and measure, although their combination with nature is unparalleled. However, the biggest problem is with "continuity" (συνοχή), which first appears in philosophical usage in Aristotle and becomes common in later Greek philosophy, notably in Proclus and Damascius. Interestingly, Simplicius in his commentary on the *Physics* passage mentioned above (*in Ph.* 1355. 8–9), while explaining the Pythagorean association of the center with Zeus, talks of the center as suited to "the goodness of the demiurge which produces stability and *coherence* (συνηχικός)." Shortly afterwards he remarks that in Aristotle's system the motion of the fixed stars is the *measure* of other motions. These may be chance similarities to the epithets in Aetius, but they suggest how those epithets could have been generated out of commentary on an original Pythagorean epithet such as "guard-post of Zeus." Thus, in light of the very suspect use of συνοχή and the fact that they are not paralleled in the early testimonia, the last three epithets in Aetius should be regarded as later additions. That the doxographer should, after first mentioning Philolaus' name(s) for the central fire, go on to introduce a list of all the names which he has encountered in a variety of sources seems very plausible.

(2) The arguments against the authenticity of the second part of this testimonium are numerous and strong, and Philip's characterization of Burkert's rejection of it as "an arbitrary simplification" (1966: 118–19), without any attempt to respond to Burkert's arguments (or Heinze's [1965: 74.1]), is incredible. It is likewise hard to see how Guthrie (1962: 285) can blithely assert that the testimonia about Philolaus' astronomy, including this entire testimonium, "present a single coherent system." The first part of the testimonium describes a system with the central fire in the middle, around which move ten bodies, including the earth and the counter-earth. We are explicitly told that the center is "first by nature" and the central fire is assigned this honorific position, although another fire is located at the periphery of the world. Aristotle's reports about the central fire also make clear that the center of the cosmos was regarded as the highest-ranking position and, as was mentioned above, he teased them for wanting to "guard" it (*De caelo* 293a15ff). The second half of the testimonium, on the other hand, makes a sharp distinction between the perfection of the heavens which surround the universe and the earthly region with its lack of order at the center, a distinction which is prominent in Plato and Aristotle and the pseudo-Pythagorean writings (see Philolaus F21). This clearly presupposes a geocentric system, and cannot be made to fit with the center of the cosmos as a position of honor occupied by a central fire, as it was for the early Pythagoreans whom Aristotle describes. Boeckh (1819: 101–2) did away with the contradiction by suggesting that Philolaus only considered the earth and its atmosphere to be the realm of change and disorder – but what then becomes of the counter-earth and central fire? The most distinctive features of Philolaus' astronomical system would be left out of consider-

ation in what is clearly presented as an exhaustive threefold division of the universe. This serious contradiction between the two parts of the testimonium is enough to lead to the recognition that they cannot be part of a coherent system and, since the central fire system of the first half is attested by Aristotle as early Pythagorean, we have no choice but to regard the latter half as a later system fathered on Philolaus.

(3) The names themselves, which are given to the three divisions of the universe, are all perfectly possible for someone of Philolaus' date and there are contemporary and earlier parallels for the use of "Olympus" to refer to the outermost part of the heavens (Parm. F11; Hes. *Th.* 689; Hom. *Od.* 20.103, *Il.* 15.193; Emp. F44). However, the terminology of the second half is inconsistent both with the first half and with the terminology used in the genuine fragments of Philolaus. In the first half of the testimonium the outermost body which circles around the central fire (i.e. the fixed stars) is called "heaven" (οὐρανός), but in the second half of the fragment not only is the outermost part of the universe called Olympus, but "heaven" is oddly given as the name for the innermost region, the region around the earth. Diels tried to eliminate this contradiction by excising "heaven" from the text of the first half and replacing it with "the sphere of the fixed stars," but this is unjustified and will not do away with the more serious conceptual contradiction between the two parts of the testimonium. In Fragments 1–6 of Philolaus, which set out his basic metaphysical principles and whose authenticity is vouched for by agreement with Aristotle's reports on the early Pythagoreans, "cosmos" is consistently used to refer to the universe as a whole. Thus, in F1, which we are told is the first line of Philolaus' book, he refers to the whole cosmos and everything in it as fitted together out of limiters and unlimiteds. It would be very odd for Philolaus to have then gone on later in his book to give us a division such as is found in the later part of this testimonium, where "cosmos" has the very restricted sense of "planets, sun, and moon" and includes neither the fixed stars nor the earth.

In the *Epinomis* (977b) the heavens are praised as giving us knowledge of number, and people are urged to study them whether they call them Cosmos, Olympus, or Uranus ("heaven"). The use of just these three terms is at first sight striking, since they exactly parallel the names given to three parts of the cosmos in the second half of the testimonium about Philolaus. Some have thought that their use in the *Epinomis* shows that that dialogue presupposes the tripartite division, and hence that the division could go back to Philolaus (Zeller 1923: 548 n. 1). Closer examination shows that this is unjustified (see Heinze 1965: 74.1). The *Epinomis* passage treats the three names as synonymous and alludes to no division of the universe.

(4) The parallels for the details of the threefold division assigned to Philolaus in A16 are found in the early Academy, and all indications

suggest that such systems arose from interpretation of the *Timaeus* and were later projected back on to the early Pythagoreans (Adrastus in Theo 148.22; Anon. Phot. 439b17 = Thesleff 1965: 239.2; Xenocrates F5,15,18, and in Plutarch, *Quaest. Conviv.* 745a – see Heinze 1965: 75). The notion that the outermost part of the universe is "the purity of the elements" (εἰλικρίνεια τῶν στοιχείων) is paralleled in the Neoplatonic commentators on *Timaeus* 32b3ff (Proclus, *in Ti.* 2.43,44,49).

(5) Finally, some of the specific language of the last part of A16 is clearly impossible for Philolaus. Both Boeckh (1819: 100) and Zeller (1923: 548 n. 1) recognized this. They explained it away by maintaining that, although the language was later, it was being used to describe conceptions that go back to Philolaus in the later part of the fifth century. The phrase "change-loving generation" (φιλομεταβόλου γενέσεως) is very reminiscent of the distinction between the unchangeable and the changeable in the pseudo-Philolaic F21 (see especially μεταβάλλοντος γενατοῦ). φιλομετάβολος is late, first occurring in Sextus (*M.* 1.82).

Testimonium A17b

Aetius, 2.4.15 (332 Diels = Stobaeus, *Eclogae* 1.21.6d, 1.186 Wachsmuth) τὸ δὲ ἡγεμονικὸν ἐν τῷ μεσαιτάτῳ πυρί, ὅπερ τρόπεως δίκην προϋπεβάλετο τῆς τοῦ παντὸς ⟨σφαίρας⟩ ὁ δημιουργὸς θεός.

3 ⟨σφαίρας⟩ Diels τῆ ... ⟨σφαίρα⟩ Heeren

[Philolaus locates] what is controlling in the central fire, which the demiurgic god set down under the sphere of the whole like a keel.

AUTHENTICITY

This report is given by Stobaeus after an account of how Philolaus explained the nourishment of the world (A18). It is this context, along with the mention of the central fire, that shows that the report is in fact about Philolaus. It is clearly the case that much of the vocabulary in it is derived from later Greek philosophy (Burkert 1972: 246 n. 38; Boeckh 1819: 96ff; Wilamowitz 1920: 2.88). τὸ ἡγεμονικὸν "the controlling factor" is clearly Stoic and is probably derived from the rubric heading in the doxographers (i.e. "Where is the controlling factor located?"). Similarly, ὁ δημιουργὸς θεός ("the demiurgic god") is clearly Platonic and thus cannot belong to Philolaus (on δημιουργός see Classen 1962). Boeckh argued that, despite these intrusions, the central idea is Philolaic, as is, perhaps, the image of the central fire as a keel. However, it is hard to see how the image of the central fire as the keel of the universe makes sense unless a demiurge of some sort is assumed. The keel is the first thing the ship-builder constructs (for the image see Plato, *Lg.* 803a3–5), and to call the central fire the keel makes less sense if no builder is assumed. However, other than this report (and the surely spurious F21) we have no evidence that Philolaus invoked anything like a demiurge. Aristotle assigns no such view to the Pythagoreans. It seems most likely, then, that the image of the keel is also introduced by a commentator and that the whole testimonium is not so much a report of Philolaus' views as a description of the role of the central fire in terms of later philosophical conceptions. The only thing Philolaic about this report is the simple mention of the central fire. For the supposed image of the universe as a ship in Pythagoreanism see the commentary on F12.

6. FRAGMENTS ON SOUL

Fragment 14

Clement, *Stromata* 3.17 (2.203.11 Stählin) ἄξιον δὲ καὶ τῆς
Φιλολάου λέξεως μνημονεῦσαι· λέγει ὁ Πυθαγόρειος ὧδε·
    μαρτυρέονται δὲ καὶ οἱ παλαιοὶ θεολόγοι τε καὶ μάντιες, ὡς διά
τινας τιμωρίας ἁ ψυχὰ τῷ σώματι συνέζευκται καὶ καθάπερ ἐν
5 σάματι τούτῳ τέθαπται.

It is worth mentioning the text of Philolaus as well. The Pythagorean
says the following:
    The ancient theologians and seers also give witness that on
account of certain penalties the soul is yoked to the body and is
buried in it as in a tomb.

Compare:

Plato, *Gorgias* 493a1-3 ἤδη γάρ του ἔγωγε καὶ ἤκουσα τῶν
σοφῶν, ὡς νῦν ἡμεῖς τέθναμεν καὶ τὸ μὲν σῶμά ἐστιν ἡμῖν σῆμα...

Once I also heard from one of the wise that we are now dead and
that the body is our tomb...

Plato, *Cratylus* 400c1-7 καὶ γὰρ σῆμά τινές φασιν αὐτὸ [σῶμα]
εἶναι τῆς ψυχῆς, ὡς τεθαμμένης ἐν τῷ νῦν παρόντι... δοκοῦσι
μέντοι μοι μάλιστα θέσθαι οἱ ἀμφὶ 'Ορφέα τοῦτο τὸ ὄνομα ὡς
δίκην διδούσης τῆς ψυχῆς ὧν δὴ ἕνεκα δίδωσιν, τοῦτον δὲ
περίβολον ἔχειν, ἵνα σῴζηται, δεσμωτηρίου εἰκόνα...

For some say that it [the body] is a tomb [σῆμα, a play on σῶμα,
"body"] of the soul which is conceived of as buried in our present
life... However, it seems to me that the Orphics most of all adopted

402

this name since they thought that the soul was paying a penalty for what it had done and that it has this covering [i.e. the body] so that it would be kept secure [σώζηται, a play on σῶμα, "body"], just as in a prison.

Athenaeus 4.157c   Εὐξίθεος ὁ Πυθαγορικός... ὥς φησι Κλέαρχος ὁ Περιπατητικὸς ἐν δευτέρῳ Βίων ἔλεγεν ἐνδεδέσθαι τῷ σώματι καὶ τῷ δεῦρο βίῳ τὰς ἁπάντων ψυχὰς τιμωρίας χάριν, καὶ διείπασθαι τὸν θεὸν ὡς εἰ μὴ μενοῦσιν ἐπὶ τούτοις ἕως ἂν ἑκὼν
5   αὐτοὺς λύσῃ, πλείοσι καὶ μείζοσι ἐμπεσοῦνται τότε λύμαις. διὸ πάντας εὐλαβουμένους τὴν τῶν κυρίων ἀνάτασιν φοβεῖσθαι τοῦ ζῆν ἑκόντας ἐκβῆναι μόνον τε τὸν ἐν τῷ γήρᾳ θάνατον ἀσπασίως προσίεσθαι, πεπεισμένους τὴν ἀπόλυσιν τῆς ψυχῆς μετὰ τῆς τῶν κυρίων γίγνεσθαι γνώμης.

Euxitheus the Pythagorean ... as Clearchus the Peripatetic says in the second book of his *Lives*, used to say that all souls were bound to the body and the life in this world in order to be punished, and that god decreed that if they do not remain here until he willingly frees them, they will meet with more and greater torments. Therefore everyone, keeping in mind this threat of the divine, is afraid to leave life of their own accord and only welcomes death in old age, convinced that this release of the soul is in accord with divine will.

Aristotle F60 = Iamblichus, *Protrepticus* 8 (47.21 Pistelli)   τίς ἂν οὖν εἰς ταῦτα βλέπων οἴοιτο εὐδαίμων εἶναι καὶ μακάριος, οἳ πρῶτον εὐθὺς φύσει συνέσταμεν, καθάπερ φασὶν οἱ τὰς τελετὰς λέγοντες, ὥσπερ ἂν ἐπὶ τιμωρίᾳ πάντες; τοῦτο γὰρ θείως οἱ
5   ἀρχαιότεροι λέγουσι τὸ φάναι διδόναι τὴν ψυχὴν τιμωρίαν καὶ ζῆν ἡμᾶς ἐπὶ κολάσει μεγάλων τινῶν ἁμαρτημάτων. πάνυ γὰρ ἡ σύζευξις τοιούτῳ τινὶ ἔοικε πρὸς τὸ σῶμα τῆς ψυχῆς. ὥσπερ γὰρ τοὺς ἐν τῇ Τυρρηνίᾳ φασὶ βασανίζειν πολλάκις τοὺς ἁλισκομένους, προσδεσμεύοντας κατ' ἀντικρὺ τοῖς ζῶσι νεκρούς, ἀντιπροσώπους
10   ἕκαστον πρὸς ἕκαστον μέρος προσαρμόττοντας. οὕτως ἔοικεν ἡ ψυχὴ διατετάσθαι καὶ προσκεκολλῆσθαι πᾶσι τοῖς αἰσθητικοῖς τοῦ σώματος μέλεσιν.

Who, then in light of this [the transitory nature of human affairs], would suppose that he is happy or blessed? Right from the beginning we were all constituted by nature for punishment, as they say in the initiation rights. For it is an inspired saying of the ancients that the soul is undergoing punishment and that our life is chastisement for great sins. For the yoking of the soul to the body is very like something of this sort. For just as they say that the Etruscans often tortured captives by binding corpses face to face with the living, matching each part to each part, so the soul seems to have been stretched through the body and fastened to all the sensory organs of the body.

AUTHENTICITY

The best discussions of this fragment are found in Burkert (1972: 248), Wilamowitz (1920: 2.90), Frank (1923: 301), and Bywater (1868: 49), all of whom consider the fragment spurious. I regard the fragment as spurious, but for different reasons than those given by other scholars. It is quoted by Clement immediately after a quotation of the passage from the *Cratylus* given above.

(1) This fragment differs from many others whose authenticity has been attacked in that it does not contain any doctrines that are peculiarly Platonic or Aristotelian. Indeed, as the parallel passages from Plato and Aristotle show, all the doctrines mentioned in it are perfectly possible for Philolaus' lifetime. Thus, if it is a forgery, the motive must be something other than an attempt to claim that Philolaus anticipated Platonic and Aristotelian doctrines, although it could have been part of a larger work which as a whole had that goal. Nonetheless, scholars have thought that the similarity with the Platonic and Aristotelian passages suggests that the Philolaus fragment was forged with those passages in mind. Burkert thinks that the similarities with Aristotle's *Protrepticus* are particularly damning. However, despite some clear similarities in general conception, the only word actually shared between Aristotle and "Philolaus" is σύζευξις/συνέζευκται (yoking/yoked), and Aristotle does not even mention the σῶμα/σῆμα (body/tomb) equation which is central in Philolaus. This equation does occur in both Plato's *Gorgias* and *Cratylus*, but of course this does nothing to prove that the Philolaus passage is a forgery, because the use of precisely these words is dictated by the etymological play. The precise combination of ideas found in F14 (body as tomb and this life as punishment) is not clearly paralleled in the other passages. However, I suggest that the similarities between these passages are just what we would expect from four different authors all describing the same point of view held by earlier thinkers, and there is no basis in the wording of the passages to conclude that one is based on the others.

One important connection that is made in the passage ascribed to Euxitheus is the tie between the view of this life as punishment for the soul and the prohibition on suicide as an attempt to avoid our divinely ordained penalty. This even suggests an argument for the authenticity of the Philolaus fragment. One thing we know for sure about Philolaus from Plato's *Phaedo* is that he preached a ban on suicide. F14 with its emphasis on this life as punishment for the soul would serve very well, then, as a basis for the ban on suicide for which we know Philolaus to have argued. But other features of F14 show that it is spurious.

(2) A second set of arguments that have been given against the authenticity of the fragment are based on its vocabulary and style. In vocabulary most doubts have been raised about the use of the word θεολόγοι. θεολογία is first attested at Plato, *R.* 379a, but Vlastos (1952: 102 n. 22) has shown that this passage does not at all suggest that Plato is coining a new term, but rather the opposite, since it is not marked in any way as unusual and is introduced by Adeimantus and not Socrates. Vlastos also points out that similar formations, like μετεωρολόγος, φυσιολόγος and μυθολόγος are common and Empedocles (F131) uses the phrase ἀμφὶ θεῶν λόγος. Wilamowitz felt that the style was not archaic, and Frank said that under some surface Doricisms there was an Attic clarity of style that belongs to a Platonist and not a Pythagorean of Philolaus' date. It is true that F14 has a clear style which is at odds with the more tortured structure of F2 and 6. However, it is simply too short, and our evidence for Philolaus' style is too meagre to be confident that it could not have been written by Philolaus.

(3) Since the equation of the body with a tomb is shown by the Platonic passages not to be Orphic, it is usually assumed to be Pythagorean. If this is so, the form of F14 is odd in that it would seem to refer to early Pythagoreans and Pythagoras himself as "ancient theologians and seers." Such language might be appropriate for Plato, who was not a member of any Pythagorean society, but seems awkward for someone who is a Pythagorean, as it suggests that the author looks on the view as in some sense removed from himself. Still we do not really know how a Pythagorean of Philolaus' age saw himself in relation to early Pythagoreans. He might have seen himself as an independent thinker in the tradition. The adjective "ancient" (παλαιοί) can have the connotation of extreme old age and is usually used this way in Plato, but it also can mean something like "of old," and could be applied by Philolaus to Pythagoras, who lived seventy years earlier (see Eur. *Alc.* 212).

(4) The greatest barrier to accepting the fragment as authentic is the way in which the word ψυχά (soul) is used, for it is clearly used, as it is in Plato, as a comprehensive term embracing all the psychological faculties. We might suppose that Philolaus had anticipated this usage except that in F13

it is used in a much narrower sense as one among many psychological facul-ties, and meaning something like "life." Indeed, this is one of the strongest reasons for accepting F13 as authentic, since it is hard to conceive of a forger writing after Plato using the word in this restricted sense. Thus, it seems very unlikely that F14 can be genuine as well. This argument still has force even if the views ascribed to the ancient theologians are not those of Philolaus himself, since what is at issue is his own use of the word ψυχή. Whether he is using it to describe his own views or those of others is irrelevant.

Fragment 15

Athenagoras, *Legatio* 6 καὶ Φιλόλαος δὲ **ὥσπερ ἐν φρουρᾷ** πάντα ὑπὸ τοῦ θεοῦ περιειλῆφθαι λέγων καὶ τὸ ἕνα εἶναι καὶ τὸ ἀνωτέρω τῆς ὕλης δεικνύει.

And Philolaus, in saying that all things are encompassed by god **as if in a prison**, shows that he is both one and also above matter.

Plato, *Phaedo* 61d6–10 τί δέ, ὦ Κέβης; οὐκ ἀκηκόατε σύ τε καὶ Σιμμίας περὶ τῶν τοιούτων [the prohibition against suicide] Φιλολάῳ συγγεγονότες; – Οὐδέν γε σαφές, ὦ Σώκρατες. – Ἀλλὰ μὴν καὶ ἐγὼ ἐξ ἀκοῆς περὶ αὐτῶν λέγω. ἃ μὲν οὖν τυγχάνω
5 ἀκηκοὼς φθόνος οὐδεὶς λέγειν... (61e6) ἤδη γὰρ ἔγωγε [Cebes speaking], ὅπερ νυνδὴ σὺ ἤρου, καὶ Φιλολάου ἤκουσα, ὅτε παρ' ἡμῖν διῃτᾶτο, ἤδη δὲ καὶ ἄλλων τινῶν, ὡς οὐ δέοι τοῦτο ποιεῖν· σαφὲς δὲ περὶ αὐτῶν οὐδενὸς πώποτε οὐδὲν ἀκήκοα... (62b2) [Socrates speaking] ὁ μὲν οὖν ἐν ἀπορρήτοις λεγόμενος περὶ
10 αὐτῶν λόγος, ὡς ἔν τινι φρουρᾷ ἐσμεν οἱ ἄνθρωποι καὶ οὐ δεῖ δὴ ἑαυτὸν ἐκ ταύτης λύειν οὐδ' ἀποδιδράσκειν, μέγας τέ τίς μοι φαίνεται καὶ οὐ ῥᾴδιος διϊδεῖν. οὐ μέντοι ἀλλὰ τόδε γέ μοι δοκεῖ, ὦ Κέβης, εὖ λέγεσθαι τὸ θεοὺς εἶναι ἡμῶν τοὺς ἐπιμελουμένους καὶ ἡμᾶς τοὺς ἀνθρώπους ἓν τῶν κτημάτων τοῖς θεοῖς εἶναι.

What, Cebes? Have you and Simmias not heard about such things [the prohibition against suicide] in your association with Philolaus? – Nothing definite, at least, Socrates. – But even I speak only what I have heard about them. However, what I happen to have heard I do not mind telling...

For I [Cebes speaking], to answer the question you just asked, have already heard, both from Philolaus, when he was spending time with us [in Thebes], and earlier also from some others, that it is not right to do this. But I have never yet heard anything definite about it from anyone... [Socrates speaking] What is said in the mysteries about these things, that we men are in some prison, as it were, and it is not right to release oneself from this nor to run away, seems to me to be something grand and not easy to see into. Nonetheless, this, at least, seems to me to be well said, Cebes, that the gods care about us and that we men are one of the possessions of the gods.

AUTHENTICITY

In order to understand the extent and nature of this fragment it is important to get clear about the context in Athenagoras. In *The Embassy for the Christians* (c. 177) Athenagoras is defending Christians against three charges, the first of which is atheism. In sections four and five Athenagoras suggests that this charge has arisen because Christians say that God is one and that God is a distinct being from matter and completely separated from it. He then shows that these doctrines have been held by ancient poets and philosophers without their incurring the charge of atheism. Philolaus is the first philosopher mentioned, and is followed by mention of the Pythagoreans Lysis and Opsimus before Plato and Aristotle are introduced.

Consideration of the Philolaus fragment in this light shows that it is very likely that the statement that "...he shows that he is both one and also above matter" is Athenagoras' own language, since this is the language he has used in section four earlier to describe Christian doctrine (ἡμῖν [Christians] διαιροῦσιν ἀπὸ τῆς ὕλης τὸν θεόν, καὶ δεικνύουσιν ἕτερον μέν τι εἶναι τὴν ὕλην ἄλλο δὲ θεόν... ἐπεὶ δὲ ὁ λόγος ἡμῶν ἕνα θεὸν ἄγει τὸν τοῦδε τοῦ παντὸς ποιητήν...). Thus the only part that can be Philolaus' own words is the statement that "...all things are encompassed by God as if in a prison." Even there the parallel with the *Phaedo* passage suggests that it may be only the expression "as if in a prison" that is being ascribed to "Philolaus." Now that the context of the fragment in Athenagoras is clear, the following points need to be made:

(1) If all that is being ascribed to Philolaus in F15 is the image of the prison (φρουρά – for this translation see Strachan 1970), it becomes doubtful whether it is based on any part of a book by Philolaus. It is more likely to be derived from a reading of the *Phaedo* either by Athenagoras himself or by his source. It is true that the *Phaedo* only talks of human beings as in a

prison, but the switch to "all things" being in a prison would be easy in the course of the tradition.

(2) Although Athenagoras thus appears to have read the *Phaedo* as saying that Philolaus used the image of the prison for our life on earth, it still remains a question as to whether this is a good reading. Does the *Phaedo* passage really give us warrant to say that Philolaus used the image of human life as a prison as the basis for his argument against suicide? The text does not allow us to be absolutely sure about this, but close reading of it shows, so I believe, that Plato, at least, is not ascribing such a view to Philolaus.

The name of Philolaus is introduced when Cebes asks for an explanation of the prohibition against suicide. Socrates is surprised that Cebes had not heard an explanation of these matters from Philolaus, but Cebes says that he has heard "nothing definite." Socrates then points out that he himself only speaks about them from hearsay, but that he will not mind telling what he has heard. This in no way suggests that what Socrates will report from hearsay is derived from Philolaus. The opposite is rather implied, since there is no hint that Socrates himself has even met Philolaus. His whole tone is of one who expects (with typical irony) to be informed by them, since they have had contact with Philolaus as he has not.

Cebes then asks again for clarification of the reasons for the prohibition against suicide, admitting that he has heard that suicide is wrong both from Philolaus and others, but repeating that he has not yet heard anything definitive on the topic from anyone. Socrates tells him to be of good hope as perhaps some day he will hear such an explanation. Socrates then suggests that perhaps there is some reason to the prohibition and refers to the story told about suicide "in mysteries" (ἐν ἀπορρήτοις), which is where the idea of life as a prison and human beings as possessions of the gods is introduced.

I submit that there is absolutely no connection made between Philolaus and the story that is told "in mysteries" here. If it is Philolaus' doctrine, Plato has done an amazing job of submerging that fact in his presentation. Cebes is called on as the one knowledgeable on Philolaus, and when he says he has heard nothing definite on the topic from Philolaus, there is no hint that Socrates is going on to tell us what Philolaus thought. Rather, the clear implication is that he is going to report what he knows of by hearsay as an explanation of the prohibition on suicide. When he presents that hearsay account he presents it as what is said in the mysteries. Guthrie (1962: 162) would have us believe "what is said in mysteries" refers to "the well known reticence of the Pythagoreans," but it is much more likely that the mystery religions and in particular the Orphics are meant (see

Xenocrates F20). Furthermore, the whole passage contradicts the notion of Pythagorean reticence. Socrates clearly expects that Cebes and Simmias have heard teachings of Philolaus and would be free to tell them, if he had said anything definite on the topic.

(3) This is perhaps the best place to discuss one other aspect of the presentation of Philolaus in the *Phaedo*. On the basis of the fact that Cebes asserts that he has heard "nothing definite" (οὐδὲν σαφές) from Philolaus on the reasons for the prohibition of suicide, some scholars have concluded that Philolaus was a muddled thinker (see especially van der Waerden 1979: 385–7, who labels Philolaus a "Wirrkopf" partially on this basis). While there is no way to turn the passage into a great compliment to Philolaus' philosophical acumen, to take it as the basis for writing Philolaus off as a dunce is an incredible overreading.

First, what does the expression οὐδὲν σαφές mean for Plato? Both Burnet (1911: on *Phd.* 57b1 and 61b8) and Adam (1902: on *R* 511c) point out that the translation "clear" does not capture the full force of σαφές. For Plato the adjective implies that an account is not just clearly expressed, but "definite" (Gallop) or "certain" (Burnet) in that it gives a sure or trustworthy (in a philosophical sense) explanation of something. In the *Republic* the levels of the divided line are distinguished σαφηνείᾳ καὶ ἀσαφείᾳ (509d9) and in the *Philebus* Plato joins τὸ σαφές with τἀκριβές and τἀληθέστατον in describing the highest art, so that Adam concludes that it often approaches the sense of "true." In light of this, what Cebes seems to mean is that he has not heard from Philolaus an account of the prohibition against suicide which he finds philosophically sound (see also *Gorgias* 451e1). Olympiodorus in the scholia to the *Phaedo* passage (DK A1a) thinks that the remark in the *Phaedo* is a reference to Pythagorean teaching through riddles (δι' αἰνιγμάτων), but given the wide use of the phrase elsewhere in Plato to mean "nothing definite," this is also an overreading that would need to be supported by some reference in the text to riddles.

With this understanding of οὐδὲν σαφές in mind, it can be seen that there are two primary ways of reading the remark. First, Plato could be indicating that he did not find Philolaus' account of the reasons for the prohibition on suicide philosophically sound. If this is so, Philolaus obviously had a lot of company, since Cebes says that he has never heard anything definite from anyone else either, and Socrates' remark that he should "remain hopeful" suggests that in Plato's mind no one has given such an account. Certainly no philosophically definite account of the prohibition is given in the *Phaedo* and doubtless Plato considers the Orphic story of life as a prison sentence given by god as still something that is οὐδὲν σαφές. The other way of reading the passage is that Cebes heard nothing definite, not because of any failure in Philolaus' account, but because of his own inability to understand. The tone of mock surprise in Socrates' question to Cebes could just as well be a joke at Cebes' expense as at Philolaus'.

Fragment 22

Claudianus Mamertus 2.3 (105.5 Engelbrecht) Pythagorae igitur, quia nihil ipse scriptitaverat, a posteris quaerenda sententia est. in quibus vel potissimum floruisse Philolaum reperio Tarentinum, qui multis voluminibus de intellegendis
5 rebus et quid quaeque significent oppido obscure dissertans, priusquam de animae substantia decernat, de mensuris ponderibus et numeris iuxta geometricam musicam atque arithmeticam mirifice disputat per haec omne universum exstitisse confirmans, illi videlicet scripturae consentiens, qua deo dicitur:
10 mensura pondere et numero omnia disposuisti...
   2.7 (120.12 Engelbrecht) nunc ad Philolaum redeo, a quo dudum magno intervallo digressus sum, qui in tertio voluminum, quae περὶ ῥυθμῶν καὶ μέτρων praenotat, de anima humana sic loquitur:
15 anima inditur corpori per numerum et immortalem eandemque incorporalem convenientiam. item post alia: diligitur corpus ab anima, quia sine eo non potest uti sensibus. a quo postquam morte deducta est, agit in mundo incorporalem vitam.
   non ego nunc rationum tramitem et nexuosissimas quaes-
20 tionum minutias revolvo, quibus haec probabilia quo voles adversante Philolaus efficit. in quae si quis vel curiositate vel studio forte flagraverit, de ipso scilicet fonte hauriet.

13 ΠΕΡΙ ΑΡΙΘΜΩΝ ΚΑΙ ΜΕΤΡΟΥ G

2.3 The opinion of Pythagoras must be sought from his successors, since he himself wrote nothing. Among these I find that Philolaus of Tarentum was the very most distinguished. Teaching very obscurely in many volumes about understanding reality and what each thing signifies before he gives a pronouncement about the substance of the soul, he discusses in a marvelous way measures, weights, and numbers along with geometry, music, and arithmetic, confirming that the whole universe has come into existence through these. He clearly agrees with the scripture in which it is said of God: "You have arranged all things by measure, weight, and number [*Wisdom of Solomon* 11.21].

2.7 Now I return to Philolaus, from whom I have now digressed a great deal. In the third volume, which he titles *On Rhythms and Measures*, he speaks in the following way about the soul:

The soul is put into the body through number and a harmony that is immortal and at the same time incorporeal. And a little later: The body is loved by the soul because without it, it is not able to use the senses. After it has been drawn out of it at death, it lives an incorporeal life in the world.

I do not now repeat the course of the reasoning and the involved details of the investigations by which Philolaus makes these things credible, no matter who the opponent is. If anyone is inflamed with regard to these matters by curiosity or zeal, he will undoubtedly draw from the source itself.

AUTHENTICITY

Claudianus Mamertus' report presents a number of puzzles concerning both the evidence he gives about Philolaus' writings and also the contents of the fragment that he quotes. The goal of Claudianus' book (*De statu animae* – 5th century AD) is to show that the soul is immaterial. While Claudianus is a Christian, he cites Philolaus, Archytas, Plato and others as pagan support for this doctrine. The most detailed discussion is to be found in Bömer (1936: 143–54), but see also Guthrie (1962: 311–12), Burkert (1972: 247), and Gomperz (1932: 156). Burkert regards the fragment as spurious as does DK, but Guthrie, while having doubts about the wording of the fragment, takes it as presenting views that are possible for Philolaus.

(1) The first problems for authenticity have to do with the sources which Claudianus seems to have used for his citation of Philolaus. He refers to Philolaus as having written many volumes, although the best evidence we have suggests that Philolaus only wrote one short book (see the introduction). Second, he cites the fragments as coming from the third of Philolaus' many volumes and says that the title of the volume was *On Rhythms and Measures*, a title which is unattested elsewhere. All of this certainly makes it look as if Claudianus is using a collection of Philolaus' works that included a number of spurious writings. This is not surprising since we have fragments from these forgeries, and most of the Pythagorean forgeries are likely to have been completed long before the fifth century AD. Furthermore, that Claudianus' source was clearly influenced by pseudo-Pythagorean writings

is shown by the fact that he quotes a spurious fragment of Archytas immediately after quoting Philolaus (2.7 [121.5 Engelbrecht]). It is, of course, still possible that one of the works that Claudianus had access to was the single genuine book of Philolaus, but clearly it was mixed in with spurious works as well, and the fragments that Claudianus reports must be subjected to careful scrutiny.

(2) What connections are there between F22 and fragments which are likely to be genuine? It is noteworthy that there is no mention of limiters and unlimiteds, but the fragment does give an important role to number, and most importantly focuses on *harmonia* which is a central topic in Fragments 1–7. However, a focus on harmony is common to both the genuine book of Philolaus and the forged Pythagorean writings, so that its presence is hardly decisive. However, the use of *anima* (ψυχή) in the fragment does not jibe very well with its use in F13. There it was used in a sense very close to "life," while here in F22 it clearly indicates the soul as the seat of all psychic activity. This in itself is a strong reason to doubt the authenticity of the fragment.

(3) The idea that the soul is put into the body through number and harmony sounds plausible for Philolaus, but the description of that harmony as "immortal and incorporeal" is problematic. No such honorific titles are assigned to harmony when it is discussed in F6. The tone of Fragments 1–7 rather suggests that harmonies do come into being and pass away than that they are immortal. Of course it could be that it is only the harmony that establishes the soul in the body that is immortal. But since its function is precisely *to join* soul and body, should it not in fact perish when the soul is separated from the body? At any rate the adjectives "immortal and incorporeal" are reminiscent of the hymnic quality of the pseudo-Pythagorean literature and the spurious F11 and F21 of Philolaus.

The most controversy has centered upon the use of the word "incorporeal" (ἀσώματος) to describe the soul. Aristotle's testimony about the early Pythagoreans (e.g. *Metaph.* 987b28) indicates that they did not distinguish grades of being and thus, for example, did not assign separate reality to numbers as Plato did (Burkert 1972: 32 n. 21). This suggests that it is unlikely that they recognized any sort of existence other than corporeal existence, and hence that Philolaus could not have used the word ἀσώματος. The word is not found in the fragments of the Presocratics, although later commentators starting with Aristotle use it to describe e.g. Xenophanes' god or Melissus' being.

More significantly, the word is used in Plato's *Phaedo*. One of Socrates' arguments for the immortality of the soul is based on the affinity the soul has with what is divine, intelligible, and unvarying, in contrast to the body which is said to have affinity with what is human, non-intelligible, and never constant. At *Phaedo* 85e3ff Simmias, who has been identified earlier in the dialogue as having heard the teaching of Philolaus, is sceptical of Socrates' argument and responds by pointing out that someone might describe the harmony of a lyre as ἀόρατον καὶ ἀσώματον καὶ πάγκαλόν τι καὶ θεῖον ("invisible and incorporeal and something very fine and divine"), and thus as having affinity with the immortal. Yet, no one would want to say that the harmony continues to exist once the lyre is smashed, and in fact the physical lyre and strings seem to persist longer than the "divine and incorporeal harmony." Simmias then goes on to say that he suspects that Socrates realizes that a harmony of the hot and cold and dry and wet is what "we" take the soul to be. Here we have a description of a harmony that is incorporeal and which is idenfitied with the soul, just as in F22, given by someone identified as having close connection with Philolaus. This is enough for Gomperz to conclude that F22 is genuine and states the views of the historical Philolaus which Plato was drawing on when he put these words in Simmias' mouth. Further, he argues that ἀσώματος in F is used in a "pre-scientific" sense of "separate from the body," which also supports its authenticity.

But what is really proven by the undeniable similarity between what Simmias says in the *Phaedo* and the contents of F22? The first point to emphasize is that there is also an important distinction between the two passages. Simmias implies that he would accept a doctrine of the soul as a harmony of the four opposites that constitute the body, and that he regards such a harmony as something incorporeal and divine. However, the whole point of his introduction of the example of the incorporeal harmony is to argue that it is *not* immortal. So that Simmias' words in the *Phaedo* are in direct contradiction with the description of harmony as immortal in F22.

Burkert argues that the addition of "immortal" to "incorporeal" in the description of the harmony in F22 in fact shows that it was written in response to the *Phaedo*. The later forger recognizes, in the light of Socrates' further arguments in the *Phaedo,* that the soul cannot be the type of harmony that Simmias describes, and while maintaining the view that the soul is a harmony "corrects" it to emphasize that it is an immortal harmony, thus hoping to avoid the problems raised by Socrates.

(4) There is in fact considerable support for the idea that F22 was forged with the *Phaedo* and the commentaries on the *Phaedo* in mind. It is the most prominent place where Philolaus is mentioned in ancient literature, and would be a natural source for later forgers to draw upon. Moreover, there are two more significant parallels between the *Phaedo* and Claudianus' report. First, it is striking that Claudianus' emphasis on the obscurity and amazing nature of Philolaus' work is paralleled in the scholium on the *Phaedo* which derives from Olympiodorus (= DK A1a). In an attempt to

explain Cebes' comment that he had heard "nothing definite" (οὐδὲν σαφές) from Philolaus, the scholium asserts that "he taught through riddles (δι' αἰνιγμάτων), as was customary for them." Second, the noteworthy description of the soul in F22 as loving the body, because without it it cannot use the senses, is strikingly paralleled by Socrates' descripton of the soul of the sensualist as "loving" (ἐρῶσα) the body (*Phaedo* 81b).

The similarities between the *Phaedo* and F22 which are discussed above are such that it is hard to believe that these texts are independent of one another. Either F22 is from Philolaus' book and the similarities to the *Phaedo* represent Plato's borrowings from Philolaus, or F22 is from a work forged in Philolaus' name and largely based on the *Phaedo*. Guthrie supports the authenticity of the fragment on the grounds that nothing in its substance is unparalleled in pre-Aristotelian Pythagoreanism. However, even Guthrie admits (1962: 312 n. 4) that the use of ἀσώματος = *incorporalis* reflects the language of a later period. But when this is admitted, what is meant by saying that the fragment is authentic? Is it that it presents the "thought" of Philolaus in later dress? This is very problematic since the language used to convey an idea is clearly integral to the thought conveyed. If all that is meant is that the fragment gives a prominent role to harmony and number, as we know Philolaus did, this is true of a multitude of pseudo-Pythagorean writings. In this vague sense much of the later forgeries can be said to preserve some of the substance of early Pythagoreanism, but this is not the issue here. The issue is whether the fragment that Claudianus presents as a verbatim quotation of Philolaus, albeit translated into Latin, can be regarded as from the genuine book of Philolaus. The usage of the terms ψυχή = *anima*, and ἀσώματος, show that it cannot be.

If we were to suppose the fragment genuine, it would mean that much of Socrates' argument for the immortality of the soul on the grounds of its affinity to what is divine and changeless (78b4–84b8) was drawn from Philolaus, including the specific phrase that describes the souls of the sensualists as loving the body. At the same time the doctrine of soul as harmony presented by Simmias will have to be seen as influenced by Philolaus' language describing the soul as put into the body through an incorporeal harmony. Thus, Plato will have drawn on Philolaus to support points presented both by his putative pupil Simmias and by Socrates. All of this seems very hard to swallow, and it is much more plausible to believe that a later enthusiast for Pythagoreanism, in his zeal to produce information on Philolaus and defend his honor, borrowed from the *Phaedo* in this haphazard way.

7. MISCELLANEOUS FRAGMENTS AND TESTIMONIA

Fragment 9

Iamblichus, *in Nic.* 19.21 ἑτέρου γὰρ καιροῦ διερευνᾶν ἐπὶ πλέον πῶς καὶ τετραγωνισθέντος ἀπὸ τῆς στιχηδὸν ἐκθέσεως τοῦ ἀριθμοῦ οὐκ ἐλάττονα πιθανὰ ἐπισυμβαίνει **φύσει καὶ οὐ νόμῳ**, ὥς φησί που Φιλόλαος.

It belongs to another time to investigate further the no less impressive things that result **by nature and not by custom**, as Philolaus says somewhere, when the numbers leading up to a square number are set out in sequence.

AUTHENTICITY

Iamblichus has been commenting on Nicomachus 1.8, which says that each number is half of the sum of the two numbers on either side of it (e.g. 4 = half of 3 + 5). He then digresses (16.11–20.6) to discuss the way in which the number 5 embodies justice. 5 is considered as the middle term if we set out in a series the numbers leading up to 9 (ἐκτεθέντων γὰρ στιχηδὸν τῶν ἀπὸ μονάδος μέχρις ἐννεάδος ἀριθμῶν – 16.18–20), the first square number that is odd. Numbers above 5 are seen as having more than their share and committing injustice, and those less than 5 as being deficient and treated unjustly. Towards the end of this digression Iamblichus says that he will put off to another time further investigation of "the impressive things that result, by nature and not by convention, as Philolaus says somewhere, when the numbers leading up to a square number are set out in sequence." Since everything else in this sentence refers back to language used by Iamblichus in the preceding pages, it is clear that only the phrase "by nature and not by convention" is being assigned to Philolaus. Further, the addition of που ("somewhere") makes it sound very much as if Iamblichus is simply quoting from memory.

The use of the distinction between nature and convention seems perfectly plausible for Philolaus in the second half of the fifth century, since it is reflected in the literature of the time, such as Aristophanes' *Clouds,* and Burkert accordingly (1972: 267) regards F9 as authentic. However, the idea that the properties of number are natural and not conventional would fit well in a hymn to number such as we find in the spurious F11. When dealing with such a brief statement it is impossible to be confident of its authenticity or spuriousness. Moreover, such a phrase, when considered independently of any context, tells us virtually nothing about Philolaus' philosophy.

Fragment 10

A Nicomachus, *Arithmetica introductio* 2.19 (115.2 Hoche) ἁρμονία δὲ πάντως ἐξ ἐναντίων γίνεται· **ἔστι γὰρ ἁρμονία πολυμιγέων ἕνωσις καὶ δίχα φρονεόντων συμφρόνησις.**

3 σύμφρασις GP συμφρόνασις CΓ συμφρόνησις SH

A Harmony in every way arises out of opposites. **For harmony is the unification of what is a mixture of many ingredients and the agreement of the disagreeing**.

B Theo Smyrnaeus 12.10 καὶ οἱ Πυθαγορικοὶ δὲ, οἷς πολλαχῇ ἕπεται Πλάτων, τὴν μουσικήν φασιν ἐναντίων συναρμογὴν καὶ τῶν πολλῶν ἕνωσιν καὶ τῶν δίχα φρονούντων συμφρόνησιν.

B And the Pythagoreans, whom Plato follows in many ways, say that music is the combination of opposites, a unification of many things, and the agreement of the disagreeing.

AUTHENTICITY

This fragment is not attributed to Philolaus by Nicomachus or Theon (or by any ancient authority), and Burkert (1972: 249) is right to say that there is no reason to do so. Boeckh (1819: 61) suggests that it should be ascribed to Philolaus, but gives no compelling reasons. It is true that just a few lines before this Nicomachus (114.13) quotes the first line of F2 of Philolaus. But there is no hint that he has turned back to Philolaus here.

Furthermore, the language and style of the definition suggest that it is a product of the pseudo-Pythagorean tradition. ἕνωσις does not occur

416

before Aristotle and is found only three times in the Aristotelian corpus (see *GC* 328b22). Moreover, it is found four times in the pseudo-Pythagorean texts collected by Thesleff (pseudo-Archytas 20.4, "Hippodamos" 99.17, 22, "Megillos" 115.21), usually in combination with a word for harmony. The rhetorical pairing of words with the same or opposite roots (πολυμιγέων – ἕνωσις, φρονεόντων – συμφρόνησις) is more suggestive of the high-flown style of the pseudo-Pythagorean writings, including the forged fragments of Philolaus (e.g. F21), than it is of the genuine fragments.

Fragment 19

Proclus, *in Euc.* 22.9 διὸ καὶ ὁ Πλάτων πολλὰ καὶ θαυμαστὰ δόγματα περὶ θεῶν διὰ τῶν μαθηματικῶν εἰδῶν ἡμᾶς ἀναδιδάσκει καὶ ἡ τῶν Πυθαγορείων φιλοσοφία παραπετάσμασι τούτοις χρωμένη τὴν μυσταγωγίαν κατακρύπτει τῶν θείων δογμάτων.
5 τοιοῦτος γὰρ καὶ ὁ Ἱερὸς σύμπας λόγος καὶ ὁ Φιλόλαος ἐν ταῖς Βάκχαις καὶ ὅλος ὁ τρόπος τῆς Πυθαγόρου περὶ θεῶν ὑφηγήσεως.

Hence, Plato teaches us anew many wonderful doctrines about the gods through mathematical forms, and the philosophy of the Pythagoreans using these as screens conceals the secret doctrine of their teachings about the gods. For, such is the whole *Sacred Discourse*, as is the *Bacchae* of Philolaus, and the whole manner of Pythagoras' instruction about gods.

AUTHENTICITY

This is, of course, not a fragment, but simply a reference to Philolaus. It is interesting for its reference to a book of Philolaus' called the *Bacchae* and for its characterization of the contents of that book. Proclus had just discussed the value of mathematics for philosophy in general and turned to consideration of the contribution it makes to the study of the various parts of philosophy. This application of mathematics to philosophy is part of the Pythagorization of the Neoplatonic tradition that was first developed in detail by Iamblichus (O'Meara 1989). Proclus considers mathematics' role in theology first, and the reference to Philolaus comes at the end of that paragraph. His characterization of the Pythagoreans as using mathematics to teach secret doctrine about the gods fits well with his general attitude towards them elsewhere. O'Meara (1989) has shown that, while Proclus regards Plato and the Pythagoreans as revealing the same truth, he tends to give Plato more credit than some Neoplatonists did, and sees him as more scientific than the Pythagoreans, who are presented as more mystical (O'Meara 1989: 148, etc.). This emphasis on Pythagorean mysticism is relevant to the evaluation of the likely contents of the book Proclus assigns to Philolaus, the *Bacchae*.

Stobaeus is the only other author to mention the *Bacchae*, and he lists two fragments under that title (F17 and F18), the latter of which is lost except for the heading. It is likely that F17 is genuine, so that we cannot easily say that this work was a later forgery. It is possible that Philolaus' book, which originally had no title or was known as Περὶ φύσεως (*On Nature*), was given this title in the later tradition. The other possibility is that the tradition about one genuine book is wrong and that Philolaus wrote other books including the *Bacchae*. However, the fragments from the *Bacchae* in Stobaeus deal with Philolaus' cosmology and astronomy, which surely must have been treated in Philolaus' book Περὶ φύσεως, so that it is hard to see the *Bacchae* as a separate book.

Since Proclus elsewhere gives us the information about Philolaus' dedication of certain angles to the gods (A14), that material may be what he is referring to when he talks about Philolaus using numbers as a screen to cover the mystic doctrine about the gods. If this is the case, since the material in A14 is unlikely to belong to Philolaus, it becomes more plausible to think of the *Bacchae* as a book forged in Philolaus' name (perhaps as early as the late fourth century BC – see the commentary on A14). Certainly the title would fit well a book that was devoted to giving mystic teaching about the gods. In that case what are we to do with the references to the *Bacchae* in Stobaeus, and in particular with F17, which on internal grounds appears to be genuine? It seems to me not impossible that the attribution of F17 to the *Bacchae* in Stobaeus is simply a mistake. It may be that Stobaeus was aware of a book called the *Bacchae*, that some of the spurious fragments which he preserves come from it, and that from some confusions F17 was assigned to it.

Testimonium A30

A Athenaeus Mechanicus 4.12 (Schneider 1912: 10) τουτὶ γὰρ ἄν τις ⟨εἰς⟩ πραγμάτων λόγον ὠφεληθεὶς ἀπέλθοι, ἐπιμελῶς ἐπιστήσας ἑαυτόν, ἐκ τοῦ Δελφικοῦ ἐκείνου παραγγέλματος ἢ ἐκ τῶν Στράτωνος καὶ Ἑστιαίου καὶ Ἀρχύτου καὶ Ἀριστοτέλους
5 καὶ τῶν ἄλλων τῶν παραπλήσια ἐκείνοις γεγραφότων. [The Byzantine paraphrase gives a different list of authors (Schneider

1912: 53):... Φιλολάου καὶ Ἀριστοτέλους Ἰσοκράτους τε καὶ Ἀριστοφάνους καὶ Ἀπολλωνίου ...]

A Therefore, for [the composition of] a treatise for practical use, someone would benefit more from giving close attention to the famous Delphic precept, than from the writings of Strato, Hestiaeus, Archytas, Aristotle, and all the others who have written similar works. [The Byzantine paraphrase gives a different list of authors: ... Philolaus, Aristotle, Isocrates, Aristophanes, and Apollonius ...]

B Theophylact of Ochrida, *Ep.* 71 (Migne *PG* 126, 493A–B)
πῶς δ' ἂν στρατιωτικὴν καὶ γεωμετρικὴν εἰς ταὐτὸ συνήγαγε καὶ
συνῆψε τὰ μακροῖς θριγγίοις ἔκπαλαι διειργόμενα μετ' Ἀρχύταν,
μετὰ Φιλόλαον, μετὰ τὸν Αἴλιον Ἀδριανόν, μετὰ τὸν ἔκπτωτον
5 ἡμῖν Ἰουλιανόν.

B How could he have united military science and geometry and joined together things long separated by great walls, following on Archytas, Philolaus, Aelius Hadrianus, and our banished Julianus?

AUTHENTICITY

These two Byzantine sources (the Byzantine paraphrase of Athenaeus and Theophylact [*c.* AD 1100]) both ascribe some sort of theoretical work on military science to Philolaus. Theophylact seems to be thinking of a work that combined the science of geometry with military matters (one thinks of the discussion of education in *Republic* 7), while Athenaeus (1st century BC?) was probably referring to a work on siege machinery, since that is the subject of his own work.

As Schneider notes (1912: 53), it would appear that the Byzantine excerptor replaced names which he did not recognize in the list of Athenaeus with other names that were better known to himself, even if they appear to make little sense as authors of treatises on siege machines. Thus we can have very little confidence that this report has its origin in anything other than the fact that Philolaus was a name venerated at the time the paraphrase was made. There is no good evidence that Philolaus ever had any practical experience as a military man (the reference to his attempt at tyranny in D.L. 8.84 is a mistake). The inclusion of Archytas' name on the list does make some sense, since he was a successful general at Tarentum (D.L. 8.79) and is known to have both written on mechanics (D.L. 8.79) and been interested in mechanical devices (A10). It is tempting to think that Philolaus comes to be mentioned in such contexts simply because he was regarded as the teacher of Archytas (A3), and hence was supposed to be a master on the topics in which his pupil excelled.

BIBLIOGRAPHY

Adam, J. (1902) *The Republic of Plato*, 2 vols. (Cambridge)

Annas, J. (1976) *Aristotle's Metaphysics Books M and N* (Oxford)

Barker, A. D. (1978) "Hoi kaloumenoi harmonikoi: the predecessors of Aristoxenus," *PCPS* n.s. 24: 1–21

(1984) *Greek Musical Writings*, vol. I: *The Musician and his Art* (Cambridge)

(1989) *Greek Musical Writings*, vol. II: *Harmonic and Acoustic Theory* (Cambridge)

Barnes, J. (1982) *The Presocratic Philosophers*, 2nd edn. (London)

Becker, O. (1957) *Zwei Untersuchungen zur antiken Logik* (Wiesbaden)

Boeckh, August (1819) *Philolaus des Pythagoreers Lehren nebst den Bruchstücken seines Werkes* (Berlin)

Bömer, F. (1936) *Der lateinische Neuplatonismus und Neupythagoreismus und Claudianus Mamertus in Sprache und Philosophie* (Leipzig)

Bouché-Leclercq, A. (1899) *L'Astrologie grecque* (Paris)

Boudouris, K. J. ed. (1989) *Ionian Philosophy* (Alimos and Athens)

Boyance, P. (1963) "Etudes Philoniennes," *REG* 76: 64–110

Burkert, W. (1961) "Hellenistische Pseudopythagorica," *Philologus* 105: 16–43, 226–46

(1972) *Lore and Science in Ancient Pythagoreanism*, tr. E. Minar (Cambridge, Mass.), 1st German edn. 1962

(1985) *Greek Religion*, tr. John Raffan (Cambridge, Mass.), 1st German edn. 1977

Burnet, J. (1911) *Plato's Phaedo* (Oxford)

(1915) "The Socratic doctrine of the soul," *Proceedings of the British Academy* 7: 235–59

(1948) *Early Greek Philosophy*, 4th edn. (London), 1st edn. 1892

Burns, A. (1964) "The fragments of Philolaus," *C & M* 25: 93–128

Burnyeat, M. F. (1978) "The philosophical sense of Theaetetus' mathematics," *Isis* 69: 489–513

(1987) "Platonism and mathematics: a prelude to discussion," in Graeser 1987: 213–40

Bywater, I. (1868) "On the fragments attributed to Philolaus the Pythagorean," *Journal of Philology* 1: 21–53

Calder, W. M. (1983) "Diogenes Laertius 3.6: Plato and Euripides," *AJP* 104: 287

Cameron, A. (1938) *The Pythagorean Background of the Theory of Recollection* (Menosha, Wis.)

Capelle, W. (1925) "Älteste Spuren der Astrologie bei den Griechen," *Hermes* 60: 373–95

Cassio, A. C. (1988) "Nicomachus of Gerasa and the dialect of Archytas, Fr. 1," *CQ* n.s. 38: 135–9

Casson, L. (1971) *Ships and Seamanship in the Ancient World* (Princeton)

Cherniss, H. (1935) *Aristotle's Criticism of Presocratic Philosophy* (Baltimore), repr. 1964 (New York)

(1957) *Plutarch's Moralia*, vol. 12: *Concerning the Face Which Appears in the Moon*, tr. with notes (Cambridge, Mass.)

(1959) Review of Saffrey, *Gnomon* 31: 36–51

(1976) *Plutarch's Moralia*, vol. 13:1, incl. *Platonic Questions* and *On the Generation of the Soul in the Timaeus*, tr. with notes (Cambridge, Mass.)

Classen, C. J. (1962) "The creator in Greek thought from Homer to Plato," *C & M* 23: 1–22

Claus, D. B. (1981) *Toward the Soul* (New Haven)

Coxon, A. H. (1986) *The Fragments of Parmenides* (Assen)

Delatte, A. (1915) Etudes sur la littérature pythagoricienne (Paris)

(1922) *La Vie de Pythagore de Diogène Laërce* (Brussels)

Denniston, J. D. (1954) *The Greek Particles*, 2nd edn. (Oxford)

Dicks, D. R. (1970) *Early Greek Astronomy to Aristotle* (Ithaca)

Diels, H. (1879) *Doxographi Graeci* (Berlin)

(1890) "Ein gefälschtes Pythagorasbuch," *AGP* 3: 451–72

(1893a) "Über die Excerpte von Menons *Iatrika* in dem Londoner Papyrus 137," *Hermes* 28: 407–34

(1893b) *Anonymi Londinensis ex Aristotelis Iatricis Menoniis et aliis medicis Eclogae*, *Supplementum Aristotelicum* 3.1 (Berlin)

Dillon, J. (1973) *Iamblichi Chalcidensis in Platonis dialogos commentariorum fragmenta* (Leiden)

(1977) *The Middle Platonists* (London)

(1985) "Xenocrates' Metaphysics: Fr. 15 (Heinze) reexamined," *Ancient Philosophy* 5: 47–52

Dodds, E. R. (1951) *The Greeks and the Irrational* (Berkeley)

D'Ooge, M. L. (1926) *Nicomachus of Gerasa: Introduction to Arithmetic* (New York)

Dooley, S. J. (1989) *Alexander of Aphrodisias On Aristotle's Metaphysics 1*, tr. (Ithaca)

Duminil, M.-P. (1977) "Les sens de ichor dans les textes hippocratiques," in R. Joly ed. *Corpus Hippocraticum* (Mons)

Düring, I (1934) *Ptolemaios und Porphyrios über die Musik* (Göteborg)

Festugière, A.-J. (1945) "Les mémoires pythagoriques cités par Alexandre Polyhistor," *REG* 58: 1–65

Frank, E. (1923) *Plato und die sogenannten Pythagoreer: Ein Kapitel aus der Geschichte des griechischen Geistes* (Halle)

Freeman, K. (1971) *Ancilla to the Pre-Socratic Philosophers* (Cambridge, Mass.)

Fredrich, C. (1899) *Hippokratische Untersuchungen* (Berlin)

von Fritz, K. (1940) *Pythagorean Politics in Southern Italy: An Analysis of the Sources* (New York)

(1945a) "Nous, noein, and their derivatives in Pre-Socratic philosophy," *CP* 40: 223–42, in Mourelatos 1974: 23–85

(1945b) "The discovery of incommensurability by Hippasus of Metapontum," *Annals of Mathematics*, 2nd ser. 46: 242–64, in Furley and Allen 1970: 382–412

(1955) "Die ἀρχαί in der griechischen Mathematik," *ABG* 1: 13–103

(1973) "Philolaus," *RE* suppl. 13: 453–84

Furley, D. J. (1956) "The early history of the concept of soul," *BICS* 3: 1–18

(1987) *The Greek Cosmologists* (Cambridge)

Furley, D. J. and Allen R. E. eds. (1970) *Studies in Presocratic Philosophy*, vol. 1 (London)

(1975) *Studies In Presocratic Philosophy*, vol. 2 (London)

Gallop, D. (1975) *Plato: Phaedo*, tr. and commentary (Oxford)

Gillespie, C. M. (1912) "The use of εἶδος and ἰδέα in Hippocrates," *CQ* 6: 179–203

Goldstein, B. R. and Bowen, A. C. (1983) "A new view of early Greek astronomy," *Isis* 74: 330–40

Gomperz, H. (1932) "ΑΣΩΜΑΤΟΣ," *Hermes* 67: 155–67

Goodwin, W. W. (1965) *Syntax of the Moods and Tenses of the Greek Verb* (New York)

Gottschalk, H. B. (1971) "Soul as harmonia," *Phronesis* 16: 179–98

Graeser, A. ed. (1987) *Mathematics and Metaphysics in Aristotle. Proceedings of the 10th Symposium Aristotelicum* (Berne)

Graham, A. J. (1964) *Colony and Mother City in Ancient Greece* (New York)

Grensemann, H. (1968a) *Die hippokratische Schrift "Über die heilige Krankheit". Ars Medica*, Abt. 2, Bd. 1 (Berlin)

(1968b) *Hippocratis, De Octimestri Partu. De Septimestri Partu. Corpus Medicorum Graecorum* 1.2.1 (Berlin)

Guthrie, W. K. C. (1962) *A History of Greek Philosophy*, vol. I (Cambridge)

(1975) *A History of Greek Philosophy*, vol. IV (Cambridge)

(1978) *A History of Greek Philosophy*, vol. V (Cambridge)

Harder, R. (1926) *Ocellus Lucanus* (Berlin)

Heath, T. L. (1913) *Aristarchus of Samos. The Ancient Copernicus: A History of Greek Astronomy to Aristarchus* (Oxford)

(1921) *A History of Greek Mathematics*, 2 vols. (Oxford)

Heidel, W. A. (1901) "Πέρας and ἄπειρον in the Pythagorean philosophy," *AGP* 14: 384–99

(1907) "Notes on Philolaus," *AJP* 28: 77–81

(1910) "Περὶ φύσεως: a study of the conception of nature among the Presocratics," *Proc. of the Am. Ac. of Arts and Sc.* 45: 77–113

(1912) "On Anaximander," *CP* 7: 212–34.

(1940) "The Pythagoreans and Greek mathematics," *AJP* 61: 1–33, repr. in Furley and Allen 1970: 350–81

(1941) *Hippocratic Medicine* (New York)

Heinze, R. (1965) *Xenokrates* (Hildesheim), repr. of 1892 edn.

Holwerda, D. (1955) *Commentatio de vocis quae est ΦΥΣΙΣ vi atque usu praesertim in graecitate Aristotele anteriore* (Groningen)

Howald, E. (1924) "Die Schrift des Philolaos," in *Essays on the History of Medicine Presented to Karl Sudhoff* (London): 63–72

Hübner, W. (1980) "Die geometrische Theologie des Philolaus," *Philologus* 124: 18–32

Huffman, C. A. (1985) "The authenticity of Archytas Fr. 1," *CQ* 35: 344–8
(1988) "The role of number in Philolaus' philosophy," *Phronesis* 33: 1–30
(1989) Philolaus' cosmogomy," in Boudouris 1989: 186–94

Hussey, E. (1990) "The beginnings of epistemology: from Homer to Philolaus," in S. Everson ed. *Epistemology* (Cambridge)

Jones, W. H. S. (1947) *The Medical Writings of Anonymus Londinensis* (Cambridge)

Junge, G. (1958) "Von Hippasus bis Philolaus: Das Irrationale und die geometrischen Grundbegriffe," *C&M* 19: 41–72

Junge, G. and Thomson, W. eds. (1930) *Pappus, Commentary on Euclid X* (Cambridge)

Kahn, C. H. (1960/85) *Anaximander and the Origins of Greek Cosmology* (Philadelphia) (1st edn. New York)
(1968/9) "The thesis of Parmenides," *RM* 22: 700–24
(1974) "Pythagorean philosophy before Plato," in Mourelatos 1974: 161–85
(1979) *The Art and Thought of Heraclitus* (Cambridge)
(1985) "Democritus and the origins of moral psychology," *AJP* 106: 1–31

Kerschensteiner, J. (1962) *Kosmos: Quellenkritische Untersuchungen zu den Vorsokratikern. Zetemata* 30 (Munich)

Kirk, G. S. (1954) *Heraclitus. The Cosmic Fragments* (Cambridge)
(1955) "Some problems in Anaximander," *CQ* 5: 21–38, repr. in Furley and Allen 1970: 323–49

Kirk, G. S., Raven, J. E. and Schofield, M. (1983) *The Presocratic Philosophers*, 2nd edn. (Cambridge), 1st edn. 1957

Kittel, G. ed. (1965) *Theological Dictionary of the New Testament*, tr. and ed. Geoffrey W. Bromiley, vols. 1–4 (Grand Rapids)

Klibansky, R. and Labowsky, C. (1953) *Plato Latinus* III: *Parmenides: Procli commentarium in Parmenidem interpr.* G. Moerbeka (London)

Kühn, J. H. (1956) *System- und Methodenprobleme im Corpus Hippocraticum. Hermes Einzelschriften* II (Wiesbaden)

Kühner, R. and Gerth, G. (1897) *Ausführliche Grammatik der griechischen Sprache II, Satzlehre* (Hanover), repr. 1966 (Darmstadt)

Langerbeck, H. (1935) Δόξις ἐπιρυσμίη. *Neue philologische Untersuchungen* 10 (Berlin)

Lesher, J. H. (1981) "Perceiving and knowing in the *Iliad* and *Odyssey*," *Phronesis* 26: 2–24
(1983) "Heraclitus' epistemological vocabulary," *Hermes* 111: 155–70

Levin, F. (1975) *The Harmonics of Nicomachus and the Pythagorean Tradition* (Philadelphia)

Lloyd, G. E. R. (1963) "Who is attacked in *On Ancient Medicine*," *Phronesis* 8: 108–26
(1966) *Polarity and Analogy* (Cambridge)
(1975) "Alcmaeon and the early history of dissection," *Sudhoffs Archiv* 59: 113–47

(1979) *Magic, Reason and Experience* (Cambridge)

(1983) *Science, Folklore and Ideology* (Cambridge)

(1987) *The Revolutions of Wisdom* (Berkeley)

(1990) "Plato and Archytas in the seventh letter," *Phronesis* 35.2: 159–73

Lonie, I. M. (1981) *The Hippocratic Treatises "On Generation." "On the Nature of the Child." "Diseases IV." Ars Medica* Abt. 2, Bd. 7 (Berlin)

Mansfeld, J. (1971) *The Pseudo- Hippocratic Tract ΠΕΡΙ ΈΒΔΩΜΑΔΩΝ ch. 1–11 and Greek Philosophy* (Assen)

(1975) "Alcmaeon: 'physikos' or physician?" in J. Mansfeld and L. M. de Rijk eds. *Kephalaion: Studies . . . offered to C. J. de Vogel:* 26–38 (Assen)

(1979/80) "The chronology of Anaxagoras' Athenian period and the date of his trial," *Mnemosyne* 32: 39–69 and 33: 17–95

(1983/86) *Die Vorsokratiker*, 2 vols. (Stuttgart)

Marg, W. (1972) *Timaeus Locrus. De Natura Mundi et Animae* (Leiden)

Martin, T. H. (1872) "Hypothèse astronomique de Philolaus," *Bolletino di bibliografia e di storia delle scienze matematiche e fisiche* 5 (Rome)

Merlan, P. (1968) *From Platonism to Neoplatonism*, 3rd edn. (The Hague)

Minar, E. (1942) *Early Pythagorean Politics* (Baltimore)

Mondolfo, R. (1938) Edoardo Zeller, *La Filosofia dei Greci nel suo sviluppo storico* 1.2., tr. (Florence)

(1956) *L'infinito nel pensiero dell'antichità classica* (Florence)

Mourelatos, A. P. D. (1970) *The Route of Parmenides* (New Haven)

(1979) "Some alternatives in interpreting Parmenides," *The Monist* 62: 3–14

ed. (1974) *The Pre-Socratics* (Garden City)

Neugebauer, O. (1957) *The Exact Sciences in Antiquity*, 2nd edn. (Providence, Rhode Island), 1st edn. 1952

(1975) *A History of Ancient Mathematical Astronomy*, 3 vols. (Berlin)

Newbold, W. R. (1906) "Philolaus," *AGP* 19: 176– 217

Nussbaum, M. C. (1978) *Aristotle's De Motu Animalium* (Princeton)

(1979) "Eleatic conventionalism and Philolaus on the conditions of thought," *HSCP* 83: 63–108

Olivieri, A. (1921) "Osservazioni sulla dottrina di Filolao," *Riv. indo-greco-ital.* 5: 29–46

O'Meara, D. J. (1989) *Pythagoras Revived. Mathematics and Philosophy in Late Antiquity* (Oxford)

Owen, G. E. L. (1960) "Eleatic questions," *CQ* n.s. 10: 84–102, repr. in Furley and Allen 1975: 48–81

Philip, J. A. (1963) "Aristotle's source for Pythagorean doctrine," *Phoenix* 17: 251– 65

(1966) *Pythagoras and Early Pythagoreanism* (Toronto)

Powell, J. E. (1966) *A Lexicon to Herodotus* (Hildesheim)

Raven, J. E. (1948) *Pythagoreans and Eleatics* (Cambridge)

Richardson, H. (1926) "The myth of Er," *CQ* 20: 113–33

Robbins, F. E. (1921) "The tradition of Greek arithmology," *CP* 16: 97–123.

Ross, W. D. (1924) *Aristotle's Metaphysics: A Revised Text with Introduction and Commentary* (Oxford)

Rothenbücher, A. (1867) *Das System der Pythagoreer nach den Angaben des Aristoteles* (Berlin)

Ryle, G. (1965) "The *Timeaus Locrus*," *Phronesis* 10: 174–90

Sachs, E. (1917) *Die fünf Platonischen Körper* (Berlin)

Schaarschmidt, C. (1864) *Die angebliche Schriftstellerei des Philolaus und die Bruchstücke der ihm zugeschriebenen Bücher* (Bonn)

Schiaparelli, G. V. (1876) *Die Vorläufer des Copernicus im Alterthum*, tr. F.M. Kurze (Leipzig)

Schneider, R. ed. (1912) *Griechische Poliorketiker*, vol. 1. *Abhandlungen der Königlichen Gesellschaft der Wissenschaften zu Göttingen, Philol.-hist. Kl.*, N.F. 12, no. 5 (Berlin)

Schofield, M. (1980) *An Essay on Anaxagoras* (Cambridge)

Schwyzer, E. (1939) *Griechische Grammatik* I (Munich)
(1950) *Griechische Grammatik* II (Munich)

Scoon, R. (1922) "Philolaus Fragment 6 Diels," *CP* 17: 353–6
(1928) *Greek Philosophy Before Plato* (Princeton)

Shipton, K. M. (1985) "Heraclitus Fr. 10: a musical interpretation," *Phronesis* 30: 111–30

Sider, D. (1981) *The Fragments of Anaxagoras* (Meisenheim am Glan)

Siegel, R. (1968) *Galen's System of Physiology and Medicine* (Basle and New York)

Snell, B. (1924) *Die Ausdrücke für den Begriff des Wissens in der vorplatonischen Philosophie. Philologische Untersuchungen* 29 (Berlin)
(1953) *The Discovery of Mind. The Greek Origins of European Thought*, tr. 2nd German edn. by T. G. Rosenmeyer (Cambridge, Mass)

Stenzel, J. (1933) *Zahl und Gestalt bei Platon und Aristoteles* (Leipzig), repr. Darmstadt 1959

Stokes, M. C. (1971) *One and Many in Presocratic Philosophy* (Washington, D.C.)

Strachan, J. C. G. (1970) "Who did forbid suicide at *Phaedo* 62b?" *CQ* 20: 216–20

Szlezak, J. A. (1972) *Pseudo-Archytas Über die Kategorien* (Berlin)

Szymanski, M. (1981) "On authenticity of Philolaus' Fr. B 20," *AGP* 63: 115–17

Tannery, P. (1889) "Sur un fragment de Philolaus," *AGP* 2: 379–86, repr. in *Mémoires scientifiques* VII: 131–9 (Paris)
(1904) "A propos des fragments Philolaïques sur la musique," in *Mémoires scientifiques* III: 220–43 (Paris)

Tarán, L. (1981) *Speusippus of Athens* (Leiden)

Taylor, A. E. (1911) *Varia Socratica* (Oxford)
(1928) *A Commentary on Plato's Timaeus* (Oxford)

Temkin, O. (1951) "On Galen's pneumatology," *Gesnerus* 8: 180–9

Thesleff, H. (1961) *An Introduction to the Pythagorean Writings of the Hellenistic Period. Acta Academiae Aboensis, Humaniora* 24. 3 (Åbo)
(1965) *Pythagorean Texts of the Hellenistic Period. Acta Academiae Aboensis, Humaniora* 30.1 (Åbo)

Timpanaro Cardini, M. (1946) "Il cosmo di Filolao," *Riv. d. storia d. filosofia* 1: 322–33
(1958–64) *I pitagorici: testimonianze e frammenti*, 3 fascs. (Florence)

Verdenius, W.J. (1947/48) "Notes on the Presocratics," *Mnemosyne* s. 3. 13: 271–89; s. 4. 1: 8–14

Vernant, J.-P. (1969) *Mythe et pensée chez les grecs* (Paris)

Vlastos, G. (1946) "Parmenides' theory of knowledge," *TAPA* 77: 66–77

(1952) "Theology and philosophy in early Greek thought," *PQ* 2: 97–123

(1953) Review of Raven 1948, *Gnomon* 25: 29–35

(1975) *Plato's Universe* (Seattle)

DeVogel, C. J. (1966) *Pythagoras and Early Pythagoreanism* (Assen)

Wachsmuth, C. (1882) *Studien zu den Griechischen Florilegien* (Berlin)

Wackernagel, J. (1970) *Sprachliche Untersuchungen zu Homer*, repr. (Göttingen)

van der Waerden, B. L. (1943) "Die Harmonielehre der Pythagoreer," *Hermes* 78: 163–99

(1951) "Die Astronomie der Pythagoreer," *Verh. d. kon. Ned. Ak. v. Wet. Afd. Natuurk.* 120.1

(1979) *Die Pythagoreer* (Zurich)

Wallis, R. T. (1972) *Neoplatonism* (New York)

West, M. L. (1971) *Early Greek Philosophy and the Orient* (Oxford)

(1980) "The midnight planet," *JHS* 100: 206–8

Wiersma, W. (1942) "Die Fragmente des Philolaos und das sogenannte Philolaische Weltsystem," *Mnemosyne* s. 3.10: 23–32

Wilamowitz-Möllendorff, U. (1920) *Platon*, 2nd edn. (Berlin)

Winnington-Ingram, R. P. (1928) "The spondeion scale," *CQ* 22: 83–91

Wright, M. R. (1981) *Empedocles: The Extant Fragments* (New Haven)

Wuilleumier, P. (1939) *Tarente, des origines à la conquête romaine* (Paris)

Zeller, E. (1923) *Die Philosophie der Griechen in ihrer geschichtlichen Entwicklung* (Leipzig) I⁷, ed. Wilhelm Nestle, repr. Darmstadt 1963

Zhmud', L. JA. (1989) "'All is number'?" *Phronesis* 34: 270–92

INDEX LOCORUM

INDEX OF GREEK WORDS

(1) Select Index of Greek Words and Phrases Discussed in the Text

434

(2) Index of all words except the article occuring in the genuine fragments of Philolaus (Fragments 1–6, 6a, 7, 13, 17)

GENERAL INDEX

No attempt has been made to list all occurrences, especially of common terms (e.g. limiters and unlimiteds) or names (e.g. Burkert). Reference should also be made to the Index locorum for the names of ancient authors.

above and below, 211–12, 215–26
Academy, 30, 35, 349–50, 352–3, 363, 370–4, 377, 385; attitude to Pythagoreanism, 23–5, 152, 386, 391
Achilles Tatius, 267, 269
acusmata, 55, 248–9, 352
acusmatici, 6, 7, 11, 12
Aelian, 162–3
Aelian the Platonist, 378–9
Aetius, 166, 269, 394, 396–8
air, 130, 145, 213, 215, 265, 295
Airs, Waters, Places, 184
aither, 145, 393, 395
Alcmaeon, 9; as a Pythagorean, 10, 11; writings of, 15 n. 25, 95; skepticism, 125–7; puts intellect in the brain, 318
Alexander of Aphrodisias, 180, 255–6, 280–2, 284–8
Alexander Polyhistor, 218–19, 310
Anatolius, 170, 315
Anaxagoras, 9, 11, 39, 42, 50–1, 65–6, 95, 104, 108, 127–9, 132, 145, 152, 200, 287; attacked by Philolaus, 49, 123; use of γιγνώσκειν, 117; astronomy, 241, 248, 257–9; on the moon, 271–4; puts intellect in the brain, 318
Anaximander, 49–51, 81, 94, 104, 123, 202, 214, 218, 260, 287, 300
Anaximenes, 50, 108, 123, 214
angles, 385, 387
animals, 307–9, 311–12, 315, 318
Anonymus Londinensis, 291–4, 297–8
antipodes, 217–19
Apollo, 338
Apollodorus of Cyzicus, 4

apotomē, 160, 369, 374–7
Archippus (?), 2, 3
Archytas, 6, 7, 8, 10, 19, 31, 32, 54, 57, 156, 168, 198–9, 339–40, 347, 356, 419–20; knowledge of means, 168–9; music theory, 365–6
pseudo-Archytas, 25 n. 9, 27, 80, 143
Aristaeus, 168
Aristotle, 8, 14, 45, 167; account of Pythagoreanism, 17 n. 1, 28–31, 38–40, 44, 47 n. 1, 56–64, 70–3, 76, 100, 106, 159, 170; and the *Timaeus Locrus*, 19; and pseudo-Pythagorean writings, 20; on the relationship between Plato and Pythagoreanism, 21, 24, 159, 166, 373; failure to mention Philolaus' book, 26, 31–4; used Philolaus as a source, 28–31, 34; reference to "so-called Pythagoreans", 31–4; says that Pythagoreans thought all things were numbers, 56–64, 173; use of ἀρχή, 79–80; on Pythagorean epistemology, 114–15, 172; on Melissus and Parmenides, 121; Pythagoreans talk only about physical world, 127; music theory, 153; knowledge of means, 168; odd and even in relation to limiters and unlimiteds, 179–85; on the Pythagorean one, 186–90, 202–9, 340; on Pythagorean cosmogony, 202–13; on above and below in the cosmos, 222–6; on Pythagorean astronomy, 242–52; exhalations, 265; moon creatures, 272–3; harmony of the spheres, 280–2; on positions of numbers in the cosmos, 283–8; on disease, 291; psychology, 309, 318; on the navel, 311;

CPSIA information can be obtained
at www.ICGtesting.com
Printed in the USA
BVHW031311020821
613420BV00004B/10